W9-DJF-283

Mary Butts

Scenes from the Life

Mary Butts

Scenes from the Life

A BIOGRAPHY BY

Nathalie Blondel

McPherson & Company, Publishers
Kingston, New York

Published by McPherson & Company, Post Office Box 1126, Kingston, New York 12402. Typeset in Palatino with Bernhard Modern titling. Printed and bound in the United States of America.

The publisher gratefully acknowledges the assistance of a publishing grant from the Literature Program of the New York State Council on the Arts.

First edition.

1 3 5 7 9 10 8 6 4 2   1998 1999 2000 2001

Library of Congress Cataloging-in-Publication Data

Blondel, Nathalie
Mary Butts : scenes from the life : a biography / by Nathalie Blondel.
p. cm.
Includes bibliographical references and index.
ISBN 0-929701-55-0 (hardcover : acid-free paper)
1. Butts, Mary, 1890-1937—Biography. 2. Women authors, English—20th century—Biography. I. Title.
PR6003.U7Z57 1998
823'.912—dc21 97-41973
[B] CIP

The line drawings on pages i and 556 are by Gabriel Aitken.

To Cecily, Charlie and Nathaniel
(in the order I met them)

Do you know where it is, the Hollow Land? I have been looking for it now so long, trying to find it again, the Hollow Land...

William Morris
'The Hollow Land: A Tale', 1856

There are episodes and moments in books and people we all want to know more about—not just the sequels, but anywhere. Round the corner in the looking-glass: the end of the looking-glass lane.

Mary Butts
Diary entry, 16.11.29

I shall find what was cold
Warm blood in the stone.
You shall have what I have
Know also what I have known.

Mary Butts
'Frère Doue Amye', 1927

CONTENTS

ILLUSTRATIONS

FOLLOWING PAGE 332:

GENEALOGY OF MARY BUTTS

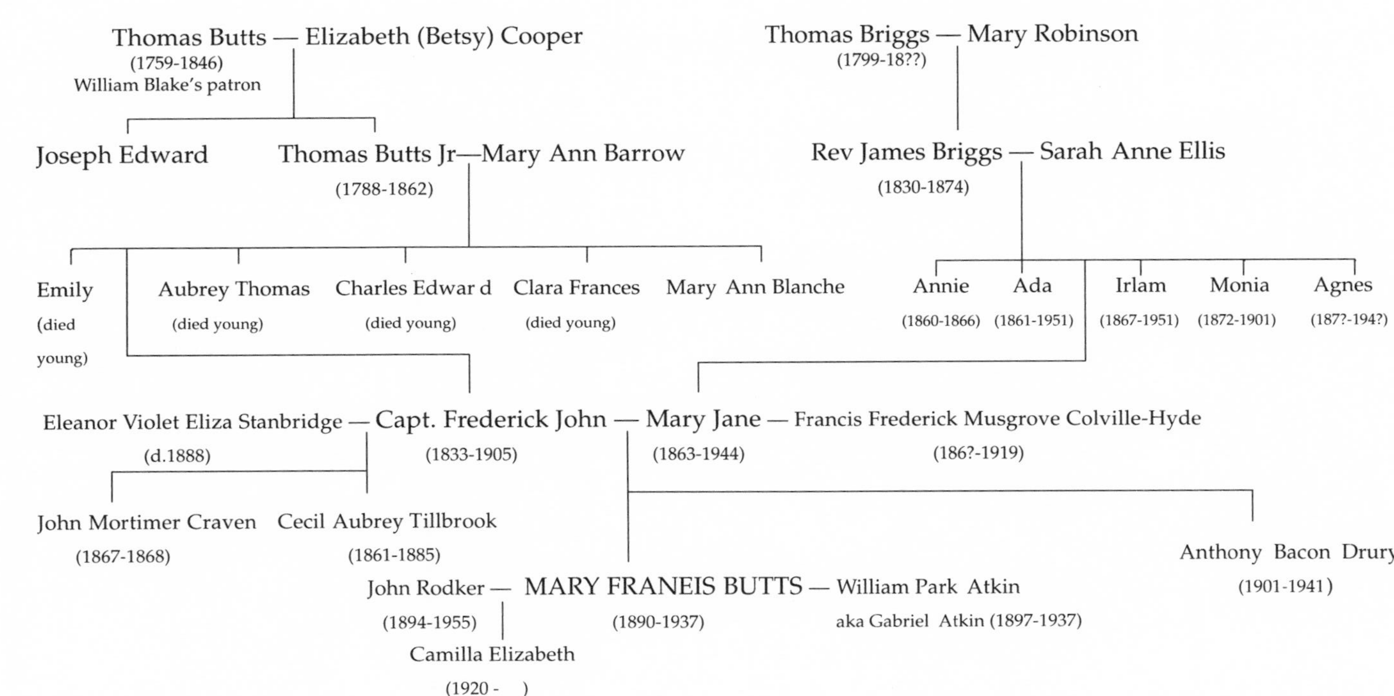

FOREWORD

MARY BUTTS was born in Dorset in 1890 and died in Cornwall in 1937. Despite her early death and the neglect which still overshadows her work, her contribution to twentieth-century English literature is impressive in terms both of quality and quantity. Mary Butts was no marginal figure on the Modernist scene. She published three novels, three volumes of short stories, a novella, poetry, two historical narratives, two pamphlets, several essays and articles, a partial autobiography and a considerable number of reviews. This forms only part of her substantial body of writing. As this biography explains, some manuscripts have been lost, but there are still many important works which have yet to be published.

A large number of her more famous contemporaries admired and praised her work, including Ezra Pound, E.M. Forster, Ford Madox Ford, H.D., T.S. Eliot, Bryher, Marianne Moore, Virginia Woolf, F. Scott Fitzgerald, Douglas Goldring, Charles Williams. She knew these writers personally, exchanged ideas with them and influenced their work, without ever belonging to any one circle or group. It is already ten years since Sheri Benstock in *Women of the Left Bank* pointed out that "to retrace the literary history of a period is to open that history to question.... Feminist criticism directed towards rediscovery and revaluation of the work of women writers has already altered our view of Modernism as a literary movement.... It has exposed the absence of commentary on women's contributions to Modernism and has rewritten the history of individual women's lives and works within the Modernist context." Yet Mary Butts's contribution to Modernism has still to be properly recognised. Again and again she has slipped through the net of literary histories of the period, often appearing only as an inaccurate footnote.

Mary Butts's formative years at the turn of the century were spent on the Dorset coast in a house containing a substantial number of works by the Romantic painter, poet and mystic, William Blake. (Her great-grandfather had been his patron.) She was an active pacifist during the Great War when she met her first husband, the writer and publisher, John Rodker, and was closely involved with his Ovid Press between 1919 and 1920. At this time she also knew Roger Fry, Nina Hamnett and Wyndham Lewis, all of whom painted her portrait. In the early 1920s, after the birth of their daughter, she left her husband and was based in Paris with other expatriate writers, such as Djuna Barnes, James Joyce, Robert McAlmon, Ford and Bryher. She 'studied' magic with Aleister Crowley, the self-styled Great Beast 666, at his Abbey at Cefalu in Sicily. She also became close friends with the French artist and writer, Jean Cocteau, who illustrated her work, and was one of the habitués at the Welcome Hotel in Villefranche on the French Riviera. In 1930 she married the painter, Gabriel Aitken, and they settled in England's most westerly village, Sennen Cove, Cornwall, where she lived until her death. In the mid-1930s she converted to Anglo-Catholicism.

I first read Mary Butts's work (in this case her 1932 novel, *Death of Felicity Taverner*) on a beach in the French Riviera. The power of her writing was such that I was immediately transported to the rich green land of south Dorset, the setting of that novel — no mean feat, given the intrusive sounds and heat of a bright French coastline. Mary Butts was a writer for whom place was paramount…and how you lived in that place: "…to some extent I think I shall be remembered as an English writer," she declared towards the end of her life. Again and again her writing evokes and celebrates the English countryside (she was an early ecologist and conservationist) whilst conveying with wit and vibrancy what she saw as the increasing "spiritual sterility" of modern life. If these warnings seem ever more prescient, her narratives are also funny, lyrical, moving. For she was a brilliant storyteller.

Mary Butts kept a diary from her mid-twenties in 1916 until her death at the age of forty-six. She knew its value even as she was writing it, commenting in the summer of 1929:

> For years I have kept, not a diary, but a note-book, in which, most days (and when I remember the date I add it) [I record]…what has interested me, or struck me, or happened to me as the times pass. There are volumes of them, fat, durable, marbled french volumes, part commonplace book, part satires, part business, ideas, events, sketches. Perhaps my fame, if I have any, will rest on someone…who has their editing.

I have quoted extensively from the diary (retaining her occasionally eccentric spellings) throughout the biography, because it is central to an understanding of how Mary Butts lived and viewed her life. Furthermore, this fresh perspective on the Great War and most of the "long weekend" which followed it will appeal to any reader interested in the minutiae of life during those years. Relying on the diary for its structural framework, *Mary Butts: Scenes from the Life* is a purposely chronological account which allows the reader to discover this writer's progress and achievements as they happen. Mary Butts was a difficult, complex, fascinating person and when portraying the often contradictory aspects of the woman and the writer, I have remained speculative rather than judgemental. One friend of hers wrote that "again and again Mary had her secrets from us all, and to seek to lay bare her whole personality is to find she has a way of escaping us a little. One can never know all about her because she never told all, guarding herself well." To write a biography is to be made aware "again and again" that you can never know all about anyone.

ACKNOWLEDGEMENTS

Work began on this biography in 1990. A small bursary from Liverpool University, who gave me the honorary status of Mary Butts Research Fellow, enabled me to make my first research trips to London. When I moved down to Bristol, the University of the West of England conferred a similar honorary title on me and, in addition to providing unlimited photocopying and postage (which were essential to the project), UWE funded a number of trips to the British Museum and the Tate Gallery. A crucial stage in my research took place when in 1994 I was successful in obtaining a £1900 travel grant from the British Academy which enabled me to visit places where Mary Butts had lived (Villefranche, Paris, St Malo and Sennen Cove). These trips were central to my understanding of the importance of place in Mary Butts's work, inspiring me to write those parts of her life which related to each location. I would not have been successful in obtaining this grant had it not been for my referees, Dr David Seed and the late Professor Donald Davie. I am particularly sorry that the latter as well as Robert Medley and Quentin Bell are not alive to see the finished work.

The research for this book has been possible only because of the generosity of a number of people. My greatest thanks are to Camilla Bagg who, in addition to making all of Mary Butts's papers available to me (including letters, notebooks, a certain amount of unpublished material and, of course, the diary) has given me a great deal of her time and insight. It is, I feel, all too often forgotten by writers and readers of biographies that their subjects have relatives. While this book is a celebration of Mary Butts's achievements as a writer, I am aware of the immeasurable generosity and integrity of her daughter, who has often had to delve into the sometimes painful aspects of her past in order to answer my questions. I would also like to thank the following people for the trouble they took in providing information, enthusiasm and encouragement: the late Harold Acton, Peter Bailey, Frances Beech, Anne Olivier Bell, the late Quentin Bell, Robert Bertholf, Véronique Blanc, Jean

Blondel, Michèle Blondel, John Bodley, Mary Brown, Sara Bursey (as she then was), Martin Butler, Robert Byington, Tina Coulsting, Andrew Crozier, Valerie Eliot, Kent Fedorovitch, Kate Fullbrook, George Garlick, David Gascoyne, Jane Grubb, Ann Hancock, Charles Hobday, Denise Hooker, Richard Ingleby, the late Frank Ingram, Chris James, Jess, Alan Judd, Meta Lindsay, Dawn Lloyd, Isabelle Masquerel, Pat McCrea, the late Robert Medley, Geneviève Monin, Stephanie Norgate, Ros Pesman, the late Sir Laurens van der Post, Mrs Priest, Joan Manning-Sanders, Glen Morgan, Ian Patterson, Penny Roberts, Joan Rodker, the late Michael Rothenstein, Derek Scott, David Seed, Charles and Nora Sisson, Dr Janet Sondheimer, Dominique Tiry, Christopher Wagstaff, Geoff Ward, John Wieners, Margaret Ross Williamson, Andrea Wittum. Librarians and archivists and second hand booksellers: Michael Bott and David Sutton at the University of Reading, Pierre Caizergues at the Fonds Jean Cocteau, Kendall Crilly at the Music Library, Yale University, Colin Harris at the Bodleian Library, Gina Dobbs at Random House, Adrian Glew at the Tate Gallery Archive, Peter Jolliffe and Peter Ellis at Ulysses Bookshop, Marius Kociejowski at Bertram Rota, Françoise Martin-Vrel and George at the Galérie Jean Cocteau, Anselm Nye at St Mary and Westfield College, Katherine Reagan at Cornell University Library, John Thompson at the National Library of Canberra, Australia, Jean Rose at Heinemann. Additional thanks to the staff at Somerset House and at the following libraries: the British Museum (Russell Street and Colindale), Liverpool University Library, UWE Library.

I am particularly grateful to the following persons who acted as readers for me in the final stages and gave me invaluable advice: Andrew Crozier, Helen Dunmore, Sue Habeshaw, Jeremy Hooker, Robert Kelly, Bruce McPherson, Ian Patterson, Dominique Tiry and Patrick Wright.

Except where noted within the text, all translations are mine.

I would never have accepted this commission had it not been for Paul Evans, who always took it for granted that I could write the biography and was only sorry that he had let first editions of Mary Butts's books pass through his hands in the 1970s before he met me and realised how central she would become to our lives. His conviction and support were total until his sudden death in 1991, and if I continued with the project against all odds, it is partly as a tribute to all we believed in. On a happier note, I would not have transformed the enormous amount of data and archival material into its present readable shape without the unstinting, discerning and enthusiastic assistance of Charlie Butler, who, I am delighted to say, through the hours of discussions about the biography has now a café habit almost as strong as my own. Finally, I want to thank my daughter, Cecily, for her help in indexing and photocopying parts of the manuscript and even more for her patience when I was writing the biography instead of being with her.

In writing this biography I wanted the people involved to speak for themselves as much as possible. I am extremely grateful, therefore, to Camilla Bagg for her generous permission to quote from a range of unpublished writings by Mary Butts as well as letters by Mary Butts and her relatives. All reasonable attempts have been made to trace and contact relevant copyright holders and I wish to thank the following individuals and insititutions for their permission to quote extracts from letters to Mary Butts (unless otherwise stipulated) by the following authors and artists: The letter from Djuna Barnes © Copyright The Authors League Fund, as literary executor of the Estate of Djuna Barnes; the letter from Clifford Bax reprinted by permission of the Peters Fraser & Dunlop Group Ltd; Anne Olivier Bell for a letter from Quentin Bell to Nathalie Blondel; University of Liverpool Library for a letter from Mary Butts [Colville-Hyde] to John Sampson; Mary Butts's letter to Edward Titus quoted with the permission of the Poetry/Rare Books, University Libraries, State University of New York at Buffalo; The Harry Ransom Humanities Research Center, The University of Texas at Austin for letters from Mary Butts to Hugh Ross Williamson and one to Kirk Askew; H.D. letter to Richard Jones used by permission of New Directions Publishing Corporation; Valerie Eliot for letters from T.S. Eliot to Mary Butts and Angus Davidson; Prof. François Lafitte for a letter from Havelock Ellis; Joan Floyd for her letter to Nathalie Blondel; The Provost and Scholars of King's College, Cambridge, for E.M. Forster's letters to Mary Butts and Gabriel Aitken; Polly Bird for letters from Douglas Goldring; Ronald Blythe for letters from Benvenuto to Lett Haines, Odo Cross to Cedric Morris and Cedric Morris to Mary Butts; Dominique Tiry and the Fonds Jean Cocteau/Fonds Mireille Havet du Centre d'Etudes du XXe Siècle, Université Paul-Valéry, Montpellier, for diary extracts and letters from Mireille Havet; Meta Lindsay for letters from Jack Lindsay; The Library at Queen Mary and Westfield College for extracts from the college register and unpublished diaries of Constance Maynard and Marion Delf Smith; Gregory Brown and Susie Medley for Robert Medley's letters to and an interview with Nathalie Blondel; Permission for quotations from Marianne Moore's unpublished letters granted by Marianne Craig Moore, Literary Executor for the Estate of Marianne Moore. All rights reserved; Letters from Ezra Pound to Mary Butts and Margaret Anderson Copyright ©1988 by The Trustees of the Ezra Pound Literary property Trust. Copyright ©1997 by Mary de Rachewiltz and Omar S. Pound. Used by permission of New Directions Publishing Corporation; Dr. P. Jane Grubb for a letter from Edgell Rickword; Rosemary Summers for letters from R. Ellis Roberts; Aitken & Stone Ltd for letters from Naomi Royde-Smith; Joan Rodker and Dominique Tiry for letters and unpublished comments by John Rodker; Lord Sackville for letters from Edward Sackville-West; Curtis Brown on behalf of the A.J.A. Symons Estate for letters from A.J.A. Symons; Donald Gallup for a letter from Carl van Vechten; Margaret and George Hepburn for the letter-poem by Anna Wickham; Oliver Wilkinson for a letter from Louis Wilkinson; David Higham Associates on behalf of the Estate of Charles Williams, ©1997, for letters from Charles Williams; Margaret Ross Williamson for letters from Hugh Ross Williamson.

PROLOGUE

The Diary Begins

The Diary Begins

The Zep has just passed almost over the house—travelling N[orth] like a great red caterpillar. We saw two bombs drop, heard dozens, put out our light, on some clothes, forgot your respirator, seized matches and a latch key, and went out into the square to watch. Everyone was there in nighties & pyjamas lending their cellars. All the late buses were empty inside, thick as bees on top. Are we down-hearted? No.

—MB, letter to Ada Briggs, 12pm, 9.9.15[1]

As I wrote, [Eleanor] seized me with memories of past ecstacies transcended. There will have to be a secret ms. seeing that no one can write openly about these things. —MB, diary entry, 3.9.16

BY THE TIME Mary Butts started keeping a diary on a regular basis on the 21 July 1916, she was twenty-five years old and living in a flat at 27 Ferncroft Ave, Hampstead, with her lover, Eleanor Rogers. They had been together for two years. There is only sporadic information about Mary Butts's life before the diary opens and this is contained for the most part in letters and poetry.[2]

Her relationship with Eleanor was strained by the fact that she had met John Rodker, a writer from the East End of London, four years her junior. They were slowly falling in love and Mary Butts was caught between her passionate feelings for John Rodker and her now-fading love for Eleanor, who was furious at the change in her affections. The situation was complicated by the fact that Rodker, a conscientious objector (or CO), was in hiding from the authorities.

Mary Butts later recounted that "the first part of the war I spent working for the L.C.C. [London County Council] among the derelict homes of East London".[3] Until September 1915 she had worked at Hackney Wick, when she collapsed from exhaustion. "There's really nothing wrong, only I haven't any store of vitality to fall back on once I'm tired. I 'spect this last dreadful year has used it all up, with that of many better people," she wrote at the time to her aunt, Ada Briggs. But Eleanor had insisted "that I was to take a rest, and then I was to get transferred to an office nearer central London, and not waste 2½ hours daily travelling. I gave in."[4] In Hackney Wick Mary Butts had done voluntary work on the Children's Care Committee with the Australian painter, Stella Bowen, who had come to England the previous year.[5] In her autobiography, *Drawn from Life* (1941), Stella Bowen recalled that at 19 she was "immensely grateful" for the friendship Mary Butts, six years her senior, offered her "at a period when I was seldom at my ease with anybody". She remembered Mary Butts as "a flaming object in that dreary office, with her scarlet hair and white skin and sudden, deep-set eyes.... Mary...had a vast set of very definite views of her own, about which she was extremely vocal." Stella Bowen considered her friend to be "an aristocratic anarchist rather than the socialist she then imagined herself" despite, or perhaps because of, her attempt "to endoctrinate [sic] me concerning the potential splendour of the Working Man and the inept futility of our Royal Family".[6] The two women spent considerable time together during the war, along with mutual friends, such as Phyllis Reid, who had worked for the suffrage movement, and the socialist Margaret Postgate, who, after her brother Raymond's prison experiences as a CO, had begun working in her spare time for the Fabian (later Labour) Research Department.[7] In spite of the war, there was still the excitement of parties, the Proms, walks in Kew Gardens and socialising at cafés, clubs and restaurants, such as the Blue Cockatoo, the Petit Savoyard and the Clarissa Club.

Whether Mary Butts was still involved with the Children's Care Committee in 1916 is unclear, but by July she was working in some capacity for the "NCCL". Set up in 1915 as the National Council Against Conscription, the broader name of National Council for Civil Liberties (NCCL) was adopted in 1916. It was a small organisation, with an uneasy relationship with officialdom: "In its various offices around London, the organisation appears to have enjoyed the close attention of the police authority acting under the Defence of the Realm Act, and reports in contemporary newspapers such as *The Times* are of police raids, and the removal of incriminating publications and records. For most of its existence this first NCCL[8] had an Advice Department, which assisted several thousand enquirers, and a Record Office, which gave information to speakers, writers and others on subjects within the Council's scope."[9] Mary Butts's work was done mainly in an office in Bride's Passage, just off Fleet Street. On the 5 August she noted: "applied more work NCCL". She also attended a number of the Tribunals for COs, including that of the Secretary of the NCCL, Bernard Langdon-Davies, on the 12 September, when she was impressed by his "purpose and fine intelligence".[10] Looking back in the mid-1930s at her war work, she wrote:

> Youth takes the injustice of nature hardly. This was a desperate attempt to find something to do the basis of which activity was just. I remember walking back from the office, office of the National Council for Civil Liberties, under a high, ghostly winter sky, out of which,

> every other night, there dropped bombs. Explosions of human rage, valour and skill and science, but in what we had to do I found some peace in the sense of historic continuity.... I walked on,...and believed that in our thankless task, by our perpetual appeals to Parliament on behalf of the helpless, we were also a public service. And was comforted. Caught up in what one understood, if only for an instant, was high civic duty, in our appeal to the ancient sanctions hated by a people at war, yet, if once lost, the meaning has gone out of victory.
>
> ...The Council would be ineffective, not only on account of the appalling difficulties that beset it or because the Police might forbid it, but because the power that might make it effective was not yet generated enough on earth.... [I] work[ed] very hard, energizing all youth's fierce sympathy with the undermost underdog. For I had not yet got my society straight, who had received the war for measuring-rod.[11]

The national registration of all able-bodied men had been introduced in July 1915. When this did not result in enough men signing up voluntarily, the first Military Service Act was passed in January 1916 which introduced conscription for all unmarried men between the ages of 18 and 41. Given England's heritage of religious and social liberties, there was a great deal of opposition to conscription. Individuals who voiced their opposition were often linked to organisations, for example: Ramsay Macdonald, the leader of the Independent Labour Party (ILP), the journalist E.D. Morel, spokesman for the Union of Democratic Control (UDC)) and on behalf of the Non-Conscription Fellowship (NCF), the philosopher and agnostic, Bertrand Russell. In response to public pressure the Local Government Board set up Local and Appeal Tribunals in February 1916 with the following instruction:

> While care must be taken that the man who shirks his duty to his country does not find unworthy shelter behind this provision, every consideration should be given to the man whose objection genuinely rests on religious or moral convictions. Whatever may be the views of the members of the Tribunal, they must interpret the Act in an impartial and tolerant spirit. Difference of convictions must not bias judgement.... Men who apply on this ground should be able to feel that they are being judged by a Tribunal that will deal fairly with their cases. The exemption should be the minimum required to meet the conscientious scruples of the applicant.[12]

Records show that there were sixteen thousand registered Conscientious Objecters in Great Britain during the First World War. Known derisively as "conchies" or "pasty faces", their position was often a difficult one, as was the fate of the organisations which tried to protect their rights. The NCF, for example, suffered continual harassment from the government. Its London offices were frequently raided by the police, and its members prosecuted under the notorious Defence of the Realm Act

(DORA). Bertrand Russell was himself taken to court for writing a leaflet (published by the NCF) in which he gave an account of a young socialist CO's experiences at a tribunal hearing and subsequent imprisonment. E.D. Morel was imprisoned after arranging for two of his pacifist publications to be sent to the French writer, Romain Rolland, when he knew that the latter was in a neutral country.[13]

By July 1916 John Rodker was hiding at 'The Shiffolds', Holmbury St Mary, Dorking, Surrey, the home of his friend, the poet Robert Trevelyan.[14] Mary Butts supported his position (they corresponded almost daily), remarking on the "collective insanity that has come over the world". On the 22 May a CO in Swansea Prison, Jack White, wrote to thank her for her "admirably wise" letter. White praised her for being "the first of my visitors or correspondents to see to the root of my position and swell by the testimony of a human mind, the generous comfort which God gives me direct. ...I need hardly explain to you that I hate violence in any shape or form. It is just for that reason that I am here now —Moral force is greater and more powerful than physical force, but moral force may be either good or evil. ...This week in prison has done me a lot of good, though my soul darted itself about like a caged bird my first night in the police cells. I've done nothing they can shoot me for yet nor indeed I think anything that gives them any right to imprison me."[15]

Mary Butts would become good friends with Jack White who inspired one of her most successful stories, 'Deosil' (later renamed 'Widdershins'), written after the War. Through him and doubtless other COs Mary Butts met or wrote to, she was well aware of the danger John Rodker was running in evading conscription. In contrast with her pacifist sympathies, Eleanor wanted "everyone disenfranchised who did not help in the war. Bertram [sic] Russell, the Trevelyans" (9.8.16).[16] Throughout 1916 Mary Butts increased her understanding by reading books about different aspects of the war, including Rose Macaulay's *Non-Combatants and Others* (1916), a book on "the state regulation of disease", Bertrand Russell's *Problems of Philosophy* (1912) and E.D. Morel's *Truth and the War* (1916).

In September there was the "chance of permanent work" at her office, which she viewed with a certain amount of resigned despondency:

> If I take that work I shall sit all day at the window at the wooden desk and look out across the alley to the high Church-wall. Round its base are cut old inscriptions, men who died in 1750.[17] Between my work I shall learn them, and only very high up is there any sky. The clouds are upon one round the tower before one has imagined them blown up the sky.... There is a tree too and a court. Not till the end of the war will there be any time for art or love or magic again. Perhaps never again.

It was doubtless with some relief that she noted three weeks later: The "job at the office definitely off". From then on she made only occasional reference to her daily work which was by turns, "interesting" and "dull". She in no way thought that she played any heroic part. On the contrary:

> The war like a monstrous inconvenience in every room of the house —a wall crawling with deadly catterpillars[18] which sometimes drop off and go for one.
> One goes on living in the middle.
> Frieze-figures 'doing our bit' even in pacifism.
> A barbarous compulsion.
> A room with a snake in it, always liable to turn up.
> 'Professional consolers'.
> The horror of the monstrosity its *essential irrelevance.*

Notwithstanding her war-work, Mary Butts's major preoccupation was her writing and the very first words of a diary she was to keep for the next twenty years opened triumphantly with: "Finished CO story." She revised it over the following week before sending it (on the advice of Edward Garnett) to the publisher, Hutchinson, on the 27 July.

The previous day she had visited John Rodker and organised a longer stay for early August. Eleanor was furious at the news and issued an ultimatum: either Mary Butts abandon her holiday with John Rodker or Eleanor would leave and "tell 'all she knows'" (presumably about Rodker and his whereabouts). Mary Butts knew that Eleanor was only bluffing because, although "impossible" and "hysterical", she needed her friend. The relationship would continue until the following April, a cycle of bitter recriminations in which Eleanor was often violent: 2 October: "E… hellish…she raved and screamed and struck my breast, and tore at my eyes and hair"; 14 October: "E hysterical, poured water on my sheets, cried, raved, etc." These outbursts were interspersed with moments of their previous intimacy. 31 August: "I heard her cry in her room and went down and came into her bed and held her tired and loving, too tired to hurt any more." Yet such tenderness was only temporary and the railing and violence would begin again, lessened only in the short periods when Eleanor was involved with other people.

By late July Mary Butts had decided that Eleanor "must be treated with the patience and indifference fit for an animal or a vicious child. Her behaviour is hardly human with odd fits of penitence. She was kinder that night. She can't be well—the war is very heavy on us all." The immediate problem of the visit to John Rodker was solved when Eleanor fell ill with tonsilitis. In nursing her Mary Butts felt both frustrated and more tender: "Remembered my throat paint. Tried it, did E good. We sat and watched her cough up matter into the basalt bowl. Normally it would have made us both sick, as it was we were wild with interest." When not looking after Eleanor, Mary Butts read some stories by the American writer, O. Henry, but decided that they were "no good as a pick-me-up. Tried gramophone—better." After several days Eleanor's condition had become so serious that she had to be sent to a nursing home. At first, alone in the flat Mary Butts could not "bear it. I can go to J now, but it hardly counts (it will tho' later). I can't go up to our room that she's slept in. There are books there and flowers, and the basalt bowl and the bottles —oh it's making me cry out of all reason. Just before she went she smiled —like she used to last August. Six months since she smiled like that— longer than that. . ." To assuage her guilt she bought Eleanor a dressing gown of flowered crêpe de chine, and took it to her along with grapes and roses. She then returned to the empty flat, wrote letters, suffered because of the "curse"[19] and waited to "discover…whether the flat alone is endurable or not."

"Flat very endurable," began the next day's entry and after a day spent at a Tribunal and visiting Eleanor, she returned home to read Russell's *Problems of Philosophy* and "the Sonnets [Shakespeare] for the first time, first series. Sheer treasure trove. 'But thine immortal lustre…' The intimacy of them…" The following morning brought renewed doubts about Eleanor, however: "When she comes back will this begin again or shall I have a chance to love and live and work in peace? It's up to us now to fight, the older men are perishing fast. I must never give in to her any more… Ought to be writing again. Will there ever be a chance?"

The long weekend which she spent with John Rodker from the 4th to the 8 August was delightful. "A month of sleep and fine air and sufficient food have increased his beauty past recognition. I never knew how beautiful he was before, now he's brown with haymaking, supple with swimming and dear past understanding." They went for walks "along the road with cypresses and stars" and during the mornings when John Rodker worked, Mary Butts read *Emma* and Bertrand Russell's book and worked at a new story (not named). There was a frightening moment when "a policeman [called] to see registration cards, especially J's. Mrs Trevelyan saved us all, engaging him in light conversation. Card given back without comment.… Tried to appear 'calm and well-bred'. Doubtful success." When the lovers parted at the door that evening "I was holding a candle in a brass candlestick looking at J and feeling for the bolts. He said 'Psyche looking for Cupid' and I 'this Psyche has found her Cupid, and will never let him go'. Then we both knew. 'Eros, Eros—'." The next day Mary Butts felt "uncertain" when "'The' question [was] discussed", but on her last day with John Rodker, after a walk around the Roman camp and a picnic lunch there was:

> further discussion. Sonia, then the real trouble. Finances, the style overlooking the Weald. All I can ever say is an approximation of this. I tried to keep my head as clear as my heart. Understand J as well as persuade him. I hardly knew myself whether I was a wise angel with a sword, or a devil out of hell tempting him. I want us to try it for a year or so, to give us both a chance to work and love in peace, and poverty mitigated by a certain security. He has starved and fretted long enough. He knows that but because I am his lover—I think he will accept me now. When we had come to a decision a great joy liberated us both. But he can never claim that he proposed to me....
> Back to London. E very bitter but sorry later.
> All well.

"Sonia" was Sonia Cohen, a dancer at Margaret Morris's school before the war. John Rodker had lived with her in 1914 and in May 1915 their daughter, Joan, was born. In February 1934, Mary Butts described her marriage to John Rodker as "one of those War-marriages between very young people". In 1918 when they married, Mary Butts was 27 and John Rodker 23. This was hardly "very" young; what this description also omits and the 1916 account shows is that they were deeply in love.

From the time they were together Mary Butts would support John Rodker and provide money for Joan as well as still paying for Eleanor until April 1917. By the previous December her relationship with Eleanor had become so strained and difficult that she commented on the "useful-if-expensive [fact] that one can buy one's peace":

> She [Eleanor] was subdued by the thought of the gift. We had tea, and started to look for it. I watched myself and her. I was bitter with her, I did not want to please her much. I wanted to buy peace. I could not afford it. I wanted money to spend on J—'necessaries' too not 'frills'. I wanted to go quietly into shops of my old kind, and spend money carelessly in sumptuous places on goods that would be perfect. If only as a protest against perpetual buses, ink, cooking and roast chestnuts for breakfast.
>
> So we went to Morris' in Bond St. There was oak panelling, a soft carpet and a remarkable selection of cigarette holders....I was cold, body and mind. E chose one, pale clouded, a shell or a flower, the end opening like a calyx, held together by a gold band round its middle.
>
> I jumped at the price, but once out in the street was reconciled. A lovely thing[20] had left a shop and become the property of one who would appreciate it, and E became adorable again! She kissed me—in Bond St—and moaned rapturously about the toy, and sadly about the price—bought Vasso with which to initiate it, and made up my amber necklace for me when I got home.
>
> Oh Eleanor—are you wholly and only to be bribed with gifts, or do you understand love so little that you do not know that it is there unless you have it made articulate with costly things?

PART ONE

The Early Years

CHAPTER ONE

Salterns
1890-1916

The family was of considerable importance in the reigns of Richard and John. I still have in my possession deeds in good preservation, dated October 11th 1170, in which the King leases large estates in the counties of Suffolk and Essex to his 'wellbeloved John and Mary Butts'.
—Undated 'Note by F.J.B. [Frederick John Butts]', 'Pedigree of the Butts Family'[1]

It's my native place and I worship it.
—MB, letter to Glenway Wescott, 1923[2]

ON THE 29 SEPTEMBER 1888 Captain Frederick John Butts (born 16 February 1833) of The Salterns, Parkstone, Dorset wrote to Mrs Sarah Anne Briggs, also of Parkstone:

> I have written to your daughter Mary to ask her whether she will, after a time, be my wife, and I have preferred writing to speaking, to give her more time for consideration. I am only too well aware of the great difference in our ages, I being 55, but marriages of this class often turn out very happily...I can give her a good home, close to her own family, and I believe I could, and would take all imaginable pains to make her life happy.... The life I am now leading is a wretched one, for, as I have told her, I am really alone in the world, since the loss of my poor wife and Aubrey. I do not know, nor does it matter to me whether she has anything of her own. If she should have, it would be my wish to have it settled upon her and her children.[3]

The object of Frederick Butts's affections was Mary Jane Briggs (born 22 January 1863). Her father, James Briggs, had been the son of Mary Robinson and Thomas Briggs, a jute merchant from the Manchester area and an ardent Free Trader. After James Briggs died young following a short illness in 1874, his wife was left with a fairly small but comfortable income for herself and their five daughters:

> The widowed mother seems to have left a great deal [of the work] to the eldest, Ada, fourteen at the time of the father's death, but somehow the girls became educated and, better than merely that, cultivated. Ada was devoted to literature and hoped to become a writer. She wrote several novels, one of which was published. She began to take part in local affairs and, in 1919, became the first woman alder-

> man on the Poole Borough Council, at that time an impressive achievement. Irlam became a painter of considerable stature. Agnes was an excellent violinist and miniaturist. Monica had a lovely singing voice but she died young, in mysterious circumstances.[4] If any of these gifted, energetic, young women could be said to be less interested in things of the mind, it was the second sister, Mary, but she was known as the prettiest, and practical with it.[5]

When Frederick Butts made his offer of marriage, he was a very wealthy man. He owned his large family property in Parkstone as well as Railway debentures, consols and Bank of England stock which together averaged (less Income Tax) £3266 per annum, or, as he put it, "£1550 apiece". This was a considerable fortune in 1888. "In addition," explained Captain Butts to Mrs Briggs, "I have £5000 of my own, which it is my intention to settle upon my wife, for her life, for her pin money, to do what she likes with, and upon her children at her death."[6]

Mary Jane Briggs accepted Frederick Butts's offer and they were married on the 29 April 1889. She was 26 and he was 56. A retired Army Officer with a distinguished career, Captain Butts had served as a young man in the Crimean War. When Mary Butts used to relate this to her friends, they put it down to her love of dramatic exaggeration. It was in fact true.[7] Frederick Butts's first wife, Eleanor Violet Eliza Stanbridge, had died on 5 March 1888. She was predeceased by their two children, John Mortimer Craven (7.1.68 in infancy) and Cecil Aubrey Tillbrook in a boating accident in Poole Harbour on the 19 November 1885.

Eighteen months after their wedding, on the 13 December 1890, at 7:45 a.m., the first child of Mary and Frederick Butts was born. She was christened Mary Franeis Butts.[8]

* * * * *

> All day long the empty space of the home-land
> Blowing wind, the shining tide of the harbour,
>
> . . .
>
> Sweet past count the song of bees on the thyme-spray,
> Strong past thought the naked curve of the downlands
> Laid like a sleeping woman bare to the sunshine
> Bare to the starlight.
>
> — MB, 'Sapphics', July 1911

> Passages have played a great part in my life. The corridors at Salterns were green and white. Great places to run in, but they never met. One ended in glass.
>
> — MB, 'Rites de Passage', 1931

THE SUBTITLE Mary Butts gave to her autobiography, *The Crystal Cabinet*, was *My Childhood at Salterns.* Salterns was the name of the house in Parkstone, bought by Frederick Butts in 1863 and in which Mary Butts was born. Set in its own grounds of 21 acres, 2 roods and 6 perches, Salterns was "the largest...property...round about".[9] It remained all-important throughout Mary Butts's life and she wrote of it as a *temenos* (sacred enclosure) where as a child she "possesses and is possessed" by the surrounding land stretching round to the Isle of Purbeck to the south and the prehistoric site of Badbury Rings to the north. She learnt to know "the ancient garden of Salterns,...the woods,...the salt-marshes [which gave the property its name]...and the sea" by exploring them repeatedly as a child and a young woman "very much as primitive man did".

Nor was it only the setting of her home which so impressed her:

> Sometime in the eighteenth century Salterns had risen modestly, of white plaster and a slate roof. A large porch and large sash-windows, wood-divided into smaller panes; a long stone-flagged hall, and a conservatory stuck on the side that looked out over the hills. The central core, the old morning-room and library, later all one library, probably part of a much older building, with the eighteenth-century additions at each end. A lofty double drawing-room and a dining-room, the first one whole end of the house, and both rising straight up to the lofts under the roof. At right-angles to all this, the servants' hall and kitchen; the new wing, and this three storeys high, built by my father in my infancy, stuck on at the angle of joining.
>
> The rest of the house was its hall, entered by the front door, flagged and wide, airy and shadowy, a delicately drawn staircase rising round three sides of it, lit by tall windows; and at night by a huge iron lantern, with bottle-glass doors, each with a coloured and one with ruby eye. Victorian-Viennese-Gothic, and much later replaced by a brass candelabrum, hung like a pale gold crown, to burn acetylene candles, at that time an exciting innovation.... It was a profoundly English life.[10]

The house was full of beautiful furniture, books and possessions, a "strange accumulation of spoil" which included:

> King Charles I's watch and key
> His queen Henrietta Maria's Seals
> Numerous minatures of our family....
> A very ancient Egyption Fragment in oriental stone in many strata representing a Priest who is consulting the sacred serpent by an arch of Triumph carved with hieroglyphics: it belonged to Belzoni....
> Beau Brummel's watch, given by him to Cornet Butts when they were in the 10th Hussars together.[11]

And thirteen grandfather clocks, whose ticking reassured the small girl growing up at Salterns.

Most important to Mary Butts was the unique collection of thirty-four Blake watercolours, engravings (including his engraving cabinet), portraits and sketches at Salterns. These included *Nebuchadnezzar, Newton, Pity* and *The Lazar-House.* Her great-grandfather had been Captain Thomas Butts, the patron and "artistic guardian"[12] of William Blake, and addressee of Blake's poem which opens: "To my friend Butts I write / My first Vision of Light."[13] There was a Blake Room in Salterns which displayed his pictures.[14] In *The Crystal Cabinet*, whose very title came from a poem by Blake, Mary Butts praised her parents for insisting that she should from an early age "make good use of her eyes". Added to this training was a skill or quality which she claimed was acquired by her close examination as a child of the Blake paintings. Gradually she absorbed "the kind of seeing that there was in William Blake", which would have a far-reaching effect on her writing, portraying as it does the surface of things whilst also intoning their resonance, their place in a pattern underlying and transcending the merely phenomenal world.

Inwardly, Mary Butts felt her poetic vocation from an early age. Growing up in Salterns at the turn of the century however, she was rigidly constrained by the late Victorian mores of what was seemly and acceptable for young ladies. In her review of *The Crystal Cabinet,* the writer Bryher [Winifred Ellermann] found in the autobiography restrictions familiar from her own childhood:

> In the early nineteen hundreds, so many harmless things were forbidden us. We might not feel water nor sand nor earth, when "two kinds of drawers and two kinds of petticoats, a pinafore and serge frock imposed, as I can still remember, a very real strain on one's vitality." Prohibitions were imposed for whose reason we might not ask. We were pruned of every form of self-expression, like the single flower on an exhibition stem, until everything in us went into a single desire, freedom, which we saw only in wind or in the breaking waves and as we could not hold these, into what was nearest to them, poetry. I do not think that the present generation [of 1937] feels literature as we did. They love it, of course, but they have no need of our intense and concentrated passion. They sunbathe at two, have some of their questions answered. It was, however, the sign of our age, the identification students will tag to us, when we are dug out, as the Elizabethans were in the nineteenth century, after the night of forgetting almost sure to come.[15]

The tone of this passage displays Bryher's bitterness towards the repressions of her childhood. In its linking together of nature and poetry, it echoes the sentiments of an unpublished poem 'To Δρακοντι', written by Mary Butts in 1909. In it, the young poet claimed kinship with mermaids rather than humans:

> Help me, o my friends,
> Not to grieve, not to cry to the stars,
> Not to judge, not to seek men's approval,
> Nor even to pass where life sends
> All joy into dull agony.
> But to laugh in men's teeth very shrill
> To pass over decorous observance
> And pour out my youth at my will.
>
> So poor am I!
> A stranger possessed with a devil,
> A child come out of the sea.
> But the wind is my friend, and the sky
> My mother who sent me here,
> Who swept me down from above,
> And gave me the gift of gifts
> Through glory and shame I can love.

Mary Butts had rather an isolated childhood, one which she later described as "saturated with arts" and in which she made her own taste. On a "bright March morning" in 1901, when she was in her eleventh year, "I was taken into my mother's room, and they said she was very ill, but her bright eyes didn't look it. And in the room next door there was lying in a cot as perfect a baby as the world had ever seen. It slept, then for a moment opened eyes of the unspeakable translucency of the newborn, bubble of jelly into which it is hardly inaccurate to say that, in northern babies, the colour of the sea and the sky are distilled. Leaning over it, I loved it. A love I almost watched. A love I knew was there, had come in suddenly but, as it were, full-grown. That would never go away, standing beside me there, quickening in the quiet of the old low-ceilinged bedroom".[16] Her brother Anthony Bacon Drury (Tony) was born.

Mary Butts was educated at the two local schools, The Haven and Sandecotes, until her father died in 1905. She was fourteen and Tony only four. She later wrote that on her father's death it was "as if a strong, small, gold sun had set. Gone as we so often saw it go, set into the cup of the hills behind Arne, a gold disk, a wafer in its paten, a Grail-image."[17] Closer to her father (in *The Crystal Cabinet* she called him Daddy whilst her other parent she called rather more formally, Mother), Mary Butts felt his loss keenly: "I do not remember a time when I did not know that my father and I stood with the same support beneath our feet. ...we were woven of the same piece."[17] She described him as "something of a scholar" with "brilliant gifts" and a "superiority, unconscious as a noble child's, to meanness, spite, self-seeking, jealousy, snobbery or any of the common pretensions and defences of men".[19] Compared with his perfections "...my mother, with her vigorous, romantic, emotional nature, truly religious, but uncoordinated by the least touch of subtlety of intellectual love, was far from that understanding. It is true that she learned from him; but no one can learn what they cannot learn, and to try is a sure way to error."[20] Mary Butts later claimed that "for my girlhood, even after my father's death, my mother and my aunt [Ada] were sufficient."[21] However, the death of her father seems to have brought to a close her sense of Salterns as a "perfectness". On the 26 January 1907, fifteen months after Frederick Butts's death, his widow married an old friend of the Captain's called Francis Frederick Musgrove Colville-Hyde (Freddie).[22] They adopted the name Colville-Hyde from then on. Mary Butts liked her stepfather and called him Tiger-Tiger, after the poem by Blake. (He was a heavy drinker, however, and the marriage lasted only twelve years, as Colville-Hyde died on the 15 August 1919.) With his arrival and her own "transit" from girlhood to adolescence, her relationship with her mother deteriorated. "From the beginning, to be given a real education was the one desire of which I was sure"[23] and when the opportunity was offered, the young Mary Butts exchanged the soft climate of her beloved Dorset for the harsh, ascetic rigours of St Andrew's, Scotland, where she went to St Leonard's School for Girls. Whilst enthralled by the study of literature and religion at school, it was an unhappy and solitary period of her life, which she would convey in her short story 'Angele au Couvent' and, much later, describe in great detail in *The Crystal Cabinet*.[24]

When proposing to his future wife in 1888, Frederick Butts had written that "should there be a family, I can only leave her the house and contents, with the interest of the £5000 settled upon her, and about £1000 more, but the £1550 a year would not be lost to her, as it would go to our children, who would not be likely to let her want, and in the event of my dying and leaving a family of minors, my widow would be allowed by the trust, the whole, or a large proportion of the income for their keep and education until they attained their majority."[25]

It would seem that Mary Colville-Hyde was not adept at managing her family's finances. "For various reasons and to meet death-duties",[26] she put up the Blake pictures for sale at Sotheby's only a few months after the Captain's death. It was their financial rather than their aesthetic value which concerned her, as she wrote to her lawyer on the 26 February 1906: "When it came to writing a cheque many of Blake's admirers cooled off and the largest offer in *writing* was £7000—which Sotheby will not let me take at present. I should [sic] propose for your approval the following scheme. That I settle the Salterns on Tony—in such a manner that I am free to deal with it as I think fit during my lifetime [and] that we take the value of the Blakes at £7000.... Would it be of any use to let the Judge know that the estate was not put into Chancery to protect the children—but that my husband died under the impression that I was free to do exactly what I thought right in every way."[27] The Blake Collection was sold to W. Graham Robertson in April 1906. He eventually bequeathed them to the Tate Gallery which owns them today.[28]

Once they were sold, Mary Colville-Hyde wrote to her mother on the 27 April 1906: "I have received part of the Blake money, and as I felt I could not look on a tenth of this, as my own or the children's, I am proposing to enlarge and decorate the Chancel of the Chapel[29] with part of it—and I have given myself the happiness of paying in £200 to your deposit account at your Bank. I wanted to do this, because it always grieved me so when I was a girl and your bank book came in and you used to feel it so if you were a little overdrawn—but by placing this sum on deposit you will (D V) [God willing] never have this worry again."[30] This shows how generous Mary Colville-Hyde could be. Mary Butts's resentment towards her mother greatly increased when the Blake paintings were sold. At fifteen, she was too young to do anything to prevent the sale; she was old enough, however, to realise their value and irreplaceability.

As well as this heart-breaking loss, in August 1906 Mary Colville-Hyde drew up a settlement with regard to Salterns, in accordance with her proposal to her lawyer a few months earlier. She was to be the owner during her lifetime. If the property remained after her death, Tony would inherit it and after him his children. Only if they had all died would Mary Butts inherit (followed, on her death, by her children). Given her father's will, it is not surprising that Mary Butts felt disinherited of her "lovely quickening home".

Nineteen-six was, however, the beginning of Mary Butts's life as a published writer when she had a poem and an essay, 'The Poetry of Hymns' accepted by *The Outlook*.[31] The poem already shows the influence of Blake:

The Heavenward Side
by Mary F Butts

One having moved from his clay tenement
Was passing softly in a rapture sweet
Through the new country of the soul, and came
Upon a sudden radiance of bloom.

He stood before it wrapped in reverie,
Till someone touched him, saying, "It is yours
You sowed the seed on earth and watered it
With bitter dew of tear. Do you forget?"
The spirit wondered at the thing he heard:
Too far he was from Sorrow, now, to see
Her bleak, sad shadow. Breathing breaths of balm,
All bathed in joy, he scarcely understood
The angel's meaning when he softly said:
"This is the heavenward side of your great grief."[32]

At school she took the exams for Cambridge but failed and moved back briefly to Salterns in 1908. This put a considerable strain on her already bad relationship with her mother, as can be seen in a letter from Ada Briggs to her niece following yet another altercation in late September 1910:

> My darling Bo [Mary Butts's family nickname from her childhood]
> The position of affairs between you and your mother is a far more serious thing than you know. I wanted to speak to you about it when you were calmer, but perhaps writing is easier. It is a truly horrible thing to have anger and certain feelings towards anyone in one's heart and towards one's mother makes it far, far worse....
> My darling you *must* learn to love your mother, to feel very tenderly and kindly towards her, find out all the good qualities in her and dwell only on those. You ought to think of her very pitifully, especially just now, and not with any shade of bitterness. It is absurd to think it a fine thing to go out to help the sorrows of the world outside, and *make sorrows* by your attitude and want of love in the home to which you are specially called.
> I do not think you at all realise what a difference it would make if instead of setting yourself against your mother, you tried to make her life happier and be considerate and patient in little things.
> Don't be proud darling, pride is weakness, and true humility is strength. Pride is the sin that loses peace to the soul more surely than any other. Don't be afraid to make the first advance, however difficult this may be.[33]

It is unlikely that Ada Briggs's homily had much impact on the young rebellious Mary Butts, coming as it did from a Victorian perspective, which she was busy rejecting.

* * * * *

Take this thing by which I live,
Take and if you can — forgive

. . .

Better than you dream I see your soul stand clear,
On the earth death's shadow thrown,
Poets see the sky star-sown.

— MB, 'To G.I. with the earrings from Cyprus', [early 1910s]

It is difficult to trace Mary Butts's movements precisely between finishing school in 1908 and the start of her diary in 1916. What is clear from the poetry written in her late teens and early twenties, however, is that her Sapphic life did not begin when she met Eleanor Rogers. In 1910 she wrote 'A fragment from Sappho'. This was followed by 'Sapphics' in July 1911 in which the poet speaks of "Beauty as sweet as rose-leaves—ancient desire/ swept and held me."

The Register of Students at Westfield College, London shows that on the 13 October 1909 Mary Butts was accepted there as a "General Student". The idea was "to read for a degree, as I chose, or not."[34] She attended for three years and later paid tribute to her teachers at Westfield not for the subject of their teaching but for the fact "that there I learned ...*how* to learn, I do not doubt."[35] At Westfield she made several close friends, including Margaret Schleselmann, Ida Binks, Megan Myfanwy Owen and a member of the non-resident staff called Gwen Ingram. Her feelings for these women are displayed in a number of poems, several of which bring together London topography and classical figures. One of her poems, for example, was called 'Artemis, Victoria Station' (5.3.13). In another, 'The Adventure', the poet declares: "I've left a place where the trees toss/ to look for Gods at Charing Cross."[36]

Mary Butts's interest in the classical world dated back to her childhood. Her father had been been a powerful storyteller and with "the tang of his irony...the cycles of antique story-telling...pleased me as they please all children, the first pleasing that never wears out, only deepens and re-quickens, like resource to a well-spring, a hidden source of loveliness and power."[37] Some of the stories revolved around Greek myths and this resulted in a lifelong familiarity with and use of classical imagery in her work. Thus her 1932 novel, *Death of Felicity Taverner*, opens:

> A young man who had arrived uninvited from France lay under the green slate roof of the verandah perfecting the idea he had suggested to his hosts, that, if he had not come, they would have sent for him.... And already the sister and brother and the sister's husband were reinstating him ...into his position as a cherished family curse. Scylla, his hostess, did it best. "He is our ring of Polycrates," she had cried out suddenly in the hour of spiritual angularity just after he

> had appeared. "We are infinitely well-off here." "Polycrates exactly," said Felix, her brother. "It didn't end there." Still, after that, the situation had run more easily; for with a certain kind of English person a classical allusion has the weight and function of a text. Instantly their minds had gone out to sea: Samos; the Thalossocrats...[38]

Mary Butts's knowledge of Greek places her writing outside the educational experience of her female contemporaries.[39] She later wrote: "Only in Homer have I found impersonal consolation—a life where I am unsexed or bisexed, or completely myself—or a mere pair of ears" (3.1.19). Strangely, Virginia Woolf used the very same word (impersonal) when she gave the fact that "Greek literature is the impersonal literature" as the reason why she found it so alien.[40] The widespread neglect of Mary Butts's work up until a few years ago, is indicated by the fact that Shari Benstock omitted it from her 1986 *Women of the Left Bank: Paris 1900-1940,* an otherwise extensive study of the period. "Need it be noted," wrote Benstock, "that the knowledge of Latin and Greek was not to be taken for granted among women educated in these years? H.D., Natalie Barney and Renée Vivien learned Greek on their own in order to read the fragments of Sappho that became available in the 1890s, and the one woman Modernist whose writing consistently turns on classical sources of English words is Djuna Barnes, who received no formal education at all and who learned etymology by reading *The New English Dictionary.*"[41] And yet in 1919 Mary Butts's knowledge was such that she noted: "To remember Greek life is not to adventure into a delicious ideal but to go home to something so familiar that it can bore me."

In 'Psychology and Troubadours' (1916), Ezra Pound described his understanding of why the Greek myths arose. It is a description which is reminiscent of the theories of Jane Ellen Harrison, a widely admired archaeologist and scholar of the period. By 1913 Mary Butts was already familiar with Harrison's *Prolegomena to the Study of the Greek Religion* (1903) and *Themis: A Study of the Social Origins of Greek Religion* (1912).[42] Since Pound's essay was written before he had met Mary Butts, she cannot be one of the people alluded to. Yet his account describes her perspective:

> I believe in a sort of permanent basis in humanity, that is to say, I believe that Greek myth arose when someone having passed though a delightful psychic experience tried to communicate it to others and found it necessary to screen himself from persecution. Speaking aesthetically, the myths are explications of mood: you may stop there, or you may probe deeper. Certain it is that these myths are only intelligible in a vivid and glittering sense to those people to whom they occur. I know, I mean, one man who understands Persephone and Demeter, and one who understands the Laurel, and another, who has, I should say, met Artemis. These things are for them *real.*[43]

In an untitled poem of 1913 Mary Butts wrote: "We were Gods once, behold our steadfastness!/ The one low cry we make in our distress,/ O for a kind Fate, and forgetfulness!"[44] There is no doubt that from childhood, she responded to features of the Dorset landscapes in the manner described by Pound: "At Salterns, at the dawn of my life, Power and Loveliness walked naked over East Dorset, side by side. Lay down to sleep together like gods on Purbeck, rose out of the dawn-washed sea." Indeed she "could not think of" the Isle of Purbeck (which she could see from the house) "as anything else but a live thing…a true daimon, as the young of each race first see power. Something like the Greek stories my father gave me and sometimes told me, only not in a book." Salterns was a place where "the wind was different, and a goddess called Artemis …shot with the new moon". And when she looked "across the threshold into a garden", she saw "the Golden Bough growing from the Tree of Knowledge, not yet of good and evil, but of true knowledge". "With Adonis and Atys and Osiris"[45] Mary Butts was led to Frazer's *The Golden Bough* (1895-1905), the anthropological study which would have a profound influence on her writing.[46]

* * * * *

AT WESTFIELD Mary Butts wrote poems continually. In 'Ad Maiorem Margaritae Gloriam'(1909) a poet who has been in London "the past-year long" is in love with a woman called Margaret [Scheselmann]: "With tangled hair and restless hands/ In her lonely room above,/ In the winter evening shadows/ Lies alone the friend I love." Margaret is a *flaneuse,* "a child of the streets", and the poem is both an emotional defence of her existence and an attack on the hypocritical society which condemns her openness about sexuality:

They lie, ten thousand-fold they lie, who say
Her laugh is evil and her life astray,
Her glory tawdry, and her strength decay.

Their shapeless bodies they perforce much scan
Her dear young limbs, her head so lightly born[e],
Her eyes as bright and changing as a faun.

Their modesty rears up so at the sight,
The mute reproach of excellence so bright,
Their purity they vindicate in spite.

They talk of love of music manifold
Yet when they hear her voice of pearl and gold
They turn their eyes away and murmur "Bold!"

'M.M.O. [Megan Myfanwy Owen] Westfield 1911' opens "Megan of your courtesy/ underneath an orchard tree/ lift your scarlet mouth to me." In 'Ida', also written in 1911, Mary Butts declared: "A star, a star, a merry star/ A golden girl was she,/ A star that fell in an orchard close/ Sunny and green, and the blossom blows/ Out on a sparkling sea." A notebook containing poetry written between July 1911 and February 1914 was entitled "Poems by Mark Drury", a pen name she adopted presumably because of the Sapphic nature of a number of the lyrics, but never used in print. (Given her affection for her brother, Tony (Bacon Drury), it is probably not a coincidence that Mary Butts chose Drury for her pen name.) She also used poetry as a vehicle to lament the powerlessness of women compared to men: "How long, O Lord, in mercy Lord how long?" she asked in 'Vacation Christmas 1911':

A man may go apart, winning his peace
In outer lands—on unseen glowing wings
Devouring fires of terrible knowledge sweep
And burn his soul and fashion it anew,
But men they busy round us like small flies
Crawling upon our skin and through our hair,
Fire that would strip our flesh from off our bones
Scarce even that could make us clean again.

O dainty, flowery, aimless life of ours!
The nice poise of small issues, painted wings
For those vast pinions outstretched on the hills
Rising to life the world up in their flight
They cut our wings, and bound our hair with flowers,
They stripped and set their seal between our breasts,
Soft shoes, fine raiment, and mock reverence.

A number of Mary Butts's poems were inspired by what she was reading. 'After reading Olive Schreiner's *Woman and Labour* [(1911)]' (autumn 1911), is an angry poem on behalf of this "Skillful player at all subtle games/ of easy life,—too wise to set her store/ on fine behaviour, and on easy names." Dissatisfied with the poem, Mary Butts decided that it was not worth typing up. The following spring she wrote verses 'Suggested by some of the later poetry of Mr Rudyard Kipling'. The poem initially praises this "Master of might and mirth" who is "Comrade of every star and heart/ A Captain and a child." Yet as it progresses, Kipling is blamed because:

You took your winged and holy words
Your nameless, deathless things,
Gave them for meat to carrion birds,
Which are the awe of kings.
They took the goods you had to sell,
They praised you for your part—
O poet, Lord, they paid you well
To prostitute your Art!

Know you the Lords of Death and Life
Are never cheated thus?
You have cast out your Art your Wife
Your starry song from us.
Never again that high, sweet song
Shall break our heart, or heal our wrong,
We leave you to your lust.

In fact Mary Butts's youthful intemperance did not prevent her from a life-long admiration for Kipling, whose stories she reread a few weeks before her death.[47]

In the summer of 1911 she spent some time with Gwen Ingram in Scotland, whence she wrote to her Aunt Ada:

> There are no words to describe the goodness of this place, full of fascinating books and the loch in the woods is glorious with a big boat to row in. I can now row quite respectably, and trout rising all round one.
>
> Yesterday Gwen…and I went down to the Tummel Falls below Bonskied. The river was low so we crawled down till we reached a rock close beside the main rush of the water.
>
> I can't describe it, the river was like some fierce living thing, and a thin mist rose from the pool below and hung like smoke.…
>
> All round the hills came down close, often sheer rock, covered with silver birches, and then above naked rock and heather, the clouds sweeping over the topmost points. The river is coloured deep gold as clear as crystal.[48]

It is probably no coincidence that the letter was to her Aunt rather than her mother, with whom Mary Butts was still getting on very badly. From the 13 December 1911, when she was twenty-one, she began to receive the small allowance her father had settled upon her and was released from her mother's guardianship. She would never, however, be financially independent of Mary Colville-Hyde.

On the 10 June 1912 Constance Maynard, the Principal Mistress of Westfield, noted in her private diary: "There has been a sad thing in the College, a deep-laid and deceitful plan between one Student and one of the non-resident Staff to go to Epsom on the Derby day and see the race.

I have been in deep waters about it, and have had to speak as never before. As to poor M. Butts the responsibility is lightened by her having before now proved herself something of a 'mad idiot', and there is no holding her to a thing anywhere; but for Miss Ingram I feel keenly. I shall never forget her face positively green with fright...when she saw I had guessed the whole truth."[49] The whole truth as reported by another staff member fifty years later, was that Mary Butts had "wanted to go to the races, always strictly forbidden by the college rules. She had become friendly with [Gwen Ingram]...and between them a plan was made to evade the rules. The student asked and received permission to visit the lecturer at her flat, and to stay there over-night. Next day, they both went to the races, but by some means (not divulged) the news reached the college authorities, who took a very grave view of the matter."[50]

As far as Constance Maynard was concerned, the facts that Gwen Ingram "loses a post worth over £100 a year, and Mary is to be sent down before the Term ends" were entirely the fault of the "glowing red-head, Mary Butts":

> It was she who coaxed and begged and got the expedition done, and her conscience seems impenetrable. On Wed. last I had to tell the Council, (without her name of course) and said confidence was the mainspring of the College, and she had broken it, and I proposed to send her down a fortnight before the close of the Term. Lord Alverstone looked hastily round the assembled faces — "The Mistress has the thorough support of the Council", and the work was done. This morning she left. I think only 5 students know anything about it, for she slipped off, and left her room as it was, leaving a maid to come later and pack her things.... She looked in with a sharp, "Goodbye, Mistress", holding her arm and hand rigid that I should not kiss her ...Never have I had such a parting; it strikes a cold chill through me to think of it. Three years here, and all in vain. It is very sad.[51]

From a 1990s perspective, the expedition seems harmless enough; it certainly shows the young Mary Butts's disregard for conventions and rules, who in 1911 had written a poem called 'The Masters', dedicated "To all governors, teachers, spiritual pastors and masters—from a rebellious scholar". Whilst it might be thought that the disgrace of leaving Westfield without a degree would have done little to endear her to her "people", on this occasion they seem to have been sympathetic.[52] Yet familial relations continued to be strained and Mary Butts wrote a poem around this time called 'To My Own People. On behalf of G.I. [Gwen Ingram]'. The specific context was not hers, but it was *akin* to her situation in the same way that Bryher had found her own childhood conveyed in *The Crystal Cabinet*. The poem is a plea for freedom and understanding:

Before you cast me out, men of my house—
Before you say I break your hearts, and sell
My birthright, have for ever cast away
The nobleness of life, honourable days,
High reverence, and seemly ordinance—
Here my defence in this wild act of mine.
This time I speak, then ever hold my peace.

Whether Mary Butts defended herself to her family is unknown. What is clear, is that she still at this period retained the sympathy of her Aunt Ada, who took her and her Aunt Agnes to the Continent in the autumn of 1912. They travelled via Belgium and Paris to Italy, where they visited several cities, including Rome, Florence, Milan and Venice. Mary Butts continued to write poems. In 'Milan' she wrote:

When we came to Milan town
We dreamed of Roman palaces,
And women swaying in the sun—
All these and other fallacies,
For draughts of deep red country wine
And wide-horned swinging-footed kine

We spent our whole time dodging trams
And courting death in Milan square,
Small, vicious, yellow trams like wasps,
Above in deep blue, quivering air
White shafts of immemorial snow
Mocked at our passing to and fro.

If she saw it, the devout Ada would probably not have approved of the last stanza of 'Milan', where the poet declares: "A pagan heart could make no prayer,/ In all that dim and blood-stained light./ Gave praise for the shrill outer air./ Young Italy at work outside,/ Her Church as drift left by the tide."

From the Casa Petrarca in Venice, Ada wrote to Sarah Briggs in September: "We have a charming view from the front of this house and are quite close to the Rialto, historic spot! Browning's Palazzo and Byron's too, we pass nearly every day… The gondolas and gondoliers of the private houses and large hotels are very smart, they usually have 2 men dressed in white with crimson, blue or yellow sashes and scarves but the ordinary cab variety is not quite so gay.… Bo [Mary Butts] is a great darling, she simply couldn't be sweeter or nicer."[53]

Venice seems to have made Mary Butts melancholy. Her poem to the city was reflective, bleak and moving. It opens:

The streets of Venice, silent, cool and clean,
Water as green as jade, and pearl-bright air,
Lace work of marble palaces serene—
Death holds this city like a crystal vase
Of frozen still perfection—stars, lost stars,
White dreams, a memory of what was fair.

Death broods upon the narrow water ways,
The light waves washing on the shallow stairs,
Torn shutters hanging loose through the gold rays.
From those high crazy walls, and round the bridges
House refuse drifts in scum and pools and ridges—
The unwashed babies laugh away one's cares.

At the end of September the three women travelled on to Florence which by train was "about 6 hours' journey" from Venice in 1912. No letters exist from their stay in Florence, but it drew an enthusiasm and quasi-religious fervour from the young Mary Butts, who felt that:

Some God took half the beauty of the world
And spilled it down in handfuls as he trod
O little town! here brooding his wings furled
He made you swift and subtle, without care,
So your sons learned that Art's as good as prayer.
And both are just another name for God.

On a return visit there in the winter of 1923 she wrote to her "dearest Aunt" Ada: "I've been down here for some time trying to escape the worst of the London weather. Florence can imitate it to perfection, with snow and yellow fog.... All the same it is the loveliest city in the world, and I prowl round all the places we went to together. Do you remember Santa Croce, and the Baptistry, and the Arno nearly always yellow and dirty?"[54]

* * * * *

If taking Mary Butts to Italy was an attempt to make her forget her Sapphism, it failed. By October 1912 she was back in London, miserable, poor and unable to work at her writing because of unrequited love which seems to have been for Gwen Ingram. As was her custom at this period, her unhappiness was detailed in her poetry. "You've tramped the streets of London all day long,/ Left your work when it was red-hot to your mind/ For a slender bitter woman—hence this song/ It's all the comfort you are like to find" ('December 1912'). It was the old, old story:

Her devilries she tells you one by one,
Some are fit to print and some aren't—talk of whips
When the most you do is listen and be dumb,
— She'd kill you if you spoke or touched her lips.

You're poor, she's poorer, and you're both alone.
She's the utmost pain and glory of your life,
You'd give her bread and all she asks a stone,
And tries to cut your love out with a knife.

The poet knows her own folly, but cannot heed her friends' warnings:

'She's running you for just what she can get,
She holds you in contempt—a plaything hired.

For you to take her out, and stand her treats.
And bear with her and give her pleasant things—
You pour your life out at her tired feet,
And break your heart to see her broken wings.'

It may be true, and then again it mayn't,
You can't tell, and you needs must go on blind,
You're her lover and you aren't no frozen saint,
You're aching once to see her—mind to mind.

Just hear her say for once. 'Old girl, we're friends,
Stick close to me, perhaps you may see done
All you desire for me before we end
Even my life fulfilled, my kingdom come'.

I don't think! but there're times when your desire
Is just to break down all that iron wall
She's hidden under—break it down with fire
Shew her your passion and make up for all.

In the spring of 1913, Mary Butts was still writing poetry to her unnamed lover. For all her misery, she cut a dramatic figure describing herself as "Poet (the worse for you)" who was: "clad in a sheath of gold,/ Delicate, devil fair/ One rose thrust in my hair/ My mouth for kisses set/ Through the smoke of my cigarette/ Skin for a man to hold" ('Spring 1913'). In the spring of 1913, according to the poem, 'To a Young Lady on her Approaching Marriage', her belovéd was married. Mary Butts seems to have recovered remarkably quickly, as in November 1913 she wrote 'Dionysiac', a love poem dedicated "to Hal" which opened:

I have my joy that tender is and rare,
And yours unspoken trembles on the air,
Yet there are few things we do not share.

One day we shall be Gods and know all things,
All the Earth's quiet, what our white star sings,
One with the nameless, dreaming splendid things.

One with the deathless sun and holy bees,
One with the great cats and the steadfast trees,
One with the patient splendour of the seas.

From what land do you come, O Wanderer,
That your bare presence makes my spirit stir?
(The day we met I wore a leopard's fur

Covering my breast and drawn across my back
—A holy fur), what God stood in our track
And sealed us both? a Dionysiac—

Child of the mysteries am I my Lord,
The cup wherein a strange God's wine is poured,
A winnowing-fan, a thyrsos, and a sword.

I am your Wife, who once initiate,
To Dionysos priestess consecrate
May know not fear or scorn or pride or hate.

This poem reveals once again the way in which Mary Butts saw herself through classical images. As to being Hal's wife, this is no poetic licence, since in a 1920 diary she noted that Hal had been her first male lover.

Being in love and writing poetry were far from her only activities. In October 1912 she began to study at the London School of Economics from which she graduated in June 1914 with a Social Science Certificate, the equivalent of the present-day Diploma in Social Work. She then began "working in the East End to get practical experience of social conditions as a sequel to her studies" on the Children's Care Committee.[55] Some time in 1914 Mary Butts met Eleanor Rogers, about whom nothing is known, except that she had dark hair and was a writer.

Then the First World War broke out.

PART TWO

The London Years

1916/1920

CHAPTER TWO

Facing Both Ways
1916

The greatest healer of all—the blessed sea
The land-stained traveller comes home alone.
Our earth gives bread, and you have only stone,
Yet from desire of bread you set us free.
—MB, 'Warbarrow Bay. Summer 1911'

I want the sea, the sea.
—MB, diary entry, 30.7.16.

IN AUGUST 1916 Mary Butts went with Eleanor to spend three weeks at Salterns with her mother, her step-father and her younger brother, Tony, on holiday from Eton. She had not been there for a year and found Salterns "very brilliant with silver and flowers and all lovely things —my room adorned". The day after her arrival a diary entry hints at the strained relationship she had with her family: "It has done no harm, this year's absence. It is now possible to look at this place, once my home, with detachment. I don't want to reform them any more. It is possible to shrug one's shoulders and accept, and believe in the good one finds, and know it partial at best, and love all one can. J[ohn Rodker] has drawn some of the power to do this out of me, I think that it was probably there before, but E[leanor] always discouraged it, and he doesn't. *Caritas—caritas, sed perfect caritas.*" Stella Bowen's blithe remark that Mary Butts "was at loggerheads with her mother, who was always opening bazaars and never (she alleged) gave straight answers to awkward questions" does not sound that serious.[1] In fact this moment of *caritas* or love was one of the very few which Mary Butts felt towards her family and especially her mother for the next twenty-one years.

The stay at Salterns had its glorious moments. Mary Butts spent most days reading, writing a new story, corresponding with John Rodker, swimming and going for walks either with Eleanor and Tony or, more often, alone: "Walk in the wind on Salterns pier," she wrote on the 13 August, revelling in the fact that she "bathed in the sea which came in shouting". This was wonderfully refreshing after the dry London streets, and especially for Mary Butts, who had addressed the sea five years earlier in 'Warbarrow Bay':

> You are our first and our most perfect lover,
> Yours is the clear, yours the unfailing singing—
> Water on clashing rocks for ever ringing.
> Yours the high song of gull, and tern, and plover.

In August 1916 she wrote exultantly: "It would not be possible to live long anywhere without the power to be alone. In solitude everything clarifies, and in doing so becomes inessential again. It is like walking down under the sea, erect, one's chin lifted, one's hands pressed to one's sides." In contrast, Mary Butts felt "very seedy" on the 17th, partly as a result of over-smoking[2] and partly because of her "idiotic [decision] to go bathing with a chill". She also mentions having a painful knee. Throughout her life she suffered from a recurrent "affection of the kneecap, probably hereditary" which began when she was a small child but "whose treatment in those days was very little understood, nor indeed did my family realise how serious it was".[3] Several later photographs show her walking with a stick. Despite this disability, she walked enormous distances whenever possible and the summer of 1916 was no exception. With Eleanor and Tony, she roamed around south Dorset, going to Purbeck and Littlesea, into Bournemouth for "records and cigarettes", and to Tucton. She tried to write "a sketch" about the latter on her return to London, but was dissatisfied with the results. A walk along the coast on the 14 August prompted the following entry:

> Explored round the docks, crossed over the tollbridge with E to Hamworthy. There we found a railway yard LSWR a sloping desolation of trucks and sleepers. We went up and found on the other side a beach with the sea breaking, and all the harbour up to Arne and Ower luminous-grey in the flying sun and wind. We saw Corfe Castle[4] sitting like a black crown on a bright hill.

Initially her relationship with Eleanor improved at Salterns: "Things are better between us...on this night we recreated our time of last August. I shall not forget the assent she gave." There were the odd occasions when E's "bitterness" came to the fore, but when Mary Butts saw her off on the 21st, she commented "all's well". Such contentment did not last, however.

At Salterns Mary Butts was "very bored with too much company" which included visits to her aunts, with whom she had little patience. Even her Aunt Ada was criticised: "Difficult to talk to her. Her fanaticism grows with age. She is now a typical specimen of the ancient virgin, clamorous for blood. One feels that she is ever conscious that the Army is out to protect her chastity. One is left wondering what she would take if they didn't..." Whatever her private feelings at this stage, in later years Mary Butts would strive to impress her aunt with her learning and literary successes. In August 1916, however, she felt too frustrated to be charitable. "I've not opened a book, or written a word or done half an hour's clear thinking for days. I hate the whole damned crowd of them," she raged, as the holiday came to an end and the earlier truce with Mary Colville-Hyde broke down. Her bitterness was also sometimes directed at Tony, because she felt that "in any trouble he'll be mother's man".

Mary Butts's relationship with her brother was always intense and never easy. A friend from her later years described Tony as "her adored brother in younger days".[5] This was no exaggeration. In 1916, in moment of reflection, she wrote about her fifteen-year-old brother: "Tony nearer again, more intimate— Now I can send him paper clips and cash with meticulous care, where before I sent him fire and ecstacies. He very sensibly likes that best." As an adolescent, Tony was extremely impressionable and Stella Bowen gives an account of how his sister tried to influence him. This very vivid description illustrates Mary Butts's love of what she would call a "lark":

> She loved a good fight, and spread considerable desolation in her home by wrestling with her mother for the possession of her young brother Tony, then at Eton. As part of Tony's education, Mary decided one fourth of June [1918] to take a party to visit him composed of people calculated to explode the stuffy, upper-class conventions under which the boy was supposed to be languishing. The party consisted of a Hindu student called Chanda, a young Jewish poet and pacifist called John Rodker, a Greek male ballet-dancer of great beauty called Jean Varda, a lovely friend of mine called Phyllis [Reid], and myself. I was wearing a pair of exquisite spike-heeled shoes which someone had given me and which pinched horribly, so we all went on to the greensward beside the river so that I could take them off, and we danced on the grass, for the edification of the decorous groups who were strolling about with their top-hatted offsprings. Then our poet [John Rodker] took us all to call on Aldous Huxley, who at that time was housemaster, and he simply hated us. But since we liked him, we stayed quite a long time. After tea in Tony's rooms,[6] we felt that we had done Eton all the good in the world. I must say that young Tony bore it all very well.[7]

After Mary Butts had died and his own health was failing, Tony wrote to the painter, Cedric Morris, who had known them both: "My dear, something's changed inside me: I no longer feel much doubt that one will see people again, tho' I'm not over-keen on bumping into the possessive Mary—...for I'm at least sure of one thing; and that is that if one's Ego, one's personality, survives death, that it remains the one we lived with.... Mary and I will still be the same creatures alas. Still, if we meet, she shall have got [the] message!"[8]

What made this sibling-relationship so problematic was the suspicion that Tony was the son not of Captain Butts but of Mary Butts's stepfather, Freddie Colville-Hyde. This suspicion was never openly acknowledged by their mother, nor by Captain Butts who recognised Tony as his son. He never, however, recorded Tony's birth in the family Bible, as he had done with his three other children. Whilst no proof exists, this may well have been the subject of Mary Butts's argument with her mother in 1910, since Ada concluded her placatory letter to her niece: "I cannot think that what you said about Tony was more than a momentary impulse in the heat of the moment when a very, very evil spirit had for an instant possession of your heart."[9] Tony would have been only nine when this argument took place and it is difficult to imagine what he could have done which would be so terrible. His sister, by contrast, would have been nineteen and well aware of the significance of these rumours. In terms of their inheritance, this fact had considerable repercussions, particularly with regard to Salterns which Mary Butts loved with such passion. Whatever the truth of the matter, her first published[10] novel revolved around a younger brother inheriting a property very like Salterns despite his illegitimacy.

On the 17 August Mary Butts wrote in her diary:

> E and I discussed the new epic—to be written with French brevity. Arnold Bennet's pitch too drab to sustain its occasional ecstacy.
> Part I Dad—down to T[ony]'s birth.
> Part II T.T. [Tiger Tiger]—down to today.
> Part III practically the unlived future.
> E will write it I hope.

This was, in fact, the first reference to Mary Butts's novel, *Ashe of Rings*. Two months later she considered writing "a study in growing madness of a tortured world. The war in another aspect—no day is wasted in which comes such an idea." The very next morning on her way down to visit John Rodker, she "thought out novel in train. To begin writing at once, or wait and let it simmer?" The first version of *Ashe of Rings* was written between 1916 and 1919. The initial five chapters were published in *The Little Review* in 1921,[11] but it would be published in book form only in 1925. Looking back in 1933 she wrote to a friend: "I couldn't write anything so passionate, or so ragged now. I was very young—full of prophetic as well as retrospective fury about my mother."[12]

On the 26 August 1916 Mary Butts remarked on "Mary Colville-Hyde's curious fit of hysteria, culminating in her old jealousy. Tony can take care of himself, we've had several straight talks—not sorry to be going. An idle useless day largely spent in circumventing M C-H and playing round with Tony." She "avoided church" on her last day and was delighted when she was "free again" and in London on the 28th. Even Eleanor was "adorable" and she settled back into her life of reading, working and seeing John Rodker at weekends. And, inevitably, clashing with Eleanor. Mary Butts knew that Eleanor's raving and cursing were "a kind of madness—because, because [sic] all the time she was crying 'love me' inarticulately", but this was little consolation for the strain. She visited John Rodker in Surrey on the 1 September and whilst there read the novel he had been working on.[13] She found it "erotic, nebulous, in parts a work of genius. Full of clichés with lapses into flamboyancy and bombast and then irresistable." Even as she enjoyed herself—"We went over to the T[revelyan]s. Good"—Mary Butts could not stop feeling guilty about Eleanor, who "is alone in London, still ha[s] the Curse and... racked with pains. I'm not [t]here to tend her. The End is bound to *come* soon."

But the end was not yet in sight. The days passed with Mary Butts trapped between her two lovers. On the 5 September she noted: "J came. Nothing can spoil what we have between us." Yet when she went home, Eleanor "was there, bitter-sweet. Ended in each other's arms." Mary Butts was caught in a deadlock which threatened to "shatter my heart and I shall fall down in the wet path annihilated, and...crawl into the sand". She had begun to read Dostoevsky and Tolstoy and it showed in her style. By the end of September she was "very tired with office work. Sick to death in fact." Nothing had changed, the war continued to rage and all she had managed to do was not to bite her nails for 4 or 5 days...

For the next six weeks she continued to work for the NCCL and attend tribunals. On the 31 October she was impressed by a speech given by the writer and pacifist Goldsworthy Lowes Dickinson, who made the "meeting good for the perfection of [his] form, even apart from its content."[14] Her relationship with John Rodker deepened, whilst Eleanor continued her cycle of tenderness and hysteria. As Mary Butts commented: "Something separates us—not infinite space, but an immensely long wall hung with felt." Yet when her story, 'Making of a CO', was rejected on the 11 October, Eleanor was "adorable. 'Think how often it'll happen again,' she said and cheered me. Talked about the war, first time in months. Our disagreements fierce as ever. Still, Peace Egg." Despite her disappointment, Mary Butts continued to write poems, began a story called 'Nostalgie' and sketched out her novel. She also read widely. In her childhood she was allowed to "make her own taste" from the huge library belonging to her father. In London during the war, she continued this eclectic practice, moving between Madge Mears' *Sheltered Sex* (1916) and Tolstoy's *23 Tales* (1919), George Gissing's *By the Ionian Sea* (1901) and Sir Thomas Browne's *Religio Medici* (1642), Dostoevsky's *The Brothers Karamazov* (1880) and E.M. Forster's 'The Celestial Omnibus' (1911). On the 19 October she "sealed Blast's fate with half-a-crown". Blast was a stray cat which she and Eleanor had found in the autumn of 1915, when Mary Butts had written to her aunt that the "reasons [for the name] are many and painful... She is a better kitten now."[15] She went to see an exhibition of C.R.W. Nevinson's paintings on the 10 October which she enjoyed, and at the end of the month attended an (unnamed) play by Bernard Shaw which was "good in bits". Never adept at saving money, she made a gesture towards it on the 20 October: "Economy! don't leave a line between entries." This fine resolve was rather undermined by the following sentence which announced: "Bought 2 pairs [of] black shiny stockings, one pair grey, fine silk, one white with black stripes, one thick white wool with checks, one emerald green. Very hard up." But Mary Butts's money was not just going on tasteful clothes. On the 20 October she also "paid for Joan" (Rodker's daughter).

Visiting John Rodker in Dorking that weekend, she remarked the:

> Difference between J's mind and mine.
> He sees a girl standing on say—a curb and notices the 'impossible brilliance' of lipsalve and writes a poem. I'd want to know where she'd come from, and what she thought about.
> So I'm likely to be the poorer artist, unless I can walk through the mirror of understanding and out into the garden beyond.

This entry was only one of many Mary Butts made about the craft of writing. She thought about it continually: "At the office talked about the 4th dimension. Mr F. [unknown] interesting. He holds that all our consciousnesses are piercing into this new dimension. As a matter of fact mine is. We went out and there was a high moon and light fast-travelling clouds. On the pavement off the Fulham Rd waiting for a 31 Bus I nearly came through." Dostoevsky's work was beginning seriously to influence her thinking by this point. She noted on the 10 November: "I can watch E and myself, and sneer and sneer, and indulge envy, hatred, malice, and all uncharitableness. New sensations these, quite in the Russian mode." Nor did she limit her interest to the literature itself:

> *Middleton Murry on Dostoievsky*[16]
>
> Can it be like this. If his work is to be compared to a 'power in the fourth dimension functioning in the third'. ...What is Dostoievsky's question?
> That 'truth, and goodness, and beauty' are only a tiny fragment of reality. They are continually thrust aside—he chose Christ but had more than a belief that Christ was 'outside the truth'.

> These powers, inimical to man's life, are they absolutely evil? Not of necessity, there may be no such thing. But, whether of their own volition or no, they will destroy man. But not if we are philosophers. There are brains which would never reel... Was Dostoievsky merely the reaction from the commonplace postivist reformer, cursed obvious optimists?

Clearly Mary Butts was becoming very interested in the occult at this time. When working on the two main female characters in *Ashe of Rings*, she described them as: "*Vana* living (unconscious or not?) in a further dimension" and "*Judy* straining *unconsciously* and relapsing into sheer materialism." "Get some occult books," was the reminder on the opposite page. Many writers of her generation became interested in the occult; Mary Butts undertook a lifelong study which was both theoretical and practical.

Perhaps her life would have continued along these lines until the end of the war, had it not been for the fact that, on the 15 November, as she and Eleanor "crossed the square in the moonlight, John Rodker ran down the dark steps and out of the shadow, across the road to meet us.... It was amazingly difficult. [Eleanor] made a few efforts, raved, collapsed, went out of the house. I did not let him stay. That I owed her, but my self-respect will never recover from it. One does not easily tolerate a world where one must drive the desolate from one's door."

* * * * *

> There were a great many Military Police at Paddington, but they did not look at me.... My first action was to go into the heart of town;... I told myself that I had been forced to desert because they would not court-martial me. I believe that at that time the C.O.'s fate was still in the balance.... I went off to my sweetheart, and the house was dark, but I waited on the step and by and by she came up with the girl she lived with, and was astonished to see me and terrified I might want to hide with her, so I went away, and I had no money and I walked along the Embankment and it was cold, and this time I was horribly vulnerable but no one stopped or questioned me, and I was longing for her and the safety of being near her all that long night. I had some coffee at a stall though I dared not stay long, but fortunately the nights were short...and later in the day I met her again, and I said the night had been a good one, and she was glad to have me back.... I don't remember if I was bothered about money or not, but I must have been, for odd friends lent or gave me money,...but chiefly it came from Muriel.[17]

WHILE THIS EXTRACT sounds extraordinarily like Mary Butts's diary entry of the 15 November, it was in fact written by John Rodker in his novel, *Memoirs of Other Fronts*. Published anonymously in 1932, it was clearly inspired by his own experiences as a CO and by his relationship with Mary Butts, the Muriel of the novel.

From the day after his arrival in London, Mary Butts helped John Rodker, who was taking an enormous risk returning to London as a deserter. Stella Bowen later wrote: "I have always thought...that if one were ill, destitute, a refugee, or in any really spectacular mess, Mary's doorstep would be the right doorstep on which to be found in a fainting condition. She would receive you and your woes with open arms, without question and without caution. No nonsense about deciding whether you were a deserving case! Mary would thrive on the drama of the situation and you would thrive on her championship."[18] And so it was. Eleanor's "complete lack of nervous courage" and the fact that she could not "rise to the situation" irked and disappointed Mary Butts. She knew that Eleanor was "insanely jealous of J" and his presence in London meant that she was "instantly deposed from the centre of the picture". In fact, John Rodker's presence forced Mary Butts to choose between him and Eleanor. Notwithstanding regrets and remorse, she chose John Rodker.

Eleanor did not make it easy. The 19 November was a "desperate day. The bitterness within matched the icy sleet across the square" when Mary Butts offered Eleanor the "studio"[19] only to be met with "more hysterics" and the threat to turn John Rodker in. Mary Butts tried to carry on—there was still the "office, hard work... Committee, then home again in dread and weariness." She continued to see Stella, Phyllis, Margaret Postgate and other friends and read Wilma Meikle's *Towards a Sane Feminism* (1916), remarking that "such a book renews one's courage more than wine." John Rodker's nearby presence brought not only comfort but intellectual stimulation as they both worked on their novels. He also introduced her to other artists, including Nevinson and the Wadsworths. On the 23 November after dinner with friends Mary Butts was exultant: "I believe that in some sort of way I am arriving. I was certainly the attraction that night... It was good, keen minds and open, free discussion, and a sense, on my part, of power. Life flowered for me, delicately like a strong garden flower in spring, my skin is marvellously better, my mind was tranquil, ardent, and very clear. I pleased—I may even have convinced." Despite this her mood was often gloomy. Her youthful anguish is visible in her exclamation the following day: "J is quite right. 'You should make good poems out of all E has done to you.' I shall—but not out of the joy I had [with] her—or that only as an auxiliary—but out of the bitter grief and wrong—Oh Life!"

Mary Butts's relationship with John Rodker was not always straightforward. On the 27th she noted: "News about the baby [Joan]—sick fear

— reunion, forced unnatural between J and S [Sonia Cohen, Joan's mother]". Given this and her difficulties with Eleanor, Mary Butts decided at the end of November: "I won't get so deeply committed with J, marriage or no. My relations with him are not so devastating— that makes them jolly. Jolly is what they are, quickening, stimulating— But I don't believe that my mate is born, or the mates for women like me." Such self-assurance was not always present, however:

> There are times when I am wholly confident in the destiny of Mary Butts.
> There are others when I find that I am
> Superficial
> Cowardly
> Facing-both-Ways
> Receptive and quick to see relations, but not Creative.

At this time Mary Butts read a book of poems[20] by her friend, Anna Wickham, as well as Havelock Ellis's 'Ars Amatoria',[21] about which she commented: "Gods! What fine teaching for husbands and wives." She also noted that it was "useful—if expensive—to know so well that one can buy one's peace." For on that day in early December 1916 she had taken Eleanor to the West End and bought her the cigarette-holder. The following day she went "to J and the oldest of consolations. Amber beads in the firelight and my hair."

CHAPTER THREE

The Usual Hell
1917

Not much new year for me. Very seedy, Dakers [shop] the only comfort. Jewelled combs and the violet wrap. 'Fig leaves' on the slips. Sales — balm.

—MB, diary entry, 1.1.17

Why should I go on hoping that E will suddenly see, understand it all and change. On no grounds, rational or intuitive whatever.

—MB, diary entry, 7.1.17

AFTER THE 6 DECEMBER Mary Butts made no further entries as "the love of keeping this diary died". By the 3 January 1917 she "wanted to recall things again, at least events" and looked back over the last weeks of 1916. There had been fun with Tony at Eton as well as parties in London. There had even been peace with Eleanor who had been off on her "own adventures — recreating her, stirring us all". Professionally, there had been the exciting news around the 13 December that her story 'Agnes Helen' had been accepted.[22] Unfortunately, this joy had been offset by Mary Colville-Hyde's "loss of the Chancery savings". When Mary Butts went down to Salterns (perhaps for Christmas) it was "no good" and she returned to London to see in the new year.

When the diary reopened Eleanor was once again making "the usual hell". Mary Butts was getting on well with John Rodker, but not seeing him every day. When he did not come on the 3rd and 4th, she reassured herself by remembering: "I've worried too often to do so now." Anyway, she had another visitor, the CO with whom she had corresponded the previous year: "Jack White turned up, and all went well. Soaked in *The Possessed* [by Dostoevsky]".[23] Long conversations with Jack White prompted her to assert in her diary: "I don't believe our life differs so much from that depicted as Russian. Our angle of approach is different, but the events and temperamental agonies are much the same. All these days could be written in the Russian mode." She poured all these feelings into *Ashe of Rings*. Not surprisingly one reviewer alluded to the Russian connection by describing it as "Dostoevski served with a little milk".[24]

Mary Butts kept her diary only sporadically during the first quarter of 1917. Despite minor ailments (she suffered from knee pain and neuritis in her elbow), she continued to work ("Office—full of cheer"), write and see her friends. The painter Nina Hamnett, "pure Greek, slim as an 'ephete'" made her first appearance in Mary Butts's entry of the 19 January. Born in the same year, the two women became close friends and Mary Butts later wrote in her diary: "Nina in a ring of light. There is the perfect way to love. I do not want to see her—least of all by myself. I know her 'sins, negligence and ignorances', but I have no pleasure like the quick remembrance that she is alive or the waiting for her to come into the same room" (14.1.19). For her part, Nina Hamnett painted Mary Butts's portrait.[25] On the evening of the 19 January Mary Butts went out for a walk: "The snow was falling. Evening on streets its whiteness seemed to make radiant.... Suddenly the warm rooms became insignificant, the silent dazzling world significant.... I saw that the falling snow was millions of white silent bees. Bees are the soul. I walked in pure spirit." She would incorporate and expand on this experience in *Ashe of Rings*:

> The roads were silent, deep in snow... Round a corner, the wind stood still and he met the snow.... The flakes whirled, and in each lamp's path he could see them, myriads falling, fluttering, rising, spinning, folding him. He moved slowly. They fluttered on his forehead and cigarette-stained hands. They mounted on his shoulders, and crystallised his hair. They cooled his face, falling on his eyelids, brushing his lips. He tasted them, and still they flew. Then they appeared to him as bees, white bees, comforters, souls.[26]

By the 17 March Mary Butts could bear the strain of living with Eleanor no longer. If Eleanor did not leave, she would. "It is done now. We move today week. I can hardly realise my joy. I'm afraid that I shall not be able to rise to the height of my liberty and my solitude. Has E spoiled me? Have I wasted these years? Now it seems that I may have wasted the first in its comparative happiness, but not this last with its hell of disappointments and frustrations. When John came, he made all things new, and the white magic prevails."

1 Glenilla Studios, NW3, a half-hour walk from the flat in which she had lived with Eleanor, would be Mary Butts's home for the next two years.

* * * * *

MARY BUTTS celebrated the beginning of her "Vita Nuova" on the 1 April by starting a new short story, 'Speed the Plough'. What she wanted was "J, and solitude and infinite time to play with my place. I drink in solitude like rain. This place is cold as hell, and without is the spring snow, but I don't care."

Sadly, this new-found joy was brief. Four days later she moaned: "There has now passed eighteen hours since I heard of J's arrest. 12 hours for the passion, and now— Am I reconciled? No—in the ghastly half-state when one prays to suffer and cannot. I have done everything I can." As she waited for news, she turned to her books. More than anything else she longed for Harrison's "*Prolegomena* again, and *Themis*. One's lovers die and there remain certain immortal words. Perhaps it is only through pain that natures like mine live most keenly. In happiness I am shy, sceptical, acquiescent.... I want all the Greek things again." Although her knee was "very bad", she did what she could for John Rodker. On the 11th she "moved his things" and discussed matters with Sonia Cohen. And waited. She read Arthur Symons's *London Nights* (1895), but these poems of "the nineties [with] their sterile weakness" did not impress her. Later, she admitted that anxiety had affected her critical faculties and wrote opposite this entry: "Bad judgement, some of the poems are exquisite."

She was staying in Salterns on the 25 April when she heard the "bad news":

> Ghosts of J in infinite discomfort aching, unsolaced, unfed. Why don't I lie on the floor tonight? Partly because I hate discomfort, partly because I hate sentiment and futility. Partly because I recognise in the impulse a heritage from M C-H. It is conventionally pretty, but since my mind is wretched why make my body sore? Besides I loath cold and discomfort. Yet my easy bed shames me. It is all a matter of relative satisfactions. Salterns maddens me now. Outside it J and I and all the youth of the world turn in agony. Here they strut and fume, and bicker and prop up their party cries and sentimentalities over the starkest realities. They know nothing of our passion and would not be sorry for it. In the long run, it is our day, not theirs.
> I can't reach J. I can only smoulder over what I know to be happening, and comfort myself with fantastic imaginations. I should be mad if I thought much. Hatred of E revives. Her letter this morning gave the note. I want to get back. I'm nearer him in Town than here.
> He is weak, every hour he grows weaker, and is in pain. I can do nothing. My body is weighted with lead. This is the house of death. Tony is good to me.

Prisons in war-time England, with their rule of silence and inhumane conditions, had changed little since the 19th century. In *Memoirs of Other Fronts* John Rodker's CO, imprisoned in London, goes on hunger strike to prove himself unfit for active service: "And to make the time go I smoked a lot and shut myself closely up, clenched myself upon myself, and lived in that room as from a distance.... My brain was horribly clean and brought Muriel intensely near; the skin of my face was literally stuck to my skull, my eyes had gone very deep in the dark pits they had made for themselves and any effort made my heart thump like a wild thing. My finger-nails at their bases got crinkled and flecked with white. So passed eleven days, thus twelve without food...and next day they had me down for the doctor." He is taken to the "mental ward" of Devonport Military Hospital where "the orderlies...understood everything...and told me I was sure now of my 'ticket'...and the doctor...weighed me and asked a lot of questions, and I sat on the scales and said my piece and got very hot and confused about it, and told them too much about my girl and they asked why I had been sent to the Mental Ward and I said because I refused to eat and they thought it was a good reason, and said: 'Well, it's clear you're no good to anyone,'[27] or so I thought they said, and I went back to the ward and this time I was sure they would let me go... But I forgot I was still a deserter."[28]

In London Mary Butts waited to hear and felt useless: "I'm torn, with every impulse dragging me to my work, stale to the Council—What have I done? Very little. Struggled with the horror of E and my own mind—all I'm fit for. The rest pis aller, CC, NCCL and the rest. There still remains the novel, poems, my craft. I'd stand by that at the last and defy every voice of the pack. Then J—I'm making him—but I haven't filled a cartridge, or nursed a sick man—I'd have liked that, or sped a plough, or fed a pig, or [filled] a man's seat in an office. I've economised, had to—suffered some. Thought...and I'm still muddled. With E I've failed." On the 7 May, whilst she had still heard "nothing from J" and suffered from "much bitterness, a restless mind and craving body", she consoled herself with the thought of her freedom from Eleanor, and her flat: "I think here that I have recaptured something of the 'Vie Athénienne'...I can look at my books and my flowers, my bare walls, and painted jars, and lovely clothes and heaped cushions and bare feet, my utter liberty and contrast it with my memories of Lesbos and be glad."

After this, no entries for four months until the 18 September.

* * * * *

IN THE ABSENCE of correspondence, diary entries or other evidence, this quarter can only be surmised, very generally, from the 'data' incorporated into *Memoirs of Other Fronts*, in the section entitled 'A C.O.'s WAR: 1914-1925':

> And after two months [June/July 1917] I was allowed to write a letter. I wrote it very small on a double sheet and it took a long time,

...and then there was a letter from her and a photograph and her shoulders were bare and moved me very much,...she told me she loved me too and that when I came out we would do all the walking, seeing things, we had talked about,...and she said she was coming to see me and one day I went down, and she was on the other side of the wire grill and there were tears in her eyes, and she tried to put a finger through for me to kiss but couldn't,...somehow we were just looking at each other with nothing to say and I couldn't bear it...and then we were talking in bits and haltingly and somehow [the twenty minutes were]...up and we had said nothing to each other, fixed nothing and I went back to my cell and it was dreadful...and next day I was thinking six weeks more, and there will be another visit...[29]

At some point during the summer, the CO is taken before "the Salisbury Committee with Lord Salisbury presiding, very serious round a table...and they asking me what I had against war, and I said it was a futile mess and solved nothing and they agreed with each other I had a conscience and asked me would I take work of National Importance and I said yes and weeks later...a van took a number of us to the station... The train passed through Mutley drawing into Plymouth.... At Plymouth we changed."[30] When the CO reached his unnamed destination, he was told that he would have to report "'with the Tor Royal Party, as from tomorrow, December 4th'...[where he] was given a card stating that [he] was on work of National Importance and therefore exempt from military service."[31]

In 1922 the Quaker John W. Graham published an study entitled *Conscription and Conscience: A History 1916-1919*, in which he described the experiences of COs during these years, and provided a large number of contemporary testimonies and articles. In the chapter on 'The Home Office Scheme' (which managed the work of National Importance undertaken by COs), sections 6 and 7 are devoted to the Work Centre at Princetown on Dartmoor which had been converted in March 1917 from a "large convict prison". 'Princetown's Pampered Pets', 'Coddled Conscience Men', 'The CO's Cosy Club' were the titles of articles published by the Harmsworth press, aimed at presenting the life of the COs at the Centre as idle and self-indulgent. According to accounts adduced by Graham, the conditions there were in fact grim: "The complete uselessness of the work set to these men...causing utter waste of their energies, was a cause of constant irritation to men of character and spirit."[32] He reprinted extracts from a letter published by *The Manchester Guardian* during the war by Lydia S. Smith in which she attacked the inhumane conditions at the camp:

The agricultural work is penal in character, that is to say, it is organized on exactly the same lines as for convicts, when, labour being only too plentiful, the main object was to make work, the harder and more physically tiring the better.... The crushing of oats is performed with antiquated machinery of the treadmill type arranged for hands instead of feet.... The spades, barrows, etc., are all prodigiously heavy, with a view to tiring the users, and all the appliances and methods are of the most antiquated nature...the food is poorer and the hours of labour longer than under the old regime when convicts filled the prison...[33]

Mary Butts visited John Rodker in Dartmoor, not in December but mid-November. While there she did not write directly about him. Her heightened reaction to the landscape seems, however, an oblique description of his physical and mental state: "On Hessany Tor. I had never seen such places before. They rose out of the moor, the skeleton of the earth where the flesh had peeled off, evil shapes, like words of power. 'Widdershins' perhaps like the spiritual boils and cancers which afflict not only Dostoievsky's people but us all. But what we conceal, lie over, gild, suppress, here nature gives the main significance. The tors are the flowers of Dartmoor."

By the time she visited John Rodker, she had been keeping her diary for almost two months. It reveals that she had been reading Yeats's poetry and working hard at *Ashe of Rings* whilst the war raged outside her flat:

> October 1st
> Last night's raid. The Hampstead gun barking overhead, blood pale flashes like summer lightning. The place shook, there was a lull. I heard in a house across the back yard 'A Broken Doll'[34] played faintly, in bad time, but persistent. Why do I stay here instead of in that friendly Tube? Intellectual superiority and a desire to annoy Eleanor...? No.... I feel as though I were obliged to 'get above' my fear. I can only do that by daring it to do its worst, hugging it close to me, letting it glare me in the face. I slept profoundly once it was over, and am curiously weak today.
> Bodies can't prevail over that which is in the sky every evening between eight and ten. It seems that mind must or spirit. If we are of the Sixth race we believe that we are pure spirit and unconquerable. The logical sequence to this is that one does not hide down Tubes.

Whilst Mary Butts stood her ground in London on principle, she longed "for the country so. The sun and the moon are making the earth a miracle." Yet she was "afraid to go alone" and so did not leave the capital.

Most of the October entries which do not refer to the novel are taken up with a discussion she was having about "consciousness" with her friends, especially Edwin G, whom she could talk to with "more exaltation and detachment". It is uncertain who Edwin G. was; Mary Butts only described him as "a great man—or perhaps a great Titan fettered in his sick body". For Edwin G., consciousness came from and resided in the intellect. According to Mary Butts it resulted from

> Τονοσ—tension—life, love, desire, vitality. It is like a thin cord, a nerve, permeating every film of our being. It becomes taut and thrills, and we live. The stimulus continually short-circuits. There are, as it were, several stages through which it must pass in order to produce a complete re-action. It must act through our bodies, it must be an intellectual thing, it must become an emotional thing....
> Here lies possibly a real difference between masculine and feminine psychology. Men may be more likely to obtain complete isolated, especially intellectual reactions than women who are 'more of a piece'. Hence the breakdowns in masculine philosophy with all its profundity. They have not worked out their metaphysical speculations in their bodies, above all their love affairs.

On the 26 October she considered "EG's way and mine: Contrasted broadly his outlook is rationalistic and pessimistic, mine mystic and in some way an optimism. We argue together because our 'pace' is the same, but his tension acts through a broken and indifferent instrument, and for my part, my health makes optimism possible." What lay at the heart of her philosophy was Sophrosynê, a "yard-stick" which she used throughout her life and mentioned repeatedly in her writing. When "Edwin G. accuses me of hedonism because I accept everything as it approaches me, and if I must choose, choose where there is least renunciation for any part of nature," her response was to:

> appeal to two things, one a wholly non-rational vision, and the other to an empiric yard-stick whose signficance would hardly be admitted—not by Edwin G.. In his *Rise of the Greek Epic* Gilbert Murray[35] approaches what I mean....
> "The East took its asceticism in orgies as it were, in horrors of self-mutilation, bodily and mental, which are as repellent in their way as the corresponding tempests of rage or sensuality. Greek asceticism, though sometimes mystical, was never insane. It was nearly always related to some reasonable end and sought the strengthening of body and mind, not their mortification."
> Herein is an antithesis, not mine, certainly not EG's but it leads on to the explanation of my yard-stick for all conduct, that elusive quality the Greeks called Sôphrosynê. "It is something like Temperance, Gentleness, Mercy, sometimes Innocence, never mere Caution, or tempering of dominant emotion by gentler thought."
> To this I would add—good form, fine breeding, humour, a sense of shapeliness—these guide choice. In all, this virtue is σοφον—'with saving thoughts' contrasted to ολοφρον—'with destroying thoughts'.

On the 3 November Mary Butts met Ezra Pound for the first time. She was by no means over-awed: "At last my most intimate convictions have been focused and justified, neither scholar, nor poet, nor philosopher, but a most kindly romantic, a competent sometimes witty critic."[36] They would become close friends, and as he did for many other young writers, Pound recommended and praised her work whenever the opportunity arose.[37] After Mary Butts had died and her work was for the most part forgotten, Pound continued to urge people to read and publish her books.[38]

By the 19 November when she may well have been staying in Dartmoor visiting John Rodker,[39] Mary Butts agonised over another "triangle" of emotions in which she was trapped: "Do I regret what I have done? No, but I wish I could tell J now, at once. Either I should have told him all immediately—or nothing. As it is, I pave the way. Why have I not told him? It would be too much, and I have committed myself by my silence, but equally because words are impossible. The affair is inchoate still, uncrystallised. I *cannot* surmise the future. As a story it would not shape —it would sound like a repeated humiliation. It may be that yet." Mary Butts did not name her "lover", but it may have been Edwin G, since in late October she had written: "I am so irresistably drawn to him that I think if he would trust me, I could save him." In late November she wrote: "With Edwin a man, with John a woman, subject to him, 'ware of him, subtle, passively sensual. He baffles me, intrigues, fascinates me. I am afraid lest he should warp my freedom. Often we do not focus—but there are times. I am on my mettle, no I am really afraid.... I shall always need Edwin to reassert my virility." It is unclear whether the affair was ever a physical one. At all events, Mary Butts was prompted at that time to write 'Lettres Imaginaires', an epistolary story, featuring "a woman in love, half gratified, then violently turned down, without explanation. Humiliation, bewilderment, horror, gradual reassertion of her will, until the adventure thus deflected, and the consummation, physical and spiritual not achieved, are achieved by herself in a delicate profound detachment. In love one can sometimes have the adventure by oneself." The story was published two years later in two instalments in *The Little Review*.[40]

Between late November 1917 and mid-May 1918, Mary Butts's diary entries are sparse. The few which were made show that she had been rereading Shelley and Wordsworth as well as Norman Douglas's *South Wind* (1917) and Freud. She was also spending time with the writers Ford Madox Hueffer (he would change his name to Ford Madox Ford in 1919) and Violet Hunt, Ford's partner at that time. Mary Butts visited them at Selsey, where they spoke of love: "In love the worst crime is to outrage the lover's sense of beauty. A 'sentimentality'? (V.H. Selsey)." To which Mary Butts added her own condition: "let one another alone, and let one another alone, and go on letting one another alone." They also discussed the craft of writing. Their concerns were those of most Modernists: "Not to describe a great occasion in the grand manner, but to make the crossing of a street equally significant (FMH—Selsey)." This was a characteristic Ford Madox Ford had already incorporated into his 1915 masterpiece, *The Good Soldier*. After one of her discussions with Ford, Mary Butts commented: "Up to now we have had writers who have been marvellously close, with complete realism of detail. What we want is a new way of seeing—a complete new attitude of approach. In fact a new imagination. The analysis has been made, now for a new synthesis. Joyce, Eliot, Lewis—?" As well as her discussions, she noted in February 1918 that she had completed another short story, 'Madonna of the Magnificat' (in fact she revised it in 1921 and 1922).

CHAPTER FOUR

Ivan, Ivan

1918

We have known each other for years—he knows most people worth knowing in London. We 'pair' beautifully, he is very handsome. We are extraordinarily happy.

—MB, letter to Ada Briggs, 22.5.18

On the 17 May 1918, Mary Butts wrote to her Aunt Ada about something which she omitted to mention in her diary: "A letter to break to you the fact that I'm married. I did it quietly and said nothing at first, but now that Tony's blessing has been amply showered on us, feel that I can make it known.... We are very happy. I've just broken it to Mother!"[41]

In the fictional world of John Rodker's *Memoirs of Other Fronts* the CO had had enough of doing work of National Importance:

> On a dark mist-laden morning, in a high exposed field... I at last made my mind up.
>
> During the lunch interval I changed my clothes and walked to Tavistock.... Outside Waterloo the train was held up for two hours because of an air raid.... There were crowds of Military Police on the platform. They did not look at me.... The first maroons were beginning to go off, and I hurried, determined to get to Muriel, and I did... and she was surprised but very glad indeed to see me, very shy of each other we were, strangers after the long separation, but the guns got nearer, louder, and in the intervals the whirring of aeroplane propellers was very menacing, and following close on them an immense shuddering bang shook the house and there was silence, awful, and she fell trembling in my arms, and suddenly there was no more barrier between us.... And that night I stayed, but afterwards took a room out and when we met it was still fearfully, fearful of ourselves and of each other and of the world outside, because we were living in sin, everyone an enemy, possibly to part us; and then she was pregnant, and furious with me because of it and to comfort her we married, and it was extraordinary the difference it made knowing everyone was our ally, that we went to bed with the fullest approval of the Church and State... Thus for half a year, till the end of the war, in fact, I was a

> deserter, walking through the peaceful empty streets,...or in the country, and all the time I felt safe, safe.[42]

John Rodker was back in London in January 1918. They were married at the Hampstead Register Office on the 10 May. From then on they lived together in 1 Glenilla Studios. She consented to be called Mrs Rodker but kept "'Mary Butts' for professional and most other purposes."[43] Ada must have replied in shock, since five days later Mary Butts wrote again and, anxious to recover her aunt's approval, justified the secret wedding:

> Please please forgive me and understand. I know that you think me a brute (and possibly a lunatic) to get married first and tell people afterwards— But I loathe the conventional fuss on which my mother would have insisted, the questions, the want of privacy which would have attended... So we did it—in fact we did not intend to tell anyone until the end of the war. That wasn't possible when all hope of peace seemed to vanish, and one or two intimate friends found out. So we waited for Tony's visit to make it public and talked it over... I did not tell you until I had told [my mother]...because the offence given would have been indescribable.... John's politics and mine and hers are likely to form a barrier... For the rest you and he ought to love each other...[44]

"When all hope of peace seemed to vanish" is as close as Mary Butts gets to referring to the German offensive of March 1918, which for a time threatened to turn the war against Britain. Characteristically, she is more concerned with her personal life than the world events beyond its ken.

Already in August 1916, she had referred to John Rodker in her diary as "Ivan, Ivan". In line with the myth-making for which she would be best remembered, Mary Butts described John Rodker to her aunt, in her letter of the 17 May, as "Russian". In that of the 22 May, she expanded on or rather embroidered this 'fact': "John...is well born (his people are anything but pleased with him for marrying me!). Their money has largely disappeared in the Revolution, and they have been on the usual parent-and-revolutionary-son terms for some time. He's been invalided out of the Army, but since then his views have changed." Mary Butts's lie about John Rodker's true relationship with the Military can be justified in terms of a desire to save him from awkward questions. Her description of him as Russian is pure whimsy, part of a growing love of all things Russian. The son of Jewish immigrants, John Rodker's family did come from eastern Europe, although Poland seems to have been their origin, not Russia. Mary Butts may have spun this tale, rather than admit that he was Jewish, because she knew that her family would have wanted her to marry a Christian.

Noticeably absent from the letters is a rather more pressing truth; like the fictional Muriel, Mary Butts was indeed pregnant. When she resumed her diary in mid-May, it was, in fact, her major consideration. There is no mention of her being "furious with [John Rodker] because of it" (as *Memoirs Of Other Fronts* suggested), although she was finding pregnancy an unpleasant experience both physically and intellectually: "Tight across stomach, like leather belt continually drawn in—pressure continuous. Hunger and thirst—complete isolation.... I cannot afford sentiment, but to J...I have become automatically sainted. Not my beauty or wit or compassion mattered to [him] as my mechanical function as mother. It's a bitter joke." Both prospective parents seem to have been pleased. What Mary Butts was most concerned about was the "external terror and fury lest I'm condemned to infinite drudgery". Her mood was variable during May and she attended seances and visited a medium to consider her situation. Whit Sunday found her in an irritable state: "Phyllis, Stella, John, nostalgie—sickness, tight back-throat. Can't take things lightly. Thin summer frocks are six inches too long, uneven about the ankles. It gives them away. Bored. Envious of Phyllis. Forlorn, no success possible." As the days passed, so she felt

> more tired, tireder and tireder. Today culmination, sheer temper ending in intemperate kisses.... Sickness now, slight, and a dizzy touch, depression, a want of lightness and illumination. John adorable. Every day I'm more glad. Tight tummy better or less noticed. Nipples like two hard red roccoco door knobs. But I wanted to cry so much. Difficult to 'disassociate' from worries—mechanical exercise harder —less conviction following, less peace.... Better tonight.

By the 27 May Mary Butts noted an "appalling clairvoyance". Perhaps she was thinking of this when, towards the end of her life, after reading an essay by Aldous Huxley, she would dispute his disparagement of mysticism on the grounds that it was felt by pregnant women. "The answer is—'why on heaven and earth not?' At—given a mystical mother —the moment of a child's quickening?" (26.6.36)

* * * * *

> *Over. The lean solitary feeling has come back—no more drain of blood from my brain into my womb. All alone and wretchful. I could spring, not cower like a guarding hen. I cried because 'Michael was dead',*[45] *but now I'm thin and virginal, skin over a core of steel.*
> *Gentler.*
> *It must happen again, and soon. But I love this freedom. The crystal wall has closed again, my sheath dances with me.*

THUS WROTE Mary Butts on the 16 June 1918. The following day, now no longer pregnant (whether after a miscarriage or an abortion is unclear), she was left with "nothing to be written, only the ache to write".

On the 29 June, she felt the need to go to the country. Before leaving London for the summer, she wrote: "Out of this world we both need to leave there have appeared certain persons whose form is significant." These included the painters Nina Hamnett and Walter Sickert (both members of the London Group), as well as the Greek dancer Yanko [Jean] Varda, with whom Mary Butts and others had gone to visit Tony at Eton on the 4th. "All the rest are painted boards beside these," she commented. She was having trouble working because of the attractions of socialising: "The elation that follows a dissipation—one feels that one can work—get something out—finds one is fatigued quickly—and that the elation is so fine that one wants to talk and sing, or dance it away, not kennel it at a desk by a pen and ink." In early July she did begin 'Fantasia', a "sketch for development of greek 'nameless' personalities in modern mysticism". Like a great deal of her early work, it remains unpublished.

Perhaps because it would not immediately affect her, Mary Butts made no reference to the passing of the 'Representation of the People Act' in June. Franchise was extended to all women over thirty (Mary Butts was only 27). Yet she would still be able to vote before John Rodker in the 1922 General Election since a harsh term of that Act disqualified COs from franchise for a period of five years. Eleanor's wish that pacifists be penalised had been at least temporarily granted.

A few notes made in a separate notebook reveal that Mary Butts and John Rodker went to Maiden Bradley in Somerset on the 7 July. They stayed in the area for a week, visiting Wells, Glastonbury and Axminster. Mary Butts was delighted to be in the country: "Extreme energy — pleasure in the tiniest detail," she declared in the medieval city of Wells on the 8th, finding "the large wind, the full green hills, the square stone houses unreal. People live in slums and squares and move in buses and in and out of tube stations, not in this roaring sea of glass." It was not just the landscape which inspired her, but its ancient, mythical history of "Avalon and the Sanc Graal".

The Sanc Graal was to a be a potent influence on her work and imaginative life. As a child she had read Tennyson's *Idylls of the King* (1859-1885) and William Morris's *The Defence of Guinevere* (1858), poetry arising from a 19th Century revival of interest in the medieval legend of the Holy Grail. Through her father's friendship with Dante Gabriel Rossetti she was also familiar with painterly representations of the legend by the Pre-Raphaelites. This renewed fascination with the Arthurian legends was not confined to intellectual and artistic circles. In 1907 a newspaper article had described the purported "discovery" of the cup of the Holy Grail in a well in Glastonbury. In response to this article, the supernatural writer Arthur Machen wrote 'The Secret of the Sangraal' (1907) in which he gave an account of the legend:

> Logres, that is Britain, is supposed to be in the doleful condition of enchantment; physically and spiritually the land languishes, and the keeper of the Graal is sick of a mystic wound. All that is required is for the chosen knight of the adventure to come to the Graal Castle; and then the holy vessel is borne before him as he sits in the hall. He must then ask what the Graal is and whom it serves; whereupon the evil enchantments will be annulled, the sick keeper will be healed, and all that is broken will be made whole. For one reason or another the knight does not ask the question on his first visit; consequently the doleful state of Britain continues and the wounded keeper of the mysteries is sometimes called the King Fisherman, sometimes the King Fisher; this title, be it noted, is not the smallest of the many difficulties in this extraordinary tale.[46]

There are many versions of this legend which has its Christian counterparts, recorded by what is called 'high History'. Mary Butts wrote that as a child she "had not yet struck Malory or the 'high History'. Chiefly taught by a book not written for children, on the 'matter of Britain', a gift of my father's and mostly unintelligible. A book which must have grounded me well, but its name even, except that it was a learned one and made me feel grand, is lost."[47] She may also have read two later books belonging to this tradition which were published when she was a young adult: the occult writer A.E. Waite's *The Hidden Church of the Holy Grail: its Legends and Symbolism* (1909) and *The High History of the Holy Graal,* published by Everyman in 1910. Ezra Pound's 'Psychology and Troubadours' and Arthur Machen's 'Mystic Speech' were first delivered as talks to The Quest Society in London before being published as essays, another sign of the widespread interest in the Grail. Certainly by the time she was visiting Glastonbury in the summer of 1918, Mary Butts was familiar with several aspects of this complex legend. Seated on the "ruin of Edgar Chapel" she decided that: "all commentators on wrong lines" about the power of the place. It was "not XVIII c[entury] vistas of 'sublime prospects', not the tragedy of the reformation, not the medieval church, not the inanities of modern Anglicanism, nothing but the source of 'mana'[48] crystallised. Joseph of Arimathea, the Larks of Wonder, Anthem, Sanc Graal, Holy Thorn... Origins, the mystery of whose cycle may be approaching its completion."

In 1920 the anthropologist Jessie L. Weston would publish *From Ritual to Romance,* a study which claimed that the grail myth derived *both* from ecclesiastical writings and popular tales. In terms of its scholarship, *From Ritual to Romance* was quickly superseded, but not before it had influenced or at the very least inspired a number of Modernists to apply some of its idioms and ideas to a modern setting. Probably the most famous is T.S. Eliot's *The Waste Land,* published in 1922. In the mid-1920s Mary Butts would also start to write her own account of the significance of the myth, one which would challenge the Freudian perspective, by then prevalent. It would be a novel called *Armed with Madness,* which I discuss below.[49]

* * * * *

JOHN RODKER did not find Somerset as awe-inspiring as Mary Butts, although they got on well, despite poverty which forced them to go "hungry to bed" in Axminster, since they were "in pawn here with no cash". Opposite this entry is a small drawing entitled 'Portrait of a Gentleman *pensive* on learning that Wife's income was less than his expectation'. By the 14 July they were at Salterns for the first time together, where "J is making good, but I'm in a horrible state, comparable only with my adolescence. A state of tension, unbearable, as though my bowels were tied in knots." This may well have been caused by the fact that her husband was well liked by her family, despite the awkwardness of his introduction. Mary Butts was not reconciled however. She described the atmosphere of Salterns as "this placid malevolence.... Microcosm of the world's state of being after four years of War." Unfortunately she did not expand on this oblique comment, except to say in a letter to her Aunt Ada: "I can't describe our exit from Salterns on paper, but the whole story is one of the best and most painful jokes our unhappy family ever perpetrated."[50]

Whether the married couple stayed over a month at Salterns or went elsewhere also is not clear. Certainly they "came back" to London on the 20 August, when John Rodker went off to visit friends and Mary Butts was left alone reading Strindberg's autobiography.[51] She was impressed yet confused by Strindberg's "correspondence between the objective and subjective life", but was "convinced that I shall get this clear in the right time—that the explanation sub-consciously sought will come—books, words, a sudden shifting and clearing. Harmony—a rhythm and pattern which we not only discover but make." A few days later she recorded how she "fell asleep 'in fairy thrall'. Then that great knock—terror. When I went into the kitchen still dazed with sleep, full of formal courtesies—I was alone. Behind me the gas ring roared, under the running tap the earth ran off the potatoes. I stood surrounded by the elements. In the studio [next door] they played *L'après-midi d'une Faune*.[52] The fear became ecstacy—I almost saw." Like her experience on the Fulham Road when waiting for the number 31 bus, this was one of Mary Butts's many mystical experiences which she tried to set down in her diary.

Writing to her Aunt Ada that autumn, she declared that she was "having a wonderful time" in London, for it was the period of the Russian ballet.[53] She was also writing a great deal, and had a short prose poem entitled 'Vision' published in *The Egoist* in September.[54] "If only the war would stop and we all had enough to eat!" she grumbled to her aunt. "It isn't easy to do good work on beans boiled with onion and an egg every other day. But I've no doubts now as to my eventual success... We went out the other day to a friend who gave us horse. It wasn't half bad, and the first meat we'd tasted for a week. There is none to be bought here—I know why I dislike vegetarians, meat keeps one fierce, and they are all mild like their precious macaroni."[55] This witty letter gives no clue to the dissatisfactions Mary Butts had begun to have since late summer with John Rodker. On the 16 September she noted:

> The old trouble—I make demands—so does he, inimical to each other. As he said—it is good to be with you—while you would have it I could live without you, but find it heaven to be with you.... The crux for me is—I shall be left with some surplus energy—(if I don't use it all in leaving him alone) am I to use it as I please independent of him?... It was as the bus swung round by Arthur's Corner that I divorced him. Then—I was very hurt, and there was an enormous half-moon to illustrate London. I learned our limitation one with another, the stopped road. There may be others—but as we crossed the Harrow Road I said—"It's all right—I will be brave, I will take my chance." I said it to him, humbly, impersonally, and he hated me in silence. But I'm going to do it. It is not an equitable bargain that I should deny my need to make demands on him, forego that adventure, and then be equally condemned by him for fitting the rest of my life where I can.... It is not his fault or mine.... I will take my chance.

It would be over two years before she and John Rodker actually separated. But the relationship was crumbling.

In the meantime Mary Butts used her diary to voice her discontent. By night there were dreams of "sweet sensuality—a heady honey-drink"; by day there was "an accompaniment of good friends... Yanko and Anwil, Mark Gertler, Hester [Sainsbury] and [her lover, the Japanese dancer,] Khori, Rudolph". She finished another play, but had "bad news" from the publisher Grant Richards which was presumably the rejection of a manuscript. On the 21 September after reading G.K. Chesterton's observation "that no one knows the cause of the change in woman", Mary Butts considered the "woman 'question'":

> Wherever there has been an upper strata of society where the bare needs of life were automatically satisfied there has been a class of free or insurgent women. A woman 'question' or no need for one.

> Woman's jobs: (i) children; (ii) home—food, clothes; (ii) has been taken out of her hands as a *sex*—growth of middle class and artisan class, ie spread of ease. One job passed out of her hands as a sex. All to the good—reproducing what has always been in aristocratic society. *Now* nearly all women want what once one class had—She has no longer become vital to keep things going. Must find new fields to conquer. Drudgery *for its own sake* no solution.
> Discovery that childbearing is 3 parts unnecessary work to the destruction of its creative element. Lesson learned from co-op production—foreign trade. Now left with a lot of free time. Search for vital occupation.
> The function of motherhood does not consist in changing napkins.
> If men will not solve our problems for us—they must leave us free to do it for ourselves.
> John is fair—bloody irritating, but pitifully fair.

The problem was that Mary Butts wanted to have a child, but was afraid of the repercussions for her work, her freedom. When she thought she might be pregnant at the end of December, she was torn:

> I feel this: the accidental quality of becoming a mother is worth more to [John Rodker and Yanko] than all that is me—wit, looks, compassion, chiefly my power to do the same work as they. I want to write —I can write. My creating is to be out of my mind. If my men were to acknowledge that—I could throw in a baby or so. I want a child. I wish they would understand that it is not worth doing unless out of it came more philosophy, more art. I mean that girl children and mothers are to have more to do in life than reproduce themselves and be nice to their men... But I want a child.

* * * * *

There are no diary entries between the 24 September and the 7 December, so that Mary Butts makes no record of the end of the Great War...

* * * * *

> *So all life is a perpetual freeing of one's vital energy (élan vital) from the forces which inhibit it.... It is hard to do so—to break the taboos one invents reasons, deifies courage etc. Having done that one goes ahead. Then the élan —tonic to the soul and antiseptic to its sores.*
>
> —MB, undated diary entry, Christmas 1918

When the diary reopened, Mary Butts was recovering from flu. "Should do reviewing if only to keep me to it. None to do. Will keep this then." She was afraid of the poverty she and John Rodker found themselves in, and on the 11 December, two days before her birthday, was in a "queer state of nerves. I could sleep all day and I dream all night. Sexual excitement, tears, depression. No work done. Nearly 28 and no work done." In the autumn of 1916 she had lamented the fact that she was "nearly twenty-six and I've done nothing except write 26 in letters so that future readers of this shall not deplore my style." By 1918 she felt too miserable even to worry about her style. Despite her lack of self-confidence, during December she completed another story, 'The Saint' and "talked over [her] play with Harold". (This may well have been Harold Monro, who held weekly readings at his Poetry Bookshop.) She also read a great deal. On the 12th there was "*Erewhon Revisited* [(1901)]. A tiresome man [Samuel] Butler. Would as soon be without him as with him." She was delighted by some Yeats poems (including 'Shadowy Waters') which she read at a friend's on the 16th and decided "Yeats's *Poems*, 2nd Series (1909)" had to be bought. After a short visit to Salterns for Christmas, where she described Tony as "Nietzsche's young shepherd", she commented on Boxing Day that she had "done little else than read Jung—I think that I am a fair example of libido rising freely into the conscious."

Mary Butts's interest in libido was not only a theoretical one. On the 15 December, after returning home from the ballet productions of 'Carnaval' and 'Scheherazade' with Tony, she asserted in her diary: "Polyandry a most natural affair". She then added: "I may just deceive him [John Rodker]—RF not a vulgarian—but I love John so. Why should I have to choose?" The initials RF stood for Roger Fry, the painter and art critic who was at the heart of what Mary Butts would later call "Old Bloomsbury". She may have met Roger Fry through Nina Hamnett who was going out with him at this time. As she sat for a portrait during December they had talked about 'significant form' in art and considered analogies between painting and writing.[56] Gradually Mary Butts was falling in love with him.

CHAPTER FIVE

Disenchantments
1919

John says that if I lived 1,000 years I would not know then if I loved him as much as I thought I did.
On the other hand —

—MB, diary entry, 16.2.19

I MUST STOP THIS introversion," Mary Butts told herself on the 10 February 1919. Yet she was unable to do so, for 1919 was a troubled year, which began with her worrying about her work, her possible pregnancy and her poverty.

On the 3 January she declared in her diary: "I know nothing about writing. John's criticism at last understood—my poems all rot." This was particularly distressing for she believed that there were "two biological aspects to man's[57] relations. He is a member of the kingdom of this world with other men. Their good is common. On the other hand, equally for his preservation's sake he is opposed to every creature. Another's gain is his loss.... Physically on a large scale, one has everything to gain from co-operation—it's one's creation in process that must be done alone. And Creation is what matters." The "blessed haemorrage" which began the following day and which at least dispelled her fear of pregnancy, did not raise her spirits for very long, as she was preoccupied with the couple's continued poverty. In February she described a bank as "not a superhuman potency, a behemoth, and unsleeping lion, but a convenience where money is stored. Like a penny-in-the-slot machine, if you can shake out more you can." All her life Mary Butts would try to borrow money whenever she could. It would not only be from banks.

Poverty, as well as the desire to be out of London, may well have been why the couple went to Cornwall on the 17 January with their friend Yanko. It appears that they stayed there for about three months. Unfortunately, once in Cornwall, Mary Butts's preoccupations did not disappear: "I worry about money—I used to worry lest my sexual escapades were found out. Now I need not—so the irritation 'running free' expresses itself there." Her passion for Roger Fry had clearly not been reciprocated by this time, since she declared on arriving in Cornwall: "Roger ought to be here. How my nerves would be quiet if we slept together once or twice, cemented our friendship in the most objective way, and settled down to our intimacy. John only wants me to be quiet, quiet and slightly decorative."

Yet it was good to be in the country again. "Outside the little house there was a patch of violets; ten gooseberry bushes at the back and a butt for rainwater. I liked it. I liked it so much that I felt the leaves like a cool plaster on a sore spot." It is not clear exactly whereabouts in Cornwall they stayed, but it was somewhere on the coast as Mary Butts chided herself on the 8 February for the "many exquisite things that one does not write down—the green rocks where the water would be over our heads. Yellow shells." It was hardly a holiday, however. "'Ladies and Gentlemen,'" opened Mary Butts's imaginary speech on the 21 January:

> 'I will now explain to you the difference between men and women.' They were willing—these two boys to move to the other bungalow, and failing Mrs Levenna, let me cook and clean and arrange and order while their lordships played chess and waited for inspiration. They forgot that it was my holiday, my respite from these things, my working time. I do not love them at all.

Along with a sense of injustice, Mary Butts also felt guilty at the fact that "we were overeaten today with roast pork—and in Europe they starve —they starve".

On the 8 February she drew up a list of her complexes, remarking: "It is extraordinary the inhibition that arises when one tries to write these down." She was haunted by the feeling that Tony would die prematurely. "There I dramatised the early death of my talent," was her Freudian interpretation of this dread.[58] There was also her snobbery, her "suppressed veneration for my rank" which shamed her. Most of all there was the continuing "internal conflict whether I should have another lover beside John". The conflict would preoccupy Mary Butts for the following eighteen months and was based on:

> *Fear*. Fear of breaking taboo, fear of hurting him [John Rodker]—fear of losing him.
> It all centres round the physical act, which is wholly absurd.
> I have 'committed adultery in my heart' with R[oger] and there I cannot feel that I have done wrong. Yet it is not so much Roger as the general question.
> All my sexual—or affectionate—libido cannot centre round John. He only needs a limited supply.

Since John Rodker did not satisfy Mary Butts sexually, she wished he would agree for their marriage to be an open one. In her uncertainty about whether to take a lover anyway, she looked to Jung's writing for reassurance and found it: "Where some great work is to be accomplished before which weak man recoils…his libido returns to that source—and this is the dangerous moment between annihilation and new life. If the libido remains arrested…then he is practically dead or desperately ill. But if the libido suceeds in tearing itself loose, and pushing up into the world alone, there a miracle appears."[59] This quotation cheered her and she concluded that her "malaise" was the result of "something desperately, definitely wrong with the main course of my life, a really frustrated libido". Viewing her London life from Cornwall she decided that her past passion for Edwin G. was "resolved, written off". Her present passion for Roger Fry, however, was only "shelved, but in process of enjoyment. I had better not fail there," she added.

When Tony came to stay in Cornwall in late March, Mary Butts felt "with health for a time". Reflecting on her behaviour towards her husband, Yanko and Tony she decided that:

> As a female animal—social training for centuries… I submit to men. I try and please them—'cock an eye for approval', am worried if I do not please them, or *must* not please them. This apart from my reason, my clear affection—a brutal physical fact. It shames me. It shames very many women (who sensually enjoy their irrational abasement)…. However free we think ourselves, we are caught that way each time —most times. Thus the woman who goes into a convent. The woman who gives syph[ilis] to every man she can.

She concluded: "There is a difference in nature. God help me." Her very small comfort lay in thinking: "Most women worse than me" and she cited Eleanor and Yanko's partner, Val.

Back in London towards the end of April Mary Butts and John Rodker spent the evening of the 23rd with Stella Bowen. Two weeks later Bowen wrote to Ford Madox Ford (with whom she had become involved) that "Mary and John are giving a large party in their new home tomorrow evening, & Mary was here this afternoon & fully expects us both to turn up…. There will be 60-70 people. Also Sickert may be there."[60] The new home was a maisonette at 43 Belsize Park Gardens, Hampstead, just round the corner from 1 Glenilla Studios.

Mary Butts's next entry was on the 3 June. By this time she had become very good friends with a woman called Fitz Taylor. "Fitz, the pleasantest, most stable association, woman with woman and friend with friend. 'There is love, there may be friendship.'" Two comments added later reveal a lessening in her delight at this 'perfect' relationship:

"21.11.19. Pleasant but stable now? She has her moods of Eleanor." And almost two years later: "9.3.21. Not much good." Apart from spending time with Fitz, in June 1919 she spent a great deal of time studying Occult literature. This included a detailed analysis of the French nineteenth century magician Eliphas Lévi's history of magic, *Dogme et rituel de haute magie* (1861),[61] as well as reading Jung, Freud and the Irish poet, AE (George Russell), on the subject. There was also her "vital friendship" with Philip Heseltine (also known as Peter Warlock), who, according to Mary Butts, "induced me into the study of magic".[62] Her interest resulted in an increased "clairvoyance as to the future.... Power has come, recurred rather, great energy, some languor... A sense of certain objects charged with their past, or as foci for evil—[e.g.] a worn farthing." At this time she began to believe more strongly in a "doctrine of signatures, principle of correspondence", similar to that described by the French poet, Charles Baudelaire, in his poem, 'Correspondences' (1861):

> The pillars of Nature's temple are alive
> and sometimes yield perplexing messages;
> forests of symbols between us and the shrine
> remark our passage with accustomed eyes.[63]

Increasingly, she experienced sensations of enlightenment: "at the 'psychological' moment I came across the book [by Lévi], the information even the experience and the person I should have most wished to enjoy. They rose like bubbles. [Likewise] Strindberg, whom I had so long evaded". In these early years she found an analogous description of what she experienced in Frazer's *The Golden Bough*, Harrison's *Themis* and *Prolegomena* and a number of occultists. It would be over eight years before she found a qualitatively different but equally powerful explanation in the writings of the mathematician and philosopher, J.W. Dunne.

Mary Butts's study of magic gave her a new perspective on her relations with men: "There's more divine life in me than in any man I've known," she decided. "That's why there is no peace with John.... He wants me dull. He will not praise or stimulate— He does not want the divine life in me." She was particularly interested by a review she read at this time of Frazer's *Totemism and Exogamy* (1910), noting "that exogamy is a male attempt to secure his free sexual choice—totemism the female attempt to limit it and establish family life—and restricted intercourse. Hence the primitive sex war—*environment* favouring one party or the other at haphazard."

She also continued to work on *Ashe of Rings* in the summer of 1919 and commented that it was "a difficult labour but is coming well. Grasp of the technique of free association of ideas, plus a stuctural unity." As mentioned earlier, her 'Lettres Imaginaires' was printed in the October and November 1919 issues of *The Little Review*. Ezra Pound and John Rodker were successively foreign editors of this prestigious American little magazine (edited by Margaret Anderson), and Mary Butts had become a subscriber in 1917.[64] She would also write three reviews between the summer of 1919 and the spring of 1921, including one on a book of poems by the imagist, Richard Aldington, and more a general article on the seventeenth-century hermetic philosopher and poet, Thomas Vaughan.[65]

On the 20 November 1919 Mary Butts announced that she had "finished [the] book" and began to give the manuscript of *Ashe of Rings* to her friends for their comments. The problem was that she was suffering from a new complex: "I cannot endure to look at my writing… in print. I dislike to see my own in typescript. In print it is agony.… In development from this I cannot bear spoken criticism. Good or bad, e.g. Ezra today. *good and bad* was torture.… As I squirm at the good it can't be all vanity. Help!"

* * * * *

December 1919, London and Sussex

> *Relations with the world:*
> *I am a good acquaintance. I last. Not a good friend—intimately I belong only where I belong and that circle is large, but with few stars in it. I am angry with pleasant persons for not being large stars. What can I expect.*
> —MB, diary entry, 8.12.19

> *I wish Ford did not tell so many lies*
> —MB, diary entry, 29.12.19

In December 1919 Mary Butts was extremely sociable. Quite apart from seeing her usual friends, Roger Fry, Nina Hamnett and Philip Heseltine, Jack White was back on the 20 December. "In half an hour we found our old continuity unbroken," she enthused. As a result of her occult studies, she felt that they were able to meet "for the first time with relative equality". This was high self-praise since she felt that "of the men and women I've known he has the most mystical power."

Two days later, there is the very first mention of an older writer who would become an intimate friend. The Anglo-Irish writer Ethel Colburn Mayne (187?-1941) is little known today in spite of being during her lifetime a well-respected novelist, short-story writer, biographer, translator, journalist and reviewer. Her first short story, written under the pseudonym, Francis E. Huntly, appeared in the *Yellow Book* in 1895.

Her first book of stories written under her own name was *The Clearer Vision*, published in 1898. She was an extremely versatile writer whose publications included a two-volume study of Byron (1912), a translation of *Dostoievsky's Letters* (1914), the novel, *One of Our Grandmothers* (1916) and *The Life and Letters of Anne Isabella, Lady Noel Byron* (1929). In three years' time, signalling the attention Mary Butts's work was beginning to attract, her short story 'Speed the Plough' would be included alongside Ethel Colburn Mayne's 'Lovell's Meeting' in *Georgian Stories, 1922*. Other writers represented in the anthology were Violet Hunt, E.M. Forster, Algernon Blackwood, Katherine Mansfield, D.H. Lawrence and May Sinclair.[66]

Mary Butts knew Ethel Colburn Mayne as early as May 1918 when the latter had been one of the witnesses at her marriage to John Rodker. She may have been introduced to her by Violet Hunt, since these two women were very close friends. (Ethel Colburn Mayne was to have been Hunt's literary executor, but pre-deceased her.) Mary Butts quickly realised that in Ethel Colburn Mayne she had found a soulmate. Three days before Christmas 1919 she wandered into town with a "heightened colour sense. I want those jade stockings with the silver fleur-de-lys. I saw the sky go pink and primrose and dull violet." She then went to see Ethel Colburn Mayne, and found her understanding: "When I was a child I wanted to put everyone in the way of the good life. I would conduct little revivals à deux at school. Like a returning cycle the power is in me again. And I'm wiser. I could tell Ethel. The words are so hard, but it is… something that can be put out with every part of my nature."[67]

In her autobiography Stella Bowen describes how Ezra Pound had first introduced her (and perhaps Mary Butts also) to Ford Madox Ford in early 1918. Bowen and Ford had begun to live together soon afterwards and moved out to Red Ford, "a tumble-down cottage near the South Downs" in Sussex in May 1919.[68] "We often had visitors for the week-end. Herbert Read and his wife came, and Francis Meynell, and Ray and Daisy Postgate, and Phyllis, of course, and Mary Butts, now married to the young poet, John Rodker."[69] It was at Christmas 1919 on a visit to Red Ford that Mary Butts showed Ford *Ashe of Rings* with the hope that he would suggest that Duckworth publish it. She did not enjoy the experience, noting on the 27th: "Ford… a kind of laying out to a mutilated corpse." Almost ten years later, in early August 1929, she would still remember the pain of the rejection: "A memory: John and our first break, when I took the ms. of 'Ashe' down to Ford's. He was perplexed by it, irritated, jealous even. Turned it down. And John turned on me, tired after a year's work, proud, starving for love and a little understanding and praise."

In December 1919 Mary Butts was relieved to return to London and to the sympathy of Roger Fry:

> 'My dear,' said Roger, 'how did it take your critics? You say they all had fits. That is a very good sign—there is no better sign than for competent judges to become irrational, and declare that that sort of art has no business to be produced. It means there is something there. Allow me to read your book.' He knelt down on the floor, put his arms round me and kissed me. I laid my cheek against his, let it be there. One forgives Roger anything for sympathy like that.
> I had not thought of that. Yet it's so simple—knowing the rules of the game. Anyway it seems like part of the truth.

She must have voiced her disappointment to her friend Anna Wickham, since amongst her papers there is an undated letter-poem from the latter. From its contents, it may well have been sent to reassure Mary Butts after Ford's negative reaction:

> *Comment ça va!*
>
> My Butts—
> I hear you have denied me.
> A blackguard has defied me
> With taunt of your apostasy
> When most I needed amity.
>
> My Butts—
> For honour's sake
> Remember Blake—
>
> Had the glories of your house
> Been the glories of a louse
> He had redeemed you—
> Long ago I dreamed your
> Transcendence in his sphere
> O Mary dear.
>
> In the old days
> I saw a flaw
> In your decor
> But never in your Phrase.
>
> Now I am justified
> By him to whom I was denied
> He twisted a contemptuous nose
> At your fine prose.
> He said that your new book was *better*
> As one who sees an infant form a letter

My Butts
For honour's sake
Remember Blake.

Trust taste
Though it make waste
Though it be bad
Though it run mad
It is a surer friend
A juster tool
Than a fat fool.

Would it be so ludicrous to suggest that Ford was the "fat fool" of the poem's final line? Whatever the truth, Mary Butts seemed in high enough spirits to give a New Year's Eve party with John Rodker. "We never gave a better. Blot, blot, blotto," she sang out on the 1 January 1920.

* * * * *

WHAT IS STRANGE, unless she misremembered the event, is that Stella Bowen's account of Ford's reaction to the novel is very different: "I can very well remember Ford Madox Ford's enthusiasm when I first showed him a manuscript of Mary's. It was *Ashe of Rings*, I think."[70] Ford also wrote to Ezra Pound on the 20 July 1920 saying that amongst the small group of (contemporary) writers whose work he admired there was "of course Mary Butts".[71] Thus Mary Butts's reaction at the time may just have been a result of the oversensitivity she had admitted to in her diary. Certainly she and Ford remained very close friends and he later published work by her in his prestigious magazine of 1924, *the transatlantic review*. He would also remember her as having "a streak...of genius".[72]

On a lighter note, Mary Butts praised Ford's cooking but grumbled about the "discomfort" of Red Ford in December 1919, where the living conditions were basic.[73] Her parting comment—"I wish Ford did not tell so many lies"—is a wonderful example of the pot calling the kettle black. As Stella Bowen points out, Mary Butts and Ford shared many characteristics, not least the belief that their position *qua* writers meant that their views should be taken seriously. They also had a 'failing' in common:

> Ford could take a fact, any fact, and make it disappear like a conjuror with a card. All his art was built on his temperamental sensitiveness to atmosphere, to the angle from which you looked, to relative, never

> absolute values. When he said, 'It is necessary to be precise,' I used to think that he meant—precisely truthful. Of course, what he really meant was that you must use precision in order to create an effect of authenticity, whatever the subject of your utterance, in the same way as the precision of a brushstroke gives authenticity to an image on canvas, and need have no relation to anything seen in fact. Words to Ford were simply the material of his art, and he never used them in any other way. This created confusion in his everyday life, for words are not like dabs of paint. They are less innocent, being the current coin in use in daily life.[74]

Stella Bowen also wrote of Mary Butts:

> She was always full of turgid, high-pressure enthusiasms and indignations, and it was essential to her to devise suitable objects for the exercise of these faculties.... In a word, Mary was an artist, and the fireworks were often extremely beautiful.... She was a born writer of great sensitiveness and distinction, with a capacity for rich and sensuous imagery that was just a gift from Heaven. But she never offered me a coin of wisdom that did not ring false, and wisdom, alas! was what I then sought. I was bothered by her fiction-writer's capacity... to take some fact, and fabricate from it a dramatic grotesquerie in which she appeared firmly to believe and about which she would weave a whole tissue of dark and magical meaning, rife with spells and portents upon which she was quite prepared to act... If I had been as wise then as I am now, I should have known that the way to enjoy any artist is to attend to his work and not allow one's self to be confused by that lesser thing, his character.[75]

CHAPTER SIX

A Daughter and a Lover 1920

I have the makings—the materials to hand—collected from a miserable youth —for a severe, entrancing, witty, profound middle-life (not 'age' yet). I am learning my trade. I am twenty-nine. I have red curls, I have cut, well I think all, allow for some of my wisdom teeth.... I am finding formulae for non-essentials, defining first principles. I can dance. I was never so handsome. My work is getting known, and my personality to illustrate it. I can write this for the benefit of all future editors.

—MB, diary entry, 13.1.20

NINETEEN-TWENTY was a watershed in Mary Butts's life. In this year she would try, in vain, to get *Ashe of Rings* published (al though in November *The Little Review* did agree to print the novel in instalments); undertake the practice of magic in earnest; spend several months in France; have a child and take a lover.

In May she decided that there were two kinds of reading: "Reading for contemplation—even a kind of vision, and reading for information. For the first only the best will do, for the rest—then one can let in anything one would like to read in the world." Early January found her in the act of a contemplative reading of Turgenev's three tales, *Lear of the Steppes* (1870). "First story very good. Second bad—interesting material skimmed. Third—male observation of himself curious. But the first is a masterpiece." About her own novel, Mary Butts felt dejected. Bim (one of her names for John Rodker) was driving her "frantic" and she looked elsewhere for support over the novel. On the 4th she described how the previous evening she had visited her friend Sally B., a writer who lived with her lover, Cecil Maitland, off St Stephen's Square in Bayswater. "I was ill and wretched. They read me their stories. They spoke about mine. I took courage, talked about *Ashe of Rings*, well at first, badly towards the end, or weaker. But they were held. 'Sympathy' of my own generation. There is virtue in one's true spirit. Half a dozen words were enough and Maitland's eyes—I left them well, gay, quickened even to my moving about the cold streets." This appears to have been the first time Mary

Butts met Cecil Maitland whom she described as having "a Russian character, there's ferocity in him, but a push might land him in good will. He drinks because he likes it. Such a little push, and the eyes beseeching. He slaves for Sally. I see myself projecting myself as a light and health-shedder over blighted lives. What mawkish vanity. What unsophistication." Mary Butts may have felt it vain and unsophisticated to want to be a "light and health-shedder" at twenty-nine; it would become, however, one of her most prized attributes from then on.

Her characterisation of Cecil Maitland as Russian shows the degree to which this inscrutable man intrigued her. Her attention was temporarily deflected, however, when a few days later she met the painter, writer, editor and inventor of Vorticism, Wyndham Lewis. He had written to her on the 4th apologising for not having been able to attend her New Year's Eve party. In his note he asked whether she could come for a sitting for a portrait the following Wednesday. They could have lunch together first. On the evening of the 9 January Mary Butts wrote: "Wyndham Lewis is the first man I have met whose vitality equals, probably surpasses mine. But he manages it badly—like a great voice badly produced. He is the most male creature I've met. I can just keep going with him—or rather have just got going with him.... A pleasure to be raped by him— Yes, that's true." Reflecting on the "erotic relation" between human beings, she decided later in January that "men are such fools at love. Bim drives me frantic and he may be better than most.... Go away and flirt with Wyndham Lewis. Bim will come prowling after. I shall let myself be won back. How often! Do I care a pin for either of them? Or for some idea of love for which they are the funnel? Flesh loves flesh. What does the mind love? *Cor ad cor loquitur* [heart speaks to heart]. But what is the heart?" In fact, there is no record that she had any affair with Wyndham Lewis, who tended to be vocal about his sexual life. They would meet occasionally, although in February Mary Butts noted that there was a possibility Lewis would not after all paint her portrait. Certainly none seems to have survived. What has, however, is a fleeting portrait à clef of Mary Butts in Lewis's 1930 satire, *The Apes of God*, where "a big carrotty anglish intelligentsia...and buxom heiress" is briefly married to Julius Ratner (John Rodker).[76] Lewis is famous for his unkind (if accurate) word-portraits of his friends...

Mary Butts met another writer for the first time in the new year. She had sent a copy of the manuscript of *Ashe of Rings* to May Sinclair who read it with "extraordinary fascination". Sinclair did have some reservations which she detailed in a letter, concluding: "It is so good that it would be worth while working at it. So very little would pull it together—a little tightening here—a little clarifying there. It's very original. You must not imagine I don't admire it because I'm finding fault. It's so good that I'd like it to be faultless."[77] In a postscript she invited Mary Butts to tea the following weekend. From then on the two women spent time together occasionally.

Mary Butts was less impressed when she met Edward and Fanny Wadsworth. "Both are serious and accomplished artists,"[78] she conceded, but could not warm to them. She "allow[ed]" that it was in part "J's attraction to Mrs Wadsworth" which put her off. It was also a result of her own snobbery: "It would be interesting to explore why the Wadsworths are detestable. On my soul I don't know—when they talk bawdy—they do it very well. I dislike it—and her laugh is loathsome—a squawking explosion. Aristocrats and 'low lots' are all right—these two are the cream of the middle-classes. Middle classes nefas (my mother came from them —but she would *never* laugh like that)." Given her disdain for her mother, to be compared to Mary Colville-Hyde and found wanting was condemnation indeed. It may well have been that she was put off by something Mrs Wadsworth said, or rather, the *way* she said it. For Mary Butts commented on one of her own character-failings in April 1920 when Cecil Maitland "discovered in me today an idiosyncracy I had long shunned —that on certain subjects, or attitudes expressed to subjects—a word contrary to my own conviction will serve to turn my warm liking, my respect, my love into complete indifference and contempt.... There have been people at school—at college—everywhere. A phrase and opinion —either I'm off for good like wood-cock, or my whole opinion of them is changed. A little worm of contempt, or indignation. They are not forgiven."

Mary Butts was doing more than writing and meeting the literati and artists during January 1920. On the 10th she memorised a speech she was intending to make: "'Look here. We are doing our best. The business is very poor and struggling. We have no capital. Give us time etc'. (Got it said, a little toned down, *not* so injured. Bill moved to tears at the time.)" Quite apart from proving her dramatic gifts, this conversation (which she had on behalf of herself and John Rodker), was financially crucial. It concerned a press which they had bought (but not yet completely paid for) from Bill [no surname]. The Ovid Press, with a dramatic colophon designed by Edward Wadsworth, was just one of several which John Rodker would own (including The Casanova Society in 1924 and, much later, the Imago Press), but it was the only one in which Mary Butts was involved. She gave not only her time but a substantial amount of money, raising £600 on her own estate. The press also received financial support from May Sinclair (£25), Dan Ingram (£75) and "£10 from America", whilst Ezra Pound raised a further £50. Ezra Pound had a vested interest since his poem, *Hugh Selwyn Mauberley*, was published by the Ovid Press in 1920, as was T.S. Eliot's second book of poetry, *Ara Vos Prec*.[79] John Rodker's own poems in a volume entitled *Hymns* came out on the 8 April.[80] He dedicated them "to M.B." Sadly, like many other small publishing houses, the Ovid Press did not survive.[81]

In February Mary Butts felt lonely. She was getting on very badly with John Rodker whom she described as a "faun". "It is difficult to love fauns—much more to make fauns love you." Might it have been different, she wondered, "if tonight he had not wanted to go to the pictures, or drink beer at the Monico, or tea at the Armenian?[82] If he wanted to stay here, and play with me, and revive me after flu, and chase off the grey devils?" She felt that they needed a holiday from one another — "no chance of that," she lamented on the 19th. She read a "nasty story" by Arthur Machen[83] in mid-February and decided that "Jimmy may be one of the people of the abyss."[84] Mary Butts had several discussions with Cecil Maitland about what she understood by the 'abyss':

> The other side of the phenomena, the vortex, is the abyss or the nothing. This 'nothing' seems to have inhabitants which are a 'something'. It does not seem to be synonymous with antithetic ideas of good and evil. It has signatures in the external world. Beardsley's drawings. Possibly some of the Goyas. In Eleanor's orison of malice.... Maitland has looked into it.... One sees it in persons who have no creative employment. Not WL [Wyndham Lewis] though one might think.

She had tried to portray the abyss in *Ashe of Rings*, but to her disappointment she "could not get that through. I tried with Judy's face in the glass for an image. It is all how it is looked at. Even Cecil who hangs over the abyss didn't see her as I saw her.... I saw. I shall never be free from the haunting."

By February 1920 she had realised the extent of Cecil Maitland's knowledge of magic. Little is known about Cecil Maitland, other than what is given in memoirs of the period, especially accounts by the writer, Douglas Goldring, who knew Mary Butts and Cecil Maitland well. In *South Lodge: Reminiscences of Violet Hunt, Ford Madox Ford and the English Review Circle* (1943), Goldring devotes an entire chapter to 'Mary and Cecil'. It should be pointed out, however, that Goldring was often inaccurate, particularly about dates—"I can make no attempt at exact chronology," he conceded.[85] Whilst he should be praised for being one of the first people to write at length about Mary Butts, he was also to some extent responsible for the misinformation which continues to surround her. According to Goldring:

> Cecil's father was an Anglo-Catholic clergyman who for years lived perilously on the brink of Rome, occasionally slipped over the border

> and became in consequence a layman, but ended up where he began. I do not know whether Cecil was sent to a Roman Catholic school...[but] it seem[s] probable.... Everything to do with esoteric religion and its practitioners, everything to do with Magic—black or white—had a peculiar fascination for Cecil, in spite of the fact that he was naturally sceptical and like most Scots, hard-headed. As a boy, scarcely out of his teens, he had attended a Black Mass in Edinburgh and found it a dull performance.... As a young man he went out to Malaya to plant rubber and acquired a taste, which never left him, for Singapore gin slings. He was in the Black Watch during the war of 1914 to 1918 and was, I believe, severely wounded at Gallipoli. His war experiences seemed to have given him a profound disgust for life and to have exaggerated his natural tendency to cynicism.[86]

In 1920 Mary Butts resumed two friendships from her Westfield College days. One began in April after she received a letter from Ida Binks "with her thanks for teaching her to read poetry, 'the best thing I ever learned.'" Mary Butts looked forward to seeing Ida again. The other old friendship, that with Gwen Ingram, which had ended on a sour note when they had both been asked to leave Westfield College eight years earlier, was renewed in mid-January: "After five years we meet again after our quarrel with our contact worn down to a stone which I do not think will wear away. Like a low altar between us, a worn stone, not engraved which only we could recognise." Mary Butts decided that "Gwen's coming" was a "signature"; the "outcome [of] Maitland magic ...after I had told him the mystical story about her". By this time she had begun to associate her destiny with Cecil Maitland, which led her to present everything to do with him as part of a pattern in her life, a "design" which she was only just beginning to comprehend: "Everywhere in this business of the unseen I sense a design, part arbitrary, part significant, over which I tumble as over a carving whose design is to be judged in the dark. Bring a candle and all is simply evident." This conviction was increased when she learned that Cecil Maitland knew Eleanor and, what was worse, that "Maitland and I ought to have met when the Eleanor business was at its worst. It seems also we tried to meet. As he said 'Something went wrong'. He could have saved me and developed an adventure. What went wrong? It shows that the circles can be broken. It makes me cry it's so futile and sad." As a result of her growing friendship with Cecil Maitland, she began the practice of automatic writing, which she would undertake at regular intervals throughout her life. She was not displeased with her first attempts and decided that she had a gift for it: "What feeble 'subliminal uprush' the scrawls without form make with increasing facility, and the deep recognitions of apparently unrelated phenomena which rise also automatically, and are among the first formula of creation." The practice certainly seemed to rouse a creative force within her and increase her self-confidence:

> To-day there came back as I slept and alternately listened to the birds in the spring rain, an intuition of the creating way, I have forgotten. Not the early innocence, not the despair, the negation of the will, the unreasonable, disproportionate idea, the slavery that shrieks and sneers, but a fusion of the energy of the one with the wisdom of the other. A third power. I don't suppose I shall command it, but it would dissolve and resolve into manageable proportions everything, even the baby, even John's alien strangeness, his depth and his slightness.

The baby mentioned was hers. Having asserted on the 25 February that she was "very tired, *convinced* that delayed curse is not pregnancy"; by the 29th Mary Butts had to concede that she was "probably pregnant". She was indeed.

* * * * *

> *I want bread and they offer me a stone. This child is a stone.*
> *My book is bread. I don't want to have it. Yet, when it comes to going to Leicester Square and buying a pill I am paralysed.*
> *No money to pay bills. Let alone a baby.*
> *A prey for the life-impulse....*
> *It should be a matter of indifference whether I bear or am barren. So long as the spirit is not barren. And if the spirit should be barren.*
>
> —MB, diary entry, 12.3.20

VERY FEW WOMEN would be "indifferent" to being barren. Mary Butts certainly was not. As in 1918, she was afraid, however, of the slavery of motherhood. An old friend, Margaret Schleselmann,[87] came to visit her unexpectedly on the 5 March. Mary Butts was appalled: "She was horrible, who was once the brightest object. Shall I turn into that sort of thing?... She died to rear her babies. Is that necessary? I will not let it be so." In January she had considered the question:

> If we resent the tyranny of our acquaintance over our emotions, how much more that of our friends, lovers, husbands, *children*. Women resent children, the pity and love for them that *must* be there. No escaping the little wretches. At the same time there is that hunger 'to be loved' that is the root of all association.... I want to be alone (one state). I want to be loved (various states).

There was the rub. As we shall see, Mary Butts solved the problem cruelly by having a child and then leaving her to the care of others...

At the beginning of March she immersed herself in her work whilst nature took its course. She worked on an essay, which has not survived and does not seem to have been published. This is a pity since the subject as sketched out in the following notes has remained an important one:

> The War is not to be considered in this case as a producer of literature except in the sense of moeurs contemporains. The significant literature produced by the war—having any quality of permanency—will appear in ten or more years' time. The war influence is negative, hinders, deflects, stops, does not create: Consider its influence in a negative way. Might begin with the bright side-lights, the moeurs contemporains (and the collapse of the Georgian writers as such) then the permanent stuff.

There are few entries for March until the 22nd when the painter "Marie Bashkirtseff has wound me up to begin this again. So little has happened and so much.... The bitterness of this 29th year and the utter failure of my work. The cursed child grows. I am slow with the pain of my failure and quick with the pain of it. Often I am tranquil and humorous, tender and gentle, fond of plain food and sugar and salt, hating tobacco." She reread Sologub's *Little Demon* (1916) but found it disappointing. "I *could* write, but I won't," she noted.

"A large foul lively beast that Herbert Cape," she expostulated on the 31 March. This may well have been on hearing that Cape had rejected *Ashe of Rings*, since on the 6 April she sent the manuscript on a "visit to Middleton Murry. Will that be delusion?" Murry's reaction seems to have been unenthusiastic, for on the 2 May she noted that John Rodker had reminded her "to take Murry with a pinch of salt". While she waited, she "finished an essay for *The Athenaeum*—gifted women writing on secondary phenomena". Since Murry was the journal's editor, it may well have been that he invited her to do so. The essay has since been lost but was probably submitted for the '"Athenaeum" Essay Competition', for which, as one of the runners-up, Mary Butts won £3.[88]

* * * * *

Some day I shall be an adept.

—MB, diary entry, 12.4.20

In late March Mary Butts concentrated on her studies of magic and announced dramatically: "Maitland and I are in love with the 4th Dimension." They sealed their partnership in magic by ritually slashing crosses on each other's wrists: "We sucked each other's cuts and kissed them, and lay back licking our own wrists." Her initiation had truly begun.

She drew up an extensive *Bibliography of Magical Books* with marginal comments. She found *The Secret Commonwealth of Elves, Fauns and Fairies* (1691) by Robert Kirk a "captivating book", particularly the sentence: "Her heat and radical moisture seemed to be equally balanced like an unextinguished lamp, and going in a circle not unlike the faint Lyfe of Bees, and some Sort of Bird that sleeps all the winter over." Louis Martonie's *Piété au Moyen Age* (1855), a study of devil worship in the Middle Ages was "entertaining [but] slight". Reginald Scot's *Discoverie of Witchcraft* (1584) was "picturesque, but with a good writer's elegance". She also read Henry Krämer and James Sprenger's *Malleus Maleficarum* (1489), a book which she would try to obtain from John Rodker when he republished it in 1928.[89] These are just a selection of the wide range of books which she read (many in French) in April in the British Museum, where she declared on the 9th: "Lie back in your chair and let the Reading Room dome pour over your head, you will get an extraordinary sensation." In 1914 she had written 'British Museum'. Although never published, this celebratory poem is a fine tribute to the building's power to inspire and revitalise, felt by so many of its visitors:

> The perfect presence of fine stone
> Bare pure and calm the strong shafts rise
> Rain-scored, alone.
>
> In their long ranks they fulfil
> All harmony, the great roof broods
> Expression of our will.
>
> The City of the Violet Crown
> Bears you in marble lifted up
> In London Town.
>
> Strange peoples mount and slip you through
> Dear columns, faintly pours the sun
> But there is blue.
>
> Rain-filled and high and tremulous
> Behind you still and the birds wheel
> The light of us.
>
> O London storm, Athenian gold,
> We men pass up the stairs we build
> And grow not old.[90]

Before addressing herself to her more theoretical studies, Mary Butts began in March a list of what she called *Literature of the 4th Dimension*: It "anywhere in Dostoievsky" and W.B. Yeats's 1918 autobiography *Per Amica Silentiae Lunae*. It is uncertain whether by 1920 Mary Butts had yet bought her own copy.[91] Either way, she felt moved to write out the following quotation because it articulated her own views:

> I think that all religious men have believed that there is a hand not ours in the events of life, and that, as someone says in *Wilhelm Meister*, accident is destiny; and I think it was Heracleitus who said: the Daemon is our destiny. When I think of life as a struggle with the Daemon who would ever set us to the hardest work among those not impossible, I understand why there is deep emnity between a man and his destiny, and why a man loves nothing but his destiny... I am persuaded that the Daemon delivers and deceives us, and that he wove that netting from the stars and threw the net from his shoulder. Then my imagination runs from daemon to sweetheart and I divine an analogy that evades the intellect.[92]

Not surprisingly, during these weeks Mary Butts had "magical perceptions". "In the night I lived as though the barrier of my perceptions was rubbed thin. It came with a noise. A crying thin shrill that dissolved, and in the middle of the night a small vibrating bell in the high lavatory ceiling. The air looked different—outside was a high moon and running clouds." As in 1918, "this pregnancy appears to be good for clairvoyance." There were also heightened dreams. In December 1919 she had dreamt: "An amourette with dark boy.... Pure ideal.... Usual Freudian imagery, but what made it interesting was the emotion of ideal physical passion that accompanied it. If I saw him now, I should be in love with him. We didn't actually embrace—but I remember his kisses on the back of my neck more than many I have had given me." On the 2 April 1920 the dreams were more specific: "Lately I have dreamed of Cecil (he is sitting beside me) as my lover—each time, with less and less inhibitions. To-day I want it *while he is here*. Some time ago when he wasn't, earlier *only* in sleep. Only it is better in sleep than it would be. Fantastic—but of a quality. Wiser to leave it at that!" she concluded. This resolution would not last very long.

By mid-April John Rodker had deteriorated from a faun to a "larve". The couple were not getting on well. In a bid to improve their relationship, they planned a three-month trip to France starting in mid-May. "Mountains, mountains, we're going away, fall south through Europe," she enthused. She was getting tired of her studies: "These books on occultism with their bastard words, credulities, falsities on facts, emotion and aesthetic falsities, inwardly revolt me. Maitland and I have a mutual imaginative dislike for the Cabala. Their way back is Jewish, Old Testament, Christian, superstitious, bastard in point of *elegance*. The symbols, save when they were purely numeral and abstract, weened but poor correspondences." She felt frustrated until:

> I came back on a sudden turn. I remembered the *Prolegomena* and the others, the profoundest study of my adolescence — I know about such mystery cults from Thrace to Eleusis. I remembered the Bacchae. There are my formulae, there my words of power.... I am rereading the *Prolegomena*—it reels off before me in plain script (all the more because it was written, *by a woman* with no magical thesis to prove.) There I know I shall find the way. Demete Anesidora and Dionysos of the Flower, Bromios, Sabazios, Master of the Voices of the Night, Thyad, Lyssiad—Dithyrambos.

These were the magic words for Mary Butts; it was in "the Hellenic grace" that she found a "vast tranquillity and assurance".

On the 27 April there was "the worst of temporal disasters" when Fitz Taylor "withdrew her offer" of money which had "meant health and leisure and ease, *I had begun to enjoy the thought of the child.*" (It is not explained what the money was for, perhaps the Ovid Press.) The result was anxiety and desolation as Mary Butts worried about the future. Yet at the same time there was "Maitland's declaration". She pondered the question: "We have, as it were, a thin glaze of sufficiency. This [money from Fitz] meant something soft and rich. Do I want it to break my contacts with the world? Cecil offers love." In her uncertainty, and increasingly cynical about diary-keeping, she turned to reading cards and to Dostoevsky.

> I have re-read *The Possessed*. It was worth a stiff knee to compel one. One has undergone again the most awful illumination the mind, no the soul, can undergo.... Suppose the European is half right, suppose man can be surpassed by hard work and taking thought. It leaves the attendant pain, the past miseries and injustice where they were. Only to live it over again and live it over right. So the Russian is right after all. Whatever the future, there's no forgiving the past.

She conceded that Dostoevsky's "people seem, as [Wyndham] Lewis says, a little heavy souled", yet this was preferable to the European insistence on respectability.

Mary Butts had finally made up her mind. She wanted both John Rodker *and* Cecil Maitland: "I have learned half that I know from him [John Rodker]. He's never been my accoucheur [midwife], but my surgeon. Cecil is the gentlest midwife that ever lived. And I wanted Cecil to kiss me. That very tender love is surely my right. Between them both I can be a little happy. A fine intellect stunting a fine perception, and a marvellous perception because it sees these by itself. One tortures and one irritates. I love the first best, the second is pure comfort." Inevitably, things would not be that simple. By the 6 May, Mary Butts wrote that "there are two reasons why my love for Cecil is not physically consummated yet. Because of the child, but likely to be...[and] a sense of unfairness to J". She no longer thought that the dreams of passion with Cecil Maitland were idealised:

> Suppose I were to die this autumn without one last fling for my body. I'm satiated with the *thought* of his embraces. I want to lie with him in that room and leave there a patch of ivory and gold—whichever we do, we shall regret, but we would have the lovely certainty of that embrace. I feel 'too much the mother', too much... the miserable furious earth. (When I am dead, and someone edits these—how many phrases will be picked out to illustrate my bad taste?) Just to use my body once more before its beauty goes—perhaps for ever. And I shall have broken a taboo. One's body says such plain common-sense. Love shall adorn you.
>
> I want to move about in that other blessed world where the light is a sparkling flood counting time in its pulse and the mind is the creator.

She decided that she knew all about marriage now—"men marry, as Ethel says, to be rid of the exalted side of passion... Once the child is born and weaned, I shall have run the gauntlet of marriage—no more of it, lovers and solitude for the rest of my life!"

But this was not quite how it would be.

* * * * *

"Mountains, Mountains, we're going away"

> *St Bertrand de Comminges is a decayed town on the spurs of the Pyrenees, not very far from Toulouse, and still nearer to Bagnère-de-Luchon. It was the site of a bishopric until the Revolution, and has a cathedral which is visited by a certain number of tourists.*
>
> —M.R. James, 'Canon Alberic's Scrapbook' (1894-5)[93]

> *And I can't catch hold of any solid truth except that we are a pair of very gifted, quite decent persons who are terribly intimate and quite unsuited.*
>
> —MB, diary entry, 9.7.20

By the 19 May the couple were in Paris. Mary Butts was unsettled and waited for letters from Cecil Maitland. On a visit to the Louvre she noticed that "a dove of Astarte in lapis and gold quivered as I passed her glass cage. So I sent her to [Cecil Maitland], and the blessing returned". According to an itinerary sketched out at the back of her diary, the couple journeyed down from Paris to the Pyrenees over a few days in order to visit the ancient cities of Arles, Nimes, Carcassonne and Avignon. Their destination was St Bertrand de Comminges and they arrived at the end of May. Perched on the top of a huge rock, the important Roman city of Lugdunum Convenarum had been ruined in the sixth century and by 1920 was a small village with a population of just under six hundred. "Here we are, and here I think we shall stay till the end of July," she announced to her Aunt Ada from the Hôtel de Comminges shortly after their arrival. The hotel was at the heart of the village, opposite the towering cathedral built between the eleventh and sixteenth centuries. From the terrace at the back of the hotel there was a panoramic view of Gargas Mountain. It was cheap, idyllic, isolated; in short:

> the most adorable place in the world. We can live here at a maximum of £5 a week (on the present exchange) in a perfect comfort verging on luxury...
>
> We have an enormous room with two carved walnut beds, and mirrors and deep arm-chair, and unlimited hot water and refined sanitation, and a garden on a terrace with a twenty mile view, knee deep in flowers you can pick. The Cathedral bells play a carillon half the day, and the country-side is like the garden of Eden. Only we have this Paradise to ourselves. Apparently the people come over later—in July and August to see the church (stuffed with unique works of art), but no one stays, and the place cooks like the Ritz! Oh the eggs and the wine, the asparagus and the cheese, the cutlets and the trout from the Garonne—long vanished from the English menu!... If surroundings count that child ought to have a chance. We're under the snow peaks, and the Garonne comes down like a streak of light. All round us are foot hills covered with an endless forest. In the valley are vineyards and olives and cherry and apple, and acacias and palms! There are grottos and Roman baths, and gothic churches, and solitude—a wise friend of ours Ezra Pound put us onto it.[94]

The letters to her aunt from St Bertrand de Comminges show Mary Butts at her most witty and blithe. The tone of most of the diary entries is melancholy and restive. This disparity is fairly characteristic, but would lead to a misconception in the memoirs of her friends, who were rarely aware of her less affable moods of gloom and dejection. There is also a third tone of voice—sometimes bitter, sometimes remorseful—which is interpolated between her diary entries. In January 1917 Mary Butts had recorded: "J said 'I'd never keep a diary, I'd have to put down the true nasty things *only*, and then you might see it and be awfully hurt.'". In 1921, after Mary Butts had left him, John Rodker was made all too aware of the truth of his statement when he 'borrowed' and read her 1920 diary.

Mary Butts's joy at being in St Bertrand de Comminges was not feigned. On the 14 June she reported: "I went out this evening on the hills.... A swallow that flew straight at me like a blue and red bee (so foreshortened). Caterpillars. The bird with the red back, dove front, black patch on sides of head, dark tail, very slender. Knew it and couldn't name it.... One magpie—for sorrow and I watched the black and white against the blue—a transparent turquoise, black and white—two for mirth. Then the blue poured over me and I climbed the hill much better." Such contemplative calm was occasional rather than continuous, however, and dependent on her physical well-being: "Yesterday as I sat by the mountain river and looked up at that hill streaming with sun, and felt myself so heavy with child that I could scarcely walk the two miles home. I understood how women, with child-bearing always on their mind, had at whatever cost, to tame their men, by fraud, force, cajolery, anyway, anyhow to protect them, feed and provide for them while they were with young. The instinct explains so much of the worst things we do."

Throughout her stay she continued to have "dreams very magical and serial", but was disappointed at not being able to "command either perceptions, 'magical' states or dreams.... I can tap the subconscious by the ritual of 'letting go', and I can detach myself for sleep or even light trance. But I don't seem able to keep quiet enough to induce light enough trance—without sleep—to let the images rise. ...as Yeats describes in *Per Amica*." She decided to try "Yeats' suggestion, scented leaves on pillow" and was pleased when she "never slept sounder." They had brought few books with them, so that she had to read what she found at the Hôtel de Comminges. It was an odd selection: "a french prose Tasso, mercifully some Stendhal and some Baudelaire, somebody's doctor's thesis on early Greek philosophers!"[95] She did not mention M.R. James's 'Canon Alberic's Scrapbook' which is set in St Bertrand de Comminges. Perhaps she had not yet come across this writer of supernatural tales. When she did, she became a passionate admirer—and James would have a profound influence on her work. Mary Butts's aunt generously paid for *The Athenaeum* to be forwarded. "*The Athenaeum* is a great blessing," she wrote in thanks on the 23 June, especially since "the heat has come here with a rush, between the hours of 1 and 5 it is hardly possible to go out. We sleep and go for long walks at night."[96]

Mary Butts's letters to her aunt were concerned with more than just describing her holiday. She discussed dates and arrangements for their return trip. They were due in Cornwall on the 2 August, and by the 10 July the plan was as follows: "Jimmy [who] has left the press in the hands of a maniac-embezzler because Cecil Maitland fell ill and had to leave it. ...must be in town no later than July 31st to put things straight. The flat is let, all our friends are away, hotels vile and dear!" The suggestion was that he would sleep on "the floor of a friend's studio" whilst she spent two nights with her aunt in Poole, travelling on to Cornwall by train from there.[97] It was also a clever means of avoiding her aunt having to see them together, since the harmonious intimacy presented in Mary Butts's letters was exaggerated. They were getting on only moderately well and whilst waiting impatiently for letters from Cecil Maitland, Mary Butts remarked: "The life I lead here in these mountains, lame, weather-bound, is one of such intense inner concentration on Cecil and what is behind Cecil, that I feel as though I were preparing in great ignorance an enormous event."

She was again anxious about money. On the 24 June she confirmed her earlier analysis that "the worrying about bills [is]...simply the projection of my fears of the world's revenge on my broken taboos. I've broken most as it suited me—without at the time much strain. Over this point of credit I'm rather objectively vulnerable—supposed forgotten years have poured into it as with a mould." She became ever more preoccupied by this theory. By the end of the month she decided that "behind each sorrow is fear":

> All our life is spent dodging fear and braving it. Now and then one says 'the worst will happen' and one waits. When it is over one is greyer and tireder—and they talk of the gospel of cheerfulness and the cure by the wind. They're all right. They help one to live. But nothing will make one forget the truth of what one has seen. And what we've seen is bad enough to create the great image of Fear—while the good we have seen—temporary Gods and charities, which pass. But fear doesn't pass. It was with the stone age man and it's here with us. The God that doesn't die... we throw it off—but it creeps up our backs again.
>
> Perfect love—so it does for a bit, but fear comes back and dries it up. We are like the flies on the paper squirming away, casting out our eggs in a white stream behind us—all our taboos and our joys—to get rid of fear, and we stay squirming fast glued down as ever—a little nearer our death. I am afraid. The only thing left is to try to understand.

Mary Butts's statement hints at the basis of her disagreement with Freud, whose work she had been reading since the 1910s. In a 1933 review she would write: "I am old enough to remember what it was like when the theories of Freud first escaped from the study and the clinic, and the great game of Hunt-the-Complex began, to the entertainment and alarm of a war-shattered and disillusioned world."[98] Such a prevalent interest in and antagonism to his work warrants a short explanation.

Two of Freud's most famous texts, the *Psychopathology of Everyday Life* and *The Uncanny* had been published in English in 1914 and 1919 respectively, and Mary Butts would incorporate a refutation of a great number of his ideas into her work. The fundamental distinction between their perspectives lies in their attitude to progress. As Mary Butts's statement shows, she did not believe that the fears of the stone-age had in any important ways passed away. In *Psychopathology of Everyday Life*, by contrast, Freud is "sorry to confess" that he has never been subject to any supernatural experiences and utterly "repudiates" the existence of all phenomena such as "omens, prophetic dreams, telepathic experiences, manifestations of supernatural forces and the like".[99] In *The Uncanny* Freud writes of the "superiority of rational minds", as compared with the "residues of animistic mental activity". If we have a "primitive fear of the dead" it is because we think "as savages" about this subject.[100] According to Freud, this is a great error: "When human beings began to think they were obviously compelled to explain the outer world in an anthropocentric sense by a multitude of personalities in their own image; the accidents which they explained superstitiously were thus actions and expressions of persons... Only in our modern philosophical, but by no means finished views of life, does superstition seem so much out of place: in the view of life of pre-scientific times and nations it was justified and consistent."[101]

This view of history enabled Freud to simplify the perspective of the "pre-scientific" primitive or superstitious person and hence reduce its force at a time when he was developing his theory of metapsychology. According to this theory "a large portion of the mythological conception of the world which reaches far into the most modern religions *is nothing but psychology projected into the outer world.* The dim perception...of psychic factors and relations of the unconscious was taken as a model in the construction of a *transcendental reality,* which is destined to be changed again by science into *psychology of the unconscious.*"[102]

Historically, however, his account was wrong. If we consider the situation of the ancient Greeks, their gods are not the outcome of anthropocentrism; on the contrary. J.E. Harrison points out in *Themis* (1912) that in the subject of religion the "cardinal question" revolves around "what... we mean by the word 'sacred'". "In bygone days," she agrees, "the answer would have been prompt and simple, the thunderbolt is sacred because it belonged to a god. The god is presupposed and from him comes the sanctity." This is indeed Freud's position. "But," argues Harrison, "we now know from a study of the customs and representations of primitive peoples, that, broadly speaking, the reverse is true, a thing is regarded as sacred and out of that sanctity, given certain conditions, emerges a *daimon* and ultimately a god. *Le sacré c'est le père du dieu.*"[103]

This changes the whole equation. It is qualitatively different to maintain, as Freud did, that superstitious people *explained* the outer world by a range of deities based on a belief in anthropocentrism, and Harrison's conclusion that the gods were a *response* to, rather than an explanation of, natural phenomena and noumena. It is Freud's position, in fact, that is based on anthropocentrism in a "man-fabricated world". Mary Butts's position was that of the Greeks and the 'savages', and her writing reflects this. In July 1920 she tried to interpret the significance of her dreams "now especially with Freud uncontaminated with Jung about, and so popular. It is undignified to run the gauntlet of anal eroticism-criticism. Yeats has protested, more protests and quick."

Freud is pertinent to the problems in Mary Butts's marriage to John Rodker, who was extremely sympathetic to his ideas and dwelt firmly in a three-dimensional world. On the 20 July Mary Butts added to her "list of '4th world' writing. 'The Ancient Mariner', 'Christabel', 'Kubla Kahn' [all by Coleridge], 'La Belle Dame [Sans Merci]' [Keats],...some earlier poems of [William] Morris, and his prose romances." She then had a discussion with John Rodker which summed up their contrasting attitude to poetry:

> He said 'you say I know nothing about 'magic'—but that kind of poetry is the only poetry, the quintessence of writing to me. Milton and Shelley are just frills beside it and all gay, dancing poetry. Poetry to me is a matter of minor rhythms—some of which you say are the key of another world to you. But I don't call it another world, I just accept it, and can't have too much of it and would like to write like it'.
>
> That reminded me of what Cecil has said, and I always tacitly recognised, that the Larve had an instinctive knowledge, less curious than ours but as instinctive. ... It is all mixed up with the chastest appreciation of quintessential poetry—often with ballads which have no specially magical content at all.

As she had noted on the 9 July, the truth was that "there is a dreadful sterility in living alone with him without friends, without anything to break our au fond unsuitability." By the end of the month, when they were about to leave St Bertrand de Comminges, she and John Rodker were both emotionally exhausted. This was because in early June Mary Butts had "told John how nearly 'physical' my relations with Cecil had been. There was very little need, only I knew that he did not know." From his response, she felt that whilst he had been grieved by the disclosure, "it did not come out by way of jealous or wounded love (I do not believe that he felt that.)" In 1921 John Rodker added in the margin: "This is wrong. You broke my heart when you told me! It came out that way because I wanted to humiliate you." At the time Mary Butts felt that she had been "a fool not to leave well alone." But it was too late. From then on they repeatedly misunderstood one another. "I could be tolerant, a little bitter, and deceive him tranquilly. And he can go—I see that it must come to that, go and *no* marriage left, not to get away to work with the essentials left — like a row of canopic jars." "But I will not be an eternal husband," responded John Rodker. "I want love too— Passion, what you gave me at the beginning." On the 9th Mary Butts wrote: "I feel degraded by his perpetual indifference to everything that warms and stimulates me. His is an active sneer—last night there was another disappointment. We had talked once before about the education of children, on one evening in town in Fitz's flat when he loved me and it had seemed a marvel of sympathy and agreement. It had remained one of my best memories of our life. I reminded him of it—he had said 'you must have a child if you know all this'. He has forgotten it—couldn't recall it." In 1921 John Rodker was full of remorse: "I'm sorry you suffered so. I know I've been a dreadful brute. Forgive me." In her sadness, she consoled herself with the thought: "Well, there is Cecil and writing, and an interesting child (possibly). Order 2, 1, 3". Her child would come a very poor third; writing as ever came first.

On the 17th she had the exciting news that her short story, 'Speed the Plough' had been accepted by the prestigious American little magazine, *The Dial*. It would be over a year before the story appeared, but in July 1920 she was euphoric. She received £8.15s in payment: "My work [is] going to be recognised. Oh the feeling of being started. The Bank will swallow every penny in an overdraft I didn't know I had but *The Dial* wants more work. How noble is labour. How much better to earn money than to inherit it. How strong I am beginning to feel." In a burst of enthusiasm Mary Butts corrected her story 'The Saint' and continued work on a play begun a few days earlier. It was to be "on Sally… [a] sketch for great comic character". Prospective publication had lightened her mood considerably. A week earlier she had been convinced that Sally had been affecting her "indirectly… telepathically…. Sally said that she had power and would turn my love from Cecil and his from me…. I can see my love rising as if out of a well. God grant it will not be a corpse when I pull it out…. I want to love him all the time, but I can only love *swans*." To which John Rodker responded mournfully: "You had a unicorn in your menagerie but you have sent it away."

Mary Butts's characterisation of Cecil Maitland as a corpse was not, in his case, dramatic hyperbole. By the 21 July she had become almost frantic after days had passed with no news from him. She sent a desperate wire to her aunt for more money and then, a little more calmly, wrote in a letter:

> My dearest Aunt,
>
> To explain our wire and apologise. Our money has apparently arrived in England—but Cecil Maitland is more or less in extremis. He has been very ill, and a few days ago his great friend committed sui-

> cide. It is very obscure—we heard, with a few ghastly details, nothing clear. We knew him well. ...the matter is serious—Cecil has been so ill that this last shock may have bad consequences—we don't know what was said at the inquest—but 'temporarily insane' is what Cecil may very well become.[104]

Little is known about the suicide victim, Johannes F. On the 23rd Mary Butts finally heard from Cecil Maitland. "So he is still alive, but the note conveyed such forlornness, such despair as might well have accounted for my feeling. He said that between Johannes's death and *everything* that had been before, a great gulf was fixed...there is nothing to be done but wait for money, and dash off to Paris—sixteen hours rumble and stink for a journey which should take eight." Ada had to wire her niece some money, since theirs, apparently, was "*all* at 43 [Belsize Park], in the shape of unendorsed cheques".[105] This was only one of the many occasions when Ada would bail out her niece. "Many many thanks. We have just heard from Cox's and leave tomorrow," Mary Butts wrote on the 27 July.[106] She was relieved to be going. "Do I understand [John Rodker] then, sympathise with his needs? It is no answer to say 'he never asks me to'". "Yes, I always wanted you to," commented John Rodker. "But you were stupid and I was too proud to explain."

The couple returned to England via Paris, where they stayed at 3, Rue de Beaune, Quai Voltaire and met James Joyce. When their boat docked on the morning of the 30th Mary Butts was pleased to be back: "Southampton water like a true pearl. Sea, six o'clock sun. Tea and bacon and eggs. English air met crisp, sparkling, *tasting*." She went straight to Ada's house in Milnthorpe, Poole, two miles from Salterns. She felt safe because in "my Aunt's house... I have not a single bad memory.... My old room, a long way below Aunt Agnes' violin." Whilst there she walked to Salterns (to visit her mother and brother), sat on a hill overlooking the house and wept. The occasion inspired her short story, 'Change', written in late September and published in *The Dial* in 1922.[107] Frederick Colville-Hyde had died the previous summer. Widowed once again, Mary Colville-Hyde no longer wished to live at Salterns. In 1920 she had already begun the process of selling off parts of the land and the tenancies adjacent to the property. It would be three years before the house itself was sold and its contents put up for auction. In early August 1920, however, Mary Butts knew it was almost the end of Salterns. She would never forgive her mother.

* * * * *

Welcombe House, Welcombe, Near Bude, Cornwall
August 1920

THE MORNING AFTER her arrival at Welcombe House in Cornwall on the 3 August Mary Butts wrote a "depressed wail" to her aunt: "It's a lonely place, fourteen miles from *anywhere*. At the moment all are a little desolate owing to catering difficulties, *etc.* Cecil thin as paper, very quiet. Jimmy fit. So am I but it's a terrifying place—huge cliffs and utter desolation."[108] She apologised the following day: "We have got over the place's desolation—it was a shock after the rich loveliness of the Pyrenees, rocks and heather and an awful sea. Now we're happy and shaken in—the house is delightful—I never felt better in my life."[109] Certainly the practical difficulties were soon sorted out; the emotional tangles of the threesome were rather more difficult to resolve.

There are few diary entries for the month of August, except those sketched out in "a Case of apparent possession" at the end of the year. According to this account Cecil Maitland and Mary Butts (describing herself as MR) engaged in occult practices. John Rodker did not take part.

> 11.8.20. CM at Welcombe. Violent suicidal impulse. Perception of JF [suicide victim] as an infuriated devil demanding that he instantly destroy himself. Distrust and dislike for MR who felt herself miserably helpless.
>
> [12.8.20] CM exhausted—like a man who had been fighting for his life. In the evening MR felt the chill in the corner where CM was sitting—at that moment aware of what was called 'the Chinaman'. (He had 'seen' him there once before on his arrival some days previously…)…
>
> 18.8.20 Mary Rodker and Cecil Maitland. Séance with glass and alphabet after lunch.

On the 19 August Mary Butts decided that Cecil Maitland was "a man under a doom. He has had from his childhood the perception of the dark place in reality, what we call the Abyss." The strain caused her to have "frightful pains in my inside [and] I thought the baby was going to be born." Fortunately, it was a false alarm. "I know what it was," she claimed to her aunt. "It was the mental stress at the new contact with Fitz and Peter [Taylor], repressed, and upsetting my inside through my nerves."[110] There are no references in her diary to being upset by the Taylors, but such an explanation was doubtless more acceptable than the truth. Mary Butts did tell her aunt in a separate letter that she and Cecil Maitland were "making a record of psychic manifestations", but did not go into more detail.[111]

By the beginning of September Mary Butts and John Rodker had returned to 43 Belsize Park Gardens. According to her doctor's calculations, the baby was due at the end of October and she had decided to have it, not at home (the cheaper option), but in a nursing home. This was possible because Ada had offered to lend her the money for the fees. In order to raise the necessary sum, Ada sold a portrait by the eighteenth century painter, John Zoffany R.A. In 1921 Mary Butts did send her aunt some of the interest on the loan, but given her bad finances, it is unlikely that she ever completely repaid this debt. Yet even this was far from being the most generous action which Ada would undertake for her niece.

Whilst she waited for the baby to be born, Mary Butts informed her aunt that she was "very well, taking long walks and writing and seeing old friends and improving my mind".[112] The friends she saw during the autumn included Ezra Pound and his wife. Mary Butts commented on "the beauty of Dorothy Pound in a silver-blue cloak and round hat of curled feathers and fur at her wrists and neck and shoes of grey crocodile skin." In late October she saw May Sinclair several times. After noticing a book about teleplasm at her house on the 21st, she had the idea of Sally as a succubus and considered writing a story based on the notion of "Sally by means of a teleplasm sucking at [Cecil Maitland's] life". She also wrote to her aunt on the 24th to say that they had been invited to dine "with May Sinclair. She is a member of the S.P.R. [Society for Psychical Research], and lends me books. She has the new one on the 'materialisations' in Mde Brisson the French sculptor's studio—with the most extraordinary photographs. Unless it is a stupendous hoax here is something that can't be telepathy or the 'subconscious' at last.... If the child hasn't come!... I'm to have it... [otherwise] John will go without me and borrow it (very sceptical) and read it with avidity, and lend it to Cecil Maitland, and I shan't get it for weeks!"[113]

Apart from these visits, Mary Butts spent most of her time with Cecil Maitland who was getting on very badly with Sally. The latter had written a play in which (as Maitland explained to Mary Butts on the 4 September), he figured as "Wilfrid...who comes in drunk. There is a long discussion on suffering. She made me out as a kind of Christ." The play depressed him. Mary Butts and he spent the evening sitting on Primrose Hill where they had their "old argument that either [Sally's] an innocent, high-minded idiot, or a most malevolent cunning and dangerous she-fiend". Mary Butts knew which interpretation she favoured: "it is now quite clear that whenever Cecil Maitland is in contact with M.B. he is restored and tranquillised. It is equally clear that any time spent with S.B. is disastrous to him, as though his system were absorbing a poison." On the 19 September she decided to write a story on "Sally's horror".

Whilst it remained unwritten, her resumé gives an interesting account of the way in which she transformed fact into a fiction of Russian proportions:

> It will want rather more narrative. A young woman who has seen her lover as a 'kind of Christ'[114] —sexual motif in the crucifixion story. Through sensual worship of his torment arrived at a very delicate, profound adoration, a very friendly and helping love. There will have to be a solid 'invention'—how did he get like that? And it might be nauseating. And it must be candid.
> The rest is easy, another woman gets the idea (how?) and travesties it to his lover... Her knock out. Finis.

But she could not sustain the necessary energy, as her pregnancy was making her "much less concerned with people's feelings and opinions, much brusquer, remoter than I used to be." Money worries prevailed at this time and prompted her to draw up a list of what "we have to *hope* for". The list included unexplained references, such as: "sale of press; Blandine; Wadsworth;[115] [and] John's father—pram? Apart from that we have very little income."

When Tony came to visit some time that "hot close autumn", she wrote to her aunt to complain about his attitudes. Heavily pregnant, she was impatient with him. Her letter also reveals the breakdown in communication with her mother:

> He was very nervous, exaggerated fearfully, looked very ill, nearly cried, tried to defend himself, but the substance of his complaint was money, money, money, its absence, his need of it, his *right* to it (without doing any work) the vile way life was treating him— etc. ad lib. It fretted me but I listened.... I can't make out what is going on at Salterns —Tony's account was so obviously distorted—they've sold the Bristol tea-set (I was shocked). Mother had run herself into debt *on her own account*— life was a conspiracy to ruin them. (As if the universe hadn't something better to do.)

The selling of the Butts possessions continued for the next twenty years. Ada had clearly been trying to reconcile Mary Butts to her mother, but it was in vain, since Mary Butts could only reply: "As to mother—give me time. I don't know what to think—your principles are all right—I don't know if they *could* be put into practice now."[116]

As the day of the birth drew nearer, she felt she had somehow let Cecil Maitland down: "I no more give him life and I have none. The child is eating it. He had none of his own. Through me, he saw his 'driving idea'. I went away. JF killed himself. He tried to save himself without me. He is drinking and whoring (which doesn't matter) and despairing again. He is dying.... The larve is good to me. But only I saw Cecil in his divine shape, last May." She waited for her child to be born: "October 22nd. No infant yet.... October 27th. No infant.... November 3rd. No baby." The next entry, dated the 8 November announced:

> Camilla Elizabeth born Nov 7th at 5.35 evening.[117]

* * * * *

> Julie had a troublesome birth in a London nursing home on November 29th [1920]. There seems to be a conspiracy of silence about the horrors of childbearing and a pretty legend that the mother forgets all about it as soon as it is over. The hell she does!... Mary Butts also had a baby almost on the same day as myself, and hers was simply colossal and very difficult to manage. Mary was quite unable to deal with her and left her to John to look after. John, being a Jew, had the paternal sentiment very well developed. Mary, on the other hand, was away in some sort of cloud-cuckoo land of her own and could not come to terms with anything so stupendously natural and immediate as a large and necessitous infant.
>
> —Stella Bowen, *Drawn From Life*[118]

Mary Butts did not find motherhood easy. In the nursing home she wrote that "the birth was soon over, three days subsequent horrors of discomfort, and tears every morning. I cried when they woke me — brought in the baby at seven." When she returned home, things did not improve: "Well, I could do without her. It is no ecstacy but a job." Stella Bowen's account seems to have been accurate, for she added: "Here and for ever it can be said that Jimmy has helped me as not one father in a thousand (or any father I have heard of) ever helped. Then he loves her more than I. 'A little girl child' he said." For her part Mary Butts was preoccupied with Cecil Maitland: "I must get well—to go out to him," was her refrain. She was also in shock: "[Camilla] had been born ten days when he told me about the poison he had taken. 1 bottle chlorodyne, cocaine 6 grains and the two narcotics had neutralised and half killed him," she noted in November. Cecil Maitland's suicide attempt was not his first, nor his last. At this point in their relationship it appealed to Mary Butts's sense of drama and she believed she could and should save him. As she remarked on the 11 December: "I love Cecil because of the delicious states he evokes in me."

With regard to John Rodker, by contrast, she decided on the 9 December that their marriage had been solely the consequence of her having

> 'sought a burden'. That is, I went out to look for reality. It was not in politics or in the poor or learning or lovers or economics. Then John came along and said 'wear my yoke'. I've worn it proudly... And I've

> learned—a kind of fundamental aesthetic and vision. *Ashe* was the last fumbling, Cecil the adieu. I'm through. There remains however a month old girl child for the figure in the outer world, a number of debts, and a 'situation' between Jimmy and Cecil. It will delay the winding up.

"No," objected John Rodker, when he read her diary in 1921. "It has wound up.... I have been reading your old letters to me. There is nothing you say about your lover that you have not said to me or about me."

* * * * *

MARY BUTTS and Cecil Maitland became lovers in December 1920. Even before their relationship was consummated, the power of their mutual attraction surpassed her expectations:

> I remember the taxi coming back when I lay conventionally in his arms and then knew that he was in extasie of his own and held my breath. I remember the drink and the fun and the long peace over the fire. I remember the blind spells of passion. I remember though we could not have each other when I made him lie down beside me and what happened. It was like falling into a thick dark cloud, and enduring at the same time a physical sweetness I have never before conceived of. It was unthinkable—a consummation of the completest sort when only our lips touched and our ankles. Talk of Joyce! When we got up—sixty seconds later—we could not stand, but clung waving on our feet. He took me up to the glass. "Look at yourself." We looked in side by side...we were so young and drunk with bliss.

Interestingly, it was at this very point, when she turned from John Rodker to Cecil Maitland, from life in the 3rd to life in the 4th dimension, that Mary Butts noted: "Birthday tomorrow. Twenty-nine or thirty." Never uncertain, John Rodker would add: "December 1890". In the years to come and, subsequently, since her death, the age attributed to Mary Butts has varied considerably.

Mary Butts and John Rodker did not separate immediately. Instead, on Sunday the 19 December, when "we were two lovers in the plenitude of our passion (*at least I was*)", Cecil Maitland tried to commit suicide with JF's revolver. "*I knew nothing* (where is our telepathy)," cried Mary Butts. "He was taken to Paddington Hospital where he is now. It is not supposed that he will die. He wrote to me. This afternoon...I went there and a nurse turned me away 'because it was not convenient'.... I came home and wrote to him. I do not know what will become of us." Still she did not give up on Cecil Maitland; still she felt she could save him. Attributing his suicide attempt to the evil hold Sally was exerting over him, she waited impatiently for him to leave hospital.

PART THREE

The Wild Party in London and on the Continent

1921/1925

CHAPTER SEVEN

A Year of Magic
1921

It is an affair complete in both worlds. I suppose all affairs are, but what makes this unique, is that I can, to an extent, watch it in both. To keep watch and experience passion in two worlds—I do not envy any adept.

—MB, diary entry, 3.1.21

TO THE OUTSIDE WORLD Mary Butts and John Rodker continued for some weeks to pretend that their marriage was untroubled. They engaged an "Irish maid" who took over the care of Camilla, giving Mary Butts the opportunity to read the poetry of the French symbolist, Arthur Rimbaud, and muse on Cecil Maitland. On the 3 January 1921 she commented: "I have had an eternity of emotion with a man whose life voluntarily—is not worth six months" and she characterised her lover as:

> A sensual intelligent boy, clairvoyant but only to the 'dark perceptions'. *Suggestible*— ...because of a certain pace and madness in him, he worked average preoccupations to intensity.... I know what followed—his ghastly illness, drink, cocaine, more brooding, more agony, a feeling round after death.... To see his beauty re-emerge, to watch him lift his head, to see his eyes 'come out'.... What I have given, he gives me back—I'm so little used to that, I'm afraid to receive it.... Soon I shall be alone with him.

By the 13 January the pretence was over. In a letter to Ada, Mary Butts blamed the breakdown of their marriage on John Rodker in order to retain her aunt's sympathy: "When I married John I was in love with him and prepared to take him at his own valuation as an artist, and I was willing to support him in order that he should be free to do his own work. However, I soon learned that he had no intention of working seriously, that all he wanted was to flirt with the arts, and with the attractive women of our set."[1] Mary Butts did not tell Ada that Cecil Maitland was her lover; instead she wrote that, as for her "friendship for Mr. Maitland, John introduced us, encouraged it from the first, and only discovered that he disliked it when it became convenient to him to use it as a weapon against me. Maitland is a queer, neuraesthenic person who needs care and kindness..." The letter concluded: "With regard to the future, I am arranging with John to be made Camilla's guardian. For the moment I have put her into much better hands than mine, and have gone away for a month to regain my health. To safeguard myself from possible annoyance I have left my address, and the sole charge of my affairs with Mrs [Fitz] Taylor, 9 Taviton St, WC1." In January John Rodker went away to Spain. It was whilst there that he read Mary Butts's 1920 diary. His notes provide some indication of his contradictory feelings about the break-up of their marriage:

> Finally you go away with your lover and though you are at 2, The Parade, Swanage and though I had meant to take you away (now reading your diary I haven't the courage to commence all over again with your âme incomprise) and it would no doubt happen again. You did me a great wrong when you married me, for that made life together intolerable and I have lost in you the most precious thing I have had.... there are instances of unpardonable behaviour [which include]... Asking Fitz not to let me have Camilla's address when you know what she is to me.

Mary Butts paid a friend to look after Camilla from 1921 onwards. Her lack of interest in and concern for her daughter is revealed by the fact that Camilla is mentioned only *once* in her diary for the whole of 1921. She was apparently not on speaking terms with Mary Colville-Hyde, since her letter of the 13 January to Ada concluded: "If my mother cares to send me a written invitation to Salterns for a week I am quite prepared to consider it when I come back."[2]

The diary is silent for the next few weeks, reopening on the 20 February in London with the following summary: "John read this [diary]. He left me. I waited three days and went away with Cecil Maitland. We stayed in a furnished room [in Swanage]. Its balcony overhung the bay. The spray flew in at the windows. John came back. His letters were like pieces of teleplasm spewed out of the Grey Thing." One of the letters included a passage about "the 'whores he (C.M.) had tongued'. When I got that card," wrote Mary Butts in her diary," I told Cecil to take my wedding ring and throw it into the sea. There was a storm. He went out. When he came back and said 'it is done', a cold breath blew across me. I thought John was a demon." One of the letters revealed that John Rodker had told Ada about Cecil Maitland. This prompted Cecil Maitland to write to Ada himself. It is a letter which, perhaps not surprisingly, highlights "Mary's unhappy life with Rodker". At the very least, it shows how unsuited they were in temperament and attitude and that the problems in their marriage were complex:

> You know that [Mary] is marvellously sensitive and she believed that the fact of her living with me, would upset you terribly. I felt therefore that it would be most unwise to tell you [about our relationship] before she recovered, for distress on your part, possibly accompanied by tears and remonstrances which could have availed nothing, would have been a fresh torment....
>
> In no sense is this to be taken as an apology for conduct of mine. We love each other and both of us consider that love alone justifies and makes beautiful sexual relations.... For my part I would never have told Mary what I felt for her, had I not seen that Rodker had starved her of love until she no longer felt it for him, was constraining her to a relationship against which she revolted to gratify his own casual passions and treating all the finest part of her nature with a cold contempt that imperilled its existence.... I believe that I have made, and shall in future be able to make Mary happy.
>
> Mary is very fond of you, that is why I am writing. If you love her enough you will understand that she is the one to be sympathised with, not that contemptible person Rodker, who can find nothing in his heart but reproaches for a woman he exploited and estranged till he drove her into her present position. He had not even the spirit to attack me openly, but only behind my back in mean, miserable and sometimes obscene letters to Mary, full of insinuations that would not enter the head of anyone in our class.

Cecil Maitland concluded: "You hardly know me, but I ask you to believe that I love her and want to make up to her for the unhappiness she has been through."[3] Such a letter, to a woman with conservative Christian principles as Ada Briggs was, did little to allay her fears and probably shocked her a great deal. From then on, until the end of Mary Butts's life, Ada would "watch, wait and pray and...hold out a hand of love without reproach, and yet without approval".[4]

On Mary Butts's return to 43 Belsize Park Gardens John Rodker had moved out into a flat at 13 Avery Row, Bond St. At the beginning of March she and Cecil Maitland travelled to the Continent where they would spend the next six months. They went first to Paris where they stayed in a studio let to them by an (unnamed) Italian. On her arrival she declared: "I am now going to have the best part of my life."

* * * * *

Paris, March—July 1921

This life with him suits me— I am twice the woman I was, or ten times.
—MB, diary entry, 1.6.21

I have an idea all the time that any man is only separated from his perfection by a razor's edge.
—MB, diary entry, mid-April 1921

If Mary Butts did not at this stage share John Rodker's grief, it was because she did not believe that their relationship was over. Even after these troubled weeks and whilst she was living in Paris with her lover, she could assert: "My will is to love Jimmy for ever. And Cecil. And myself. And that I should be the conductor of Jimmy's illumination as I am for Cecil's. That some day the 'sphere should break' for Jimmy and let out me. That we may be three souls together. That is what I want." It might have seemed possible from Mary Butts's 4th dimensional perspective; it certainly had no basis in three-dimensional reality. Stella Bowen may well have been right to describe Mary Butts as inhabiting a "cloud-cuckoo land of her own", since on the eve of her departure for Paris she left a rose and the words "belovèd Jimmy" on an envelope in John Rodker's flat. He responded with "an envelope full of bills. On the back of one was written—'your tenants haven't moved in yet.'" It is a measure of her naive self-absorption that Mary Butts was surprised. The mention of tenants referred to 43 Belsize Park Gardens. Until the end of her lease of the house in the spring of 1924, Mary Butts would sublet the property to several artists and writers, including the actress, Elsa Lanchester, the sculptress, Gladys Hynes, and the writer, Douglas Goldring. But this would be later...

Once in Paris Mary Butts met a great number of people, probably in part, through "the lively and stimulating...Nina Hamnett, who knew everybody who wrote or painted, introduced newcomers to each other as well as to earlier arrivals and generally acted as informal hostess at the Café du Dôme, the 'Select' and the other cafés which acted both as meeting-places and clearing houses."[5] Memoirs about the roaring twenties provide the greatest number of accounts of Mary Butts. It is also the decade from which most of the misrepresentations would arise.

Certainly Mary Butts would spend time with Nina Hamnett. One of the first people she mentioned on her arrival in Paris, however, was the writer, painter, arch-magician and adept, Aleister Crowley, who called himself the Great Beast 666. Nina Hamnett described this eccentric as "quite bald, with the exception of a small bunch of hairs on top of his head, which he twiddled into a point. He shaved the back of his head and appeared entirely bald."[6] In 1917 Mary Butts had quoted in her diary St Augustine's maxim "Love and do what you will." From March 1921 she began to cite Crowley's precept: "Do what thou wilt shall be the whole of the Law." According to his biographer, Crowley had derived it not from Augustine directly but from the sixteenth century French writer, François Rabelais.[7] Born in 1875, Aleister Crowley declared that his "task was to bring Oriental wisdom to Europe and to restore paganism in a purer form".[8] He believed his most recent previous incarnation had been as the French occultist, Eliphas Lévi, whose work Mary Butts had studied the previous year in the British Museum. (By the 1940s Crowley believed that his previous incarnations had included William Shakespeare.)[9]

In March 1921 Crowley's reputation was already formidable. He was about to leave Paris for Cefalu, a fishing village on the north coast of Sicily. There, the previous year, under the names Sir Alastor de Kerval and Contessa Léa Harcourt, Crowley and his "Scarlet Woman", Leah Hirsig, had signed the lease for a villa perched on a hillside half a mile outside Cefalu. This very ordinary villa was the Beast's Collegium ad Spiritum Sanctum and he had renamed it the Abbey of Thelema (the name of Rabelais's imaginary abbey in *Gargantua and Pantagruel*; Thelema means 'Will'). "And my house is going to be The Whore's Hell, a secret place of the quenchless fire of Lust and the eternal torment of Love", was Crowley's "demoniac vision" of the Abbey.[10]

Before he left Paris, Aleister Crowley instructed Mary Butts and Cecil Maitland in some of his magical practices. "I believe the Beast to be a technical expert of the highest order," Mary Butts declared several months later (18.8). Yet from the outset she was not overawed, commenting on the 31 March that "Alastair is an assistance, not a road nor a card". Crowley taught them about the gnostic cross, yogic asanas and pranayama (postures and breathing techniques) and mantras. These were all aids to "astral journeys", on which the practitioner would enter higher levels of consciousness. Mary Butts and Cecil Maitland began to undertake astral journeys, often while smoking hashish. During one such 'journey', Cecil Maitland 'saw' John Rodker working on a play in the tiny village of Sennen, West Cornwall, where he spent several weeks in the spring of 1921.[11] Mary Butts's journeys, which she described in great detail throughout the year, often involved landscapes around Salterns: "Aleister Crowley says that in certain places...there is a leak from the astral (accounting for 'the place you wouldn't spend the night in if you were paid'). People can be leaks. Salterns" (18.7). Already in May she was increasingly convinced that *Ashe of Rings* had been "all prophecy" and in her entry for the 25th, she traced the lineage of "A priestly house. Alkmaionids—Eumolpidae[12]—Blake—I—Camilla—?" (This was her only reference to Camilla for 1921.) In September she pondered in relation to her 'journeys' whether this "incursion perpetually of Salterns is itself an astral leak?" By the time she came to write *The Crystal Cabinet* in the mid-1930s, she declared that she had inherited the Butts family "secret":

> A secret concerned with time and very little with death, with what perhaps medieval philosophers called *aevum*, the link between time and eternity. With which goes an ability to live in two worlds at once, or in time and out of it. Even in a further dimension of time. A secret which might make us devout. Or might not. Incline us to mysticism, as in the case of my great-grandfather, Tom Butts, an official at the War Office, and one of those eighteenth-century types who combined respect for the Archbishop of Canterbury with the introduction of Swedenborg to the drawing-rooms of Fitzroy Square.[13]

She claimed that it was this "secret" which had led her great-grandfather to realise the mystical importance of William Blake and hence become his patron. In 1921 Mary Butts herself was certainly inclining to mysticism.

In April she and Cecil Maitland discussed "what we really wanted 'in magic'". Mary Butts had seven aims which show that her interest was bounded by her dedication to her writing:

> I. I want to study and enjoy, and to enter if I can into the fairy world, the mythological world, and the world of the good ghost story.[14]
>
> II. I want by various mystical practices and studies to produce my true nature, and enlarge my perceptions.
>
> III. I don't only want to find my true will. I want to do it. So I want to learn how to form a magical link between myself and the phenomena I am interested in. I want power.
>
> IV. I want to find out what is the essence of religion, study the various ideas of God under their images.
>
> V. I want to make this world into material for the art of writing.
>
> VI. I want to observe the pairs of opposites, remembering that which is below is as that which is above. From this I wish to formulate clearly, the hitherto incommunicable idea of a third perception. This is a perception of the nature of the universe as yet unknown to man, except by intuitions which cannot be retained, and by symbols whose meaning cannot be retained also. I want to fix it in man's mind.
>
> VII. I want to write a book not about an early theocracy and fall of man,...but a book written about the subject, *historically, under terms of human fallability without deification of Pythagoras or the writers of the*

> *Kabala*.... A book to show the relation of art to magic, and shew the artist as the true, because the oblique adept.

Mary Butts added a dark personal coda to this ambitious search for knowledge: "I have an intuition, that, if, I ever know it, I shall have to cross a threshold of some frightful impersonal suffering or horror before I get it."

In May her intuition was tested. "*Ashe* is not to appear," she noted and tried to minimise her grief by watching herself in pain. She was referring to a conversation with Ezra Pound, who had explained that *The Little Review* would not, after all, be able to publish her novel. As he wrote to Margaret Anderson on the 21st: "I have told Mary we probably wont [sic] be able to use her novel = Certainly we cant afford to be suppressed at any time during the coming year. = Cost of reprods. forbids. = also 5 times is enough. Let someone else come for'ard. = If you want to do Mary's novel, it wd. mean 32 pages extra per number. = & corresponding increase in price which wd. make it too high."[15] *The Little Review* had suffered enormous costs and suppression for indecency, following the publication of chapters from James Joyce's *Ulysses*. Understandably, it was a blow to Mary Butts, who did not even seem to know that the first instalment of the novel had been printed in the Jan-March 1921 issue of *The Little Review*. It was James Joyce who informed Cecil Maitland of this, leaving a copy for Mary Butts with Sylvia Beach at her Paris bookshop, Shakespeare & Co.[16] The next few chapters would be printed in the Autumn 1921 issue.

Things did not improve when Cecil Maitland fell ill and his eyes were seriously affected. Mary Butts "grudged him his preoccupation with his illness—I did not trouble to lie well. I allowed myself quilt. I did my duty with great contempt." Aware of his dependence on her, that she "had to hold everything together without the privileges of the leader, or the protections of the child", she commented on the "commonplace insanity of our position" and craved solitude. At such times, she felt that there was a curse on their happiness, but such feelings were only transitory. Two days later, when he was better, she declared: "Cecil is giving me life now and I have advanced a grade in adeptship." There were also many enjoyable evenings spent with friends. "Last night was amusing, [Tommy] Earp, Dodo, Hilda [HD], Berenice [Abbot], Cecil and I. The three cabarets...I saw my beauty in a hundred mirrors, it wore well. I could dance and I drank," she enthused in early June. After such a cheering occasion she wrote that "the curse upon C and I has lifted."

Her feelings were again tested when John Rodker arrived on the 19 May. They spent the next month talking as they wandered around the

Luxembourg Gardens, the Parc Montsouris and other Parisian haunts. Nothing was resolved however. By the beginning of June Mary Butts and Cecil Maitland had decided to join Aleister Crowley at his Abbey of Thelema. She gave her reasons in a note to John Rodker: "Cecil and I have something particular to do together.... I'm going South to Sicily with him to find out what it is. I shall learn and live and suffer. He will learn and suffer and perhaps die. I'm not speaking of our personal passions just now."[17] John Rodker did not leave Paris until the 19 June. By this time Mary Butts's astral journeys had been so successful that she began to view herself as a "secular Isis" and in their last meeting, although in some ways lucid, was clearly absent in all but body:

> Jimmy and I went out. I took him to the Parc Montsouris. He started 'going over the case'. The futility wore me down. It had all been said. At best we are waiting for an event. I remember the white hot, rough stones on the terrace above the Rue des Artistes—I said to the daimon 'this is nothing'. He said 'take it piece by piece'.... We lunched. I tried to be cold and remember my wrongs, but we got friendly. I saw that *whatever* he was, my grievances were phenomenal rubbish. We went for a stroll, and sat on a concrete rock and he clung to me. I felt a time had come, and nothing had come to fill the time. I shall remember what followed. The sun was behind the concrete rock. The path was covered with little pebbles. I turned a little away from him and stared at them, still speaking to the daimon. There was the shadow of my head in my wide hat, very black and large and less of his head, he was sitting back, near it. There was this black shadow, the stones, and the sun. I looked into the small stones and understood... I looked twice, and twice he pulled my arm, and said, 'what are you thinking?' and I answered, 'about a magic.'

A few days later the lovers left Paris for Cefalu. Mary Butts had been right. They would both suffer during their ten-week stay there.

* * * * *

Cefalu, late June–16 September

> *A.C. shews me a desolate path.*
>
> —MB, diary entry, 7.7.21

THE ABBEY OF THELEMA, up a narrow mountain path above Cefalu, was in an idyllic setting. Crowley described its breathtaking panorama: "We are high on the neck of the peninsula and can see West of Palermo, East over the sea, North is the mighty rock of Cephaloedium and behind us to the South rise hills, green with trees and grass."[18] According to Mary

Butts, the weather during the summer of 1921 was equally "enchanting. High winds...huge clouds, an audible sea up here, on the hill-side. We've bathed in rollers, not in a crystal toy. We've slept out night after night, seen the stars move across... The other side of the rock is a huge sea with spray columns and rainbows."

The living conditions in the Abbey were not so pleasant, however. When they arrived at the Collegium ad Spiritum Sanctum, Mary Butts and Cecil Maitland had to undergo initiations in order to begin their search for their true will. Mary Butts recorded that she was forced on more than one occasion to "go back into the cave. There was a rug on the floor with a diamond pattern, black and yellow. A round window looking onto a cove and rocks at low tide with dark green weed. There was an odd bird-reptile squat-looking thing on a shelf. It changed, I could not make it talk, I tired, and I came back." As for Cecil Maitland, Crowley's biographer states that he "went for a swim in the bay (the Caldara) with the Beast, who seems to have tried his best to drown him. He saved his life by climbing the rough rocks to the cliff top, losing only portions of his skin."[19] The discipline at the Abbey was harsh. There was little food and very little privacy or free time. The initiates had to rise at dawn and perform asanas and astral journeys by meditating on specific magical symbols decided upon by Crowley, often with hashish, opium or cocaine. (Mary Butts commented that the drugs were not necessary in her case, which seems to have been true.) The Beast also gave lectures (she noted one on the tattras in early August). "Everyone in the temple had to write their diary every day and everyone else was allowed to read it."[20]

Soon after their arrival on the 5 July, Mary Butts and Cecil Maitland participated in a two-hour initiation ceremony. Crowley gave an account of this gruesome ritual in his Magical Record:

> 2.00pm. The ceremony of preparing the Cakes of Light. A young cock is to be baptized Peter Paul into the Catholic Church by C.J.A. Maitland,[21] the son of an apostate Romish Priest, and therefore the ideal 'Black' Hierophant. Mary Butts and I are its sponsors. Peter and Paul are the founders of the Christian Church, and we want its blood to found our own church.... The cock is slain in honour of Ra-Hoor-Khuit [Horus], who is invoked before the killing.[22]

Despite their appealing name, cakes of light were made of excrement. To Crowley's surprise, Mary Butts refused to partake of them. Strangely, she was not put off the Abbey immediately by this bizarre ritual and Crowley soon admitted that her clairvoyante capacity was well-developed. Part of the regime at Cefalu involved the rigorous analysis of complexes (also called masks) in order to remove them. This practice led Mary Butts to reflect on how she used to fear the supernatural:

> I remembered the quality of that fear, and was on the edge of applying it to all that I see and do here. Then I saw what horrors that would open up, if I feared this place, as others fear, and I used to fear 'the supernatural'. One grinds on explaining, but it is a horror. This one fear was part of the rim of one wheel. Another brought anguish of mind about Cecil, another a horror of physical sounds. Behind these wheels each with its horror point was a wheel that was all fear. There was another called Trance-of-Sorrow. But the fear of fear was like going over an edge, and I felt that I was suffocating.
>
> (A.C. said next day that I may have been attacked by an astral shape, *or* be on the verge of remembering my last death, which had been violent—drowning?)

Crowley himself later paid tribute in his autobiography to Mary Butts's knowledge of the occult. Whilst she was at the Abbey, he was revising *Magick*, a treatise which was published in 1929:

> I showed the manuscripts to Soror Rhodon [Mary Butts] and asked her to criticise it thoroughly. I am extremely grateful to her for her help, especially in indicating a large number of subjects which I had not discussed. At her suggestion I wrote essay upon essay to cover every phase of the subject. The result has been the expansion of the manuscript into a vast volume, a complete treatise upon the theory and practice of Magick, without any omissions.[23]

Personally, Crowley's memory of Mary Butts was far from complimentary, however: he described her as "a large white red-haired maggot".[24] According to his biographer, Crowley felt threatened by Mary Butts and did not like it.

He was probably also annoyed that her will was not easily made subservient to his, as she continued to write whilst at the Abbey. Certainly confidence was not lacking: on more than one occasion she "saw...something about myself. I may be an image of the great work, and those who love me have to comply with my conditions, I have to comply with them myself." She revised *Ashe of Rings*,[25] wrote poetry and stories. Several of her astral journeys provided material for her fiction. For example, on the 11 July she noted "the astral journey—blue water, a solid lapis-lazuli stuff pouring about the base of a rock, or out of a rock like a basin on a pedestal and splashing round.... Young man... shewed me a round mirror on the floor, which had a bright sky in it—white, with shaking boughs. I could see nothing. Got tired, and came home." In her two-page tale, 'Bellerophon to Anteia' published in 1923, the hero describes his exile in a place where "I stood on stone at the edge of a round pool that was open to the sky.... I was so pleased with the double circle of sky and water, a blue lid over a blue plate..."[26] Another astral journey on the 20 July included "a dark cave, a furious sea breaking through it...

water sucking through a kind of blow-hole. Then the open coast and black rocks and white sea rising, a frightful place." Such a blow-hole, "worked in a jet with the strength of the Atlantic behind it",[27] would provide the climax of her novel, *Death of Felicity Taverner,* as well as occurring in the opening paragraph of *Armed with Madness.*

Whilst at the Abbey she continued to study the occult by reading "*Liber Aleph,* half the commentary on the book of the Law and begun to learn the Hebrew letters and their numerical correspondences." Aleister Crowley clearly did not approve of reading non-occult literature, since Mary Butts noted on the 16 August: "Read—when my three day's vow not to is over—Some Verlaine, *Bouvard et Pécuchet* [Flaubert], Aphra Behn... *Tess of the d'Urbervilles.*"

Very soon after their arrival, Mary Butts began to feel that Crowley was trying to destroy her relationship with Cecil Maitland. On the 7 July he read their destinies in the Yi King.[28] About Cecil Maitland, Crowley "said: 'His will is set vehemently in things he has not the resolution to attain'. To me he said, 'You must realise that human beings are animals to be trained'." Mary Butts felt that this was a "precise account [but] implies a relative inferiority in Cecil to myself which...breeds resentment in him and impatience in me". It was certainly not conducive to the couple's intimacy and Mary Butts lamented the following day that before coming to Cefalu "we moved with most exquisite facility to a common end. What I would give to have that back."

By August she was beginning to have serious doubts about the Abbey of Thelema and the Beast's methods. The positive aspects were its library and Crowley's "technical knowledge". But these were far outweighed by the appalling living conditions and Mary Butts made a list of sensible suggestions for transforming the Temple into a "miniature university". These included proper sanitation facilities (when she recorded "filthy streaks in the life here", she was not being metaphorical; the absence of toilets meant that human excreta littered the grounds); more provisions (on the 16 August she gave 200 lire to Crowley to buy food); the abandonment of unnecessary regulations, such as limiting the initiates to two cigarettes a day. This was having a particularly debilitating effect on Cecil Maitland: Crowley "offered us every drug in and out of the pharmacopaea, and tried to take away Cecil's cigarettes. This to a man who had recently cured himself of what looked like dipsomania and had reduced his count of fags from fifty to twenty-five a day." She also wanted the abolition of the Beast's disturbing practice of using children in sexual rites. Crowley was not impressed by her suggestions.The final straw came at the end of the summer when Mary Butts and Cecil Maitland witnessed an attempt at copulation set up by Crowley between the "Body of Babylon [Leah Hirsig] and the Virgin He-goat." In the event the goat refused to co-operate. However, according to Crowley's biographer, "immediately afterwards, the Beast had cut the goat's throat and the blood had spurted over Leah's bare back. In an aside, she asked Mary, 'what shall I do now?' And Mary had replied, 'I'd have a bath if I were you.'"[29]

By the time they left the Abbey on the 16 September, Mary Butts had decided that the place was a "sham" and Aleister Crowley a fanatic. On their return to Paris, according to Nina Hamnett's 1932 memoir, *Laughing Torso*: "They looked like two ghosts and were hardly recognisable".[30] (*Laughing Torso*'s claims about Crowley would lead him to sue Nina Hamnett for libel in April 1934. He would lose.)[31] As a result of her experiences at Cefalu Mary Butts declared:"I guess my judgement is made—I'd sooner be the writer I am capable of becoming than an illuminated adept, magician, magus master of this temple or another." After all, "Isn't one page of *Per Amica* [Yeats] worth every *Equinox* [Aleister Crowley's occult journal] considered as the thing in itself?"

* * * * *

London, September–December 1921

> *I do not want, I do not mean to be side-tracked into mysticism—*
> *I'd sooner be a Villon than Æ.* —MB, diary entry, 17.11.21

FROM THE 28 SEPTEMBER Mary Butts was back at 43 Belsize Park Gardens with Cecil Maitland. Already renting rooms in the terrace house at this time were the sculptress, Gladys Hynes, her brother Hugh, their nurse, Aly, and Val.[32] Back in her "delightful room" (she and Cecil Maitland had separate rooms in the house), Mary Butts pondered her stay at the Abbey of Thelema. In retrospect she claimed that she was "never once objectively convinced" by the evidence she had found there to prove "an intelligence in the universe other than man's intelligence". Rather, "three months I spent...in heat and filth and starvation and fever and insolence and fatigue and sickness and contempt and there was nothing shewn that might not have been produced by my mind...or Cecil's or the Beast's." Her depressing conclusion was that "whereas before I suffered from complexes (fear-of-the-crowd principally) I now know I do, and suffer double."

Mary Butts's health did not improve on her return to London, where she continued to eat little and took large quantities of heroin, which she called by Crowley's euphemism, "basil". She complained of "fever" and sickness on several occasions during the autumn. Yet far from abandoning all of the Beast's teachings, she continued the practice of astral journeys and under the title *Examination of the Astral Plane* recorded "extraordinary results" at the beginning of October. These included astral journeys where:

> III There is a high, brilliant world very white where are the archetypal shapes.
> IV There is a heightened image of the world we know—woods were brilliant, cliffs higher, darker seas.
> . . .
> VI There are places no imagination can picture or retain, celestial fields, people no people were ever like, echoed in literature in Fiona Macleod and Morris, in Ballads. Also the Good Friday Parzival music.

"I should prefer III," commented Mary Butts. "It's purer and more profound, but I long for VI. I have been there two or three times." In mid-November she decided that she had lost her former idealism: "I had standards, I knew the world did not 'live up' to them, but imagined that it wished to and paid them more than lip-service... I believed. I had faith." Despite this phase of despondency, she continued to search for VI all her life. It was the world conveyed in her poems and narratives and the reality she tried to force others to embody. "I can live in ideal beauty," she claimed on the 25 November. Others could not. Mary Butts keenly felt their 'failure' to do so, in spite of her decision to "never blame people. It produces a re-action in them—everything gets out of proportion." She was right, but could not live up to this difficult resolution.

That Cecil Maitland lived in a series of heightened Dostoevskian dramas continued to attract Mary Butts. There were moments, such as on the 27 October when "we kissed and praised each other and behaved like a hero and heroine of a novel of 'strong passion in the open'". Yet she did have doubts when depressive moods made him morbid and distant. Then she knew that "explorers of extremes without any provision are less than men and more." "Perhaps he is no good," she mused in early December, or "perhaps I like his type even if he died of dope in my hands." This was extremely shrewd if fugitive self-knowledge.

Mary Butts was drawn to her lover, principally because he inspired her imagination: "For weeks Cecil Maitland and I have played at being forlorn children or a prince and princess on a long phantasy of living in a fairy world and its place-on-the-edge of the star-world." All the while she knew that "we did this to gild our position of a worn-down hard-up man and woman", but this in no way detracted from the power of the fairy tale. In the autumn and winter of 1921, however, the practical reality of living at Cecil Maitland's drugged tempo was affecting her capacity to work: "I find writing difficult, but I think I can work it back. Ideas...I'm racing to catch up" (8.10). Two days later she had to concede that whilst she "want[ed] to try writing again, can't begin". Sensibly, she redirected her frustration on that day by making "the house lovely and tranquil again". But such fits of concern for her surroundings were rare at this point in her life. To spur herself into writing she decided the following day to "go through mss. and send to papers", an activity which, to judge from her letter to Ada in December, was fruitful. When she was not working at her story, 'Madonna of the Magnificat', she read the *Occult Review*, saw friends, went to hear Carlotta Mosselli sing and attended a "good" lecture on socialism in China by her adored Bertrand Russell.[33]

On the whole, however, her attention in these months was taken up with fighting what she described as a "grey patch". Crowley continued to send Cecil Maitland and Mary Butts astral predictions and she felt that, in doing so, he was pursuing his "wanton obstinacy to separate" them. She dated a series of "bad astrals" from the arrival of a letter from the Beast and claimed on the 15 October: "From the phantasms we raised out from past discarded selves, real potencies are exchanged. We have won so much that *instead* of the weak fears we forced down, real demons are after us." This would not be the last time that she felt Crowley was trying to hurt her, or that he was "a conductor for potencies that could break up the soul" (11.1.22). Perhaps some of her paranoia (which included a belief that the house was haunted) was increased by excessive drug-taking. Yet she had the self-possession to note the dangers on the 11 November:

> Sick—depressed.
> I know now why people take drugs.
> Why people do not stop taking drugs.
> I know how easy it is to think of suicide.
> But not yet how hard it is to do it.
> I know how hard it is to stay the course.
> I know how lazy, fearful, timid and contemptuous
> in all but action I am....
> I trust no one and fear the lot....It is horrible to know oneself.

* * * * *

THERE ARE NO diary entries for a month after the 8 December. It is uncertain where or how Mary Butts spent Christmas or the New Year. The only evidence is a rather breezy letter to Ada from 43 Belsize Park

Gardens on the 19 December. It is a letter in which Mary Butts portrayed herself as a hard-working writer: "Very busy writing…I've another story coming out in the States and two here."[34] And a devoted mother: "Camilla is adorable. She can walk a little, and has just got her crib. It's a beauty—with close polished wooden bars she could not possibly get her head through. She also has an eiderdown with elephants on it, and all sorts of beasts. She is very well."

Perhaps it was with a degree of bravado that Mary Butts ended her letter: "I'm very happy—happier now than I've ever been in my life."[35]

CHAPTER EIGHT

The Riotous Life

1922

In each man there is a power, I call my daimon, that seems to be an unlimitable source of peace, pleasure, rhythm and even truth. This can be evoked and must have something in common with the thing in itself, for what it shews is always, and in a vital manner, true. I think that here by true, I mean true for action and life. —MB, diary entry, early February 1922

I think that I am at the beginning of more serious writing than any I have done. —MB, diary entry, 1.5.22

IN EARLY JANUARY there was a "good sequence" in Mary Butts's relationship with Cecil Maitland. During the first two months of this year they practised magic, including seances and using Abra-Melin squares to predict events in the near future, with a certain success. On the 21 January Mary Butts declared: "There is 'magic' about.... Not at all horrible, something that passes between light point and light point—that is carried, embodied by light points. The six glass balls from Cecil's ceiling do it, and the mirrors and shined things in my room, even oiled wood." In this mood she polished an African fetish, or, rather as she put it, she "gave [it]...beeswax. It was most noticeable how he liked it," was her animistic comment. Often the lovers undertook their magical experiments in Cecil Maitland's room, the Old [Ovid] Press Room in the basement. "Even C.M. who is really clairvoyant is uneasy. Neither of us would sleep down there," noted Mary Butts, who felt that his room was "undoubtedly haunted between 5 and 7, and indeed most of the time". But this fact did not prevent her from having a very productive astral journey there, which took her to her beloved Dorset and showed her how to continue her story, 'Madonna of the Magnificat', which had been troubling her. It also left her in a very strange mood:

> Listened to the 'magic' rising in Cecil's room. Watched the ghost trap on the ceiling. Hypnotised by the silver glass ball—saw, but not in the ball, my coast, and grey sea, and rocks, the other side of the martello tower at Kimmeridge, where I have never been. Saw a large red-brown beam washed up. Went tranquil—then half-stunned to sleep. Lay down in arm-chair to sleep. Could not. Looked at balls, this time ex-

> pecting a perception, got none. Rested, smoked with pleasure. After some time I thought of a 'clou'[nail, linking idea] for the magnificat story, and came round rested into normal activity.
> All the time, the ghost tide is washing in.
> About 2 hours, from being very busy just before tea, tea, then over-tiredness, then this, now normal again.

These experiments did not appeal to all their friends: "Why on earth do you want to raise any devils, Cecil?" asked Douglas Goldring on seeing the "pentagons and magic circles...chalked on the floor". "Oh. I just wanted to see if they'd come and if there was anything in it," was his blithe reply.[36]

It is uncertain exactly when Goldring resided at 43 Belsize Park Gardens. As he later admitted: "A biographer...would find it difficult, if not impossible, to keep track of me between 1919 and 1928."[37] Whether or not he was a tenant there by 1922, Goldring was close friends with Mary Butts by that year, since she would write to him in August: "My dear Douglas...you have done so much for my shaky belief in myself."[38] Some time in the early 1920s he introduced the writer Alec Waugh (brother of the now-more-famous Evelyn) to Mary Butts's work.[39] A close friendship between Mary Butts and Alec Waugh arose,[40] but more than this.

As mentioned earlier, Mary Butts's story about a shell-shocked First World War soldier, 'Speed the Plough', was one of the twenty-two stories to be included in *Georgian Stories 1922*. The anonymous editor of this annual anthology stated in the preface that the aim was "to produce a collection which shall be thoroughly representative of the modern short story as it is being written in England today".[41] The response to this collection, and to Mary Butts's story in particular, was enthusiastic. *The Daily News* spoke of the "excellent selection" (unfortunately a misprint gave Mary Butts as Mary Bates!).[42] A long article in the *Times Literary Supplement* described 'Speed the Plough' "which is a piece of sharp originality, lucidly imagined" as "one of the best stories in this volume, possible the best of all".[43] Even the negative review, 'Nasty Georgian Fiction', by Winifred Blatchford for *The Clarion* found Mary Butts's story "remarkable".[44] When the *Best Short Stories of 1922* came out early the following year, reviews in several papers, including *The Observer* and *The Weekly Westminster Gazette* lamented the exclusion of work by D.H. Lawrence, Katherine Mansfield and Mary Butts...[45] *Georgian Stories 1922* was published by Chapman & Hall. This publishing house (which published the work of Charles Dickens) was owned by Alec's father, Arthur Waugh. Alec, who worked part-time at the press until 1924, may well have been responsible for suggesting 'Speed the Plough' for inclusion in this anthology. What is certain, is that he convinced his father to publish Mary

Butts's first book. *Speed the Plough and other Stories* appeared from Chapman & Hall in 1923.

Another newly-established resident at 43 Belsize Park Gardens commented on how Goldring "who was a tenant for a short time was almost stupefied with love for...Gladys Hynes", who lived "upstairs" with her sister, Sheelah (thirteen years her junior).[46] This quotation comes from the memoirs of Elsa Lanchester, later a famous actress, but only twenty years old in 1922. She had studied dance in Paris with Raymond Duncan (the brother of Isadora Duncan, one of the pioneers of free dance) and just after the war set up a nightclub with Harold Scott at 107 Charlotte Street. Goldring gives an account of their Cave of Harmony, which seems to have satisfied the "post-war craze for dancing":

> Evenings at the Cave consisted of dancing from about nine till midnight, followed by an hour's cabaret and further dancing until 2 a.m.... The cabaret shows put on by Harold and Elsa consisted of singing and dancing, but on one occasion a one-act play by Aldous Huxley was produced and drew a semi-fashionable audience, including people like Arnold Bennett. It was at the Cave that Elsa made one of her earliest successes with the touching Victorian ballad, "Please sell no more drink to my father." Among the early frequenters were Mary Butts and her brother Anthony, Pat Kaye, then a pupil of Mme. Astafieva and subsequently known to fame as Anton Dolin,...Alec and Evelyn Waugh, that genial pundit...J.W.N. Sullivan, and a host of others...[47]

In her autobiography, Elsa Lanchester described how she moved into "a very large room with a piano, a camp bed, and quite bohemian kitchen privileges in a large mid-Victorian stucco house owned [it was in fact leased] by the writer Mary Butts".[48] According to Lanchester, the life led there ranged from the "odd" to the "riotous" and had a garden to match: "Behind these mid-Victorian houses were long gardens with some nice trees and bushes, but behind No.43 the garden was unkempt and usually rather muddy, with some rank grass. Even in summer the bushes looked the same as in winter, yet not exactly dead. Someone gave Mary Butts a white chicken, which was named Charlotte the Harlot, and this garden was her home."[49] Lanchester described Cecil Maitland as "thickset with a rather red skin and black hair. He was either drunk or seemed to be most of the time, but maybe he was sniffing something. I didn't like Maitland at all. He frightened me."[50] But she did like Mary Butts, in spite of describing her as "strong meat for anyone... Over time I seemed to survive the power of her talent-personality. She remained a friend, though rather an out-of-focus friend due to her drug habits, I'm sure. She often came to my very large room with the piano, to watch me practice dancing and create numbers for the Cave of Harmony shows. I often noticed her sniffing the back of her hand. She was a vague but fascinating person, with or without cocaine."[51] Whilst a resident at No.43, Elsa Lanchester was invited to have tea with Mary Butts and the lawyer and writer E.S.P. Haynes, whom Elsa Lanchester found to be "lecherous"; Mary Butts also introduced her young tenant to the writings of the psychiatrist Krafft-Ebbing. Elsa Lanchester designed a dance based on his Case no 74B of Zurich.[52]

What Elsa Lanchester omitted to mention, but which a fellow dancer, Anton Dolin, paid tribute to, was the fact that "Elsa, like the rest of us, was not very rich, and often it was Mary Butts who would give her food."[53] At this time Anton Dolin rented a room only a few streets away in 25 Belsize Crescent. A fellow resident was the ballet enthusiast, Poppoea Vanda (Poppy). Dolin was first introduced to Mary Butts when he was invited to a party "Poppoea gave…at the house of her friend Mary Butts, the writer.… And so I went to my first…literary 'do' after the theatre."[54]

Mary Butts and Dolin would become life-long friends. Poppy was even more important in Mary Butts's life at this time. Not only did they share a passion for the Russian ballet; it was Poppy who looked after Camilla as a baby in her flat, thus freeing her friend to lead her "riotous" life. Mary Butts explained the arrangement to her aunt: "Poppy is magnificent for infants. I shall have her directly she is past that."[55] She did not.

In March Mary Butts, Cecil Maitland, and Gladys Hynes spent a fortnight in S. Egliston Cottage, in Kimmeridge on the Dorset coast. Mary Butts took Camilla who was looked after by Gladys's old nurse Aly. Tony also came to visit. She showed her friends her favourite places in the area, such as the Tower at Kimmeridge, Creech Barrow, the village of Corfe Castle and Badbury Rings. The importance in Mary Butts's imagination of these three concentric prehistoric rings surrounding an ancient pine wood cannot be overstated. They inspired the eponymous rings of her novel which she was still trying to get published. Even earlier, after one of her visits to this site in her early twenties, she had written a poem celebrating the power evoked 'On Badbury Rings'. It begins:

The earth appoints her place for our return,
A moor, a tree, a curved and lonely bay,
The hollow of a stream, hill perilous,
Where open walks the shape of night and day,
The dance of living air miraculous—
On Badbury Rings.

Up from the sea over the hill's high tower
On breathless autumn days there whistles light
A ghostly breeze. Their immemorial crown

Makes audible in the gaunt tree-tops' height.
Red glow the slender pine-shafts of the down
On Badbury Rings.

Broad be the girdles of the Holy Wood
Bare ramparts of lean grass close menacing,
That all but trembles on our sight, who made
Some passion of dim Gods therein out played
Or the vast act of a forgotten King
The imminent wonder, nameless luminous
On Badbury Rings.

Her visit to the Rings with her friends on the 12 March 1922 provoked a magical "sequence". In describing it, she explained the significance of the site:

> On Badbury Rings.... We went up the hill to them. I walked first saying *it is I who have given them life*. Then inside the first fosse is steep, and I leaned on Cecil's shoulder and said *I need you to enter the Rings*... There was the quiet. I lay stretched out on the ground, and understood that the Rings' signature is written in its quiet. Its quiet is made audible by the sound in the grove. I saw the fir-tree tops on their red shafts and the bunches of needles that pass sideways. They have the sensual, distinct beauty of Japanese or Chinese silk-paintings.

But a "distinct beauty" was not all that Badbury Rings evoked for Mary Butts:

> Now this place is enchanted—technically—concretely—if there is such a thing—by reputation, by experience, by tradition. I have felt them—but I have never seen anything but trees and grass and wind and their accompaniments. I have no sign I can tell. Obliquely I retold what I had seen in *Ashe*, but the communication and translation are oblique. They have affected my mind and because my mind is that sort of mind—they have made an aesthetic restatement.

* * * * *

ONCE BACK IN LONDON by the 17 March, Mary Butts resumed her practice of magic, which included automatic writing and drawing inspired by her "electric blue quicksilver ball". The atmosphere at No.43 was heightened and troubled by the presence of Leah Hirsig, (Crowley's "Scarlet Woman"), who had arrived in February. By March Mary Butts had decided that Leah's presence was part of Crowley's attack, the plan of "an erotic old megalomaniac [who] wanted you, and your money, and the prestige your personality would give him. Your lover prevented this. He has *not* yet quite given it up and has sent a subtle fanatical sweet, accommodating woman to see what she can do." As far as Mary Butts was concerned, Leah and the Beast were "two people who are *living* the book of Revelations". Yet, although Leah was "charged with occult power", even she was "*uneasy* in the Press room, like everyone else". By the time Leah left on the 27th, Mary Butts, who had taken "25 grains of quinine in 3 days", admitted that she was "not normal". Unable to stop herself, she began to do automatic writing in the Press room. The results were unclear; the whole "uncleanly business" left her feeling "gaga" and she "quarrelled hysterically with Cecil". But she could not stop and felt trapped: "In disliking the practice I seem to have felt as others have done, and like them I do not know what it is I have done. I have still a strong instinct to leave it alone, and a nervous impulse to continue it."

* * * * *

Titisee, bei Freiburg, Baden, Germany

> *There are places that are signatures. I do not mean where one has lived continually or where important affairs have happened but a place felt to be significant and passionately cherished... There is this place.*
>
> —MB, diary entry, 9.4.22

In an undated letter to Ada, probably sent in April, Mary Butts apologised for not writing earlier, "but I have been travelling about and putting things off. I've at last found a place that does my malaria good—I was getting it again badly and this place [Titisee] which is up at the top of the Schwarzwald, very nearly mountains, seems to be killing it."[56] Malaria was Mary Butts's private name for drug-induced ill-health. A letter she sent to Douglas Goldring on the 9 April from the hotel in Titisee was rather more specific: "After some crowded hours of glorious life in Paris, we found this place. Hundreds of miles of black trees and snow, very quiet, which after unlimited cocktails in Freiburg at one penny each, is just as well. It costs half-a-crown a day to live in the solidest comfort and we shall stay a long time and work."[57] In fact they stayed two months.

On arriving in Titisee Mary Butts had a recurring intuition that she had seen this place in her adolescent dreams. It was partly the pine trees: "I have seen pine trees, loved them, and their properties and their God since I was a child. They were material for my secret reveries, my first technical magical practice. They are on Badbury Rings. Cecil lived among them. We came, by accident to live among them here." All her life Mary Butts felt an alternating affinity with trees and the sea, and had declared the previous November: "I should like to be a wave coming up again and again, or a tree that I could watch the web for ever...the web the world throws off, the pattern that flies glittering in the dark air over our heads."[58]

In Titisee in late April 1922 she sensed that the pine trees "sigh to me, they trouble me, their ranks stand down the valley, dark, with snow banked round their roots, when the sun comes out between the snow flurries, they glow as they do in mid-summer, especially when their crests have been dusted with snow". This kinship explained, she thought, her favourite perfume: "*My* scent is Chypre de Coty. It transported me before I knew that it was made from moss 'gathered at certain times in the woods'. The moss is arm deep in these woods, feather-moss and club moss. I have a little Chypre with me. It would be appropriate to make a libation?"

Another 'magic' of which Mary Butts was keenly aware in Titisee that spring was her red hair: "*My life is in my hair*. It *is* my chief beauty." Nine years earlier she had immortalised its power in the final verse of her love poem, 'Dionysiac': "Blood of my heart I give to you, the world/ Turns on us—see before this strength is hurled/ My hair a banner on the wind unfurled." During the summer of 1916, when she, Eleanor and Tony had been together at Salterns, Mary Butts had noted that at one point Eleanor "cursed us all horribly, even the colour of my hair". It certainly seems to have been her most striking physical feature since almost all accounts of Mary Butts comment on her hair. For Elsa Lanchester, she had "thin carrot-coloured hair that was almost pink"; for Constance Maynard, she was a "glowing red-head"; for Douglas Goldring, her hair was "red-gold"; for Stella Bowen it was "scarlet"; for Iris Barry it was "vermillion red". Even Aleister Crowley, who saw her as a "maggot", described it as being "red-headed".[59] As we shall see, almost all the friends Mary Butts made in the following years were struck by her hair...

Despite the restorative climate, the lovers were not always well in Titisee. Cecil Maitland had various ailments and recurrent nightmares, while Mary Butts was consumed with hatred for her mother and "went mad" at one stage, convinced that Cecil Maitland no longer cared for her. Yet for all this, their stay in the Schwarzwald seems to have led to a greater intimacy and "complete harmony" between the lovers, even when they took 'basil': "C took some...for his neuralgia, and I a little 'to keep him company'. I did not sleep. There was a great tension—as though there was something wicked, nearly visible, walking about in a dark glass world filling our rooms. Then he called me. 'Darling, you are the great magic.' That broke it. I went in and lay in his arms...and then we slept. I have rarely known a glory like it." Whilst she continued to believe that her relationship with him was fated, part of "a huge significant design", she noted: "The psychologist [would] say: two exceptional suitable natures in unhappy circumstances met and had the realism to stick to one another." Mary Butts's response was: "One can only observe the sequences coming out." After all, "sometimes...we see structures, sometimes there is a new perception that can be co-related, sometimes a phantasy which can be related to nothing, and is terrifying and enchanting. The psychologists must name that quality and account for it." To her aunt, she wrote on the 19 May: "I am getting my health back, my talents, my nerve and courage. I am happier than I can ever remember to have been. This I owe to Cecil Maitland. He has comforted me, taken care of me, taught me how to help myself, analysed the dark patches in my mind, praised me, believed in me, loved me as no one has ever loved me before. We are as likely to separate as two streams that have run into one another."[60] There is no doubt that Cecil Maitland and Mary Butts were suited.

While in Germany her "disgust with the occult that followed...[the] automatic writing in March" led to the desire to "clean" herself though reading non-supernatural literature. This included "the only book to read in this hotel", J.G. Lockhart's 1837-38 biography of Sir Walter Scott. Given her love of Scott's poetry and fiction, it was an enjoyable experience, particularly when she came across his argument with the Earl of Lauderdale, since, apparently, Cecil Maitland was Maitland of Lauderdale and the Earl had been his great-grandfather.[61] (She also noted in Titisee that Cecil Maitland was born nearby, in Davos, Switzerland.) In addition to the Lockhart, she reread one of her favourite poems, John Milton's *Comus, A Maske presented at Ludlow Castle, 1634*. It would have seemed particularly pertinent, being set "under the spreading favour of these pines"...[62]

The last diary entry at Titisee was on the 17 May:

> ...the spring has settled in and we have found sheets of violets in the woods. I picked a bunch to-day for him to wear. We are talking of going back to France for a month. I think it would be a good thing—this series has been run through. I can even write down results which are also beginnings. We have both found that we can be well again and have taken the resolution to be well. This is a great thing for Cecil to have done. I feel able to deal with my obsession over my mother, he has begun to write again.[63] From examining ourselves and each other we have re-based and reaffirmed, grown our love. We are conquering sadness. We have got some of this out by using 'basil' discreetly, not as a substitute for thought or feeling, but to elucidate it. Finally, the daimon said when I was out for a walk alone one evening in the hills, 'Adorn and admire your tree, don't dig it up at the roots'.

And with this oblique instruction, they left Titisee.

* * * * *

Holy and cold I clipped the wings
Of all sublunary things

—William Blake, 'Of the Sexes' (circa 1818)[64]

After this entry in May, Mary Butts made only occasional notes in her diary until the following February. She and Cecil Maitland did return to Paris, where, on the 13 June she declared that they had stopped taking "basil" and had been feeling better until Leah reappeared, "lean, mad, lecherous as ever", and threatening that "we should come to harm if we did not give Crowley some money. We laughed at her, but later Cecil gave her 100 francs because she looked starved, making it very clear that it was a personal present. She then vilified us, and went to [Crowley in] England." A few days later "a horror did come…[which] did not succeed but it bruised", as Cecil Maitland took an overdose of veronal [a barbiturate] in early June. Although he was recovering, Mary Butts commented on the 13th that "he is not quite normal yet and I (near my period) am sad and wild and a streak of me hardly responsible". She was left "guarding [them] both", uncertain whether his action had been a result of Crowley's intervention or a genuine suicide attempt. "I have perpetually to speak to the daimon, and reaffirm my will. '*Holy and cold I clipped the wings/ of all sublunary things*'" was her response to the traumatic situation.

A week later she was back in London, alone for three days and determined to finish some stories. Two of them, 'In the Street' and 'In the South', would be included in her first published collection. 'In the Street' may well have been inspired by her anger towards Mary Colville-Hyde, which she had experienced so strongly in Titisee. It is a monologue by a woman on her way to a tube station after a ballet in London during a wintry rainstorm. As she walks she maligns her mother whose actions have forced her into poverty: "It's all because of you that I'm out ill in the rain, or I would be laughing at it. You horrible old woman. I get that out of it, the appropriate words for you…. You great gilt and pink idol down there in the South." The story ends: "Impudent old woman. Here am I, and I drift about in the night saying that an old pink witch is murdering me. I am turning you into an *immortal house, imperishable, starlike*. Who said that the old have peace? Not if I can help it.'"[65] 'In the South' is an account of renewed understanding between a brother and sister as they wander around "the small, steep hill and its ruin that was the hub of all the long hills and shallow valleys, out of which they had come,…where everywhere, as the wind fell, the sea could be heard knocking". This landscape, although unnamed, is suggestive of Mary Butts's beloved Corfe Castle in South Dorset.[66] In this story the sister:

took a deep breath. There was something to say that would be difficult, but which must be said because there had been a hole in the temporal foundations of their life.

"Do you know, cher ami, that I think it is time that the family habit of quarrels should stop. Look at us. Why should we bang cursing out of each other's doors? And when has there been a time when we have not? Quarrels about aunts, about politics, about nothing, about cash— "

"About sisters, about brothers." He took her hand. "I agree. I agree. It comes to this. There is only you and me left. We're the last that's left of our rows and lovers. The saga ends with you and me. We're the last word of the genius of our race. They will die, and there will still be you and me—.[67]

The reality of July 1922 was rather different from this idealisation. There is only one entry for this month, when Mary Butts was on the Dorset coast in "a cottage at the top of the sacred wood under Tyneham Cap with the wind blowing and the sea running."[68] There she read the manuscript of Douglas Goldring's novel, "Nobody Knows", and waited to see if Tony would accept her invitation to come "to the place appointed for another beginning and another end". The now twenty-one-year-old Tony was more wary of his sister and had his own life to lead. He came but "he would not stay" and as he left, the desolate Mary Butts "turned her back to the verandah and stayed still...a long time". If she did send Tony the letter drafted on her return to London, it is not surprising that he was a little cautious: "What avails it if I have written *Ashe* and better,...and saved a man's life and know magic, if the Bee Brother does not care for these accomplishments, not enough to come to town and see my little word made flesh.... I'm going off on an astral journey to wail and gibber all night round your bed."[69] No doubt, this was meant to be funny... Certainly, even if he did not conform to her ideal of him, Tony remained on very good terms with his sister at this stage in their lives.

* * * * *

"WE HAD A GREAT holiday in Germany," commented Mary Butts in November 1922. This was her only mention of a summer trip with Cecil Maitland and Sheelah Hynes to Germany and then on to Austria where they stayed in Sankt Anton in the Arlberg. In *The Nineteen Twenties* Douglas Goldring reprinted the one surviving letter written to him in August from this ski resort, where he appears later to have joined the holiday-makers. The letter is both informative and a fine example of Mary Butts's witty epistolary style:

My dear Douglas,
Good luck and blessings to you! Details as to the journey... Once you are over the German frontier you spend very little. Be careful that the lunch car which is hitched on at the frontier is not unhitched while you are peacefully eating so that your luggage goes one way and you another. That happened to us. You'll have a four-hour wait at Frankfort. Opposite the station, between the theatre and the Hotel Bristol is a majestic pub called, I think, the 'Hotel of the English'. The lift-boy is a dream of classic beauty and nearly lost us our train... Between this hotel and the theatre there is a large street, and about 100 yards down on the right a lovely little dancing-cabaret. It says Amer-Drinks on its window, and has a jolly band and pretty boys and girls. Very simple and merry and *cheap*. You might do worse than put in an hour or so there... Try and reserve a place in the Munich train. We had to sit up half the night and stand the other half.

The trains were late. We arrived S. Anton about seven o'clock on Wednesday evening, found the party stuffing chicken and champagne... The place is glorious. So is the whole valley. We shall probably not stay in S. Anton but move two or three miles down the valley to Petneu, where there is a jolly, simple gasthaus. The hotel here is frankly profiteering without being really comfortable, let alone chic.

We play beaver everywhere—Sheila champion—and we're always hungry and we drink Tokay at a shilling the bottle, and tramp all day and get hot but never dirty and in the intervals I read Jung's *Psychoanalysis [Psychology] of the Unconscious....*

Could I ask you to bring letters from 43 with you?... Also Cecil wants a bottle of strychnine pills—Easton's syrup pills is the family brand—but he says you know of another. Either would do... Forgive this scratch, but I'm unsettled with heat and drink.

Our love to you, Mary.[70]

No doubt when Goldring joined Mary Butts, he gave her some of the positive reviews of *Georgian Stories 1922*, which were then appearing.

While the holiday was a happy one, Mary Butts recorded that she and Cecil Maitland quarrelled over drugs after their return to London. "I was afraid he had 'taken to' dope instead of amusing himself with it. He shewed me again his will to lead the life we imagined together. I am not absolutely at ease but have checked impatience and too great idealism.... Remember, I failed him in Paris, ceased to be able to bear the pain and stress of our intercourse once its joy was gone. He had to resent that and get over the resentment. I had to let my shock wear off—or run down. It is over. May we have a joy to equal it" (11.11).

* * * * *

A FEW OF Mary Butts's movements in October can be gleaned from accounts by Douglas Goldring and Virginia Woolf. In his article, 'A London Bookman's Day Book', for the American newspaper, *The Sunday Tribune*, Goldring referred to Mary Butts at length, a fact which suggests her name would have meant something to an American readership:

> MONDAY, OCTOBER 9
>
> Mary Butts, who is just home again from Germany, came to dinner with me this evening and we debated the question as to whether English writers "talked literature" when they got together as much as writers of other countries. I didn't believe they did and Mary—who knows—was inclined to agree with me. "We gossip about our friends and enemies," she said, "and about publishers and editors, and we talk a good deal of pure and unadulterated shop. But in London I hardly ever find myself let in for a full dress literary discussion. There's something about us which makes us shy of that kind of thing—I don't know why it is."
>
> It was jolly to see Mary's bright eyes and her flaming mop of red hair after her long absence from London. She told me she had brought back with her from the Baltic a sufficient number of short stories to make a volume and promised to let me see them as soon as they were typed. Her contribution to the recently issued volume of *Georgian Stories*—it was printed, I fancy from *The Dial*—was much the best thing in that curious collection. She has real originality and if she can only succeed in forgetting *Ulysses*, she ought to make a name for herself as soon as she gets known.

It may well have been on seeing them typed that Goldring recommended Mary Butts's stories to Alec Waugh. He mentioned her again in the same article in two other 'entries':

> I went this evening to a little cabaret called "The Cave of Harmony",...and spent some quite amusing hours. Edgar Jepson, the novelist, was there with his wife and daughter, but the only other writers I noticed were Mary Butts, Alec Waugh and Thomas Earp, the poet. Dancing, for some reason or other, isn't the done thing among our literary highbrow. I suppose they think it undignified or perhaps they can't dance. There were plenty of painters, however. Walter Sickert seemed to be enjoying himself and was busy making sketches and Augustus John looked in for an hour or two.
>
> SATURDAY OCTOBER 14
>
> This afternoon I went to the private view of the London group exhibition held in Heal's gallery. I went there with Gladys Hynes, the painter and designer, and we picked up Robert Dell and Mary Butts and her brother, Anthony Butts.... I was delighted to see Ford Madox Hueffer looking very fit and well.... The show gave us an appetite for

> tea and my rooms being close at hand we bought buns and took them home and ate them. It was Sunday morning before our party finally broke up.[71]

On the 29 October Virginia Woolf wrote in her diary that Mary Butts had come to tea that day. The latter had sent the Woolfs a copy of *Ashe of Rings* in the hope that their Hogarth press would publish it. Unfortunately Virginia Woolf rejected the novel which she described as an "indecent book about the Greeks and the Downs".[72] Mary Butts was still without a publisher for the novel.

* * * * *

ON THE 11 NOVEMBER Mary Butts noted that "Crowley has had no success in London.... I dislike this book and all that it is about." She was referring to Crowley's novel, *Diary of a Drug Fiend*, which was published that autumn. It is an account of addiction to cocaine, heroin and opium in which the first person narrator, Peter Pendragon (based on Cecil Maitland), introduces an unnamed character who is clearly modelled on Mary Butts: "a fat, bold, red-headed slut. She reminded me of a white maggot. She exuded corruption. She was pompous, pretentious, and stupid. She gave herself out as a great authority on literature; but all her knowledge was parrot, and her own attempts in that direction the most deplorably dreary drivel that had been printed even by the chattering clique which she financed."[73] Mary Butts's work is later alluded to in equally contemptuous terms in what is an obvious reference to her stay with Cecil Maitland at Crowley's Abbey the previous year. Peter Pendragon has arrived at King Basil Lamus's Abbey and is being warned about the dangers of laziness by Athena, King Lamus's pupil. She declares:

> We had two people here last year, absolutely hopeless rotters. They called themselves writers, and imagined they were working if they retired solemnly after breakfast and produced half a page of piffle by lunch. But they didn't know the meaning of the word; and the place nearly drove them insane. They were bored with the Abbey, and bored with each other, and were very insulted because everybody laughed at them. But they couldn't see the way out, and wouldn't take it when it was shown them. It made them physically ill, and they went away at last to every one's relief to an environment where they could potter about indefinitely and pose as great geniuses.[74]

Mary Butts was appalled and decided to divulge to the press details of her "Sicilian Expedition", as she euphemistically called it in a letter to her aunt.[75] The result was an anonymous interview published on the 26 November in *The Sunday Express* under the title 'Complete Exposure of "Drug Fiend" Author'. The article increased the Beast's notoriety by declaring that "the stories of bestial orgies conducted by Aleister Crowley in July [1921] sound like the ravings of a criminal lunatic."[76] As a result of the adverse publicity, Aleister Crowley's publishers were forced to let *Diary of a Drug Fiend* go out of print.[77] Mary Butts had had her revenge.

On the 1 December Ethel Colburn Mayne wrote to offer her congratulations on Chapman & Hall's interest in publishing Mary Butts's stories: "I hope that firm will undertake them. Few things in my literary life have given me more pleasure than the notices of your 'Speed the Plough' in *Georgian Stories [1922]*; and in my view those notices were thoroughly deserved by the story which, as you know, I had always thought both original and beautiful.... I have a strong faith in your powers. You have a style which, if you trust in it sufficiently...will give you a distinguished place in letters. From the standpoint of an interest in the development of what are called 'short stories', I believe that work like yours is not only significant but in itself possesses value and real beauty."[78] Such a letter would have done much to boost Mary Butts's self-confidence.

Throughout the whole of December Mary Butts's diary was silent, as she worked on the volume of stories (due to come out the following March). She did however, give public voice to an issue of wide-reaching concern. In contrast to her anonymous interview with *The Sunday Express* the previous month, she gave her name when interviewed on the 20 December. It was in connection with a court case where she and two other women were included on the jury. The case of Nelson versus Moir was one of slander in which the plaintiff Nelson claimed that the defendant James Moir, a heavyweight boxer, had accused him of committing "an act of indecency" with the defendant's son. The defendant denied damages. Since the case would involve "evidence of the most unsavoury kind", the three women on the jury were given the option to "retire"; an option which Mary Butts and one other woman declined. It was, she declared in *The Pall Mall Gazette*:

> ...a question involving several important principles. It is not enough for a woman merely to take advantage of the judge's permission to retire if the case is such as he thinks likely to offend her susceptibilities. There is much more in it than the factor of delicacy alone.
>
> To begin with, it does not at all follow that because a woman knows and hears many of the unpleasant facts of life she is thereby coarsened. In any case women know a great deal more than they are credited with knowing, and are quite capable of forming a reasoned judgement on the facts.

> Women are now taking a continually increasing part in public life, and they must, if any good is to come of it, take their part thoroughly. There must be no shrinking or shirking.
>
> ...I consider it most necessary that there should be a frank and adequate knowledge on moral and criminal questions. The law's decisions will be hampered and women's usefulness will be rendered abortive unless all obscurantist prejudice is done away with.
>
> And this view is one which is more broadly held than the mass of the public are at present aware of.[79]

When the case came up for appeal the following February, it was rejected, but not before the issue of women jurors in 'unpleasant court cases' was once again raised. Supporting the right of the two women to stay, the presiding judge, Lord Justice Bankes was reported as saying that "whether one agreed or disagreed with them, one could not look on their motive in remaining in the jury-box to listen to disagreeable statements otherwise than as an honourable motive and he refused to draw any conclusions from the fact that these two women did not retire... In any case there were only two women on the jury, against ten men."[80] The judge's own sense of propriety may not have been offended, but he nevertheless felt the need to reassure the public that the imbalance in the numbers of women to men on the jury would ensure that their presence constituted no threat to 'justice'...

CHAPTER NINE

The Wild Party Continues 1923-1925

What is the age's formula?... Movement, the continuity up and down, in and out's the thing. Passion for the ballet. How does the mind move to Einstein's physics? What is the correspondence? That is what art is to sound like, written art. —MB, diary entry, early October 1925

MARY BUTTS'S ONLY diary entry in 1923 was on the 6 February when she had lunch with E.S.P. Haynes in London, after which she wandered around Lincoln's Inn Fields. This place would figure prominently in her story, 'Brightness Falls', which she wrote in 1925.

Her journal for the period between February 1923 and November 1924 was, according to its keeper, later stolen. The loss is all the greater as it would have recorded the beginning of Mary Butts's literary recognition. Certain of her movements and social activities in these two years can, however, be pieced together from various letters, diaries and memoirs of the period.

There were two major events in Mary Butts's life during 1923. The first one was positive and involved the publication of *Speed the Plough*. The writer and editor, Kirk Askew, had written to Mary Butts early in the year to praise her story 'Speed the Plough' and ask her for a list of her published works. She replied, thanking him on the 25 February and announced that a volume of stories was about to come out, adding that she had been obliged to "'pad' this book with work I would rather not pass, or Chapman and Hall would never have taken it."[81]

Speed the Plough was one of the books on Chapman & Hall's spring list (along with Douglas Goldring's *Nobody Knows*). Mary Butts paid tribute to Ethel Colburn Mayne by dedicating the volume to her, with the words "...mais un cadeau peu digne" (a present not worthy of its dedicatee). The publisher advised in its advertising blurb: "It is not everyone's book; no book that is worth anything is. It is modern both in its choice of subject and in its style. But it is a style that is as much a part of twentieth-century civilisation as the telephone and typewriter. *Speed the Plough* introduces a writer who should go far." The nine stories included in Mary Butts's first collection were 'Speed the Plough', 'In Bayswater', 'The Saint', 'Bellerophon To Anteia', 'Angele au Couvent', 'In the Street', 'The Golden Bough', 'In the South' and 'Madonna of the Magnificat'. The book was widely reviewed both in London (*Sunday Times, Times Literary Supplement, Evening Standard*) and beyond (*The Scotsman, Irish Times, Liverpool Post, Empire Review*). It was included in *The Daily Telegraph*'s 'Books of the Week', those "which are specially worthy of attention".[82] The overwhelming response was that the nine stories in the collection were "cleverly written" (*Country Life*).[83] For *The Daily Express* the stories were "sometimes so vivid as to be blinding, sometimes so sparing even of the essentials as to be totally incoherent. They have beauty, excellent characterisation, but little humour. They are, we feel almost too clever."[84] This was a common response: "We duller folk...[need] a key or glossary to the idiom of *Speed the Plough,*" declared the reviewer for *The Nation and Athenaeum*.[85] And *The Irish Times* felt that Mary Butts had been influenced by James Joyce: "No doubt these stories are very 'clever'; but there is no use in being clever if you are clever beyond your audience."[86] Brodie Fraser writing for *The Sunday Times* was enthusiastic and defended the book's difficulty: "The impressionist school has some disciples of genius. For example, such tales as those by Mary Butts in *Speed the Plough* are in the ultra modern style, but any 'obscurity' is redeemed by the brilliance of the writing."[87] Similarly the review in *The Daily News* declared that "Miss Mary Butts...has that touch of brilliance which makes one overlook a good many weaknesses."[88] Such support was needed, for in belonging to what J.B. Priestley called the "new impressionistic method of presentation" (*The London Mercury*), her stories were placed with those which "find more inspiration in a dustbin than in the stars" (*The Bookman*).[89] In the first but not the last stinging criticism of her writing, Gerald Gould declared in *The Saturday Review* "that Miss Butts has, it is clear, a gift. Perhaps one day she will use it."[90] Gerald Bullett in *The Challenge* believed, by contrast, that of the nine, "two tales are entirely successful and should alone suffice to make one sieze with eagerness upon Miss Butts's future work".[91] The two stories referred to were 'Speed the Plough' and 'Angele au Couvent'. Together with 'In Bayswater', they drew the most attention from reviewers:

> Told in a curiously abrupt, disjointed fashion, the nine sketches in Miss Butts's book are all powerful and interesting. 'Speed the Plough' with a vein of satire running through it, is the story of a broken soldier who was sent to do farm work, as the one possible treatment for shattered nerves, when what his soul cried out for was the handling

> business to deal with in a fashionable milliner's. 'In Bayswater' describes a peculiar, neurotic family, father, mother, son and daughter, and their mutual fear, suspicion and hatred. 'Angele au Couvent' is the meditation of a girl at school, apparently in St Andrews, too acute to accept life without question, but whose inability or disinclination to conform to routine is mistakenly regarded as dullness or indolence. It is a curious, clever book[92]

The Scotsman was alone in liking all three. On the whole reviewers tended to have a favourite: 'Speed the Plough' was praised by *The Liverpool Post* as the "easiest and most effective" story, which *The Observer* felt evoked the reader's "sharp sympathy".[93] The reviewer for the *Bolton Evening News* also praised 'Speed the Plough' in which Mary Butts "cleverly suggests the encounter of an urban and artificial mentality with the plain processes of Nature [as] much the best thing in the book".[94] As for 'Angele au Couvent', K.K. in *The Evening Standard* thought it "a rather hysterical sketch of a schoolgirl" and *The Westminster Gazette* maintained that despite "a thwarted, sensitive affection...the story gets nowhere, not even in the eventless region of the mind."[95] Three writers, two established, one yet to make her mark, disagreed. Conal O'Riordan felt that the "*paysage* of the Fifeshire coast in winter is worthy of [Robert Louis] Stevenson... There is no direct indication on what segment of the long Fife littoral Miss Butts has placed her scene; but, for me this stark prose reconstructs my memory of St. Andrews as I saw it two and thirty years ago."[96] Reviewing *Speed the Plough* in *The Daily News*, Rose Macaulay felt that "the best thing is a sketch of a schoolgirl at a Fifeshire school. This alone would establish Miss Butts' claim to be seriously considered as a writer. She has the imaginative power which sees and feels, and can transfer her vision and sensation to the reader. She can call up before us cold winds, sharp colours, sharp realities." Macaulay felt that with "a little more sincerity, a little more fusion of surface realism with deeper truth, a little less straining after the grotesque.... Miss Butts might be a very good writer indeed... As it is, she is distinguished notably from the common run of story-tellers."[97] In her memorial article, 'Recognition Not Farewell' (1937), Bryher would claim that the story had inspired her to begin her own literary career: "I read 'Angele au Couvent' and, because of identical experience, wrote."[98]

With regard to 'In Bayswater', one reviewer claimed that it should be renamed 'In Hell' and another 'In Moscow' since "if Dostoevsky had had no faith, he might have written some of it."[99] The story which provoked the most disapproval was Mary Butts's account of the annunciation in 'Madonna of the Magnificat'. The reaction ranged from the belief that "though it has the air of an irreverent exercise—there is a certain power", to condemnation of it as "an offense against good feeling for which there is no kind of excuse," and even "blasphemous".[100] Yet when the American writers, Zelda and Scott Fitzgerald read it, they declared it was one of their favourite stories by Mary Butts.[101]

There is no doubt that the stories caused quite a stir. Two long articles discussed the collection. Without mentioning Mary Butts or her book by name, A.N.M. wrote with mock humility in the *The Manchester Guardian*: "I read some short stories the other day, and, as they appear to have gained applause, far be it from me to say that there is nothing in them." After all, "it may be some cryptogram to which I haven't the key". Yet A.N.M., who declared: "I don't want to stop innovation, I can even find something to admire in the later work of Mrs. Virginia Woolf", did not appreciate the new kind of writer who said: "You shall follow the vagaries of my mind. I will not seek common ground with you; it is for you to come to me."[102] By contrast there was a eulogic critique in *The New Witness* by the writer Conal O'Riordan:

> To a man of letters who loves his calling there is always a fine thrill in the opening of the very first book of a new author…seldom have I seen a more appetising book, with its mustard cover stinging the palate of your eyes, and its handsome and distinguished print. Let me say at once that a book of this sort needs to be well printed, for not a line of Miss Butts' writing can be taken as read. So clamant is she for the mental collaboration of her reader, that the occasional misprints, few indeed, seem almost to lacerate the brain.…

Whilst he had some reservations about infelicities in style, O'Riordan claimed that "there is no page in which the literary mind may not take pleasure".[103]

Public opinion was not so kind however. Perhaps Mary Butts's two newspaper interviews had irked the guardians of civil morality in some way. Ostensibly it was the "absence of normality and health" and the "offense against good feeling" evoked in the stories, which led to the banning of *Speed the Plough* from public libraries for indecency.[104] This act was heralded by Frank Vernon who included it, alongside Aleister Crowley's *Diary of a Drug Fiend*, in an article for *John Bull*, entitled 'Books We'd Like to Burn'.[105] On the basis that all publicity is good publicity, Mary Butts's first book had done very well…

* * * * *

THE SECOND MAJOR event that took place that year, was, by contrast with her literary success, an unforgettable and unforgivable blow for Mary Butts. On the 27 and 28 June "at eleven a.m. precisely each day", there was an "important sale by auction of the High-Class Antique and Modern Equipment" in Salterns, Parkstone-On-Sea. Five hundred and sixty items were for sale over those two days, including "a 3ft mahogany writing or painting table on shaped legs and castors, with pull-out writing slab and secret compartments (used by the Muster Master General of the Forces Temp. of George III", "an antique toilet mirror with hinged shaving mirror attached in inlaid frame on turned column and circular base support, by Chippendale", "a very rare old map of London with letterpress in gilt frame by The Society Antique, 1737, re-engraved from map dated A.D. 1560 (a similar map in Westminster Abbey)", "A valuable Charles II Grandfather striking clock with ormolu mounted silver dial, second hands and calendar, in burr walnut case, with brass mounted fluted columns, supporting top and 3 brass globe ornaments, by William Allam, London" and "a 7ft Chesterfield settee spring and hair stuffed, upholstered in old gold tapestry and crimson Utrecht velvet with loose cover"... Lots 392 to 427 were books from Frederick Butts's library.[106]

The sale comprised, in fact, almost the entire contents of Mary Butts's birthplace, which had been sold earlier that year. Doubtless she was devastated.

* * * * *

Little information exists about Mary Butts's movements in the late spring and summer of 1923, which she probably spent for the most part in London at 43 Belsize Park Gardens. On the 28 August she and Cecil Maitland completed their joint novel, "Backwards from Babylon". Mary Butts wrote on the handwritten manuscript: "not to be typed". It never has been. In September *The Dial* carried a three page review of *Speed the Plough* by the American novelist, Glenway Wescott, whom Mary Butts knew by this time.[107] The review opened with the following eulogy:

> Miss Butts' collection of stories can be likened only to master-work: *Dubliners* [by James Joyce] or Mr Lawrence's *England, My England*. It is the announcement of a new intellect, acute and passionate, to scrutinize experience with an unfamiliar penetration and to substitute for it, as it ceases, new form and light.

The rest of the article, about an author who is "English to the core", was as enthusiastic as the opening. Wescott described Mary Butts's dialogue as a "work of genius" and compared its power to that of the Restoration dramatist, William Congreve. He singled out 'In Bayswater' for particular praise because "the absence of praise or blame gives a terrific tragic tonality to the whole; one choir of instruments stilled for a purpose. The purpose is an artificial savagery, deliberate and strong; furthered by Miss Butts' refusal to employ any modern convenience of interpretation or terminology." Of the book as a whole, Wescott wrote that it was

> an irresponsible evocation; the first and strangest resource of the human intellect, and, in our literature, longest in abeyance. Of all forms of utterance, narrative, the description of a mobile cluster of experiences, is the least easily comprehensible; the contrary appears to be true only because debased romancers have too long imitated a redundant theatre. The latter's devotees are bound to find "that which is done" in these stories much overlaid by that which merely is, the plot of something as displeasing as poetry. Their demands are in fashion; but fine writers have always differed from petty by understanding that the relation between experiencing itself and mere events is exactly that between the music and text of an opera.... This moody haughty mind, essentially religious, collects no drawing-room symbols; but gathers exactly the sense of ploughs, blades, and blood. It is rich in the scholarship of a golden bough, of a stamen of wood twelve feet long hung with a fox-pelt and feathers, of a dark grail. Strictly contemporary experience is lit by an antique fiery light; life an "infernal saga...coming up-to-date". The racial memory, the animal memory, has been strangely extended; and memory is the identifiable soul.[108]

In a letter later in the year Tony wrote that "Ethel Mayne told Clifford Bax the other day that she thought that you were a better artist than she."[109] With such high praise and understanding from contemporary writers, Mary Butts could justifiably feel that she was 'arriving'.

* * * * *

> *One of the circumstances which enhanced the rapture of being alive in the 'twenties and young enough to enjoy oneself was the opportunity, created by the high value of sterling, of going abroad. Life was cheaper almost everywhere in Europe than it was in England, and in congested Paris—in spite of the Yankee invasion—an English pound note went three times as far as it did in London.*
>
> —Douglas Goldring, *The Nineteen-Twenties*[110]

MARY BUTTS made the most of the high value of the pound during the 1920s by living the greatest part of the next seven years on the continent. In early November she once again left for Paris with Cecil Maitland. Before going they attended a party given by Douglas Goldring at his house at 7 St James Terrace. "Wasn't Douglas' party a success?" exclaimed Tony on the 8 November, when he wrote to wish her "a marvellous time" abroad. Judging by the letter Mary Butts sent to Goldring just before her departure, she certainly seems to have enjoyed it:

> What a party! A fruity mixture indeed: we were all so happy. We owe you a bottle of drink which shall not be forgotten, but we haven't bought it yet—because we're starting out in much the same condition as you when you left for Minorca!
>
> If you feel you could, would you send us an introduction to Norman Douglas? I know it is the sort of thing you are perpetually asked, but we are likely to be in Florence some time. Poste Restante there, till we have a settled address. All love and good luck— from us both....
>
> What a party! What drink! What company! It will become a classic example ...[111]

Mary Butts and Cecil Maitland seem to have enjoyed themselves in the French capital where they saw several friends, including Nina Hamnett, the painters, Cedric Morris and Lett Haines, and Duff Twysden. Goldring recalled that "Lady Duff Twysden, who was almost as tall [as Mary Butts] but dark, slant-eyed, long-nosed and of slighter build, made a perfect foil for her."[112] The two women became close friends and Mary Butts generously lent Duff Twysden £300 in 1925. Twysden had "a storied past, a notable capacity for drink and a string of admirers which included Pat Guthrie, one of the [Montparnasse] Quarter's celebrated playboys".[113] (She is usually remembered today as the model for Brett Ashley, the heroine of Ernest Hemingway's novel, *The Sun Also Rises/ Fiesta* (1927).)[114] Stella Bowen and Ford Madox Ford were also around, having by then settled in France. The latter, according to Mary Butts, "was in magnificent fettle, but I always behave stupidly with him and fear that the impression I left was none the best. Paris was a dream. We didn't go to bed for a week, and spent *all* our money on such binges! The last thing I remember was dancing solely supporting myself by the lobes of Cedric Morris' ears."[115] Mary Butts need not have worried about her impact on Ford. In November he announced the imminent birth of a new journal which he was to edit from Paris:

> *The Transatlantic Review*, the first number of which will appear on 10th December, 1923, will have only two purposes, the major one, the purely literary, conducing to the minor, the disinterestedly social. The first is that of widening the field on which the younger writers of the day can find publication, the second that of introducing into international politics a note more genial than that which almost universally prevails. The first conduces to the second in that the best ambassadors, the only non-secret diplomatists between nations are the books and the arts of nations.[116]

In the early years of the twentieth century, Ford Madox Ford (or Ford Madox Hueffer as he was then) had been editor of the prestigious *English Review* which had published "the first words of Mr. D.H. Lawrence, Mr. Ezra Pound, Mr. Norman Douglas, and many other writers now established...and the first of the longer sociological novels of Mr. Wells who will contribute also to the *Transatlantic*. So too will Mr. Joseph Conrad. The ever moving film has now progressed by a reel and it is such writers as Mr. James Joyce,...Mr. E.E. Cummings,...and Mr. A.E. Coppard that with the assistance of Mr. Ezra Pound, Mr. T.S. Eliot, Miss Mina Loy, Mr. Robert McAlmon and Miss Mary Butts, to mix our liquors as singularly as possible—the *Review* will energetically back."[117]

On their way to Florence in November, Mary Butts and Cecil Maitland stayed at the Pension Select in Rapallo in order to visit Ezra Pound. From there she wrote to Goldring:

> How good it was to see your blessed handwriting and your good meaty letter full of real news.
>
> Until the day before yesterday, there was no need to envy us for climate. It rained and rained and rained, winds howled, several at once, and that tactless brute of a Mediterranean that never goes in and out soaked us both with iced spray every time we put our noses out of this anything but Select Pension. Also I've been wretchedly, unspeakably unwell. I ran down like an overworked mainspring and am only just beginning to feel better. Also I missed my dear friends, tho' we've made some new ones, and a precious queer lot they are.

There was also the good publishing news to report: "Ford's Review (*The Transatlantic*) paid me £4 for a 3,000-odd word story."[118] This was for 'Deosil' which was published the following March and would have a success even greater than 'Speed the Plough'.

From Rapallo, the couple travelled to Florence where they stayed over four months at the Pension Balestra,[119] overlooking the Arno, near the Ponte Vecchio and the Uffizi gallery. As mentioned earlier Mary Butts wrote to Ada from Florence with her reaction to the city itself. Mindful of the recipient of her letter, she gave a rather formal description of the people with whom she was spending her time: "We are a party of friends, Mrs Aldington, I think I've told you about, and Cecil Maitland, Mrs McAlmon and her husband....[and] Norman Douglas, do you know his books?... People we know are always passing through, and if it were not for the plague [of influenza], we should be having a great time."[120] Amongst friends and literati, Mrs Aldington was better known as H.D.; Mrs. McAlmon as Bryher and "her husband" as the writer and editor of *Contact*, Robert McAlmon. Mary Butts had known H.D. for some time, but it was only the beginning of her friendship with Bryher and Bob McAlmon. As with so many reminiscences, Bryher was immediately struck by Mary Butts's hair: It was "blowing and rough for Florence, when a cab came beside the Arno, stopped, and my first, my lasting impression was of Mary's hair, flaming and red, no Tuscan scarlet but the torque-gold of windy islands."[121]

Mary Butts had obviously also written to Tony at this time, as on the 12 January 1924 he wrote back: "My dearest—It was good to hear from you again. I only saw Bryher...once at the Eiffel Tower [a restaurant in London] and not liking Bob—to me the supreme arriviste was also darkly suspicious. Americans are queer and usually no kind of formula to them. I don't like Bob—I reiterate. His work is bad which doesn't matter a damn and what exacting women like you, if you do...see, I can't conceive. However, Norman Douglas, poor old darling, I was rereading [his 1921 travelogue] *Alone* just when your letter came....get Norman D. to take you to San Gimignano...and Fiesole."[122] Whatever initial suspicions Mary Butts may have entertained about Robert McAlmon, a year later in Paris he published her first novel...

Tony kept his sister informed about the social scene in London and hoped to be able to come out to Florence. In early February he wrote: "I miss you so. How long are you likely to be in Florence?" Both sister and brother must have been having knee-trouble at this time, as Tony added in a postscript: "I hear that an operation removing the cartilege of the knee is absolutely safe—and not painful and removes any trouble of any kind. I am contemplating this for myself—as my knee [pain] has begun again. The surgeon says that our knee trouble may become very serious in middle life."[123]In Mary Butts's case, it certainly did.

In the spring of 1924 the lease for 43 Belsize Park Gardens was due to expire and Mary Butts had done nothing about it, even though it meant that her sub-tenants would be made homeless. She must have written in panic to Tony to sort it out, since with friendly but clearly-felt exasperation, he wrote in late February: "I have been twice to see your Landlord—twice equally he has been out. I am trying to obtain his telephone number from the Enquiries. Failed that. I wished to write to him. But, my heart, why in the name of all that is sanctified, why did you do nothing while there was yet time? I cannot see that you have any position at the eleventh hour. I will do anything that I can. Gladys I gather has only enough rooms as it is for the immediate Hynes galaxy. Elsa too, has nowhere to go. Unfortunately I have as little time in the evenings, the only time when I am free. When I hear anything I will wire you."[124]

* * * * *

> *Paris was the new frontier....if you wanted to be a publisher and have a little magazine the printing costs were cheap.... It offered the climate, the ambience, the importance of the recognition of the new for the artist.... By ten in the evening the [Latin Quarter] would take on the fullness of its own life with the terraces crowded and the well-known drunken poets or painters, celebrated for their stupor rather than their art, wandering across the road from café to café...*
>
> —Morley Callaghan, *That Summer in Paris: Memories of Tangled Friendships with Hemingway, Fitzgerald and Some Others* (1963)[125]

> *If I could take hold of life more firmly, if I could take life more easily, I might get through.* —MB, undated diary entry, late 1924/early 1925

IT IS VERY difficult to give an accurate account of Mary Butts's whereabouts between the spring and November 1924 when she began the next volume of her diary. What is clear, is that she travelled between France and England. Until April her address was still 43 Belsize Park Gardens. Correspondance dating from October is addressed to her at 7 St James' Terrace, where at some time after April she had begun to rent the first floor flat from Goldring in the "large, semi-derelict house" he leased by Regent's Park.[126] The ground floor flat continued to be his home when in London.

In fact she may well have spent most of the summer with Cecil Maitland in Paris, probably at the Hôtel Foyot, where along with Tommy Earp, Robert McAlmon and George Moore she is reported to have lived "from time to time".[127] The Foyot (which was pulled down in 1938) was then on the Rue de Tournon in the Latin Quarter near Sylvia Beach's bookshop, Shakespeare & Co. It is quite likely that Mary Butts and Cecil Maitland stayed there with H.D. and Bryher, who were booked into the Foyot by Sylvia Beach on their return from Florence in the spring of that year.

In 1920 the American writer, William Carlos Williams, had set up and co-edited with Robert McAlmon the short-lived but exciting journal called *Contact*. In 1924 he came to France for six months and noted that in Paris during May he attended a small drinks party with the expatriate writers, "Harold Loeb, the Birds [William and his wife], Bob [McAlmon], Mina [Loy...and] Mary Butts".[128] Cedric Morris also painted his garish portrait of Mary Butts in Montparnasse during 1924.[129] Stella Bowen gave an account of a party she and Ford Madox Ford threw in their studio in Montparnasse that year. On the Left Bank "if you gave a party, you could not hope to know more than half the people who came... This made it ever so much more exciting," she declared.[130] Sometimes even too exciting, since most of the expatriate writers attended this particular party and all seemed to be going well until

> ... at midnight...I saw through the open front door that Maitland was in the garden with his face all covered with blood. Now Maitland was a young man who was said to be always trying to commit suicide, and Mary Butts, who had brought him to the party, was usually able to prevent it.... [then] I found out that it was nothing worse than a bloody nose, inflicted by a hefty American [unnamed].... It appeared merely that a person called Pat [Guthrie] had smacked Mary unceremoniously as she danced past him, and she had demanded that Maitland should avenge her. But Pat's friends pointed out that he was much too drunk to defend himself, so the American stepped forward and offered to take Maitland on instead.[131]

Yet Mary Butts was not always perceived by her contemporaries as gregarious. The writer, Edouard Roditi, remembered "two very strange writers in Paris". One was Mary Butts and the other was the American writer, Djuna Barnes. According to Roditi, "they both led very odd solitary lives—extremely neurotic lives."[132] Mary Butts may well have met Djuna Barnes by this time: they certainly became good friends in Paris, where they both had work published in Ford Madox Ford's *transatlantic review*. As mentioned above, Mary Butts's short story, 'Deosil' was published in March and Ezra Pound wrote to Ford asking for more work by her.[133] Her poem about the Delphic oracle, 'Pythian Ode', came out in the September issue.[134] Both would be republished. McAlmon later claimed that "shortly after Conrad's death [3.8.24] Ford Madox Ford sent wires to a number of writers asking them to do an article on Conrad's place in English letters. Of the ones with whom I later spoke were Mary Butts and Hemingway. Each of us thought that our article was to be the sole article.... Ford, however, edited that issue of *The Transatlantic*, so that the glory which was Conrad's appeared but a reflection of Ford's glory."[135] No account of Mary Butts's reaction (nor her article) has survived...

On the 25 October she wrote to *The Dial* offering a new story, 'Friendship's Garland', for their consideration. A month later the American writer, Alyse Gregory (then Managing Editor), reluctantly returned the manuscript on the grounds that the magazine had no room for it at that time.[136] Mary Butts made no reference to her disappointment in her journal; perhaps she consoled herself with the fact that 'Speed the Plough' had been selected for a book-length anthology of *Stories from the Dial*, which came out in 1924.[137] Other contributors included Conrad Aiken, D.H. Lawrence, Sherwood Anderson and Padraic Colum as well as Paul Morand, who reviewed the book.[138] Mary Butts provided a biographical notice for this anthology in which she stated that she was born in 1892, instead of 1890.[139]

Mary Butts may have been back in England by the end of October. She was certainly there at the beginning of November as she was spotted at the "Film Society's Inaugural performance" by a reporter for *The Sketch*.[140] Evelyn Waugh noted in his diary that on the evening of the 6th he went "to Mary Butts', who is sweet".[141] By the 25 November she was back in Paris, where she saw Jules Romain's play, *Knock* (1923), at the theatre on the Champs Elysée and travelled by rail to Chartres (taking note of "the picnic habit in the corridors of french trains") to see the "most feminine of cathedrals" there. In November 1924 she was in good spirits:

> In the state of mind when one could write anything, when everything is worthy of notice, and one can choose nothing to put down, or get as far as conceiving one thing separate from another. A pleasant state, and a principal excuse for idleness. A day possible to be all pleasant. A little work might be done—but one is diverted by the pleasures of friendship, a little study and war [sic]. Also beginning to feel well again.

In spite of this self-criticism, Mary Butts was working very hard. In her diary she jotted down an idea for a novel. It was to be "derived from the quartier: End of 19th century idealism. the last refuge of amenity and freedom, *freedom* from inhibition. U.S.A. results. The growth—the laboratory where a new idea of human life and relationship is being tried out. A scientific kind of poetry. Waste products. It would have to be rather like a ballet." Stumbling and undeveloped these notes undoubtedly were; they carried the germ, nonetheless, of what would become her second published novel, *Armed with Madness*.

Mary Butts also drafted a number of poems in her diary at this time, including 'Corfe', which she had first started to write in March 1922. Also known as 'A Song to Keep People out of Dorset', this poem (as the titles suggest) is a defence of the "Hollow Land"[142] of her "sacred South" and would be first published in 1932. In addition, she wrote a series of what she called "tunes" or "little songs" and a poem entitled 'Victorian', all of which convey her feelings in late 1924. Tunes I and III run:

> Paris sighing with light pain
> The Foyot—The thin rain
> What'll I do?
> What'll I do?
> The crimson roses have black thorns
> A stigmata without pain.
> Oh heavenly pain of chaste love
> Not quite chaste affection without disillusion or regrets.
>
> Aurelius said that lovers
> Keep an emerald
> A little stick

To remember each other by.
I have nothing of yours
And am too cautious to ask.

The breakdown of her relationship with Cecil Maitland is made plainer in 'Victorian' which opens:

We have been quarrelling now six months,
In love some years.
Drifting about the rainy quays
Remembering—
It had been as inevitable as love,
Remembering—
Our admirable, bloody pride.
Remembering—
That we could never forget
Accompanied
By the smart terrier common sense
That takes old lovers on new walks alone.

This melancholy poem concludes: "I saw where we were./ In another place on no business of our own—/ There was our life,/ There were our fantasies." In the margin she wondered whether to change the final two lines to "There we were doing something./ Here nothing at all." As their relationship waned, Mary Butts once again described in 'Tune VI' the impossible ideal she was continually seeking:

Always looking for Plato's image
In the persons of young men.
I am under nature's law:
Necessity:
And all that:
I don't complain, but am invariably surprised.

Her dissatisfaction seems to have been precipitated by the fact that Cecil Maitland had begun to have other lovers and she moaned to herself:

> Cecil does not care much for me, and is a disappointing man; because I am afraid of him, because I am unjust to him, because I love him, most of all because he has humbled my pride, because he is dear, and inconceivably stupid, and so strong for his own ends, because I have put my life into him, and need him. If I were loved, I might get through. Any love that was love, and that would do its share. Then I could punish Cecil and love him secretly, by myself, and not tell him, and make him want me, and not have me.

> Or if he came to me and said that he was sorry, that he understood, infinitely sorry. Then the pain would stop.
>
> He will never do that because he does not understand, and does not understand because he does not love, and does not love because he admires himself, and is very willing to make me a bloody sacrifice on the altar of that admiration.

Perhaps she remembered the proverb she had quoted in 1916 that "when a friendship is dead, do not turn back to look at the corpse". Certainly for the next few weeks her diary is concerned primarily with books and her work. She noted that she must get Lafcadio Hearn's *Japan, an Attempt at Interpretation* (1904). In the meantime she read widely: James Breasted's *History of Egypt* (1906), Roger Fry's *The Artist and Psychoanalysis* (1924), *Studies in Dreams* edited by H.O. Arnold-Foster and the fictional biography, *Peter Whiffle: His Life and Works* (1922) by the American writer, Carl van Vechten: "In this last part...he is on the old game of the black occult. Why does that so continually come up?" Under the heading *Art and Occultism*, she drew up a list of "artists whose works have affinities". Her list included the painters Goya, Breughel, Burne Jones, and Rouault as well as the writers Machen, Dostoevsky, Blake, Melville, Bulwer Lytton and W.B. Yeates [sic]. Whilst omitting the supernatural writer M.R. James, she commented rather cryptically: "May Sinclair (marks a new departure)." In addition to this list her diary for the twelve months between November 1924 and November 1925 contains a particularly large number of her own occult and hypnogogic experiences: "'Border state' in dreaming; after fatigue, or with slight fever the drifting images of the still conscious mind suddenly become clear, so 3 dimensional as to appear solid as they drift along. They are inclined, along with their distinctness to be a little abnormal and fanciful.... The first of these dreams that I remember I think I was six or seven." A note of these dreams together with *Art and Occultism* were part of a systematic examination of the occult, which she explained in early 1925:

> Five years ago I first became anxious to make a study of phenomena I felt were not explicable by understood physical laws. I date this *conscious* wish from my first acquaintance with C.M., though previously I had studied 'occultism' and found it stirring, but unsatisfactory, a maze of blind alleys. I made various attempts, scrying, automatic writing, read up spiritualism, mystery cults, some neoplatonism and to no conclusion. Crowley, if anything, would have convinced me there was nothing in it. After five years, and lately I have not interested myself so much, I realise that I have observed, all my life, a series of phenomena, not all subjective, not technically related to the problems, but which I now believe to be part of a series though the connection between them is not clear. There are no conclusions as

> yet, only observations, and the observations may be incorrectly given, but it is impossible to realise them without emotion, for I know now that they are the cardinal events of my life.
>
> The stage I have arrived at is to connect these events with each other, and to arrive at a theory for them. I have no doubt of them (as I might have doubted if I had seen an 'angel' in the blue glass ball) and my realisation has come slowly like a growth in nature, not an attempt to pry.

She was convinced that if she could "relate these, and describe the relation,...the result will be an account of another order of Life, an extension, not contradiction of this."

By the end of 1924 Mary Butts and Cecil Maitland were back in London at 7 St. James Terrace, where he remarked that her room looked like "the BM [British Museum] aranged by a cocotte [tart]". They were very sociable at this time. Mary Butts remarked on an evening spent at the Eiffel Tower restaurant with friends and having long conversations about Einstein with the scientist and philosopher, J.W.N. Sullivan. He was among a list of people she drew up (which also included the actors Harold Scott and Geoffrey Dunlop) who had failed to return books she had lent them. All her life she was very generous about lending books and felt dismayed if they were not returned. In January 1925 she wrote some 'House Rhymes' with Cecil Maitland, amusing light verses in which they both figure, although Goldring is the main protagonist. The couplets refer to Goldring's inept management of his financial affairs, but could just as well be applied to Mary Butts:

> The Douglas Scheme—this we insist on
> 'S a monument of human wisdom.
>
> He wakes to run his daily race,
> And ruin stares him in the face.
>
> . . .
>
> Then to the Bank to see the boss,
> Explain he's not a total loss;
>
> And that the cheques of yesterday
> Are being met in cash to-day.

The poem cycle also highlights the difficulty of getting a hot bath at home, given the nocturnal habits of the residents:

> The bathroom at S. James Terrace
> Is a convenience and a menace.

At eight o'clock the water's hot
But then by noonday it is not.

At eight o'clock we are asleep,
At noonday from our rest we creep.

There is a light-hearted account of the changing love affairs at 7 St. James Terrace, in which Mary Butts has no part to play:

Within these walls erotic life
Is mother of erratic strife.

Douglas has several mistresses,
And more than several witnesses.

Cecil has two whom he neglects,
Mary has none and so objects.

We mingle discontent, possession,
With singularly small discretion.

Each nourishes his simple hopes
Controlled by Doctor Marie Stopes.
. . .

Each hears the embraces of the other
A sound no earthly walls can smother.

The poem comes to its sad conclusion with Douglas Goldring about to take up a lectureship in Sweden (which he duly did although surely not in the manner attributed to him):

The Douglas credit system's done
The landlord and the Bank have won

The cheque that met the cheque is dead
And Douglas goes to lay his head

In Sweden where the Banks are green
In Sweden where his sheet is clean.

Trade for the butter on his sandwich
His faultless knowledge of our language.
. . .

And Douglas' temperament is such
I don't think he will teach them much.[143]

In Sweden Goldring would meet his future wife, Malin, who became good friends with Mary Butts.

Such witty verses show that Cecil Maitland and Mary Butts were still capable of having fun together. By February 1925, however, they had separated. Less than two years later Cecil Maitland would be dead.

* * * * *

February–November 1925

> *To make poetry out of these last few months, not verses, one has to abstract them; or get out equivalents for a, b, c. Unpersonalise the thing without reference [to] any ecstatic states, prevent 'any sort of meaning' from looking intense.*
> —MB, undated diary entry, May 1925

BETWEEN NOVEMBER 1924 and February 1925 Mary Butts had been working steadily. The following are three ideas for stories which she jotted down:

> The dinner at the Lunns' flat, the half memory of the scene before with B.L. When C[M] shot himself and he wouldn't. Might be a 'tabu' story—you can take another woman's man, but not let another man use a gun etc.[144]
>
> Another Tabu-story: going out with Pat [Guthrie] and Duff [Twysden] and being bored, and Duff reading Plato, and neither getting near each other.
>
> As a 'psychic' story through 'character['s]' eyes. A man describing what happened to two women—wife and friend. On the story I told myself coming over Primrose Hill in the fog.

Against both the first and the third idea, she wrote 'Done'. The first became 'The Dinner Party' and the third 'Brightness Falls'. Both stories were published in 1932. Mary Butts never transformed the second idea (although after Pat Guthrie's death, she would be asked to do so). As well as this new fiction, she revised older work for possible publication. She extensively redrafted a novel she then called "A.H." (perhaps based on the short story 'Agnes Helen') which probably became her unpublished 300-page novel, "Unborn Gods". In addition, she collected together a volume of her latest stories (including 'Friendship's Garland' which *the Dial* had refused) and sent it to Ford Madox Ford for consideration by Duckworth. She also posted a copy of her story then called 'Menesthius'[145] to both Duckworth and *The Criterion*, the little magazine edited by T.S. Eliot. Unfortunately they were all rejected.

Despite these setbacks, in 1925 her fiction received its greatest recognition yet. Early in the year there were reviews of a 1924 anthology in which a story by Mary Butts appeared. A new journal was started, with a story by her in its fourth issue; yet another of her stories was anthologised and, after five years, her novel *Ashe of Rings* was finally published. In the meantime, she spent the summer and early autumn in London where she fleshed out her idea for *Armed with Madness*, enlarged her poem, 'Corfe', and wrote some more stories. She also led a busy social life, made new friends, attended the theatre and numerous parties (some of which she gave), fell in love, had a holiday in Dorset and moved to France on a more long-term basis.

After going to the theatre on the 19 January Evelyn Waugh remarked: "We went to Elsa's with Mary Butts who joined our box on finding her mother two seats away from her. It was bitterly cold and we all stood about for hours over the fire sipping gin. Eventually more people arrived and we started dancing."[146] Mary Butts was clearly not getting on any better with her mother.

Exactly a month later, when Mary Butts recorded that she was ill in bed, *The Yorkshire Evening Post* nominated *The Best Short Stories of 1924*, edited by Edward O'Brien and John Cournos, as "Our Book of the Week".[147] Mary Butts's 'Deosil' (from *the transatlantic review*) was included, alongside stories by A.E. Coppard, Dorothy Richardson and T.F. Powys.[148] The book and 'Deosil' in particular provoked a certain amount of critical attention, including a complimentary review of the anthology as a whole in *The Scotsman*.[149] The reviewer in *Cassell's Weekly* liked 'Deosil', "the story of an exile returning on leave to his ever beloved London and finding it all strange and changed, and the woman whom he loved now quite remote and estranged from him. There is deep pathos here."[150] Whilst Henry Baerlein in *The Bookman* described Mary Butts rather coolly as "a most competent practitioner", the *Times Literary Supplement* was extremely impressed: "'Deosil' by Mary Butts, is a corrosive study of an egoist who wanted to get men 'to see their cosmic significance'. It is an admirable piece of work. The cleverness of the story is justified by the author's swift and dispassionate perception—a perception which indicates more than intellectual integrity."[151]

In May Mary Butts was busy; she found it "strange" to go backstage before a performance of Bernard Shaw's new play, *St Joan*, in which her friend Harold Scott (the originator with Elsa Lanchester of the Cave of Harmony) was acting the part of the Dauphin. "The smell of incense, sitting on a dress-basket, watching the [actors] pass. It was two worlds. Back in the middle-ages… Homage to inspiration. Odd dressing Harold. It was a sort of ritual." This experience together with the arrival of Arthur

Waite's book on the Grail ("received to-day from the B.M.") prompted her to sketch out her own play in which the protagonist was modelled on Duff Twysden. It would have a prologue and as well as the Girl, the characters would include two Aunts, a Rationalist Young Man and a Celtic Twilight Young Man, both "up to date". The play, set during a country house party, would revolve around the discovery of an object. "Might be a Keltic jewel, might be something Aunts think of [as] the Grail cup. Awful fuss about it. Ceremonially installed in the house." This play à la Noel Coward called "A Play in Three Acts and a Prologue" was completed that year. Never published, its ideas would become central to the plot of *Armed with Madness*.

Initially she was unimpressed by Waite's *The Holy Grail* (1909): "Imagine the subject treated with scholarship, omniscient information and personal belief by a sentimental hen reincarnated as a maiden aunt. Dead Waite." However her opinion quickly changed: "Waite is not always like a hen. He sees how Logres is an image of our desolate hearts. I am living there, so I know. Once the Grail left Cecil and me." She made extensive notes from Waite's book, which were useful as she had already decided that her "New Book" was to be about "where we all are, the obvious answer to the futility of [Aldous] Huxley's last chapter of [*Those*] *Barren Leaves* [(1925)]. Two themes, the Sancgraal story and the windings of the inferiority complex."

Mary Butts's studies were suddenly interrupted, however: "A dream last night.... incoherent... That was yesterday. It might as well be seven thousand years, so much I must be in love." The object of her passion was a young actor and friend of Tony's, Geoffrey Dunlop. Elsa Lanchester remembered him from the late 1910s as "bitter about everything (mostly himself)".[152] In Mary Butts's eyes, he was "a Latin Kelt...absolutely intellectually truthful, graced and gifted" and she wrote poems to him in her diary. After a walk in Kew Gardens together she declared:

Geoffrey remember:
The Kew-chinoiserie. The peach-leaves and the bird
That fell, straight
Lifting its fall just perceptibly
At your feet.
Remember Geoffrey
. . .
The way you laughed
. . .
Oh Geoffrey, Geoffrey, wasting here I see
Your thin skull and the blue cords of your hands.
A piece of stylisation, almost art.

Elsewhere she wrote: "You are an actor/ I am a courtesan./ You are a scholar,/ I am a child./ You are well-born./ I am well-born/... Play with the ghost of you/... Oh Geoffrey—Geoffrey." The following lines make it unclear how far Geoffrey Dunlop reciprocated: "You will not see/ These songs or my breasts:/ Fifty-fifty thankfulness, unthankfulness." She wanted "to make poetry out of these last months," but lamented: "It's no good, I can't do it yet. I'm still drunk on living it. Finish the play for practice and discipline... Oh hell." Caught up in her turbulent emotional life, Mary Butts made no comment when in June her story 'The Later Life of Theseus, King of Athens', a first person narrative based on the Memoirs of Menestheus, the Erecthid, came out in the fourth issue of *The Calendar of Modern Letters*.[153] This monthly journal (price 1s 6d) was edited by the writers, Edgell Rickword and Douglas Garman, who paid the contributors three guineas per thousand words. This issue also included a story by Stella Benson, a critical article on Arnold Bennett by Edwin Muir and a review by the composer and writer, Cecil Gray. Like 'Speed the Plough' and 'Deosil', which were acclaimed and respectively anthologised in *Georgian Stories 1922* and *Best Short Stories of 1924*, 'Theseus', "in the style, almost of Dr. Garnett", as one reviewer described it, was later included in *Georgian Stories 1927*.[154]Other contributors selected for this collection of eighteen stories included Osbert Sitwell, Storm Jameson, William Gerhardi, E.M. Delafield and Mary Butts's dear friend, Ethel Colburn Mayne.[155]

Mary Butts continued to see Geoffrey until she left for France in October. When he disappointed her by not living up to her expectations, she was resigned: "There is always a time when one's friends are good, better than themselves, 'see', are, I like to think, more their real selves. I bank on that. They won't be able to keep it up, but I'd sooner remember them for that. It leads one into no worse trouble than this unfriendly, suspicious disillusion that is so popular. It takes some time to find out that they won't keep it up. And then one has to remember that, with luck, it will return; and anyhow, it is my way." Douglas Goldring, Glenway Wescott and a rich young man called Peter Morris were also in London for Mary Butts to "play with". But she did not only play; she also worked on 'Corfe', her new play and novel as well as writing the story 'Honey, Get Your Gun'. She re-read Bury's *History of Freedom of Thought* (1913) and Ethel Colburn Mayne's latest book of stories, *Inner Circle* (1925), copying out a passage from her story 'Black Magic'.

During the summer while she was in London, her novel *Ashe of Rings* was published in Paris by Contact Editions. Ford Madox Ford pointed out that with William Bird's Three Mountains Press (which also printed the Contact Editions books) "these two printing establishments formed a centre and established between young writers contacts precisely that were in the early twenties more than invaluable."[156] Contact Editions (1922-1931) was owned by Robert McAlmon, who ran it from his room at the Foyot Hotel.[157] When announcing the birth of the Contact Publishing Company, he declared: "We will bring out books by various writers who seem not likely to be published by other publishers, for commercial or legislative reasons."[158] Other writers published by this press were H.D., Bryher, Mina Loy, Ernest Hemingway, William Carlos Williams, Djuna Barnes, Ezra Pound and Gertrude Stein. Three to five hundred copies of each book were printed. In 1938 McAlmon noted about Mary Butts: "I had published her *Ashe of Rings* and she was most effusive. Her hair, which looked as though it had been soaked in red ink, framed her white face and full thin-skinned liquid lips."[159] Looking back on Contact Editions after its demise, McAlmon felt that the "venture was not a cheering affair. It was not only the customs; reviewers in America were ruthless against them. They would not comment on them as books; they were always mentioned as expatriate and Paris publications even when the authors never saw Paris. Since, some of the books have been republished in England and America and have been greeted with praise."[160] In fact all the authors except McAlmon himself were republished fairly quickly by commercial firms. *Ashe of Rings* was published in America by A.C.Boni in 1926 and a new edition was brought out eight years later in England in 1933 by Wishart & Co.

* * * * *

Ashe of Rings

> *We are spectators of a situation which is a mask for another situation that existed perhaps in some remote age or in a world outside time.*
>
> —MB, *Ashe of Rings*[161]

MARY BUTTS reworked the ending of *Ashe of Rings* for the Contact publication, because she felt "the book's finish should be more sober". Years later she described her first published novel as a "War-Fairy-Tale". *Ashe of Rings* is a Modernist text in that it is neither wholly realistic nor fantastic. Rather, it combines elements of both characteristics in a narrative which, whilst unfolding in time (Part I is set in 1892, Parts II and III in 1917), also defies historical temporality by aspiring to a position of mythical timelessness. Early on in the novel Anthony Ashe asks his wife, Melitta: "Can you feel how time is made sound and we listen to it, and are outside it? Have you thought what it is to be outside time?"[162] Melitta, however, does not share her husband's preoccupations. Later, Melitta's sister Vera declares cryptically: "We are spectators of a situation which is a mask for another situation that existed perhaps in some remote age or in a world outside time."[163] She understands.

As mentioned on several occasions, the novel is concerned with the significance of the prehistoric Badbury-like Rings of the title, which give their name to the Ashe home nearby. The story opens with the following dramatic metaphor:

> Rings lay in a cup of turf. A thin spring sun shone on its stones. Two rollers of chalk down hung over it; midway between their crest and the sea, the house crouched like a dragon on a saucer of jade.[164]

To a large extent, *Ashe of Rings* is an allegory, a battle between those who understand the significance of the age-old landscape of the Ashe family and who thus see themselves as the Eumoldipae (inheritors of the Eleusinian Mysteries)[165] and the forces which are antagonistic to it. These forces are portrayed through the "masks" (in the Greek sense of the word) of the other characters. Anthony Ashe and, on his death, his daughter Vanna, become guardians of the Rings. Ashe's wife Melitta's indifference to their power is such that she defiles them by having sex with her lover on them. Vanna's friend, Judy Marston, personifies the destructiveness of the Great War which overshadows the whole novel. There is also Serge Fyodorovitch, the Russian artist who, whilst he tries to understand the significance of the Rings, cannot see beyond their surface appearance of "wet grass and high trees...a cold wet place [where he] chewed on wet leaves and laid on stone".[166]

In First-World-War London Serge and Judy are locked in a mutually destructive sexual combat. When their relationship breaks down temporarily, Vanna rescues Serge from his near-starvation and encourages him to resume his painting, taking him away to the countryside of her birthplace. There is no passionate relationship possible between them as Vanna is preoccupied with regaining possession of Rings, from which she has been disinherited by the birth of her brother, born of the relationship between her mother (Melitta) and Melitta's lover. Meanwhile Judy becomes involved with Peter Amburton, Vanna's neighbour, who has been discharged from the war because of shell-shock. As a result of her (misplaced) sexual jealousy of Serge and Vanna, Judy persuades Peter to rape Vanna on the rings at night. Like the Lady in Milton's *Comus*, the virginal Vanna thwarts this plan by the force of her chastity. She lies naked on one of the stones so that Peter is terrified by the sight of her and runs away. In this way Vanna atones for her mother's earlier defilement of the Rings and the novel ends with a reconciliation between mother and daughter which re-establishes Vanna in her rightful place as the guardian of Rings. Whilst contemporary in its powerful evocation of war-riven London, the novel is written in the Modernist idiom, in that it draws on imagery from a medley of literary texts—from the classics to Frazer's anthropological study, *The Golden Bough*. It is a measure of McAlmon's regard for *Ashe of Rings*, that he published it, given the fact that he did not like the way "Pound and H.D. ... went soft at the mention of antiquity."[167] Virginia Woolf was right to point to the centrality of the Greeks and the Downs to the novel (although the supposed "indecency" is debatable). Indeed, classical images as well as references to the Dorset of her childhood are recurrent motifs in this as in most of Mary Butts's work. Yet the American poet, John Wieners, was closer to the spirit of her writing, when he wrote years later that Mary Butts "called around her, called down the fine spirits, whose every book is a re-affirmation of life, who says in every book that that other thing has to be fought".[168]

Compared to her other books, the Contact edition of *Ashe of Rings* was not widely reviewed. (The following account also includes reviews of the American edition of 1926.) *The Manchester Guardian*, as McAlmon later claimed, "had slight suspicions of English-speaking books published in Paris" and disliked even the name of the press: "Contact with what? Not reality—not beauty."[169] Another reviewer writing in *The Liverpool Courier* considered *Ashe of Rings* under the ominous title of 'Futurism in Fiction: The Nightmare Prose of "The Moderns"'. Like the work of Mr. James Joyce and Miss Dorothy Richardson, the book was seen as "another bad case of Futurism", except worse: "If you can imagine the stylistic influence of James Joyce, combined with Miss Richardson's soliloquising method on a writer whose theme has the incoherence of a nightmare, you may realise how bad and mad is *Ashe of Rings*, by Mary Butts."[170] Several reviewers compared her style to that of other writers in an attempt to convey its quality. *The Saturday Review of Literature* spotted May Sinclair as the "chief influence"; an article in the same newspaper the following year claimed both that Mary Butts was "almost as precise and pictorial as Elinor Wylie"[171] and that "*Ashe of Rings* sometimes suggests the Lawrence of *Women in Love*. There is the same lyrical writing and consciousness of beauty; there is the same stripped reality side by side with a turbid guesswork of motive and action; there is something of the same perverted types of humanity."[172] As mentioned in an earlier chapter, Cecil Boulton in *The New York Evening Post* found in the power of Mary Butts's writing the influence of Dostoevsky: "Bound with a subtle arrangement of relationships, these people dance and spin about to get on each other's nerves all through the book, are reconciled and get away from each other, hold spiritual jamborees and call each other names, and are, altogether, delightful and interesting. Dostoevski served with a little milk."[173]

The critical response ranged from the enthusiastic ("The chronicle of the Ashe Family...is of a fluent, restless intensity, and a concrete, clear-cut visualization that is a joy to read.");[174] to the derogatory ("The novel seems to us to be interesting only in so far as it is an attempt to depart from the ordinary and the mundane.");[175] to the more measured ("Miss Butts is a short-story writer of ability... If that talent were integrated, it might produce something above the ordinary.")[176] Whether positive or negative, all the reviewers agreed that the book was difficult. "Bewilderingly fluent," was the judgement of *The New Criterion*; whilst other critics found it "impressionistically, elliptically written" and "certainly no book for casual readers." One reviewer even provided a delicate metaphor for Mary Butts's style: "She skips from point to point of her narrative with the agility of a literary chamois."[177] Others found that "the sentences are choppy", that "the obscurity is not all necessary for the fulfilment of the theme, and has been a little exaggerated for swank" and that "the thought sequences are guilty of occasional non-sequiturs".[178] Yet there were plaudits also. "One is often charmed by the pure virtuosity of her attempts. She writes like a genuine poet. Occasionally her words and phrases seem forced, but much oftener they have a freshness, a vividness, a precision which deserve high praise."[179] Cecil Boulton wrote lyrically of the book as:

> A tale told in vivid lightning flashes, inspired by the glitter of knives and sunshine, by a tapestried background of ancient things and the desire to continue an existence already snatched up by the greedy clouds of a restless creation.... Freshness of exquisite imagery, uncanny delineations of character,... *Ashe of Rings* is a work of highly poised emotional intensity...the author's grasp is strong with the strength of fine steel; her words walk surely, lightly, fantastically, stepping in a rhythm that charges its way to curious paths.[180]

As to the plot of *Ashe of Rings*, it was described variously as "fantasy and...psychologized witchcraft", or set in "a rather Satanic atmosphere; it is in the suggestion of this Mephistophelean element pervading Rings and its owners that the book chiefly excels." The book was also said to resemble "the communications of a medium".[181] Two American reviews accurately pointed out that the novel was the work of an "inescapably" and "peculiarly" English writer.[182] In a long review in *The Calendar of Modern Letters*, Edwin Muir felt that "Miss Butts has made the mistake of trying to express the age instead of herself which means that the *Zeit Geist* is not immanent in her, and has to be treated as subject-matter rather than expressed as content."[183] The reviewer in *The Springfield Republican*, by contrast, felt that the novel's combination of ancient and modern was pertinent: "Miss Butts has recognized...in her story of the 20th-century inheritors of the ancient estate...their ties with a violent tragic and superstitious past, and their family present, impinged on by internal and external ambitions and selfishness expressed in modern realities, including the Great war. The result is a story of people of our times, some dominated by an idealistic mysticism and some by motives neither idealistic nor mystic."[184]

All in all, Mary Butts's first novel provoked strong reactions in the reviewers. If they were not all positive, if some of them had "fits", that, as Roger Fry had reassured her six years earlier, was proof that her writing hit a nerve. When drawing attention to Mary Butts's novel, *The London Mercury* of September 1925 also commented on the "recent" publication of "the *Contact Collection of Contemporary Writers*, which includes twenty stories, poems and essays by some of the firm's authors."[185] In fact the volume included both Contact and "unaffiliated" writers and ran to 338 pages. Mina Loy, Gertrude Stein, James Joyce, Ford Madox Ford, Havelock Ellis, May Sinclair, Edith Sitwell, Ezra Pound and Norman Douglas were amongst its contributors. It was here that Mary Butts's story 'Friendship's Garland' was first published. The autographed copy given to Sylvia Beach on the 5 June shows that Mary Butts was in illustrious company.[186]

* * * * *

I don't know what I shall do, try to get away at once, but I should like to see you once again, not to talk about money and our wrongs, but to try to be real friends in, and forget the way we've hurt each other.

—MB, undated letter to John Rodker, late 1925

ON THE 10 SEPTEMBER Eugene O'Neil's play, *The Emperor Jones*, opened in London with Paul Robeson playing the lead. It was well received. A few days later Mary Butts gave a party in Robeson's honour at 7 St James' Terrace. Unfortunately "he had a fit in his dressingroom and would not come" but many other people did. Her guests included Evelyn Waugh, who noted: "The party at Mary's was quite fun.... [There] we found some very odd painters quite drunk and rather naked. They were for the most part what Mary called 'Paris Queers'.[187] ...After a time complaints came from the man above...and the party broke up." Waugh and his friends "stayed on for a little while talking while Mary disappeared and we heard unmistakable sounds of something from the lavatory. We thought it was time to go"... [188]

Mary Butts was herself soon to leave England. She recorded that John Rodker spent the nights of the 2 and 3 October at 7 St. James' Terrace although their differences over money and the care of Camilla were not resolved. However much this upset her, she continued to work and play. Earlier that year she had become friends with the young brilliant ballet dancer, Rupert Doone. During the autumn she noted his advice about how to do her hair: "Comb it on one side like that, Mary, over your forehead, so that it looks as if God had drawn his finger across it." As well as with Doone, Mary Butts mentioned spending time with Anton Dolin, Geoffrey Dunlop and the poet, Tommy Earp. On the 20 October she sent a story and a poem to the American poet, Marianne Moore, who was now editing *The Dial*. The poem was rejected and the story 'A Week-End' was accepted only if cut.[189] Yet Marianne Moore took this opportunity to express her admiration: "Your [story] 'In the South' is a permanent pleasure to me as is so much else of your work."[190] Indeed Moore was one of the writers who would remember Mary Butts after her death. By the time she sent this letter on the 10 November, Mary Butts had already left for Paris, where she met up with her friends and wrote 'Scylla and Charybdis', a story about the "contrast in temperaments, Russian, English". No doubt she also went to see Josephine Baker who had begun to perform in *La Revue nègre.*

But she did not stay in Paris for long. She was off to the Riviera...

PART FOUR

The Years in France

1925/1930

CHAPTER TEN

Villefranche
November 1925–April 1926

Mary Butts first went to Villefranche in November 1925 and stayed there until late April the following year. It was to be one of her magical places and she would return for two lengthy visits in 1927 and 1928. Together with surrounding towns it inspired a great deal of writing, including the poem 'Juan les Pins', the short story, 'The House-Party', and the essay, 'A Small Town', which she wrote in June 1928, after her last visit. "This sketch," as Mary Butts called this never-to-be-published essay, "is meant for an attempt at some description of the curious society, or rather the society of curiosities which has somehow come to settle at Var-les-Roches [her pseudonym for Villefranche]". "Remember," she wrote elsewhere in the essay, that this "small settlement somewhere between Cannes, Nice and Monte Carlo, the Three Towns of the Blue Coast…has been there since the curtain was rung up on the mediterranean scene.... Greeks and Phoenicians have unloaded on its stones: Moors and Genoese cut each other's throats on them." In Villefranche she began to write her second novel, *Armed with Madness*. And whilst in the Riviera older friendships were tested and new friends made, including Jean Cocteau, Mireille Havet, Gabriel Atkin and Harcourt Wesson Bull, all of whom would have an enduring impact on her life. From her diary entries during her sojourns there, it is clear that the fabric of the place had a powerful effect on her, which would be equalled only by the seascapes of Sennen Cove in the so-called "English Riviera" when she moved there in 1932.

* * * * *

On this winter [1925-1926]
Divided into three periods
I. Arrival. Roy part, Murray, at a distance. Estrangement from Glenway and Monroe.
II. Cocteau's coming. Loss of G and M. Murray close-up.
III. Broken period. Trouble over Murray. Main event, a certain amount of opium with Jean, but principally, with Auric.

—MB, undated diary entry, Spring 1926

First of all...I am not coming back to England to live, not at least for years.

—MB, undated draft of letter to Tony, April 1926

"NOT NEARLY ENOUGH notes made: sheer idleness," Mary Butts castigated herself after arriving in Villefranche in November 1925. She was unhappy about the breakdown of her relationship with Geoffrey Dunlop and whilst in Villefranche socialised a great deal in order to raise her spirits. Very quickly this small medieval resort caught her imagination: "The wind here in the arches—blown over the peaks blazing with snow, warmed to traditional zephyrs, over the foothills and the sea, then wandering in and caught in the alleys, under the arches, where the sun has never been, or becoming perfectly still." She attributed the power of the place partly to its Mediterranean climate, nestled as it is on the south-eastern coast of France, and throughout her visits there she commented on the light reflected and refracted in the sea and skyscapes: "The weather I think," she later wrote, looking out over Villefranche bay in the spring of 1927, "is the purest of human pleasures. To-day sun and high wind, and a tendency to white light in the sky. The Mediterranean quivering, shaking, light blue and silver-winged. Dust storms, palms roaring." And then in May that same year: "Dawn at Villefranche, the lace of cloud over gold, east, above the mountains; blue-black, silver patched water, a few late lights in the town. The holy calm."

Mary Butts had a bird's-eye view over the bay of Villefranche, for she stayed at the Hotel Welcome. The small station where she alighted was and remains tucked inside the hillside providing a breathtaking view of the sea. After clambering down a steep zig-zagging path and walking along the waterfront, there is no sign of the Hotel Welcome with its impressive and majestic facade until moments before it is reached. In 'A Small Town' Mary Butts described it as "the hotel on the quay, still the only possible one in the place, and worth a moment's attention":

> The basis of the hotel's success was solid comfort, set in a place where beauty is glorious, even sometimes strident; fair and augmenting

> prices, and a 'flair' for small things one does not usually get in a hotel of that class. Pleasant liberties like the freedom to use on urgent private escapades, the back-stairs through the kitchens down to the bar on the quay, where the fun went on, and the place's reputation was made. Outward decorum was beyond reproach: in the salon above the colonel's wife played bridge; but down on the quay came all the sailors from all the fleets and the girls who follow them. And all the gentlemen and ex-gentlemen of Europe who follow such distractions. And such gentlemen among those gentlemen who like artists, and bring them along too.

In the opening to her short story, 'The House-Party', set in Villefranche, the Hotel Welcome is lyrically described as: "The sea-washed, fly-blown, scorched hotel along the coast, whose walls were washed primrose above the blue lapping water, where one mounted to bed by a plaster stair outside above the shifting sea, under the stars shaken out in handfuls." Paul and Essie Robeson, who were also staying for the first time at the Welcome, were equally charmed. It is "the most enchanting spot in the world —so far as we know," wrote Essie to Carl van Vechten and his wife; "Paul and I are as happy as can be."[1] Alec Waugh was another writer who had fond memories of the Hotel Welcome: "Some of my pleasantest writing hours have been on the terrace of the Welcome Hotel in Villefranche, at a round blue-topped table with friends breakfasting all around me." The reputation of the clientele at this hotel is conveyed in Jocelyn Brooke's fictional-autobiographical novel, *Conventional Weapons* (1961), where the narrator spends two weeks at the Welcome. In order to convince the night-porter to provide a dunken friend, Nigel, with a room, he "had to explain that Nigel was *un artiste-peintre anglais très célèbre*, who had been eating bad shellfish—at which the porter, though he granted...[my] request, looked sceptical, as well he might."[2]

Today, literary histories of the Hotel Welcome tend to revolve around the French writer and artist, Jean Cocteau (1889-1963), who went there for long periods from 1924 until his death. As he wrote in his *Portraits-Souvenirs* (1935): "The hotel Welcome in Villefranche-sur-Mer with its pale blue rooms above the gulf...is a source of myths, a place which today's youth, with their delight in lyricism, should transform into an altar to be covered in flowers. All kinds of poets of different nationalities stayed there and by osmosis turned this extraordinary small coastal town with its untidy sheer rocky edges, into a focal point for fables and inventions."[3]

In her enthusiasm for the fishing village itself, Mary Butts commented in February 1928 on the "sense of design at Villefranche. Who has made a map, let alone a model of this hill-side,...old town, and then the slope, its wicked darts of track up to the second Corniche, its mule-paths, road slips, brick paths, sentiers,...each on a separate level, utter irregularity of rock-shelf. Ups, downs, overhangings, set back, a constant, broken facade of plaster of ugliness above the clustered loveliness of the old town." And a few days later: "Villefranche at night: road round the sea from the station above the rocks, part open, part cut out of the living rock. Changes in the pavement; stone oblongs polished or 'facetted' different angles and sizes. In the old town, the ribbon of thin red tiles."

Quite apart from the French writers and artists who stayed in Villefranche during Mary Butts's first visit, there were a number of expatriate English and Americans in residence. Amongst these were various young men whom Mary Butts got to know, including Murray Goodwin and Roy Martin, the writers, Glenway Wescott and Monroe Wheeler, who had a villa in the hills above Villefranche,[4] Paul Robeson of whom Mary Butts "remember[ed] the veins on his hand, like a smooth, perfect prehistoric tree",[5] the dancer, Isadora Duncan, and the American painter, Eugene MacGown.[6] Later Cedric Morris and Lett Haines joined the party. It was a very sociable time for Mary Butts; when she wasn't sitting in cafés talking, she was exploring with friends the neighbouring villages and countryside. She took a taxi to the nearby resort of Beaulieu; she wandered in the pine wood off St Hospice; she climbed up to the Citadel above Nice and gazed over the Mediterranean. "And the sea," she commented, "thirteen ways of looking at a piece of jade."[7]

She travelled inland to the medieval walled city of St Paul de Vence at the end of April 1926. Her affinity for the pine forest at Lou Contour prompted the following tribute: "The avenue of old figs: the grass on each side, rather raw and dull, springing with a kind of lily like lords and ladies. The wind that was more than singing, that brushed through millions of trees. I have never known anything like it. Could never leave it, once I had lived there. Shall go back. Have not found a name for it. The wind came and went, ebbed and was there all the time; turned the wood silver; was the wood. And the trees were wind, and the scent went through." It is a measure of Mary Butts's delight with and reverence for woods that her initial working title for *Armed with Madness* was "In the Wood".

Mary Butts commented in her diary that Villefranche formed the stage for "silly indiscretions" by its residents. "Murray Goodwin was in love with Roy, and trying to keep friends with me from affection and interest...and Roy was angry with me because he has no courage, and a little too much inclination in Murray for him, and so against me, had worked him up. And so he would not speak to Murray, nor be plain to me. And P de L [unknown] hated me because I had red hair, and her young man liked me because I had. And I loved some, and disliked no one much, and wished for peace." In fact she gradually fell in love with Murray Goodwin (a young man about whom little is known).[8] Whilst she spent a great deal of time with him, this 'love affair' seems like earlier ones to have been mainly imaginary: "On the M[urray] of-the-imagination. 'He's a darling. I always love him. He and I have awful fun together. But then he's my lover too.'" The real relationship was rather more frustrating, as can be seen from her notes for a letter to Murray in December:

> It is now or never. That it is up to him [to] 'faire les belles choses' because, mysteriously, the job of being my helper and my comfort, over the worst, is his. He can't do too much, because in some way, my 'genius' depends on it. I've been through a crisis since I was ill, and I've an idea of the burden that is being put on him. He should do it for more than his own sake. (Of course it's a way of getting him to sleep with me; but there's more, in this case, I think, than that.)

Although this relationship elated and depressed her by turns, it never stopped her from working. By January 1926 what she wanted was "to see a pattern between the groups here, well, if there is one, I'm the bead running on that string… Beads that do not click all together. And," she continued, showing as usual that all her socialising was feeding her imagination: "I wish I knew how to begin the novel. I know all it is to be about; no plot." In fact, very quickly, she developed her ideas into a definite plot: "I think it shall begin with 'boys and girls' finding the Grail cup. At S. Egliston." A little later she commented on the need to "get the Yank as a person, and *not* protagonist. Alter stresses for that." These are the essential descriptions of the storyline in *Armed with Madness*. Mary Butts not only produced a first draft in Villefranche; during these weeks she also wrote a number of poems including 'Picus Martius: Here lies the woodpecker who was Zeus'.[9]

* * * * *

> *When Jean [Cocteau] said: 'that some people had real fairy-tales in their times, friendships and things like that; but that they had to pay for them, I knew what he meant.*
>
> —MB, undated diary entry, February 1926

THE PERSON whom she met at this time who would have the greatest impact on her life and writing was Jean Cocteau. As mentioned above, the effect of Villefranche on his work and life has been widely documented by French literary historians; however, as Pierre Caizergues declared in *Jean Cocteau et le Sud* (1989), these accounts are far from exhaustive:

> Should we have followed him through all his travels from north to south between 1924—when he first stayed in Villefranche—and March 1963—when he left Santo Sospir for the last time? That would be an impossible task given what we know today of Cocteau's biography and not really worth the effort.
>
> Indeed as the poet himself often told us: even though nations or individuals develop through history, it cannot capture their essence, for "history is made up of truths which become lies through the passage of time whilst mythology is made up of lies which eventually become truth."[10]

Cocteau's friendship with Mary Butts began in January 1926. Later he would provide illustrations for two of her books. Their relationship seems to have been one of mutual respect, stimulation and support right up to and beyond her permanent departure from France in 1930. Yet even in more recent accounts of Cocteau's life and work their friendship and publications have passed unnoticed, undocumented, which underscores Caizergues's comment.

Mary Butts had been looking forward to meeting Cocteau, writing the draft of a poem in her diary which included the lines "en esperance/ on attend JC" (waiting and hoping to see JC). When they did meet in early January 1926 she was in no way disappointed: "JC 1st impressions: that like all people who are developed and good for something, he is utterly agreeable, and without pretension. Gay,...witty, sincere, and wholly intelligent. ...Aged and suffering, Latin quicksilver quality—I like him, not at all afraid of him. He improves G [the composer, Georges Auric,]—perhaps 'touches nothing that he does not adorn'. I think that's the phrase. Yes, France's Brightest Boy." Very quickly she sensed an affinity between them: "*Remember*, his beauty when he talked about the theatre; a description of what I wrote in the 'Week End'.[11] That he is doing what I was too lazy, too disencouraged to do, a revision of Greek tragedy." Here Mary Butts was referring to Cocteau's play, *Orphée*, which was to be first performed in the summer of 1926 in Paris. "I shall see that," she decided in her diary when Cocteau described it to her in February. During their conversations, she was greatly impressed by "his gift...his power of making fairy-tales out of the silliest commonest properties. The lost shirt, the glass crocodile, the fried fish."

One of the ways in which she felt a closeness with Cocteau was through his sense of persecution. In a letter to his mother at that time he declared: "The more I think about it, the more I believe that the strange hatred shown by the Surrealists is not only plain hatred but mixed with magic and sorcery. It is since they first appeared first appeared (dada) that my life began to take on an unlivable quality. Prayer alone will save me. Pray. Pray. Let us pray."[12] This extreme sense of being up against supernormal rather than human forces was one Mary Butts understood. Perhaps she recalled at this time Aleister Crowley's "interference" shortly before Cecil Maitland's suicide attempt in Paris four years earlier and how "when it happened, I heard the daimon say—not what you think has happened, but something else and dangerous" (13.6.22). In Paris in the autumn of 1926, this feeling would return: "I remembered that I had seen Crowley at the 'Select' and the evil he had tried to do me, or that had arisen from him (had it?). And I was afraid. Of everything. Pure fear. It waved in, or marched in like a wall. Receded—I feared society, myself—what that old man could do." Also by the time she came to Villefranche for this first visit in 1925, she was beginning to feel that Mary Colville-Hyde, Tony and to a certain extent John Rodker were forces of evil against her. It is not surprising, then, that she felt a certain empathy with Cocteau after a conversation on the 25 February. (They spoke in French; the following are her notes):

> He talked to us of what is technically envoutement [enchantment]. Not a moving or emotional conversation. Gene [MacGown], having listened to as much as he could take in, left. (Memories not all remote, for me, *Ashe*, Eleanor, my Mother, JR, things seen in London. What possessed Cecil Maitland etc.) Facts (via Jean Cocteau), they [the Surrealists] practise technical magic. Soupault.... Aim: to destroy Jean's life and creation.... That they half succeed. He said they were killing him.

"This story did not make me emotional," she commented. "There was no 'rapture of the intellect at the approach of the fact'. I had to be dry as Jean is dry, unable to comfort him, convince him. Only try to make notes, with the usual difficulties." Her lack of sympathy for the Surrealists may well have been the result of Cocteau's presentation of them. Goldring commented that "their alleged disgusting vices profoundly shocked Mary, who was usually tolerant in such matters."[13] Stimulated by Cocteau's company, she wrote a number of poems at this time, including 'Prayer for Jean Cocteau', (which he liked); 'The Little Party' (in which Cocteau is described as the "Bird-Catcher"[14] and Georges Auric as "the most respected friend alive");[15] 'Thinking of Saints and of Petronius Arbiter' and 'Rites de Passage' ("L and C [Lett and Cedric] as well as Jean Cocteau. Part of the rite—which ought to be into 'reality', what the world is.") From 1926 she referred to the Achilles Set in her poetry, where Achilles was Cocteau and his circle of friends were his Myrmidons. She and Cocteau also copied out poems, the latter even translating a poem into English. He was a perceptive critic of a weakness of her poetry: "Jean said: about my poems, that he thought I tried to be modern, and when I was modern, it was a thing dated and in time, not before and after and outside time as when I wrote about Delphi and the land: [and, elucidated Cocteau,] 'When [the Futurist] Marinetti said that Thermopylae was like a train, it was as bad as Annunzio saying a train was like the battle of Thermopylae.'" Yet Cocteau himself was also aware of their affinity, declaring in a comment which is characteristically lyrical yet cryptic: "Like me, you look for chiselled words, not coloured ones."[16] They had several conversations about poetry, in one of which Cocteau said that the "image [was] like cutting holes in folded paper, pulled out, made lace. That poetry was seeing things like a part of the paper unfolded—more or less. About never using an image for the sake of an image—like calling a boat yellow." Mary Butts disagreed and reported that "I said '*then* you'd have to tell everything about the boat'. He said 'like saying a woman had a left eye.'"

Whilst she was working hard at this time on *Armed with Madness*, they clearly had time for fun or "larks". She noted the night of the 3 March in particular, to which she gave the title *"Nuit de Pavot"*. "Remember: Jean and Auric here after dinner.... Jean threw on my hat and a scarf, found an easel, and painted me on the blotting paper, ancient style artist Montmartre. The acting.[17] How ill he was."

Pavot, the French for opium poppy, was a reference to the drug which was central to Cocteau's life. According to Monique Lange, one of Cocteau's biographers: "People smoked a lot of opium in those days when they were rich, colonels or sailors. Opium was one of the curses of Cocteau's life. It plays as large a part in the poet's biography as his childhood, his writing and love."[18] At this time Jean Cocteau was drawing pictures, such as *Le Mystère de Jean, l'oiseleur* (1925) which had a particular style influenced by the opium he was taking. Among Mary Butts's papers there are a number of his sketches in this style and which probably date from this period. Monique Lange also points out that "opium addicts like to convert others with whom to share what they believe makes them happy."[19]

While this was undoubtedly true for Cocteau (Robert Medley cited it as the reason why Rupert Doone had broken off his affair with him),[20] it was not the case for Mary Butts. Cecil Maitland had introduced her to opium early in their relationship, and although she smoked it for the rest of her life, there are several testimonies to the fact that she never tried to convert anyone. Harcourt Wesson Bull, a young American writer who first met her in Villefranche in 1928, wrote in a memoir: "Be it to Mary's great credit that she never directly suggested I begin smoking; the temptation may have been strong since it could have meant another to share the expenses, or even to provide them."[21] Quentin Bell, who met her in Paris in the late 1920s, confirmed this: "Although Mary believed strongly in the value of this drug as a means to inspiration, contending that there was hardly a single good poem in the English language which was not produced under the influence of [opium], she never—and this is rare amongst addicts whom I have known—attempted to 'convert' me."[22] It is clear that her knowledge of the drug was considerable, for in October 1927 she wrote a fascinating semi-fictional account of the complicated mechanics of opium use, entitled 'Fumerie'. Her aim in this still-unpublished essay was to provide "some notes it has amused me to make, hints from the Travel Bureau, the opium Baedeker, which, so far as I know, has not been written cheerfully enough in the western world", although she does praise the work of de Quincey and Baudelaire.

'Fumerie' is in many ways a cautionary tale: "It takes a year's practice to make a pipe", necessitating specific materials—"the tray: the needles: THE LAMP. The moistened rag or piece of sponge. The Pipe: its bowl… Tape. The dross-box and palette—and a great deal of patience." Mary Butts's clear familiarity with this activity is illustrated in the witty rhetoric of the following passage: "Is it a sub-conscious protest, relic of a mis-applied sense of sin," she asks, "which so frequently inhibits the purchase of oil and wick? You are in a hotel, and a descent into the salle à manger at mid-night to rob a cruet is hardly the best preparation for your bed-time pipe. Nor is a strip cut out of your finest wool sock a convenient and economical substitute for the 'mèche' [wick] which should be the smoker's first care." 'Fumerie' gives advice not only on how to prepare the drug but also how to transport it:

> You are going away for the first time with It. Probably it will not have occurred to you that the problem of packing now presents serious developments.
>
> In default of a travelling set you have followed the usual course in the case of extraneous objects, and your smoker's outfit is secreted in socks, between handkerchiefs, in a shoe. Lucky for you if you have committed to the sponge-bag the bottle, tin, flask or jar on which all depends.
>
> If you have not, on unpacking you may find a morass; chemises, or shirts, tooth-brushes, make-up and books gummed together by an inseparable, uncollectable mass of semi-solidified opium.
>
> Useless to repine: you will probably soak each article in your wash-hand basin, bottle the result collected by means of your douche and drink it day by day.
>
> NEXT TIME, [we are reminded] YOU WILL HAVE LEARNED: that opium has the qualities of treacle, glue, quick-silver and india rubber.
>
> ALSO: that liquid, blown to bubbles, cooked to paste, to dust, opium is a living substance, a magic extract. One that knows its own business and who are its own people—if you do not learn its ways, it will leave you, and leave ruin behind it.

Mary Butts translated a number of poems[23] for Cocteau and during this first visit to Villefranche he asked her to translate his play, *Orphée.* "Accepted", she wrote in her diary and announced it joyfully in a letter to Rupert Doone.[24] Yet from the draft of a telegram to Cocteau in April 1926, it would seem that her task was in fact to edit an English translation already in existence and which left her unimpressed: "A curse on your translator, I've corrected 40 pages. He invents, he lies, he works at finding clumsy words. He likes quotation marks. He loves stylistic errors. Your beautiful correct sentences, as elegant as Poe's appear as if they had been dipped in molasses. I've changed many things." She concluded the telegram with the salutation: "I remain your faithful and furious friend. Marie."[25]

CHAPTER ELEVEN

"High up in the arms of Paris" *April – December 1926*

For Sergei: the knight's move.
He has to do nothing, he has only to know (and he will not).

—MB, undated diary entry, summer 1926

It is all very well to say: accept the world for what it is.[26] *Who can? It is too indecent. Take this life at Montparnasse—where there is no love, no honour, no generosity of strength. Not a single real friend here, no lover, nothing, a rather bad good time dust and ashes. No courage.... No one to tell anything to. Have I even to square that up, to be an artist? Absolutely alone. Hope I suppose, is left; but I am become a little hysterical. Without words, only pain.*

—MB, undated diary entry, late April 1926

IN MID-APRIL Mary Butts wrote to John Rodker to send all her correspondence c/o Lett Haines at 29 Rue Liancourt, for she was returning to Paris. By the 27 April, she was living at the Hotel Royal at 212 Boulevard Raspail in Montparnasse. During the spring she took Camilla away from Poppy Vanda, saying "she would return her in a week."[27] In fact she never returned the child to Poppy who had been looking after her for the past four years, ignoring Poppy's urgent pleas for money owed to her. Yet Camilla was not to live with her mother, who placed her in a pension outside Boulogne. "Please let me know by return," she wrote to John Rodker in London from the Hotel Royal on the 1 May, "exactly how far you are willing to go in helping Camilla and myself either in acknowledgement of parental obligations or by the repayments of debts of honour."[28] His reply was evasive, although the problems were partly caused by the General Strike which was then at its height: "At the moment I'm so hard up that I don't think I can stand the cost. I need what little money I have to start again and the strike is holding up everything and probably will for some time after it's finished.... You're fortunate to be out of all this." He refused her request that he become her publisher.[29]

As can be seen from the diary entry quoted above, Mary Butts was unhappy at this time and tried to forget her own problems by reading works by Emerson and the historian, Arthur Weigall.[30] Yet for all her true anguish, her diary records a great deal of socialising in the Dôme and the Rotonde which were only a hundred yards or so from her hotel. She also frequented the Select which was a little further away. In his autobiography, *Drawn from the Life,* the English painter, Robert Medley, described his first evening in Paris in May 1926 (he was then 21 years old), when his lover Rupert Doone introduced him to the Bohemian centre in Montparnasse. There he found "the unprecedented invasion of international and polyglot artists of all kinds that swarmed in post-war Paris had adopted the studios and the cafes and the cheap hotels of the 6e and 14e *arrondissements* as their stamping ground." Medley recalled that:

> The most crowded of the cafés were the Café du Dome, with its ranks of tables on the pavement, and on the opposite corner across the boulevard the Rotonde, which before the Revolution had been frequented by Lenin—or so it was said. For some reason the Rotonde was falling from favour...[and] the café frequented by our circle was new, small, and aptly called the Select. The decor was nondescript art deco. The first to see us and be seen as we entered was Mary Butts—easily recognized by the tangled mass of flaming gold-orange hair that refused to remain tidy. She had a clear pale complexion, small, bright green eyes, zany red lips, broadly rouged in a carefully chosen colour, and an infectious giggle. Her bangles slipped down to her elbow as she waved a welcome with a cigarette held in a long ivory holder. Sitting next to her was Mary Reynolds, a quiet intelligent American lady, then living with Marcel Duchamp. Cedric Morris and Lett Haines swept in on their way to a party and arrangements were made for us to meet the following day.[31]

As with so many of her friends, it was Mary Butts's hair that Medley recalled with such vividness. Elsewhere he expanded on "Mary's 'giggle'. Mary's 'laugh' was a 'giggle', *the mischievous conspiratorial giggle,* the special privileged share in the joke."[32] The bangles Medley mentions are clearly visible in the fabulous photograph of her taken by Man Ray in 1927. Mary Reynolds was a close friend of Mary Butts's, who described her as "the world's most charming woman".[33]

Another of her favourite haunts was a nightclub called the Boeuf Sur le Toit. Named after Cocteau and Darius Milhaud's 1920 tango-ballet of that title, the Boeuf had opened its doors on the 15 December 1921. Cocteau himself presided at its grand opening when it moved a few weeks later to the Rue Boissy-D'anglas on the 10 January 1922. "The premises were minute with a dance floor the size of a pocket handkerchief", yet you could get a wonderful meal for only 25 francs.[34] During the twenties, "the decade of illusion",[35] the Boeuf's music was provided by "the cocktail pianists Jean Wiéner and Clément Doucet [who] were said to...'play like angels and looked like Mutt and Jeff.'"[36] Indeed "word soon spread that the only place to meet celebrities was at the 'Boeuf'. People wore evening dress or gray flannels. High society mingled with artists in jerseys. Businessmen talked with writers. Everyone knew everyone else… No evening was complete that had not been rounded off by a visit there" and so of course Robert Medley was taken to the Boeuf by Rupert Doone, Cedric Morris and Mary Butts shortly after he arrived.[37] In *Drawn from the Life* Medley recalled how on that particular visit to the "Boeuf sur le Toit…Mary, a regular smoker of opium at this time, was disappointed not to find Cocteau. Weiner and Doucet, the cult classical pianists, were improvising jazz duets, and here we ended the evening, and my first experience of Paris by night."[38] The following year Mary Butts would write 'Le Boeuf sur le Toit', a poem which opens:

From one side of the Boeuf to the other
Raced Achilles' set
From the great bar, square and black
To the little bar, yellow and red; a slip of a bar
To meet in and set the pace.

Speaking for himself and Rupert Doone, Medley recorded that Mary Butts was "our closest friend" in Paris at that time, and he would look after her during a period of detoxification in November 1928.

In the spring of 1926 Mary Butts's relationship with Murray Goodwin was going nowhere. A sense of her disillusion can be gained from her poem entitled 'Prayer (for MG)':

O God who created them to laugh and steal cherries
O God who made them to laugh and do what
they like. Direct Murray whose toys
are stolen, who fell down and was bruised, and
who was not mended by Your easy grace.
So that forgetting to laugh he could not love; and
not loving he could do as he pleased.

At the beginning of May Mary Butts also recorded remarks Murray made to her in her diary: "Murray said: 'there is a patch of yellow and there is lightening—when the lightening is gone, the yellow patch will still be there'. Adding that I wasn't lightening, but like something in nature, a sun or a moon or something, sometimes behind a cloud but not changing. These distressing banalities, but I like the first." Whilst the actual relationship could not satisfy her, she was able to transmute aspects of it, in true Modernist fashion, into her writing. Thus she incorporated Murray's remarks in her poem 'Rites de Passage' which she was then reworking. In the poem Murray's words are attributed to a theatre usher or waiter:

> A garçon de promenoir once told me:
> 'There is a yellow patch and there is lightening: When the lightening is gone, the yellow patch will be there.'
> Adding kindly: 'You are not lightening. You are something natural that keeps on turning up—that is never and always there. You know I don't like women...'

The poem was first published in *Pagany* in 1931. One of Murray Goodwin's other comments showed an astute understanding of Mary Butts's attitude to the people she loved: "M[urray] said: 'you have no judgement; you're romantic; always seeing people as you want them to be'. The only answer being that I want them to be what is in them, what only a poet sees." Not regarding this as a criticism, she used the remark as the basis of her reply two years later when interviewed by *The Little Review*. It was in response to a questionnaire sent to all the contributors (including H.D., Marianne Moore and William Carlos Williams)[39] and published in the final issue of the magazine in May 1929. When asked, "What do you like most about yourself?" she replied: "My faculty for seeing, as a whole, as one sees a work of art, the best in people." When asked what she disliked most in herself she answered: "Lyrical rage when they don't keep it up all the time."[40] This mythologising characteristic would be revealed most strongly in her relationship with a young expatriate Russian, Sergei[41] Maslenikof, whom she met later that spring...

In late April Mary Butts recorded how she was partly "cured" of her despondency at a party given by Antonio de [Tony] Gandarillas in his flat at 60 Avenue Montaigne, a few streets away from her hotel in the Boulevard Raspail. This Chilean diplomat (well-known for his "lurid and fashionable life") housed, fed and supported a friend of hers, the impoverished English painter, Kit Wood.[42] She knew most of the people who attended, including Lord Napier Alington [Naps] (whom she had known as a child in Dorset), Cocteau and Georges Auric. Characteristically, she noticed not only the people, but the beautiful objects around her:

> *Remember*: black lacquer tables with the crystal and rose quartz.
> Naps running down-stairs.
> The bed with the blue cover. The lamp, the confusion of lacquer, jade, orange ivory—The people on the bed—The people on the floor... We might be at Salterns: Tony in his hair—fixing cap—Jeanne[43] in my arms—Auric with his toys—fragile Jean so light in my arms—Naps angry and softened by the drawings—Tony [Gandarillas] saying he was a kind of saint. Talking softly with Tony on the bed...the coromandel screen at last.

Mary Butts was particularly happy at this party because Gandarillos's flat evoked something of her beloved Salterns and she wrote 'Avenue

Montaigne' in celebration. In this lyrical poem, the coromandel screen she admires there forms a metaphor which conveys the flat's magical timeless atmosphere:

> No more time in that house
> No time at all
> Times and spaces folded in and out
> Tenfold on the tall
> Coromandel screen that folds the wall
> Between the light room and the room kept for night.
> . . .
> High up in the arms of Paris.[44]

The Coromandel screen would make a small but crucial appearance in her short story 'Brightness Falls', where it forms part of Mary Butts's examination of Freud's *lapsus linguae*.[45]

She attended the opening night of Cocteau's *Orphée*. A mutual friend wrote to Lett Haines on the 15 June 1926: "Tonight occurs the new Cocteau play, to which everybody is going. The Surrealistes are, of course, going to make a fuss. Mary Butts is able to live in an atmosphere so splendidly melodramatic that she is perfectly happy fevering over the possible effects of it all on poor Jean's health."[46]

There is scarcely a mention of *Armed with Madness* in her diary for these months, as she was principally engaged in a study of Ouspensky's, *Tertium Organum* (1923, 2nd ed.) for the "redaction Surrealiste" (unexplained). She was fascinated by the Russian philosopher's discussion about the need for a new kind of perception, noting in her diary: "Ouspensky says: 'furthermore, it is necessary to understand that all objects known to us exist not only in those categories in which they are perceived by us, but in an infinite number of others in which we do not and cannot sense them. And we must learn first—to think things in other categories, and then so far as we are able, to imagine them therein.' This is a problem," she commented, "in every art and every development or change in the form of any art, notes, lines, words, colours. We have to 'break up their lazy family habits' before we can create, ie approach reality, and do living work again". She concluded that "Ouspensky is least convincing when he writes about our closest approaches to reality, love and art. There he slips into sentiment and is too tentative, tho' he never says a thing that is not true. Because perhaps he has not had time for love, and is not an artist."

The theme of love particularly concerned her at this time for she had recently become friendly with a White Russian exile, one of many to be found in Paris during the 1920s. "Sergei Maslenikof had never had any money," recalled Robert Medley. "He was an extremely talented designer and he designed the elaborate embroidery of 1920s frocks, ...diamanté...all the applique designs of 1920s dresses...he made designs for the very best houses... He never seemed to do any work except when he hadn't got any money...he was always broke, but a very sweet and charming man, very nice but always broke... Ah Sergei Maslenikof, I ought to think of him because Paris was full of Russian refugees at that time; there were dozens of them..."[47] In *Death of Felicity Taverner*, Mary Butts's third novel (which she began to write the following year) she elaborated on the fact that

> Russian emigration is making a world within this world. Persons whose position in society has been taken away with their goods, and who lack the chance or the will to re-establish themselves. Slavs who have given in to the slav character...[and forming] the under-tow of the world's tides. ...not properly charted, and little of any value is known or has been written about them to-day—though the picaresque novel, from the Satyricon down, is full of them. For their picture-making qualities are obvious...[48]

Trying to get closer to Sergei and point him in the right direction, as she saw it, became her overriding preoccupation for the next three years. She described her role in July: "That he is dispersed—loving in one direction, laughing, working, thinking, also desiring in others; his idleness the common factor, his pride off at another tangent: that he is all aristocracy and one penniless boy. ...there is nothing greater than Sergey for Sergey. If I had the 'right' to control him, that is the power. I would take him away into the hills and the sea. Consider the parable of the talents. All his are buried. He can be teased with that." Stella Bowen confirmed that Sergei was typical of the many Russians in Paris, who "drove taxis and...ran restaurants and snack-bars. They sold their heirlooms and they made amusing things of glass, and silk and leather. They designed clothes and stage-sets and they sang haunting songs to the balalaika."[49]

The fact that Russians often sold their heirlooms provides an interesting cameo-example of how Mary Butts transmuted a small yet significant detail into her fiction. In mid-January 1928 she reported in her diary: "After dinner heard one of S[ergei's] discourses on russian history. Our Lady of Kazana—story of the other Madonna, ikon of whom his mother had hung round his neck and he'd lost with the grand-duke Serge and a tapette in Constantinople. I said 'your bad luck began then, Sergey.' He said, 'don't frighten me'. But I made him listen: 'that's how magic works. You lost your ikon, conductor of your mother's good magic, with and because of drink and fancy boys. And it's those things which have almost killed you. Until another woman, another 'Mary' if you like, happened. Don't you see? 'Magic' works through natural things.' I hope he did." She worked this incident into *Death of Felicity Taverner*:

> From the dreadful moment when he had been tempted to abandon [his mother]...[the Russian, Boris] had felt that he had come under a curse...his belief in the curse was confirmed by what had happened to him later, explaining a gesture his friends noticed, as though feeling for a chain or a ribbon that was not there. There had been a ribbon once, because, before they parted, his mother had given him an ikon, an ancient one that was also a jewel, had hung it round his neck and told him never to take it off. Never to give it away or to sell it in whatever distress; still less never to lose it or allow it to be stolen. Good mother-magic. But in Constantinople, not six months later, he had gone out one night to get drunk....
>
> All he remembered [of that night] was waking up on a seat in the gardens at Pera. It was winter and still dark, and as his hand went up to his throat to feel for the ikon, it was not there. Feeling down his body, he had mistaken the edge of a button for the jewel where it had slipped, and the horror of disappointment had done something to make him mad. In his waistcoat pocket he had found a packet of cocaine. He had traded his jewel for that? He did not know. He could never remember what had happened at the "dancing". Nor could he ever forget. Nor be persuaded that his vital misfortune, something very like the ruin of his soul, had not begun that night. On that night something had been settled about him.[50]

The significance of Sergei for Mary Butts, and the reason she supported him financially and emotionally during her years in Paris, was partly explained by her in a letter to a friend in July 1928: "His personality is curious, like the King of Sweden who was called 'the Janus King'. Most of the time he makes me fairly unhappy, then suddenly he shows a side of himself, half-saint, half-child, half-prince. I've got a lot out of this, as you know."[51] In an unpublished poem 'Frère Doue Amye',[52] written in the early summer of 1927, she compared Sergei to "A chinese tree straightened in Europe...a soldier without a sword...a rider without a horse...a prince with two faces...[a] cub out of Byzantium." Nine months after their difficult relationship began in the summer of 1926, Mary Butts commented on the discrepancy between the Sergei of her imagination and his real counterpart: "Long play today and last night with the imaginary Sergey" (27.3.27). A few days later she added: "If one could know the relations, if they are not *wholly* fortuitous, whatever that means, between say: my game with the Sergei of my imagination [and] my account recited to-day of what the real one had done." The Sergei who inspired her writing from then on and for the rest of her life, was the "imaginary Sergei". In 'Frère Doue Amye' she wrote:

I set traps for light
. . .
Glass for a trap to catch your spirit, make
Your image seen in the glass of the imagination
Come true.[53]

During the summer of 1926 Mary Butts went on a number of enjoyable outings around Paris and in Normandy with Sergei and other friends. The trips prompted her to write several poems, including 'Chateau Galliard'; 'On Vexin' and 'Surprise Song'. Yet by the time she returned to Paris in the autumn, her relationship with Sergei had settled into what would become a regular cycle of elation and dejection. At that time she suffered from hysteria and heightened perceptions: "I felt as if I saw shapes, the abstracts of the madness: evil: despair: fear that is going about the world now. A thorned white thing." Whilst despondent about other friendships, the following description of her squabbles with the real Sergei, shows that their relationship was her major preoccupation:

> I am busy sewing, with a rhythm on the seam. S plays the gramophone next door, and does not take the record off at the end. I say: 'S, do take it off.' He does not answer. I do it and mention it. He says: 'when I was ill in bed today, you put on this, and I got up each time'. I deny this: honestly (once possible). Go back. Ask a minute later, what *has* happened about the electric light. Say that the workman S had said would do it, knows nothing about it. And I have worked hard, and Sergei is never decent. Can't even see two lamps are fixed when [he] knows I can't work at my table without a reading lamp. (Imagine myself going blind). He says. 'you do like to complain, Mary'. I turn away feeling excitedly sick. He goes away. Comes back, (he has left the lamps). Says: I have a friend coming to tea I think. If you are indisposed, stay here. I say: 'Surely you tell me off too often. You do not know how to get the best out of people.'[54] He shouts at me for the char-woman to hear. I leave it at that, cynically. And sick. I think of his drunkenness, his evil words, the nuisance he is. The demands, 'sendings ups', little brutalities, the manque d'amour. ...later... Explanations—my apologies (to a child) warm. His cold. And troubled. All over, a little frost for bloom.

This passage has a quality of the relationship between Peter Pendragon and his lover in Aleister Crowley's *Diary of a Dope Fiend* (1922) and the hypersensitivity Mary Butts expressed is probably partly due to alcohol and drugs. There is no doubt that she supported Sergei financially, and several of her friends thought that she was being exploited. Harcourt Wesson Bull later wrote that "Sergei, the protagonist of Mary Butts's *Imaginary Letters* [was]...an idealized portrait of him: the real Sergei was less attractive and far more of an incorrigible ne'er-do-well than one would have dreamed possible."[55] Robert Medley, by contrast, understood the attraction Sergei held for her, describing him as "sad, lovable and funny" and, like most Russians, "possess[ing]...a special combination of intellect, intuition and mysticism."[56] As we have seen, Mary Butts had been attracted to these Russian qualities since the 1910s.[57] She may have been often frustrated and angered by him, yet she continued to be inspired. This is most visible in her epistolary narrative, *Imaginary Letters* (mentioned by Wesson Bull), which she extensively redrafted in September 1926,[58] at a time when she was reading *Science and the Modern World* (1926). The latter was a series of lectures given the previous year by the English philosopher, Alfred North Whitehead.[59] Mary Butts quoted from Whitehead in an epigraph to *Imaginary Letters*: "We must not expect all the virtues. We should be satisfied if there is something odd enough to be interesting."

As the title implies, this 60-page novella is, like its predecessor 'Lettres Imaginaires' (1919), an epistolary fiction. The unnamed female narrator addresses a number of letters to the mother of her lover, Boris, a Russian emigré, who, as the poet, Robin Blaser, pointed out: "will not stay still...[being] unstable, lost, homosexual, unavailable".[60] "God forbid that I should give away the young to the old," the narrator declares in her first letter, adding: "but as you will never read this...I do not think it will be impertinent of me to talk to you, as if you were a living ghost."[61] These never-to-be-sent letters are in a fact a kind of diary in which the narrator tries to understand the magical, incongruous and inescapable power of love, however hopeless. *Imaginary Letters* is a lyrical prose "sequence",[62] evoking all the qualities, faults and mysteries of what Russia signified to Mary Butts. It was published two years later in November 1928, with illustrations by Jean Cocteau.

* * * * *

14 Rue de Monttessuy

BY SEPTEMBER 1926 Mary Butts had begun to rent a flat on the second or third floor at 14 Rue de Monttessuy, a short street in Paris on the edge of the 7th arrondissement, close to the Seine. In December 1926 a friend wrote that in this flat "she writes feverishly...under the shadow of the Eiffel Tower", which stands at the end of the street.[63] Other flats in this terraced house were rented at various times by friends of hers, including Mary Reynolds and the American writers, Kitty Cannell and Harold Loeb. 14 Rue de Monttessuy became Mary Butts's home for the next four years until she left Paris for the last time in June 1930. Today, as then, the "street door [of this unassuming town house] opens with a press button". In January 1930, she noted that the house was built "40-50 years ago—cheaply, stupidly without one trace of attention to man's wants or respect for his health or his imagination.... The dim memory of a tradition, the pure and eloquent french line, saved him [the architect]—in the stairline mounting from floor to floor, while there are red tiles, six-sided, to wash and even my salon floor is laid in wood-strips—tile-hard—the years of wax and weight have locked into one, and given each its own relief, and knot and grain stand out set together in one brown-glass floor pool." Douglas Goldring described the sitting-room as "characteristic of its owner":

> It contained an enormous divan, piled with purple cushions, three or four rickety chairs, a bright green piece of sculpture by Ossip Zadkine, two flower-pieces by Cedric Morris, a water-colour by Kit Wood and a clever portrait-drawing of Mary by Jean Cocteau. One wall of the room was taken up by book-shelves which stretched from floor to ceiling and were crammed with the literature in vogue. Sex, sociology, Loeb translations, Abramelin, Lévy's [sic] *History of Magic*, *The Golden Bough*, the *Chansons de Maldoror*, T.S. Eliot, Virginia Woolf's latest,[64] Aldous Huxley, Jean Cocteau, Radiguet's *Bal de Comte Orgel* —in short, all the "period exhibits" of the future. On the divan, on top of the purple cushions, lay the sky-blue bulk of *Ulysses*.[65]

In a less descriptive but more atmospheric account, Mary Butts's flat forms the setting for 'Frère Doue Amye':

> These memories of the four rooms we found
> A nakedness of plaster, splintered boards,
> Tails of stripped paper in a common house
> In a common street a hurrying step to make
> The Eiffel Tower accessible, just off
> The high-hung, long-flung magical streams of Paris—
> Rue de Babylone, glorious Rue de Grenelle,
> Exiles forbidden doors. Yet with our luck
> Out of four rooms we made four magic boxes,
> Accessible and inaccessible.
> Step of the earth, a refuge, an address—
>
> On the knight's move the old creating trick
> The door to open on two worlds at once.
>
> Begun with a bed, a blanket and a chair.
> Four glasses, a red tray lacquered with stars.
> The concierge lent a table, waxed the floors
> My goods came overseas, woke me at dawn
> Who had been all night dancing. So began
> That play inside four boxes built in air.

The poem is a paean to the magical qualities this flat acquired for Mary Butts, where "time here/ Brims in a cup all times to trap your spirit/ The daimons invited in, lured back/ Aidos and Nemesis left our earth for good". The spirit addressed is Sergei's and the poem is a magic spell, an incantation to make him "know…love…remember":

Until: Between the birds, the embroideries
Between the wine and the jar
The eye in the glass, the ships and the Eiffel Tower
Between the fetish and the Buddha
Between the jade and the cup
The seal with my shield, knots in the web of power.
Between the wood cut on Badbury Rings,
the green tree girl
The knife of gold, steel, silver and mother of pearl.
Inside the ivory box
The tooth and the stone
The bird-blue linen, the scarlet curtain, the white lace
The wood and the bone
By the dancing-girl on ebony sticks with her body
curled
The crystal before the ikon, the visible world
Clouds, illuminate, set—
I shall find what was cold
warm blood in the stone.
You shall have what I have
Know also what I have known.

Getting Sergei to understand what she "knew" was her continual aim. Occasionally she felt she had succeeded: "Sergey said: 'How I am changed. I was like an untidy flat and you came in and gave me doors made of crystal which open onto a garden full of beautiful things… I can breathe now.'"[66] Yet for the most part he eluded her plans for him.

In her diary in early November she repined: "I find it almost impossible to write well—or even without affectation when I wish to deal 'straight' with what we call beautiful or good." She used the metaphor of the knight's move in chess to convey both the necessary oblique manner of writing and the qualitative change conveyed by supernatural transformations. In July 1929 she explained this metaphor which recurred throughout her work[67] and is central to her conception of herself as an artist:

> The correct analogy is in chess the knight's move, more perhaps than a mere analogy. The implications of that motion of a piece of wood or ivory across a given number of squares and its effect on a given number of other carved pieces, different in name, shape and power, are to

> be extended over a number of events caused by man and nature, in infinite, not arbitrary relation. This has to be translated back into a number of γρaηατα. 'Scratches' on paper, one of whose ends is to form a base of that 'science of mysticism' J.W.N. Sullivan has considered possible.[68] The problem is in part the artist's, to express an unknown in terms of the known.
>
> And so, my scratches, chiefly arbitrary and some questionable by the weight of memories and associations they drag with them, out of the lost ages of the world and through our histories — will have to do.

In a letter to a friend in the 1930s, she would ask: "Does the question of what is called 'mystical experience' interest you? It means almost everything to me—I mean as a thing separate from any practice, from love or the arts or work of any kind, the pure quiet sudden thing, like a fire—no, a light.... Yet it is extraordinarily hard to write about, to examine to describe. Language wasn't invented to deal with it; so it mostly gets out by indirections, obliquely, something like the knight's move in chess."[69]

In common with many other writers, not least T.S. Eliot in *The Waste Land*, Mary Butts used the metaphor of a game of chess to describe life. In *Ashe of Rings* Melitta says to her husband, "You pretend that there are other ways of looking at things which have nothing to do with Christianity." He replies, "Little Melitta, Christianity is a way, a set of symbols, in part to explain, and to make men endure the unutterable pain that is in the world. There are other sets like chessmen. But only one game."[70] It was also a metaphor used by Jean Cocteau, whose illustrations for 100 deluxe copies of *Armed with Madness* (1928) on hand-made paper included one with the words: "La vérité du jeu d'échecs" (the truth of the game of chess).

Mary Butts spent time with Kitty Cannell, Duff Twysden and Harold Stearn, the continental scout for Boni and Liveright, who may well have been responsible for A. & C. Boni publishing *Ashe of Rings* and *Armed with Madness*. She recorded the various intrigues and disagreements played out between them: "Duff's deplorable and lovable follies—retranslated into conduct of the dirtiest, and cause of more of the misery *common to us all*"; "follies" which are difficult to decode for an outsider. She read Sisley Huddleston's *France and the French* (1925)[71] as well as Gide's *Les Faux Monnayeurs* (*The Counterfeiters*) (1926). On the 15 October she had the decree nisi of divorce served on John Rodker, although she made no mention of it in her diary. Their divorce would come through the following year. Generally time passed pleasantly enough. She took Camilla to play with Stella Bowen, and Ford Madox Ford's daughter Julie on several occasions during November.[72] In early December, however, Douglas Goldring told her of Cecil Maitland's suicide and for the next few days she was stunned:

On Cecil's death:

> Thoughts which have occurred to me out of the chaotic anguish; the ones that help me—I do not know if they have any prompting outside myself, do not dare hope they have.
>
> That, partly, I left, deserted him, because he was making me unfit to mother Cuddy [Camilla][73]—Also for my work. And seeing her strong and beautiful, and knowing how hard he made it, helped me the first day. Then I thought I felt him about smiling, as I loved him (no sense of conviction there).
>
> I thought in the taxi, on the morning of the second day that we were one young scamp to the less, better dead if he would only live to hurt us.
>
> Then, later in the day, I was 'bad' in the kitchen, crazy with weeping, and I felt as if I saw his face in misery, down somewhere on the ground, and understood that I was making his suffering, for, if any of the theories are right, he would suffer—worse. (He has made us all so suffer who loved him that in any justice attendant on his survival he would suffer—I won't run to that kind of sentimentality.) Then, almost as if he were near me that I was not to grieve for that increased his pain.[74] I asked Sergey if he had heard it said that over-grieving made it hard for the dead, and he said 'Yes, we say that in Russia. It was I who told you'. Rather cross. Then it was like a murmur which has changed the quality of my crying: 'forgive me and I shall be forgiven'.
>
> I can't quite yet, but I shall sleep now, and tomorrow go out and get my hair waved, and try and live again.

Duff Twysden was extremely supportive during this time. When Mary Butts had a frightening vision of Cecil Maitland suffering and "fading away behind...a live obscene corpse—ghost...and trying to dodge it and it was like a mask," Duff consoled her. Her comforting words prompted Mary Butts's last entry for 1926:

> Duff said also 'I knew he was a man with something great to expiate even when he was alive', and I have got some idea about an expiation within an expiation, and remember the night Duff was fey and her story of what happened in Scotland in the XVI century, the murder they did, and how she knew who he had been. 'That God may / burn his hell up speedily / and bring our souls to his city.'

CHAPTER TWELVE

The Storm Goddess and Her Un-rest Cure
1927

Mary was an Englishwoman of gentle birth, a roisterer, and a writer of intensely personal fiction.... I used to call her "the storm goddess" because she was at her best surrounded by cataclysms.... We had lovely times together, warmths, clarities, and laughter. Then the bickering began; and though our separation was not casual, by the time the year was out we were not meeting. That was in 1927. When she died in 1937 I felt almost like a widower. —Virgil Thomson, *Virgil Thomson* (1966)[75]

Shall I ever make a poem out of this spring day with the sun shifting in through the shutters, the warm coolness, Paris humming at a distance; and tears because there are fairy tales in which the pain stops, a miraculous right-about-turn of misery into accomplishment, that never happens;...and Sergey my wretched fairy tale, who, all the same, is a prince, and...William James 'adorable genius' calling me to order?

—MB, undated diary entry, late March 1927

Mary Butts spent the first three months of 1927 in Paris, preoccupied with finding an expiation of and meaning to Cecil Maitland's death. In January she did a great deal of automatic writing which she felt brought her messages from him. She shared W.B. Yeats's belief that "the dead, as the passionate necessity wears out, come into a measure of freedom and may turn the impulse of events, started while living, in some new direction, *but they cannot originate except through the living*."[76] Cocteau sympathised with her sense of loss because he had been broken in a similar way when the young writer, Raymond Radiguet, had died of typhoid in December 1923. "One odd thing," she noted: "Cocteau said how Radiguet dead led him to books and passages in books. I opened a volume of the *Encyclopaedia* [*Britannica*] and was stopped by the name Ker, the Jacobite spy. With a feeling that I was meant to look."[77] As she later explained in the introduction to her historical narrative, *The Macedonian* (1933), the Greek word Kêr has a specific meaning which is linked to the word "daimôn".

> I have used two greek words which may be unfamiliar, but for which english has no exact quivalent—daimôn and kêr. Daimôn—from which our 'demon' but with a specifically bad sense—is a potency,

> never a god; though some of the great daimones attained personality and became gods. A daimôn is sometimes as definite as a season personified, such as Winter and Spring; but usually it is the sheer force that lies behind the manifestations of life—the 'mana' even of a dead man or a tree or the sea or the wind, or in an idea such as Plenty or Nemesis or Luck.
>
> Kêr or Kêrês is a less developed form of the daimôn idea; more a folk-image, less philosophic; represented in popular art as little fluttering winged bodies, and imagined as a cross between a bacillus, a bogy and a ghost.[78]

Nor was this the first time she used the term in her writing, for it occurs in her short story 'In the House', written in the autumn of 1929.

A newfound spiritual relationship with Cecil Maitland would stay with Mary Butts for the rest of her life and she felt inspired and enthusiastic in the early months of 1927. She saw a great deal of her Paris friends including Kitty Cannell, the American painter, Eugene MacGown, and the French writer, Jean Guérin, as well as two new friends. Malin (recently married to Douglas Goldring) was alone in Paris in the spring of 1927, and Mary Butts came to "love [her] as much as" she loved Goldring. He later wrote of his gratitude to "the loyalty of a few friends of whom Mary Butts was one."[79] Her other new friend was the American composer, Virgil Thomson, then 30 years old and studying in Paris. Not only did he and Mary Butts have an intense relationship in 1927 (she called him her "un-rest cure"[80] and he called her "the storm goddess"); Virgil Thomson was responsible for her work becoming known in America. At this time he was the European editor of Sherry Mangan's *Larus, the celestial Visitor*. This magazine and its unexpired subscriptions were shortly sold to another magazine called *Pagany* (named after William Carlos Williams's *A Voyage to Pagany* (1928)), edited in Boston by the American writer, Richard Johns. A number of Mary Butts's poems and short stories were published in *Larus* and *Pagany*. Virgil Thomson would never forget Mary Butts; it was at his suggestion that Paul Bowles included poems by her in a 1973 issue of *Antaeus*.[81]

Mary Butts worked hard at *Armed With Madness* which she had started to call 'People Among Trees', a title suggested to her by Virgil Thomson. Whilst she was frustrated at having to look after Camilla, who was ill, she still found time to read and comment on Oswald Spengler's *Decline of the West* (1926), John Buchan's occult story, 'The Smoking Leg', William James's *The Will to Believe* (1897) and unnamed (but probably supernatural) narratives by Henry James. She found the latter particularly helpful: "I felt that it was [Cecil Maitland] gaining more and more power to influence me right; who has made me see that my fault lay in allowing free entrance to evil thoughts, not so much native to me, but coming from others.... (I can only use banal (ghostly) expression, lighting my way). Anyhow, I have found out, thanks largely to rereading Henry James, that there are thoughts, almost thought forms one must refuse to entertain emotionally. I don't mean not understand, 'get' them, but strictly entertain them."

Camilla had been suffering from poor health for a number of months and her mother was advised that the climate of the south of France would be beneficial. At the end of March, therefore, they travelled down to Cannes where Mary Butts settled Camilla at the Villa les Sablons before taking the train on its 36km journey to Villefranche. To this day the coastal route is idyllic, passing through Golfe-Juan, Juan-les-pins, Antibes, Cros-de-Cagnes and Nice before reaching Villefranche. Mary Butts stayed not at the Hotel Welcome but at the smaller and cheaper Hôtel de la Colline[82] on this her second visit to the French Riviera, from late March until the end of May.

On the train between Cannes and Villefranche she recorded a discussion with Glenway Wescott in which she had perceptively analysed their role as writers in the late 1920s. In it she referred to Gertrude Stein's now famous remark about their being a "lost generation": "Conversation with G on the necessity of our memoirs, of our age. Are we a lost generation? Courage to publish, necessity to be more than novelists not memoir writers to earn our bread. So much more to tell than Pepys; for example—New Saint (!) Simons we could be, for the new aristocracy we are looking for, watching arrive, creating?"

A few weeks later while still in Villefranche, she described this "new aristocracy". It was part of a long consideration of her credo as a writer. What often irritated Mary Butts's contemporaries were her affectations and her decidedly aristocratic mannerisms. These contributed to the misleading impression of her not being the hardworking and dedicated writer which she actually was. Yet Virgil Thomson, who was intimate with her, noted that "every day...she wrote with pen in large note-books. ...and roistered only when the day was done. What Mary liked most...come six of an evening, was a long pub crawl—going with loved ones from bar to bar, dining somewhere, then going on, tumbling in and out of taxis, fanning youth into a flame. Come midnight she would as leave go home and write."[83] Indeed her critical self-appraisal in the spring of 1927 illustrates the seriousness with which Mary Butts viewed her responsibilities as a writer. She headed the entry: "UN RAPPEL A L'ORDRE [call to order]":

> What I believe, after ten years, I am coming to see... What interests me—up to now, I am an unsuccessful writer, lover, dubious mother, of no social distinction—well liked, but my looks are going and to a certain extent, my health. Well, I can write and I want to, should never

> want to *do* anything else. What for? To present reality under ideal forms. Just for the art's sake? yes and no. In the old cant phrase, I want to shew people beauty—soundness. Now the best work cannot be made up wholly from the ugly and the unsound. And our world is both. I begin to understand several things, labelled bolshevism, surrealism, eccentricities of pederasty, the Paris *Daily Mail*, my husband ...the Jew-boy here, the decline of good will, charity, friendship, erotics, the bankruptcy of religion as practised and not practised, defended and attacked everywhere.
> What apart from the specific work of writing is what interests me? Nothing but spiritual development, the soul living at its fullest capacity: using itself....
> I have not got it yet, but I am beginning to know what is wrong with the times. And many of the things we do are not wrong, it is our way of doing them. They are very good things—Paederasty and jazz and opium and research.

Now that he was dead, she believed that "the only time this desire of mine worked, while it worked, perfectly, was with Cecil Maitland. It is odd that since his death, I have begun to understand so clearly." She went on to ask herself: "This mysticism of mine, enough for me because I 'get' and 'know' things which I cannot describe or explain, on what is it based? To make, under no matter what image or indirection, a living clarity of it, great art and great power—life giving—would flow through me, enough at least to refresh my generation." The conviction came from what she termed her "lever", a belief, which would enable her "to keep so-and-so steady, and myself in relation to them, in this frantic life, with the rot getting into the liveliest minds and spirits. In with this works my conviction about Sergey and even the Murrays...what I have called then 'the foundations of a new aristocracy'."[84] When she came to write her autobiography shortly before she died, she was able to explain what set her apart, by protecting her from the anguish of the Lost Generation. It was her memory of Badbury Rings, the prehistoric concentric rings of her native Dorset. Thus towards the end of *The Crystal Cabinet* she described how in her late teens:

> Often and often I walked to Parkstone Station, took the train to Wimborne and, my lunch in my pocket, walked out there. A long way, a dull way, under great trees, all along beside the park of Kingston Lacy...
>
> *'Without God there is no man: without supernature there is no nature; without philosophy there is no psychology; without theology there is no science; without mysticism there is no common sense'*[85]
>
> All this is truth and all the truth; but truth that our age has chosen, clause by clause, to reverse. With the results we are beginning to appreciate. ...in after years it was because of [Badbury Rings] and what they showed me there, that I remained, however uncertainly, critical

> of that reversal. ...there, once and for good, the complaint was stilled, at which man grumbles, of the equivocal nature of the contact between visible and invisible, the natural order and the supernatural, between time and eternity. Experience that would provide in the end, not the answer, but the way to the answer—to all the materialists, from Voltaire's 'racking wheel' to Mr Aldous Huxley's dealings with Pascal's *Feu*.
>
> In short, without the Rings, I know what would have happened to me—whirled away in the merry-go-round of the complex and the wish-fulfilment and the conditioned reflex, with Jung and Pavlov, Julian Huxley and Bertrand Russell, in group-consciousness of the post-war young. On those rocking-horses I might have pranced for ever, with the rest of us, at our version of Vanity Fair.[86]

* * * * *

VILLEFRANCHE WAS AS popular as the previous year: "Glenway is here and Munro, Virgil Thomson, Phil Lasell, and up and down the coast half the world." Virgil Thomson wrote that "Philip Lasell...was a playboy of wondrous charm. For him I served as guide to the intellectual life, though he used in this way Jean Cocteau, Mary Butts, and the young French novelist René Crevel. ...It was through him that I came to know Mary Butts."[87] She was not just playing: "I...work night and day revising the book, now finished. Called either 'In the Wood' or 'People among Trees'. Much in the order of 'When it was Dark', erroneous find of the importance of the Sanc-grail—reactions in a country home, the Foyot and the Boeuf sur le Toit."[88] In fact a diary entry at the end of May shows that Mary Butts toyed with several other titles ('The Egg and the Cup'; 'The Egg in the Cup'; 'Landscape with Birds'; 'Bees under the Roof') before finally settling on *Armed with Madness*, which she noted in her diary was Glenway Wescott's suggestion. The book was published a year later in June 1928.

As ever, she was enthralled by the Riviera: "*For a poem*: the sea's edge here in bright weather: the cacti along the de Maleissye terrace in their variations. Two ways of looking at the same thing. Crete. Happy here." She celebrated the event by writing the poem, 'Juan-les-Pins':

> At June the pines
> In the restaurant built out over the water
> permitted to remember Crete.
> . . .
> Glancing perpetually at the sea
> Crete I prayed

Set your stage and terrify them
Who, seated at your sea's hem
Omit the ceremony
the salt-line has spelt
To your memory.[89]

The way in which the coast of the south of France reminded Mary Butts of Greece was yet another characteristic she shared with Cocteau.[90]

* * * * *

Is there a person among our 'ever widening circle of friends' who is not smoking, wishing to try, about to give up, giving it up, gives it up, starting again, or superciliously denouncing the practice.

—MB, undated diary entry, June 1927

From New York Herald: *'Virile Australian Vegetarian Tears Telephone Book in two'.* (cutting kept) —MB, undated diary entry, June 1927

BY THE 3 JUNE Mary Butts was back once again in Paris where her social circle was "widening": the young Scottish artist, Vivian Ogilvie, is mentioned in her diary as well as the fact that she attended a party given by the American writer, Natalie Barney, at her house in the Rue de l'Université, not far from Rue de Monttessuy. Virgil Thomson also took her to meet Gertrude Stein at her flat in 27 Rue de Fleurus. In November 1925 Mary Butts had noted that Stein's work was impressive. After the visit she only listed (à la 'Tender Buttons') Stein's possessions which she coveted. Later, however, the visit prompted a "real row with Virgil Thomson…I don't want him to be an old lady's tame musician, just a salon composer. A wide cast of the net brought strange information about Gertrude. I can only repeat and repeat and repeat and repeat that a real relation is worth the effort to retain." Her antagonism towards Gertrude Stein would be fictionalised some years later in her short story, 'From Altar to Chimney-piece'.

From the very beginning Mary Butts's relationship with Virgil Thomson was not easy because, as he subsequently recorded: "There was no evil in her; her magic was all tied up with religion and great poetry. But she was strong medicine.… And she was sovereign against my juvenile reserves, my middle-class hypochondrias, my 'pessimisme américain'…" Yet, "I still did not like having my emotions manipulated [by]…a greedy and determined 'femme de lettres' some seven years older. The mental powers were too imposing, the ways inflexible."[91] Thwarted by Thomson, under-fed and smoking a great number of opium pipes, Mary Butts turned her attention once again to the spiritual and imaginary rather than actual living people. "I think I shall soon be in a position to compose on little or nothing to eat, or smoke," she declared, as she was, as usual, writing. In addition to a number of poems, she wrote 'Our Fumerie', which would form the basis for 'Fumerie'. When not writing or socialising she was continuing her crusade to convert Sergei and had a measure of success which she headed *A Miracle*. Shortly afterwards, however, she was depressed when he fell seriously ill. She also spent a great deal of time 'contacting' Cecil Maitland, either alone or with Tommy Earp and other friends. Her latest attempt involved the "Sortes Virgilianae". In his *Oxford Companion to Classical Literature*, Sir Paul Harvey explains how "Virgil's fame grew after his death into superstitious reverence. ...He came to be regarded as a magician, and miraculous powers were attributed to him. The *Sortes Virgilianae* [Oracles of Virgil], attempts to foretell the future by opening a volume of his works at hazard, were from an early date widely practised (even by the emperor Hadrian)."[92] Mary Butts's own attempt produced the reaction "Not bad!", when it resulted in "2 passages [from] volume of Shelley picked at hazard because I felt my elbow impelled."

According to her diary, by the 17 July she had travelled with Camilla to Pramousquier, a tiny resort on the South coast of France, near le Lavandou. There they stayed for about two weeks at the house of American millionairess and art collector, Peggy Guggenheim, and her husband, Laurence Vail. In her autobiography, *Out of this Century* (1979), Guggenheim described Pramousquier, which her mother "always mispronounced as Promiscuous [as]...not a village or a town. It merely possessed a railway station and a few houses. A little train passed eight times a day, four going from St Raphael to Toulon and four from Toulon to St Raphael."[93] Mary Butts was just one of the many guests (including the writers, Mina Loy and Robert Coates) invited to Pramousquier during the 1920s.

The house was in an idyllic setting, with the beach just below. During the summer months "about two o'clock we ate lunch on...a terrace, which was...sheltered by trees and built on an overhanging cliff that was swept by pleasant breezes."[94] As in Villefranche, Mary Butts revelled in the proximity of the waves: "The sea at Pramousquier: in bed at night the water on the open rocks below makes several sounds, glass music, knocking very imperative and broken, a sound like talking, a drone that rises to a roar, almost a train noise, of, I think, pebbles drawn under and back."

It was both a productive and a troubling visit: whilst there she wrote 'The House-Party',[95] one of her most powerful stories, set in Villefranche and dedicated to Cocteau. She also read a number of books, of which she made a list under the heading *Mind Improvement at Pramousquier*. These included Wyndham Lewis's *The Lion and the Fox* (1927), Yeats's Introduction to Blake (1905), "Wells' little book on Russia" (*Russia in the Shadows* (1920)), Trollope's *Framley Parsonage* (1861) and E.M. Forster's *A Passage to India* (1924). Also on the list were a number of French books and some detective or "'tec" fiction, not least the manuscript of Laurence Vail's *Murder! Murder!* (1931).

In the draft of a letter to Virgil Thomson dated 23 July, she referred to her sadness at some recent altercation between them and also explained why her visit to Pramousquier had suddenly become nightmarish. The fact that she prefaced the letter with the heading: "Virgil now promoted to *the family horror*" (the title she gave to letters to her mother), shows that their relationship had become strained:

> Dear Virgil
>
> I wrote to 44 Rue Jacob with the Pramousquier address. It is blazing hot here, blue and classic, with the sea just under the terrace—Rather tragic suddenly, a cable for Mrs Vail [Peggy] that her favourite sister had died in child-bed, both.
>
> Cuddy is gloriously well, and I désintoxiquée, fit, working, quite detached. There is good news of Sergei. My own affairs none too prosperous.
>
> ...Must go and dress—and hear Cuddy her prayers.
>
> Very tired in spirit and unrefreshed but I think I've managed a letter almost as 'sec' as yours, ~~which is a bit of a triumph some sort of success.~~ And I suppose what I mean is that I'm still sorry it should be like that. M.[96]

By her own account, Peggy Guggenheim was "slightly off [her] head" as a result of her sister's death and whilst sympathetic, Mary Butts did nothing to help by choosing this period to ask for financial support.[97] She did realise the insensitivity of her timing, yet described herself at this time as "stunned...in a morbid state...a little mad". While conceding that "it is hard luck on Peggy to have had such a proposition made to her at a time when she is suffering herself", she felt "contempt and strain" at "the future with all its complexity and promise to be faced without a cent, or clothes or the dentist I need, or Cuddy and some debts" in the absence of Peggy Guggenheim's "cheque of deliverance". Very like Joyce, Mary Butts always felt convinced that life somehow owed it to her to give her money. Nowhere is this more visible than in 'Waiting', written in early 1928. This unpublished poem is amusing, although the reality was not, either for her or her family and friends:

Days when the head
Is a pot of beads without thread
If the money comes—
Will the money come?
Is it still debated?
Refused?
A letter to say no?
A cheque to say yes?
Is it in a mail-bag?
On a ship?
Thrusting through a gray Atlantic?
In France?
In the concierge's lodge?
Roaring down here?
Lying still in Antibes post-office?
Lost?
If the money doesn't come, God help us!

When the money comes
Sergey will play on the movies and my pen
Cover book in book out leaves of
white sheets, ruled-blue and margined red.
The pools of the word will be pricked by
a double, sharp splash.
The Sun of Solvency will rise
on an earth
to be weighed, to be divided, to be *chosen*.

Chosen a ring
a silver dress and pointed shoes
greek revived in a brain, words made
into more words
duly arranged in tunes
And from tunes airs, more music to become action
    for people.

(A child's life will shoot-up.)
Sergey will be on a horse
I in a car
There will the child in hydroplane,
speed-roar shooting the mild stir of the Mediterranean.

To Ajaccio
Where Napoleon jumped off
There will be peace, stillness, toys,
If the money comes

Let the money come
(less than they would pay for a horse or
a room decorated in american-renaissance—
their state rooms here and back)
It will change
petals of a flower to fruit shapen from Russia
from the 'wrath-bearing Tree'
A fruit-grain will fall into warm earth.
A child will not need to know
What I know
(No pleasant knowing to live with for one must live.)

It will unite
Fair objects to fair bodies to produce fair actions
fair thoughts.
It will be changed into Life.

By the time Peggy Guggenheim came to write her autobiography over fifty years later, her memory of Mary Butts was of a self-obsessed and selfish person:

> In the summer of '27 Mary Butts came to stay with us and brought her daughter Camilla, a charming child but neglected by her mother, who was always up in the clouds. One day she got sunstroke and was very ill. Doris and I had to look after her. Mary took a whole tube of aspirin in one day when her opium gave out. She believed in black magic and was perpetually trying to initiate Laurence into her mysteries. He loved the atmosphere she produced and she was extremely clever at flattering him.[98]

* * * * *

> *Une Ronde, la Ronde de Reubens. Love. Friendship, a little work, some cash (much less opium* needed.*)*
>
> —MB, undated diary entry, September 1927

ON HER RETURN to Paris in early September, Mary Butts gave the following resumé of the rest of the summer in her diary, opening with the declaration: "This is the happiest period I have spent in years, since the first time with Cecil." From then on her 'memory' of her relationship with Cecil Maitland would be used as the yardstick against which to measure others. "It began after Pramousquier where I was wretched (money and bad auras chiefly) at Antibes, Juan les Pins...with my friends [Mary Reynolds, Bob Chandler, Eugene MacGown and Walter Shaw], when I was penniless and didn't care." Before returning to Paris, she visited Brest, Tréboul and Douarnenez on the west coast of France.[99] She wrote to Goldring from the Hôtel du Coteau in Tréboul: "Cuddy recovered from her illness and safe at Cannes. We've just passed a month together in the Midi. Divorce absolute from J.R. Alimony not yet settled. Finance awful, but prospects bright."[100] The resumé in her diary concluded: "Carried forward here [Paris] to the lovely night with Virgil when 'our union was blessed'." Although she was still "suffering" because of Sergei, she believed that "illumination went with that" and felt surrounded by friends. Not only were Virgil Thomson and Phil Lasell there for her to play with; Jean Cocteau, Douglas and Malin Goldring, Val Goldsmith and Pierre de Massot were also in the capital. Of the latter, Mary Butts noted in late December:

> I think that lately we may have all been 'envoutéd' [bewitched] a little by Pierre de Massot's true but elaborately cultivated griefs. Sketch of a boy; mature young frenchman, small as a boy, black hair, ivory skin burning, short-sighted eyes. Desolate, ragged, abrupt. Thinned with years of unrest, bad food, suffering, cabotinage. It is all true, all his sufferings are; but by now so stylised, produced *repeated* that it acts on us like a hysterical play we are bound into our seats to watch.

This comment was just as applicable to Mary Butts herself. Although she did not say much about Val Goldsmith at this time, she was saddened and sympathetic when his wife committed suicide in early December 1927.[101] Generally, the autumn was a difficult time for Mary Butts and her friends as Malin's sister and brother-in-law in Sweden also committed suicide. "Douglas said: 'the year 1927, a wash out'. Just; but I pointed out that he'd married Malin in it."

Mary Butts spent the rest of the year in Paris from where she offered 'The House-Party' to *The Dial*. Her novel was now finished and she was already pondering the next one: "Carry on from the last, *Armed with Madness*, which might well have been called 'The Waste Land'. Eliot always anticipates my titles." In late December she expanded on this claim: "T.S. Eliot...the only writer of my quality, dislikes me and my work, I think. But what is interesting is that he is working on the Sanc-Grail, on its negative side, the Waste Land. Up to now, he has been before me with my titles, *The Sacred Wood, The Waste Land*." These ideas for a new novel were the beginning of what would be published five years later as *Death of Felicity Taverner*. When not working, she read Charles Baudelaire's *Les Paradis Artificiels* (1860) with pleasure and in September bought Cocteau a picture of a Kingfisher, which she felt was a "magic" act, since, "we are looking for the Sanc Grail." Two months later he gave her a drawing "which began as a portrait of [Edward] Titus, and ended as 'the truth about chess'. Darling," she commented (see above p.174). She also delighted in the "flowers Virgil sent in the red and gold jar, dahlias pale violet and rose against the yellow wall, on the corner, a door for imagination to come through." In a moment of happiness at their intimacy she commented on "my hunch that I saw GS as evil because she made me clairvoyant to an evil thing, so, suspecting her as wishing to take VT away from me, I identified her with 'It'. She may well, I see now, be good." This feeling of good-will towards Gertrude Stein did not last, however. At the end of the month Mary Butts reported a "bitter-sad" day with Sergei and another argument with Virgil Thomson: "Last time he was with [Gertrude Stein] the same series, only worse. Throat bad also. Has it any connection?" Certainly, by the end of October she believed that "Virgil is with GS and all against me" and her relationship with Thomson continued to deteriorate, partly because he refused to give her any more money.[102]

All through this period Mary Butts was smoking opium. In September she had blithely described it as "the rather easy opium fight, as if we were laughing at one another, pushing an adored friend reluctantly and temporarily out of the house." In the latter months of 1927, however, she was often unwell. "Remember this day: opium down to 7 pipes,"[103] she declared in mid-October, with an air of triumph which can only sound hollow to non-opium addicts. More and more withdrawn, she felt threatened when Aleister Crowley appeared in Paris and several diary entries refer to messages from both Cecil Maitland and her father. In the midst of this, on the 11 October, she completed the moving short tale, 'After the Funeral', inspired by an anecdote Mary Reynolds had told her during the summer. Mary Butts dedicated the story to her friend and it was first published in *The London Mercury* in December 1932.

In late October she saw Fritz Lang's new film *Metropolis*, which she described as the "best camera picture I have ever seen". The 1 November brought the return of her friend, Roy Martin, whose beauty in Villefranche two years earlier had inspired her poem, 'Picus Martius'.[104] "A moment in the taxi when the sweetness came back too, the magic," she enthused, until they arrived at the Boeuf where:

> Mary [Reynolds was] drunk, jealous, intolerable. Whispered conversations and 'histoires' and too much drink. And the sight of Roy utterly no good now, a lean white death's head, who was nice and strong, attractive man, full of mana and bird fun. So much for another so called 'Achilles set'. I sometimes think I have no one, but the two dead, no one on this earth, but Daddy and Sandy [Cecil Maitland]. 'Free among the dead' and that only there love is.

Her depression was increased a few days later when she received a letter from Marianne Moore rejecting 'The House-Party, not on the grounds of its style, which Moore described as "felicitous", but because its content was "out of harmony with *The Dial*".[105] This may well have been a coded way of saying that the explicit portrayal of homosexual relationships in the story was too risky for the time given the legal battles faced by D.H. Lawrence and James Joyce.

The publishing history of 'The House-Party' sheds light on how some of the confusing 'facts'about Mary Butts may have come about. It would be included in her second collection of stories, *Several Occasions* (1932), but before this it was published in *Pagany* in January 1930. This occurred because it was one of the stories and poems which Virgil Thomson took back to America when he returned there at the end of 1927. *Pagany* lasted from 1929 to 1932 and published work by H.D., Robert McAlmon and William Carlos Williams, amongst others. What is significant about Mary Butts's inclusion is not the fact that its editor, Richard Johns, recognised her work as having "international importance," adding "Mary Butts' two novels, one the exquisite *Armed with Madness*, ha[d] introduced her to a select audience in this country."[106] Rather, it was the claim by *Pagany*, underlined by its subtitle—'A Native Quarterly'—only to publish work by Americans.

In his 1969 study of this little magazine, *A Return to Pagany*, Stephen Halpert commented on how the publication of work by writers such as Jean Cocteau revealed that non-Americans were included. Yet he continued: "One dictionary definition of native, 'belonging to, or natural to, by reason of the circumstances of one's birth,' would certainly have included such writers as Ezra Pound, Gertrude Stein [and] Mary Butts...who despite their present expatriate status were born and bred in [America]."[107] This statement is all the more ironic for anyone who knows Mary Butts's work, since her attitude to America as a nation (although she had a large number of American friends) was unequivocally derisory. As the young American writer, Harcourt Wesson Bull, remembered:

> There was one bad evening with the brother[108] of Edgell Rickword, a contemporary of Mary's, in his cups, accusing me, an American, of being responsible for so many of their generation being killed in the War. "It's your fault for not coming in sooner!" he savagely reiterated over and over. Mary, for once, didn't come to my aid. "I'm afraid he's right, Harcourt," was all she said. She was momentarily carried away by her own memories, although she did retain some of the anti-American sentiments fashionable in her youth and after. "Keep the American from our shore," is a line in one of her poems.[109] She had interjected, however, when she read it to me: "No offense meant", and I cannot believe that this feeling was deepseated.[110]

In fact, Wesson Bull is being rather generous here. Humphrey Carpenter's comment in his 1987 study, *Geniuses Together: American Writers in Paris in the 1920s*, conveys her attitude in a way which also reflects the widespread ignorance not only of Mary Butts's work, but also of her existence on the scene. We are told: "Someone called Mary Butts" points out to the writers Robert McAlmon and Scott Fitzgerald their necessary *qua* American lack of understanding of European culture by saying: "But you don't know the depths of Europe. What will become of us all?"[111] In a review of R.B. Mowat's *Americans in England* in February 1936, Mary Butts expressed her views on the subject unambiguously:

> This very charming book traces the adventures over more than a century of distinguished visitors to Europe, and to England especially. From Franklin to Gouverneur Morris, Talleyrand's friend, to the later diplomats and to Woodrow Wilson. A story of the pleasantest and most generous interchange, the fairest spirit of give and take. If all the Americans one has had the privilege of introducing to various aspects of England and country life had been made of the same stuff as these open-minded and enthusiastic travellers, all ready to meet one half-way....
>
> Here the chief criticism rises. With few exceptions all these men were New Englanders of standing or from equally traditional parts of the South. That is to say, they were one and all English by descent and more than conscious by the continuity of their culture.
>
> Already it is no longer like that. Americans are arriving here without root or memories of any kind in this land. Other forces are at work—in letters alone you can see the change, the breakaway from the New England tradition. Already one has read a few of the young writers who have never heard of Wordsworth. (What are Mr. Hemingway's views on "natural piety"?) When the descendants of all those races who in the last century have poured over into the States arrive and begin to express themselves, what will they have to say about us?[112]

What she saw as a fact, she reflected in her fiction. The narrator of the story 'Mappa Mundi' declares that "American boys...their imaginations having less historic exercise than ones over here [in Europe],...are inclined to be superficial—that is, romantic."[113] This is certainly true of Dudley Carston, the American in *Armed with Madness*, who repeatedly finds himself out of his depth in the very old Dorset landscape, when his hosts, the Taverners, think they have found the Holy Grail. "Once he had lived in America," muses Carston, "but that did not count any more. That theatre was as another earth, and the plays were not the prologue to this play. For this play there had been no rehearsal and he did not know his part." The result is that he is constantly having to "translate" what is said around him, while his major preoccupation remains how to seduce his hostess, Syclla Taverner.[114] The inclusion of Mary Butts's work in

Pagany helps to explain how her work came to be taken up by the American poets, John Ashbery, Frank O'Hara and John Wieners,[115] and especially the Berkeley poet Robert Duncan, who as early as the 1940s was instrumental in introducing her work to fellow poets[116] at a time when she had been buried and forgotten in England.

However, in early November 1927 Mary Butts could not have been aware of the posthumous debt she would owe Virgil Thomson. By this time she had discovered the supernatural fiction of M.R. James and it was with excitement that she received her copy of his *More Ghost Stories of an Antiquary* (1911). She wondered why her

> idea of an Anthology of 'Magic' poetry or prose has never come to anything; meaning by that of pieces and passages when the actual *state* was evoked, as in 'Lully, Lully' or certain stanzas from 'Kilmeny' *'in yon green wood there is a wake'*, in contrast with most of the rest, the vision of Mary Queen of Scots, for example which is telling, not evoking. Eliphas Lévi or *The Faerie Queene* [Spenser], (mostly) in comparison with certain ballads, *some* of Yeats, the choruses of the Bacchae, part of 'the High History of the Holy Grail'. It seems to me, that I have not studied our literature of ghost-stories for nothing. I have always followed them, since I was a child—since 'the Haunter and the Haunted' [by Bulwer Lytton] and anything I could pick up anywhere. Till I halted several years, in the perfection of Professor James.

In fact, Mary Butts's long-term interest would lead to several publications in the 1930s, including a study of supernatural fiction in early 1933 and, the following year, one of the first critical articles to be published on M.R. James. She also received a contract from Methuen to publish a selection of writers' supernatural experiences in January 1935, but although the questionnaire was sent to E.M. Forster, Havelock Ellis and others, this intriguing idea came to nothing.

In November 1927, all this was a long way off, and on the 20th she chastised herself in one of her moments of lucidity for having "taken too much opium dregs. Not done enough work, played with ideas instead of getting down to it. Justly reproached by Mary [Reynolds]. Been sorry for myself, because of my poverty." Perhaps she was thinking of her conversation with Stella Bowen two days earlier. The latter referred to it in a letter to Ford Madox Ford:

> Today there came…Mary Butts, with her head tied up from a motor accident [unexplained], who wanted me I think to have Camilla to live with us for £3 a week! When I had conveyed to her that it would be impossible, she asked for another loan with the most distressing humility. She had paid back 600 frs of the 1000 she had before & wanted me to give her another 1000 in exchange for a cheque for 1400 payable Dec 3rd— The cheque seems all right & of course I'll see that it is

> presented on the exact day—I can perfectly easily lend 1000 frs for a fortnight but if there is any hitch with this cheque, she can never ask me again & that will be that—She does so give me the creeps & I always feel with her "there but for the grace of God" etc & I long to earn money—[117]

Whilst her financial difficulties had been settled, at least temporarily, Mary Butts reflected on the breakdown of her relationship with Virgil Thomson:

> Have not understood Virgil; perhaps have not wanted to understand him. He said, and it made me cry, that if I wasn't always thinking what he could or might do for me, we should get on better—I should get more out of him.... There must be something wrong in me. At least I haven't taken him *as he is*. Do I love him or want him, *as he is?* I wanted someone to be good to me. I should like to understand, but I'm too tired to care. (And I waste time over Sergey Sergeyitch). But I was happy, when I thought he loved me. And I worked. He seems too hard and cold a man now—I know I am somewhere to blame; at least there is a bitter spirit in me I half encourage. From tomorrow I will start again. Paint my face, be gentle and gay with my friends, discipline myself— Hope that light will come back.

Unfortunately December brought no real reconciliation in spite of a letter she sent Thomson suggesting that they try again—a letter which (despite their separation) he always kept.[118] Whilst it seems clear that she was partly to blame for the breakdown of this relationship, some of her friends saw faults in Thomson also. Mary Reynolds's words were comforting: "Forget him, Mary. He's a shrewd man. Men hate love and responsibility. Women snatch at it." And Cocteau said: "Virgil is a man who has nothing to do, those kind of people always make scenes, create difficulties...imagine traps which don't exist."[119]

Whatever the truth, she felt disconsolate during the final months of 1927, especially when in December she heard from Boni that there would be "no money in advance for the books".[120] She was still capable of some characteristically wry humour: "YESTERDAY'S GREAT THOUGHT. You can't be seduced when the bath-room is out of action." Yet in her unhappiness she turned increasingly away from her friends to books and Cecil Maitland for consolation. She was not disappointed. During the night of the 23 December she felt that "it came in like a frieze, a design...as from Cecil Maitland that my life was not a failure." On Christmas Eve she had another "gift" from him: "I was stumbling through the last chapter [of Rudolf Steiner's *Outline of Occult Science* (1914)] and came upon, among the arid, dogmatic, unpersuasive polysyllables, a paragraph about 'our' search being the search of the Sanc-grail—Eliot—I. Just at the moment that Hans came in, south german boy from Munich, the country Sandy loved; *at* the time when I was steeped, half haunted by *The Ugly Duchess*.[121] Hans came, as fair a slip out of the Waste Land as I've ever seen. Pitched himself into my bed; and I remembered Cecil saying that we think of Germans as hard Prussians or genial Barbarians, but if we want temperament we should try the light, black type with a cross of latin blood, I'd felt before that Hans was 'a present from Cecil', who has a twist towards Germany. Certainly I'd written *Armed with Madness* without reference to Steiner, and *The Ugly Duchess* heralds the south german boy. Cecil," she apostrophised, "your unworthy lover begs you to arrange her finances, and the way is open at last."

Sadly, Hans did not live up to her expectations and she turned once again to Sergey with whom on New Year's Eve 1928 she sped down by train to her magical south and her last stay in Villefranche and its environs.

CHAPTER THIRTEEN

Mary Butts and Mireille Havet 1928

Is this true, o eternal preoccupation 'that our air is disturbed, as Mallarmé said, by the trembling of the veil of the temple, or that our whole age is seeking to bring forth a sacred book?'.

—MB, undated diary entry, late February 1928

MARY BUTTS DID NOT GO directly to Villefranche. Instead she stayed for several weeks at the Hotel Antipolis opposite Vauban's fortress in Antibes,about 15 km away.[122] There she spent time with Sergey, Hans and a young rich Frenchman, Philip Lavastine, who paid for treats such as her trip in a hydroplane in Antibes harbour.[123] She also had Camilla with her who delighted her mother by calling her "ma princesse". On the 6 January Mary Butts was "exceedingly happy...[with the] snow down the mountains, foothills in a kind of cloisonné, round crystal moon, towers-tiles-roofs of the old town, stairs and sea ripple, a flounce drawn along the sands. Nature imitating Cezanne indeed!" she scoffed. "Imitating Homer and a mid XIXth Century academician."

But this delight soon turned to despair, as she was of necessity only peripherally involved in the homosexual adventures of her friends. Also, the rains came: "These notes made on a wet soft Mediterranean morning," she wrote on the 16 January, when "steady wind and rain driven from the mountains, doubling a short sea back on itself, a little irritated; the rock and olive land a cup of *wet*." Short of money, she sent letters to her mother and friends. Part of her worry centered on her daughter's education. She was impressed by a new school Bertrand Russell was setting up in England, where Camilla had been provisionally accepted. However the fees were high, John Rodker claimed to have little money and Mrs Colville-Hyde wrote back in mid-February to say that she would provide no more finance. According to McAlmon, Mary Butts's own 'poverty' was debatable:

> Miss Butts purportedly came south because her darling child, poor lamb, needed a good, sweet, pure, clean air, and sweet, fine country

> butter and a wholesome healthy life as befits an English child. Of the various people from whom Miss Butts borrowed money to this end few ever saw the child, but Miss Butts ("what will become of us all?") was seen dashing from Villefranche to Nice, Cannes, and Monte Carlo, and always in taxis. Sometimes there were mutterings because Miss Butts displayed an expensive wardrobe obtained from the best coutourière [sic] in Paris and before other ladies who had loaned her money for that poor lamb of a child.[124]

On the 15 January she finished a notebooks and began a new one: "'Anna Perenna'[125] it has been whatever that means. Emaintos, a year-in-year-out year. All that there is in durée, time dipped in eternity. Since Sandy's death years have been inlaid into me, or rather dip after dip into life where there are no years." It was no exaggeration when she announced in her diary: "Sandy, whose death has become more than life", since her memory of him, her sense of communication with him, was her anchor and when the contact was broken at this time, she felt distraught. "Forget pain in work, not work in pain," she urged herself. Whilst "hope and the evidence of things unseen...had...died, life hasn't died where the work is, that continues, almost joyfully. And I guess I'd better get on with it." She continued to work on the first draft of *Death of Felicity Taverner* and completed 25,000 words by March. She sent her amended proofs of *Imaginary Letters* to Edward Titus, the American publisher in Paris, whom she was paying to print the narrative. It was to be published in November. On Douglas Goldring's advice she accepted the offer by Edgell Rickword as editor for Wishart & Company to publish *Armed with Madness* in England. Ernest Wishart, who had funded Rickword and Garman's journal, *The Calendar*, also provided the money for the Wishart press which Garman and Rickword established in the spring of 1927. Like Contact Editions, its aim was to bring out "all the good literature that was being rejected by commercial firms".[126] Wishart became Mary Butts's main English publisher. During January and February she worked on the proofs of this novel for both Wishart and A.& C. Boni (her American publisher). She was also writing poems. 'Waiting' (quoted above) was written in Antibes as was 'On an American Wonder Child who translated Homer before she was ten years old'.[127] As well as writing Mary Butts reread one of her favourite books:

> *Themis* was one of my chief quarries...[and] a quarry still, but how fast our interpretation begins to differ from victorian rationalism, is just beginning; when it comes in full, there will be a spate. Ten, twenty, fifty years? JH's [Harrison's] *Reminiscences* chiefly interesting for its omissions. How did she get through the current opposition to women's education? What made her give up search 'for the scientific proof of immortality'? Why was it once inspiring, and now death 'una

perpetua dormienda'? One senses that there was, some time in her life, a final step she would not take...

Mary Butts's first entry in the new journal was concerned with her continuing interest in co-incidence in the synchronic Frazerian sense of the term.[128] It also provides a comment on the intrinsic hermetic nature of diaries, even to their keepers: "Last year's book began with CM's [Cecil's] death. First page said 'Tony Gandarillas script best'. Not what it said, and the *name* is forgotten, the script good as lost at the de Malleissye's. And in the paper I read that the London floods had destroyed all or lots of Conan Doyle's psychic records. I have observed this so often. It is odd."

At this time she read and reflected on a number of mystical works in order to test what she described as her "pet theory that man's 'highest' or 'most magic' qualities have remained constant through history' ie. for example that the impulse of mysticism, in high civilisations has remained constant, evoked but not dependent on religions, or, and this is more provable, that most formulae have produced the best art." To this end she reread Stanislas de Gaeta's work, which she liked, John Buchan's *The Dancing Floor* (1926) which left her unimpressed, and Aldous Huxley's *Two or Three Graces* (1925) which delighted her: "Blessed man. ...not a master of form or language—magic language—but clear, hard, witty, observant, pitiful, aseptic—like the sound of wood of a chippendale chair.... I finished it with the words ringing; 'it's the truth: it's the truth: it's the truth.'" She discovered that John Rodker was republishing *Malleus Maleficorum*, the fifteenth-century attack on witchcraft, and wondered whether she would be able to "wangle a copy" from him. She also pondered whether to see a medium: "I sometimes wonder if I shall die young because of these pre-occupations of mine." Yet characteristically, her curiosity distracted her from such morbid thoughts.[129] "Comparative study of the death-rate and qualites of such people would be interesting—probably a question of 'who the Gods love'", she concluded as she remembered how "Yeats has stuck it out."

Although she did not move to Villefranche until mid-February, Mary Butts went there in late January to spend time with Cocteau and meet his new lover, Jean Desbordes. She also wrote to H.G. Wells: "that though I have not seen him for years by his books he has been part of my life continuously, as though we often met."[130] Wells wrote back on the 26 February, inviting her to his house, Lou Pidou, at Grasse. If Mary Butts did go, she made no note of it.

Once back in Villefranche she was delighted to find herself at the Hôtel de la Colline where the previous year "in the dawn-room...I wrote *Armed with Madness.... Remember* light clusters on the battle-ships out on the silk-black Villefranche harbour," she enthused, adding, "that it was good the undressing, fresh pyjamas, here in bed within sound of the sea". She continued her conversations with Cocteau about writing. Prompted by their shared love for Villefranche, she suggested he write a novel about it. He replied that he was only capable of poetry or memoirs about the place, believing that "all achieved art...[is] a complete assimilation, reborn as something else." For herself, Mary Butts noted: "The business of art is to tell the truth...that by lighting-up our imaginations it made us aware of reality by further means than by the ordinary exercises of our senses: that it retuned those senses to a higher path... Shelley got it all in: 'Poetry redeems from decay the visitation of the divinity to man.'" Cocteau claimed that "it's worth having written at all since something in what I wrote brought me Jean Desbordes." To which she replied in her diary: "Dear Jean, wish a JD for me."[131] The absence of a lover or a companion was a matter of recurring sadness to her. Reading Yeats's autobiography, *The Trembling of the Veil* (1922), she remarked how she wished for "a 'Lady Gregory' to take care of me, a place where I could live in peace". She would never have a Lady Gregory, but when she moved to Cornwall in 1932 she did find a place where she could live in peace.

In March 1928 she reread Shakespeare's tragedies, particularly *Macbeth*, which she found awe-inspiring: "One has not noted one hundreth's part of the relations. The play is infinite." When considering the form of *Death of Felicity Taverner*, she thought it "might open with a flock of letters to stir up the english set. A post-poem has never been written."[132] Around Easter Sergei introduced her to the English painter, Francis Rose. She found him a "very remarkable young man" and enjoyed his company: "After the walk [together] in the hills to Orvula brought me back to the sense of sanctity (The fig-trees green hands with the sun through. The grey plant, the cherry flowers). True love, such wisdom, ignorance, expression, innocence 'Out of the mouth...'" Francis Rose was a "comfort after Sergey Sergeyitch", and she began to teach him literature, musing: "If I'm to be a director of souls, and the role seems to come more and more my way, I wish I knew more technical psychology." Whilst it was a role which Thomson very much resented, Francis Rose recalled in his autobiography, *Saying Life* (1961), just how much he owed to Mary Butts. In an account which also provides a vivid painterly portrait, he remembered her as:

> very pale and English in her appearance. Her fine voice was cultured and high-pitched, and was as much a part of her personality as the wheel of pale green jade that hung from one of her ears, generally tangled in her untidy red hair. Mary lived between her studies of perfect English (in general via Fowler), and the dramas of her friends.

> When she arrived at Villefranche she was accompanied by Nina Hamnett, the fashionable artist of the Bloomsbury set. Nina Hamnett was perfectly dressed by Chanel without entirely hiding her famous figure, which was already known as the 'Laughing Torso'.[133] She was ...incredibly neat.... One could not imagine her...travelling with the untidy dramatic Mary Butts,...[who] between writing, smoking opium, arranging misamours of Igor [sic] her muscular, hysterical boy-friend, managed to teach me a great deal about English poetry.... Many evenings were spent in her room reading aloud Shelley and Keats and translating some works by Cocteau. I owe a great deal to Mary Butts. She taught me to find delight in the sound of English words and to see poetic resonance in a Blake-like way.[134]

"Someday I shall make my own prosody notebook, working guide for young poets," she decided in early May. A fortnight earlier she went on a short trip to Corsica with Rose and was enraptured by the island, on which she rambled and danced. "The country is a mountain range rising out of the sea, coloured bright blue. I never saw a bluer world," she declared. "Clean, airy, untouched, blue hills out of the blue Mediterranean. All the blues. The Gods keep it so." On her return in late April, she produced a reading scheme for Francis Rose and considered writing a series of essays on the contemporary scene. (The only one extant is entitled 'Vision and Belief' and was completed on the 14 May. It has never been published.) Yet her attention was diverted shortly afterwards by the arrival of Douglas and Malin Goldring[135] as well as two new friends, Mireille Havet and Harcourt Wesson Bull. The latter recalled:

> It was at the Hôtel de la Colline during luncheon on the day of my arrival in late April or early May that I first laid eyes on Mary Butts. She was not unbeautiful with her sandy-red bobbed hair and fair skin, and certainly "interesting" in her pale green boucle dress and one extremely large, light jade pendant earring, mill wheel shaped. (Later I saw just a touch of green make-up on her eyelids.)[136] She was sitting alone and reading, but I knew she was taking one in—we had heard of each other. I had read *Ashe of Rings* in college and was pleased and impressed to be meeting her. I was twenty-three and she a decade, more or less, older.[137]

More rather than less, as Mary Butts was, in fact, in her thirty-eighth year, although by this time she herself believed her own legend. On the 28 July 1927 she had noted: "I am now 35", although she was a year and a half older. Wesson Bull became a stalwart friend and many years later wrote '"Truth is the Heart's Desire"',[138] a moving account of their friendship from 1928 up until and beyond her death in 1937. In this essay Wesson Bull provides a great deal of insight into her character, chameleon personality, what he called her "'reticence' and when [I felt] impatient, her 'secretiveness'." With hindsight he remarked that he "had no good conception of this in the Villefranche days with her when she threw herself so vigorously, boisterously like a little girl, into having fun, laughing hard. *Everything* seemed shared." What Wesson Bull realised after her death was that "again and again, Mary had her secrets from us all, and to seek to lay bare her whole personality is to find she has a way of escaping us a little. One can never know all about her because she never told all, guarding herself well."[139] Yet already, in Villefranche in the spring of 1928 he was aware that "there were times when friends of a different set descended on her, and she simply disappeared for two or three days." One of these friends was the French writer, Mireille Havet, whom Wesson Bull described as an "agitated, vivid young woman".[140] For the next two years, Mary Butts had an extremely intense friendship with Mireille Havet, who recorded it in her own journal.[141] Before passing on to this relationship, however, it is helpful to have a sense of Mary Butts's state of mind at the time of their meeting.

She had just finished correcting the proofs of *Armed with Madness* and had turned to her longstanding preoccupation which in 1921 had made her spend time at Crowley's Abbey at Cefalu: her desire to try and link up the third to the fourth dimension. By the time she got to know Mireille Havet in Villefranche, she had become absorbed in the work of J.W. Dunne, whose work on serialism, *An Experiment with Time,* had come out in 1927. She was also focusing her energy and attention on what she considered to be the supernatural potential of her relationship with Sergei. By May 1928 she was frustrated: "Shall I try an explanation which I believe is more than pseudo-scientific: on the physical link between the seen world and the unseen, the 3rd and the 4th? How we are, once hunger and fatigue and physical sex are satisfied, refreshed, made over, made new by harmonies that strike the senses and the imagination direct. Music or the sight of somebody loved. That there is another way, between say Beethoven and a good meal, the contact of bodies—sex apart—between 2 people who love each other; interchange of some fluid, which is a medium between the 4th and the 3rd. (Rules of the game and we didn't make them.)" Her sadness over her relationship with Sergei was due to the fact that he was a homosexual. As a result there was a barrier between them "because I am not allowed to do what I was sent to do... If we can't develop—in the 4th—our relation further, we had better separate. We mustn't bruise ourselves against a rock which we are intended—*rule of the 4th* to pass through."

* * * * *

Mary Butts and Mireille Havet meet

IT WAS IN THIS troubled state of mind that Mary Butts first met Mireille Havet in Villefranche in April 1928[142]—a meeting which initially did not seem propitious: "Why does that woman make my hackles rise?" commented Mary Butts in her diary. "Like a well-bred fox terrier and I'd do a lot to avoid her; but went. Curious series. Here last year, warned against her... Now Robbie [Mireille Havet's lover] gone for good; victory of Scots temperament, I suppose. Curious affair. No, it's Mireille who is curious and I repeat I don't like her." However a few days later she changed her mind and commented on the characteristics of Mireille Havet which attracted her: "Best 'goose' I've stuck in years. Polished steel wits. I am going to like her. I like those people with bright open passions. (They suffer for them too). Within limits there are very few things she would not understand. Yes, good luck to her—distinctly—yes. Visit had a touch of 'signature' about it."

The fact that Mireille Havet's full name was Mireille Havet de Soyecourt and that, like Mary Butts herself,[143] she had a family crest, would have appealed to the latter's snobbism. Born in October 1898, Mireille Havet was the daughter of the painter, Henri Havet. Originally from the Pas de Calais, by 1908 the family were living in a flat at 51 Rue de Raynouard, Passy, in Paris, where they hosted a number of soirées attended by French artists and writers including Philippe Berthelot, Auguste Perret, Paul Fort, Guillaume Apollinaire and Jean Cocteau. Mireille and her older sister, Christiane, were present at these gatherings.

According to the diary of Ludmila Savitsky, who acted as a kind of guardian angel, supporting her financially as well as emotionally for most of her short life, Mireille Havet received very little formal education, principally because Paul Fort convinced her parents that her poetic sensibility was such that it should be allowed to flower naturally. As a consequence she left school in her early teens and immersed herself in the literary and artistic circles of Paris of the 1910s. Her father died in 1913 and her mother in 1923, after which Havet continued to live in the flat in Passy, where her life revolved around passionate sexual affairs, drugs and writing. When she was about sixteen there was talk of her marrying the poet Alexis Léger [Saint-John Perse], but she already showed more interest in lesbian relationships. In 1928 when Mary Butts met the 29-year-old Mireille Havet, this gifted and precocious writer had already published some poetry in Apollinaire's journal, *Les Soirées de Paris*, a collection of prose poems entitled *La Maison dans L'oeil du Chat*, which first came out when she was only 16 and was later republished with an introduction by Colette, and a novella entitled *Carnaval* (1922). In so far as she is remembered at all today it is as a protegée of Apollinaire and friend of Cocteau. According to Savitsky, Cocteau's influence on the young Mireille Havet went beyond the poetic sphere, as she cut her hair very short and had clothes made to look like his. This account is confirmed by Eugene MacGown who remembered Mireille Havet as "as a man in travesty, who always wore tight-fitting, very tailored, masculine clothes and men's hats. She was, nevertheless, 'pretty as she could be,' and 'bright as a cricket,' with a husky voice."[144]

Cocteau chose Mireille Havet to play the part of La Mort in the original stage debut of *Orphée* which opened at the Théatre des Arts in Paris on 15 June 1926, and which, as noted earlier, Mary Butts attended. This role was ideally suited to (whilst perhaps reinforcing) Mireille Havet's tendency to morbidity, a mood dominating her diary entries which evoke a sad pattern of failed lesbian affairs and the consequences of her drug addiction to opium and then heroin. Characteristic of her gothic imagination was the diary entry for the 16 September 1929 where she recounted a dream sequence in which she was with her lover, Norma: "I beat Norma with a candle which broke in two—then we dined together in the cemetery at Passy among tombstones veiled in wild grass and weeds."[145]

Mireille Havet's interest in obsessive unrequited love affairs was explored in *Carnaval*. This 93-page novella, published when she was only 23, deals with the tortuous relationship between a twenty-year old man called Daniel and the older and more cynical married woman, Germaine. "I would never have thought that someone like you could exist," declares the naive Daniel when they first meet. Yet she replies to his exalted passion with a worldweary admonition: "You're lying… You are so young that you believe in the supremacy of youth over those who have already suffered from love, but what you say does not affect me. I have heard and said the same things myself too often in the empty chance enounters which only lead to more egoism and silence. I am not asking you to love me, I know more about love than you do, it's a terrible poison which you should drive away, a drug more powerful than any other. Do not speak of it so lightly…"[146] Inevitably Daniel does not listen, cannot understand what she is saying until it is too late and he has suffered as Germaine has done, so that by the time she realises the genuine nature of his affection, it has passed. At the end of the novella Daniel learns that Germaine has died alone, unloved. Mireille Havet's own obsessiveness is reflected in Daniel's. As she admitted in a letter to Mary Butts early in their relationship, it was a trait which she felt had driven away all her previous lovers: "I am a heavy burden [because]…I do not accept—nor can I bear *when I am present*...being forgotten. I want to be everything or nothing."[147] In March 1932, four years later, Mireille Havet died, officially of tuberculosis but actually from her long-term drug addiction, at the Sanatorium in Montana, Switzerland. She was only thirty-three.

My precis of Mireille Havet's life is sketchy because not enough is recorded about this powerful writer, whose work is all out of print. Whilst she clearly deserves her own biography, her involvement here will be weighted towards her relationship with Mary Butts, and particularly what their friendship reveals about the latter's position and sense of herself between 1928 and 1930.

Since both women knew Cocteau, it is fitting that their first proper meeting should have been in Villefranche, a place where they felt at home. On the 13 June at 3 o'clock in the afternoon (she was much more precise in her journal entries than Mary Butts) Mireille Havet wrote: "It's really the calm here, this setting, this room, this view of the sea and my dear Cap Ferrat unbroken by suburban rooftops—which I need... V holds particular memories for me...I have loved and known it for 8 years—and sadly I spend less and less time here—but despite all this...it is in this old town that I have left something of myself, something which I know now is essential, different and unlike any other aspect..."[148]

During May the two women saw each other a great deal and Mary Butts wrote in her diary that there was "a whisper of luck turning". The month culminated in over a week of days and nights spent together:

> 29.5.28: Yesterday. Odyssey with Mireille: in the fiacre: to the wine shops in the cellar: in the street... Dinner after: grey sea and moon clearing. Its edges becoming distinct. A triangle of cloud passed through, cut across.... She is another study in 'the decline and fall of an old family': last of the Soyecourts-Race. Not erudite at all, and her catholicism a passion. More to be expected of her within the classic french limits. More to be expected of her? She wants more. We drink something of each other. In no way, so far as I can judge, vulgar or common, and too hurt by the world to have been completely depraved by it.... It seems that we are waking up love again: spray in our faces and over us from that fountain at least. S[ergei] not pleased. Nor M's friend, [Germaine].
>
> 31.5/1.6.28 Les jours foux [wild days]: First at Mireille's—a lovely night—the balcony windows open over Nice and the sea, the authentic night blue panel—It is as if the life and sap of France enters me with Mireille in my arms... She was very beautiful in the night, without make-up—pale olive, black eyed, dark-red mouth, all smooth.

Mireille Havet was equally drawn to Mary Butts: "And there has been M[ary]—o nothing troubling—much less than with Germaine certainly—but an extraordinary honest gentleness and a sincerity neither repressed nor feigned of 2 nights spent side by side—in the warmth and friendship of a loved one...in the silence of a small room lit only by the moonlight which watches us through the half-closed shutters—the gentleness—her two arms chastely and so tenderly clasped around me and under my cheek...sending us both to sleep... I had never imagined M. could be so sensitive and tender... I had never imagined I would spend 2 of the sweetest nights of my life [in her company]."[149] A few weeks later Mary Butts wrote in a letter to her French friend: "One day I will find a way to thank you for some of the best hours of my life."[150]

Despite the lyrical sensuality of these descriptions, the mutual attraction between the two women was not primarily physical. Mireille Havet confided to her diary on the 30 May: "My love for M is not sexual, there is no question of that, not for a second neither on her part nor on mine."[151] Although the following days did lead to some passionate exchanges, what underlay their relationship was the magical quality their physical proximity unleashed for both of them. The novelty of this relationship for Mireille Havet, used to a more straightforwardly sexual passion, was conveyed in a letter written on the 4 June in which she referred to the unaccustomed inarticulacy their love created in her:

> I dream of communicating with you other than through my body... which is my only means because I cannot talk to you about it, and feel that I must not force myself and thus shatter this extraordinary silence too early—in which the miraculous peacefulness which is entirely new to me is born in your arms...[a peacefulness] which surrounds us in the night like a magic cage, a circle drawn around our happiness... My good one—Mary—it's Heaven itself which made our paths cross—and I believe that it is God himself—and this is in no way blasphemous—who drew me to your arms.[152]

Mireille Havet believed that they were setting out on a "mysterious" and "destined" journey.

A journal entry Mary Butts made in the spring of 1927 illustrates how much Mireille Havet's interpretation of their relationship would have appealed to her: "What do I love, outside writing and clothes and opium and the weather and my friends?" she asked herself and replied: "I have always had since I can remember an incomparable pleasure in finding someone psychically sick, and hearing about it and seeing if there is a way out. This feeling very much mixed up with sex, bed not necessary, but makes things work better, ie, any powers I have seem to work better in that relation. I've always wanted to make my lovers well, sense powers liberated in them, fears in the dustbin, raw life taken in and coming out translated." As she went on to admit, there was "plenty of egoism in this".

This entry and the fact that she was able to declare when her relationship started with Mireille Havet: "so that's begun"—show how much Mary Butts was the stronger, more dominant (because more detached) partner in this friendship. Her diary entries illustrate clearly how aware she was of the benefits of Mireille Havet's company, especially in the face of her ongoing sense of failure with Sergei: "Night with a live flower branch in my arms. A snuggly beast too. Exquisite sleep. Life being distilled into me. M is a good talker and a good listener. A lesson in several ways for me" (late May). "Greatly strengthened last night in M's arms, in the white dark before dawn, 'rappel a courage', tranquillity, measured energy, spring" (3 June). "Mireille 'ronde'. I know what I am for her, her first contact with 'l'etranger'. She needs to get out of her tight french classic formula, Robbie served that turn first, and I next. She is not the first french *man* but the first *woman* I have known well, and her 'shape' has value for me. It is being a good exchange. And I adore her letter;...she is happy with me, and life is looking up again... Bless her!" (5 June). A few days later she added: "Mireille 'ronde': it appears to me often that France, especially Paris, makes some sort of holocaust-sacrifice of its loveliest and most gifted girls to an almost infernal Aphrodite. They are trained for nothing outside sex, the home and a little art. M's life for a woman of her gifts a waste, a sacrifice to a dressed-ape painted animal eroticism, called l'Amour."

Mary Butts's greater self-confidence and self-reliance came in part from the fact that at 37 she was over eight years older than Mireille Havet when they met. It was also the case that whilst both had suffered from failed love affairs, Mary Butts was able to distil her experiences into fiction whilst Mireille Havet was increasingly overwhelmed by them. Even at the outset of their relationship Mireille Havet's dependence on drugs (opium and then heroin) was much more debilitating for her than for Mary Butts. According to Eugene MacGown: "Mireille...played a pivotal function in Mary's later drug addiction by introducing her to French sources of supply that would not otherwise have been available to her."[153] Both women underwent detoxification cures during the two years of their friendship. But whilst Mary Butts never stopped reading, writing and publishing, Mireille Havet was increasingly destroyed by her addiction. In the four years between the beginning of their friendship in 1928 and her death in 1932, Mireille Havet published nothing, although in a letter of the 9 April 1931, she described her grandiose plan to collect and publish all her poems in a volume to be called *L'Amour de L'Amour* as well as three volumes of essays and memoirs.[154]

Notwithstanding MacGown's rather cynical interpretation of their friendship, in early June 1928 Mary Butts was sincere: "I think things will go well; because my feeling for her is based absolutely on affection, tenderness and interest in what she is and represents, can do and be. I am beginning to understand Catholicism, her kind and Jean [Cocteau]'s." However, by the time Mary Butts left Villefranche for Paris on the 20 June, Mireille Havet's drug addiction had greatly increased. Although she had dictated her last will and testament to Mary Butts on the 13 June, the positive intensity of her feeling for her English friend had turned to a sense of paranoid disillusionment. Clearly there had been some kind of misunderstanding between them, although it is difficult to tell how much was due to drug-induced perceptions.

In the overnight train from Nice to Paris Mary Butts noted: "*Train notes*: Clairvoyant days: approach to sudden active period I think.... For the artist—any sort—whether he knows it or not—experience [is] a *sensation*. His art is the repossession of it, its frame, cadre, extension, translation.... Can finish the 'small town'[155] now." At the very moment that she was omitting any mention of Mireille Havet in her diary, the latter, by contrast, was confiding to her journal:"I refuse to believe for one moment the hateful and absurd possibility that M might have left without seeing me again—without saying goodbye... She is not mad—does not love me with the kind of passion which made Robbie fear me...I refuse to believe it...and yet I tremble with worry...am overwhelmed by the terror—that this is a real fear. Ah if Mary whom I believed to be a real friend...has dared to do this—then down with England..." The entry concluded, rather melodramatically: "If it's true, Mary, that you have left me without saying goodbye—if that's true—you will never see me again..."[156]

In fact, this was by no means the end of their relationship; over the next two months they wrote to each other regularly. Mary Butts's tone was almost always gently admonishing: "Mireille, if you agree to be patient with me, our friendship will be a very beautiful one. Things will work out magically for us (I know more about this magic arrangement of things than you do.)"[157] She was unstinting in helping to sort out Mireille Havet's affairs: undertaking to find out where Robbie had gone to, sending money as well as arranging for Cocteau and other friends to pay her debts and subletting the flat in Passy to Clinton King, an American recently married to their friend, Duff Twysden. Repeatedly, she encouraged Mireille Havet to leave Nice to return to the capital in order to write near her: "Come back to Paris. Start your work again. (Everything that I'm writing seems so hard.) But you are so gifted, so proud, so beautiful, so adorable, so well-born, that you should be hard on yourself."[158] In spite of occasional bouts of self-pity, Mary Butts did follow her own ad-

The infant Mary Butts with her mother, Mary Butts (later Mary Colville-Hyde), 1891.

The Salterns, Parkstone, south Dorset, where Mary Butts was born in 1890.

An outing aboard the Captain's yacht, The Vanity, circa 1898. Front row, left to right: Captain Frederick Butts, Mary Butts, Mary Butts (Mary Colville-Hyde). Standing behind the captain is Mary Butts' aunt, Ada Briggs.

LEFT: *Mary Butts, circa 1894.*

BELOW LEFT: *Mary Butts, circa 1902, in 18th-century clothing.*

BELOW RIGHT: *Formal studio photograph of Mary Butts in the 1910s.*

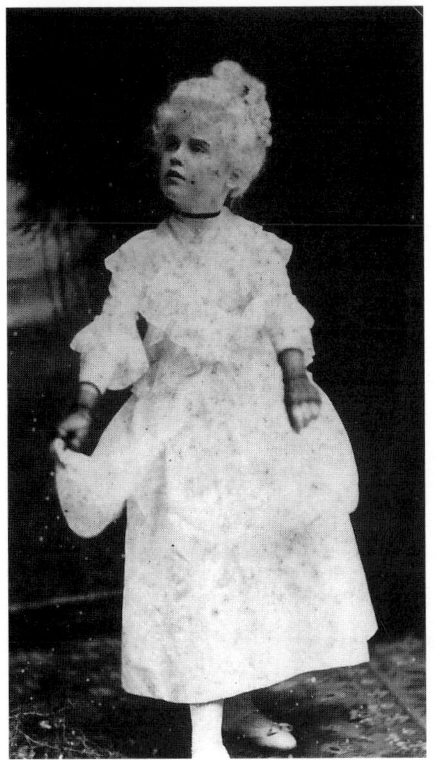

Mary Butts' first husband, the writer and publisher John Rodker (1894-1955)

Mary Butts, age 29 in 1919.

Mary Butts' brother, Anthony Butts, 1919.

Fatalité. *Mary Butts's mother, Mary Colville-Hyde, early 1920s at Saltern*s.
[Note: captions in roman type are Mary Butts's.]

left: *27 Ferncroft Avenue, Hampstead, London, where Mary Butts began her diary on 16 July 1916.* right: *43 Belsize Park Gardens, London, her home from 1919-1924.*

Corfe Castle on Purbeck, south Dorset.

'Death of Felicity Taverner'. *Mary Butts standing on Dancing Ledge, Dorset, 1922. Notice that she is already using a walking stick.*

ABOVE LEFT: *Sketch of Mary Butts, 1920s, artist unknown.*

ABOVE RIGHT: Carte d'identité. *Passport photograph, early 1920s.*

LEFT: *With Cecil Maitland on the continent, possibly in Italy in 1921. Mary Butts dedicated* Ashe of Rings *to him.*

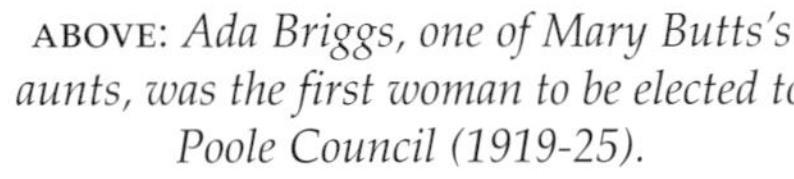

ABOVE: *Ada Briggs, one of Mary Butts's aunts, was the first woman to be elected to Poole Council (1919-25).*

ABOVE RIGHT: "Vous avez l'air plus jeune que la fillette, Marie" J.C. *[Cocteau}. Mary Butts and her daughter Camilla at Cannes on the French Riviera, 1927. Virgil Thomson may well have taken this photograph.*

BELOW RIGHT: *The English writer Douglas Goldring and Mary Butts on the continent, 1920s. Mary Butts dedicated* Several Occasions *to him.*

Rue de Monttessuy, Paris, as it appears today. No. 14 is at the right far end.

The Welcome Hotel, Villefranche, on the French Riviera, 1920s.

'La mort de l'ange Heurtebise'. *French author and artist Jean Cocteau, circa 1926-27.*

LEFT: *Pegeen Guggenheim, Camilla and Mary Butts at the summer home of American heiress Peggy Guggenheim and her husband Lawrence Vail, at Pramousquier on the French Riviera, July 1927.*

ABOVE LEFT: *The Russian émigré, Sergei Maslenikof, 1920s. Maslenikof was the inspiration behind Boris in the novella* Imaginary Letters *and Boris Polteratsky in the novels* Armed with Madness *and* Death of Felicity Taverner.

ABOVE RIGHT: *[To]* Harcourt Wesson Bull, from Mary, Villefrance Spring 1928. Soyez sage et simple. *[Butts family motto]*

Mary Butts, right, possibly with the French writer Mireille Havet, French Riviera, 1928.

'Ole man river" Villefranche 1927. *With American actor and singer, Paul Robeson, and unidentified friend. Actually the photograph was taken in 1925.*

The English writer and editor, Hugh Ross Williamson, 1941. Mary Butts dedicated Death of Felicity Taverner *to him.*

Mary Butts had Jean Cocteau's elegant 1926-27 line drawing made into a Christmas card in 1931.

vice to work whatever the circumstances right up to her sudden death in March 1937.

Whilst Mireille Havet's letters tended to be self-centred and aggressive, Mary Butts's reveal an unflagging generosity and patience:

> My dear Mireille,
>
> Listen darling and remember that it is difficult for me to reply in French.
>
> First, a lot of what you have written is *illegible.* But you are so dear to me that I understand your words by some kind of divine inspiration and above all I know that you are angry with me for returning to Paris.
>
> Mireille, I am a loyal friend. My days and nights are full of thoughts of you. But, small love, you knew from the outset that I would have to come back to Paris as soon as possible. It was because of you that I stayed down south so long, for the exquisite pleasure of your company.
>
> But think a moment about my situation. I am a writer...and Camilla's mother...my duty...is to be here and lead a regular life, work on a daily basis, take up contacts again with editors, publishers and people who could be useful.[159]

As with so much of her correspondence, this was part-truth, part-bravura. Yet compared with Mireille Havet who was watching herself slip further and further into her drug dependency, Mary Butts remained extremely active.

CHAPTER FOURTEEN

Back in Paris

June 1928 – June 1929

One need not read Mary Butts if one has not a feeling for feeling.

—Marianne Moore, review of *Armed with Madness*[160]

She wished the earth would not suddenly look fragile, as if it was going to start shifting... There was something wrong with all of them, or with their world. A moment missed, a moment to come. Or not coming. Or either or both. Shove it off on the war; but that did not help.

—MB, *Armed with Madness*[161]

ARMED WITH MADNESS was published in June in England and America with the dedication "To Peter and Paul".[162] The writer, Elizabeth Madox Roberts, wrote to A. & C. Boni to thank them for sending her a copy of the novel. Madox Roberts preferred *Ashe of Rings* which she felt had a little more clarity. Nonetheless she was "delight[ed]...in the work of Mary Butts...she etches events and persons with delicate hair lines, leaving to the active mind the process of filling in the color and heft. So that reading her book is a delicious exercise, as if one experienced mind as an actual mechanism, within his own person."[163] In general, the critical reception to *Armed with Madness* was divided between those who enjoyed and those who resented being made to "fill in the color and heft" when reading the novel, whose complicated plot was helpfully given in the *New York Times Book Review* :

> *Armed with Madness* is the story of five Englishmen and one girl during a week's life. Scylla and Felix are brother and sister, high-born and poverty-stricken, and Picus and Clarence are two friends and distant relatives who live in a house near by. These four, with an aloof fairly normal man named Ross, constitute a kind of highly and diabolically sophisticated group, with their own code, their own gestures, their own recondite ways of making themselves understood. A sixth person, an American named Carston, comes down to visit them, and finds himself the intended victim of a strange practical joke thought out by Picus, an unscrupulous kind of sadist with a perverted sense of humor. Picus buries a cup in a well, brings it up with a sword, supposes it to be a relic, and invokes the symbolism of the Holy Grail. The appearance of this cup proves strangely upsetting and leads to

> all sort of emotions and happenings just this side (and sometimes just the other side) of madness. A kind of diabolic malice and subtlety begins its interplay among these people, with their queer attachments, their quick jealousies and their unconventional attitudes. Before the end is reached Scylla has been tied to a statue and pierced with arrows, Clarence has tried to commit suicide, Felix has gone to Paris and brought back a hungry young Russian noble, and Carston has had his eyes opened to things undreamed of in his philosophy.[164]

Marianne Moore was impressed by the novel where "there is much to notice", praising Mary Butts's style and the fact that: "There are gruesome things here, as there were continually in the minds of the maddened conversers—'While high over them the gulls squalled like sorrow driven up.' But there are many graces. And it is a triumph for the author that it is a mistake to recount anything she writes without recounting it in her own words."[165] Several reviewers commented on the power of her writing. *The Morning Post* declared that she had "a fine sense of words"; Eugene Lohrke in the *New York Herald Tribune* stated that she was "an admirable word artist...[who wrote] beautiful and admirable prose", while even Gerald Gould conceded that she "can, when she chooses, write well...[and] render real experiences with exactitude and force."[166] The reviewer in the *New Age* parodied Mary Butts's tendency to chiasmus: "Yes, this is all right, but there is no need to be so beastly clever in making words halt and bump each other.... Most of it is written in that way—written, it is in that way, most of it. Some of the descriptions are first class, and the general sensation—atmosphere—of something fey, brooding, uncanny, is extraordinary. If only the sentences would not get themselves knotted up, cryptically."[167] Yet several reviewers commented on the poetry in *Armed with Madness*: Mary Butts's "web is spun out of words which she uses much as a poet uses them, for their texture and overtones. Woven in eccentric, fantastic patterns, they set up vibrations in the reader," declared the *Aberdeen Free Press*.[168] The long review in the *New York Times Book Review* was categoric:

> There is no question that Miss Butts is a poet, and hardly more that she is a writer of often distinguished prose. And once you enter her world, if you can accept it as a world unto itself, what goes on becomes exciting and unpredictable, Aldous Huxley and William Blake walking hand in hand, with what results one can perhaps imagine.[169]

While *The Librarian* found it "idiosyncratic", the *New York City Times* was not alone in looking to other writers for stylistic resemblance.[170] The *New York Sun* noted: "There is a great deal of identity between her people and the people that are created by Huxley, [Michael] Arlen and the Sitwells."[171] The *New York Herald Tribune* found a similarity with Rabelais, whilst in

'Join the Ladies' (where *Armed with Madness* was reviewed alongside works by Naomi Royde-Smith and Storm Jameson), Mary Shirley referred the reader to Henry James's tale, 'The Last of the Valerii', with the claim that "the book is a brilliant and subtle, if rather chaotic expression of this Age of Jazz...and might be described as Henry James in the idiom of 1928."[172]

The degree to which the novel was praised tended to depend on the relationship perceived between form and content. For one reviewer they made a strange combination: "Throughout the whole book, runs a note of cruel and decadent sophistication oddly in contrast to the freshness and brightness and the beauty of the writing, with its amazing imagery, its clean, natural sensuousness, its occasional pregnancy of significance."[173] For the *Times Literary Supplement*, the characters were "not so much armed with madness as entirely composed and compacted thereof: their language, their habits, their actions appear alike demented." For this reviewer, their "case" was "impaired by the author's method of telling their story. For by a desperate stroke of consistency she describes this carnival of lunacy in a style no less disordered—in such a series of jerks and shocks and abrupt surprises that the reader, emerging from the wild experience, can be expected to offer no lucid account of it."[174] The difficulty of the book lay not only in its style but in the symbolism; there was general agreement that it was not for the "average reader" or "simple soul", for, when Picus "fishes an antique chalice from a well[,] there is much discussion of its origin, references to the Holy Grail and the Spear, with their related symbols from the emporium of Herr Professor Freud."[175] This symbolism did not prevent the *Aberdeen Free Press* reviewer from enjoying the novel in terms of its presentation of a complex love tangle: "A strong woman [Scylla], who opens doors that every sane person knows are better shut, is surrounded by men—more or less real, but mostly neurotic. How the one seemingly real man [Carston], among them fails to achieve his desire is the root of the story. He fails because he cannot get inside the lives of this strange, psycho-agonised set, and because the most agonised of them all [Picus] is the one upon whom the woman's choice falls."[176]

Armed with Madness can very well be enjoyed at this level; a more profound interpretation, however, was given by the American reviewer, Libbian Benedict, who contrasted American and English attitudes:

> All the European influences to which American expatriates subject themselves cannot eradicate the naive, essentially hopeful outlook which their own country instilled into them....We also have our lost generation, but it is a generation which is lost somewhere on a fresh fruitful prairie. There is no need to worry about it.

> In England, however, this is not true. The lost generation there is lost for good; it is dying of autointoxication.

According to Benedict, the characters were representative of a type: "It is the madness of a group, of a handful lifted at random from a still larger group. It is the madness of decline, of unified decay. Miss Butts's people, with one exception, are all English." No surprise then, that "Carston, the American, a child of a more simple civilisation, cannot grasp the story, but the mystic quality of it taints him also. Besides, he wants the girl Scylla, who has been the mistress of Picus."[177] Several reviewers felt that the book lacked substance: that the reader was left "in the air"; that Mary Butts had constructed a spire but no foundations; that the ending was incomprehensible.[178] Gerald Gould wondered whether *Armed with Madness* was about "everything and nothing, or only nothing", resting his case with her own words: "'People who had come for a week had been known to leave next day.' When you have finished Miss Butts's book, you won't blame them."[179] Or perhaps it was a case of beauty being in the eye of the beholder, as Marianne Moore concluded: "'There was something in their lives spoiled and inconclusive like the Grail,' she says. Some would say nothing in them was like the Grail. But Miss Butts is not palming anything off on us. We may make what we may of it. It is sympathy she offers us in Carston's reply when the vicar wonders 'whether a true picture of the real is shown by our senses alone.' 'All I can say is that I've never been so bothered, never behaved so like a skunk, never so nearly fell dead in my tracks till I got down here and began to think about such things. It's unfashionable now, you know.'"[180]

In a letter to her mother, Mary Butts responded to what she saw as Mary Colville-Hyde's tendency to conflate autobiography and fiction when reading *Armed with Madness*: "I would like to point out, that along with my old ones, my new book is neither a portrait of myself, nor, except for certain minor characters, of any of my friends… Your mistake, if I may say so, is a very elementary one, and very common. The book is part of a gallery of portrait types of our age, the kind of people you meet about… None of the incidents ever happened and Scylla Taverner is no more me than she's you. I may say that I know my job too well for that." With a somewhat condescending astuteness she added: "But people think like that, judge works of the imagination whose truth lies in their picture of a state of human society, and I suppose they will till judgement day…"[181] This biographical interpretation of her work occurred rather more widely when she published her next novel, *Death of Felicity Taverner*, in 1932.

* * * * *

> Remember: *On return small things like painting the flat, putting cherries in a dish, going to buy drawing pins in the stationery shop and cheese were like poetry.* (A POEM ON THIS and *the S[ergei] loss). And that my friends here are all very unhappy. Heroin has arrived; which may be a ghastly finale to our pleasant opium days.*
>
> —MB, undated diary entry, end June 1928

MARY BUTTS WAS happy to return to her flat at 14 Rue de Monttessuy. Harcourt Wesson Bull remembered it as "small: a sitting-room, bedroom and kitchen only, and I don't remember noteworthy furnishings, but it was Mary's, and there were a few interesting objects about. I especially remember a 'snow-storm', a glass-domed paperweight ornament made...by Man Ray, its 'scene' a large painted eye in a triangle...."[182]

Quite apart from dealing with Mireille Havet's affairs (there are a few letters, but in real terms the relationship abated for a year), Mary Butts socialised with a number of French and expatriate artists. Wesson Bull's account of her during the summer of 1928 shows her in several different moods, from the homely, to the exuberant, to the darkly prophetic:

> It was interesting to see Mary in a domestic role, one had never thought of her like that. She could prepare a meal easily and simply, deft with salads. Sometimes we sat quietly talking while she sewed.
>
> Of course we went out together often, Mary in her bee earrings and a Chanel dress, the skirt all ribbon streamers... At a time when sheer pleasure-seeking was neither shaming nor dull, many bars saw us, and the night-clubs and cafes one frequented in those days: the "Boeuf," the "Grand-Ecart," the "Select," where Mary sat with a paper bag of...raw opium at her feet. (It was to be picked up by someone.) We danced "chez Bricktop". Bricktop called her "Miss Mary",...she...liked to be amused—and be amusing; sometimes we laughed over very simple things, the names she gave people. A friend of mine to whom she was not drawn, the German painter, Helmut Kolle, she called "Monsieur Faux-col";[183] another, Peter Teigen, whom she found attractive, became, of course, "Nice Mr. Peter Tiger." But we had many, many serious discussions, and I think she was observing me as well, "one of the new young batch America was sending over." In a way I can see there was something of the mentor and pupil in us. She knowingly taught; her mind was always at work.
>
> I told her of my impressions of Paris and how I sensed the change from what it must have been like in the years just following the '14-'18 War: the now well-known artists and writers of that wonderfully creative period yet unknown, it must have been vital, and certainly "magic." Mary agreed, "and we were all 'copains' then, and poor."
>
> ...There were other quiet moments together; I remember sharing one of Mary's "signatures" with her. We were sitting talking in her flat one night when suddenly we heard an unusually frightful hu-

> man cry in the street below. We look up, startled and sobered. "Terrible days are coming, my Harcourt," Mary said like a sibyl. "Can you shoot? Strengthen your hand. Strengthen your long brown hands". My hands are neither long nor brown (if presumably then tanned), and the admonition sounded too dramatic, but her prophecy, made in all seriousness, could not have come more true as history turned out. (Mary showed a perspicacity in international and political affairs I hadn't looked for. She spoke discerningly on the problem of the Polish corridor.)[184]

From this account it is clear that, just as in her relationship with Francis Rose, Mary Butts liked to be a "mentor" to Harcourt Wesson Bull or, as she described herself rather more loftily, a "director of souls". Also, as Wesson Bull related with gratitude, she quickly introduced him to her Paris circle of friends, including Robert McAlmon and the American writer, Kay Boyle.

She continued to read widely. She also corrected the final proofs of *Imaginary Letters* (which was to come out in November), worked at *Death of Felicity Taverner*, completed a number of poems, wrote some essays and reflected on how "three or four years ago I said would be a good short note as well as letter writer. That I've done. For years have wanted to improve on system of notation, to make the printed page convey more to the eye, some sort of psychological arrangement of word or type. Am *beginning* to see how to set a page, here and there in these notes. And I said I would be a writer, and I am." She also started a systematic study of ghost stories, entitled 'Use of the Supernatural in Fiction'. "It is to be noticed," she wrote in her journal, "that the best class of [ghost fiction] assumes the most...eg. 'Haunters and Haunted' [by Bulwer Lytton] and the wide mystical common-sense assumptions of May Sinclair.... Whilst Poe, eg, takes an abnormal situation—'Fall of the House of Usher'—and works up from that;...[M.R.] James takes the most normal situation, the most normal people, and lets things happen in the most prosaic way. "*But* James takes some things for granted, a blood-drenched wood, satyrs etc. Attempts no explanation. He assumes a lot."

Mary Butts completed the study in September and dedicated it to her brother. "Your study is enchanting, your prose more sensitive, incisive, more luminous than ever... Your summing up is exquisite in sensibility, sense and style and I thank you for it from the depths of my heart." Tony's letter also made clear that, as with *Ashe of Rings* and another work,[185] Virginia Woolf was not interested in publishing this study. "One can see that it isn't perhaps conventionally quite what the Hogarth habitually publish," he commiserated, "but that absolutely fails to explain their rudeness in not acknowledging it."[186] If the study was unacknowledged, then it is understandable that Mary Butts would have found the snub wounding. It was eventually published in *The Bookman* between January and April 1933 under the wonderful title of 'Ghosties and Ghoulies'.

Jean Desbordes and Cocteau asked Mary Butts to translate Desbordes's *J'adore* (1928) and she worked on it on and off throughout the autumn of 1928. Sadly, the translation has been lost. Her enthusiasm for the work was such that in a letter to Edward Titus she tried to persuade him to publish her translation: "I think it would go well. People are getting bored with the cold, hard, damp objectivity of a lot of the most modern work and the book's like a spring morning."[187] However nothing came of this suggestion and the English translation was never published.

J'adore is a curious work and rather difficult to characterise because the forty essays and prose pieces contained in its 200-odd pages blend together fiction, autobiography and reviews. It is a celebration of different kinds of adoration and passion for religion, sex, sensuality, nature and literature. Indeed Desbordes claims an equivalence between semen, words and the love of God. "Ecrire l'amour," opens the essay entitled 'Faiblesse des Forts' ('The Weakness of the Strong Ones'): "Is there any love other than one's own? There are hours of love on my paper alone. Where are you, who could love to the degree that I love with my ink?"[188] Elsewhere he declares:

> He who does not love, who doesn't adore according to his heart and his senses only needs the light bread of our House, the Church.
>
> Tranquillity in love insults God. Was God's love ruled by lack of warmth?
>
> God gives love because he is blind love.[189]

Sex, for Desbordes, is the glistening filament linking men to angels: "Sex doesn't come into the laws of love but sex is love because it is life and warmth and simplicity. It gives itself, it exalts and the state in which it puts human beings is a state of an exhausted angel, but an angel all the same." Thus "know that to love love is to love God, and enjoy his calm on his shoulder. You will grow wings and in your hands angels and men will be one."[190]

Anyone who is familiar with Cocteau's work and its almost obsessive reworkings of images of men and angels, God and gods will immediately understand why he and Desbordes should have been drawn to each other's writing. Not only did Cocteau write an intelligent eulogic introduction to *J'adore*; the work itself contains an essay entitled 'Jean Cocteau' and three discussions of two of Cocteau's plays, *Antigone* (1922) and *Orphée* (1926). One would be wrong to see this as displaced narcissism; rather, there was clearly a true empathy between these two writers, which when they first read each other's work must have felt like seeing themselves in one of Cocteau's magic cinematographic mirrors.

This marriage of true minds would have embodied what Mary Butts searched for all her life. The magical visionary affinity which she felt she shared with Cocteau on an imaginative plane simultaneously reminded her of the impossibility of any kind of equivalence on a sexual plane because of Cocteau's homosexuality. The American poet, John Ashbery, has pointed out rightly that her writing about homosexuals is sympathetic.[191] She enjoyed their company until the end of her life, feeling simultaneously drawn to yet inevitably excluded from any kind of fulfilling relationship with each one individually. She was also well aware of being an outsider:

> I note with amusement and curiosity touched with alarm, that my popularity will dwindle if I begin to criticise paederasty. Even to criticise. I see now that before I was accepted, among other things, as a useful champion, a good-looking and gifted woman who didn't care, who was sympathetic etc.
>
> Now I find that I must go canny.... I shall find most criticism will make me enemies—always with the retort ready that I make it through jealousy: thwarted desire for the young man criticised...! There might be much vileness. *And* I mean to say what I think...
>
> Thank God I was on that jury.[192] (August 1929)

The ways in which Desbordes evoked and adored the natural world and celebrated the awakenings of sexual desire (not only homosexual but also heterosexual) would have greatly appealed to similar instincts in Mary Butts. For example, in *Armed with Madness* we are told that whenever Scylla Taverner is troubled, she lies on a branch of a tree and plays "an old game, that she was lying out on the wood's roof: translating the stick and leaf that upheld her into herself: into sea: into sky. Slowly back into wood, flesh and sea."[193] Desbordes's narrator of 'L'amour au jardin solitaire' ('Love in the solitary garden') engages in a similar phenomenological metamorphosis: "Under my thighs, the earth yielded to let my body enter its body.... My body enveloped the earth and the earth filled my void."[194]

Mary Butts would have been particularly drawn to the essay 'Les plus beaux garçons de la terre' ('The Earth's most beautiful boys'). It is a eulogic essay about the untouchable beauty embodied in a particular kind of young man (such as Sergei Maslenikof, Roy Martin and Gabriel Atkin):

> They will say, "What's the matter? Are you sad? I love you, don't worry. Are you happy?" They will not show goodness but they will show love. We will not know that they are self-centred because they will appear not to be. Splendid and silent they will fill the void, swell our hearts, put life on a higher plane without knowing what they do, what they are, what they love; and then they will go and have their

> fortune told, they will say, "I will try to understand everything. I would so like to help you; with so much love I think I can give some."
> They will be the earth's most beautiful boys.[195]

These are the young men she wrote of in poems and stories as her Achilles set, the Kouropidai.[196] There is a melancholy, solitary tone in *J'adore* which occurs also in her work, where her characters feel lonely, uncertain of being heard or understood, for example the narrators of *Imaginary Letters* (1928) and the earlier 'Lettres Imaginaires' (1919) which are avowedly not-to-be-sent-letters. Similarly Desbordes's 'Lettre Anonyme' ('Anonymous Letter') concludes with the narrator asking: "Do you exist? Am I talking to anyone? Am I only crying in the desert? Is it perhaps a star which I surround with my dreams?"[197] He assumes that each person is alone because that is the quintessential fact of human existence: "How similar all things are," we are told in 'La Maison' ('The House'), where the narrator sits by his mother's bedside as she lies dying. "We speak to you, God, in just the same way that we make love or remember; we are sick as desperately and with the same loneliness. He who loves, loves alone. He who makes love, makes love alone and he who prays, prays alone."[198] Desbordes was writing against this fact of solitude, searching for a love which is not merely sexual possession, in which the lover remains alone; instead he was aiming at a state where love is absorbed rather than absorbing so that a kind of detachment remains: "Breathe in the stars which love makes you produce. Take love by its roots. Be detached from worldly things, calm enough in the heat of things, orderly enough in heaven itself, to absorb love wherever it is."[199] This amorous detachment was what Mary Butts felt for Mireille Havet and this is why their relationship gave her so much confidence, unlike her love for Sergei Maslenikof.

As for most of her adult life, much of her time on returning to Paris in June 1928 was spent writing letters to her family and her solicitors. These letters were mainly requests to 'borrow' money, which she usually felt she was owed, although often there was little basis for this belief. With regard to her family and particularly her mother, there is no doubt that she suffered from delusions. Tony once commented to her on a financial dispute she was having with Mary Colville-Hyde: "I know that you genuinely believe what you say in this matter, just as I know that you are genuinely mistaken."[200] Mary Butts's attitude was based on a belief that (like James Joyce and Ford Madox Ford) she was owed special dispensation from the rules governing ordinary people: "My untruthfulness he [Tony] and Mother hark on is often over subjects that lie deep: that I'm trying to see with all my nature: subjects where my genius if I have any is engaged. Poets and artists are always excused of that. Was Shelley lying when he let his subconscious rip?—hasn't that in him been proved part of the 'vrai vérité' ever since?" (11.8.29). Several examples have already been given to show that whenever Mary Butts had any money, she was extremely generous with it. This was much to Mary Colville-Hyde's chagrin, who when she chided her daughter, was told: "If…my money, or a little of it has gone and will go on helping people in great need, is that a crime? At most a folly; but perhaps not even as silly as it sounds. For it's part of the essential me to help people: sometimes I am helped back."[201]

* * * * *

ONE OF THE PEOPLE Mary Butts encouraged in 1928 was the English artist, Gabriel Atkin, whom she had first met in Paris and got to know better in Villefranche earlier that year before he returned to his native Newcastle. He wrote to her from there: "For the loveliest of letters, all my thanks. It made Paris sound like Heaven and brought a ray of sunshine… If I do get a book published, I've been thinking of all the people I really know whose initials are SS, so that a pleasant ambiguity should accrue. E.g.… Siegfried Sassoon, Sergey Sergevitch, Sacheverell Sitwell, Sebastian Sprott…etc, etc. It really ought to be, however: To Mary Butts."[202] During these months she not only encouraged Gabriel Atkin to work hard; she also asked for sketches to pass on to Dodie Todd, then in Paris and looking for articles. Whilst these have not survived, Gabriel Atkin's witty letters to Mary Butts contain several finely-drawn sketches.

Tony came to stay in early July and they visited some chateaux in the Loire valley. She enjoyed the visit but lamented to Mireille Havet in a letter on the 5 August: "My brother will not help me. He gave me a beautiful dress and a few days in the country, but that's all."[203] She explored this feeling of abandonment in her fiction, especially in the figure of Felicity Taverner in *Death of Felicity Taverner*[204] and in a short story of a few pages which she wrote in the autumn of 1929 called 'In the House'. It opens:

> So it is to be like that again: hunger, no, not exactly hunger, because when the brother one loves has gone away in cold anger, one is not hungry.… God knew quite why he had gone away, and with the pain of his going left a thousand little pains, fluttering like Pandora's *kêrês*[205] through the rooms which had done their best to be made lovely for him.[206]

She was hopeful about an advance for her next book of stories when she had lunch with the American publisher, Mr Boni, who had brought out the American editions of her first two novels. However, from the draft of a letter to him in late October 1928 it is clear that this came to nothing. "My race has been with time," she declared a year later, "time and material things are telling on me. I may pass out or pass away purely through that." By the end of July 1929 a combination of grandiose ambition and self-pity was present in her lament: "I am beginning to understand my piteous, passionate need of money. If I had been put down in another society, happy, on an even keel; not *war-shocked*[207] and contemptuous and glutted and famished; I should soon have found my feet.... But alone in chaos, who love cosmos, who might be able to help restore cosmos, I need some artificial security. I feared these as excuses. In honesty now I see them to be true."

Already in the summer of 1928 she was depressed. It was partly a result of desperation over Sergei who at the end of August entered a mental asylum on the edge of Paris for several weeks. She visited him there and was relieved to find him looking better:

> 4.9.28 *Sergey Sergeyitch chez les Fous*
> ...To-day we took a walk in that great park—of a lunatic asylum—as a pair of landed proprietors, admiring the prospect, taking down and putting up—a tree here and a garden seat there... Sergey playing the nobleman; but much licked into shape. My little lamb. God bless thee.[208] ...Strength come back to him, his will greatly and evidently fortified. We might have done worse. I dare not hope. Some sort of peace.

In September she spent a fortnight in London—in part to see solicitors about finances and to organise her daughter's schooling, although this was not in fact sorted out. Mainly it was the literary life of the capital which captured her attention. She had tea with May Sinclair, visited Nina Hamnett, shopped at Selfridges and dined at the Ritz. In a state of heightened sensitivity she made repeated references in her journal to perceiving, in London and the surrounding countryside, the kinds of atmosphere evoked in the writing of Arthur Machen and M.R. James.

On the 1 October she returned to Paris. A few days later she delighted in meeting the Surrealist writer, Max Jacob, a friend of Georges Auric's. Yet she also lamented the change in atmosphere and attitudes which she felt were transforming the city: "(I had been talking about the virtuosity of Djuna Barnes' *Ryder* [(1928)], the lovely language and rhythm: consecrated to bawdy jokes, bottoms and 'pipi'—etc). He [Walter Shaw] said (I had said 'why use such lovely language about ignoble things—Never about fortitude or chastity or Aphrodite')—'Because they don't believe in such things any more.' True." Mary Butts also felt that an equal deterioration had occurred in the newly redecorated Boeuf sur le Toit, in the Rue Boissy-D'Anglas.

> The New Boeuf is gloriously beautiful, lit like some lovely 'futurist' stage, smoke veiled, shrill apple-jade, lights in oblong glass [tops], the electric wires and boxes strewn in a corner, scarlet, sea-blue, gold, crimson—purple—mirror upon mirror upon mirror, even the doors disguised in looking-glass (cf Chanel's house). A good dancing floor, the bar high on the right up black steps.
>
> *But*, where is the little side bar for the family-party? Where the comfortable shabby old beauties? Where is the Boeuf that was our party-place? It was beautifully decorated, none the worse for being a little old and worn.
>
> *And* people come out of the street, *disappear* in it, a sea of black bodies and grey faces, all alike. It was difficult to recognise one's nearest and dearest, *all* colour *stripped* off them: quite *too tenebrous*... We may be a bad crowd, but why reduce us to what we shall all look like when we've been dead a bit? I painted my face like a Petruchka doll and carried myself straight up and I was only one degree less spectral.

"Our Boeuf", the entry concluded, "is dead".

Now no longer in existence, the Boeuf formed the setting for several scenes in Mary Butts's fiction, even when not specifically named. Hence in *Armed with Madness* when Felix returns to Paris, we are told that: "He turned up the Rue Boissy d'Anglas and found himself indoors again.... The café walls were black, filled with mirror panels squared with small red and gold lights. Like an old mirror that has a circle of miniature mirrors inlaid in its glass, the place reflected and repeated a great deal of what is going on in the world."[209] Mary Butts spent a great deal of time in the Boeuf and it was central to her imaginative map of Paris; she was concerned however that her presence at its tables should not be reported to her brother as a sign that she was doing no work.[210]

By the autumn of 1928 her drug addiction, which had been steady whilst with Mireille Havet in Villefranche, had increased dramatically. A comment in which she compared herself to de Quincey on having managed "one day without," shows that such abstinence was a rarity. She was later amused to find out through the course of her reading that "the use of our 'dopes' is more ancient than I had supposed: that the heathen in their beastly devices used opium, hashish with datura, hemlock—& others at all times. In Greece there were immortal or divine names amaranth, athanasia & Morpheus gave the poppy and an Egytian gave Helen stuff to make her first parties go off well on her return from Troy—opium, henbane, bugloss, mandragora" (6.8.29). Robert Medley remarked that in the summer of 1928, it was unknown to most of her friends that her "drug habit...had escalated from opium—which she shared with Cocteau—to heroin."[211] Throughout the autumn her senses were heightened by addiction: "I am becoming more and more sensitive to the quality of paper that I touch. Certain note-papers—the new buff block with the scarlet address I dislike though it looks well once the ink is dried to black; but my paper-cutter is not sharp enough. It 'chiffons' out the margins of the new Strachey [*Books and Characters*]. This paper [of the diary itself] is supportable but I like best the thin, transparent, cheap indian block—One might be writing upon vegetable glass. This has a relation with my childhood's nervous—almost sickening—pain at the *idea* of running my nails along a soft whitewashed wall. The sensation returns to me now."[212]

When not inside the flat reading and working, or out visiting friends, she wandered around Paris. Her drug addiction combined with a lack of food was making her increasingly susceptible to psychic experiences:

> Remember a Walk: After lunch, equinox, the air—gulf Stream pouring in over Paris—June warm, rain flying—fairly *straight* down, leaves yellow, wet and still crisp.
>
> I lunched out of doors—a number of things happened, some strange, all agreeable... The rain held up—I walked to the mysterious PO in the Rue Amélie for a parcel: Down the rue S Dominique. The rue S D has been there a long time. Its 'line' is exquisite, and there are courts off it, I have explored a few. That there are more courts I know—old houses *plastered on* over older houses.... First because the rain had brought out the colours and the wind made walking delicious and this...makes me sensitive and glad...cobbles and plane trees... I felt—well—definitely 'psychic' at a patch on the round, uncomfortable stones. As though when I stood at a spot, on a group of them, a dark went up my legs to my knees. (The stones were no darker, but they felt darker.) I took a pace or so back to them. This made me more sensitive.

Such experiences did not frighten her; on the contrary, they confirmed her belief that she knew Paris and "its psychic auras...magically". On a trip there in 1921 she had found one such spot: "Explored the part of Paris that lies behind the Quai S Michel, between Chacornac's shop and Notre Dame. There is a magical relation between that shop and the church." This knowledge lies behind her short story 'Mappa Mundi' which she started in 1936 and completed only two months before she died. Its forbidding yet tantalising atmosphere is present from the opening paragraphs:

> Paris is not a safe city. It is never supposed to be, but so often for the wrong reasons. Perhaps the only place in the world that is really and truly both a sink of iniquity and a fountain of life at one and the

> same time; in the same quarter, in the same place, at the same hour, with the same properties—to even the same person.
>
> It is no use, or not much use, to know it only as a spree, or as an aesthetic jolt, returning very sophisticated about it. Like all the great feminine places, behind its first dazzling free display, you come quickly upon profound reserves. After the spree a veil is drawn, a sober, *noli me tangere* veil. Isis whose face on a first swift initiation you think you have seen, even to the colour of her eyes, Isis you believe you have kissed, withdraws, well wrapped-up, grown instantly to her own height—as is the property of a goddess. Colossal, as Apuleius saw Hecate, and made of stone which is goddess's material; and for lover and mistress you are left with an image, remote as St Geneviève where she stands looking up stream, an inviolable city behind her.[213]

In this ghost story an American disappears—the implication is that he is dead—because he did not take enough care in the secret magic areas of the city.

Around this time she tended to see significance in what other people might see as coincidence: Feeling ill on the 1 September and "very near collapse" she believed that her "cure came…picking up the P. to the S. of the G. R. [*Prolegomena to the Study of Greek Religion* by Jane Harrison] to look up a word for the poem. Opened at the Orphic tablet, & it is as if the water from that well, almost physically, refreshed me.[214] Like a dew. There is almost a consciousness of JH about, as an awareness, 'her mild and gentle'—& how much more 'ghost'." Other sensations were more worrying: "I am afraid for J.C. [Cocteau]. Because of what I know. Because the glass over his picture broke to-day."

In spite of ill-health, her life did not slow down. A few days in Chartres in late October with a drug-taking American companion, Walter Shaw,[215] brought renewed enthusiasm for the Cathedral where, as she noted, the Belgian writer "Huysmans came and sulked about his soul." She celebrated its power in a review of Henry Adams's *Mont-Saint-Michel and Chartres* in June 1936.[216]

Back in Paris at the end of the month, she had Sergei (who was now out of the asylum) bring back the almost eight-year-old Camilla from the Pension in Cannes to stay for a few days with her at the flat in 14 Rue de Monttessuy. "Heaven with my girl," she declared in early November during a short-lived outburst of enthusiasm for motherhood.[217] All too soon it was displaced by a much more familiar preoccupation with Sergei. Her frustrated passion for him found a brief outlet in "the comfort of Benvenuto", an aspiring writer then in Paris. All this time she was still writing: "The new story—written itself—to have been an essay, l'Inconnu," she declared in a tantalising entry. She wrote to Marianne

Moore at *The Dial* to recover a copy of her story 'Change' which they had published in 1922. On receipt of the story, she declared to Moore: "I am very glad that 'Change' has been recovered; but for you it would have vanished off the earth; and I hope to bring out a book of short stories in the spring."[218] In fact, *Several Occasions* (her second collection of stories) came out not in 1929 but in 1932 and 'Change' was not included. Despite acclaim, it has never been republished.

By the 4 November, Mary Butts's drug habit was dominating her life more and more: "*Remember*, exquisite fatigue and rest after the 'shot', illuminated repose, eyes shut, a moment, a minute before I am writing this." As the month progressed, however, so her health deteriorated. On the 12 November Sergey was arrested for soliciting and given a three-month prison sentence. Mary Butts declared on the following day: "There is nothing for me but work, work, work." Whilst she still saw a few friends, including Mireille Havet who had returned to Paris, by the end of the month the diary fell silent as she began her detoxification cure.

In Nice in June 1928, Mireille Havet used her diary to consider how she had come to be a drug-addict. It is a sensitive portrayal of the illusions to which she, Mary Butts and no doubt other drug-takers have been prey:

> For a long time I said and could say without exaggeration or arrogance...that drugs are not a danger for me. I have my head screwed on and sufficient instinct and common sense and control over my body...to be able to calculate exactly how much I consume, and to declare this to a doctor with honesty and accuracy. [The doctor]... will be able to use this information as a basis which he can trust and thus cure me easily and with my full cooperation... I could even reduce my intake by myself if only opium were involved....I know that now for the first time in my life—I wish to write it here as I could die of drugs not intentionally but by chance and much more quickly than I realise—which would vex me a great deal and be the cause of my eternal damnation which would be no more than my infernal pride deserves... I no longer admit to myself how much I take...no longer want to control the amount...and I would not admit the quantity to any doctor nor friend—for the simple reason that I don't know how much I take and I don't want to know and anyway... I know that I am no longer an accomplice...but a prisoner bound by blood and breath to my favourite drug—and that this unnatural relationship—so good in the beginning...has left me...like deaf people who will not listen or drivers who lose their way on purpose although they know the route by heart... I have lost my free will and am now only an animal, a slave amongst slaves.

The confession ends with the following lament addressed to Mary Butts: "My life is now only a series of withdrawals and self-abuse... I will no longer write any stories, Mary. I like stories too much—before writing them I wanted to live—and reality has substituted itself for the creation—my life for the work I should have written in my life. My death... substituting itself for the imaginary death of the ends of chapters and—to end on a bad pun—heroin for my heroes and heroines..."[219]

* * * * *

FROM LETTERS AND other memoirs it is possible to piece together Mary Butts's movements in these months, principally from the account by Robert Medley who looked after her and Walter Shaw in her flat during November 1928.[220] Coincidentally, Cocteau began a detoxification cure himself at St Cloud in Paris a few weeks later. His account entitled *Opium* (1929) would result from this—curiously, Mary Butts is not mentioned.

Even by the end of December she was not much better, admitting in a letter to John Rodker that it "will be a matter of time...before my health is restored".[221] He came to Paris at this time and convinced her to let him take Camilla to stay with Mary Colville-Hyde in London in January 1929, initially "for a week or so".[222] In fact Camilla did not return to France and Mary Butts followed her daughter to her mother's flat at 3 Buckingham Gate in late January. After a brief stay there, Harcourt Wesson Bull found her a flat to rent a few streets away at 22 Clarges St, London W1 (now demolished) and she was based there until her return to Paris in mid-June 1929. According to Wesson Bull it was a time of wild parties in London:

> Mary was completely in her element at the time of the Greek Party in the early spring. I had introduced her to some of the so-called Bright Young People I had met, in this instance Elizabeth Ponsonby,...Eddie Gathorne-Hardy, Brian Howard, who asked her to plan their costumes: there were feathered caps and almost indecently high tunics. Mary tried, without success, to persuade Jean Cocteau to come over from Paris... I regret that 'flu kept me away from the Greek Party; I would have liked to have remembered Mary in her long chiton and high headdress and blue wig a caryatid or goddess. I have a photograph of her taken at the party by Olivia Wyndham...and she is lovely. I heard that she had a wonderful time and was seen under a table with the octogenerian, Harry Melville.[223]

In October 1928 Marianne Moore had commissioned her to write a long review of Glenway Wescott's new book of stories, *Good-bye Wisconsin*. Mary Butts finally sent it over in March 1929 when, always conscious of her reputation, she preferred to describe her "serious illness" to Moore as "flue" [sic] rather than the result of drug addiction. At all events Moore did not think that the 'flue' had affected Mary Butts's ability to write: "It pleases and rather terrifies one, that you should have perceived so much more about our country than is written down, and we are grateful for the substance with which you endow the book."[224] Mary Butts was paid the substantial sum of $30 for the review, which came out in *The Dial* in May 1929.[225]

In March she took the 09.30 train from Waterloo to Parkstone (w/e return ticket, 17s 9d) to visit The Haven, her old school which she wanted Camilla to attend. Although her knee was troubling her at this time,[226] she walked from the station to the school in "about 1/4 of an hour" and was "welcomed like a lost child" by her old school teacher, Miss Lawrence. Being in Dorset brought back her enthusiasm for her childhood landscapes: "It is the happiest place, in a pine-wood high up, looking out straight over Poole Harbour to the Purbeck Hills."[227] Camilla attended this school from April 1929, but disputes between her mother, father and grandmother over the continued payment of her fees were a continual source of epistolary acrimony right up to Mary Butts's death.

Before returning to Paris in June, Mary Butts made a couple of short trips, one to Bruges in late April, where she spent time with Sergei and wrote an essay on Aldous Huxley,[228] and one to Dieppe in late May. In a letter to Cedric Morris at this time she wrote that she hoped to buy his painting of two gulls and a duck with money she was soon to acquire.[229] This money was to come from the sale of a Holbein painting which Mary Colville-Hyde first mentioned to her daughter in a letter that year: "You remember the picture of Sir William...well the experts now say it is (as the family always said) by Holbein you will remember. I bought it from Henry Butts myself for £450—I will let you know if the cleaners reveal the Holbein underneath."[230] The portrait was of Sir William Butts, "the eldest son of Henry VIII's physician, and a man of distinction like his father. He was an ardent friend of the Reformation and became a favourite of Queen Elizabeth, whom he entertained at his manor house of Thornage, in Norfolk, in 1563."[231] Not only would the minutiae involved in the sale of this painting be documented in Mary Colville-Hyde's letters to Mary Butts from that time on; it quickly became part of the myth the latter elaborated on for her friends. It is central to the anecdote about her by the barman[232] James Charters (Jimmie) in his 1934 autobiography, *This Must be the Place: Memoirs of Montparnasse*:

> Mary Butts was an English writer whom I used to see frequently. Once she told me a about a portrait of a Colonel Butts painted by Holbein, which had been in her family for a long time. She said the family had been offered £80,000 for it, but refused to sell.
>
> 'You know, James,' she said, 'I'll tell you a secret. There are about five brush strokes in the left-hand corner that were done by a PUPIL

> of Holbein's. You mustn't tell anyone! It's a big secret.'
> It was a 'big secret' all right. I never said a word, but I found out later that she had told the same story to everyone she knew, always cautioning them about secrecy.[233]

In fact the sale of the Holbein painting would be complicated and protracted. Yet this did not prevent Mary Butts from borrowing money on the basis of her share of the fabulous sum the portrait was expected to fetch.[234]

CHAPTER FIFTEEN

The Epoch of Excesses Draws to a Close
June – October 1929

> *While the evening gathers, perceptibly for the first time earlier, and the Paris night arrives to hang jewels over the bends of this river where man has decided that there shall be light, by preference coloured light, but light.*
>
> —MB, diary entry, 3/4.8.29

By the 11 June Mary Butts was living once again in Paris. Mireille Havet was also back after a four-month stay in New York where her love affair with Norma had broken down. Characteristically she then began (like Mary Butts) to idealise the relationship in her journal. Mary Butts had let her flat in 14 Rue de Monttessuy to an American, Guy Allen, and so stayed with Mireille Havet in her flat in Passy. Situated at 51 Rue de Raynouard (Paris 16), it was only a twenty-minute walk on the other side of the Seine from the Rue de Monttessuy in the 7th arrondissement. The original house no longer exists, having been pulled down in 1932 and replaced by a building designed and inhabited by the French architect, Auguste Perret. When arranging to rent it out on Mireille Havet's behalf during the summer of 1928, Mary Butts had noted that the flat had "2 big rooms, kitchen, bathroom etc. 'phone, attic, *View*, phonograph. servant 500 a month.... All gas, wood stoves. Maid fed at midday, stays to do dinner." By the time she lived there for a few weeks from mid-June 1929, Mireille Havet could no longer afford to pay a servant. Whilst not describing the interior, Mary Butts did note the flat's view and surroundings:

> 'Our haunt': 30 years ago, Passy was a village. Yesterday I went down the steps—hill-village steps—towards the river, & came out in the lane in front of the house & below it. I looked up at our house, in which M's flat lies. The garden—or half of it, has been levelled to make a modern block of hideous flats, & our house stands now on a cliff, twice as high as seen from our Rue Raynouard with its ruelle-like village lane it once was. "I saw it, high, old & grey—'panelled' with grey shutters—But for no colour and no washing, it might have

been a mediterranean tenement. And the look of it made me afraid—the same impression, without the awed beauty, of the pine-tree high above the low wood at Salterns, with the ivy and the huge cones and the blue sheen in its crest. Not *quite* the same—more 'ghostly' & *as though I had seen it before.*

At first, being with Mireille again recreated the intensity of their original relationship in the South of France and supplied Mary Butts with examples of what she called "Paris poetry: the night M & I went to look for Elise, & I sat on the tenement stairs in the dark with the stair-tap dripping, & struck matches as the workmen came up & down in the dark & their dogs jumped over me.... Later, the rondeau in the night-chemist's shop." However she soon became annoyed with her friend, mostly for the very characteristics which they had in common: "M's egoism, certain high vibrations[235] in her voice: her female inability to go out and come in when she says she will." In an entry on 9 July she mused somewhat condescendingly on reports of how Mireille Havet had annoyed mutual friends: "What I expected, M had killed her own goose: presumed: taken for granted: been a bore. The old story." Yet Mary Butts was not only critical of others; she also used her diary to exhibit flashes of astute *self*-knowledge: "When I began to complain it occured to me, for this time, *at once* of how little I have to complain of—a little hurt, rather over-worn, waiting for material deliverance to come from 2 sides, neither far off. This in comparison with many of those I love." This measured tone was short-lived.

Since Mireille Havet did not keep a diary during these months, there is no information about Mary Butts's effect on her; for her part, Mary Butts increasingly felt sapped by both her French friend and her flat:

These weeks at M's are my first in an admittedly haunted house—(M's father)
I. Woke up with throat and considerable fever & said that I felt I'd been fighting something all night.
II. Vitality dully and fairly continuously sapped.
III. Endless creaks, taps and little noises; & in spite of loneliness inside and out, one could easily be scared alone at night.

She was relieved to be able to return to 14 Rue de Monttessuy. Once there, she countered her sense of loneliness with her characteristically high level of activity. She read widely, making extensive notes on a number of books: Gilbert Murray's *Ordeal of this Generation* (1929) ("Yet honestly to few men do I owe more, do I more bless in my heart than that old scholar and gentleman");[236] an edition of Thomas Macaulay's *Essays*, Lytton Strachey's *Books and Characters* (1922); Burke on the French Revolution; Wyndham Lewis's *The Childermass* (1928). All her life Mary Butts was a bibliophile and her journal is full of lists of books. Ideally she would have "3 editions of the best loved—a) An old one to read. b) The newest edition with full notes. c) A pocket one for travel."[237]

She socialised both with friends and other writers. For example, on the 1 August she had lunch with Mireille Havet; on the 5 August she attended a farewell supper for Cocteau ("our Ariel") with Walter Shaw and Jean Guérin, at the latter's flat. Among her papers there is a drawing by Cocteau signed "Souvenir du bon vieux temps (sic) Jean à Mary 1929" which may well date from this period (in addition to the 1929 drawing of Mary Butts by Cocteau reproduced in *A Sacred Quest*). On the 10 August she had an enjoyable lunch with Carl van Vechten whom she had met the previous year and it may well have been during these weeks that Lett Haines did his drawing of her, 'Mary Butts Paris 1929'.[238] Yet, just as in the early 1920s, when her socialising in Montparnasse had led Harold Acton to believe that she was not working, so in 1929 she continued to work indefatigably whilst sustaining a hectic social life.

On the 27 July she noted how that day she had made "13 pages of notes, summary etc… That with letters, a morning's money-chase, a long interview, some reading, 3 pages translation *and* Mireille". As she concluded herself, that was "not bad". She also commented on a system of marginal notation which she continually reworked over the years. Coming across the omega character "used in margin for 'work in progress'", she remarked in her diary: "That will do, being my raison d'être in life." Whilst aware that "these signs are but arbitrary and childish", she saw them as "no more than reminders to catch the eye and prevent repetitions while I try and work at what I am learning, … to convey not only what I have seen and half-divined, but the exquisite subtlety of its mode of happening." Ever resourceful, she accepted Edward Titus's request that she become the sub-editor of the little magazine, *This Quarter*, although for some reason it was Samuel Putnam who took up the post at the end of the year.[239] She made notes for an article about the use of stimulants and in late August wrote a long disquisition which she described as "a study of our times" and to which she gave the somewhat clumsy working title of "View of the Present State of Civilisation in the West". She dedicated it to Tony Butts and Walter Shaw, but never published it. "Think of me as the siammese [sic] twin who had *not* married" she wrote in her preface to Tony, a self-description which reveals her continuing obsession with him.[240] Never complacent about her work, she mused in early August 1929: "It has taken me all my life to fix the little of which I can be sure, arrive at such poor theorisings from them as I have—while I am haunted that they slip by me each day in millions." Although it would be another ten months before she left Paris to live permanently in England, Mary Butts was aware that the frenzied pace at which she was living could not last much longer. As she put it: "My epoch of excesses is an end" and later wrote a story about this, entitled 'Ford's Last Dancing'.

At the end of August she moved back briefly to 51 Rue de Raynouard to look after Mireille Havet who was once again in the throes of excessive drug addiction: "Think of a niece bending over a sick bed, thermometer in one hand, iced drink in another, a pen between her teeth and League of Nations[241] in her head," she wrote to her aunt. By the 10 September, Mireille Havet had moved into 14 Rue de Monttessuy and Mary Butts informed Ada rather breezily how "just after I wrote to you, my nose began to hurt, right up at the top &...[Mireille de Soyecourt] came in limping, saying that her knee hurt. We couldn't think of a reason for either phenomena. I compressed her knee but what can you do for a nose? Her knee got worse. I put her to bed and sent for my doctor. He said it was...slight abscesses of which there is a plague in Paris now."[242] In fact, both abscesses were the consequence of heroin addiction and for once the graphic description which Mary Butts gave her aunt about how a certain Dr Tivel lanced Mireille Havet's abscess without anaesthetic are not epistolary hyperbole. Many of the details are corroborated by the latter's entries in her diary which she started writing again on the 10 September. The first page carries the following facts: "At Mary Butts's home 14 Rue de Monttessuy during the 5th abcess on my knee drained by Dr Tivel."[243]

Like those of the previous year, Mireille Havet's journal entries are for the most part concerned with past love affairs, sexual frustration, her need for money and the minute details which absorb a bed-bound convalescent suffering from heroin withdrawal. She commented on the sounds coming through the window of Mary Butts's flat: the bells of a nearby church, the advertising jingles of the Bon Marché Department Store a few streets away, road sweepers and people beating their carpets and throwing dirty water into the gutter. Among these outpourings and minutiae are instances of Mary Butts's generosity towards her:

> 11.9, 9 in the morning Wednesday:...without Mary's impressive generosity I would be in an anonymous iron hospital bed.
>
> 13.9, midnight: Chance has not really failed me—I have found this fraternal and extraordinary friendship in Mary, who is looking after me here in her home with unfailing devotion and good humour despite being poor and tired herself—what would I have done at home—alone—the charity hospital would have been my only option.
>
> 14.9: Dear Dr Tivel. Miracle. ...lanced my knee 8 days ago and Mary has drained and dressed the abcess every day since then.[244]

On the 10 September Mary Butts wrote to her aunt:

> ...as we've no money for nursing-homes and hospitals here are impossible, I'm nursing her here. If you ever have a septic wound to be dressed, come to me. I'm very proud—[Dr Tivel] said that he could not do the dressings better himself. He also dealt with the other side of my nose—which is still troublesome. And horribly disfiguring. It's as well I can't go out much.
>
> Mireille still suffers a great deal: but never complains. The dressing of her knee is a long job, and as hideous to look at as it is to feel. But she only thinks of me. Sleeps in the little salon, and every day the concierge carries her onto the big divan in my room and back at night. We tell each other stories, and translate some Plato— [245]

As with John Rodker twelve years earlier, Mary Butts was once again proving her capacity for responding to a friend "in a really spectacular mess". The following extract from Mireille Havet's diary written during the night between 16-17 September conveys not only Mary Butts's unstinting encouragement and enthusiasm, but also her ability to inspire her friends:

> But my confidence, at the very least my curiosity and my interest in life in general and in my own life, are almost recovered thanks to Mary's genius and what she makes me glimpse and morally define as a sudden and secret way out, in so far as it might be imagined only by her at this stage in the history of poetry. I admit I do not understand yet but I know that from the very moment when I understand, it will transform my youth, my faith, my audacity; bring back my fighting spirit and that I will not have enough minutes in a day to express myself, discharge my new duties and achieve in all spheres—social, affective and finally literary—by writing it out in order to give to the world what might be one of the first translations and interpretations—and then my work will be inspiring and come from God alone and my guardian angel. But until then, it is so wonderful, such a new and unfamiliar perspective, for my head to conceive, such a poetic service of our life and universe—my task at last! How clumsy and hesitant I am in what is becoming for me and my ignorance the shadow of blinding formulae and heavenly truth which Mary is giving me as if it were the most natural and commonplace thing in the world.
>
> Her genius crushes my poor mind which has learnt nothing for years and all the cogs are rusty through lack of use or the vilest and vulgar train of thought and mere sentimental preoccupations and disappointments.
>
> I must get used to this magic alphabet and that slowly there grows in me the theory of the new signs which will help me to spell out and herald the new poetry of the world and its true eternal truths.[246]

Mireille Havet stayed at 14 Rue de Monttessuy until mid-September. There were moments of intimacy and exhilaration, such as on the 5 September when Mireille Havet recorded how they had spent the night discussing poetry. They also took part in a number of more or less successful seances at which Mary Butts's friend, the artist Vivian Ogilvie, was sometimes present.[247] On the 14 September Mary Butts became very excited when the letters "J A C M" were rapped out. These were the initials of Cecil Maitland's full name (James Alexander Cecil Maitland) and it was perhaps in memory of this that when *Ashe of Rings* was republished in England in 1933, she changed the original dedication from "To CM" to "To J.A.C.M". On the 15 September she thought that she had seen a man standing at the end of her bed in the early morning. Later she believed this figure to have been her father when young. For the most part, however, she felt tired and depressed because there was "no money …no holidays, no air, no rest, great heat, rarely much food: the abcess in my nose!" Both women were grateful when Mireille Havet was well enough to move back to 51 Rue de Raynouard, and Mary Butts was able to nurse her sense of abandonment by her mother[248] and brother in private. In a lucid diary entry later in the month she realised that if her brother failed her it was because she expected too much: "I call him to a service which is not his." However she still wrote defensively to him: "You despise my complaints—but I have worked well."[249] Reflecting on the previous six weeks she referred to her long study, "View of the Present State of Civilisation in the West": "The book done: the closest account and *demonstration* of the new perception yet given: the 'awareness', in its naturalness, simplicity, simplification, comprehension—the start—to put it in one way—to realise what is true Present, the basis of the science of mysticism." By the time she reread it with less passion and more detachment the following year, she saw its faults.

In late September as the weather cooled a little with the onset of the "exquisite autumn", Mary Butts revived. She read Hugh MacDiarmid's poetry and Merezhkovsky's biography of Akhnaton[250] as well as David Hogarth's *Philip and Alexander of Macedon* (1897). On the 25 September she noted—"Hogarth's *Alexander* finished, and my Alexander still in the making: farther off, since I've been forced to shed some fancies; but each day nearer, since I approach him. Before I have done I shall not be far-off seeing him face to face. *Peace comes by strange ways* and light. So Athens draws by a thread her lovers, by the fine cord Heirmamenê."[251] This was her first diary entry to refer to what was clearly a long-standing ambition to write a study about Alexander the Great which she completed in eighteen months, although it was published only in 1933.

During September she noted Mireille Havet's comment that she was "sursensible"—oversensitive. Mary Butts had realised this fault in herself years earlier, describing it as "an abnormal sensitivity" (16.6.20). In 1929, however, she noted: "I believe that we miss, all of us, what we are looking for, by its 'staring us in the face' = by our perpetual use of what so far we have not given a name [to]." On the 28th she tried to articulate what she meant. It began after a

> day in hell: won out of *by myself*— An hour's high fever in which I saw nothings,—as I have seen them lately several times—in a medium I can only describe as exquisitely 'pointed'—a sharp, dying sweetness, a source of tears: never joy, magnificence, 'clarté', victory. Only an ineffable sadness. Something it may be well for me to feel—because by it I may understand what others feel, what it occurs to me that Sandy may have felt. It's not an emotion or an 'approach' common to Achilles' set—more 'keltic' I should call it, 'the beech-leaves cold'. Also a sensibility I have not allowed for it—for it flutters and hovers, while mine soars.
>
> It has nearly escaped me now, so alien is it to me when I am strong...

Yet Mary Butts was not strong, for on the 1 October she recorded that she had a fever with a temperature of 102°F, during which time she read Perry's *Children of the Sun* (1923). This led her to wish to write a book on 'mana' and animism and to assert, in contradistinction to H.G. Wells's beliefs, that all thoughts had some basis in reality. As to people, she felt disappointed by Mireille Havet and began to detect a "bad streak" in her. However she gave no further details as she then received a postcard which changed the course of her life.

CHAPTER SIXTEEN

St Malo
October – November 1929

Couronne de pierre dressée sur les flots
[Crown of stone rising out of the waves]

—Gustave Flaubert on St Malo

Saw each other side by side in the ward-robe mirror—laughter and tears and play and plans. All of which may God fulfil for us. Another blue-bird prince warmed to life so quickly it seems half miraculous.

—MB, diary entry, 23.10.29

ON THE 30 OCTOBER 1929 Mary Butts wrote to Anne Weir that her nephew, the artist Gabriel Atkin (whom she had met in Villefranche the previous year) "sent me one of his post-cards to Paris [from St Malo]. I had been over-working for months and came down gladly to join him."[252] On the 5 October she travelled by train to St Malo, the medieval harbour town on the emerald coast of Brittany, and remained (with a short break) until the 22 November. Whilst there she and Gabriel Atkin stayed at the Hôtel Central[253] in the old part of the city, the Intra Muros. "(I have a snob-longing, sometimes, to write a snob-address.) c/o The Dalai Lama, the Palace, Lhassa—for example; or X Faubourg St Honoré. It never seems to be gratified. Meanwhile, and this is punishment: 'Hôtel Central—St Malo'," she later wrote with regret, for whilst the hotel was situated on the Grand'Rue[254] or High Street, this was in the poorer area of the city. During her six-week stay in St Malo, her deepening love for Gabriel Atkin and awareness of the magic qualities of this town combined to create for her "a very slow recovery to normal life, ie: augmenting vigour: perspective. Enjoyment: curiosity." For the sake of clarity I shall present them separately, although Mary Butts's diary conveys that her strong supernatural perceptions and new-found love were intertwined in her mind.

* * * * *

St Malo and the supernatural

As a 'magic' town S Malo is taking hold of me. The sequence runs — General pleasure in it and a sense of being on the keltic border: the marches between France and what is not France.

—MB, diary entry, 20.10.29

Eternity isn't a quantity, it's a quality.

—E.F. Benson, *Visible and Invisible* (1923)

MARY BUTTS was greatly affected by the atmosphere of St Malo and became absorbed in the history of her new surroundings. In medieval times the Grand'Rue (which was only about a hundred yards long) had derived its name from the fact that it was the main thoroughfare from the Grande Porte (or Porte de la Mer). This harbour gate was originally the only entrance into St Malo, a walled city of about 45 acres, whose ramparts, begun in the twelfth century, still provided a scenic promenade for its occupants. Indeed in 1921, eight years before Mary Butts's visit, the ramparts had been classed as national monuments. The Grande Porte was flanked by two vast towers built in 1582 on which the inhabitants had placed cannons which successfully repelled attacks by the English in 1693, 1695 and 1758. On the town side of the Grande Porte were two stone staircases leading down to the Place Poids-du-Roi, so called because in 1582 Charles II of France had ensured the city's maritime prosperity by giving it a charter to set up weights, scales and public measures.

Above the gateway, tucked in a niche below the towers stood the painted granite statue of Notre Dame de la Grand'Porte or Notre Dame de Bon Secours. This 1.92 m high statue was of the Virgin Mary who carried in her arms the baby Jesus holding a bird. According to local legend she had been found in the seventeenth century floating in the waters off St Malo by a fisherman who had hauled her in, and from then on she had become the patron saint of the city. By the time Mary Butts came to St Malo in 1929, a glass casement had been installed at the front of the niche to protect the statue, and every year on the 15 August (St Marie's day) the Malouins went on a torchlit procession round the city ending at the Grande Porte to venerate her. Notre Dame de la Grand'Porte gazed up the Grand'Rue.

The Hôtel Central was half-way up the street and at the top stood the Cathedral. Originally started in the eighth century, it was finally completed in 1866 after Napoleon III donated the funds to build the ornate spire which pierced the skyline. Mary Butts remarked shortly after her arrival: "One says 'God' very naturally in this old town, where the Cathedral...squats brooding her ancient house-cluster like a hen."

In October 1929 she was physically exhausted from her excessive consumption of heroin (and alcohol) and although she continued to take the drug in St Malo, it was in much smaller doses. Throughout her stay she tested her own experiences of *déjà vu* against the theories of J.W. Dunne's *An Experiment with Time*. On the 9th she described both her hypnogogic states and the difference between "ordinary" and "magic" dreams. As can be seen, she was resistant to a Freudian interpretation:

> On falling asleep I have often been conscious, (and, during this last great fatigue, generally conscious, *aware*) that I had 'shot off' to places and events known *always* in my dream life; and with these, relations with people I know quite differently, though intimately, when awake. (No sex in waking life *in fact wished or implied*). ... This has interested me so much as to wake me, to try and fix it—them—in my memory at least. With deep sleep all memory disappears.
>
> *Now* those dreams are, roughly, between two categories: ordinary dreams, and the high, magic dreams on which my life has been strung.
>
> . . .
>
> On this matter there is Dunne's comment in *An Experiment with Time*.... There, as I remember, he says that there is a recognised form of memory trick in dreaming, when a dream of a thing unknown presents itself as known, part of a long sequence. This the doctors have named. [in margin of diary: "look up"]. Now this touches the question...—but lots of these dreams appear as picking-up what's been going on all the time. So I recognise them when I begin to dream. 'Here we go again' I say—as if on the *common* plane of what I see and where I go *'East of the sun, West of the moon'*. Where, for example, I find the true Sergey, know the true Cecil is.

On several occasions in St Malo, Mary Butts experienced a prescient connection between a dream and a daytime activity: "Last night, a sea-fear dream—high rocks, tide-incoming. Today, sensation shell-hunting along the causeways under the sea-fortifications. Storm coming up from Dinard. Same fear" (26.10). After being there for just a week, her senses were in a heightened state: The "discovery, the 'awareness' shapes and shapes, I feel it more...a lovely sense of a new form of movement" so much so that she wanted to "relate the unrelated". She already used the margin signs [Δ] for "dreams: Dunne" and [Δ with star] "delta with a star for apprehension or hints of the future when awake: so forebodings". In addition she noted at the back of her diary that she had to think of a "new sign for the new *intellectual* perception I am beginning to get of the hitherto unknown (or misunderstood) relations between concepts and events I am beginning to be aware of—often on the edge of sleep—and lose—as I gain them—in a flash. Which I must train myself now not to lose: to set down—if I have to invent a new language." Unfortunately in mid-October she "fell off the ramparts, a 12 foot crash onto granite". "I should be dead," she remarked wryly. Shaken by the fall and in order to get money (wired there by her mother) she returned to Paris for two days and stayed in Mireille Havet's flat in Passy. She found the journey delightful:

> Coming up in the train on the 14th, I watched as beautiful a day as I have ever seen from the long *open* french carriage window. There was Le Mans, and its cathedral, the high-pitched tower wall—
> Apple trees hung with enamel balls, scarlet to cold green:[255] enamelled turf under each.
> At Chartres—the moon waxing, smoke mist in the meads ... —there were little lakes, and first it was red rock and apples, then slowly the great french landscape with its sense of 'vast horizons', slowly rising land, forest-arms and single poplars: chateaux with high-pitched roofs—and occasional modern re-constructions with a tendancy to break out into mosaic dragons and general heraldry set into slates.
> All the way up, single magpies—all but one flight of 5 or 7. *'One for sorrow'*—I sang *'waiting for the moon to rise'* out of the window song—a Sergey song and even earlier. And I blessed the Power which has filled my life with poetry.[256]

While Mary Butts made little mention of her visit to Paris, it is clear from her diary that Mireille Havet found her presence overbearing: "Mary is here for 2 days. She overexcites me, troubles me and makes me triple my doses and yet I still love her with all my heart and she saved my life."[257] What Mireille Havet could not bear was the hyperactivity (too similar to her own) which accompanied Mary Butts's drug-taking. Also, she was slowly falling in love with Vivian Ogilvie (who rented a room in her flat) and wanted to be alone with him. Mary Butts clearly did not realise that she was *de trop*, for she invited Mireille Havet to come back with her to "rest" in St Malo. Whilst tempted, the latter declined because of poverty and her "fear of the exhaustion and the nervous tension which comes from being with them both, Mary Butts and her English friend [Gabriel Atkin] who has to be prevented from drinking".[258] By 3 o'clock in the morning of the 16 October she was at the end of her tether: "Mary is always restless because of her drug-taking insomnia which is too like mine—she uses any excuse to come into my room and talk to me. Oh I'm so exhausted."[259] They argued and Mireille Havet felt sorry and guilty when Mary Butts accused her of "ingratitude", yet was relieved when her friend returned to St Malo on the 16th.

For her part, Mary Butts was very pleased to be back in "the wine-blue air here...this old town, the high stones right and left, and the memories...of many pirates, Surcouf,[260] whose name I like: the Malinois, this old, rich dear mixed, hard land." Hardly was she back when she once again stumbled. But this fall produced the following genial aside: "I fell down the stair-way of the 'Grande Porte' on the platform below the Virgin, Our Lady of Safety, who seems hardly to have been on duty that night!"

Whilst her relationship with Gabriel Atkin ebbed and flowed, her interest in the supernatural quality of St Malo only increased: "As a 'magic' town S Malo is taking hold of me." She recalled Algernon Blackwood's supernatural tale, 'Ancient Sorceries' (1908), in which an Englishman stays overnight in a medieval town in Northern France with terrifying results. On arriving there the narrator remarks: "I felt a new strange world about me. My old world of reality receded. Here, whether I liked it or no, was something new and incomprehensible."[261] St Malo, noted Mary Butts in October 1929, "is that sort of town" (in fact Blackwood based it on Laon, north-east of Paris). When expanding on this comment, her description evokes the same kind of atmosphere as she had perceived the previous autumn in Paris:

> Began to grasp it [St Malo] as a 'whole', as one, as an organism, take pleasure in its streets: sense them and feel out for spots:[262] eg. the little bare square at the top with the wooden erection.
> Last night, looked out of my window onto the moon-washed stones ...went prowling among the Malinois, also Sunday-prowling: enjoyed it. Fell upon—I felt that I should upon a ghost book, E.F. Benson, a Tauchnitz, but mostly new.

The book she found was a collection of Benson's stories called, appropriately enough for her preoccupations, *Visible and Invisible* (1923). In line with her study of Supernatural Fiction begun in the summer of 1928, she analysed Benson's stories for their supernatural characteristics under "several well-defined heads: *Fun at the Mediums, sense not scepticism,* 'Mr Tilly's Seance'; *the Man of science who goes too far—scientific overweight,* 'And the Dead Speak'; *the evil elemental,* 'Negotium Perambulans'."[263]

The collection also fed Mary Butts's imagination, her powers of perception. She was impressed by Benson's statement that "eternity isn't a quantity, it's a quality", since it corresponded with what she felt about the relationship between time and space. On the 14 January 1927 she had commented in her diary: "it is this splitting up of events into an irregular, inconvenient, positively demented time sequence that bitches things up. Why can't the relative things happen together, simultaneously or in close sequence? Instead we live like jugglers, keeping a dozen balls in the air." In St Malo she reconsidered this subject with an uncharacteristic degree of self-confidence:

> It seems to me that people like me, for I count myself among the people of genius have those fifty-fifty experiences of joy and its opposite just

> because they are pressing through all the time to the true nature of being where the pairs of opposites are united. Only, being still subject to our space-time contraptions we 'live along the line' like the rest of the world, only rarely aware, and that partially of the true nature of existence.
> Names for it—, eternity: true present: reality: the-thing-in-itself: union of the pairs of opposites : union of the five senses and their prostration (China).

While she mused in this way, she continued to meander around the city: "Went exploring on the ramparts in spring hot light—all the blues. Then in the old town where I found wynds, and a carved door, the lintel turned over in two rounds of stone—might be waves or might be roses: prospects of ancient houses and massed chimneys. Once, on the ramparts, like a wound, a gap—one of the great old houses of the Ship-masters which sweep round them—pulled down; its carved, plain hearths resting naked in the wall of its neighbour. Lots of splendid lines, and steep alleys where the rock of S Malo rushes up to its crest." On one of her wanderings outside the city walls, she felt:

> something 'coming through', an awareness, fugitive and persistent, of the nature and the relation of things. *Description* : an almost alarming indifference to 'our' time: a sense of 2 or more objects or series in o.t. [our time?] converging on one another. As out on the beach towards Paromé there were the lanes, each lane between the houses an open mouth towards the sea: the parallel tree-trunks below the sea-wall, out of the sand: the rain and cloud-steams : a bit of [William] Morris' poem—'rough wind, art thou unhappy?' : these, and others only felt, seemed to be balancing together, poised like piled matches to form a *one* : a 'thing', whose being as a unit implied an existence of a very little understood kind.

As she concluded herself, "Of course, I hadn't all the terms of the thing, as a series. I only felt a whole, or rather described some parts of a whole I could only feel and only that in part." It was here in St Malo, in this atmosphere of heightened sensitivity that Mary Butts fell in love with Gabriel Atkin.

* * * * *

Gabriel Atkin

Remember *how Gabriel slept—coolly like a child in the bed across this old, wide haunted room—if he goes on like that, there will be life again and peace.* —MB, diary entry, 24.10.29

Because love is
Because of what love is
Love is the vision in extremes
(We who know what love is)
And it is not possible to love
Any people but these.
—MB, 'Thinking of Saints and of Petronius Arbiter' (1931)

On the 5 October, as she left for St Malo, Mary Butts was still suffering from a sense of loss over Sergei and remarked in her diary: "Another Sergei odyssey, begun without him." As she fell in love with the thirty-two-year old Gabriel Atkin, so she told him of her regret over Sergei. He knew Sergei and Mary Butts's obsession with him. The previous year he had written sympathetically to her: "My dear—about Sergey. Is he with you? If he is, don't say that I asked, is he a cad, or just silly? He has talent and charm—why should he not [while] away his life with the scum of the Riviera? Amuse yourself if you like, good Heavens—but stop at a given signal: the signal that only you yourself can give."[264] Initially at least, her love for Gabriel Atkin may well have been a kind of compensation for the futility of her love for Sergei, as well as the feeling that she had in some way failed him, which continued to sadden her. In March that year she had commented in her diary: "This love that is, if not useless, unusable by SS [Sergei] must spread itself in the world. Does so without effort. *Seigneur, since it seems there to be uneatable food, send someone to enjoy it who I also can enjoy.*"

The new friend Mary Butts had to "enjoy" was William Park Atkin, who preferred to be called Gabriel. Born in South Shields in 1897, his talent for drawing was already noticed when he was a schoolboy at the Royal Grammar School at Newcastle upon Tyne. He began his art training at the King Edward VII School of Art, Armstrong College (now King's College), London, but enlisted when the First World War broke out. After the war he resumed his studies at the Slade and in Paris. His friend, Osbert Sitwell, described him as:

> by nature...an esthete.... He was boundlessly kind, generous, and, as a young man, full of humour and life; and these qualities, too, make themselves felt in his drawings and paintings. Extremely versatile, the things he admired had an inner unity, were co-related. In a time —the end of the World War and the beginning of the peace—when most people of taste looked down on such composers as Verdi and Rossini, he worshipped them, would attend any concert which included their works, and looked forward for weeks to a performance of the Barber of Seville or of Traviata. He would spend hours improvising on the piano in the manner of Verdi. In literature, too, he showed considerable discrimination, and indeed, no doubt helped to discover various talents. (He was an early admirer of Ronald Firbank, for whom he would have made a perfect illustrator)... As for pictures, he liked the English Early-Nineteenth century painters.... But most of all, he loved the pre-Raphaelites, and his drawings are some of the only English modern drawings to be influenced by them. For the rest, the Russian Ballet affected his work much more than did any contemporary paintings. But, perhaps because of this absence of direct influence, his drawings remain very individual. He was trying to follow paths of his own, along which he must be his own guide.... He was in competition with himself, and no one else.[265]

As a young man he had moved in the artistic circles of London and the Continent and is said to have been sculpted by Epstein. Certain of his talents he may have been; he lacked constancy in his personal life as Mary Butts was to learn to her cost. By the time she knew him, he had had a series of lovers, both men and women, including Maynard Keynes and Siegfried Sassoon.

Almost immediately on arriving in St Malo, Mary Butts remarked, as she had earlier in relation to Cocteau and Mireille Havet: "G's catholicism, I respect and find beautiful." From the outset she was aware of her "love—and the 'ambivalence of its emotion'", recording about their first two weeks together: "And so we went on, swinging from one side to the other of this shore and its emotions which I know to be part of my life, to be reckoned on 'for keeps'; and out of which something of enduring virtue could be made. Gabriel fulfills the saying *'let them know, let them love, let them remember'*. If in certain small ways he will direct himself, it should go well with us. Stupid and abominable and mean things have happened, and magic and bright and sweet. 50-50."

"Certain small ways" was in fact an unusual understatement for Mary Butts—a sign perhaps that she saw herself at this stage equal to the challenges facing her if their relationship was to develop. The problems originated from what she later described as the "'soft' turn" in Gabriel Atkin. "Will G come out all right?" she asked herself on the 31 October. "So I pray, desire—etc—'but what are desires...even prayers' to the set of a character?" There were three aspects of his character which troubled her: his long-term alcoholism ("we are as up against the alcohol business as ever people have been. Put one way—Gabriel still prefers Pernod to me"), his inability to commit himself to one person (a fact which was made more complicated—in Mary Butts's case—by his strong homosexual desires) and a tendency to waste his prodigious artistic gifts.

She had been excited at the thought of seeing him again after her three days in Paris: "This time twenty-four hours ahead I shall, I should be in Gabriel's arms—O Seigneur let it be so." She was therefore distraught on her return to St Malo, because, "what was he doing while I was jolting down four hundred miles and more all night to reach him? Having a boy." In her diary she tried to console herself by giving examples from his youth when he had shown a similar lack of commitment. "Just as he no doubt once preferred any light letch to Siegfried Sassoon; accepting the five years sorrow after with a sort of fatalism." And: "if MK [Maynard Keynes] found it intolerable, what re-action could Gabriel expect from me?" In *Elders and Betters,* Quentin Bell remembered Gabriel Atkin as a young man. It is not a flattering memory:

> Maynard twice ventured to bring his boyfriends to Charleston. The first occasion was a disaster; the disaster was called Gabriel Atkins. I do not remember him at Charleston, which perhaps is not surprising for the legend is that when Gabriel arrived all the regular inmates fled, leaving Maynard to deal with the situation that he had created; nor did they return until Mr Atkins had left. I came to know him well—rather too well—in later years when he was the companion of Mary Butts, by which time he had I suppose lost those charms which made him the toast of British sodom. Even so, I am astonished that he should have been Maynard's guest and catamite.[266]

Mary Butts was particularly hurt by Gabriel Atkin's "flings" because, in contrast to her relationship with Sergei, her love affair with Gabriel Atkin was also a passionately physical one. On the 27 October she recorded with delight "G and I together— A virginity gone west— Je plaisante [I'm joking], but the joy can't find words—yet. And Gabriel this morning is full of pride and swank and peace: sang 'O! Mistress mine', to me, and old songs from the halls, and carries himself with an air and a spring that is all new and wholly blessed. God keep me worthy of this fair lover. Keep us together: with adventure, with peace. For Love's sake." Perhaps here she felt that she could succeed in the desire she had noted in May 1927 "to make my lovers well, sense powers liberated in them, fears in the dustbin, raw life taken in and coming out translated." In late October on one of her walks in St Malo she spent some time "in the Cathedral—prayer for and a dedication of our lives and of our love".

Throughout the rest of their stay in St Malo she experienced "intervals of paradise", whilst being haunted by the fear: "Will G come out all right?" Seeing him asleep on their bed, she noted: "he was like a golden arrow when he was a boy. Now, I think he might have gone out with the tides if I hadn't come." A fortnight later she wrote of how Gabriel Atkin "wants me and through me, life, art, adventure. Does he want life in that relation we call 'truth'?" and answered with lucidity: "I think not." In contrast to her relationships with Sergei, Mireille Havet and Harcourt Wesson Bull, amongst others, "with him [Gabriel Atkin] I'm no spiritual leader. All the same, I love this man and know that there is quality in his love for me." However self-important this claim sounds, she was quite accurate about the beneficial effects for him of their relationship. His letters to her the previous year show how much he appreciated, indeed needed, her encouragement in order to work. Writing to her in France from his aunt's house in Newcastle, he had declared: "I grow increasingly despondent—which is the worst possible return I could give for all your gracious gifts of good cheer. It is fear that I may not justify the nice things you have said about me; but we are all apt to go through these drab moments.... Not that that's any excuse for my plaguing you with a series of unbecomingly mournful letters! I only mean to show my good intent, that the good of you stops the foolishness that had really become my course." Meeting Mary Butts in Villefranche in 1928 had been crucial: "I was really very hard up for someone to say an encouraging word to me that afternoon when we walked round the ramparts of Villefranche. It sticks for ever, my dear..."[267] Her letters have not survived, yet they clearly increased his self-confidence:

> Your letter was a supreme joy; I am too dull to compete with it, but I must write to you because it's like touching your hand—the sort of thing I suppose Tennyson meant to say. Only your voice, across the postage system, is so much alive! And it wasn't a sermon at all—there was just the delicatest trifle of a hint of a rebuke that I should be such a rotter as to grouch at being stuck here, where there are really no worries, excepting perhaps the greatest—Boredom. But you help me to conquer that, and I've done a hell of a lot of work.[268]

In yet another letter he acknowledged where his shortcomings lay:

> I am working so terribly hard on a new venture—that I feel a bit addled and stuffy; yet it's good. And if I come to Paris (for all the work is a means to an end) I hope that if you catch sight of me betraying an inclination to loiter at a cafe, you will say firmly: "go back to your garret and do a drawing." And I shall go like a lamb. And I shall feel quite pleased with myself, and you, and everybody—and even the drawing, probably. The trouble is that hitherto everyone has said "oh don't go! Do have another." Or if I haven't been there, "Let's go

> to Gabriel's—he won't mind." But I did, very often, if not often enough. It was all very funny then, but it isn't so amusing to look back upon as it might be. It does a hell of a lot of good to have a gentle kick now and then. I say all that because I'm certain that you wouldn't mind giving me the kick I needed.[269]

Despite all his good intentions, it was quite different when they were confined within the ramparts of St Malo, where Mary Butts herself remarked that she was "not in a normal state". She was acutely aware of both their faults and the incompatibility of their personalities. After one argument, she "fell into a fit of useless, nervous temper—the sort which helps no one, anyhow. We were both stupid, and I, granted my temperament, bitterly provoked. But I was silly and useless—in a nervous rage his faults provoked." On the 17 November she recorded: "G and I discover, piece by piece, all that is worst in our characters. Procrastination and Impatience—will they ever make a match of it and one correct the other's faults? They might—they could—if I could keep my tongue—'buttoned' like a sword which is *not*, in this case, to be used in a duel to the death. And also, if, Gabriel would use his common-sense about it, look at the situation with some of *his* humour and detachment. When he is hurt and upset he is apt to forget that I'm a person full of parts and passions and needs like himself.... Then I limp off like a hurt animal to hide; and like a hurt beast am very apt to snap—and worse."

When Gabriel Atkin had been sober for a few days, she was "very proud of him...the Gentlest Shepherd...and the Golden Boy and Monseigneur." However, when he would not respond to her plans for him she was despondent because her well-being was so bound up with his: "We bitched our walk, but what did my disappointment matter?" she moaned in mid-November. Yet she knew how crucial such perambulations were: "These walks are a part of my cure. As necessary to me as food: my great deterrent against taking 'stuff'." Worse than these individual disappointments was the "shock" a few days later, when she "learned G's 'anti-feminist'—rotten word—opinions, instincts, 'unreasons', prejudices". As she realised on the 20 November, "the sun has not yet risen on the day when he, unconsciously, says 'human being' first, then 'woman' as a distinction, an afterthought." It is a measure of her optimism at this time that she added: "That will come though."

In this way the days passed, see-saw fashion, as the lovers went from crisis to elation to crisis again until on the night before their departure Mary Butts recorded how "slowly, round the corner, as it happens always on the knight's move—We began to re-make and deepen our relationship. Last night I shall never forget... Over again we sealed our bargain...[to] make the new life we are constructing together. *Not* an affair, a work to be done in a day—*Not* a love-affair that I've ever had that is not of use now to help me perfect this one." Throughout the weeks in St Malo she had begun to sort out Gabriel Atkin's financial affairs. His father was now dead and the trusteeship of his affairs was held by his Aunt Anne Weir. In her diary Mary Butts wrote a large number of drafts of letters (she soon even devoted a notebook solely to his affairs) to be sent from them both in order to find out and then recover control of the capital and the property left to him. This was crucial as they had decided to marry. Mary Butts's announcement of it to their respective relatives is characteristically urbane and idealised. On the 30 October she wrote to Mrs Weir: "We are much the same age: as Jane Austen says—We have friends in common, careers, tastes, affections. I am just financially independent and hope soon to be more so. I *can* see a very lovely life ahead of us—and on my honour, he is already hardly the same man (or I the same woman) as the two who met at the station here about 3 weeks ago."[270] To her mother she announced the situation in the following manner:

> A very sweet and dear friend who has been asking me to marry him for years—goes on asking. He will be wealthy, which is something—has marvellous gifts and we have most tastes in common. I can't decide. He is delicate—almost too much in love. I *don't* believe it (nor value it as I should): a catholic: almost unselfish! A gentleman—old Asquith loved him dearly and the Sitwells do and Maynard Keynes. But he's wholly impractical. All my sanest moments have been passed in getting him to cancel powers of attorney he had given—during a long absence from England—to a set of scoundrels who have robbed him—and in comforting a grown man of my age because scoundrels exist!"[271]

The extent to which Gabriel Atkin had been denied money owed to him is unclear, although he was without doubt quite impractical; what is certain is that Mary Butts cast his familial and financial predicament in the same terms as her own. On the 14 November she wrote of the "customary opposition to our proper good...[from Gabriel Atkin's] older people, at least" and to a friend of his, Trevor Stevenson, she lamented the fact that "the marvellous chance we're offered may not be realised because of extra fortuitous difficulties thrust in on us from outside—Finance...our families."[272]

Yet she felt hopeful at the end of their stay in St Malo: "Tomorrow we go to Chartres and have our Sacre. Then Paris and our adventure." As she watched Gabriel Atkin sleeping she wrote: "It is the last night in this old, warm, ugly, large, haunted room.... In it I have loved, suffered, crept, prayed, dreamed, fought, loved. Won." And yet, she wondered: "Will our ghosts hang about this room—a film of our passion. Will future travellers hear that rare laugh of his, that laugh that haunts me. And what is this patch of eternity we have become aware of, spun-out on a time thread?"

* * * * *

IN 1944 THE CITY of St Malo in which Mary Butts had felt so much at home was almost completely destroyed in an allied bombing. It was rebuilt, reconstructed along the same lines, so that on the original site in the Grand'Rue where the Hôtel Central had stood, a new Hôtel Central stands. Yet of the St Malo where they had stayed, very little remains for Mary Butts and Gabriel Atkin's ghosts to haunt.

CHAPTER SEVENTEEN

The Last Time I Saw Paris
November 1929 – June 1930

Once back in Paris in late November 1929, Mary Butts saw her friends again, such as Walter Shaw, Mireille Havet and Jean Guérin—all, that is, except Sergey who seemed to have disappeared.[273] Gabriel moved into 14 Rue de Monttessuy as she continued to sort out his financial position. She got her old friend, the lawyer E.S.P. Haynes, to act for him and a number of letters "made and signed" by Gabriel were actually drafted by Mary Butts in her diary until the 9 December when she recorded: "Note-book set apart for Gabriel Atkin's affairs—it is rather like coming back to one's home after it has been let, to have this book for intimacies and adventures."

Although on the 6 December she had taken delight in rewriting 'Greensleeves' as

> Gabriel is my joy,
> Gabriel is my delight,
> Gabriel is my heart of Gold—

Mary Butts's "young Apollo", her "lost and wounded Prince", was not able to live up to her expectations. As with Sergey earlier, she called her relationship with Gabriel Atkin at this time her "fairy tale": "When joy comes to Gabriel it *descends* on him like a gift, a kiss from the Holy Spirit—He—It—there is no distinction, is the *cleanest* thing (purest if one likes the word)—that I have ever seen." Yet Cocteau's comment that they had to pay for the fairy tales they were living out was coming true, since her elation turned into a confession on the 9 December that she was taking "far more 'stuff' [heroin]—so as not to suffer physically" because Gabriel Atkin no longer wished to be her lover. She described his decision as one of "unwisdom", which left her "un-tuned", since "it was our physical relation which was holding me on to life—physical life. It was, apart from the infinite good the pleasure of it had begun to do my body, a sign of life, of earthly continuance. I was beginning to get into the state when one prepares the body for death by loosening all but spiritual or 'mystical' contacts with the world. In his arms I re-attached." This was by no means the end of their physical relationship, however. By the 15 December she attributed their "bad break" to Gabriel Atkin's ill-health ("[Dr] Tivel's pride in his cure") so that "we have ended this evening in…a conclusion of harmony… O Aidos! O Sophrosynê! Make me to understand the nature of his difficulty. O Daimon! whose name I search for and have not yet found, make me aware by what knight's move we may leave it behind for another move in the sacred game." The difficulties in their relationship, however, would never be satisfactorily resolved.

Mary Butts was also distressed when Mireille Havet not only refused to repay the money she had spent on her during her illness but also told mutual friends that she had taken money for herself that Mireille Havet's uncle, Pierre Corneiller,[274] had sent. Since in her own journal Mireille Havet raged against Mary Butts in much the same way (and given both women's inaccurate accounts of money owed to them), it is not possible to know who was right in this case. Several other testimonies have shown, however, that Mary Butts was generous to her friends and there is no doubt that she did save Mireille Havet's life in September 1929. She believed that Mireille Havet was jealous of her relationship with Gabriel Atkin. Matters came to a head on the 16 December when Mireille Havet refused to lend her 10 francs for a taxi when it transpired that she had over 250 francs in her purse. By the time Mary Butts left for England on Christmas Eve, her friendship with Mireille Havet had come to an end: "So much for the heroic girl I nursed here,"[275] she wrote at 14 Rue de Monttessuy on the 23 December. "Who talked like an angel, showed to me what I had shewn her of Paradise: shewn, how it was possible to create the kingdom of heaven here now: of the meaning of good-will. Since I returned [from St Malo] she has left me in shameful difficulties and shocked me, she is reversing all our past: making an evil sequence—a mystical work of evil it needs no mystic to observe and appraise."

For most of late 1929 Mary Butts's spirits were low. She found time to read Samuel Johnson's *Lives of the Poets* ("admirable set of short novels, and in judgement a warning for all time") and continued to assess her dreams and perceptions in the light of Dunne's theories. Yet apart from several ideas for poems, she did little writing and consoled herself with the comment that "while I doubt, or pretend to doubt if I shall ever write again, these note-books fill apace. The day's tiny discipline and part salve to my conscience." Depressed and demoralised, she crossed the Channel to spend the Christmas week in London at 3 Buckingham Gate with her mother, Tony, Camilla and John Rodker.

There were enjoyable moments to end the year: teaching Camilla the Greek alphabet; going with Rodker on New Year's Eve to see *Journey's End* (R.C. Sherriff's powerful play about the First World War written the previous year).[276] She also noted in her diary that she must "*remember*: walking up the Mall to the Palace, the rose-bronze, the turquoise and various jades of the sky laced with bare twigs—A strictly unpaintable picture." Whilst annoyed by "John's sick and sombre and rather mean presence", she conceded with her usual honesty:

> As to his remarks on my work. He is quite right. I wanted to explore the hitherto un-explored, and having partly done so, must now shew its relation to broad, common phenomena. Have just found the way to the relation through what I understand, and, above all, to what I am *sensible* to in the recent discoveries in physics.[277]

She was acutely aware at this time of missed opportunities. "How much I have lost in my life," she wrote in the night between the 30 and 31 December, "through over sensitiveness—which makes me prefer to give rather than to take. Now that I am desperately poor, I see the inconveniences. I should have visited more: sold my work more: acquired more gifts from my men friends while my youth was still fresh."

She and Gabriel Atkin sent each other affectionate letters—as she noted in her diary: "Absence from him strengthens my love." Yet the old disagreements with Mary Colville-Hyde continued as Mary Butts felt once again that her mother favoured Tony over her. They argued over what proportion she would receive from the proceeds of the sale of the Holbein painting and after returning to Paris she wrote to her mother: "When you say 'if I help you when the picture is sold, you'll only lead a wilder and more extravagant life'—the real answer is... Suppose you did really help me and my life had a chance to become all that it might be—having the things I need, and my health restored and some peace..."[278]

After a rough crossing Mary Butts arrived back at 14 Rue de Monttessuy at midnight on the 1 January 1930. The next five months were to be her last in Paris.

* * * * *

Adieu, Paris

> *'Every day a new adventure' [Gabriel] said one heavenly night.* Yet, *the pull* against *adventure in him is still strong, and my deadly fear is that it may prevail: write 'Finis' on our love on which so much of the adventures hang: ...it is my fear and a reasonable fear that his fear may win—finish the Prince—and incidentally me, and probably a dozen or so other people in various degrees, and finally impoverish this great, hurt, agonised world of ours which he and I among others were created to light-up and delight.*
>
> —MB, diary entry, 14.1.30

> *For Gabriel I've risked my reputation.* —MB, diary entry, 17.3.30

I HAVE ALREADY mentioned the sense of responsibility Mary Butts felt that she and her contemporaries carried with regard to their artistic vocation. In 1927, aware of the dubious reputation of the Parisian art scene, Robert McAlmon had felt moved to publish an article in its defense, entitled 'Truer than Most Accounts'. In it he declared:

> Regardless of the legend that Quarterites are unproductive, quantities of serious working writers, painters, dancers, playwrights, musicians, and sculptors were of the scene.... That Montparnasse furnishes a resident and transient background of beings futile to themselves and destructive in their false contempt of production, does not mean that the Quarter is a disintegrating force for such people as find it a convenient rendezvous for interesting encounters, or for dissipation that appears often excessive and ridiculous.

After all, as he readily conceded, "talented, hard-working and intelligent people have always had their excesses and their ridiculous moments."[279] This was certainly true of both McAlmon and Mary Butts.

Yet perhaps the American journalist, Wambly Bald, who wrote a weekly column entitled 'La Vie de Bohème' for *The Chicago Tribune* from 1929, best summed up the contradictory quality of Montparnasse in his valedictory article on the 25 July 1933. His opinion is interesting because his column was famed for its impartiality; so much so, that he had come to be nicknamed "the Left Bank's ubiquitous Boswell".[280] "Let's say Montparnasse is a handkerchief," suggested Bald in his parting column. "You crumple it up and put it in your pocket. When you go away, you take it out and wave it at your friends. It makes a pretty spot of colour on the thinning air." For Bald, Montparnasse was both "a filthy rag [and] a glad rag.... I've had a good time, I've seen them all," he wrote, giving names of the famous and not yet known artists living and working there.

"I've seen the Coupole expand over the Quarter like a mushroom or like a weight-lifter's chest, the Select go Oscar Wilde and the Rotonde Nordic. I've seen the Dôme, that palace of cheap bliss, that ugly wart on the face of the earth, turn into an American Bar. I've seen all that—..." If Wambly Bald was leaving, it was because he believed that the party was over. And his reason was summed up in the following appropriate metaphor: "You get something out of Montparnasse, and then it gets something out of you—just like bad liquor."[281]

T.S. Eliot had warned McAlmon that café-life in Paris was a "strong stimulus, and like most stimulants, incites to rushing about and produces a pleasant illusion of great mental activity rather than the solid results of hard work".[282] Mary Butts had for several years been well aware of the dangers of café society, noting two years earlier in January 1928: "A gay thought...[a friend] said...'if life were only one café after another it might be considerably worse...' For me a slight call to order, who have begun to pretend to despise them: because: the first and the best and the last of them was killed in them: by them. He who could resist, the East and the West, all pleasures of compromise and ambition, killed by a row of long-necked bright bottles in a bar without sirens." Whilst Mary Butts herself had spent many enjoyable hours in cafés and bars over the last decade, she also knew all too well on her return to Paris in January 1930 that Gabriel Atkin was potentially one of its next victims:

> I *know* the divine powers that are in Gabriel. His instincts are those of a Prince... *Only*, and in this lies my chief fear—he has not been trained to command—either himself or others: to reflect: *to reason*: to examine: be dispassionate—least of all about himself. *'Il faut être toujours ivre'* [you must be drunk all the time]—Baudelaire is right enough. Drunk—but on what? Or rather B. is half right—but with every drunkeness there must be an *equal and corresponding* sobriety. There comes the Delphic secret—that...by the creation we make of those states *contrasted*...our real—that is our immortal—Life is made. That is where our real life begins. While as to drunkeness: there is essentially only one sobriety, but an infinite choice of drunks. From the mystic blinded by ecstacy before God—to the unsteady step, sprawled body, meaningless speech, crazed judgement, *sterile* emotions. With that kind of drunkeness last Sunday Gabriel poisoned, smashed, destroyed his princely gift to me.

On the whole her last five months in France were the bleakest of her life, as her health and spirits deteriorated almost to a point of no return.

Many of her diary entries for this period focused on her relationship with Gabriel Atkin. The previous summer she had bought a record for her friends, Walter Shaw and Jean Guérin, called *What is this thing called Love?* Listening to it in mid-January 1930, she pondered the question. She knew that he had "exquisite gifts and the finest perceptions", but "oh that my Gabriel would take his life into his own hands" was her constant refrain, as he continued to prefer drink to food and work. There were still magical times, such as on the 17 January when "the ways of Providence fitted-in. The light had to be paid, the gas, the concierge—and by [the] morning's post came the cheque: the dew of solvency = the dinner at Prunier's—our first *sortie*—while as for the daimon who accompanied us—you could see the wings, their sweep and feather music." At such times Gabriel Atkin was her "Almond Tree Prince" and she his "Persephone". More often, however, she covered pages of her diary with frustration and disappointment:

> After a drunk return from a sullen Sunday's walk in black rain ... we quarrelled bitterly...and the next day—yesterday—I tortured him, tortured myself—re-wounding myself because I had allowed myself to believe again and live and enjoy. ... (He never *has* understood that psychically and nervously I'm almost as ill as he is—in some ways worse having an artist's sensibility and a woman's.)
>
> On the other hand, he has less common-sense than I—and his lack of that and his instinct to feel 'sunk' may yet sink our ship.

Whilst she wondered whether she would not be better off alone, neither of them was able to take the initiative to separate. Day by day these two talented, sensitive, disturbed people slowly descended into what Mary Butts called "hell".

She continued to see her friends, for she knew the danger of introspection, urging herself on the 22 January in stark capitals to "GO OUTSIDE WOMAN, GET OUTSIDE YOURSELF". The death of her friend, Jeanne Bourgoint, in early January had left Jeanne's young brother Jeannot grief-stricken. Like Jack White thirteen years earlier, Mary Butts felt that "Jeannot can evoke magic states and instants and accept and admit them. Voilà sa puissance! [there lies his power] (Cocteau knew this.)" Indeed Jeanne and Jeannot Bourgoint had been the inspiration behind Cocteau's novel, *Les Enfants Terribles*, published the previous year. Mary Butts spent a great deal of time with Jeannot who "came: was fed: spoiled: rested. And some daimon found a little joke to make him for a moment almost forget—when scratching behind the mirror and its frame for a lost visiting-card we unearthed—*not* the card, but 3 long nail-files, one shell paper-knife, one little 'lime' [nail-file], one Cocteau drawing, one rare stamp and piles [batteries] innumerable. But three quarter foot files! For five minutes he was a boy again." She consoled Jeannot in his grief with the same degree of sensitivity and generosity she would later show Frank Baker on the death of his friend, Marcus. In her concern, she wrote to John Rodker to see if there were any work for Jeannot in England. Because of the Depression, it was not a good time to ask. "About your young friend," he promptly replied. "I am afraid I don't know of anything; you know what unemployment is over here; but if anything should possibly turn up I will, of course, let you know."[283]

Vivian Ogilvie visited Mary Butts on several occasions during January 1930 and told her about the breakdown of his relationship with Mireille Havet. Mary Butts had not seen her since returning to Paris at the beginning of the month. "So," she commented in her diary on the 24th:

> the curtain went down [for Mireille Havet]—to rise on another act: her deadly illness: 2 new women—but this time in her even more deadly need, source after available source rejected, poisoned, used-up—or at best turned brackish—until death's door reached and there, at best, a passive tolerance more of exhaustion than love. During this it seems, except for a few insults at the start, not a word of me—for me or against me. Various angers burn round her in separate fires: her confessor it seems fed-up... God knows how many others.... But Vivien left her flat for good a staring, fleeing young man, and one whose incorruptible loyalties had been suddenly violently rejected, pitched, plunged, blown out on shrieks of her voice, tossed-out on obscene kicks given by exquisite feet into true cruelty's timeless hell.

Although she sympathised with Vivian Ogilvie—he "will recover, *not* mortally hurt"—Mary Butts "felt quite dead" towards Mireille Havet and never saw her again.

In a letter to her mother at the end of January, she wrote that "*peu à peu* I've arranged, put in order, examined, brought into line, reviewed all that I've done, am doing, could do.... Explanations won't fit in a letter—It was last summer—and a book written suddenly—that shewed me. It's as if I'd reached a place or a height and at last saw below and ahead of me the *whole* plane—country—of my search."[284] The "book" referred to was her study, "View of the Present State of Civilisation in the West" which, in her distracted state of mind, she still saw as earth-shattering. In her continuing search for "a gymnastic to catch new relations between old ideas, 'ways of seeing things'", she longed to read Bertrand Russell's article on relativity in the *New Encyclopedia Britannica* which she had glanced at in a bookshop.[285] She reread H.G. Wells's *Outline of History* (1919, revised in 1930) in February and considered why the past was so much more attractive than any future utopia:

> In E. Nesbit's book *The [Story of the] Amulet* [(1906)]—a child's book and a classic—where would any one child or not soonest be—with the children *real*, the reallest children, Cyril, Anthea, Robert and Jane,—back in the past in Egypt and Babylon or on their one visit to the greatly improved future of the world? 'Charming' as that chapter is no one would prefer either its life or its peoples to any, except *per-*

> *haps* the pre-dynastic, time we know to have been, in spite of pain, war, treachery—cruelty even.... Is this our want of imagination to *see* an actually amended, a fundamentally changed life, and changed so as to minimise pain, danger and fear. *Or* is its insipidity *not* due to us, but due to the nature of life apart from our animal-evolutionary experience of it?

It is not surprising that Wells's utopian vision should have prompted Mary Butts to comment on *The Story of the Amulet*—the "charming" chapter mentioned is itself a description of a Wellsian world. This is highlighted by the fact that Nesbit gives the boy from that future world the name 'Wells'.[286] Mary Butts's own long-standing interest[287] in Nesbit's book is visible in the following reference to it in her story 'Widdershins' (first published in 1924 under the title 'Deosil'). It is part of a conversation between Dick Tressider and his friend Brooks on the steps of the British Museum:

> 'I read a jolly fairy-story about this place,' [Tressider] said. 'Some children got a magic amulet and wished the things home, and they all flew out. Those stone bull things, and all the crocks and necklaces.'
>
> 'I remember. They found a queen from Babylon, and she said they belonged to her, and wished them all home, and home they went.'
>
> Dick looked at him with a sideways, ugly stare.
>
> 'I know. You like me, don't you, when you think I'm a fairy-boy. A kind of grown-up Puck? You like me to like rot.'
>
> 'But I do,' said his friend. 'I like the story myself, and was glad when you recalled it.'[288]

Mary Butts's account is extremely faithful to the original.[289]

In her search for answers she re-read Robert Browning's poem, 'Mr Sludge the Medium' (1864), with a sense of greater understanding and at this time Miguel de Unamuno's *Tragic Sense of life* (1913) became her most read tome. According to Mary Butts, Unamuno believed that the tragic sense of life "consists in our unquenchable desire for personal immortality and the fact that reason contradicts such hope. With him I went down like a plummet into the spirit's ocean-abyss. Reason is imperative to man, and follows him implacably to the final 'absolute' of the heart's desire and denies it. A glorious 'run over' of philosophic agonies accompanies this. From this he argues that this tragic conflict is *essential*, a fertilising mystery: that rightly seen, accepted, handled there results an austere beatitude, and even more a completeness of *living* wisdom. That the doubt of it, in fact is one of the terms of our immortality."

Given this sanction for a non-rational view of existence, and transmuting her personal life to the level of "saga", Mary Butts used the term "Ghostly Enemy" to denote anything or anyone who presented a threat to her very fragile relationship with Gabriel Atkin. Into this category came Roy Martin who visited them on the 30 January "just after the poem came out"[290] and who took Gabriel Atkin on a drinking bout. It was three days before he returned. Mary Butts fed her anxiety into the aptly-named poem 'Inquiétude' which she began at this time and which she revised on the 6 February, when she noted in her diary *"Remember for Gabriel*: when revising l'Inquiétude—he draws a picture of Mary Butts writing a poem about Gabriel Atkin by Gabriel Atkin, a valuable historical document." Unfortunately this drawing has not survived and the poem has never been published.

A visit from Gabriel's aunts in mid-February passed off tolerably but Mary Butts declared on the 22nd: "ALL THIS TIME IS THE END OR THE BEGINNING—or a part of both which has a quality not analysed." Whilst "there are times in my arms—(when it so pleases him) when he becomes flesh made in alabaster and lit from within with the first exquisite fire, the very fairness of the fairness of our God", she realised that "without a shadow of blame, he is turning again to men now. And I am utterly disarmed." Unsure what to do, she continued to watch and wait and hope that he would 'return' to her. In the meantime there were consolations. In late February on a "bright half-clouded east winded winter Sunday" she was "sustained by [the] more and more delightful and enchanting Quentin Bell", who regaled her with anecdotes. It is clear that Bell enjoyed the visits as much as she did for he wrote in his memoir that she was "a remarkable person. I read and enjoyed her books…but it was her conversation which was most enjoyable, she was tremendously good company and she helped to educate me."[291] In sharp contrast she was shocked at the "hideous, tragic piteous change" in Sergei when he turned up on the 4 March. Finally, after several years of trying in vain to help him, she was able to realise the "Secret of Sergey: that he is propitious for poetry. There is no more to be said about it or for him. Or less."

As always, she continued to write. *Death of Felicity Taverner* was slowly progressing; an unpublished poem, 'Modern Love', was written at this time, and she had the first ideas for a story completed in October 1931. 'In Bloomsbury' was published in her 1932 collection, *Several Occasions*. On the 9 March she reported that for several days Gabriel Atkin had "stayed here with me to face discomfort, hunger, harsh human contacts, every variation of the difficulties our Ghostly Enemy has thought to send. Like an almond-tree, the starved black branches are breaking into flower. From Gabriel lately I have had some very noble help: help that a man gives his mate. After these last evenings out in hell's stews, have come back to a well and a fountain of pure water."

Three black lines were drawn across the page after this entry and

Mary Butts then wrote in disbelief at midnight on the 17 March:

> Am I the same woman as she who wrote these last notes? After 9 days starvation, experience, cold, illness, despair up to this moment's respite tonight? Physically I'm noticeably changed, thinned, ivory-pallid and blue veined (not becoming.)... (Perhaps, in life, one gets one's death-wound by installments. If so, I am perceptibly nearer my end.) Learned this: Fatigue capable of producing a hitherto unknown endurance, ending in haemorrage, fever sleep of the stunned, laced with terrible dreams.
> Then: The indifference, fear, ineffective horror, avoidance, stupidity of friends...imaginative dullness...isolated—like a new kind of substance—or animal even—moving about round one. ... Evenings spent in a literal hell. (Compare with what the writer of *All Quiet*—knows.)[292] There is the March wind iced and fouled, iced liquid mud, blood-rose lights and infernal blue of Montparnasse—especially the Café du Dôme—dragged out those nights by an old woman sot—to try and find enough money so that the true life that there is in me and in Gabriel...should have enough to eat and so go on.

By March she was borrowing money from anyone who would lend it to her. On the 2nd she noted James Charter's generosity: "*Remember*: Jimmy the Barman; 'You keep your pretty things, Miss. I've known you...these seven years.' 200 francs and refused the ring.... This for a fairy-tale.... *Bless him—Bless him—Bless him. If I forget him, let this hand forget.* I don't think I should have got home tonight if it had not been for him."

In an attempt to save their relationship, Mary Butts and Gabriel Atkin travelled to Giverny at the end of March as guests of a friend, Louise Coons, who had been staying at 14 Rue de Monttessuy since the beginning of the month. Far from bringing them closer, the visit increased Mary Butts's humiliation when Gabriel slept with Louise Coons. (Until then she had thought that his other lovers were all men.) She returned to Paris in April alone and distraught. Just as with Murray Goodwin and Sergey, she was now reduced to "the dreadful game of 'making up' [Gabriel's] voice". He did not return to Paris before she left France permanently in June.

Half-starved, at times delirious, addicted to cocaine and taking "sleep-stuff", she watched herself become ever more depressed: "Dawn [30 April]: Am still up, indulging myself for the past two hours in almost acting—telling out loud at least to myself—a fairy tale." Yet even at her lowest ebb, she was partly aware of the slightly ridiculous aspects of this, adding: "J.R. would call it a dramatic compensation for a lost brother, foiled maternity, social position. So far it fits in perfectly with the freudian formulae under the circumstances." She was saved from a complete breakdown by the support of people who visited her regularly at this time, including John Rodker,[293] Jeannot Bourgoint, Guy Allen and Quentin Bell.

A friend, Agathe Paléologue, played a particularly important role in helping to translate one of her works into French. Unlike Mireille Havet and Gabriel Atkin, even at this, her weakest point, she never stopped working. Indeed the translation work led to the following declaration:

> How I owe all my failure to want of proper interest in my own proper interest. Am worn out after 3 hours with Agathe translating my own book:[294] after a chapter I got to loathe it, wonder why I had written it, while the memories made me 'emotionnée'. If Agathe hadn't held me to it, I should have run home. While her...courage and perseverance shamed me... I stuck it out.... Incidentally it appears that my prose 'runs' into German.... Every other paragraph we are held up with a thought or a turn of thought not known in french, not to be known in french or only to be admitted in french by the back-door of a paraphrase. An english felicity, if it goes at all, becomes nearly always a bald explanation—or too long, or an extravagance or an obvious translation. And where at the end is the style I've taken such years to control and vary, that virtuosity with my language where I'd reached such a point that art concealed art?

Alongside these self-doubts, she made a prediction of which unfortunately even the first part has not yet come true: "And, already, a premonition is growing up, of me translated, each work, into german, read in Germany: of a school of me in Germany: of an aging me lecturing there complete with translator and only too-profound attention: of professors driving me mad with the meaning of my meaning, and the kind of youth I don't at heart love only too ready to testify 'What Mary Butts Has Done For Me'. While, petulantly, I want Paris' favours. My snobbism *and* my heart are here."

Notwithstanding such lucid comments, her health was continuing to deteriorate. Harcourt Wesson Bull noted in his diary when he visited her at the end of May: "After I had knocked and knocked and knocked and gone down into the street again, I looked up at her window and saw a frowsy head furtively appear. At the sight of it, and remembering this was the behaviour pattern when creditors were calling, I knew on the spot that our relationship was not going to continue as before." His account written over thirty years later continues:

> Mary's flat was unkempt, she had been ill in bed, and there were medicine bottles and unwashed plates and glasses about. Immediately she asked to borrow money. Because the sum she wanted was large for me, and because I felt sure it was either for opium or for paying pressing debts that had accumulated while she spent the rent money on opium, abysmal, repeated process that meant I'd be embarrassed unless repayment were prompt, I said I could not make the loan. Indignantly, I thought it unfair of her to put me in that position.

With hindsight he felt differently about the incident. Whilst "on one level my attitude could be said to have been perfectly justified...on another level I was almost entirely wrong, and I am ashamed of this picture of the youth I was then, something selfish and hard in him, thinking of himself only, giving another no benefit of doubt, uncharitable.... 'Uncharitable', that is the key, not enough love. Mary, at the lowest ebb I have ever seen her, needed love and comfort, which I did not give and which I truly know she would have given me had our positions been reversed.[295] On that day something was spoiled, a friendship that had been good was impaired. Whatever else, it was unworthy of me, and in a sense, not worthy of Mary, either, as a matter of fact, for both of us were capable and worthy of loving one another as time was to prove, and this unhappy episode, fortunately, more than redeemed."[296]

Such redemption was a long way off however. For weeks Mary Colville-Hyde had been trying to persuade her daughter to enter a nursing home in order to recuperate. Mary Butts had continually refused, yet it was becoming clear that she could no longer stay alone in Paris. On the 31 May she noted: "These bad days—one's mind works, one can *think* as usual and feel. While it is just all one can do to put it down, a line here and there. But to externalise and *create*, one might as well be dead." A few days later she moaned: "Gabriel, Gabriel mio—you have left death sitting on the throne where we were crowned with life."

By 7 June Mary Butts had left Paris and was staying with her mother at 3 Buckingham Gate, London. She never left England again.

PART FIVE

Back to England

1930/1931

CHAPTER EIGHTEEN

"But it was Mother who saved me"
June 1930 – July 1931

FIRST DAY 'AT HOME' after these years," wrote Mary Butts a few days after her return to England in June 1930. "If Gabriel grief intolerable; a fair amount of work done—in patches—proofs, letters, corrections, notes." She wrote to his Aunt Anne in a desperate attempt to find out more about the breakdown of her relationship with him: "So much explanation and such plain courtesy I've surely the right to ask."[1] There is no record of any reply.

As to "work done"—"the *end of FT* [Felicity Taverner], what is the end?" she pondered. Apart from enjoying Evelyn Waugh's *Vile Bodies* (1930) and "one story by E.M. Forster about the machine",[2] her continued interest in the supernatural directed her reading in the early summer of 1930. Several accounts in Rupert Gould's miscellany, *Oddities: A book of Unexplained Facts* (1928), intrigued her and Nesta Webster's study of *Secret Societies* (1924) provoked admiration: "With all its imperfections, it serves me, at least, as a piece of short twine in a maze. By this I mean that her argument is literally and substantially true," she wrote on the 29 June, quoting the following footnote from the book: "'It is curious to notice how Sir James Frazer…never once refers to one of the higher adepts, Jews, Rosicrucians, Satanists.… The whole subject is treated as if it were the spontaneous outcome of primitive or peasant mentality.' This is profoundly true and for years has puzzled me and hindered me. Also JH [Jane Harrison] and almost [Gilbert] Murray," she commented cryptically.

The diary records "sickness" throughout June ending in "recovery" in her mother's flat, where "all things of beauty here I've known since I could first see and love 'as though they were persons': Mother my own Mother, back again." Re-reading this entry in June 1931, she remarked "this reads curiously" and her peace with Mary Colville-Hyde would only be brief. However, she did have the honesty to note in June 1930 that if she was alive and working, it was because "Mother…saved me." This temporary closeness led on the 1 July to her touching description: "Mother's beauty (who says she is nearly 70!) to-night in white and green, a string of jade beads and pearls. The long room sets her, and she moves about it like a goddess."

* * * * *

O Daimones, bring me one gold chance and I promise that I shall not miss it.
—MB, diary entry, 20.12.30

I'm just in love with all these three,
The Weald and the Marsh and the Down countrie.
Nor I don't know which I love the most,
The Weald or the Marsh or the white Chalk coast!
—Rudyard Kipling, 'A 3-part Song'[3]

The next entry in Mary Butts's diary is for the 19 November 1930. "For what has happened since July there is no record," she wrote darkly. She did, however, relay one rather astonishing fact: that she and Gabriel Atkin were married on the 29 October. It took place at the Register Office off Hanover Square, London. Compared to her first wedding, this was a more public affair, since Goldring wrote: "Although for the past ten years or more Mary had been carrying on a violent and noisy quarrel with her long-suffering mother, her brother Tony had patched up things sufficiently for the wedding reception to be held at her mother's flat, 3 Buckingham Gate."[4]

Once married, she signed herself variously Mary Butts or Mary Aitken. Perhaps she preferred Aitken to Atkin[5] because she felt the latter to be vulgar, with its evocation of the First World War private soldier in Kipling's poem 'Tommy':

O it's Tommy this, an' Tommy that, an' 'Tommy, go away';
But it's 'Thank you, Mister Atkins,' when the band begins
to play—
The band begins to play, my boys, the band begins to play,
O it's 'Thank you, Mister Atkins,' when the band begins
to play.[6]

In November the newly-weds "went for their honeymoon to a house lent them by Gerald Reitlinger, the painter".[7] It was a small farm in the hamlet of Little Thornsdale, Iden near Rye in east Sussex. Apart from a few short trips to London, they extended their honeymoon by making it their home until late April 1931. During this six-month stay Mary Butts slowly regained her health, spirits and a capacity for hard work which would lead to a steady flow of publications from 1931 until and beyond her death in March 1937. At that time the couple's long-term plans were vague: "We might stay in this land" she confided to her diary on the 11 January 1931 or, as she wrote to the landlord of her flat in Paris later that same month, "J'espère de me réinstaller là en mai prochain [I hope to move back in May]."[8] In fact they did neither. After leaving east Sussex in late April 1931, the couple would spend the summer in Newcastle at the home of Gabriel Aitken's Aunt Anne, moving back down to Chelsea in late August where they would stay until 1932. Only then would they settle down in their own home, far removed from both the south east and the north of England.

Unaware of the travelling ahead, in November 1930 Mary Butts was enchanted by what she called the "Apple land" of Little Thornsdale and its environs. As always, it was the joy of exploring the countryside that revived and nourished her physical and imaginative life. "Am very near the 'magical' truth of this country," she declared on the 19 November. "For example—that in the valley orchard past Little Thornsdale it is always summer. It is a hollow land,[9] and there the rabbits snub us, bobbing slowly away from us, scuts up. And, in the lane towards Peasemarsh woods there is a tragic stretch—where it runs down to the stream-bottom, before the sharp hill and the manor-house." On her fortieth birthday she expanded on the 'magical' atmosphere of the land:

> Remember, yesterday, enchantment on the marsh. First the pearl-day, then the swans: then across the grass to meet them again coming down stream—the absolute whiteness.... *Then* the green cliff that ends Oxney and on the other side of the isle marsh for ever. I have known all along that that green cliff is one of the 'places', a temenos. England once began there (until 1300c?)... And to go up it was part of the sacra, the ritual.... Back looking towards the Weald, and day going out in a storm of opal. North across the march, along the Rother. The first star came out. I was staring and it sprang out of faint blue, not there and then there. It is always like that. Why?

As the months passed so she wandered near and far, from a short stroll "down [the lane] which was like a green transparent corridor 'magically' under the sea" to a longer walk on the 6 January 1931 "from Dymchurch...through New Romney to Broadlands from lunch till starlight across the Marsh". She was continually discovering new delights such as the walk from Wittenshaw by the Marsh and Iden Castle. The experience of being "out before the snow" in early January prompted the following eye-catching description: "The distance across the March-Oxney cliffs—the high plants of the Weald were the colour of blue jade, and the trees like red veins under the ceiling-hung grey sky." Her interest in the area led her to read William Holloway's *History of Romney Marsh* (1849) as well as attending a local archaeological meeting in mid-February.

During the "perfect days" in Little Thornsdale she recuperated through these long walks and the light farming "work we have to do" which included looking after chickens ("the soft fire warmth of eggs under the hens"). The restoration of "Gabriel in his beauty and mine" in this quiet retreat inspired her to copy out the following lines from Æ's 'Ancestry' (1930) because of their aptness:

> When thy lovely sun has been
> Wasted in a long despair,
> World-forgetting, it may look
> Upon thee with an angel air.
>
> There was never sin of thine
> But within its heart may dwell
> A beauty that could whisper thee
> Of the high heaven from which it fell.[10]

Quite apart from reading poetry, she commented on the "books read of all sorts" whilst in Little Thornsdale. From studies concerned with the supernatural on which she made extensive notes (Mary Lewes, *The Queer Side of Things* (1923); Eugène Osty, *Supernormal Faculties in Man* (1923); Theodore Besterman, *Some Modern Mediums* (1930); Gustave Geley, *Clairvoyance and Materialisation* (1927)) to a range of "shockers". "Best Murders," she noted on the 7 December, were by "Dorothy Sayers, Austin Freeman, Berkeley, Agatha Christie, Fletcher, Mason—Farjeon". Mary Butts was typical of her time in her enjoyment of detective fiction and wrote a number of reviews in the 1930s.[11] However, as she commented soon after her arrival in Sussex: "To begin to work again—that is difficult. Already I've begun to live—here in the pearl-land with Gabriel. Already my mind and my imagination are stirring but a fear and a fatigue 'prevent' me from writing down poetry or thought. And thoughts—ideas and poems swarm. I believe I must go *slowly*, force nothing *and* discipline myself.... For discipline—I must put down something from now on each day under the heading: 'Remember'." This exercise became a habit she would never lose and resulted in a large number of her most finely wrought descriptions and comments.

Yet in late December 1930 she was dissatisfied with herself: "I begin to be jealous and restless because I have done more work than ever I have published. And not done enough. And am doing none. And so many others are doing what I could do better. O Daimones bring me one gold chance and I promise that I will not miss it." She began writing two stories and asked her mother to send one of her notebooks in mid-January so that she might continue work on *Death of Felicity Taverner*. (In addition she asked for the Dunne book which she needed.) It was also towards the end of her time in Little Thornsdale in late April that she had the idea for the "CW book". After her return to England, Mary Butts would learn of the death of a number of friends. 'CW' referred to the painter Christopher [Kit] Wood who committed suicide on the 21 August 1930. Mary Butts was asked by his partner, Frosca Munster, to contribute a piece on him. As she wrote to Frosca when sending her the article in mid-June 1931: "Here is something about Christopher. Will it do? Better people than I will write about his painting."[12] Never published, Mary Butts's two-page article was a tribute both to Kit Wood and to the power of Dorset.[13] In late December she also noted the death by suicide of another friend from earlier years, Philip Heseltine (Peter Warlock). Four years later she reviewed his biography by a mutual friend, the composer, Cecil Gray.[14]

These deaths were not the only cause of sadness to impinge on her rural idyll. Throughout her stay at Little Thornsdale, she continued to have a certain amount of contact with the outside world. There was her "Paris courrier" which included letters from Walter Shaw and Sergey and visits from friends.[15] Yet during December she became more fearful when Gabriel travelled north to visit relatives: "There have been fits of fear, harassment, cynicism—fused into one disproportion, and a melancholy which quickly exhausts tears," she remembered on the 7 January 1931. The main problem, inevitably, was money. "Will the Holbein never sell?" she asked her mother in early February. "We can't work if we're worried."[16] Although she announced in a letter on the 19 February that "G is doing a a set of superb drawings and my new book [*Death of Felicity Taverner*] should be ready by the end of March", this information was mainly given to persuade Mary Colville-Hyde to lend her money for doctors' fees, money which, apparently, Mary Butts's trustee, Tom Swan, would "pay…back out of my tax return".[17] No money was forthcoming, however, and it is clear that the recent truce between mother and daughter was over. According to Mary Butts, this was due to Mary Colville-Hyde's reneging on a promise made when she returned to England that she would not have to worry about money again. "I'm sorry we don't seem able to come to any sort of understanding," wrote Mary Butts on the 6 March. "Can't you see that your good relation with Tony is the result of your sympathy for him and with him, and of your tolerance. You've none of that feeling for me—while I have far more for you than you'll let me show. However, argument is no use but a very *serious* thing has happened for me." She was extremely worried as her landlord in Paris was threatening to sell all her possessions ("my furniture and books...all I have taken so long to collect and need and love so much...my pictures too and the C[octeau] drawings") for non-payment of rent.[18] According to her diary this had arisen from a misunderstanding. Apparently Agathe Paléologue had arranged to rent the flat at 14 Rue de Monttessuy during her absence, but had decided after a few days to move to another flat in the same house. Whatever the truth, "if I lose the mss, two-thirds of what I have written, not to speak of my books, there will be nothing more to be said for my career."[19] Whilst this was a real fear for her, there is no doubt that such a dramatic presentation of the facts was part of a campaign to get Mary Colville-Hyde to pay. Not only did Mary Butts write to her mother herself; realising that she was likely not to prevail, she also 'attacked' the question from another quarter by writing to Tom Swan:

> I have been thinking the matter over, and feel that if you should get in touch with my mother it might be the only way to persuade her that though she has not been able to help me as she promised, it is still 'up to her' to see that circumstances are not made too difficult for me.

With regard to asking her mother for money, Mary Butts had no scruples, for as she explained to Swan: "She has not changed her way of life in any material way, so she must still be in a position to keep things steady for me. She seems anxious now to see as little of us as possible, and this would certainly be the best way for her to ensure that."[20]

In mid-March she wrote to a relative to say that she and Gabriel would be "in B[ournemouth] after Easter to fetch my small daughter from school". This was one of only a few references to Camilla during their stay in east Sussex. One of the others had been in January when she recorded a "bad dream about the child". Far from feeling any sense of neglect in her responsibility towards her daughter, Mary Butts lamented the fact, as she saw it, that she had "a child who needs me and who I am separated from". Their separation was never her fault, but always due to others' refusal to provide financial support or, more vaguely, to fate.[21]

There are no entries from mid-March until late April during which time Gabriel underwent a cure for tuberculosis in Switzerland which involved injections of gold. When she resumed her diary on the 23 April with an account of the previous two months, her husband had returned:

> Work has seemed impossible, and not doing it frets me. I hate the use — the tactile use of a pen. What has been done? Chess, music, Eddington's *Physical Nature of the Universe*,[22] some reading and Wells' questions about the state of man realised again and asked. Nervous health better. But the uncertainty of our prospects and our future pushes through like coarse, poisonous shoots through the spring, out-of-doors, birds, friends, even Gabriel, thought, imagination.... An inertia paralyses me without lessening fear.
>
> But, all the time, like a tapestry half visible behind coarse films the pattern of one's proper life is visible, weaving serenely. That goes on happening, though I have to peer through at it. Not in sequence I remember Walter [Shaw]'s letter, the spring-dusk-passion when I raced Gabriel and Philip up through Little Thornsdale. The 'visible Pan' of this country in a series identical and unique. The downs on our way to Brighton. The exquisite and incredible Gabriel at Easter.

On one of their last evenings in Little Thornsdale, during a hail storm with the "wind screaming and rain travelling, memories of the Sacred Wood and the sea", she wrote in the draft of a letter to the writer, Harold Nicolson: "It was with great regret that we listened to your last broadcasting. Your reasons rather ought, I suppose, to prevent protest, but not thanks for the unique pleasure you gave... But I suppose that I shouldn't have written and said anything about it if you had not spoken of Jean Cocteau, also my old friend. It was of you, I think, he said once: 'comme il taquine l'éternité' [how he teases eternity]."[23] Mary Butts tended to write "sent" in the margin of her diary against letters which had been posted. In this case nothing is written.

In early May they moved away from east Sussex and spent a few days in London. There she recorded a visit to the National Portrait Gallery as well as time spent with friends, including Edgell Rickword, whose second volume of *Scrutinies*, which included her essay on Aldous Huxley, had come out a few weeks earlier.[24] It particularly impressed A.J.A. Symons, who wrote to her: "I read your Scrutiny of Huxley, which has prompted me to the intention of rereading him. I had formed different conclusions, but your case is so well stated that I feel I must have missed a good deal."[25] Particularly memorable, Mary Butts noted on 14 May as she left London for Newcastle, was her first meeting with Hugh Ross Williamson. A writer and editor of *The Bookman* (he would write the first book to give serious consideration to T.S. Eliot's *The Waste Land*), he had admired and read Mary Butts's work since *Ashe of Rings* had come out in 1925. From that time on Ross Williamson would become one of her closest friends and supporters.

CHAPTER NINETEEN

Making Contacts
1931

To get all that I can done and waste no more time: leave some name and a discovery.
—MB, diary entry, 16.6.31

'O TO BE IN England (but not in Newcastle) now that spring is here' was more or less the burden of Mary Butts's reaction to Gabriel Aitken's native city in mid-May 1931. "I think of all the places where the spring is burning: in Newcastle-on-Tyne it is put out by coal. There is a war against green, asphalt driven hot across thin grass. The green and white driven out by red. The town is a black wound, old blood and a hard scar." Yet quickly she grew to like aspects of the city, such as the "Facade of the 'Lit and Phil':[26] harsh gold sunset on the Town Moor". Two weeks after their arrival she described Mrs Weir's semi-detached house at 10 Osborne Avenue, Jesmond (from where Gabriel Aitken had corresponded with her three years earlier):

> At Aunt Anne's. The entire late-victorian-edwardian interior. Would its completeness—its whole—have an aesthetic value—say to a great-grandchild? Has it one now? Where no single object has value in itself. A pattern of brilliantly kept insignificances, vulgarities and an occasional monstrosity. (Excepted two 18th Century chairs, one fire-screen, 2 stools, a tallboy in the back bedroom which is a friendly magic. Gabriel's pictures: sounds drawn from the panio and radio-set. The fires, the wood's polish and the brass: my dressing-table.)… Yet I am glad to be here. It is a friendly house and my lover is with me.

At least he was there for part of their three month visit. At various points in her diary Mary Butts mentioned some "crisis" in her relationship with her husband which may well have involved his homosexuality. Initially they got on well: attending plays ("Remember Gabriel's touch on my hand when they played that song in the theatre"), meeting his friends and visiting his old haunts within the city, as well as travelling outside Newcastle to Tower Ty, Durham and Chesters. Their explorations of the surrounding countryside and descriptions of the industrial scars left on Newcastle would figure in the pamphlet, *Warning to Hikers*, which she wrote the following autumn.

Her overall pleasure at being at 10 Osborne Ave dissolved, however, when she recorded on the 6 July:

> What hurt last night: Gabriel had just told me that if I had not come to him he would be dead. (And I think it would be true, or else unworthily alive.) Aunt Anne should know that, yet she called me aside to explain that his aunt Margaret would not help us, nor would she help us, to find a house of our own and live in it and work and be with each other and be at peace. I know all over again that people will do nothing to help love.
>
> All this hurts with a pain like a still death. It seems as though Gabriel will not face it, vexed that the question should exist and wishing to shut his eyes to it.

With her usual semi-honesty, Mary Butts conceded that "this is egotism", yet felt what she saw as injustice no less keenly for this partial self-knowledge. To add to her gloom she learnt the following day that "Jacques de Malleissye is dead. Achilles Set less by one more", and only a day later she heard that another friend had died, this time an Englishman called Gordon Russell.

Yet, notwithstanding her personal grief and disappointment, Mary Butts's output during her three-month stay in Newcastle was impressive. On the 12 June she finished a tale started at Little Thornsdale ('Two lovers found playing chess', still unpublished), completed a second draft of 'Green' and, at the end of the month, made a list of possible stories for a collection which would be published by Wishart the following spring. As was her wont, she read and read, discovering the poetry of Alan Porter,[27] analysing stories by Sheridan Le Fanu, and praising, amongst others, Rufus King's *Murder by Latitude* (1930) and Marjorie Bowen's *Old Patch's Medley* (1930). Evelyn Waugh's book on Dante Gabriel Rossetti (1928) also caught her attention:

> *Rossetti* by Evelyn Waugh— our young man with a future —
> "The romantic outlook sees life as a series of glowing and unrelated systems, in which the component parts are explicable and true only in terms of themselves; in which the stars are just as big and as near as they look, and 'rien n'est vrai que le pittoresque'.
> It is this insistence on the picturesque that divides, though rather uncertainly, the mystical from the romantic habit of mind."
> Here, anyhow, is a mind that will never be content with less than the truth of things.

Two very different books also prompted high praise from her. The first was Naomi Mitchison's *Corn King and Spring Queen* (1931), which she reviewed for *The Bookman*. "This is a book of the greatest importance. In subject it would seem to be unique, and it is likely to endure as a work of art," began her review. She explained that the book was about "Narob, a tribe of half-hellenised Scythians, after the division of Alexander's empire and before the rise of Rome. In exquisite detail their life is evoked, crystallised in the adventures and development of their young 'god' queen and 'god' king." What attracted her was not just the fact that "it is an exciting story whose excitement is absorbed by the interest in life"; it was also because "there has been nothing like it before."[28] In a review later in 1931 she elaborated on the originality of Mitchison's work:

> The art of novel writing is in a brilliant state to-day, but there is one form of it—the story told in the setting of classic civilisation and a reconstruction of antique psychology and ways of life—which has been rarely done, hardly ever well done; yet when it has succeeded at all, both popular and significant. To-day, because of archaeology and The Golden Bough, most of all because Hellenism has been a preoccupation of our race, there are promises that this kind of story telling, with its extraordinary possibilities, is coming into full use. If this is true, work like the *Corn King and Spring Queen* of Naomi Mitichison may mark an epoch, a book whose quick, entrancing life makes us free of that new world which writers ask for and people who read.[29]

A second book which Mary Butts read at the end of May had an even more direct influence on her own writing. It was Lytton Strachey's *Portraits in Miniature and Other Essays* (1931): "He sometimes parodies himself, but quel rappel à l'ordre. It was because of his 'high intellectual tradition' that I've had to make a Greek of myself". Strachey's book may well have acted as a catalyst on her own latent desire to write a classical novel, since on the 17 June she wrote: "Alexander in my mind. What happened is quite clear: *how* it happened is difficult.... (Drawings by Gabriel?)." Now, at last, she felt ready to write her account of Alexander the Great, which she called variously the "Alexander Book", "A Book on the Education of a Prince" and "Scenes from the Life of Alexander of Macedon". Writing it so absorbed her that by early August, only seven weeks later, the first draft was complete and she decided to dedicate it to Gabriel. On the 20 August she sent the typescript and some of Gabriel's illustrations to Mr Warner at Chatto and Windus with the instruction to pass them on to Hugh Ross Williamson.[30] Six days later on the 26 August, Mary Butts and Gabriel Aitken left Newcastle and moved into a flat at 105 Oakley St, Chelsea.

* * * * *

As was Mary Butts's habit, the move to London prompted a description of her surroundings: "I have almost fallen in love with [Chelsea]," she announced in early September. "It is like a country town—if it were not for the buses in the Kings Road. Windy from the river, and full of lanes and passages and walled gardens and trees. Rebuilding is being done in keeping. The shops are small, gay, individual and friendly." An entry later in the month shows that even in the capital she retained a naturalist's eye: "*Remember*: sparrows and starlings in the sycamore tree, tapping the bark and the undersides of the leaves. Leaves breaking off, and falling softly to lie, upside down, on a lower leaf."[31]

Once back in the capital she set about re-introducing herself to its literary circles. Hugh Ross Williamson was central to this aim, not least in his role as editor of *The Bookman*. As he later wrote in his autobiography, *The Walled Garden* (1956): "My chief concern with *The Bookman* was to build up a new body of young critics, who were unentangled by the racket and unafraid of it and who would do at a different and more popular level what T.S. Eliot was doing in *The Criterion* and F.R. Leavis was starting to do in *Scrutiny*." Among "many other exciting contributors" (including not only Mary Butts's friends, Douglas Goldring and Oswell Blakeston, but also Geoffrey Grigson and F.R. Leavis himself) he cited "particularly Mary Butts".[32] Her review of Mitchison's novel for the July 1931 issue of *The Bookman* had been her first contribution. From then on she would be a regular reviewer until its demise "by being merged with *The London Mercury*" at the end of 1934.[33] In the Christmas 1931 issue Ross Williamson wrote a series of what he called 'Portraits' of contemporary writers whom he felt to be important. These included Havelock Ellis, Naomi Mitchison, Richard Aldington and Mary Butts, of whom he wrote an extremely laudatory account. But this came out towards the end of her five-month stay in London; rather earlier, on the 16 September, having read her her manuscript, Ross Williamson wrote excitedly: "My dear Miss Butts, Alexander is quite superb: it thrilled me enormously—and satisfied me: your writing always does that for me: I feel so *safe* with you: you excite and frighten and explain and reveal, but you never let the reader down by an unfulfilment or an anti-climax." He suggested a few minor changes and additions and then concluded: "I've sent the ms. with your husband's delightful drawings to Eliot and *do* hope something comes of it. I should think it would interest Eliot himself. If not, may I try again? It is too good of you to have mentioned me in the preface.[34] I am grateful for that, though you really shouldn't have troubled. But I am a thousand times more grateful for the book, which is an inspiration."[35] She was delighted. "Dear Mr. Ross Williamson," she wrote back a few days later. "I am not able to tell you the pleasure your letter has given me. I could have no greater satisfaction than that you should have enjoyed the book. If Eliot decides against it, do anything you like with it. Cape might be interested. He used to want to do something of mine. Your criticisms seem to me wholly just.... I hope it will get published soon. I've faith in it..."[36] Unfortunately this faith did not result in an early publication, as I describe in a later chapter.

However, in the autumn of 1931 Mary Butts was hopeful. She was also able to announce in the above letter to Ross Williamson, that "Wishart has just accepted a book of short stories." The collection was due to come out the following January although in the event it was in March 1932 that *Several Occasions* appeared. The agreement as to its content must have been a fairly vague one, since 'In Bloomsbury', only completed in October 1931, was included. While in London she also worked at two other stories. The first began life in late November with the following idea: "For a story. The faked ghost who comes true." This would form the basis of her splendid story, 'With and Without Buttons'. The second was 'After the Funeral', which she had started four years earlier at Mary Reynolds's suggestion. Both 'After the Funeral' and 'With and Without Buttons' were completed in 1932 and published in a posthumous collection.

Shortly after her move to Chelsea Mary Butts began to revise her manuscript, "View of the Present State of Civilisation in the West". "It was the pride and wonder of my life and should do. The question is how to revise it...transform slang and sentiment without losing its vitality. Turn passion into art without killing it." At first she wrote: "I think it can be done," and began work on "the introduction [which] is too long and repetitive." Yet after a few days' editing she began to wonder: "How much connected sense is there in all this?" Although she worked on the manuscript on and off throughout the autumn, she never created a draft which satisfied her and eventually laid it aside. On the 24 September she recorded "the kind of day on which one would write a masterpiece if one could think of a masterpiece to write." Whilst no idea for a masterpiece was forthcoming, this unpublishable manuscript did inform and inspire a great deal of writing at this time, not least the two pamphlets, *Warning to Hikers* and *Traps for Unbelievers*, which she wrote in October and November and which were published the following spring. It also led in early October to a series of notes on her *Personal Experiences of Supernormal Perception*. Under this heading she considered, amongst other examples:

> *Telepathy:* variable, sometimes frequent.... I believe I am more aware always than my conscious mind will admit, or 'let me notice' of what people are thinking or about to say.... *Future 'Awareness':* sometimes

> very strong, on Dunne's pattern.... And Major VG and his wife at Versailles.[37] Doubtful about my dreams though for some weeks I've kept a strict record.... *Automatic Writing:* Have been able to do it for years, do it very rarely now since the extraordinary spell after CM's [Cecil Maitland] death. Then, at that time only, I was *made* to do it, with the results that still seem significant....*General 'Awareness':* This by far the most common... At the hour of my step-father's death...after contact with Gabriel's aunt Margaret... On Badbury Rings.... This awareness too, seems to overlap, to include 'spots' of other classified experiences; but it is sufficient in itself. I'm then, as Emerson says, 'in vision', and such moments have had enormous importance in my life. Their memory slips in and out like fish, not their effect.[38] *Clair-audience*: None that I remember, but bells affect me, have brought an awareness to what was strictly invisible.... *Clairvoyance*: Very little. When I was eighteen, on the Fifeshire beach, but that was more disorganised vision, a whirling in the air, and awareness. The moment after I had heard of CM's death... 'Seeing' CM go into the concierge's loge.

She also adduced in this category "the change of scene on the lawn behind Lincoln's Inn Fields". This experience lies at the heart of her story, 'Brightness Falls', which she had completed by the end of June 1931.

Mary Butts's relations with her family continued to be strained in the second half of the year. "Last night, the F H [Family Horror] mitigated by high spirits that were not altogether forced. M C-H unchanged—perhaps a little aged and gallant. T. white, bald as an egg—a pointed egg. His eyes. Suspend judgement". When she did make judgements, they tended to be unfavourable, as reflected in a dream she had in late September: "In the Park outside BPG [Belsize Park Gardens]. G and I arrived in taxi. Got out there. M C-H, T. and his S.A. [South African] friend arrived in another taxi, got out, greeted us spitefully and drove off..." Tony's South African friend was the writer, William Plomer, who never liked Mary Butts.[39]

In contrast to her familial differences, being in London enabled her to renew old friendships. In particular a reunion with Ethel Colburn Mayne in October 1931 brought both women great joy. "It is good to have found one another again; I missed you—how much I did not know till you came back again," wrote Ethel Colburn Mayne on the 20th.[40] As for Mary Butts, she noted on the 18 November:

> *Remember:* last Thursday (and more shame to me not to have written this before.) E.C.M. to dinner, the low, linked laughter between the three of us—like Mozart. All that it has been to be with her again. Gabriel and I after, when it all came back. What I became aware of listening to Ethel, not only the argument *and* the voice, but all of her, the impact of her love and wit and imagination. An experience I shall never lose, and learn to use again with other people.... The harmony between G and I was her work, and the next day's joy and the life's memory.

In late November she made a list of people to whom she would send copies of Cocteau's 1928 drawing of her as a Christmas gift. It included Poppy Vanda (who had looked after Camilla as a small child), Hugh Ross Williamson, Nina Hamnett, Angus Davidson (a young Scottish writer who would become a very close friend); Douglas Goldring, Violet Hunt[41] and Ethel Colburn Mayne. The latter was delighted with hers: "You are a dear...to introduce me to 'Jean' whose drawing of the head 'à Mary' delights me."[41] Mary Butts also saw a great deal of Douglas Goldring at this time and in November she decided to dedicate the projected volume of stories to him.[42] On the 2 January 1932 they attended the French Impressionists Exhibition together. Afterwards she wrote enthusiastically: "It is an exquisite thing to find old friendship, renewed, never altered, undestructible, and to enjoy it at such a show as that. We went, as he said to love and understand, not to show off. And that I was like a good child with a new rattle."

These old friends and her new friend, Ross Williamson, did much to mitigate the bad news in November that T.S. Eliot had rejected "Episodes in the Life of Alexander of Macedon" for Faber. His reasons, transmitted in a letter by Ross Williamson, would doubtless have been some consolation: "Eliot says: 'I agree that it is a very good book of its kind, and it certainly deserves to be published. It shows both knowledge and a special enthusiasm for the subject as well as the literary ability which I expected from the author of *Ashe of Rings*. We all felt, however, that it was not a type of book which could have a very wide public and in the present state of things we do not feel it would be wise to offer to publish it.'" Ross Williamson had taken the manuscript straight to Cape who was considering it ("Capes think it might benefit by a new title with the present "Episodes in the life of Alexander of Macedon" as a sub-title. I rather agree with them. Do you?")[43] What particularly troubled Mary Butts was the "rather awful thing" Ross Williamson had to report: Gabriel Aitken's illustrations had somehow got lost between his office and Faber's. Anxious that she should not blame T.S. Eliot, and in an effort to console them both, he wrote soon afterwards: "I'll write to Eliot tomorrow and let you know immediately he replies. Failing satisfaction, I'll ask him to lunch (I owe him one, anyhow) and *talk* about it. I want the drawings perhaps even more than you do, for, as they were in my care, I feel the guilty party."[44] Although the search continued into the New Year, the pictures were never found. The only consolation was that the loss drew Ross Williamson and Mary Butts even closer to one another.

While she waited to hear what Cape thought of her manuscript, Mary Butts continued to write. As Christmas approached she amused herself by classifying the cards along her shelf: "Change in *general* taste and variations inside taste. The old priest's card (of a fashionable church), the arts-friend, the business friend, the old-fashioned gentlewoman, the cultivated aunt, the fashionable young man…" "For a story?" she asked in the margin. Unfortunately, it never materialised. However, a great change was about to take place in her life. Whilst no clear information is given, a letter from Ethel Colburn Mayne on the 31 December inviting her to tea on the 4 January included the comment: "So you are off to Cornwall—whereabouts? But you'll tell me."[45]

The move, a few weeks later in January 1932, was a permanent one.

PART SIX

The Cornish Years

1932/1937

CHAPTER TWENTY

The Move to Sennen Cove
1932

Days at Thornsdale were a string of beads, dusk & light (& all the greens) green glass? What is the Sennen string made of? Another transparency?
—MB, diary entry, 6.2.32

On the 4 January 1932 Mary Colville-Hyde wrote to her sister that "Mary and Gabriel are going into Cornwall—having had a home lent to them she tells me." The couple moved permanently to Sennen Cove in late January 1932. It is a small coastal village on the coast of West Penwith, the fifth of the nine Hundreds, the ancient areas into which Cornwall is divided. The name Penwith is Cornish and seems to have three different meanings: "the last promontory" and "promontory on the left" make sense geographically; the third translation—"the headland of slaughter"—is rather more disquieting. Ruth Manning-Sanders, a writer already in residence in Sennen when Mary Butts arrived and who would explore this Hundred with her, provides a detailed account of this mysterious land in *The West of England* (1949):

> To many people the all-but-island of West Penwith (the part of the Duchy that lies west of a line drawn through the narrow neck of land that separates the Hayle estuary on the north coast from Marazion on the south) is the essential Cornwall. The area has a character all its own. The sea is almost everywhere in sight, and always within hearing. In times of tempest its long roar fills earth and sky; in times of calm the light winds carry its throb and rumble over fields and moors as if some giant were at work, threshing corn. The whole district is thick with folklore: the flat boulders on the moors are giants' "bob-buttons", the logan rocks their quoits, the hill forts their castles, the water-worn hollows in the stones their bowls and cups, the long flat rocks their beds and tables; and the massive lumps of granite that strew the hillsides bear witness to their ferocious battles. Trebiggan, Bolster, Wrath, Holiburn, Blunderbus—their names survive; their huge shapes, received back in the earth that made them, sleep, turned to stone, among the hills and cliffs.[1]

The most famous landmark of West Penwith is Land's End. As Manning-Sanders points out: "there is something in the very meaning and sound of those two words that excites the imagination of the tramps and the tourists alike. The name is a magnet; let it but be spoken or written—'thanne longen folk to goon on pilgrimages;'...[to its] hotel on the cliff top,...over the outcrop of pillared rocks, where the waters from north and south meet in white and swirling commotion."[2] Land's End may well be at the "end of things"; Sennen, where Mary Butts was to spend the last and most productive years of her life is, in fact, the most westerly part of England to be *inhabited*. A Victorian account, Black's 1870 *Guide to the Duchy of Cornwall,* dismissed the settlement, however, in a passing parenthesis: "[Inland lies SENNEN (population 652), above Sennen Cove, a fishing station 387 feet above the sea, and boasting of an hostelry which is quaintly called, on one side "The First" and on the other "The Last Inn in England." But the "Land's End Hotel," has a better claim to this distinction.]"[3]

This terse description does not begin to do justice to the power of the stretch of Whitesand Bay above which the houses of Sennen Cove are clustered. Even today when cars have made access to its now widened coastal road so much easier, the extremely steep and curved descent from Sennen Churchtown into Sennen Cove provides a breathtaking view over a seascape stretching out from the Longships Reef beyond Land's End to the east and the rocky outreaches of Nanjulian Cliffs to the west. Directly ahead, between and beyond these irregular coastlines lies the Atlantic which seems to fall over the edge of the horizon. As Mary Butts described it: "Below the stream-cleft, bog-patched, bush-picked, flower-scattered decline of huge rocks and moist earth, the sea lay. From headland to headland, the gold crescent of coast, filled with the sea, chord [sic] of that pure circle where the sea meets the sky."[4]

Notwithstanding Black's cursory note, Sennen Cove has its historic importance also. John Corin, the author of *Sennen Cove and its Lifeboat* (1985) (who as a child may well have known Mary Butts) agrees with Black's guide that "fishing station" is the most appropriate description of Sennen Cove. Yet his account gives a far better idea of the geology and maritime life of this hamlet:

> There is no semblance of a natural fishing harbour. Indeed there is not even a cove in the usual meaning of the term, indicating a considerable inlet in the cliffs. In fact on the east of Pedn-men-dhu the high granite cliffs give way to a steep hillside rising behind a low cliff, which is not of solid granite, with a fairly large level or gently sloping area at the western end. Beneath the cliff the shore is made up of granite boulders and originally there would have been no break in

> this seafront. The present little harbour, 'The Cove', is a manmade feature. At the eastern end of the settlement the low cliff gives way to sand dunes and the rocky shore to a long beach of white sand. It was here perhaps, centred on the ancient Chapel Idne, that the original fishing community grew up, using small beach boats. In 1337 the 'Port of Land's End' paid ten shillings (50p) to the Duchy Havener. Presumably this was Sennen and the payment ranked it equal seventh on the list with Newlyn.[5]

Corin describes how Sennen's people survived by fishing and whatever could be salvaged from the wrecks which foundered on its treacherous coastline. There are feats of courage from the eighteenth and nineteenth centuries as men braved the sea to save those shipwrecked. The foundering of ships became a less common sight when the first lighthouse was installed on the Longships Reef off Land's End in 1795. This lighthouse figures in 'Look Homeward, Angel', Mary Butts's story which considers and evokes the eerie and treacherous seascape off the headland of slaughter:

> Not a sigh of air from off the Four Winds' Playground; even the sea beat inaudible for once. This with one exception: for each alternate minute the stillness was not so much broken as underlined by man's answer to the day and night terrors of fog at sea, when the siren at Pendeen answered the gun on the Longships Lighthouse, muffled thunder alternating with a strangled moan. For even these huge voices the fog had by the throat; and men heard them as you might imagine voices from the other side of death.
>
> "Queer," said Julian, "millions of drops of water a reason why large iron ships should pile up on rocks, and be ground to pieces on equally hard stones. All by more water, lots of water, pulled about by the moon. It's a queer universe."
>
> "And we live in one of its queerest patches. That's why we love it..."[6]

A lifeboat station had been established as early as 1853, long before Mary Butts's arrival in Sennen. However the breakwater which enabled a more successful launch of the lifeboat was only finally constructed in the early years of this century with the memorial stone being laid in 1908. When she came in 1932, the four pulling and sailing lifeboats had been replaced by a steampowered lifeboat, The Newbons,[7] only ten years earlier. The new boathouse with two slips to launch The Newbons was completed in 1929. Mary Butts would have been interested in all these details for she noted with pride in her diary on the 15 December 1932 that Gabriel Aitken had been elected to the lifeboat committee.

In the 1930s, according to Daphne du Maurier's *Vanishing Cornwall* (1967), "you could still ride or drive in pony and jingle about the roads and byways of 'the headland of slaughter,' even in the summer, and be the one intruder."[8] Yet Sennen was not so remote. The Atlantic Cable had first entered England at Sennen in 1881 and Mary Butts made full use of the wireless, electrical and postal systems which served this most westerly English village. The following extract from a letter to Ada shows how unpredictable the postal service was: "As only too often happens here, *both* your letters came together. There is only one post a day and they had got sent down to the Cove and held up there, as the Cove postman won't deliver letters for Sennen Churchtown… (We live between both places). It's always happening, tho' your address was perfectly correct."[9] The post office was clearly also unused to the needs of a cosmopolitan correspondent, for learning that one of her letters had gone astray she wrote ruefully on the 29 March 1933: "I can't think what happened to it. It just adds one thing more to my complaints against our PO (Run entirely by amateurs—the Post Master, a War-Veteran, badly wounded, saying quite cheerfully that he has no idea how much parcels ought to cost, or exactly how to send, let alone charge for—say—a foreign telegram!)"[10] Mary Butts made a large number of references to the importance of radio broadcasts after moving to Sennen. In April she was sorry because she had missed a broadcast by Hugh Ross Williamson, as her wireless was broken. A few weeks later she listened to the broadcast by Filson Young, the Programme Consultant for the BBC[11] about how he drove from Chiswick to Sennen Cove in a day. She later got to know him fairly well as he had a house in the area. She also listened to a great deal of music: "Last night Tchaikovsky, Sextet Op. 70. Get the record," she noted after hearing it on 25 July 1932.

For their first four months in Sennen Cove the couple lived in Sarah's Well, a house tucked into the side of the cliff, off Maria's Lane. This road, also named Mayon Cliff Lane in the Land Registry, was not then "properly metalled".[12] It lies three hundred feet above sea-level and is accessed by turning left off the sheer road leading down from Sennen Churchtown to the sea. "Somehow we got here," Mary Butts wrote to Hugh Ross Williamson shortly after settling in: "It's all blue, a return not to the earth but the air. The house is perched on the top of Sennen cliffs, & you can only see the sea & the sky full of gulls. It's as though we were hanging in a balloon. I'm beginning to be incredibly happy."[13] Ten days later she wrote to Angus Davidson about why the place made her so contented: "We got here, about 2 weeks ago, and have been enchanted with enjoyment ever since. It's a fantastic place, not in the least like England, rich and secret and haunted.… I quite understand how otherwise respectable writers fall right down and write books on Cornwall. And why D.H. Lawrence loved it."[14] While she would not write an entire book about

Cornwall, its landscapes and coastlines inspired a great many of her articles, stories and reviews from that time on.

As soon as she arrived, she began to get to know her neighbours and the habits of the locality: "The people of the cove," she noted in her diary on the 29 January, "are all cousins & watchful & hate foreigners. (Mrs R born in Ireland & only lived here 22 years.)" In *Vanishing Cornwall* Du Maurier declares that, this "reserve…in the Cornish character…[is] deep-rooted, a self-sufficiency bred in the bone through centuries of independence and being largely his own master, with a natural scepticism and suspicion of the stranger who ask[s] questions". She also adds that "despite innate reserve the Cornish, like the Irish, are great raconteurs".[15] Mary Butts certainly listened to her neighbours' stories and wrote down snatches and shorthand versions in her journal. What caught her attention were local dialect words, such as: "'quaft'= full-up re food; 'slag'= light sea-rain; 'tizz-wiz'= scarecrow; 'maunder'= round wicker basket". That there were many such words is not surprising. Ruth Manning-Sanders points out "that into the hill forts, caves, rock clefts, and underground strongholds of this farthest corner of Britain, successive waves of defeated peoples were pushed and crowded before successive waves of alien conquerors. …that before the Celts were the Iberians, and before the Iberians, heaven alone knows who. …that until the end of the seventeenth century they spoke in a foreign tongue, that the speech of the older folk is still sometimes unintelligible to a stranger, and that it is only [since the beginning of the] century that they have had much intercourse with the outside world."[16] She also comments on another characteristic of the Cornish which in some way sounds too much like descriptions of Mary Butts herself, not to have delighted her. This is a "very marked sense of humour; a humour so characteristically native that it has deceived some people (W.H. Hudson amongst them) into affirming its non-existence. He [The Cornishman and Cornishwoman!] delights in pulling your leg, and, as his imagination takes wing, his eyes will blaze and his hands gesticulate eagerly over some long circumstantial story that has no foundation in fact. It is this gift for drama, and the solemn relish he takes in 'stuffing' you, that is so deceiving. 'They tell me that in a Cleer day those in the Island [Scilly] can discern the people in the maine as they goe up ye hill to Church, they Can Describe their Clothes,' writes Celia Fiennes. Here you have the Cornishman successfully using his technique with a too inquisitive stranger. (The shortest distance between Scilly and the mainland is twenty-five miles.)"[17] Given her love of tall tales it is hardly surprising that Mary Butts felt at ease in Cornwall.

Shortly after settling in, she began to make a note of stories which had an incomprehensible, magical quality and although unpolished, her broken sentences convey that atmosphere of strangeness which pervades so much Cornish legend and literature:

> 29.1.32 The Goblin Sands—a sand-pit, inland (on the road to St Just?) full of shifting sand, hard to get out of, where the children jump for sport. [A] girl came home & talked about a box there they'd uncovered. It was a coffin with a dry skeleton in it. Inquest. Unknown.
>
> 16.2.32 Ghost at Mayon House, the servant girl who buried her baby in the garden. Herself, her sister (who couldn't bear the eyes, & didn't know (?)) Lady H & her parson son who *laid* it. 8 years ago.
>
> 29.2.32 Remember: Philips the woodseller from Sancreed, the first time I saw him & to-day when he brought the wood. Like the men who came up on the moors near Tower Ty. As if I had always known him. And he knew it. 'A face like an angel'.

Yet whilst the tales and secrets of the area intrigued her ("their funerals where the corpse is carried and everyone goes. (Find out more)"), what particularly captured her imagination were the land and seascapes around her. Her first diary entry in Sennen ran: "*Remember*: how we are suspended here above the cove, looking out to nothing but the reef they call Cow hole [Cowloe] & the sea. The sea. The sea like a blue tiger lying on its side, stretching out a paw." She developed this image of the tiger when describing the impact of the seascape from Sarah's Well in a letter to Ethel Colburn Mayne, who referred to it when expressing her thanks for a gift of Cornish cream and regretfully declining the invitation to come to stay in Sennen in early February 1932: "It is lovely of you, and Gabriel, to want me, and lovelier still of you to say it so exquisitely. Your blue tiger will live for ever in my imagination, and how blue must be looking those incredible days, which even here are paradisal."[18]

On the 10 March Mary Butts wrote: "*Remember*: Out on the cliffs by Nanquidno [2 miles down on the cliff path towards St Just]...what I saw looking down & cannot describe." In fact she was clearly able to describe a great deal of what she saw, and the blue tiger[19] was only the first of her memorable metaphors for the sea. A journal entry at the end of her first week at Sarah's Well ran: "*Remember*: the wave-turn-over, checked by a gold sand-bank. As the water rose, before it fell over, one could see the yellow sand columns, inset, like crater-smoke in the water wall." Eight days later: "Today it was the Aphrodite Sea. Almost Botticelli's, but too high, for it's winter. The cliffs in the gold dawn, pure Mediterranean, siren water." On the 26 February she commented on how "to-day, 5 o'clock, a grey-pearl, the whole world cut out of grey pearl & black, a level-floored sea, lightly incised, dead white round the Brisons when the foam lifts." And a month later: "*Remember* last night, the moon again, on its back like a boat beside its star, the emerald & citron sun-flight into the sea." Nor did her wonder at the natural scenes about her diminish with time: "Remember: this Sunday morning", she reminded herself over a year later at the sight of the "pearl-blue day, sun in his first strength—which is surely greater in Cornwall than anywhere else in Britain." Not only does her delight echo some of her earlier descriptions of Villefranche seascapes; the superlative used here is an extraordinary compliment from a writer who is primarily associated with her love for Dorset.[20] Again and again over the next five years the journal entries would reveal her gift for articulating memorable images: in the autumn of 1935 her powers of description are illustrated in her reminder to herself to "remember: Rainbow-hair on the wavecrests running in—Shocks & shocks of iris-drift."

Her interest in her surroundings was by no means confined to looking out to sea from her window. "I shall go exploring tomorrow, with luck on the hills" she wrote in November 1932 and with her Ordnance Survey map, her copy of Edward Step's *Wayside and Woodland Blossoms* (1928) and one of her newly acquired volumes of *A History of British Birds,* edited by Rev. F. O. Morris, in hand she explored most of West Penwith on foot. When trying to convince Hugh Ross Williamson to come to Cornwall in early summer 1932, she wrote: "Truly you ought to come & see this place. We could put you up—proper baths & everything, & we could go exploring. I'm only just beginning to find out how strange it all is. Round us there are untouched miles of primitive moor which have never been reclaimed, full of hollows & stones with histories & plants & birds."[21] Her diaries for her Sennen years, from January 1932 until her sudden death in March 1937, abound with botanical and topographical descriptions. As she set out on the five-mile path from Sennen to St. Just (which she was able to do in under an hour in spite of her bad knee), she no doubt looked out for "the little sweetness that is called the lady's tresses among the rough grass of the sandhills above Sennen Cove".[22] A walk there in February 1932 was described in the following way: "To-day—Horae Aurae [Golden Hours]—On the cliffs to St Just. *Remember*—the small farm with the bar, the sunk turf before the storehouse, a hollow wave, the memory of something mediaeval, or of something once known & forgotten, something with mystery to it..." Not all her experiences were pleasant ones: "Feb 24th [1933]: *Remember*: 3 nights ago, before the great wind came on again from the north, walking up from the Manning-Sanders'[23] at dusk, the awful look of the sea. Not where it broke, but the plain of it, a terrible green-black. The sky, torn gold and purple was ominous enough—but that sea-floor. And its voice. All the way up the hill, I was violently afraid. ...that night a Pan was visible that I shall not forget."

The reason that Mary Butts wrote these lengthy comments is because throughout her work, be it a diary entry, a short story, a novel, a poem or even a review, she wanted to convey, however briefly, what lies behind what she called "the enigmatic veil". "The English countryside is worthy [of] two things," she declared in a 1933 review—"the utmost love of which a man is capable and the final perfection of art." This is because of:

> the enigmatic veil with which Nature has furnished the smallest weed in the hedge, a snail-shell, a pebble; as much as the most stupendous mountain ranges, the stateliest sunset.
>
> No use to peer & try to snatch at that veil. Yet the whole life of poet or painter, no less than scientist or common man, has been determined by its lifting—if only for an instant—if only from a quite ordinary tree, a bend in a stream, a shoulder of hill, a plant, a stone.[24]

Her writing is at its most powerful when she is trying to lift this veil. No need to go far, or too far, as she felt Eliot did in *The Waste Land*: "Why catch up with the Holy Spirit when He is hovering over Asia and saying 'Shantih'? He is in a nut in a Glastonbury thicket..." Interestingly, in this same letter to Ross Williamson, Mary Butts used both a nut metaphor and the knight's move to describe the failure of her long essay "View of the Civilisation in the West": "I once thought I had written a great work about [mystical experience]. Wrote it in a white heat for someone I loved, put it away for over a year—and then when I got it out, it was like a withered shell, without even the skeleton of a nut inside! I had written it in a lightening-flash of understanding, was convinced that I'd put down something that had never been put down so surely before, and it just wasn't there. I've let it work out on its knight's move ever since."[25]

In January 1921, at the time of their separation, John Rodker had spent some time in Sennen Cove in one of the Coastguard Cottages which still stand at the very end of Maria's Lane. This may explain how Mary Butts first came to know of this part of Cornwall as well as her introduction to Ruth Manning-Sanders and her husband, George, who were old friends of Rodker's. Yet it was the very strong pull of the land which made her want to stay in "the little farthest corner of England",[26] in spite of regret from her metropolitan friends that "London has lost you, and is much the poorer."[27] What kept her there was the fact that, as du Maurier explains: "The further west [you] travel in Cornwall, the further back [you] go to earlier days and earlier ways, to a greater degree of saw and superstition, even to a change in accent and intonation."[28] Whilst Mary Butts wanted to live in the country, she felt that the sale of her family home and the changes in the Dorset landscape made it impossible to return to the place of her childhood. Thus she "found a home in the county nearest in spirit to her own",[29] where the landscape conveyed a strange, primeval quality of equal power. It was a strangeness she felt on her "first night's walk" in Sennen Church cemetery, the very place where just over five years later she would herself be buried. This fourteenth-century Church, with its tower providing a great landmark for mariners, stands beside the First and Last pub on the A30, the main road through Sennen village (or Churchtown). To get to it from Sarah's Well, Mary Butts would have walked up from the north side of Maria's Lane along a path which started at a knight's move from Tebel Vos, across a stile and through small fields in which there was a standing stone. The path leads on to the main road very near the Post Office. The Church is on the left about a quarter of a mile down the road towards Land's End.

On her return to Sarah's Well from Sennen Churchtown after that first visit, she saw "the full moon rising, shining through the wheels of the keltic crosses," and commented: "I think with Montagu James, there are things in Cornwall at night that are better not talked about."[30] Not only did she talk and read about the strangeness embodied in this landscape, she wrote about it repeatedly, hoping, as she explained to Mr Hills, the Sennen Postmaster, that along with other writers and artists, "all we strangers come to live here might do Sennen credit." At 41, she was determined to establish her reputation as a writer in England.

In October 1933 she noted that it was partly something about the siren sea-tongue on the Cornish coast which made her feel at home because it reminded her of the sounds of her childhood at Salterns: "*At Sennen*: Gabriel and I, both of us, always hearing, through the surf, a music-noise. Only through the surf, & nearly always...cheap music, like a band, jazz & waltzes or marches. But when it is quite impossible that there should be any... I think that it has been the same with me before near the sea. But why?" Six weeks before her death she again remarked on the lifelong impact of the sea on her imagination which this time she described not as a blue but a green tiger: "On the way back from Mousehole, walking from Newlyn to Buryas Bridge—*into* the gale rising from the Sou'-West. A wonder," she declared on 16 January 1937, adding: "the dark grey and the lights came out, & the Green Tiger caught me up & the music (after Salterns) seemed to have been in my ears ever since I was born, its song as familiar, as orchestrated, as full of meaning—as say the 2nd Movement of [Beethoven's] Vth." Nor was it only the seascape which was reminiscent of her native Dorset. "*Remember*," she wrote in late August 1932, "looking up the hill from the Manning-Sanders's [studio]. The burning white light and blue shadows on the cliff grass and shrub and rock.... That memory. At Salterns the ivy-strangled pine." Also, "out in the dark," she noted after a ramble in Sennen on the

5 November 1932, "in all loveliness, making me remember Salterns and when I was a child". This memory prefigures *The Crystal Cabinet*, the autobiography, undertaken a few years later in which Mary Butts wrote lyrically of the house where she was born.

CHAPTER TWENTY-ONE

Tebel Vos
1932

IN MID-MAY 1932, after four months of renting Sarah's Well, Mary Butts was finally able to move a few hundred yards down Maria's Lane into what she saw as a real home. "All that plot of land situate[d] near Sennen Cove in the Parish of Sennen in the County of Cornwall... together with the dwellinghouse or Bungalow erected thereon and known as 'Tebel-Vos'" was sold by Ernest Barton to her trustees, Fermian Le Neve Foster and Thomas Swan, for the sum of £650-0-0.[31] It was Mary Butts who had changed the bungalow's original name of 1 Marine View to Tebel Vos, something approximating to 'House of Magic'. She preferred this "good cornish" name, she explained to Ross Williamson, because it was "a translation for what we wanted to call it, which in English would have sounded pretentious." She felt that buying Tebel Vos was the "best thing" her trustees ever did for her and, whilst always prone to hyperbole, she was not exaggerating here. She spent the rest of her life transforming the house. "I wish you could see it," she enthused in a letter shortly after moving in:

> It's one of the little houses on the cliff, the people here called 'Barton's castles'. 'Castle' is what we'd call a 'Folly' in Dorset. Mr Barton made money as a London Builder. Came to Sennen and saw it as a 'plage' and the whiskers on England's Riviera cat. Bought a great strip of the cove and the cliff, bitched the lives of the inhabitants, and then, five years ago, spoiled the Inn and built these four little houses for a start. Of course, the people he wanted won't come to Sennen, and never will, God be praised. Two are still empty. But he spared no expense. The bath boils, the oven bakes.[32]

The delight is not one of epistolary effect (although she did often adopt this frothy tone in her letters), for many of her diary entries up until her death are devoted to what can be seen as a transubstantiation of an ordinary 1920s "flat, dull bungalow...which seemed to have been chucked on to the narrow shelf of [a] cliff high above the wide roaring Atlantic breakers"[33] into an extraordinary sanctuary, a kind of shrine.

The deeds reveal that the five-room detached bungalow (or "cottage" as she preferred to call it) was the first of four houses on the south side of Maria's Lane. During her lifetime the 30-by-25 foot bungalow was not structurally altered. Some rough stones jammed into the cliff to form rather treacherous steps led down to it from the lane. There were two entrances: a back door at the rear of the property and a front door set in a porch on the seafront wall, reached by walking round the right-hand side. The gardens which Mary Butts would tend with such joy were created on the side and at the back of the house on the twenty-five feet or so of sloping cliffland, just below Maria's Lane.

A fairly dark corridor led from the front entrance of Tebel Vos where the only natural light was through a glass panel in the upper part of the door. Indeed since it was set into the cliff, the whole of the house was dark and depended (apart from a few lamps) on the light reflected from the sea and sky caught in its front windows. Doors on the right and left led into the two front rooms which looked out onto Whitesand Bay and the never-ending Atlantic beyond. On the left was Gabriel Aitken's "studio" containing his baby grand and easel. There was a fireplace on the external wall, flanked by walled cupboards. The room was quickly littered with paintings and half-finished canvases. On the right was the "salon", where Mary Butts would write at her desk and the social life of the house would take place. The room was heated from a fireplace set in the external wall.

The four remaining rooms were at the back of the house: Gabriel Aitken's and Mary Butts's bedroom in the left-hand corner. None of the rooms was large and there was only space here for a small double bed, a chest of drawers and a rail for their clothes. Beside it was Camilla's bedroom, containing a single bed and shelves under the back window. To the right of her room was a small bathroom with an airing cupboard in the short passage leading to it. The back door led straight into the kitchen which was at the right-hand side of the house. There was a sink beneath the window on the right-hand wall, along which stood the range. There was a walk-in pantry along the back-wall and a small table in the centre. Here Mary Butts's maid, Lucy, who lived in Vel-an-Dreath, would come each day to prepare the meals, which would, of course, always be taken in the salon. Such 'standards' were maintained, despite the restricted space afforded by the small house. By September 1933 Tebel Vos would have acquired in Mary Butts's imagination the same importance as her flat in 14 Rue de Monttessuy and, of course, her birthplace and childhood home in Dorset: "Quiet in the House.... That this house—with others like Salterns—is a trap for more worlds than one. For *one* more any[way]: through the candles and the shine and the wave sound."

Her first journal entry in Tebel Vos on the 15 May 1932 revealed the importance of her surroundings for her: "The move here and the beautiful things come from London. (... the view from the window which would stop any quarrel.) The marvellous 'finds' unpacking, books and curious treasures and beautiful things." In 1927 she had made a list of all the objects in Gertrude Stein's flat in Paris which had appealed to her; similarly, for the next five years the small journal heading "Added to the House", later changed to "For the House", heralded her wonder and satisfaction as she set about gathering in belongings from the various places where they had been stored as well as amassing new possessions: "We have added to the house, useful things—kept as though they were beautiful, until they become beautiful—some beautiful things: a crockery mug, dogs and birds in very coarse painted relief and a white frog inside: the paper-weight; the Wyndham Lewis floor;[34] Oswell [Blakeston]'s spanish leather pouch. The beginning" (mid-July). "Sept 17th: Added to the House: old Cornish Cottage figure—2 girls each side of a jar and above it a clock. ...Several books. Brought out and displayed in the open bookcase the Borgia book and the three Dantes, velum inlaid green and red and tooled in gold—Gabriel's superb edition." Alongside the new and recovered possessions there were *objets trouvés*, such as as the "2 glass floats, pale green and black green, found on the shore, off submarine nets". Interior decorating continued apace: on 2 October Mary Butts recorded with delight how there were now "picture rails in the passage and pictures, and the high shelf, a decoration for the kitchen, lavender crockery and red candle-sticks. Blue Wedgewood and the pine-apple decanter, which is a stately piece. When Gaby put up the yellow match-box against the crocks and the black pottery cat, it looked well. Now a shelf for spice-boxes. All this," she noted, "made a little ground-bass of pleasure, a steady tune that went on playing." This was far from being merely the love of beautiful objects. All possessions and particularly family heirlooms had for her a "totemic, magical, symbolic value", as Tony put it in a letter.[35] In the summer of 1932 there was also the "*household hint*: Polish your glass as well as your brass—but it's a magical discovery really." In this way Mary Butts created a magical setting for herself, a haven within which to write.

* * * * *

THE OUTSIDE of the house also commanded Mary Butts's attention, for she was a very keen gardener and her notebooks contain detailed lists of what plants were sown and when. "A garden, gardening—the 2 words stand for the most straightforward and also the most mysterious of the occupations of mankind.... It is the way to certain basic contacts and knowledge; the entrance to the workshop of Nature and to her altar," she wrote in one of several reviews of gardening books in the 1930s.[36] If her vocabulary sounds quasi-religious, it is because she regarded it in very much these terms: After an afternoon's gardening she wrote of "a nature sacrament with the flowers and the earth and the quickening sun", and words such as "litany" and "rosary" were recorded on other occasions. Similarly, when reviewing the *Studio Gardening Annual 1932*, she wrote of "the Garden Faith", praising the book because "it has throughout something of the feeling and infection of some kindly old religion, so sure of itself, so ripe in its ideology, as to welcome all new-comers and set them to work with a blessing."[37] Gardening was important because "it would seem that in gardens there is all that we have of a nature religion left to us." It can be seen from several journal entries that gardening provided a "rest" from the rigours of writing; however, it did much more that this: "July 5th...what a lot this patch of very amateur garden is teaching me. About how to grow things, but even more about the nature—the looks and the characters, the similarities and repeats of things. Something about life-patterns; and the incredibilities and the subtleties of strength." Contact with plants was so important to Mary Butts that she declared on the 16 July 1933 how gardening that day had given her a sense of renewed "well-being—physical[38]—spiritual... Sense of the earth and the nature of each plant getting into my hands again." Although she described herself as working in an "amateur garden", the opening paragraphs of an article in which she described the impact of a spring storm on Tebel Vos, show just how extensive in three years her botanical knowledge had become. It also forms a striking contrast to the relative waste land of the garden behind 43 Belsize Park Gardens. The article was published in *The Manchester Guardian* in June 1935:

> In this house, perched on an eyebrow of bushy, flowery cliff, three hundred feet above the Atlantic,[39] one watched its awful play.
>
> It is a house in an island of garden, hollowed out and protected by turf walls and hurdle and stone, growing hedges of fuchsia and veronica, and young sycamore trees just breaking into their gold-beater's green leaf. There are lilies whose green towers the Florentine artists copied in marble and bronze; lupin and honesty and columbine, alison and sweet william, pansy and peony and carnation. At

> the back a great rock with the herb patch round it, thyme and tansy, parsley and rosemary, garlic and alisanders, mint and Corsican carroway. The vegetable garden round the herbs, raspberry, and broad bean and green pea. All divided by rock walls where the ice-plants crept, the saxifrages, while between each planting, like a corbel, a knob of house leek, blue and bloody-thorned, its flower beginning to rise like a feather in its cap. All are rather behind, what with the late winds, but "coming along handsome".[40]

Similarly, 'The Warning', a story first published in *Life and Letters To-day* in January 1935, is set in a house on the edge of a Cornish cliff:

> There, three hundred feet below, the full Atlantic poured its waters in and out of a cup.[41] There you enjoyed night and day the entire conversation of the sea.... There, in a world jutting with empty stones, and airy as though you stood everywhere at a great height, the cliffs have clothed themselves; and you look down or you look up into a crosswork of gorse and bracken, blackberry and bryony, threaded with the drip of streams. There, all summer, the rose-campion waves a scarf in its face exactly the opposite in colour to the sea. There, in the middle of the bay, the sand has blown itself together into one place, a dune thrust out from the land, a child carried upright in the belly of the earth; dunes the couch-grass has covered, the grass that never stands close enough together, so that between each blade you can see the skin-pale sand.
>
> There, round about the house at night, the hedgehogs squeak; and night and day, in every tone of voice, the sea says out loud its stupendous secret, which is the meaning of everything, the tuning-in for the music of the spheres; and men often listen attentively, understand, and instantly forget all about it; while a foot above their heads the gulls mew like cats.[42]

Repeatedly, the Cornish landscape reverberates in her writings from these years. Her stories, 'The Warning', 'Look Homeward, Angel' and 'The Guest' unfold in very real local places with wonderful names such as Nan-Dreath, Sarscathian Moor, St Enys, Carn Brea and Nanquidno.[43] The powerful quality of west Cornwall is also evoked in her reviews of books about the county. In one such review, entitled 'The Magic of Person and Place' in the December 1933 issue of *The Bookman*, she praised a work of fiction and an archaeological study:

> If it is not their native place, people have need of certain books to elucidate the piece of earth on which they live. For to know it, one must have a private map of one's own in one's mind. A magic map.... In West Cornwall you are living in a land where culture is overlaid on culture. This year two books brought out its contours. A small classic no one seems to have heard of—*The Crochet Woman* by Ruth Manning Sanders; the land seen through the glass of an exquisite imagination, the complex of stone, water, plants, air and human character on the moor the Ordnance calls Selene, the Moon-Moor.

> The second was Mr Hencken's account of West Cornwall, in the County Archaeologies series. For all its scientific precision, a work that makes one realise that, in the house under one's feet, in the garden, up the lane, across the fields, one is walking among the bones of the First Men. A people in the night of time whose life was a ritual and a cult of death; raising, without metal of any kind, thirty-ton boulders, houses for their dead. The peninsula sown thick with them, until out in the islands of the Scillies they stand like corn.... Never did an unadorned style and a strictly scientific treatment do more to reach the imagination. Curiously too it helped to enhance the isolation dwellers here feel from the rest of England. Nowhere else is one so sure that one is in a foreign land, whose significant history was over before what we call England began.[44]

Shortly after arriving in Sennen, Mary Butts informed Douglas Goldring: "I've a book coming out in March and 2 pamphlets, but this last year I've written more and I think better than I've ever done."[45] Certainly 1932 would prove to be her annus mirabilis in terms of what was published.

At the beginning of February, a few days after moving into Sarah's Well, she had received the depressing news that Cape had rejected "Episodes in the Life of Alexander of Macedon". On the 8th she wrote of her disappointment to Angus Davidson: "Thank you so very much...for your praise of 'Alexander'.... I've just read [Pierre] Jounguet's *Macedonian Imperialism* [(1928)] and find that he stresses his mixture of mysticism and common-sense just as I did, on intuition.... This makes me happy. I *know* I've got that book right. But shall I ever find a publisher?"[46] As her agent tried other publishing houses, Mary Butts's response whilst waiting was to "read, read, read". A friend remembered her urging: "read. Always read. When the heart fails and there is no health in anything, turn to your books. Always read at such times."[47] Thus she commented in her journal how she liked Yeats's introduction to Joseph Hone's biography of *Berkeley* (1931). She was so impressed by Desmond MacCarthy's *Portraits* (1931) that she made notes on his essays in her journal to remind her what to comment on in her next letter to Ethel Colburn Mayne: "Of all its excellencies," she recorded on the 10 February, "this is the chief, when you have read it, you are left with an increased sense of the dignity of man, his worth and greatness...—in his diversity." She was amused by the American writer H.L. Mencken's[48] description of Blake as "A poet and mystic who died mad and is chiefly remembered for his weird drawings à la Beardsley." In sharp contrast to her own view, she noted wryly how "'mystic' [is] a Mencken insult". The occult writer Eliot O'Donnell's account of tree potencies was more in line with what she felt. "Some trees have personality—out of hell or fairy-land," she noted in her journal. "That is why I miss them, even here—and am not sure if I know yet, or can grasp—the daimons of this land."[49]

A walk at the end of February prompted Mary Butts to muse on the difference between art and nature, specifically in relation to the Cornish landscape:

> *Remember:* The walk along the cliffs south of Land's End, the whole way one natural splendour after another, the most glorious kind of beauty. But nowhere and in no way the beauty of art; not because of repetition, for the variety was endless; not because of excess, because there could be no excess of such a world. Nor can I see art made out of it, not of its characteristics; not visual art. (Had there been? Will Gabriel? There is something in it tempting but irreducible). Nor has Cornwall produced more than folk-work.

She would later disagree with this view, being herself one of the artists who managed to evoke its powerful beauty. However this diary entry illustrates the sense of continuing frustration she felt at the gap between what she *saw* and what she was able to convey through language.

She also never stopped writing; ideas "for a poem" or "for a story" are scattered throughout her journal in spite of her lament on the 13 February that "I cannot work and I want to. I have no patience and am ashamed not to have it. Is it the fault of *Dorian Gray* [1890], reread after 16 years and I dare say that I still find it a good book?" Two days later she started to write a story which (together with 'From Altar to Chimney-piece') explains in fictional terms why she had had to leave Paris in 1930. The story is entitled 'Ford's last Dancing'—a reference to the parties given by Ford Madox Ford and Stella Bowen in a zinc bar in the 1920s.[50] She finished it the following January but it has never been published.

An anthology and a journal came out in 1932 which included some of her earlier poems. The American poet, Louis Zukofsky, included 'Corfe' ('A Song to Keep People out of Dorset') in his collection, *An 'Objectivists' Anthology*.[51] It is one of her best poems, combining wit, lyricism and a strong rhythmical beat. Ostensibly centering on the Dorset village of Corfe Castle, it resonates with even older allusion. Just as her writing about Villefranche had done, the poet refers us back to the classical world:

> But when I remember you Corfe, I remember Delphi
> Because your history is also a mystery of God.

In October 1931, Mary Butts had sent some poems to Dr K.S. Bhat for his consideration. In the spring of 1932 the third number of his journal, *Soma*, included four of her poems from the 1920s: 'Picus Martius', 'Thinking of

Saints and of Petronius Arbiter', 'Douarnenez' and 'Heartbreak House'.[52] *Soma* was a lavish production bound in black leather and embossed with a golden crescent. It was printed in England with a limited run of 500 copies of which 400 were for sale. The third issue included stories, poems and illustrations, including a short story by T.F. Powys entitled 'A Suet Pudding' and one called 'Aren't We All?' by Oswell Blakeston. A writer, critic and film-maker, Blakeston saw Mary Butts a great deal in Cornwall and later wrote favourable reviews of her work.[53] Together with Herbert Jones he also edited a small magazine called *Seed* which published her poem, 'On an American Wonderchild who translated Homer at 8 years old', the following January. *Seed* also published work by Kay Boyle, H.D. and Emily Holmes-Colman.[54]

Several Occasions

THE BOOK (mentioned in her letter to Douglas Goldring) due to come out in March 1932 was *Several Occasions*, published by Wishart. It was handsomely produced with a classical scene by Gabriel Aitken of two lovers in a bower reproduced on the dust jacket. Originally called 'Various Occasions', it is a collection of nine stories, all of which had been written before she moved to Sennen, mostly in the 1920s. Six of the stories had already been published in little magazines between 1924 and 1931, and two ('Deosil'[55] and 'The Later Life of Theseus, King of Athens') had been selected as among the best in their respective years.

H.D. found several of the stories "exquisite" and Ezra Pound wrote to Mary Butts to say that her story 'Green' (published the previous year in *Pagany*) was a "damn good job".[56] On the 10 March Hugh Ross Williamson declared: "As I've just finished 'The House Party' and am still almost quivering with excitement about it, I must obviously write to you. It is superb; I think one of the best things you've ever done." Of 'Friendship's Garland', which McAlmon had included in the *Contact Collection of Contemporary Writers*, Ross Williamson believed that its first page was "a most perfect example" of Mary Butts's style.[57]

Several Occasions was reviewed widely, both in the literary columns of the bigger organs, such as *The Observer*, *Time and Tide*, *John O'London's Weekly*, the *London Mercury*, *The Spectator* and the *Times Literary Supplement* as well as in several regional newspapers, including *The Glasgow Herald*, *The Northern Echo* (Darlington) and *The Birmingham Post*. The general response was favourable, with the continuing proviso that the collection was high-brow. "In spite of the commercial suspicion in which short stories are held, occasional high-class volumes continue to be published," declared the reviewer in *The Sunday Referee*, who praised the "very fine collection by Miss Mary Butts. This author's previous volume of short stories [*Speed the Plough*] contained much distinguished work; but of *Several Occasions* it must be said that nearly every story touches the high-water mark of contemporary tale-telling."[58] In a similar vein, *The Northern Echo* informed its readers that "Mary Butts is not an easy writer.... She is clever and to be read: but not by people who merely reach out for a book at such times as the wireless has ceased to amuse."[59] An article in *The Saturday Review* explained that this was because "Miss Butt's [sic] stories demand very careful attention. Most of their obscurity is due to the subtlety of thought and delicacy of theme, but for much her method is responsible." For this particular reviewer the difficulty lay in the fact that her "characters are never introduced to one [so that] often a second reading is required to place them." Yet the following conclusions were shared by most of the reviewers: "The reward of the reader's effort is the discovery of a distinctive imagination" and "Miss Butts's stories...assuredly have gleams of brilliance...which will repay study, and I recommend them," declared the reviewer in *The Observer*.[60] Several of the stories were singled out for particular qualities: *The Glasgow Herald* felt that two of the "most successful" were "'The Dinner Party' where an atmosphere of tense expectancy is evoked with the greatest degree of economy [and] 'The Later Life of Theseus, King of Athens', an ironic modernisation of Greek myth."[61] *The Yorkshire Post* favoured "the dramatic tale of the terrible cousins from Africa—'In Bloomsbury'" and *Time and Tide* declared that "'Green', where innocence triumphs over spite, has a charmed beauty."[62]

Two reviews were particularly significant for Mary Butts. One was by the writer, R. Ellis Roberts, in *The New Statesman and Nation*, which showed that he had read her work as it came out:

> Will the publication of *Several Occasions* make a few people realise how incomparably Miss Butts has grown in stature since her story 'Speed the Plough' was acclaimed a masterpiece—is it ten years ago? She is a perplexing, at times an exasperating author. One of her best essays in fiction—*Ashe of Rings*—has never been published in England; but *Armed with Madness*, its successor, came out, and fell, so far as I know, deplorably flat. People still ignore her work when they criticise modern novelists. That should be impossible now that *Several Occasions* is published.

As far as Ellis Roberts was concerned, "'The Dinner Party', 'In Bloomsbury', and 'Friendship's Garland' are stories which, if the generation to come shows any curiosity about our society, will take their place beside *The Waste-Land*, *The Poor Man* and *Those Barren Leaves* as documents of revelation."[63]

The other crucial review was part of a long article by the poet and essayist, J.C. Squire, in *The Daily Telegraph*. Under the heading 'The Modern Revival of the Short Story', Squire maintained that "it is undoubted that there has been a recent revival of interest in the [short story] form" and singled out Mary Butts in the following sensitive and perceptive discussion which also gives a clear account of the book:

> ...of all the numerous contemporary artists in the short story Miss Mary Butts, on the strength of *Several Occasions* seems to me one of the very best. It is much better than anything she has done before: in its kind it could hardly be better.
>
> A KATHERINE MANSFIELD?[64]
>
> 'In its kind', I may say. How indicate its kind? Rough comparisons of one author with another are usually invalid as criticism; but they may be indicative in a review, in which one is trying to convey to people whether they will like a certain thing enough.
>
> Taking this as so, Miss Butts resembles Katherine Mansfield, has less Chekhov in her than Katherine Mansfield, and more Henry James. She is unlikely to be widely read, until or unless she becomes a fashionable cult, or (later) is imposed as a classic upon unfortunate children in schools. Her characters are mostly intelligent, and even neurotic; they are perpetually aware of things unspoken; they have incomes or can sponge, or are artists, have a skin less than other people, and can afford the time to watch the reactions of the thin skin. They are not seen working; they remain in Paradise, with the Snake in attendance, as it were. They are cosmopolitans in Paris, or aesthetes in Bloomsbury, or expensively dressed clairvoyants in Mayfair, or prosperous English Anarchists, or decadent Americans with an income drawn from factory-hands overseas.
>
> Yet the material must be granted; all artists who wish to arrive at the ultimate refinements of the human soul, have to place it 'in vacuo' economically. Miss Butts is doing no more for her modern dreamers and decadents than Shakespeare did with his Lears and Hamlets.
>
> IRONIC AND HUMOROUS
>
> She succeeds wonderfully. The air in all her stories is charged with psychological conflict;... One of the finest stories in the book is 'Scylla and Charybdis'; one of the protagonists is a strong, silent (but subcutaneously neurotic) Englishman from the East; the other a workless, but charming young Russian emigre.... People in the last resort are Miss Butts' concern. Most of us do not have the time to refine things as her characters do; but, put into one of her aquaria, we probably should, and her observations are illuminating.
>
> She is in all her worlds, but not of them; at once detached, ironic, sympathetic, and humorous. She has the gift of the exact word and the pregnant image.... Take this:

> *Now that the Government in Athens has changed, as it was bound to change, it can be seen that the activities of the late King were no more than the wind ruffling the unstirred deeps of the ocean. Wherein exist those dumb and flexible powers who reigned before him, and have been shown to survive him.*
>
> Why the full-stop in the middle? If you have an ear why refuse it, merely because there is a fashion to refuse music in prose, because the last age was rhetorical. However, I do not wish to look a gift horse in the mouth. Miss Butts may live to fulfil the promise that Katherine Mansfield showed.[65]

"Squire's notice is quoted as an ad. in *Times Lit Supp*. It ought to do a lot of good," wrote Ethel Colburn Mayne on the 13 April. This comment was in a letter which opened with the gloomy news that her attempt to launch Mary Butts on a "translator's chequered career" had been unsuccessful, Putnam having turned down their proposal to translate *St Saturnine* from French. Ethel Colburn Mayne's enthusiasm for the "lovely writing" in *Several Occasions* had prompted her to put it forward for the Femina list, a literary prize for which she was one of the judges. "When I proposed it," she confided, "Rebecca West at once said: 'Oh yes—indeed we must have Mary Butts!' I fear that short stories haven't much of a chance of getting through, but *I* shall work for you, at any rate. It would be gorgeous if you got the Prize!"[66] The book was not shortlisted, but Mayne's confidence in her had cheered Mary Butts, who noted in her diary: "I'm wild for praise". In a later entry she explained why it was so important to her: "If people only knew what can be done by Praise. Praise, the wine in the cup, the 'balm to hurt minds', the blessed bread to the starved spirit.... As a generation, we are starved for praise—for the giving or the receiving of it. Gabriel laughs at me and my fan-mail, but if he only knew what praise does for me.... It has a magical power over me, and I can't help it. That's the sort of artist I am" (11.3.33). In this she was like "the Greeks, who knew most things, [for they] made a daimon of him; or, at least, an attribute, perhaps accurately, an aspect of Apollo. Paian—Παιον—the god himself. To express this, man invented a poetry; a making, the Paean." *Several Occasions* came out a few days before its dedicatee, Douglas Goldring, had arrived for a visit in mid-March. He stayed for several weeks and returned for a second holiday later that summer. On the 14 March Mary Butts noted in her diary that his presence as the "perfect guest and faultless friend" (along with the reviews by Squire and Ellis Roberts) gave her "the sense of something fairly won" and increased the "sense of release, of triumph and the delights of first recognition".

From early March onwards, she began to write regularly for *The Bookman*. It was the beginning of an impressive career as a reviewer which by the following year included frequent articles for a number of magazines and newspapers, such as *Time and Tide, John O'London's Weekly, The Sunday Times*, as well as occasional reviews and articles for *The Daily Telegraph, Crime, The Spectator* and *The Manchester Guardian*. In 1933 alone, quite apart from her own writing, she also wrote 27 reviews on a total of 43 books. By her death four years later her reviews and essays totalled well over one hundred. Even taking only her literary reviews into account, it is clear that she read the works of many of her now more famous contemporaries: Vera Brittain, Ezra Pound, Llewelyn Powys, Daphne du Maurier, James Hanley, Katherine Mansfield, Nancy Cunard, Agatha Christie and Robert Graves. Whilst her reviews were always discriminating, her own need for praise made her a sympathetic and generous reader, as the literary editor of *Time and Tide* declared after her death: "The reviews which Mary Butts contributed to *Time and Tide* will be remembered by many of our readers for their highly individual quality. Although it is true…that her natural abundance sometimes made her a misleading guide to other people's intentions, the depth of her knowledge and the essential truth of her vision gave a special value to her judgements even when she appeared to be going off at an unlikely tangent. She touched nothing that she did not in some way enrich."[67] Her literary journalism also enabled her to renew lapsed acqaintances. One of the most important of these was the publisher, writer and historian, Jack Lindsay, who would prove a crucial correspondent when she was writing her historical narrative on the life of Cleopatra in 1934. Thus whilst fairly isolated geographically, she clearly kept in touch with the literary world. In addition, from 1932 onwards she devoted whole pages of her diary every few weeks to lists of recently-published books, which she would tick off after ordering them from the Boots Library in Penzance or The Book Club.

Three nights after moving into Sarah's Well in January 1932, Mary Butts had had a dream: "Out for the evening—to dinner—with Lytton Strachey…which will never happen again.[68] One is curiously made: I realised when I woke that I send off the proofs of the Harmsworth pamphlet relieved that now it can never fall under his ironic scrutiny. And that I shall feel this again." Strachey had died a few days earlier on the 21 January and Mary Butts felt his loss keenly. She later wrote when rereading his *Books and Characters* that it was "like lying back to sip an exquisite wine," adding the lament: "O the loss of that amenity and that wit!" (9.9.33). In 1936, she pointed to his influence in her unpublished essay, 'Bloomsbury'.

Traps for Unbelievers

THE "HARMSWORTH PAMPHLET" to which she referred was one of two published in March 1932. Desmond Harmsworth published *Traps for Unbelievers* whilst Wishart published *Warning to Hikers.*[69] Although brought out by different presses, they are very much companion pieces, directly addressing the need to preserve the land and retain some sort of spiritual belief. Together they encapsulate what Mary Butts regarded as the "Nature religion" which she had commented on in her gardening reviews, mentioned above.

Coming out of an earlier article entitled 'Vision and Belief', written in Paris in May 1928, the theme of *Traps for Unbelievers* is clear from the outset: "It is continually being brought to our notice by different people in various ways, that for about the first time in history, the Western World is going about its business, to a great measure without the belief or practice of religion, organised or private." Quoting from Aldous Huxley and Rebecca West[70] who shared her views, Mary Butts stated that instead, "the word Religion with its vast connotations" either acquires "the category of the shame-making or obscene" or still worse is ignored. This "strident indifference" to belief encompasses not only Christianity but all religions; life without God(s) arising, she maintained, from the misconception that to discard God(s) will free us from the constraints of social morality. In actual fact this banishment of belief has repercussions which extend far beyond the physical and social realms of life. For whilst the decision to "dispense" with the religious attitude has been made "in the name of scientific truth, [this is] an activity, which for all its overwhelming importance, was not designed to deal with the emotion behind the experience of religion." Gods may not be needed when all is well, but:

> The time comes when something disagreeable happens, quickening often with secret and horrible vitality into tragedy; and one begins to notice what happens to natures who have only human nature to fall back on; not strengthened to meet pain by any of the old receipts and for whom no new ones are available. Receipts which linked the phenomenal world to the eternal, condemned events by reference to concepts not affected by change or by any vicissitudes of man.

By focusing on and giving priority to *human nature* at the expense of the *phenomenal world* (Nature: that within the human sphere but which is other than human) and the *eternal* (the supernatural: that realm entered through religious belief), an anthropocentric interpretation of existence has been formulated which cannot bear the tragic, the unordered, unnameable aspects of existence. What is now absent, because it has been lost, is "a very peculiar kind of awareness" which Mary Butts locates not only in religious belief, but in primitive mysticism and the occult. Whilst regarding the practice of magic as "very largely primitive science", she discerns "behind" that a kind of awareness which is, she concedes:

> difficult to describe. It has something to do with a sense of the invisible, the non-existent in a scientific sense, the relations between things of a different order: the moon and a stone, the sea and a piece of wood, women and fish. Its appellation by means of primitive guesswork is one of the most shocking records of human trial-and-error in history, but it is by no means quite so sure that all of the original guesses were unscientific or the original "awareness" quite such nonesense.
>
> This perception has no more died in man than has his sight or any other of his senses; only he does not now try it out or at least not often...

This underlying awareness or "perception" is not, as far as she was concerned, a luxurious sixth sense enabling a richer, more complex life. Rather, it is a crucial filtering process through which we can see how things are, and without which life under its disabling aspects is intolerable. Thus a character in her novel *Death of Felicity Taverner* declares: "You can get a first in Greats or fly around the crater of Vesuvius, but what you depend on for your private life is your degree in witch-doctoring. How much you can can smell out the propitious from the unpropitious."[71] It is significant that Mary Butts should find this "awareness...difficult to describe", and she made repeated attempts. Her inability to put this awareness into words, to define it, to pin it down, reveals not *her* inarticulacy, but the limitations of articulation itself—the fact that there are areas where language cannot go, or at best only go 'around' by a series of metaphors or paraphrases. We have bodies, we live in space(s) and we have language. These are not of the same qualitative order. All of Mary Butts's works are attempts at linking up the phenomenal world to the eternal sphere: "Holy, holy, holy sang our fathers and they felt better," she declared in *Traps for Unbelievers*, adding, "what they were doing was very ancient magic."[72]

"It's heavy going in spite of its apparent lightness," wrote Hugh Ross Williamson whilst reading the pamphlet.[73] Yet by the time he came to review it for *The Bookman*, he placed her polemic alongside attempts by T.S. Eliot and Middleton Murry to respond to "the apparent failure of organised religion" with a "book which in size is little more than a pamphlet, but contains more ideas than many a large volume". The scope of her overview is referred to when he wrote: "Miss Mary Butts has examined the whole situation in the light of that instinctive and inevitable religiousness, which has been part of the heritage of the race from the beginning of time, which has changed in fashions and in forms, but which rests on realities which cannot be denied."[74]

Response to the pamphlet depended on whether the reviewer found the absence of God or gods in the modern world a problem. Whilst her concerns were shared by many, there was also a readership, such as George Pendle (reviewing *Traps for Unbelievers* for *Twentieth Century*), who was "not convinced that Western Man will require any 'external' support henceforth."[75]

Warning to Hikers

Mary Butts had completed her other pamphlet, *Warning to Hikers,* in London in October 1931 after her stay in Newcastle-on-Tyne. As a result, the setting for the fifth part of the pamphlet is the countryside not of her beloved Dorset but that around Newcastle. Her comments provoked an enraged review in the *Northern Echo* entitled 'Tyneside: "A Public Catastrophe": A Woman Writer's Onslaught'.[76] Written partly in response to the tremendous rise in popularity of hiking in the 1920s and 1930s, *Warning to Hikers* warns against the increasing prevalence of a "cult of nature", the use of the countryside not as a place to live in, but simply as another source of "free" leisure. With respect to her own experience she wrote:

> If it has been one's fortune to be brought up among physical beauties, natural and created, if one's senses and tastes have been formed on them; if also one was taught their use as a standard and to reject passionately all that was not like them, adult life becomes a greatly enhanced but not an easier thing.

She compared this perception with "a kind of psychic shock or rather strain" which is endured by the dwellers of "the majority-home of England, in a town or a suburb of a town".[77] Repeatedly the people inhabiting her fictions are sharply divided between those who are "town-tuned" and those who respond to the mysterious forces of nature.[78] In view of the present increased concern for ecology, this pamphlet published over sixty years ago is both prophetic and pertinent. "I want to tell you how very much I admire the *Warning to Hikers*. It seems to me one of the best things you have ever done," wrote Tony. "It's very disquieting, as there is no kind of escape from any of your conclusions. Life is always at pains to show one what outraged nature can provide by way of punishment, in any manifestation, to those who break her rules.... You set up in the more jaded town-dweller something more than deep nostalgia and dissatisfaction."[79] His view was shared by a young writer, Louis Wilkinson, who wrote to Mary Butts: "I have read *Warning to Hikers* with both interest and fright: it brings one's own fears up to a very clear surface."[80] The pamphlet also received a boost from *The Daily Express* book critic, James Agate, who headed his review with the praise "GOOD WRITING". "Who is Miss Butts? And why have I not heard of her? This pamphlet is proof that she possesses the two qualities essential to first-class writing—the urgency to communicate something personal to her and to nobody else, and a sufficient way of telling it which is hers and nobody else's." Whilst he did not agree with all her arguments, he concluded: "It is the best shilling's worth I have read for many a long day."[81] "Did you see J.A. on me in the Daily Express?" wrote Mary Butts with pleasure to her mother on the 25 June.[82]

In his article on her work in *The Bookman* the previous December, Ross Williamson had provided a pertinent account of the privileged attitude she had towards the land and why it informed all her work. "Country-writers we have had in plenty," he states:

> There are those who turn to Nature as a highly-idealised form of escape from urbanity; and there are those, inspired by reaction from this school, who delight in exhibiting the sordidness and narrowness of rusticity by reminding us that a picturesque village may contain more squalor than a hideous slum. With neither class has Mary Butts anything whatever to do. In the first place she accepted the country without comparisons. To live there was not a mode of existence to be contrasted with the lot of the city-dweller; it gave her the only background for experience she knew. If she judged it by any standards, they were the historical ones of family tradition.[83]

Mary Butts wrote to Jean Cocteau in March 1932, asking how he and their mutual friends (Jean Desbordes, Georges Auric, Jeannot Bourgoint) were. She also rather tentatively asked for news of Mireille Havet ("about whom I'm afraid to ask questions"); in fact Mireille was at that time dying in Switzerland. Mary Butts had heard that L'Echéance (one of his publishers) had announced the imminent publication of her translation of *Imaginary Letters* with a preface by Cocteau. It would appear that this publication did not take place and unfortunately the translation has been lost.[84] Another project which came to nothing was the suggestion in May from an old friend, that Mary Butts write a book on the relationship between Duff Twysden and her lover in the mid-1920s, Pat Guthrie, who had also recently died. "Often have I thought of it but it won't shape," she remarked to herself on the 24 June. The following day she sent her condolences to Duff Twysden whom she had not seen for several years: "Duff, my dear, a friend of his aunt...has told me about Pat. We know between us most of what there is to say, so I needn't try. Nor can I ever forget how you pulled me through the worst bit of Cecil's death. How are you my dear? I'm married to Gabriel—d'you remember how we first set eyes on him one night in the Select, before too many things happened to us? He was camping around with a pot-hat on the back of his head, and you said 'who is that boy. Isn't he enjoying himself?' &, later, 'not for us'. We live here [Sennen], utterly sober and industrious. (3 works out this spring & a contract with Heinemann.) That's that. What news of you?"[85] Industrious, Mary Butts certainly was and would continue to be—the couple's sobriety, however, was a very fragile and ultimately impossible undertaking.

From March onwards she began revising *Death of Felicity Taverner* which Wishart was to bring out at the end of the year. "Nothing has happened to us," she wrote to Hugh Ross Williamson in early April, "I'm hopeless when a book runs away with me; go about with it so much in my head that I talk to myself, and only come round sufficiently to do the housekeeping."[86] Comments on writing the novel continued until July and the following extract from her journal entry for the 22 March shows the close interrelation between this book and the recently published stories:

> *Death of Felicity Taverner*
> Données—'the great war between the young & the old'. It now comes to this point: arrival of old Mrs Taverner, Adrian (opening—slight spring interlude of Boris' pranks). Mrs T like the old woman in 'Green'. Inventions for her & her son? Meet Boris & adopt him? Test of his virtue, which nearly succumbs? After all, he'd have a reaction-grievance on the other Taverners for getting the truth out of him. Is the invention their detaching game with him? It might be a resumé of several stories; the spoiling game & the death game—'Green', 'Friendship's Garland', 'The Dinner Party' (?), 'The House Party'. Also 'The House'.

In mid-April she briefly interrupted her work on the novel on learning that Heinemann was to publish her book on Alexander, now entitled *The Macedonian*. "Just a line to say how I 'drink, dance, shout' at the Heinemann news. It is *good*," wrote Ethel Colburn Mayne in jubilation on the 19th.[87] This good news made up not a little for the disappointing loss of the illustrations for *The Macedonian* which was eventually published without any drawings. June found Mary Butts happy with her lot, as she declared in a letter to Angus Davidson: "We've settled down here now,...and we've made [Tebel Vos] very lovely.... My *Death of Felicity Taverner* is in its last stages, the awful ones.... And we're brown and freckled and horny-handed, and sober and thrifty and extraordinarily happy....

Of course we're horribly poor and this is partly to ask you—Gabriel has a Modigliani drawing, description enclosed... Is it saleable? And if so, what should we do about it?" (Mary Butts did not note whether the drawing was ever sold.)[88] She concluded the letter with the news that *The Macedonian* was due to come out in September. In fact it did not appear until mid-March 1933.

In late June she heard from Wishart that in spite of the positive reviews, neither *Several Occasions* nor *Warning to Hikers* had sold well. Yet she continued to be fairly contented. "Gabriel said I look 'like a langouste with crumbs', I thought I was going brown," she laughed to herself on the 1 July. The following day she went for a delightful walk with Ruth Manning-Sanders to the nearby Penrose Farm and as the month progressed, so her happiness grew. On the 4 July she noted the following idea for a story, 'The Gertrude Stein Song': "Gertrude Stein and her house. Visit of a young woman in love. Loss of her lover. The empty ciboria. The art-snobs. Behind the curtain. A tragic tale." The story was later published under the title 'From Altar to Chimney-Piece' and is an attack on Stein's circle in Paris as well as her work and explores Mary Butts's concern at what she saw as the modern fashion for converting religious ikons into art objects, a trend she tried to reverse in her own writing and in her home. The protagonist of this story is a First World War veteran who on a visit to Paris in the 1920s is shown some "shining objects" by Miss Van Norden in her flat:

> They were all the same. About a foot high, of some common metal, gilt, rough, traditional. But the design was pure, the whole representing a flame or a star on fire, inset with a circular disk, rubbed silver-bright and painted on it in blue, the letter Chi. It was clear ...what they were: they were frames, supports, stands for the ciborium, the box—in this case a round of hollow glass, fixed on to the disk—to hold the wafers of the Host. The box taken away, they now made delightful chimney-piece ornaments. He saw it for himself and Miss Van Norden explained, and told how they had been sent her from Spain, and had once been part of the traditional altar-furniture in country churches.
>
> 'Those Greek letters are the only relic of piety about them,' she added, 'and cleaning will soon wear them off. Interesting parochial baroque—and from the country of its origin too. For they are not old.' She picked up one and began to rub it on a filthy handkerchief of khaki cotton, on which she spat. The old paint was dry and cracked and the signature of Christ rubbed off at a touch.[89]

Horrified at this lack of respect for the religious origin of the objects, the protagonist takes his leave.

Mary Butts completed the story in six months and wrote of it to Ross Williamson in an account which reveals her attitude to Gertrude

Stein's writing and to what she felt was most damaging about modern society:

> I've finished yesterday a song story (50 pages), whose real title is 'The Gertrude-Stein-Song'. Rather grim and the key to it—the mutilated altar-ornaments—I saw myself. In fact its *all* true, but nicely arranged. Of course, I had to hide who it was,—fairly well—but I'd like to learn that depraved old creature not to monkey with the English language! As you may gather, I think the story is a Wow. While no one on earth will publish it, separately I mean. Unless *The Cornhill* would do it in two installments. I'll try them. Its all about the Surrealistes and their cult of the cruel and the obscene, all about 'le culte du Moi' and living entirely in your sub-consciousness, and what happens when you do—Fay's 'mysticisme du Verbe'. I saw something of it in Paris and the trail of artificial disaster it created. (I mean artificially caused, the disasters were real enough.) I sheered off, and I'm rather sorry now, for it led into some very interesting country. I think it is spreading too.[90]

In early summer Ross Williamson wrote to apologise for his silence, but he had been asked to write a book on T.S. Eliot. Whilst not often read now, *The Poetry of T.S. Eliot* was the first lengthy critique of Eliot's *The Waste Land* and Ross Williamson confided to Mary Butts how "I nearly referred to *Ashe* in 'The Waste Land' Chapter—your use of the knife and dish as the complementary magics of lance and cup. They are complementary, aren't they? Not simply parallels. But then I thought I'd keep that till later and do another book called 'Mary Butts' in an uniform edition with 'T.S. Eliot'!!"[91] Whilst that book was never written, he did mention Mary Butts in his study of T.S. Eliot, which came out later that year. Probably thinking of *Traps For Unbelievers*, he wrote: "In one of her books Mary Butts points out that a symptom of an age's decadence is the repudiation of this idea of a God-Man in favour of a Man-God, the substitution of Deification for Incarnation."[92] Mary Butts wished him good luck with his book, told him he was right in his assumptions about *Ashe of Rings* and asked if she could dedicate *Death of Felicity Taverner* to him. Ross Williamson replied: "I can't tell you how your letter cheered me. I finished the book last night and feel depressed. It's been too hurried. Don't dare to buy a copy. You're in the "six" and shall have one immediately. But my posthumous reputation will not rest on that but on the fact that you are going to dedicate one of your books to me. I can't thank you enough."[93]

On the 13 July Mary Butts looked back at how "these last few weeks have been, no are being the happiest in my life". This was due to a sense of both personal and artistic satisfaction: "A balance of all ways, focused round the new house & the home and the life we are making. The last chapters of *Felicity*. Gabriel's paintings, Gabriel's book.[94] The exquisite *details* of the house, from the food to the objets d'art. The reviewing and perfecting of it. The weather and the flowers and this land. The books. The candle-light. The letters of our friends. Health and work and marriage, 'the plant', the sea. The great angers and griefs and anxieties are being reduced by these, a little more than a dawn battle. They are sharp enough, but there are prayers also against them. I have to learn to be really happy again, to *notice* it, to go slow and notice it."

During the summer she drew up a list of stories for a third collection (to be published by Wishart). It did not appear in her lifetime, although a third selection, *Last Stories*, did come out in 1938, a year after her death. Five of the stories from the 1932 list were included: 'From Altar to Chimney-Piece', 'After the Funeral', 'The House', 'The Guest' and 'With and Without Buttons'.[95] In September 1932, she wrote to M.R. James to ask if she could dedicate 'With and Without Buttons' to him. There is no record that he replied.[96] In her work notebook on the 21 July Mary Butts triumphantly signed her name and added the words "ista perfecit opus" [she has brought the work to a close] underneath the final sentence of her novel. That evening she noted with satisfaction: "Finished *Death of Felicity Taverner*. Never had such trouble with a book before. But it has been the utmost blessing of our marriage—how we have worked together (Gabriel on his book all but finished tonight) on these. [in margin: "done"]." A few days later she visited the Manning-Sanders, whose daughter, Joan, remembered her in the following vivid manner:

> Mary Butts...was lame in one knee and walk[ed] with a constant dipping or bowing motion—not ungraceful—rather like a yacht at anchor. She had a large round white face, bright blue eyes, usually wore a cloak, walked with a stick. Altogether a massive, formidable personality—not massive so much in size as in impact and capacity. As I recall her voice—she had a short, emphatic, way of speaking—never drawling languid or monotonous, but using and falling from high to low keys.[97]

Mary Butts wrote at that time to her mother how "the young Joan Manning S[anders]—the girl who got her first picture into the Academy at 16, is doing a portrait of me. The usual dreary thing. This time I'm a cross dumpy little woman with coarse hands. What do I do to painters that each one sees me as a different monster," she moaned, adding: "the camera doesn't".[98] Since none of the portraits by Nina Hamnett, Roger Fry, Eugene MacGown and Joan Manning-Sanders has been found, it is difficult to assess the truth of this remark. Whilst the line drawings of her by Cocteau and Gabriel Aitken are graceful, Cedric Morris's painting certainly depicts very much the surface appearance of Mary Butts, which Joan Manning-Sanders had of her as a child. Similarly, the first impressions of the writer and organist, Frank Baker (who met Mary Butts in 1933), were of "a ridiculous figure; a clumpy woman with a limp, wearing short scarlet Wellington boots, a blue beret and an old black sweater, and with cosmetics haphazardly daubed on a large round moony face".[99] It was only on getting to know her that he discovered the "formidable personality" behind the "large round moony face".

Throughout August she revised the completed manuscript of *Death of Felicity Taverner*. She also found time to relax: "Today Mr Hills and the run in his car to Penzance. Finding the two frocks and the hat. The good lunch. The way the men smiled and the women scowled at me.... The delicious unpacking of trifles.... I am enjoying such physical acts of living today and tonight. Dried Gabriel in his bath." In addition there was the company of the writer, Louis Wilkinson, who had spent a few days with them, walking and chatting (amongst other things about Rebecca West and Aldous Huxley), although the visit had been slightly marred when Gabriel was vexed by a grumbling appendix. "How kind you both were to me at Sennen," wrote Wilkinson from East Chaldon, Dorset where he had gone on to stay with the Cowper Powys family. "I am most grateful and I enjoyed those days extremely...I hope that Gabriel has had no sort of return of that ailment and that you are all very well."[100] A visit from another friend did not pass off so pleasantly. Douglas Goldring and his family stayed in Sennen over the summer and, as the month progressed, so their friendship began to be strained. By the time he left in early September Mary Butts felt only relief that "the Deplorable Visit [was] over.[101] We did not quite lose our tempers, depression, irritation, sometimes visible, infinite disappointment, but no row." She believed, however, that "the friendship [was] not broken—under a cloud only" and indeed, six months later they began their friendly correspondence once again.

A visit to the dentist on 10 September prompted the following entry: "An Interesting Day. Penzance and the new dentist. Returned less a tooth plus information about teeth and people." On the publishing front she was able to send the good news to Angus Davidson that Methuen were interested in republishing *Ashe of Rings*. She also started a new longish story called 'What the Moon Saw' and wrote a first version over the following four months. Her idea was to divide it into a number of parts based on the different aspects of the moon. "Look up the names of each Moon—Harvest moon, Hunter's moon etc," she noted on the 15th, adding a few days later: "'What the Moon Saw'. I finished. For II—what about the idea for a writing—moon-memories of this place before?" She was rather worried by the fact that she "wrote Moon I with too great facility, what *might* become a parody[102] of my style, and what is worse, of my thinking. The moons needn't *begin* with the moon—some can start with things done under the moon, moon-influenced or not. The trouble is to find 'em. What about times when the moon saw only lovely and appropriate things?" Over the next few months she noted phrases, sightings of, poems and stories associated with the moon which inspired her, such as William Morris's poem, 'East of the Sun, West of the Moon' and Aldous Huxley's numinous stone. "Remember," she wrote on 9 November, "Moon waxing. A simple light on the sands at low tides, a torch or a crescent, steady in the quiet air." A month later she commented on the "knife-moon, this December. I was right. It has slashed us, now three days with the east wind. It rides above it, cold and distant, and rarely quite clear of a blur of high brown clouds." She worked on the story-cycle intermittently over the next four years.[103]

On the 28 September she was pleased when Duff Twysden wrote to her, noting: "There is a parallel in both our lives, and what is between us is unforgettable (Answered, saying this)." Early October found her in a such good spirits that "this morning the wind, no rose, kitten's messes, a bleeding scratch, the stove, tradesmen, undone hair, bills etc, dustbin were somehow patterned and controlled." "Could we make it always happen!" she added in the margin. Later that month she wrote to Hugh Ross Williamson to ask whether *The Bookman* would be interested in publishing the article on Supernatural Fiction which she had written in Paris in 1928. "And wouldn't I just love the 'Supernatural' for the Bookman," he replied. "May I begin it in the January number? Which means at press by December 8th." The article was revised, renamed 'Ghosties and Ghoulies'[104] and published in four parts between January and April 1933.

In the same letter Ross Williamson wrote: "'Felicity' has arrived... And the dedication. Again I can't thank you enough. But may it be just the plain name, without anything else?"[105] He concluded by announcing: "And now I'm going to read 'Felicity'."[106] Mary Butts was so nervous about his reaction that she apologised for the novel in her next letter, saying that she wanted him to like at least parts of it; failing that, then the invention—the fact that it was another description or part of "our Waste Land".[107]

Death of Felicity Taverner

James Boswell designed the striking dust jacket of the novel which was published by Wishart & Co at 7s 6d. Its plot was succinctly described by Wynyard Browne who reviewed it in *The Bookman*: "*Death of Felicity*

Taverner arises directly out of the contemporary situation. The conflict in it corresponds with the conflict in the modern world," he wrote and proceeded to give the "skeleton of the story":

> Felicity, who was neither understood nor loved by her mother, was married to a Communist Russian Jew, named Kralin, and was killed in a motor accident in France. The younger and more sensitive of her relations, [Scylla Taverner, her brother Felix and her husband Picus Tracey] with the help of Boris Polteratsky, an exiled Russian aristocrat, attempt to find out the cause of her death, for which they feel that Kralin and in a lesser degree her mother were responsible. They only find that Kralin has a stranglehold on them and their land (the atmosphere of which pervades the book like a scent); that he intends to turn it into a pleasure resort of the most repulsive and profitable kind as soon as he can persuade Mrs Taverner to sell him Felicity's house[108] and some of the surroundings as a nucleus; that in order to get the house he will resort to blackmail, threatening to publish Felicity's most intimate papers as material for psychological research. But Boris, remembering an old score against him and his kind, kills him in a cave after pointing out its advantages as a curiosity for trippers.[109]

Mary Butts was greatly relieved when Ross Williamson replied in late October to tell her that he found the novel "quite magnificent; I've lived with it for two days—in tubes, armchairs and bed: read it twice; thought about it, thrilled to it and criticised it. This last as the final compliment, without which anything else I might say would not please you." These opening remarks convey the novel's capacity to absorb and exhilarate, while the following extracts from his letter with its balance of praise and careful criticisms illustrate the integrity of his reading as well as the significance he gave to their friendship:

> I think you've got right down to the depths, clarified it inside yourself and shown it to the world; show them what they *must* think—those that can think anyhow—about ultimate things. The sheer dramatic force of it is amazing; the great point, I think, is when you first hear of Kralin's plan about the land; it's so enormous (in the sense of enormity), so unexpected that it's something like the shock of surprise (only reversed; ugliness instead of beauty) that you get on coming suddenly on York Minster, towering above you, out of one of the tiny lanes where you'd never suspected its presence. Then, again, the first time they all sit down together to discuss things! Almost the feeling of aesthetic satisfaction when a clever dramatist has got all his characters, credibly, together; combined with the authentic Surreyside thrill, when the green light announces the villain. And the tension that only you can get.
>
> I pick those out, I suppose, because the dramatic always gets me (it's that partly in T.S.E.); but the atmosphere; the things observed—and how well described! and the sureness of the psychology; the pat-

> tern—detail (like the Boris-chant on Kralin at the end of chapter 14) and large design—the gradual unfolding of the general out of the particular, without the particular becoming lost; the main large issue, implicit, not superimposed; oh High Priestess, magnificent!
>
> And criticism? Two minor points only. I'm not sure that, for the general reader (and at this point *he* is important) a little of the background of the Taverners and of Boris in chapters 13 and 14 ought not to have been transplanted into chapter 1. This is uncourageous, I know; but I personally felt that by the time I'd reached that description of the Taverners (which in my book on you I'm going to quote in full as a statement of your—our—creed; it's one of the best things you've done) I didn't particularly want it. You'd made me *dig* for the Taverners; I'd dug; and then you suddenly decided to save me the trouble. (Me being in this case the General Reader, poor dove). And Boris is really hazy at the beginning—which I think he should not be. It's important to grasp him fully earlier than one does.
>
> And the second point is that I felt the need of seeing explicitly and at some length Felicity through Kralin's eyes and Kralin through hers. Almost (to go dramatic again) as if you'd done me out of the psychological *scène à faire*. But perhaps I'm wrong here? And insensitive? But I know it's all there, really.[110]

Hugh Ross Williamson was not alone amongst her friends and relatives in enjoying the novel. On the 1 November she made a list of people to be sent *Death of Felicity Taverner*. These included Ethel Colburn Mayne, E.M. Forster[111] (who wrote to say that he was looking forward to reading it), Tom Swan (her lawyer), Douglas Goldring and Filson Young. The latter was extremely impressed: "Let me say at once that it is far and away the best piece of work in what I would seriously call the modern technique that I have read.... It is the best adventure in the imaginative fiction of today that I have read; it gives me hope as well as pleasure and mental exercise."[112] He concluded the letter with the hope of visiting her when he returned to Cornwall at Christmas. On the 13 December Ethel Colburn Mayne opened her letter with the words: "Darling, with a sticky pen I must nevertheless pour out my praises of 'Felicity'—they won't be too treacly, I hope. I think it is exquisite in the true sense of the word, and more than that for more is in it—the greatness which has made you so beloved to me. Beauty and nobility informing the whole, and beauty even in the ugliness which makes the theme so painfully exciting. It is worthy of you—more so than anything else you have written; and moreover it is witty and subtle and hard with a crystal hardness." She then added: "Of course I shall put it on our damned Femina list, and if it doesn't go to France (where the prize is *awarded*: we send three books) I shall resign from the Committee, and say why."[113] In fact, *Death of Felicity Taverner* was not nominated and the prize was won by Rosamund Lehmann's *Invitation to the Waltz*.

On the 28 November Mary Colville-Hyde sent Mary Butts her "warmest congratulations on your lovely book—it makes me think of a great irridescent [sic] christal [sic] vase—filled with wind anemones and tansy and wood sorrel, I feel sure Gabriel is very proud of you."[114] Tony was equally enthusiastic, commenting on her power to evoke the atmosphere of the Dorset coast. "I want to tell you how very much I admire 'Felicity', and to give you all my congratulation on it from the depths of my heart. Your prose becomes more vivid and jewelled in each book;...each story of yours is for me something like a dream often repeated; the geography of the dream, with each landmark becomes clearer and more familiar; one is living for the time in a crystal world, where the figures of Callot, Rouault and Bérard move in the luminous landscape of Claude...your prose was never more sensitive, never sharper. Never was the air more beautifully vital with the scents of thyme and of the sea, and with the humming of bees; no house was ever more haunted by a lovelier ghost." He also commented on the fact that the novel had "achieved the seemingly impossible, in making reviewers almost intelligent".[115]

Certainly, the reviews of *Death of Felicity Taverner* were in the main extremely complimentary: "The style is exquisite, difficult, careful; impossible to skip, to tear the sense out of the page in haste," declared Gwendolin Raverat in *Time and Tide*.[116] L.A.G. Strong in *The Spectator* found *Death of Felicity Taverner* extremely well-crafted: "The novel is of a high standard, even brilliant in parts; the writing is subtle: there is a well-constructed story, with drama, conflict and suspense."[117] The *Evening News* (which reproduced Man Ray's photograph of Mary Butts) recommended *Death of Felicity Taverner* as "not easy to get into: but it is lovely and exciting."[118] Even the *Times Literary Supplement*, which was rather more guarded ("pathetic in its way," was how Ethel Colburn Mayne described this review, "so bewildered, and so afraid of showing it"),[119] commented that whilst "the problem of Felicity is not, of course, a new one... The glittering allusive method employed by Miss Butts, the restlessness of modern detail, make the story a stimulating adventure in mind."[120] The most general criticism was the old one: "Often however the writing is so conscious as to hold up the reader's attention; the way of saying a thing distracts one from the thing said."[121] For Wynyard Browne, writing in *The Bookman*, this style was due to the experimental nature of Mary Butts's writing: "*Death of Felicity Taverner* is very much more than an allegory of contemporary world politics." Rather, each character "stands not only for an attitude to the world, but a group in the world. Felicity herself, for instance, who is dead before the story begins, represents the Magical attitude, that is in fact only just dead, and stands for the group who live as though they were in a Golden Age and suffer for their innocence. The words of the characters have so many echoes, their actions so many possible interpretations, that only several readings of the book in different moods could form the basis for a complete appreciation. And so far I have only read it once." He then went on to place *Death of Felicity Taverner* at the forefront of contemporary novel-writing alongside that of James Joyce:

> It is in no derogatory sense obscure. Miss Butts writes always with clarity, if not always with the precision one expects of prose. But it has to be remembered that the modern novel is, at its best, poetic. It has taken the place of epic and tragic poetry. The problem before the serious novelist can be stated in terms of the difference between prose and poetry. Mr Joyce first made the problem plain, and he has approached more closely than anyone else to a solution. Miss Butts is among those who are working consciously to that end. This is not the place to discuss technique in detail. It is enough to say that she relies most on metaphor and on heightened and expanded dialogue. Naturally she is not yet quite sure of herself. Like every writer seriously attempting to overcome technical difficulties, she sometimes fails badly.... But in the average novel such faults are so frequent as to pass unnoticed.

His other major criticism was that "her characters though we are told explicitly the difference between them, talk very much as if they were the same." Yet what Wynyard Browne found most compelling about the novel was its refusal "merely to supply a demand". Instead it "attempt[s] something more difficult and more valuable" and its effect (as Filson Young had commented) was to "modif[y] the reader's attitudes to a remarkable extent. People or events can be seen differently in the light of it. The reader is changed as he is changed by poetry that is 'alive' or by contact with someone who is more aware than others; whose mind is growing."[122]

Mary Butts was delighted with Browne's review and felt a sense of "triumph" about *Death of Felicity Taverner*.[123] That he had responded to the novel in the way she had intended, is clear from the role she assigned the writer in 'Ghosties and Ghoulies': "It is curious," she wrote in this long study of supernatural fiction:

> Up to our age a writer, even the most detached artist, was allowed to teach. Having special love or knowledge, he was supposed to hand it on. The present world, its majority suddenly become literate, unless the subject is technical, faints at the thought. Until it is noticed that, having read any imaginative work from Aristophanes to Ronald Firbank, and taken pleasure in it, something of its quality has entered in and become part of oneself. Has made one more aware and sensible, using the writer's eyes. So that one finds out that, after all, one has learned.[124]

When writing to Ross Williamson Mary Butts commented that Browne's criticism was as sound as his praise, and that she would be more careful about dialogue in future. "And 'Felicity' is nothing to the books I'm going to do—tho' I haven't the least idea at the moment what they are."[125] Whilst the following January she toyed with the idea of writing a novel about "Scylla & co in a new set", her next narrative would be a historical one: *Scenes from the Life of Cleopatra*.

In early December her editor at Wishart, Edgell Rickword, wrote to say that he had received a letter from the "English representative of Messrs Little & Brown who has unsuccessfully been trying to get into touch with your agents about the American rights of *Felicity*. She says that she has had no reply to two letters. I tell you this, because we found them dilatory over correspondence, and it might be well for you to jog them up." (This was not the only time her agent would let her down.) Rickword was also writing to discuss her future work. The following extract shows that there was a great deal to consider. "There seem to me a number of points," he wrote in a letter which combined an astute publishing sense with respect for her writing:

> (a) Short Stories
> (b) Novel
> (c) Revised edition of *Ashe of Rings*?
> (d) Another volume of short stories, more lengthy than *Several Occasions*, then regain your rights to *Speed the Plough* and have a collected edition.
> (e) Are you going to stick to one publisher, for fiction at any rate? You see the amount a publisher can spend on pushing a book in advertising depends on the likelihood of his getting another book or books by the same author before the public forgets the name.
>
> Also, a novel is very much more easily saleable than stories (though I would never try and persuade anyone to write novels when they write stories like yours,) but from the publisher's point of view I must admit that one could give double the advance on a novel that one could on a volume of stories.... I think £50 would be quite reasonable for a book that we could have in time to publish before the end of 1933. For a novel you ought to get more. But when you say two years, it does seem a rather long while to wait.
>
> Still, only you can know what you are likely to have, and when.... I wish you were up here so we could talk it over. Is there any hope of your re-publishing *Ashe of Rings*? If so, might not that help to tide over the barren patch, and ensure a more regular flow of the base metal?[126]

Methuen's interest in republishing *Ashe of Rings* had unfortunately come to nothing. Mary Butts thus accepted Wishart's proposal. As a result, 1933 saw the publication of the first English edition of *Ashe of Rings*, *The*

Macedonian, 'Ghosties and Ghoulies', as well as a number of reviews. Yet whilst her professional reputation increased and her work brought her new friends and admirers, her personal life became ever more difficult as her relationship with Gabriel and her family deteriorated. The situation was brought to a head in December 1932 because of the repercussions of the sale of family heirlooms on Camilla's education.

La Chute

That Mary Butts believed there had been an earlier paradisal period in her life is clear from a diary entry on 5 November 1932 where she remarked on how a beautiful evening had made her remember Salterns "and when I was a child. Before MCH and Tony began to hurt." At the end of September she was not feeling charitable towards her mother: "I don't feel as if I could forgive; or, what is worse, that I want to forgive. Which is it? Is it 'can' or 'will'? How hard it is to judge where one's own fault lies, and how much easier it is to brood and fret over one's own fault—hazily—without quite determining its quantity and quality." On the whole, however, she tended to be less philosophical and lucid, and more self-obsessed. "Bad interval," she wrote a few days later, "sick and a little sorry. Not able to work and anxious to—'déprimé'... And I have hours of fury when I think of my people and all they are doing to spoil what they can. It may come this time to a final break with Tony...his subservience to his mother look as though they would give final cause enough."

The continuing cause of resentment derived from the protracted sale of the Holbein portrait. In early 1930 it had made the headlines of several newspapers and art magazines.[127] Opportunities to sell the painting had been missed through bad advice, however, and by the summer of 1932 it remained unsold. In a letter to her aunt in 1933 Mary Butts related one spectacular missed opportunity: "I happened to have been in London and I was standing by her [Mary Colville-Hyde's] side when Captain Duveen[128] rang her up to ask if he was to have the picture, I think for £80,000, and a cold shiver ran down my spine then at the tone in which she said 'I am afraid you won't have it Captain Duveen.' Some idiot had told her that she ought to hold out for £100,000."[129]

A bad return from Railway dividends in August had led Mary Colville-Hyde to inform Ada: "The Estate Accountant tells me I shall have £500 a year in all, so until the Holbein is sold I shall try and sell some of the family heirlooms."[130] In the autumn she wrote to her daughter that "we are now (under very important advice)—lying low about the Holbein as we are told this *must* be done...and try again in the new year."[131] "My affairs look very black," she explained elsewhere, "I shall be thankful when the strain of living here [3, Buckingham Gardens] is over—...I hope to take a tiny flat with a part day maid...I am selling off my diamond cigarette etc for Camilla's school fees—etc—at Sotheby's."[132] Aware of his sister's grief at the sale, Tony wrote in November about "the impending sale at Sotheby's":

> I'm not really the evil genius behind the auctioneer's throne that I may perhaps seem to be; the facts are really very simple in their origin. Mother asked me whether she should sell Charles the First's watch; I replied, not unnaturally, that such a sale would depend entirely upon neccessity [sic]; she suggested a consultation with your friend Tancred Borenius,[133] which took place in due course; he rushed about the flat like a pig after truffles...; in fact he rushed us into a sale of more objects than we either of us wished to part with.

Tony then went on to make two points which highlight his understanding of his sister's personality. The first illustrates how far her sense of identity was built upon the history of her family, to which Tony was sympathetic:

> I shall be deprived, just as much as you, of transmitting family heirlooms to my children;...to love and to desire lovely things is not a very original point of view, especially when they have a thousand associations of youth and memory behind them. And the capacity for suffering at parting with them is no more a unique possession, either; I don't doubt for a moment, though, that it has its degrees of pain.... You are wrong in saying that I don't care about them; I don't for a moment suggest that I care for them as deeply as you, but I don't think I'm indifferent to beauty. Neither am I indifferent to the families to which I belong, Butts, Briggs, Irlam, or any of the million amalgams which give us a psychic entity. Actually you are luckier than I; and must suffer more at their dispersal, since they have a totemic, magical, symbolic value for you, I imagine, in addition to their other values.

The second point shows Tony trying to pre-empt the kind of fruitless discussions which had taken place between them in previous years: "Nothing can be gained by justifying either of our attitudes to each other, in terms of our own private interpretations of life; yours may well be a far better one than mine, more true, more honest, more profound, more permanent. But," and here Tony's realism comes to the fore, "what solution have you to offer?"[134] Unlike the happy understanding between brother and sister in her story, 'In the South', Tony and Mary Butts were unable to agree on this issue.

That he had foreseen his sister's reactions accurately, is clear from her version of events in a letter to Hugh Ross Williamson on the 5 December. It is a dramatic account which also reveals the interest such a sale would have for collectors of art and antiques:

> Just now—I mean this minute, I've heard from [my brother] that he and Mother are selling the last of our things at Sotheby's. The Stuart things—we've had them since the Civil Wars—Charles' I watch and the Queen's seals, Monmouth's box and Mary Tudor's. And the Blake miniatures. All in fact that we've got left. The land is gone, the money, the Blake pictures,—and now these. There is something final about it. Now we're nothing. And that is my Mother's stewardship—she was left with all the power—of our affairs. And Tony's response—as head (and last) of our family. So that, Ross, is that. I've spent the days since I heard paralysed or else crying with futile rage and sheer misery. There's an intense—perhaps too violent—possessiveness over beautiful things in us. It's weaker in Tony, for all his connoisseurship; and my Mother has ruined us and they need ready money, how badly I hardly dare speculate, and the things must go. But it's a 'Finis' being written. I had to tell you about it, as I always tell you about important things.
>
> And Gabriel and Ruth Manning-Sanders are trying to make me see it as an end and a beginning—me being the beginning. It may be true in a way—I'll try and make it true, but...our house-saga is finished.

Two days earlier Mary Butts had described the situation in her journal as "the last 'chute' [fall] of my people" and her account to Ross Williamson with its criticism of her mother's and Tony's inattention to money, led very naturally to the following request: "Forgive me again, but it will be all right about that cheque for 'the Supernatural'? If it is, then Christmas will be all right, and the coal and a cake with nuts on and things—"[135] A cheque for £21 was sent a few days later. Ross Williamson also wrote sympathising with her feeling of loss. He then went on to pick up on Gabriel and Ruth Manning-Sanders's point that Mary Butts's writing was a beginning. "That's not bogus soothing-syrup," he declared, "but something I really believe." His explanation was based on a debate, current at that time, about the relationship between tradition and the individual.[136] "It seems to me, that in the eternal fight between tradition and individual—because it is a fundamental quarrel—there comes a point where tradition dies and the individual is born.... Haven't you been *forced* to take that step? All that the Blake miniatures in your home meant essentially is in *you*. They mean nothing more than that. You epitomise that tradition."[137] In his previous letter he had articulated the extent of his respect for her as a writer (adding the touching postscript—"Better not answer this: it might embarrass both of us!"): "You are very great. You know that, don't you? It's difficult to say this without appearing impertinent, but from the first moment I read 'Theseus' all those years ago:

through *Ashe* till now, you have been, for me a writer different *in kind*, not just degree, from nearly every contemporary. Lawrence had it too: but he denied discipline: Eliot has denied too much for the sake of discipline: I still believe that in 1950, at the latest, it will be generally conceded that Mary Butts fused the two."[138]

Camilla

> *If you have time to write books, surely you have time to love your only daughter.*
> —Camilla, undated note to MB, early 1930s

> *Of course I really and* truly *am longing to see [Camilla] and this place makes a very good change from Parkstone, now alas so spoilt. It gives her the really wild surroundings and contact with nature she seems both to need and to love. There is nothing better than that—for a child or grown up.*
> —MB, undated draft of letter to Ada Briggs, Friday, December 1932

In early 1929, after John Rodker had brought her to England, Camilla attended several schools. The move back to her native land brought about no real change in her relationship with her parents however. During her childhood she would never live for any length of time with either of them.

From the correspondence between Mary Colville-Hyde and Ada, it is clear that there were continual problems over the payment of Camilla's school fees. In August Mary Colville-Hyde had agreed to pay £75 p.a. for Camilla and in November John Rodker agreed to pay £50 p.a. providing Mary Colville-Hyde kept up her payments.[139] It appears that John Rodker wanted Camilla to live with him at this time. However, since he only rarely paid the £50 he had promised, it is uncertain how serious this desire actually was. In any case Mary Butts was adamantly opposed to the idea. She herself expressed interest in Camilla spending the summer with her at Sennen, a suggestion which worried Mary Colville-Hyde and Ada who were unsure whether she would look after her daughter properly. Mary Colville-Hyde reassured Ada in a letter: "I don't think Mary has the fare" and this suggestion did come to nothing. Indeed, Camilla spent the summer holidays that year partly with Mary Colville-Hyde and partly with John Rodker in Essex. "I am very sorry for her," Camilla's grandmother wrote to Ada. "She is pulled two ways all the time." Worry over the difficulties within the family prompted her to head this particular letter: "Burn this when read." Ada Briggs did not. According to Mary Colville-Hyde, Mary Butts was "furious" with her for allowing Camilla to visit her father during the summer, but as she confided to Ada: "What can we do?"[140]

"Camilla seems now well-settled at Sandecotes—and finds (I am told) it rather difficult to be at the bottom of the new school—instead of near the top of the old—she has been re-vaccinated—as this is a school rule," wrote Mary Colville-Hyde to her daughter in early autumn that year.[141] Mary Butts explained her inability to deal with the practical difficulties of motherhood. Her response involved laying the blame on her mother: "Your decision not to let us have the £100 a year you had allowed me since my marriage, has made our lives very much harder and more difficult. It would not be easy for you to realise how so small a sum could make such a difference, but it has—put back our clock, hindered the work we are doing—which would have given us complete freedom very much sooner.... Above all, I have had to let Cuddy [Camilla] be for a while longer. We should have had her here for this summer. Then it became literally impossible. That made me bitterly unhappy."[142] As far as Mary Butts was concerned, Camilla's education was a family matter rather than one for which the parents alone were responsible. On the contrary, letters written the following year reveal her unabated insistence that the financial responsibility lay with her mother and John Rodker to pay the sums they had promised. Problems developed when Mary Colville-Hyde's income reduced dramatically, from £500 p.a. in August 1932 to £199 in January 1933. Unmoved by this drastic reduction, Mary Butts offered the following explanation and instructions to her aunt at the beginning of 1933: "I have my mother's promise verbally and in writing, and lately repeated until just before Christmas to pay for Camilla's education...until such time as Gabriel and I shall be well enough off to take it on ourselves," her letter began, and continued:

> Don't give notice or have any bills sent to me. The holidays are all we can manage at present; tho' in a year, or so, we ought to be able to take the whole charge on ourselves...I have made it quite clear to Mother that Gabriel and I can do nothing more than the child's holidays *yet* and that with difficulty. To have a much-praised novel out [*Death of Felicity Taverner*] doesn't mean that one has made any money *yet* (forgive repetitions). I certainly haven't. Tho' I have every hope of doing so...I think it will be all right, I have her [Mother's] promise so absolutely underlined, and countersigned by Tony.[143]

Such was her sense that the responsibility for Camilla's education lay with her mother, that in reneging (as Mary Butts saw it) on Camilla's school fees, Mary Colville-Hyde was jeopardising Camilla's very existence: "Jan 15th:...I thought of the child's threatened life and loathed the woman who bore me"; "Jan 22nd:...afraid for the child"; "Jan 30th:...One step more in this terrible un-making, [Mary Colville-Hyde's] abandonment of the child." Her attitude to Camilla's father was equally unrelenting, as she explained in a letter to her aunt Ada: "Now for John Rodker. The best thing I can think to do is to make it quite clear to him that he won't see the child again until he has paid up.... I've absolute legal—and now I think moral—right to do this. If that won't bring him to his senses, nothing will. I am also writing to my solicitors for their advice if there is any further action we can take."[144]

Her own attitude towards Camilla was in part based on a belief that as a writer she should be spared the daily duties of a parent and it is no exaggeration to say that Camilla's childhood was sacrificed to Mary Butts's writing. Yet it is a depressing fact that her attitude (which involved unpredictable and always *short* bouts of interest in her daughter), combined with an inability to deal with the reality of a child's presence and needs, is by no means uncommon amongst writers: Rebecca West, James Joyce, H.D., A.A. Milne, Roald Dahl and Enid Blyton, to name but a few.[145] Not only was Camilla particularly unfortunate in that neither of her parents seemed seriously interested in her; the fact of Mary Butts's early death (when Camilla was only sixteen) meant that she and her mother never had the opportunity *together* to come to terms with her emotional neglect.

It was the septuagenarian Ada Briggs who took upon herself the responsibilities of the parent, and whilst this was admirable, it was nonetheless hard for the child because Ada's beliefs belonged to a different age. Mary Butts's general disregard for the day-to-day arrangements of her daughter's life, meant that it was months before she was aware of her aunt's central role in Camilla's life. "I had no idea of the care and interest you had taken in the child," she wrote rather blithely to Ada on the 10 January 1933. "I had understood from Mother, that you found her tiresome and difficult; got the idea into my head that you rarely saw her; had not the least conception of all you had done. I am beginning to understand now." Nor could she resist another opportunity to criticise her mother: "Perhaps I may say, frankly, that Mother has a way—unconscious *perhaps*—of making ordinary people misunderstand one another."[146] That word "perhaps" is so telling—this is no general ordinary dislike for Mary Colville-Hyde; her hatred was as intense in the 1930s as it had been in the 1910s. Early in March 1933 she listed some of the family possessions which Mary Colville-Hyde had sent her as part of her Christmas gifts: "Miniature of me when a baby in blue enamel and paste octagonal frame... Crystal seal with gold setting... A piece of amber, and a brass chinese compass etc." Yet this in no way alleviated her attitude of disdain, as only two days later she declared:

> In one thing I am clearer: I was right about my mother, when as a girl I feared her for the destruction she would bring on our house. Now she has done so, and I must hate her for it. Not quite 'hate', for I am not quite without understanding or even a kind of pity. It is like awe in a way, or withdrawing of myself entirely from our relation of mother and daughter, a looking at her. Mixed with a kind of horror of what she has brought on us. And it is good to have it so far clear.

In early December 1932 she wrote to her mother asking her to pay Camilla's £4 train fare to Sennen; Mary Colville-Hyde, who was waiting for the Sotheby sale of the heirlooms on the 15 and 16 December, was unwilling to send it. She later informed her daughter that "a great many items did not reach their reserves."[147] These included the Blake miniatures. The Charles I watch was one of the heirlooms which did sell (before the sale Mary Butts wrote to Ross Williamson that it was rumoured the King was interested in buying it). Only then was Mary Colville-Hyde able to pay back Ada for the upkeep of Camilla in that year. (Ada was greatly relieved as she had been forced to use her own capital to pay Camilla's school fees.) In late autumn Mary Butts had suddenly decided that she wanted Camilla to come to Sennen. Indeed, she was so insistent that Ada was worried she might just take Camilla away indefinitely; Mary Colville-Hyde, however, predicted with a great deal of accuracy that she would "be sick of the child before the end of the holidays".[148] Whilst she was wrangling with her family, Mary Butts wrote of Camilla's imminent visit to Hugh Ross Williamson in rather different terms: "The child is so glad she can come—have a real home here together at last. And bless your 'Bookman' for making it possible."[149] She sent him a Christmas card based on a witty and fine line drawing by Gabriel (see p. i). It shows Mary Butts "as the virgin and himself as the Angel of the Annunciation, offering to her the slightly drooping lily of purity. The droop is typical of them both, a bit of camp against themselves, which mocked them rather than the people they depicted."[150] There was also a sadder aspect to this card which its recipients would not have realised. In St Malo in 1929 "Annonce faite à Marie" was how Mary Butts and Gabriel Aitken referred to their decision, not only to marry, but to have a son, who, in deference to her regard for Milton's poem, would be called Comus. By the time Gabriel drew the card, with its obvious tribute to Dante Gabriel Rossetti's painting *The Annunciation* (1850), the decision to have a child had been abandoned.

On the 23 December Mary Colville-Hyde wrote to Ada that Camilla had arrived safely in Sennen. The first morning she woke up in her room in Tebel Vos, she looked down on the floor to see a tin of biscuits bearing a note saying "EAT ME" (as in *Alice in Wonderland*). Such a delightful gesture towards her child's comfort and needs was, sadly, uncharacteristic of Mary Butts. This first period of over three weeks together since the 1920s, which Mary Butts had been looking forward to with such "longing", did not prompt much comment in her diary. The first mention of her daughter's presence was ten days later and it is rather telling: "Filson Young called; [I] was rather proud of Camilla. She is also a darling when I want to work". The basic pattern for the entries on Camilla involved praise when she was no trouble, and excessive criticism when her behaviour was in any way contrary. Camilla being a "darling" usually meant that she was absent from the house—a fact which clearly had a lot to do with Mary Butts's last-minute decision to extend Camilla's visit in Sennen by a week:

> My dear, if you don't mind, I'll keep her.... The weather is exquisite, she is out of doors all day, wildly enjoying herself. Her health could hardly be better, her manners have greatly improved—she told me all the struggles *you've* had with them, and is trying to mend them and be less pert and cocksure and more considerate. Every day there is something fresh to do, the healthiest possible things; while we've become such friends again, that my heart will ache when she leaves. She's been away so long, that I feel I can never have enough of her. While her step-father already cares for her so much. So we're a very happy family.

Even though this was written to her aunt, rather than to one of the new-found admirers of her work, it would seem that Mary Butts could not resist producing a letter where an entertaining style was more important than factual accuracy: "Look here, I'm beginning this letter all wrong—with my family circling round me, the butcher calling, the cat trying to show me a dead mouse."[151] Effect would seem to be paramount; I raise this point because the idyllic family scene appears to have been shortlived, if her diary (which does tend to convey a more accurate account of her attitudes and feelings) is to be believed. Hence two days later on the 12 January she complained that a visit to an ancient well in the area had had to be abandoned: "Sancreed: we did not go to-day," partly because Gabriel had been ill, but partly also because "Camilla forgot the time and her watch was slow." This bristly tone is also present in the entry for the following day and shows her impatience and annoyance whenever her daughter got in the way of her appreciation of what was so crucial to her—the landscape. The very construction of the sentence (with its break to express an aside about Camilla) reflects Mary Butts's adamantine refusal to make any concessions to her 12-year-old child if she interrupted her work. The entry is all the more poignant for the fact that her description of the landscape is conveyed with characteristic vividness and sensitivity:

> *January 13th [1933]*: Went to 'Chapel' Carn Brea.[152] I can no more describe it than what it is to look into the face of a crystal. I saw—(I do not know how much the child saw, she was in a growing girl's peevish fit all day) I saw—the Atlantic: and the coast of England: and a map of very pure green fields. Then behind us and away for ever, rising higher than our hill, a brown moor, sewn with stars. Houseless, pathless: and the air was purer than imagination has words.

When she put Camilla on a train back to Parkstone on the 17 January, her first reaction was one of relief: "Camilla Elizabeth returned. Great fatigue." Interestingly, her imagination then immediately went on to transform this individual child into the 'type' (in the Jungian sense) of a girl of 12 years, rather than *her* own daughter: "Are girls comparable [to boys]? Yes, sometimes. Will Camilla be? I doubt it. But I am a little prejudiced against her when I see her as I have the last few days—from time to time pert and conceited, and, even for twelve years, almost unbelievably inconsiderate. On the other hand, I believe these will modify, have modified already, under Gabriel's influence especially. Heaven bless them both." Having dispensed with her daughter, the rest of the entry focused on her work: "I must put my inside house in order tonight, and tomorrow take up a hundred duties and some severe. Dieu, qui m'a créé artiste—give me the exercise of my genius again." Her comment to Ada a week earlier that her heart would "ache" when her daughter left, seems to have been quickly forgotten if it was ever true.

Even before Camilla's departure the family correspondence relating to her upkeep had continued without reprieve. On the 10 January Mary Colville-Hyde wrote to Mary Butts: "I have paid Camilla's last money from the sale of the watch and hope to pay the next from the same source, but it is fairly obvious that unless we make the money, I cannot pay off more unless and until the Holbein is sold." This seemed rather unlikely in the short term for she had been advised that "our only *chance* is for the market *to forget*...until D V [God Willing] the hour...strikes". Awareness of her daughter's lack of sympathy made Mary Colville-Hyde add: "You do believe—don't you—the truth of all I tell you."[153] However Mary Butts remained unimpressed, writing to her aunt that she felt "very bitter about it all."[154] Ada wrote back to say that she had once again paid the following term's fees from her own capital and in view of the lack of future money, she would have to give provisional notice of Camilla's withdrawal from the school for the following term. As a possible help she asked whether Camilla should try for the £50 scholarship which was being offered in February. It is a sign of Mary Butts's self-absorption that she waited almost three weeks before thanking her aunt for her "generous suggestion", to advance the term's fees. "It's splendid on your part to suggest such a thing," she repeated without any compunction or guilt.[155] She agreed that Camilla should try for the scholarship and repeated that John Rodker must have no contact with his daughter until he had paid up. Three days later she excused herself for not writing more often because of work and wifely duties: "Don't think that you and Camilla are ever out of my thoughts, but I am working very hard; also, for the last few days Gabriel has been in bed with a very bad cold. So I've had him to nurse as well as everything else."[156]

Marriage

UNFORTUNATELY all was not well in Mary Butts's and Gabriel Aitken's marriage. Depressed and with a slight chill she wrote on the 22 January: "Perhaps one has to be as unhappy as this from time to time—to learn all over again that one is absolutely alone." Taking the evidence of her public writings — her letters and the fact that she dedicated *The Macedonian* to her husband[157]—this may seem a strange comment. In fact, it is characteristic of the split between the way she presented herself to the world and the private reality. Whilst she was often inspired by Gabriel (that is, by the Gabriel of her imagination, the potential which she saw in his painting, his caricatures, his cartoons and his "shocker"); Gabriel the man was a constant source of disappointment to her. Part of the problem was his continued alcoholism. As Mary Colville-Hyde wrote to Ada: "Gabriel is good and charming—only he drinks too much—but it only makes him cry and everyone has a good word for him."[158] Since no letters from him survive from the period after their move to Sennen, it is not possible to know his side of this story. It is also clear that due to her unpredictability and tendency to mythologise, Mary Butts was also a very difficult person to spend any length of time in close proximity with—everyone eventually disappointed her. However, it is fair to say that Gabriel's particular weaknesses of character and his lack of dedication to his painting (although he was undoubtedly talented), were especially frustrating to Mary Butts. She was, herself, far from abstemious in Sennen although on a less excessive scale than when she had lived in Paris: she drank heavily (especially from the mid-1930s a potent drink called 'Champagne Nerve Tonic'), smoked de Retzsk cigarettes and Sobranie on special occasions as well as opium. Harcourt Wesson Bull saw a great deal of her when he stayed with Angus Davidson in Sennen between February and August 1935. The following anecdote testifies both to her fairly constant consumption of an opium infusion by that time and to her inscrutability:

> Angus and I had been carrying down to her from the Post Office many mysterious cartons, some of them quite large, sent by garden supply houses. One day a partly damaged box revealed the fact that it was full of dried poppy heads. "What's in all these boxes?" one of us, too innocently, asked. "Oh, just little bits of wood," Mary answered. From then on in the evenings there was always a brew of those "bits of wood" simmering away in a small saucepan at the back of Mary's stove, and I couldn't refrain from asking, one night while we washed the dishes, what *it* was. To be sure my question from one point of view was impertinent, but it was not meant impertinently. Knowing her as well as I did, sharing daily all we shared, being possessive about her, I wanted a truthful reply so that our intimacy and trust would be even greater. If she had said: "It's an infusion of poppy heads—a mild opium substitute," which I knew it to be, and had not treated so near a friend—childishly in this case, for she only said casually: "Something for my knee,"—I would have been content. Never once had she referred in any way to the old days [1928-1929, Villfranche and Paris] when I lay beside her as she smoked, though I gave her opportunities, and I felt it unnatural of her not to do so. To this day I have no idea why she was so reticent, actually secretive, on this subject at any rate, and at least with me who knew, and shared her laughing jokes about it. Whether she now felt shame, or a shyness, or wished to avoid criticisms and discussions, I could not tell.[159]

This revelatory account perhaps partly explains how difficult Gabriel may have found life with his wife. Yet, unlike Gabriel, however much she drank or smoked, she *always* worked. A diary entry for the 17 July when a friend came to visit, shows the deleterious effect of Gabriel's drinking on her:

> Gabriel rather bad, perfect at first—then, I will not be known as the wife of a 'gifted and charming man, pity he drinks'. *I will not*. Gabriel does not understand. He is not inside his own little group now, where being a 'bit blotto' is taken for granted. He has to come back to the world's eye, *with* a wife. And we both have careers to make. Would he be pleased for *his* friends to see *me* like that? *And he does not remember what he is like*. He is rude to me, and all his lovely charm and wit vanishes in repetitions and vague sentences which mean nothing and questions he can't formulate, and an awful pointlessness. Shame-making, above all, to me who have such pride in him. He embarassed the [visitor] and only a feeling that one of us mustn't lose any more face kept me from abandoned crying.
>
> If only he'd be shrewd enough and ambitious enough to see that it won't do. For one thing, when we have more money, how are we to go to London and into the world, dine and meet people, if he cannot be sure of himself? But the real thing is that he is risking our marriage; for I cannot endure it. I can't do more than try and put on a brave face. I cannot 'pass' it, because it is outside my powers of endurance, my moral power or force.—Even now—stories will go back

> to London, stories so common-place and vulgar, yet,—no, and, to me *unendurable*.
>
> And the one thing that really matters is that Gabriel is injuring himself, the gay, pure, gifted, brilliant, loving, adorable Gabriel will be destroyed by this. That is what matters. Not me. Not our marriage. Himself. His beauty, his mana, his art.

This entry shows not only Mary Butts's own ambitiousness, her understanding of the importance of respectability if she was to establish herself as a writer; it also reveals her belief in Gabriel's talent and an acute sense of the tremendous and inescapable waste.

By the 11 October 1932, the second anniversary of their marriage, she asked herself whether there was "equal weight pulling, 50-50 on the partnership? Is it a case [of]...painting *v* writing? Question of my respect... Opportunities to be looked for. Up to now all mine.... Portrait of me...that our failures...are bound up together. Power over my soul." Notwithstanding the delicate line drawing Gabriel had done of Mary Butts and the incoherence of the entry, the serious problems in their marriage had not and would not lessen. By March 1933 Gabriel had left Tebel Vos on the first of his visits back north. It would be the beginning of the end of this short marriage and from the end of 1934 they would never live together again. When Ross Williamson wrote to Mary Butts to announce that he had broken off his engagement, the following comment would no doubt have struck a chord with her: "It's very funny, but I'm getting afraid of this awful feeling that one must stay *alone*, so that one's fate does not involve any one else directly."[160]

CHAPTER TWENTY-TWO

Making History

1933

> *The only thing there is to do is to get to work and work and work and work. Thank God there is enough of that. I must not think of ruined things. If I have no-one to trust—I have no-one.*
>
> —MB, diary entry, 23.1.33

THE FINAL WEEK OF Camilla's stay in Sennen had coincided with a great number of letters and Mary Butts's being "rushed by proofs".[161] Wishart asked her to provide a preface for the new edition of *Ashe of Rings* which was to come out in July. On the 9 January she mused on what to write:

> *Preface to Ashe*? What can I say? That it's a fairy-tale? That life got like that at the end of the War (has perhaps been like that ever since only we're more or less used to it).[162] ...A kind of fairy-tale of our sorrows, with the good ending fairy tales must have?
>
> Anything about style? The truth is that I was tight on Joyce at the time, as we all were; and that now having found how to reproduce half-conscious thinking, most of the fun has gone out of it. Yet it can't be taken out. Say that I could do it—now—just as deeply and more conventionally now.

She put aside the introduction until the end of February to see if any ideas would come to her, turning instead to the "last proofs" of *The Macedonian* which she received on the 15 January. She praised the editor at Heinemann's, for his "exquisite work", including in the Preface to the novel her thanks "to Mr Weston Edwards, for whose wise criticism and suggestions and discovery of errors of geography and punctuation I can never express my gratitude, nor forget what the text looked like before and after his revision".[163] So impressed was she by Weston Edwards (who admired her work) that she dedicated a short story, 'The Tomb of the Snatchers', to him in the spring of 1933. Originally called 'The Hermit and the Harpy Tomb' and completed in February that year, this tale set in the reign of Constantine, explores the conflict between pagan and

Christian beliefs. While it does not appear to have been published, it reflects the interest which led Mary Butts to begin her narrative, "Julian the Apostate", two years later. After promptly correcting the proofs of *The Macedonian*, she considered the possibility of writing a sequel to *Death of Felicity Taverner*, the "Scylla and Co in a new set" mentioned above. She described the plot in her diary on the 21 January: "...on the sufferings of our age. The aristocrat who knows only the aristoi are worth having, and yet seeing the people it was his business to help coming to destroy him.... It gets in my pet 'données', especially magic." This idea was never developed.

Instead: "I want people—people and pleasant words," she noted the following day. In their absence she turned to her work. Her declaration that "there is enough of that" was no exaggeration. As well as completing one of the still unpublished narratives from her cycle, 'What the Moon Saw', in January, she also finished two stories mentioned earlier: 'From Altar to Chimney-piece' (then called 'Altar-lights') and 'Ford's Last Dancing'. Mary Butts described the latter to Ross Williamson as:

> A rowdy tale which will get me into trouble, about a party at Ford Madox Ford's—of all people! where one lady knocked another lady down and danced on her face and her nose bled, and Lett Haines took the red roses I was carrying and dipped them in the blood and sprayed the room. The lady who danced was a curious creature—did you ever hear of her—Elsa von Freitag Von Loringhoven, once married to the General's son, and he blew his brains out and she lived on blackmailing the Von F.V.L.s? An ageing courtesan—*not* a nice person. When her looks went, she shaved her head and lacquered her skull and her derrière in different colours. She's dead too now. Wrote noise-poems and they're trying to bring out an edition of them.

Mary Butts felt that the tale was "not satisfactory" and never published it—perhaps also fearing reprisals. Yet she was not exaggerating about Elsa von Freitag von Loringhoven; Margaret Anderson gave a similar account of this eccentric and ultimately sad woman.[164] Mary Butts's comment to Ross Williamson shows the degree to which she felt her Paris life was behind her: "We did have fun in Paris, tho' like Queen Victoria, I don't wish those times back again. Not because I didn't love them, but because one can't repeat."[165]

As usual she read a great deal, commenting on, amongst others, John Langdon Davies's *A Short History of Women* (1927) and Dorothy Sayers's new book, *Murder must Advertise* (1933). A fan of Sayers's work (she had written to her, though there is no record of any reply), she was disappointed by this novel: "About her worst book, a caricature of the others. What possessed her to write such a spineless fantasy. And the end was morally cruel. Sherlock Holmes knew better—the murder on account of blackmail *does not* come under normal categories".[166]

When she was not working, she saw a few people, including Oswell Blakeston and the Manning-Sanders. On one of the evenings spent with Ruth Manning-Sanders earlier in the month, she had discussed religion and the tendency for people, "O.B. and others of various sorts [to] talk, mostly windily, about 'Eastern Initiations'. *Always* Eastern, without knowing much about them, or about initiations on their savage, or social, or scientific aspects." It baffled her why "people who chat airily about isoteric Bhuddism and its advantages, never consider what Mithras or Orphism let alone Delphi or Eleusis or the Grail did—can do for men." Increasingly she saw Cornwall as not just symbolically but *actually* embodying The Waste Land. The ancient well at Sancreed was especially intriguing because, as she wrote to Ross Williamson, the Grail was "stirring" there: "Do you know—there is a most remote village here, inland, called Sancreed; where there is a holy well and the ruins of a hermit's chapel. And in the churchyard a keltic cross, ten feet high, with a device carved down one side of it, a spear coming out of a cup, which must be the Sanc-Grail. This is its part of the world."[167] As for herself, she noted in her diary: "I know my own life to be a series of initiations, under the cool, holy, adorable, sophrôn formulae of Western man." In late January she quoted George Manning-Sanders "on Cornwall and what it does to weak and imaginative people, quickening their inner perception, which, if they have no knowledge to ballast it, destroys them." This view echoed her own beliefs about Dorset and she added darkly: "One knows this story."

Indeed, it was a crucial aspect of her short story, 'The Guest', written the previous summer. Archibald Erskine-Browne, described as having an "unfed imagination", visits Julian and his wife Cynthia who live on a "flowery cliff 300 feet up from the Atlantic." He comes in part to fill "that small dreadful hole within him." However, he quickly realises "I don't belong to these people, and they sit, quiet, watching me not being part of them." When he is alone in the "haunted wood on Sarscathian Moor, where there are three woods and a *daimon* in each…in the sudden quiet [he] heard his own breath." His own limitations—his "fake glass"—make him misinterpret the interrelationships he finds there and remain completely unaware of the real dangers in the primitive wood. His tragedy, what makes him leave in sadness, is his realisation that, but for his lack of sensitivity he, like Julian, "might have been a great painter."[168]

At this time she reviewed A.E. Waite's *The Holy Grail* for *The Bookman* and wrote of "the Grail[169] and Gabriel's goodness sustaining us." A bleak comment added alongside this entry in December 1935 points to the transitory harmony in their marriage: "You see, it sometimes came back for a little—never for long." To counter her loneliness she went for long walks. It was partly the light which drew her outdoors: "We talk of the 'dreaming' summer earth, but why not the 'dreaming winter'—on a fine day of pure cold sun, with its air of illusion?" There was also her love of beach-combing: "rosy baby cuttle-fish bones; a new inlay of shell; skull of one large bird, too battered to bring home." The sea's rather more edible gifts provided, at the end of January, the focus of one of several descriptions which convey her growing admiration for the work of the local fishermen:

> *Remember:* The bass-catch. The mirror-wet sands, all Sennen at the net, the splendid fish drowning in air. Their faces at the sea-harvest, good money coming in, the sea's gift, hard-work at the tide with the sea rising to lift and let out the fish. (20 lost out of about 2,000). Every man in Sennen, splashing at the light wave edge, carting the fish back in creels and boxes and sacks. Red faces and bright eyes.

Towards the end of 1933 she described the ritualistic quality of the fishing: "This evening just off sunset, a fiery storm-sky across turquoise: watching for the fish. Two little boats tumbling in the bay & on top two Huers, speechless, directing them with gorse branches. It was rather awful. One of them stood, black against the gold, in one spot but his body & face contorted, writhing, frantic. He flung himself about, his black face glaring at the sea, stabbing & pointing with his branch of dead gorse. It looked like agony. It was magic. Women are not wanted then about. I turned up the hill.... It was more than fish-food searching. It was a rite." This last description would form the basis of an article published in *The Manchester Guardian* in March 1935 under the title 'The Seine Net: Community Fishing in Cornwall', which in turn may well have influenced Ruth Manning-Sanders's account of the 'huer' in *The West of England*.[170]

In contrast to these turbulent seascapes, Mary Butts heralded the 1 February as "Quilt Day". Quite apart from her prodigious output, her growing correspondence and reviewing, her gardening, her exploration of the countryside and her socialising, she also worked at quieter domestic miniatures. On the back cover of her 1932 diary she had noted the completion of 121 pieces of patchwork by the 1 December; by the 10th she had finished a further 44. References to patchwork and to rugmaking are scattered throughout these later volumes.

The post in late January brought fan mail. In December Ethel Colburn Mayne had written to say how she had been "delighted to read the notice of *Felicity* in *The New Statesman* for last week. There is real understanding and appreciation there; I wonder who wrote it."[171] The reviewer made himself known to Mary Butts on the 24 January:

> Dear Miss Butts,
>
> Though you may know my name, I can hardly hope that you will remember that we once met—for a minute or two only—at Ethel Colburn Mayne's—before *Speed the Plough* (the volume) was out.
>
> I am emboldened to write now as I had a message from Edgell Rickword that you liked the review of *Felicity Taverner*, which I wrote in the *New Statesman*. I was the happier at your praise of it, because I have...been a little peeved at the way in which some critics, while thank God! praising you, have produced you with an air of discovery—and one even referred to *Felicity* as your first novel. It must be some years ago since I was asked not to write on you in a well-known monthly, because your work was not known. That at least is, I hope, now quite untrue: tho' some of the notices of *Felicity* have been extraordinarily unobservant. Hardly anyone gets Boris, for instance.[172]

"That is going to begin something," was her delighted response. In an attempt to impress Ada, she enclosed a copy of the review[173] in a letter, explaining that it was by R. Ellis Roberts, "a contemporary of yours, noted for his profound and noble religious life. He...wrote to me himself, repeating his pleasure in the book."[174] A man of letters, Richard Ellis Roberts later wrote the first biography of Stella Benson, whom he had known.[175] Having been editor of *The New Statesman and Nation* from 1932, in the autumn of 1934 he took over the editorship of *Life and Letters Today* from Desmond MacCarthy. Seven stories by Mary Butts would be published in that organ.[176] Along with Hugh Ross Williamson, he was instrumental in providing her with introductions to the literati of the 1930s, including Naomi Royde-Smith and Rose Macaulay. Generally speaking, however, February was a bad month for Mary Butts. This was partly due to her nervous anticipation about the imminent publication of *The Macedonian*. "I feel all life in suspense till 'Alex' is published. Then I am certain my future will be clearer." Towards the end of the month she sent off her revised introduction for *Ashe of Rings* which was to come out in July. In her draft she justified her fairy-tale ending on the grounds that "as Lytton Strachey points out, it is essential in such stories that they end happily, that 'the lost princesses and insufferable kings' should be remembered." In the preface, published as an 'Afterword', she employed this quotation from Strachey without citing him—a typical Modernist practice characteristic of *Ashe of Rings* itself.

The final entry for February included a quotation from Charles Williams's novel, *Shadows of Ecstacy* (1931) followed by her comment: "A book, not a complete book, but all there is in answer to D.H. Lawrence. Credo." Charles Williams was an English writer and critic who worked for Oxford University Press. His writing was concerned with religious and mystical issues, often in the context of the detective genre. He is best known today for his association with C.S. Lewis, J.R.R. Tolkien and other members of the 'Inklings' group. Mary Butts's admiration for Williams's work would grow as she read *The Place of the Lion* (1931) and *War in Heaven* (1930) later that year. In 1935 she wrote to him with the idea of producing an article on his work which would have doubtless have explained his "answer to D.H. Lawrence". She would die, however, before it was completed.

The Macedonian

> *Spring must be with you by now — and I hope the evergreen for 'Alexander'.*
> —Hugh Ross Williamson undated letter to MB, late March 1933

> *One thing I must be prepared for—the failure of 'Alexander'. Instead of joyful, augmenting success, coldness, bewilderment, boredom and disbelief. It will be interesting to see how far my 'hunch' that this marks the turning point is right.* —MB, diary entry, 8.3.33

In contrast to the dejection of February, Mary Butts was able to give details of a perfect day in early March; perfect because it brought together the joy of gardening, beautiful new possessions, an exquisite seascape, fine conversation and the arrival of her copies of *The Macedonian*:

> *Morning*—gardening in spring sun, bulbs up.
> *Afternoon*—Goldsmith [a friend in Sennen] gave me a snuff-bottle. Which shall it be? The agate with the fish in relief and the coral stopper? The crystal with the peach tree, jade stopper? The sapphire glass with swastikas, coral stopper? They are all in a drawer and I can sit on the floor and look at them and choose. Oh very pleasant!
> *Evening*—after a day of pure sun, a sunset past belief. Modelling—no—a sculpture of clouds on the Atlantic. These buildings crossed by a veil of hurrying shower cloud. In its lightness and quickness it tossed a veil across them pearl-grey against their stupendous colour and darkness. It vanished *into* them; and for an hour, they stood on the horizon in the shapes of the stones of this country. Menhir and dolmen, rocking stone and standing stone. *All* the names…
> *Night*. Last post brought 'Alexander' and R M-S to supper. Good talk, warm and a feeling of joy. And so to bed. Not too ungrateful, heaven help me.

When *The Macedonian* in its chalk blue dust jacket with white lettering came out, price 6/-, on Monday 13 March, Mary Butts wanted "nothing really but to be out of doors, walk and garden and talk a little. Housekeep—not write." As she listened to a radio broadcast of Stravinsky that evening, she commented: "Who would not sooner hear his Nightingale music to the best bird solo or chorus? Nature has her place, a pretty big one; but there are times when Art can beat her on her own ground."

She did not have to wait long to receive reactions to her latest book. "My dear Mary," wrote Douglas Goldring. "I am enchanted by *The Macedonian*, which in my not very humble opinion lands you unmistakably on the top shelf. Alas the *Sunday Referee* has fallen on evil days and their reviewing is cut down to nothing.... However I'll do my best to squeeze in a paragraph of boost, every little helps.... The Book Society has made a complete ass of itself in not making *The Macedonian* the book of the month or at least recommending it. I hope to have some fun with them for that."[177] Such unqualified praise from Goldring reveals that their friendship had indeed survived the previous year's difficulties. Meanwhile congratulations poured in: "Your Alexander is magnificent. People talk about you. Really you needn't worry any more," wrote Hugh Ross Williamson.[178] Naomi Royde-Smith believed that the novel was "great because you didn't hint—you told...I *do* believe you are a great writer."[179] Ethel Colburn Mayne liked it so much she put it on the Femina List, although since the novel did not fulfil the criteria "F[elicity] will probably have to go alone."[180] Ellis Roberts expressed his admiration and enthusiasm in a long review in *The Manchester Guardian*.[181]

In her 'Preface' Mary Butts had declared that the "book is the outcome of some reading, long reflection and a great love of a period in the world's history of such importance that there seems to be a tendency to ignore it, or to take it for granted as too big to be handled.... Following Mr. E.M. Forster's lead, I have tried to shew the importance of the visit to Siwa; and I have dealt with it, and with all other events, as it seems to me that they might well have happened."[182] On the 14 March Forster wrote to her:

> I like 'The Macedonian' *very much*, and feel proud that I should have been of any help to you in it. As far as I am concerned the book chimes completely, but of course it is a far bigger concern than mine, and goes into regions outside me. I find it difficult to write about it with detachment, because you have been so very kind and generous in your references, and when this happens one's flattered and therefore unreliable; still it does seem to me than [sic] you have pulled off a most remarkable piece of work. I so much admire (to praise as coldly as I can!) the *form*; the introduction of the Callisthenes letter, all decency and common sense, in the midst of the wildness is masterly...[183]

"Non sum digna. And the loan of his book on Alexandria[184] to come. After all these years," noted Mary Butts on the 15 March. Given his high praise, it is curious that when E.M. Forster was asked about her in 1949 he "seemed to know little of her work".[185]

Mary Butts's second husband, the English artist Gabriel Aitken (1897-1937), during the Great War.

Aerial photograph of Sennen Cove. Tebel Vos (1), Esther's Field (2), Sarah's Well (3), No Place (4), Coastguard Cottages (5).

The seafront at Sennen Cove, 1930s. Tebel Vos is just visible, upper right horizon.

View of Sennen Cove today, from the coastal footpath. Tebel Vos, on left on the first ridge, is now called Namaste. The dormer window is new since Mary Butts's time.

Sarah's Well, Sennen Cove, where she and Gabriel Aitken lived from Jan. to May 1932.

Left to right: Mary Butts, Odo Cross, Gabriel Aitken, Angus Davidson, Camilla in Cross's Chrysler outside the First and Last Pub, Sennen, August 1933.

A panoramic view today over Whitesands Bay from Mary Butts's home in Sennen Cove, West Cornwall. Little has changed since she lived here between 1932 and 1937.

Mary Butts and Gabriel Aitken at Tebel Vos, 1932-3. Mary Butts dedicated The Macedonian *to Gabriel.*

CLOCKWISE FROM FAR LEFT:

No Place, Autumn 1934 Bolshie *[Burnett]* thatching.

Camilla and Mary Butts, Sennen, August 1933.

Tree-Mallow from Tidcombe, July 1935. *Mary Butts in the garden of Tebel Vos.*

Warriors resting, May 1935. *Angus Davidson and Mary Butts, gardening at No Place.*

No Place, March 1935 completed.

Jacket design (1932) by James Boswell.

Jacket design (1933) by Gabriel Aitken.

Sennen Church today.

Mary Butts's tombstone today.

The Macedonian, accurately described by one reviewer as "a series of ten scenes [in which] Miss Mary Butts has studied the personality of Alexander the Great, and more particularly his tendency to think himself a god or God",[186] sold well. Out of a print run of 1,500, 1,060 were sold between March and August 1933. It also received a great deal of critical attention, including over fifty reviews and notices from all around the British Isles. Not only were there long articles in the main newspapers, such as *The Observer, The Bookman, The Manchester Guardian, Time and Tide, The Manchester Evening News, The New Statesman and Nation* and the *Times Literary Supplement; The Macedonian* was also reviewed in *The Leytonshire Express, The Sheffield Independent, The Bristol Evening World, The Inverness Courier* and *The Gloucestershire Echo*. The response, overwhelmingly, was one of admiration, including two reviews in *The Church Times* and *The Methodist Times*. Hugh Ross Williamson was clearly not exaggerating when he claimed that people were talking about her.

There was also general agreement that *The Macedonian* displayed sound scholarship. Mary Butts's "modest claim," wrote one reviewer, "is that she has simply retold some interesting stories about [Alexander], but she conveys an impression of universal energy as well as personality; and in doing so her own scholarship has been happily augmented without affecting her artistic clear-sightedness."[187] Wynyard Browne wrote that she had "read her authorities carefully, and with a lively imagination strictly controlled. And she has succeeded in making a very probable likeness of her man."[188] In one of the most encomiastic reviews, Humbert Wolfe pointed out that the book was "not so much a novel or a biography as a gospel. That is not to say that she is foolishly rapturous, a mere inventor of vain things. On the contrary, she has studied and mastered her sources, and writes as a scholar, but as a scholar, who in the process of research, has become an evangelist."[189] *The Macedonian* was compared favourably with Walter Savage Landor's *Imaginary Conversations of Greeks and Romans* (1853) and to work by Plutarch and Anatole France; seen as more powerful than the writing of George Moore and Naomi Mitchison and "combin[ing] the rapier-like penetration of the late Lytton Strachey with a vivid, impressionistic style that can distil, in a succession of subtly contrived scenes, the essence of her subject and his times".[190] Several reviews praised the innovation of the book, whose poetic prose and episodic form made it difficult to categorise.[191] The writer Edmund Blunden described it as neither history nor biography but "cadenced psychology, very near a poem of changeful intuitions and introspections".[192] There were those who found it too difficult and too obscure, but these were in a very small minority.[193] When Joseph Sell described her as "one of the finest writers we have" in a laudatory review which included a stately line drawing of Mary Butts by Gabriel Aitken, he was echoing a number of other critics. What several reviews did include, however, were a number of errors which show that her work was still not widely known: *The Nottingham Guardian* described her as a "new writer" while *The Inverness Courier* referred to her short stories [*Several Occasions*] as published "I remember, in the autumn of 1931" (it was actually March 1932) and stated that *The Macedonian* was published by Wishart instead of Heinemann. Mary Butts found the reviews to be good but rarely intelligent. "What I mean is, no one seems to have *digested* the book yet," she wrote to Hugh Ross Williamson in early April.[194] Doubtless she was cheered by the following letter of appreciation by John Coghlan who had reviewed *The Macedonian* in *The Everyman*. Coghlan had won a prize of "one guinea for the best open letter of appreciation or criticism, in not more than two hundred words, addressed to any author named in the February number" of *The Bookman*. The winning entry was printed in the April issue:

A LETTER OF APPRECIATION TO MISS MARY BUTTS

> MADAM,
>
> I do not think that the "common reader" altogether realises what an original figure you are in English fiction. You have a strong, vivid style, a poetic imagination and a mischievous sense of humour.
>
> And how well you know your own limitations! For even in your longer stories it is the continuous, cumulative accounts of little curious happenings, mental adventures, spiritual discoveries that make your work so fascinating. Even the characters in your stories are often seen as curious beings; some of them are spectacles that appear to fascinate by their very strangeness and perversity. At the same time you have given us so much that is fine and memorable in your books that it would be ungenerous to cavil. Every artist has his (or her) own peculiar artistic vision; it is the only method of making reality fresh and therefore recognisably real. You always achieve this reality in your books, and one feels in them that one has a faithful imaginative account of experience. As a result your work is as original as that of any living novelist, as was recognised almost from the first by the critical and discriminating reader.
>
> Yours truly,
>
> JOHN COGHLAN[195]

Perhaps one of the least-known facts about *The Macedonian* is that a number of schoolchildren studied an extract from it during their history lessons from the late-1930s onwards. In 1937 *The Imaginary Eye-Witness* was published by Longmans, Green & Co. Edited by C.H. Lockitt, it contains seventeen accounts of historical events drawn from literature. The collection opens with 'Alexander the Great 325 B.C.' by Mary Butts and follows with extracts of work by Sir Walter Scott, Edward Bulwer Lytton, Charles Kingsley, Nathaniel Hawthorne and others.

Helen Moran concluded in her review of *The Macedonian*: "This is very different from her other books. What will she do next?"[196] In fact, on the 11 March, two days before *The Macedonian* was published, Mary Butts noted in her diary: "Is it—is it *the* idea? Can I now write the life of Cleopatra I have so often told myself. Yes—if this is the key—(were my family ruined to show me this?)—that she could no longer stand the degradation of the Lagidae? If that is the key to it all, in Aulêtês, in Arsinoë, in her young brother, *if I'm right*, I can do it. R. M-S accoucheuse [midwife] to this. Will it do? I feel as though all the pieces of a puzzle were falling into place. It explains Caesar, her ridding herself of her kin, her cultivation of herself." This idea (with its tribute to Ruth Manning-Sanders) was the first reference to *Scenes from the Life of Cleopatra* which was published two years later. Mary Butts began work on it the very next day.

Writing this narrative became her main occupation and touchstone for the rest of 1933. She was given a contract by Heinemann in April,[197] and the novel provided a retreat from as well as a justification of what she saw as the continuing deterioration ("were my family ruined to show me this?") of the Butts Fortune. However disproportionate the decline of the Ptolemies to that of the Butts family in historical significance, she clearly felt that a shared sense of humiliation gave her the necessary entrée into the mind of Cleopatra.

Her immediate worries centred around the still-unsold Holbein, which meant that her daughter's attendance at Sandecotes was in jeopardy. Since she continued to blame Mary Colville-Hyde for stopping her payments for Camilla, it was with relief and a certain self-righteousness that she wrote to Ada in early March: "I'd a hunch [Mother] would come round, and I believe a letter I sent to her…two months ago…*helped*. Anxious, anything but angry, but put in such a way that she could not but realise she was breaking a promise most solemnly given: that she hadn't a moral leg to stand on."[198] She wrote to Hugh Ross Williamson about the Fall of the House of Butts and he was, as ever, sympathetic: "It's a bad story, but I don't see what you can do…. It is, as you say, the *thing* much more than the money. That I don't think you need worry about. You'll be wealthy and famous—not that you care for it." In fact, Mary Butts did care very much about wealth and fame but acquired neither. "Hurry with Cleopatra," he continued, and taking the same line as he had done in 1932, suggested that perhaps the protracted Holbein sale was "purposed… Driving you more and more on to yourself, being great enough to suffer."[199] Like the reviewer of *Ashe of Rings* who felt that "the quality of her work [wa]s of more consequence than her Norman blood",

Ross Williamson's interpretation was that Mary Butts's own writing was the future Family Fortune.[200] Such a letter did much to offset "grim days" with Gabriel and her obsessive fury at Mary Colville-Hyde. "How the anger burns in me," she raged. "How can I find a way *through* the obsession of it, trying to poison this spring day, to the calm and indifference, and something more than the last which I know to lie behind it?" Unfortunately she never did. E.M. Forster's book on Alexandria arrived on the 18th ("all that I wanted") and Mary Butts found it, together with Arthur Weigall's *Alexander the Great*, invaluable for the writing of *Scenes from the Life of Cleopatra*. At this time she toyed with 'End of the Lagidae' and 'Last of the Lagidae' as possible titles for the book. Assiduous application meant that the first section of around 21,000 words was completed on the 12 June. It had taken her only three months.

Writing *Scenes from the Life of Cleopatra* was far from being her only activity in the spring and early summer of 1933. On the 30 March she read a "very excellent book on Bacon by Mary Stuart. Buy this *and* a Latin Dictionary," she decided. On the 4 April she suggested to Hugh Ross Williamson the possibility of submitting an essay on "'Private Artists' or Contemporary Illiteracy". Nothing came of these proposals, although in 1936 she wrote a long essay on Bloomsbury. She did, however, send a review of Dorothy Margaret Stuart's *The Girl through the Ages* to *The Bookman*. Hugh Ross Williamson had asked for it to be amusing, but she had been unable to because "the more I tried, the more sombre thoughts on the subject of youth, especially female youth, crowded my mind."[201] Quite rightly, Hugh Ross Williamson did not tear it up, as Mary Butts suggested, but printed the review in the May issue.

As well as a positive account of the book, her review is also an extremely insightful piece, deserving a moment's attention. It opens with the general reflection that "since the rise of Christianity there has been one subject that has never failed the man—priest, preacher, parson, monk—set in moral authority over others: one sermon he has always found time to preach—on the wanton, troubling and essentially immoral nature of the beauty of young women and the ways they choose to enhance it." As she then asks: "Why at a time when we are perpetually being warned (and when have we not been warned?) that the foundations of morality are on their last legs should…the piercing of the ear[202]…; the cutting of the hair; the covering or the uncovering of the head,[203] the neck, the arms, the breast, the back, the knees—take up so much of ecclesiastical time?" After all, "it may be taken to be as near certain as is possible in human affairs that never, never, never did these admonitions produce the slightest effect." She liked Stuart's historical survey because "her book is not only about girls, but even manages to give an impression of that charming but half useless thing, girlhood: though in her pages, down the centuries, they all appear much of a muchness. Is that because the State of Girlhood is changeless, or is it because we do not know enough about the past to tell how the changes in the temper of each age affected the opening personalities of half of the human race?" This is a question we are still trying to answer.

The concluding two paragraphs of the review refer to Mary Kingsley (who would be central to Virginia Woolf's argument five years later in *Three Guineas*):[204]

> One thing is clear. Save in exceptional families, or sometimes in the case of women of royal or noble station, few parents seem to wish their girl-children to have any education at all. One remembers Mary Kingsley, who reckoned that, while two thousand pounds had been spent on teaching her brother, not one penny—with the exception of some German lessons—had ever been spent on her. One remembers one's own case.[205] Down the ages, it depresses.
>
> In this one respect, mankind seems to have changed its opinion. If it has, if the present change has been made for good, if the majority of parents do not finally think worse of it—well, one mercy has at least been shown to the before-mentioned half of the human race.[206]

Despite all her failures as a parent, Mary Butts believed that Camilla should be educated.

Notwithstanding bouts of fever in early spring (which she continued to describe as 'malaria'), Mary Butts extended her circle of acquaintance when she and Dora Russell visited one another in early April. Dora Russell (separated from her husband, Bertrand) lived in Carn Voel at Porthcurno "surrounded by the majestic cliffs of Treen and St Levan, aware constantly of the seething Atlantic waves rolling relentless over the long white sands below."[207]

Camilla came for Easter. "Longing to see her," wrote Mary Butts to her aunt in early April, "and what about you paying us a visit yourself later on. I can't tell you how I long to see you again. Think it over, at least. This place is so gloriously beautiful. And it's an experience as well, being so unlike what we think of as England. While up to now it's kept its native character and integrity in a wonderful way."[208] Faithful to the advice given her in the early 1920s, Ada Briggs did not come to Sennen while her niece was alive. Although she never made any adverse comments to Camilla about either of her parents, she did not feel able to sanction Mary Butts's lifestyle and irresponsibility by visiting. Also, she knew all too well the discrepancy between reality and her niece's epistolary accounts. Mary Butts felt that the Easter holidays were a success. Camilla was "being marvellously good—the greatest improvement on last holidays...in such health and spirits and the life here agrees with her so well."[209]

Angus Davidson also came to stay in early April while Camilla was still there. "*Remember*: Angus's visit and especially on Sunday the walk to Penberth; and coming home with our faces to the sun and the Atlantic," wrote Mary Butts on the 17 April. However good Camilla's stay had been, her mother expressed relief after her departure: "Peace in the house with the child out of it." A few days later "on a May morning, when the country-side was one sweep of living primrose, anemone, violet and narcissus," she enjoyed watching the traditional Furry Dance at Helston, an event she recalled the following year in her review of A.K. Hamilton Jenkins's *Cornish Homes and Customs*: "As the reviewer also can answer for, the people at Helston enjoy their Furry Dance, danced as it should be to-day in silk hats and morning coats. The trouble is, as Mr Jenkins shows, that the people of Helston have also learned to exploit it. The 'movie' men are there, their cameras perched on top of taxicabs."[210] Naomi Royde-Smith came to tea on the 13 May[211] and it would seem that Gabriel Aitken behaved well on that occasion, although in general things were not good. On the 25th Mary Butts remarked "if it were not for the book, intolerable sadness. However there *is* the book."

In June she completed a story then called 'Caesar and the Pirates' which was published in *The Cornhill* in June 1935 under the title 'One Roman Speaks'.[212] It was to be one of a collection of stories for "The New Book of Classical Studies", but this project never got off the ground. In mid-June she was enchanted by the "ducks—bronze and white enamel, by the stream, in the tangle of ragged robins and large grasses and the hemlocks, *against* the sunlight". During these days she was reminded of her friend, Theobald Bartholomew (who had died the previous February), by the arrival of "two pictures in water-colour by John Hookham, of Theo Bartholomew's rooms in Pythagoras House at Cambridge. They are very lovely, and fill the house—or rather—it is filled—with Theo."[213] Now dead, Bartholomew joined Cecil Maitland to become one of Mary Butts's ghostly companions. "Tall book-shelves on the right-hand side of the fire. Edges marbled by Gabriel," were also added at this time. "Quarter-filled now—but filling…for mine?" she wondered. The seaside setting of Tebel Vos led to glass floats being placed on the shelves as "book-stops".

In early July she took a break from writing about Cleopatra and concentrated on the garden with its mass of white poppies. She was woken at 5 a.m. on the 4th by the sound of her black-and-white cat, Patrick-Paddy-Paws, "giving a song of triumph" on killing a rabbit. Mary Butts noted with amusement: "Later. Found left a kidney and one leg. P-P-P asleep. It was a large rabbit." She spent that day sending copies of the English edition of *Ashe of Rings* to friends, including Ruth Manning-Sanders, Hugh Ross Williamson, Roderick Meiklejohn[214] and Betty Montgomery, to whom she would dedicate *Scenes from the Life of Cleopatra*. While she waited for the critical response to *Ashe of Rings*, she began Part III of her book on Cleopatra on the 22 July. However work was halted by a succession of visitors: Camilla for her holidays, Angus Davidson in late July, her old friend, (Paul) Odo Cross, and his partner, Angus Wilson, in mid-August and Tony in early September. "I wish I knew how to make Gabriel happy. Of course, I could not *make* him happy, but he has the keys of happiness in his hands—and of my happiness—and lately he so often will not turn them. Angus is coming. There is hope in that," she mused.

* * * * *

> Remember: *these last days heat. The cornfield on the right, the* storm *of white butterflies, picked out with tortoiseshells, and here and there, a saffron.* —MB, diary entry, 5.8.33

THE SUMMER OF 1933 was a hot one. From the 11 to the 14 August Mary Butts, Angus Davidson, Camilla, Gabriel Aitken, Odo Cross and Angus Wilson had "A-Four-Day-Party", roaming around West Cornwall in Odo Cross's Chrysler. Mary Butts recorded the party in detail. "Joy and joy and joy and joy," she enthused:

> *First day*. dinner (not G or C—us four) St Ives by way of Zennor. At Zennor, peace in the church and magic by the great stone and friendliness at the Tinner's Arms, and the renewal of Odo's and my love for each other. St Ives—lobsters—the Inn with Two Eyes—Flight home…
> *2nd day*. All of us. St Ives and the three curio shops and gifts all round of lovely things. This was Camilla's day. She was adorable—merry, modest, joyful, wise—a girl to be proud of.…
> *3rd day*. *All* over Cornwall. Helford and *the Shipwrights Arms*—the tide-creeks and the great trees down to the water's edge. The green lane looking for Mullion. At M. the hotel, Angus' pantomime leap through the window. The happy child. The good child.
> *Fourth day*. Lunch at Sennen Cove, love and peace, farewells.…

"These tiny notes for eternal remembrance," she concluded.

After this highpoint she felt rather low when her visitors were gone, and had another attack of 'malaria'. She was despondent about *Scenes from the Life of Cleopatra*, which was not "finished and the last fifty pages appear unwritable—while the revision of so long a book with so many references and practically no library seems in my mind the kind of thing that *never* will be done."[215] Jack Lindsay came to her rescue the following year but in late summer 1933 Mary Butts felt lonely. She missed Angus Davidson particularly and clung to the "hope" that he would move to Sennen. "You see," she wrote to him at the end of August, "since some years ago when the person [Cecil Maitland] I loved—and still do—best out of all my life—died—(after a bitter misunderstanding and separation)—I've been alone in a way difficult to define. Anyhow, since I left Paris, over three years ago, I've had no one to talk to as I can talk to you. (This explanation will get the capital 'I's over.) About *some* things rather essential to me, I've had to shut up and not mind too much. Until the last month I've begun to realise that I might tell you and it wouldn't bore you. I could talk about the child and Tony" and, although she did not say it, about Gabriel, for Davidson was very much her confidant as the marriage tottered.[216] This was the first in a series of letters she wrote to him in the coming years (unfortunately, only her half of the correspondence has survived). The main subject at that time was her brother's imminent visit.

Tony had written several friendly letters over the previous months as he travelled around France. In March he had responded to *The Macedonian* in a letter of "profound admiration" which described how "exciting" the publications had been in the spring of 1933. "Well, Mary my dear, if I may say so, I certainly hand it to you, and how," he wrote from Villefranche at the end of March:

> *The Macedonian* arrived just as I'd read a quarter of *Light in August*, which I promptly laid by and forgot for the time; and I think that for such an astonishingly beautiful, terrible and nerve-searing novel as Faulkner's that's saying something; it's been an exciting spring, what with Alexander, Faulkner, and here, Céline's vile masterpiece *Le Voyage au Bout de la Nuit*, and William's frozen land-grabber, Mr Rhodes.[217] And Stephen Spender's poems. Are you going to repeat this with an Akhn Aton[218] [sic] or an Alcibiades or a Virgil or somebody? I don't really think you've ever written as beautifully, or as poignantly, to be frank. You certainly unveil the hidden life of the hero; and bring the god into sufficient line with man to make him partially understandable. One can't find any part more lovely than the whole, in your book, even with the, to me, special beauties of the section VII to the end. And when he is in the end dead there's a dry bitterness in one's mouth, as of when the god's moved away from where one is.[219]

When he went to Paris in April, Tony wrote to say that just as in London, "everyone is...talking about Alexander and how."[220] Yet when she wrote to Davidson on the eve of Tony's arrival, Mary Butts feared "something dreadful. Years behind us of love—and then years of things rather like cruelty and disloyalty." With characteristic blindness, she added: "I think one could call them that if one were watching detachedly on another planet. While," and here she was perhaps more accurate, "my own idiocy stares me in the face. Too much love and some fear and a ridiculous pride. While I don't know why he's come—suddenly—after so long."[221]

When Tony did arrive she was shocked at how much he had aged and faded even since their last meeting two years before. But after a few days of awkwardness they both relaxed and she wrote to Davidson to say how happy she was. Quite apart from his presence, Tony had brought her a "Red Lacquer Chair. A glory from China. A throne for me" which she placed in the corner of her salon facing the window. Just as with Davidson in April, she took her brother to Penberth on the 7 September, which in all its autumn "glory" reminded Tony of Renoir. However when he returned to London abruptly after only ten days she felt that "the delicate fabric of renewed confidence and intimacy [was] torn to shreds.... I hate. I despair. I weep. I dis-esteem us both." As anxious as his sister about the sale of the Holbein, since he had no money either, Tony had left in the hope that his presence might help speed things up. However, as Mary Butts had predicted, it was a vain hope. When he wrote to say "how much I enjoyed being with you both", he announced that "the H[olbein] left for the States last Saturday or rather yesterday. W[edell] thinks highly of its chance of being sold soon."[222] This hardly reassured his sister who had heard it all before.

She was also upset because Tony had not been able to organise the rescue of her possessions from her Paris flat, which once again the proprietor had threatened to sell. Her brother's declaration "I will do all I can in the matter of the rue de Monttessuy" seems reasonable and generous, but Mary Butts was not reasonable where her family was concerned. For all this, she would probably have shared Tony's amusement at his postscript, that he was about to go "to a party... given for Louis Armstrong and Bryher—of all fantastic combinations!"[223]

* * * * *

> Quiet in the House. *Camilla gone: Tony gone: Angus gone: Odo and Angus [Wilson] gone. The stillness between us very lovely, and this room looking delicate, fire and reflection, light-point answering light-point. Glass and brass and polished wood—'there is neither speech nor language'.*
>
> —MB, diary entry, 16.9.33

WITH THE QUIET LEFT by the departure of all her visitors, Mary Butts divided her time between work, gardening and cottage-hunting, since, to her delight, Angus Davidson had made a definite decision to live in Sennen. There were a number of possibilities but he eventually bought a cottage not far from Tebel Vos which Mary Butts described in a letter as: "Right by itself behind the coast-guards [cottages at the end of Maria's Lane], on the *top*-field way between our part of Sennen and the First and Last.... One storey, thatched, tiny garden, empty.... It's only 2-3 rooms...but could be attractive. All Camilla's idea by the way."[224] Her meticulous and often daily overseeing of the rebuilding of Angus's cottage (charted in the regular bulletins she sent him from then on) is a tribute to Mary Butts's generosity.

In contrast to the busy sociable summer, the remaining months of 1933 were relatively quiet. She began her first review for *John O'London's Weekly* in late September and wrote regularly for that newspaper from then on.[225] Her growing experience meant that she felt, quite rightly, that she was "improving rapidly as a critic."[226] On the 9 October she recorded how she was:

> Thrown head over heels in the shadow-half of the year. Low sky, warm, wet air-drift, and the bay—a quarter-mile fringe of torn water, ravelled into huge flounces, last gasp of some out-at-ocean hurricane. Indigo under grey, and on the cliffs the bracken like quenched fire. If only we had trees to complete the ground-cycle. You can hear, through the full-throated sea, the shriek of ground pebbles, and the skies are leaning over us, as if they were putting us to sleep. I should like to sleep too—wake with the spring. Instead, must begin our winter-works.

* * * * *

Ashe of Rings with an enchanting dust jacket depicting the Ashe home below Badbury Rings designed by Gabriel Aitken[227] came out in late summer. Its fate at the hands of the reviewers dismayed Mary Butts who recorded on the 11 October that it had been "a flop". This was something of an exaggeration. Several reviews of this English edition reveal a deepened admiration for her work. Henry Fraser in *The Everyman* pointed out that "ten years ago Mary Butts and Kay Boyle...were writers known only to the highbrow internationale that foregathers in Paris. Both had a considerable vogue and were hailed as artists of originality and power among the exiles, American as well as British, who found in Paris the understanding which was denied them at home.... But now," he added ironically, "both these novelists have been 'discovered' in England, and have been acclaimed by even the most conservative critics."[228] *The Manchester Guardian* described *Ashe of Rings* as "an exciting and often enchanting experiment" and *The Glasgow Herald* declared: "To-day we may read the work with understanding and fascination which on its first publication was too innovative stylistically," whilst "its treatment of the war...both too elusive for taste that demanded direct, almost vulgar statement, and too truthful and penetrative in its criticism."[229] Other critics, however, were dubious about the wisdom of republishing a youthful novel at this time.[230] Whilst almost all the reviews reflected the view expressed by *The Referee* that "the novel is bound to be appreciated by readers who love good writing", some, including Mary Butts's old enemy, Gerald Gould, found it affected, too intellectual and too allusive.[231] William Plomer, writing in *The Spectator*, was quietly dismissive. Like several other reviewers he misread her 'Afterword', conflating the date of the novel's completion with that of its publication in Paris.[232] "Miss Mary Butts writes much better now than she did then, but her admirers will naturally be pleased to see this early example of her talent," he wrote, clearly not placing himself among them. The best he could find in the novel was "'period' interest" and an "energetic talent", but it is clear that he was unimpressed.[233] Even so, he found her style distinctive enough to wish to parody it in *Museum Pieces.*

It is no surprise that Mary Butts was depressed by the reception of *Ashe of Rings* although friends wrote to reassure her. The writer, Clifford Bax, who had known her in London during the First World War, "venture[d] to send...these lines to say that I have greatly enjoyed reading your book *Ashe of Rings*. There is a kind of brilliant broken beauty; and often you registered a subtle impression in a clear fresh phrase. Moreover, I do not see how any who read the book attentively could forget its peculiar flavour: something which I believe to be unique resides in its pages."[234] Ellis Roberts told her to ignore the "asinine statements" by Gerald Gould in *The Observer*.[235] She wrote back to thank him for his sympathy and Ellis Roberts replied:

> I am glad indeed if my letter brought any kind of comfort. One of the worst things about the size of modern life is that people like yourself who don't live in London, or in any particular 'bunch' of people find it difficult to know how much your work is admired and held to be one of the few inspiring elements in 'modern' literature. For people who read your books and love them don't, unless they're professional writers, write and say so, because they think of you as evidently not touchable by the silly abuse of the unimaginative and cowardly.[236]

Ellis Roberts's words were a great comfort. What Mary Butts lacked at this time was the detached self-confidence of July 1931 when she noted: "what one says to oneself of the unfavourable critic: 'Drunk again'."

In early November she wrote to her agent, Leonard Moore,[237] about her publishing hopes. Whilst still interested in producing a book of classical studies for Wishart, she wondered whether they could be interested in an "interim book of stories. That I could complete quickly." She also suggested that Moore should persuade them to publish a volume of her poems (just as she had tried with Edward Titus in 1928). "Not a costly edition, but something [Wishart] wouldn't lose money on. Perhaps buying them outright."[238] Neither of these projects materialised, however.

Mary Butts's main concern during November was the sorry fact that "Cleopatra is still in the ditch"[239] and she was struggling to give it shape. It did not help when Ethel Colburn Mayne wrote to her on the 8th announcing that "the fools on the Femina Committee have voted *Felicity* off the final list; despite my (and VH's [Violet Hunt's]) admonitions that they were making a hideous mistake. This is so great a disappointment to me that I take no interest in the voting and probably shall not attend on that day." Knowing how upset she would be, Colburn Mayne sympathised: "I am afraid you will be wounded, darling—and so am I, most profoundly. I had set my heart on at least sending *Felicity* to France. However, you should have heard Osbert Sitwell talking of her the other night, admiring her so enthusiastically and discriminatingly. That doesn't mean £40, but it does mean something."[240] When she heard that Rosamund Lehmann's *Invitation to the Waltz* had won the prize, perhaps Mary Butts found some consolation in remembering her brother's comment earlier that summer: "How odd that the French, of all people, rave over the books of the beautiful Rosamund Lehmann, which are so dull, and haven't yet got onto you.... I suppose really that nothing's harder to make than an accurate judgement of foreign literature."[241]

On the 18 November several pages of the manuscript of *Scenes from the Life of Cleopatra* were damaged in an odd way; Mary Butts's witty account relays information about her writing technique as well as echoing the atmosphere of her story, 'With and Without Buttons', with a nail-biting twist:

> *A Mystery*: mutilation of 2 pages of the fair copy of 'Cleopatra'. The book lay open on the escritoire,[242] with the first draft, also open, identical books. I had left the house for half-an-hour. On returning found the 2 last pages that I had copied, bar 2 with the top righthand (or left!) corners torn off. A 2-3 inch *ragged* edge, and on one page, a slight smear. How conceivably can it have been done? The tears are unequal—one page noticeably longer than the other.
> I cannot understand and do not like this. No sign of the torn bits.

Until the final comment: "One bit found carried on a shoe into Studio—Settles mice."

While there were occasional outings such as when she had "fun with Mr Minnifee [a neighbour] at the First and Last", Mary Butts recorded a number of "bad days" at the end of the month. "In bed with a chill and the life of Nijinsky," she noted on the 28th. Romola Nijinsky's *The Last Days of Nijinsky* (1933) prompted "tears for the ballet and exquisite memories—sharp and unbearably poignant." She then added: "One reason to be glad we have lived in this century, one healing for the War—that we have lived to see and know, adore, saturate ourselves with the Ballet Russe."[243]

Mary Butts also wrote out sentences under the heading 'Flowers of English' at this time, including the following two unattributed quotations: "'a single gust of effervescing zeal set the fiddle-strings jangling out of tune' *and* 'a half-blown smile was lurking up his sleeve'." Together with her ideas about an essay on contemporary illiteracy, this activity looked back to a desire she had noted over five years earlier of writing a handbook on English prose.

In late December she sent Angus Davidson a Christmas card which, as in the previous year, was based on a witty drawing by Gabriel Aitken. This time it was of himself at his baby grand piano and Mary Butts sitting beside him quill in hand, looking pensive. "Angus love,... Forgive this late writing," she wrote on the back of the card (to which Gabriel added his "love and good wishes"), "but have been worrying at 'Cleopatra' like a dog with a bone.... A proper letter once this week is over, but Camilla comes tomorrow, and I'm overwhelmed with Christmas."[244]

CHAPTER TWENTY-THREE

The Gold Shifts So

1934

THE FESTIVE SEASON had come and gone. Mary Butts had attended the "cold church" on Christmas Day as well as the pantomime in Penzance. She had also received a long letter from Douglas Goldring which announced the possibility of his editing a new journal. "The 'brow' is to be higher than that of existing tuppenies but the appeal much broader than that of the 6d 'heavies'," he explained, adding: "if the paper materializes there should be some more or less regular and possibly useful 'bread and butter' work in it, for yourself...[since] I'd like both of you, whom I have so long regarded as among my closest and best, to be in it from the word 'go'."[245] Even though this project came to nothing, such compliments were cheering.

On the 7 January she described the first week of 1934 spent in the company of Naomi Royde-Smith and Ruth Manning-Sanders as "unforgettable—revelations, criticisms, exchanges and delights". On the 24th she was dazzled by the night sky with its "great stars like pricked lace against a grey veil. While the long band of quiet winter surf under the moon brings back blue and gold and all the business of the 'wine dark'. Why? Walking home across the fields, I could not make out. Or why the January moon and grey tiger should bring back *Hellas*." Just as the waters of Villefranche bay had done, again and again the sea in Cornwall (the darkness transforming the green and blue tiger to grey) drew her back to images of Greece.[246]

Against this inspirational scenery, she felt increasingly distressed and frustrated by the slow yet inevitable breakdown of her relationship with Gabriel. By contrast, her professional reputation was continuing to grow. No major work came out in 1934; however, a number of articles,

38 reviews and her story, 'A Lover', were published. One of the most interesting publications was her long essay on the work of M.R. James, published in *The London Mercury* in February. A distinguished academic and antiquarian, Montague Rhodes James (1862-1936) was at various points in his career Provost of Eton College, Director of the Fitzwilliam Museum, Cambridge, and Vice-Chancellor of the University of Cambridge. He is best known today for his four volumes of supernatural tales which have greatly influenced later practitioners of the genre. 'The Art of Montagu James' has since been acknowledged as "probably the first 'critical' essay" on his *Collected Ghost Stories* (1931).[247] Like the previous year, 1934 would be extremely productive: Mary Butts would finish *Scenes from the Life of Cleopatra* and begin an autobiography about her childhood; write a number of stories and correspond with several writers to their mutual profit.

Yet such an overview is naturally only possible with hindsight; Mary Butts often found the actual experience of living the year difficult and wearing. When she wrote to Angus Davidson on the 20 January, it was after a "long silence.... We have had a bad time without you," she lamented. Not only were things bad because of Gabriel; she had found Camilla difficult over Christmas and "Cleopatra is now 400 pages, and not nearly dead yet." There had been consolations, including Charles Williams's *Many Dimensions* (1931)[248] and gardening, but all in all: "A feeling too—*you* won't laugh—as though I were on some kind of spiritual trial, and it was of the utmost importance that I keep on quietly doing—or rather being—exactly right. All as part of a pattern I am only most fitfully aware of, if at all."[249] On a more material level, she apologised for not yet repaying the £10 Angus Davidson had lent her, promising she would do so in February. (In March she wrote to say that "there will be money for you *soon* soon.")[250]

In his autobiography, *I Follow But Myself*, the musician and writer, Frank Baker, devotes an entire chapter to Mary Butts. In it he describes their first proper meeting in the summer of 1933, when he was introduced to her by George Manning-Sanders. Although he described her then as "the ridiculous woman in the red Russian boots"; like several of her friends, Baker found her voice distinctive: "I can never forget the sound of her voice. Husky, slightly breathless, every word tilted slightly towards a question high above the stagnant pool of facts. She was a consummate killer of small talk." George Manning-Sanders lent Baker *The Macedonian* to read and he was instantly impressed by its power: "It was not so much the quality of the writing or the thought expressed which held me; it was the authority: the assumption that she had been there when these things had happened in Macedonia; and more—as though this was how these events *were happening*; events which had stirred man's movements so many centuries before the writer's day, or the reader's. There was nothing flamboyant in the writing; none of that vivid colouring which Mary Renault[251] gives in our time to her recreations of the ancient world. It was almost a matter-of-fact account. But always there was this wielding of authority, as though the Delphic oracle had commanded the writer thus to report these matters and lift them out of the gimcrack framework we call 'time'."[252] This latter sentence particularly would have pleased Mary Butts with its suggestion of her being some kind of Blakean Secretary or medium.

Frank Baker became a loyal friend, and a rare one in that he both attended her funeral and did not forget her after her death.[253] In his memoirs he introduced her in the following manner:

> Mary Butts was a writer, and I do not think she would wish to be called anything else. Not novelist, historian, story-teller, or critic. Writer. She handled words with an alchemist's potency, in the way Arthur Machen did, though their styles are very different. Mary wrote obliquely, often juggling words as though they were balls thrown in the air, deftly caught and changing hands and colour on the way back to her; while Machen achieved a deceptive simplicity. Both wrote with an informed passion, and never easily. I would say they had to wrestle with words. Both were writers of unquestionable integrity, and although they were in the main stream of literary tradition they leave no imitators. They had met evil face to face, lived through it, and passed beyond it; and they produced books which to a few discerning readers will always be unique. I am not seeking to balance one with the other merely because I happened to know them both at the ends of their lives. But they both passed on to me a deeper understanding of the power and the ever flexible beauty of the Word, and made me more deeply aware of the significance of the craft I had chosen.[254]

It is clear from this account, that in Baker, Mary Butts had found a young writer who was eager to learn from her.

On the 5 January 1934 she noted that "Mr Baker came. His friend is dead." Baker himself wrote: "I called at Tebel Vos. I gave as a reason that I had come to thank her for the Christmas card... And then suddenly, uncontrollably, I blurted out the news of the death of Marcus, whom Mary Butts had known slightly the previous year. By one friend to whom I poured out this distress I had been told that such loud grief was unseemly. Perhaps it was. But Mary did not receive it with any such reproof. ...she was able to share this sorrow and so take a little of it from me. I remember that she held my hand and looked at me, her eyes filling with tears. And she murmured, 'That beautiful person...' She did not need to say any more."[255] Mary Butts noted that after hearing the news, "a strange thing happened. We [Gabriel Aitken, Camilla, Mary Butts] were all in a sensitive state, awed and not thinking of ourselves. ...then he went to the studio to play and I was kneeling by the salon fire-place with Camilla standing by me; and suddenly the little green glass ball beside the Longhi figurine fell and broke in pieces in the hearth. Nothing was 'near touching it'.... When Baker first came I spoke up for the logical blessedness of our dead—against a general scepticism. Was that why the ball—?" she wondered.

"A Plenitude" was how she described the 1 February, with Dorothy Sayers's 1934 novel, *The Nine Tailors*, "and spring and its days, and the garden and a little moon and a particularly clear fire, and a peace that passed understanding—a mixture of spiritual victory with bodily bien-être." She was also struck by the sea that day, describing it as "a black and lightening sea—black crystal laced with white fire. An awful loveliness."

In a long letter to Angus Davidson in early February she discussed her attitude to Fascism and Communism about which she had been reading a great deal. The previous year she had written to Ross Williamson for advice about "this Nazi business—with particular reference to a book of atrocities I've just got hold of."[256] And in a letter to Angus she adds: "The more I live, the surer I am that Communism, with its denial of all spiritual and all *individual* values is the supreme enemy—worthy the best energies we have—for it threatens, finally and fundamentally, everything on which the good life for each separate person depends. Only it's a matter, not of indifference or shouting or anger or contempt, but for profound understanding. For, incidentally, they've done good things—given 'common' culture a chance against aristocratic—and God knows in Russia it needed it. Killed one form of class-snobbery...given women their fair chance. Blown a whole tangle of lies and superstitions sky-high. At the same time, they are as much the devil for George George as for you and me."[257]

Since Mary Butts died in 1937, it is impossible to state categorically how she would have articulated her hostility to Nazism and Communism during the Second World War. She did not support the Labour Party and was not a democrat ("The people's friendliness and good temper. One's love for them returns but why trust them with government?" (9.3.35)).[258] Yet in *The Crystal Cabinet* she referred to "how easily, as in Nazi Germany, the liberties we now take for granted may be lost."[259] Her position is more clearly stated in a letter from October 1935 where she fulminates on Germany and the Abyssinian War then raging: "Germania gone neurotic is a pretty ghastly proposition—witness the late War. Now we've got a new one—but you won't want comments about that. The only blessing I can think is that the moral issue is clear, and Italy indefensible."[260] She was furious when in a conversation about Communism and Fascism in November 1936 Angus Davidson accused her of anti-semitism. After all, John Rodker was Jewish.

In January 1934 Tebel Vos was "full of Corvo's Name. For years his books had been a special study, he had aroused an intermittent, but passionate interest; and scraps of information had been pieced together, with an ardent desire to know more. A desire gratified by the arrival of Mr Symons' book as perfectly as a wish can be." Thus she wrote in her review of A.J.A. Symons's biography, *The Quest for Corvo* (the pen-name of Frederick Rolfe) for the February issue of *Time and Tide*.[261] Symons wrote to her on the 18th: "You will, I am certain, permit me to plead the fraternity of a common interest in letters and in Rolfe in writing now to thank you very warmly for your sympathetic, discriminating and just review of my book in *Time and Tide*."[262] She also wrote a lengthy article on Corvo's work which, after being rejected by *The Cornhill*, was published in *The London Mercury* in May.[263] The article so impressed Symons that he wrote to praise this and a number of Mary Butts's books, which he had searched out in the weeks since first writing to her:

> Naturally I like them all [*Death of Felicity Taverner*, *Ashe of Rings*, *Several Occasions* and *The Macedonian*]; good writing has an irresistible appeal to me. But most of all I enjoyed *Felicity Taverner*. Kralin is insidiously sinister without the charm of the snake. Who was the original of Boris, who must be drawn from life? You have drawn one of the strangest dramas I know, with brilliant skill, and found a truly modern theme. *Ashe of Rings* also astonished me, though I found less to sympathise with—perhaps because less that reflected myself. Yet I felt all through the latter half of the book that its torments were true, which is the best that can be said of any book.
>
> I like all the short stories, particularly the long one concerning the unlucky waif in Paris (I have not the book by me).[264]
>
> In *Alexander*, on the other hand, I failed to find my own image of the conqueror. It is a scintillating book, and I enjoyed your virtuosity; yet I feel that his daimon, as you describe it, would have made an orator, not a man of action. And you seem to me too generous to Alexander in respect of Callisthenes and Parmenio. But these differences of temperament do not blind me to the poetry of your picture, the skilful contrasts and shimmering reality of your portrait. I am very grateful for your gift.[265]

Mary Butts invited Symons to Sennen and he in turn invited her to his home in Essex. Neither took up the invitation, but it is clear from their letters that they had a great deal in common. (There was some discussion of Mary Butts and Gabriel Aitken collaborating on an opera based on Corvo's *Don Tarquinio* (1905)).[266] Their shared interest in Corvo prompted Symons to send Mary Butts a copy of Corvo's *Hubert's Arthur* (1935) the following year. She was delighted with the book itself and with Symons for sending it. She reviewed it in December 1935.[267]

At the end of February she began a series of "notes I now feel I *must* make—relations between G and myself." This list of grievances, misunderstandings and disappointments makes rather sad reading. She added to them during the rest of 1934 and in spite of occasional periods of closeness, felt increasingly resigned to the demise of her marriage. "Physically very down" in March, she retreated into her work and applied to a number of magazines and newspapers for more reviewing. Ellis Roberts helped her as much as he could, suggesting amongst other things, that she write to C.H. Warren, the editor of *Everyman*.[268] He also reassured her: "You couldn't review badly—or rather you couldn't write a review badly, you couldn't write anything which wouldn't make me want to print it. But you are, sometimes, too kind, I think: but it never strikes me as un-directed kindness, only perhaps occasionally mis-directed...which may be the target's fault. The gold shifts so."[269] The previous year she had been discouraged by inaccurate reviews of *Ashe of Rings*: "E.M. Delafield, for example, takes a sentence out of its context, attributes it to people who neither said it or heard it said; *then* holds it up to ridicule. Lesson for me never to do that. It's not fair to the writer. In its context, it is quite sensible."[270] The distance provided by reviewing enabled her to show a kindness and understanding of which she was not always capable on a personal level and given the letters writers (including Ellis Roberts) sent to her, it is clear that she was far from alone in needing praise.

* * * * *

ON THE 9 MARCH she was able to exclaim: "*Cleopatra* finished —Exquisite relief. Now I can write just what I like. Refresh myself, play with the House. Adorn it and the garden. For even when I did not touch it, as these last six weeks and more, it hung over my head. Now, well or ill done, it's over. I see I do not like commissioned work." Just as after the completion of *Death of Felicity Taverner* three years earlier, she turned to writing stories and considering a new collection. Of the eleven stories listed, only two, 'The Guest' and 'One Roman Speaks', would be published. 'The House-moving and the Parents who would not Help', the projected title for an unwritten story, reveals that old grudges ran deep. A list of twenty-three books she wanted to read (including four books published that year: P.G. Wodehouse's *Thank You Jeeves*, Margery

Allingham's *Death of a Ghost*, Clive Bell's *Enjoying Pictures* and Harold Nicolson's *Curzon*) illustrates the wide range of her interests.

Having completed *Scenes from the Life of Cleopatra*, she ruminated "*on this new fashion for classical novels*" and provided her own apologia:

> For years, for centuries we have been told about these people. They are a part of 'Education'. And a damned dull education it has been—and not only for our half-wits. Then, with the growth of anthropology and archeology, it is as though a release had been made—really *it is like breaking down an inhibition* and we find it possible to believe they even happened; that they were human beings, with lives.
>
> It is all coming out with a rush. As though we and our ancestors had passed our lives in a picture-gallery, with subjects all labelled and learned by heart, but entirely unintelligible. Then suddenly *sight*—the eyes—and *formal knowledge*, in the brain, were united, and we saw that the pictures were about what we had been told they were about. In fact, we saw them for the first time, and naturally a great deal that we had never seen, not formally even. Hence excited interest.
>
> Our danger is likely to be (i) an over-stress of their humanity (ii) they have been figures of formal significance only so long, that *anything* about them is likely to be important, because it is about *them*.

"But we have been given a great treasure," she concluded. She was aware that her own narratives were part of a trend which included Helen Simpson's *Henry VIII*, Una Broadbent's *Perilous Grain*, Robert Graves's *I, Claudius* (in a review of which she expanded on the apologia given above) and Jack Lindsay's *Rome For Sale*, all of which she reviewed around this time.[271] Both Broadbent and Lindsay expressed their gratitude. Thanking Mary Butts for her "very kind and discerning critique," the former added: "While I am writing, may I also thank you for some very thrilling hours spent in the company of the incomparable Macedonian? Some of your scenes and phrases haunted me for days, apart from the general impression which will colour all my future reading on him."[272] In October Una Broadbent wrote again, because she had been rereading *The Macedonian* and liked it more than ever.

Jack Lindsay wrote: "It is heartening to read such a response to what one fondly feels oneself as the core of one's work and others seem to fail to see.... Your praise is generous and make[s] me feel more contented with my work than anything else that has come my way: which is my excuse for writing to you."[273] Their "slight acquaintance", he reminded her, dated back to 1928 when in the "Fitzroy Tavern we met and exchanged a few words about Theocritus."[274] In his autobiography Lindsay expanded on this meeting: "Careless of herself, she was still impressive with her red-gold hair, her white skin and rich blue eyes, her large naked face. In build she was rather stocky. We talked about Theocritus. She had a passionate interest in the Greeks, and every time we met we spoke of nothing else, apart from a few words about her Butts ancestor who had been Blake's patron; she considered that she had an intuitive understanding of the Eleusinian Mysteries."[275]

A shared interest in history informed a correspondence which would be of crucial assistance to Mary Butts as she revised *Scenes from the Life of Cleopatra*. Only Lindsay's letters have survived, but it is clear from these that their discussions were varied, often focusing on some finer point of history.[276] He spoke for them both when he wrote (in a statement which holds true for good biography): "my attitude about historical novels is that one is at liberty to 'fill in' as one wishes, but all known facts must be entirely respected."[277]

When he read *The Macedonian* shortly afterwards, Lindsay found that it "displaced everything till I had read it—for once I began, I couldn't put it down." His praise for the narrative was high:

> I think it is perfect in insight, that it is entirely true and beautifully divines the essentials of Alexander's life. You have got to the core, I think, of the urge to assume divinity,... that terrible need of humanity to find an image transcendent and yet immanent, a goal and yet an immediacy: the trembling edge between the race-life and the individual life, where the individual feels drawn into something greater than himself and has to fight to aggrandise individuality in order to escape the chaos of blind forces... the whole tragedy of religion which is a madness and yet a necessity. Again and again, the book wavers on that edge of unutterable contact. It rouses all kinds of emotions which one cannot express, for rightly they exist only in the definition of the words.[278]

Such praise, and a reading which was so close to her own vision of the world, would have been exactly what Mary Butts wanted to hear. Lindsay had been reading *I, Claudius* just prior to *The Macedonian* and felt that whilst "excellent... in many ways,... Graves' book... has none of the truth of [*The Macedonian*]".[279] He accurately predicted that *I, Claudius* would be a best-seller and that if *The Macedonian* was not, it was probably because it lacked a "continuing story". "This public demand is silly in its way," he conceded, stating that she had provided not only "a complete picture of Alexander—an enduring picture," but also, "the first bit of real history on the subject".[280] It is rather surprising given this wide-spread praise for *The Macedonian* that it should have had to wait sixty years before being republished.[281]

In one of his letters, Lindsay sent his "blessing... to Cleopatra". Since he was himself embarking on a novel about the Queen of Egypt, he was relieved to hear that instead of "overlap[ping]", *Scenes from the Life of*

Cleopatra and his *Last Days with Cleopatra* would be "complementary".[282] It was at this stage that he wrote to say: "If I can be of any help to you in getting your book clear, please do let me know. I should be happy to pass on any information that might be of value. I'm fairly conversant with the period now," he added modestly, "and perhaps could help with any aspect that's still evading you."[283] Several letters during the summer of 1934 provided detailed answers to a "list of questions" she sent him. When Lindsay received the proofs of *Scenes from the Life of Cleopatra*, he was even more impressed than he had been by *The Macedonian*.

* * * * *

The Marriage Dissolves

ON A PERSONAL LEVEL, things were going badly at Tebel Vos. Mary Butts was at the end of her tether about Gabriel: "He is incapable of learning—of learning—of learning. It is fatal," she lamented on the 25 March. "Only there is Angus soon." After his visit, Mary Colville-Hyde came for a short stay in mid-April, bringing her daughter a reproduction of the Holbein painting of William Butts. This visit passed off "without catastrophe, with even possibly a better understanding," she wrote to Angus in early May. The old resentments remained, however: "Only all the time I kept thinking: if she had done for me one tenth of what she did for Tony, we shouldn't be to-day a ruined family. I *know* I could have prevented it, saved the pair of them from the adventurers who fed on us. Now *everything* has gone, place, pictures, fortune, objets d'art—even the last of our plate! She remains quite wonderful, upheld by a strong religious faith, *and* because she is too old to realise anything.... Meanwhile Tony is without a cent in the world, she living in one room in a cheap hôtel, and the Holbein won't sell." With wry self-consciousness, she added: "But you've heard all this—how many times, my dear?"[284] There is no doubt that Mary Colville-Hyde was extremely gullible, and there is much truth in Mary Butts's complaint.

After her mother's departure, she worked at several stories. She finished 'The Lover who lied Story' and 'Caesar and the Pirates' which she offered as 'One Roman Speaks' to Lord Gorell at *The Cornhill* in the summer. "Certainly, 'One Roman Speaks' will do—as you modestly suggest. It is an admirable piece of reconstructive fiction, to my mind, and overcomes the great difficulties of such recapturing of the mind of the past with marked success," he replied.[285] There were two slight problems however; the story was too long, and it could not be published "this side of Christmas". Mary Butts wrote back immediately to accept both the revision and delayed publication and was paid £16.6.0 for the story, which was published over a year later in October 1935.[286] Gorell also indicated that there might be space for a short series of classical reconstructions in *The Cornhill* during 1935 and asked her to send a list of suggestions with a synopsis. This idea, unfortunately, was not taken up.

By the end of May Mary Butts was depressed about Gabriel and his effect on her:

> The bad times have begun again—God knows how long they will last. I saw it working-up days ago—when I felt ill and he was cross at getting me things.... I must remember he is not in a normal state, but a very evil nature in him—and a pretty bad one in me—shows at these times. It is hell. I have so much to do, and it takes all the strength out of one. I remember—with considerable disproportion—all he might have done and refuses to do. I'm all unnerved about Mother anyhow. Not proud of myself.

Happily, on this occasion the "bad times" did not last. The very next entry, five days later was one of relief: "3.6.34. An end came quickly to this. *Laus Deo*." She drafted her version of the family history to her mother in a letter which is a mixture, characteristically, of lucid self-knowledge and resentment: "Mother, I had hoped that after your visit, some beginning of confidence was possible between us again. I know that as a young girl I was a little beast in many ways. It was hard luck on you to have had that sort of daughter, you did not expect and didn't know how to deal with. While it has taken me years to understand—and—as I've said—most of the trouble was that you misunderstood and so unjustly accused me. While if it had been different—it's that which makes it so tragic and why I want it to stop—for if it had been different, do you suppose our Family would be in its present appalling situation?" Mary Butts felt she understood why her mother believed any gossip about her, writing with extraordinary understatement about herself: "I think I know why—judging from Tony and tendencies in myself I learned early to try to repress—and that, to be candid, is a love of dramatic stories, 'finding things out', so to speak."[287] This may well have been one of her mother's failings; there is a great deal of evidence that Mary Butts shared this particular "tendency", despite her boast that she had repressed it. "I'm our best asset," she declared towards the end of her letter, adding a rather melodramatic aside: "There—I've got this off my—etc.... I'm much more likely to kill myself with financial worries which I ought not to have."

Once again it was the natural world which cheered her: "*Remember*, as I came into this room [the salon] about 10.30—through the windows the sea and the sky in the last light—inside blue jade and pearl." Three weeks later she noted: "*Remember*. The flowering of the great poppy—its trinity of white heads streaming and tearing and flying in the wind against the white houses out to sea, white on white against blue." The summer brought not only stimulating and heartening letters from Jack Lindsay and others; it also brought a new resident to Sennen. Mary Butts began to spend a great deal of time with Marjorie Bagot, who gave her a "conical green-bottle-glass door-stop with a bubble tree inside" on the 1 July. Such a friendship was all the more important, since on the 8 July there was terrible news: "I have now found out the worst thing I have found out in my married life. Stunned and sick as usual.... Am very afraid." From the context it is clear that it had something to do with Gabriel Aitken but remains a mystery. It was all the more traumatic for coming the very day after she had noted with excitement: "THE NEW BOOK. My childhood—how God, art and magic were learned. Praise of my Father, praise of Salterns—both dead." This was the first mention of *The Crystal Cabinet*, the autobiography of childhood, which (after a difficult publishing history) would be her most popular but, sadly, posthumous book. It was by no means a new idea. Bryher remembered how ten years earlier in Florence, from Mary Butts's own lips, she had "heard the outline of *The Crystal Cabinet* then told, not written, history handed down as in the tenth century the skalds taught it".[288]

She did not start writing *The Crystal Cabinet* immediately. Instead there were "nightmare days after nightmare weeks after nightmare months. Will it ever end? And how?" Yet even in the midst of her pain the writer in her added: "For a story? (One might as well get that out of it.)" Part of the problem seems to have derived from disagreements between Marjorie Bagot and another recent resident, Christine Ashcroft, in which Mary Butts had become embroiled. She used this "nasty little storm in a tea-cup" as the basis for 'The Warning', a story which she wrote that summer. Ellis Roberts who had taken over the editorship of *Life and Letters To-day* in October 1934 accepted the story and published it the following January.[289]

August brought good news, when Odo Cross and Angus Wilson made a second visit to Sennen: "Odo's visit—'splendeurs et misères'—Gaby's faults, alas, as it has been all this year. With mine as well, but dreadful, useless and silly. But, great joys and our love for each other, the three of us, deeper and stronger than ever before." She was excited also by the prospect of a visit to their home at Tidcombe Manor, where she stayed in July the following year. Her admiration for Odo Cross was greater than ever as she perceived in him a capacity for "mediumship, if he developed it—which he probably won't".

The other exciting news was that "Angus [Davidson] will have No Place." This was the name given to the property she had described to him the previous September. To judge from her letters to Angus from the autumn onwards, it would appear that she had little time to do anything other than oversee the rebuilding and conversion of the house. She kept him informed (as he was away for at least part of these months in America, staying with Harcourt Wesson Bull) by letters which are not only a testament to friendship, but reveal the range of her interests and a wonderful wit.

In September she announced that the council had passed the plans for No Place, and discussed the laying of the drains and the creosoted Canadian pine to be used in the new walls. When the new hearth was set up, the question was whether it should be made of granite rather than plaster, or perhaps, even better, brick (Gabriel's suggestion)? On the 20 September the walls were eight foot high in the midst of terrible rainfloods. By early October the "bones" of the kitchen were visible and she was soon to start work on the garden with Christine Ashcroft. From mid-October onwards the news was all "thatch" as (Bolshie) Burnett, a local labourer and friend, was hard at work on the roof of No Place. "Thatch. Thatch. Thatch," she wrote in letters from the 19-23 October; "Thatch. Thatch. Thatch," she repeated on the 28th. Only at the end of the month was she able to announce that the thatching was complete. Her letter in early November was all about the toilet, joists and cement. On the 9th there was a problem with the kitchen. It was so small that a table would not fit—perhaps a "combined dresser-table," she suggested. The re-building of No Place caused a great deal of local controversy and on the 19 December she wrote that it would only be ready by the beginning of February. "A most magic home is waiting [sic] you—a place of infinite possiblities and one which is impatient for you. One can feel that in the stones," she declared, closing her letter with best Christmas wishes.[290]

* * * * *

> FOR MY BOOK — *This afternoon, alone in the house, above the sea, the sense of possession. Waiting for Marjorie Bagot. I know I shall never be any different—and more than that. I saw my power. There are no words.*
>
> —MB, diary entry, 10.10.34

OF COURSE, overseeing the building of No Place was far from being the only thing Mary Butts did during the autumn and early winter of 1934. In September Gladys Hynes (her old friend from their Belsize Park

Garden days) came to visit with the painter, Dod Proctor.[291] Unfortunately Gabriel was not there to see them as he had broken his arm slipping on the sheer stone steps in the back garden and was recovering in Penzance Hospital. "How is Gabriel getting on?" asked Tony when he heard of the accident. "Are they looking after him properly in Penzance?... I can't imagine anything worse for a painter."[292] Mary Butts described the accident to Angus, adding with rare praise for her daughter: "Camilla and I are holding the fort between us, and she is being a darling, every sort of help."[293]

In October she visited a medium in Penzance and made several pages of notes as she tried to distinguish between the pertinent and "the usual good luck" comments. She had found the medium to be "a woman of transparent honesty, considerable charm and overwhelming vitality.... Took me alone into a nurse's consulting-room, *v* medical—*no* aesthetics. I sat before her, facing the light. She asked for something to psychometrise. I gave her a silver bracelet. She spoke for nearly 1/2 hour, v. fast, eyes shut, sending out immense energy." The medium commented on her "immense physical mediumship, ectoplasm, healing powers. (Gave me practical, demonstrated massage for Gaby.)" With regard to Mary Butts's writing she said "Your work's 'ibrow [high brow]. It's modern work, and it helps modern people in their difficulties.... Then people trying to 'do' me over my work. The word 'wangle' repeated. Told to hold on—etc.... The usual good luck coming soon.... Then had I a new book about to appear with which I was not satisfied? Well, I was to be. Was I waiting for important news about future work? I should soon hear (These last too easy, perhaps)." On her marriage: "Then worried about a young man, ill, in a v. nervous state, my husband. That he was getting on, would get over. Healing thro' her massage (Nous verrons) Wait for February for him. Shortly a journey, unexpected (idem)." The medium also mentioned Mary Butts's father and ended with: "Had we a friend with a car—a friend under some sort of stress? Yes. Well, avoid that car. A Warning!?" Mary Butts concluded: "Now with all this it's exceedingly hard to judge. She *tore* at it, asked very few questions." But she decided to come again and "paid 4/- to her sick fund." In fact, Mary Butts did have a bad car accident the following year...

In November she started work on the final proofs of *Scenes from the Life of Cleopatra*. She received a complimentary letter from Ezra Pound in Rapallo, prompted by her recent review of his *Make It New* (1934) in *The Sunday Times*.[294] "How did jhu penetrate them parages? rape the editor, or wottell ? Or has the wyper changed hands ? who zoo in the Sunday boozuu?" During the course of the letter he recommended Alice James's diary and made the following lament: "Jheezuss/ gord wouldn't you think by 1934 there could again be a magazene AT least as good as the

Little Review was in 1917/19."[295] "So glad to get your letter," she wrote back on the 10th. She agreed that there was nothing to match *The Little Review*,[296] recommended Una Broadbent's *Perilous Grain* and wrote of her work and some of her attitudes to the literature of her time which included "not hanging by my eyelashes on the Auden crowd" and the fact that "all this Virginia Wolf [sic] worship. Not my totem."[297] Perhaps she was remembering an article published exactly a year earlier in *The Glasgow Herald*, entitled 'The Trend of the Modern Novel', which was one of the very few critiques to state that "Virginia Woolf is noticeably evident in the far finer work of Mary Butts (particularly in that little masterpiece, *Death of Felicity Taverner*)."[298]

An indication of Mary Butts's thoughts towards the end of 1934 which would find fuller expression in *The Crystal Cabinet*, is given in her review of Adrian Bell's autobiography, *The Balcony*. Praising his ability to "recapture some of the magical significance of childhood", she opens with a statement which shows her belief in the predominance of nature over nurture:

> People are beginning to be very clever about remembering their childhoods, in recalling that picture, so tiny, so disconnected, so momentous. So enduring, because the more one observes, the more one is aware of a personality that was there all along, an essential self, a being no affected by time, which manifests itself at three months or three years or thirty, in the manner appropriate to each. Impossible to say when one first becomes aware of it, perhaps the first time one hears oneself telling oneself" "My friend, you are to do this," or "you are that". This self, this watcher, is the being one comes to know better, until it becomes identified with the self, moving about in time; and the man or woman who makes this identification are in the way to become their own masters.

This sensitive review was printed in the last ever issue of *The Bookman* (Xmas, 1934) and was tucked away in the journal's final pages among the reviews of children's fiction, signed only "M.B.".[299]

Whilst there are few entries for the last two months of 1934, she provides a delightful description of her desk (which Gabriel Aitken had given to her) on the 13 November:

> My desk in its beauty. The wood after 2 years' polishing. All the niches in order—MSS, reference, letters, etc. The large square of coloured blotting-paper. Two glass pillar candlesticks; my seal, the dragon on its jade block. Pale blue Bristol ink-bottle; the stamp-box of inlaid straw; two glass paper-weights with 'magics' inside. The little cup for tags, shells, rings, precious pebbles. Last of all the glass goblet, full, to-day with wallflower and freesia. *Then* the crystal bottle that came from St Ives.... It sits there, exquisite.

On the 7 December she decided that "since life in one respect these last months could hardly have been worse, try and think of what other things have stood out." During such a moment of composure she could note that "grievances, real and faked, can become a kind of compensation, a false martyrdom." She could also find compensation in every misfortune: "The illness was bad; G's neglect and impatience and contempt even worse; but in bed I struck *Sun in Capricorn* [(1934)]." This last was a novel by Edward Sackville-West, with whom she would correspond over the next two years. She also spent many hours in the "continual companionship and sustenance of Charles Williams's two books [*Many Dimensions* and *Place of the Lion*]". By the end of the year she had begun to make notes for a long essay on his work. These and "a thousand things I have forgotten," she regretted.

Yet whatever the compensations, it was impossible to avoid the fact that she "could bear this hideous parody of marriage no longer." She was "truly sorry for Gabriel...I believe I could still help him—if I loved him enough. And it is my failure that I don't. And pride stands in the way. I have, on all human reckoning, been filthily treated, vilely miscalled, misjudged; my love *defiled*. All the gay adventure spoiled. That hurts so pitifully. And when I think what [some] people here...who think him so charming would say—if they had seen him, snarling at me in the kitchen, five minutes after they had left the house.[300] My own great fault has been impatience. No one, who knew, could blame me if I cast him out of my life after such a year. Except just a few people, and my own soul—apart from my pride—and something I can't name. It tells me now, saying 'after all, you've failed him too.'" As with Sergei, she did still feel that she should have been able to change and 'save' Gabriel Aitken. This ambitious conviction, that she had the power to direct people in the 'right' direction, was the delusion which caused her the greatest suffering. Her account on the 10 December shows just how little her efforts of the previous five years had done to erase her husband's ingrained lack of self-confidence:

> Tonight Gabriel came into my room—the room where we used to be so gay—and for the hundredth time I tried to make him explain what has come over him for this past year, and all he would say was that he was disappointed with his life. Yet how much he's already done with it. And how much was offered him at our marriage? And here? When most men have to go to an office and slave at some job, he was given liberty and beauty and freedom to do his part, and a person to love him and work for him and make the money we need. None of that has been sufficient; yet, by the irony of life, *because* he's been utterly, totally ungrateful—to God, to life and to me, he'll most prob-

> ably *create* the very thing he fears. Become a failure. For if ever a man paved the way to his own hell, it is Gabriel.

This was Mary Butts at her most insightful, most understanding. Unfortunately, at this stage in her life, her failure (as she saw it) not to be able to deflect him from his "own hell" meant much more than the fact that "our marriage is as nearly over as not." This in itself, would have been sad enough. So intertwined was her life with his, however, that she felt her "whole nature" to be affected: "And quite likely to be the death of me. For my hold on *human* life is weakening. He had the key to *my* earthly happiness and he has thrown it away." Mary Butts had used the metaphor of the key before in relation to Gabriel Aitken and it would be wrong to see this merely as a verbal hyperbole of anguish. She would live a further two years and achieve much; there is little doubt, however, that something was broken inside her from then on. Little wonder that at this disappointment in the "human" side of her life she turned her attention in a more spiritual direction. A short sentence written the previous day—"the discovery of Father Walke and a place to pray"—might belie the significance of this fact in Mary Butts's last years. Yet this "discovery" was part of a process which had become more pronounced in 1934 and which she announced in a letter to Ellis Roberts in February 1935: "Have you noticed I'm a Christian again?"[301]

CHAPTER TWENTY-FOUR

St Hilary

For myself, I speak as a Christian and a Catholic—and I wasn't one for 20 years, quite long enough to understand the difficulties.... Put it baldly, and with far too many 'I's—only one can best argue at the start from oneself—I, after years of disbelief, your kind of disbelief, ie. every fashionable kind of scepticism, magic, etc., after years of really quite hard work, came back, by entirely intellectual paths to belief again.

—MB, drafts of letters to Edward Sackville-West, May and September 1935

Once at St. Hilary's there was the Mystery to adore as I have never understood—(that's not the word) before. It lifted me clear above the agony here [at Tebel Vos]—outside it. —MB, diary entry, 9.12.34

In January 1933, Mary Butts had attended Sennen Church and wrote of having "saved [the] faith I have so nearly lost". From then on she began to write out prayers in English and Latin. Her faith was not new; she had simply put it aside since her childhood. After all, as she had her character Scylla Taverner declare in *Armed with Madness*: "there were fifty good reasons for supporting the non-existence of God."[302] In a letter to a friend in 1936 she tried to explain her renewed understanding:

> I've indicated positions; yet on the other hand, I've said less than nothing. Talked round. As though a man should give a lecture on *Figaro* instead of singing an air from it; described a ballet, instead of bringing in a dancer.... And I shall only say a little more in the same way: that one has objective (if the word has any meaning, and only a generation that has theorised itself silly would claim that it has not) knowledge of the existence of God, His exquisite care, His counsel, His terrible beauty, His love. Of which every value we prize is the dim mirror. That the years—twenty years—I spent with the 'Intelligentsia', semi-denying it were so far wasted years. A fair span out of life. Passionately I regret those years when the War and the Time-spirit caught me up, and I prattled my version of the current version you are all prattling...
>
> Only I could never quite swallow it. Yet I half wasted priceless years, and I wish I hadn't. It was history helped save me, history and the arts and my common sense; and something of the same sort of thing has happened to Pascal. Also an honesty that made me in my ignorance believe that Science really had the last word, so that I was, so to speak, on my honour not to believe what I knew.[303]

Sennen Church was not her only place of worship. In the early 1930s Frank Baker was church organist at the nearby town of St Just. A friend wrote to him after her death: "I remember Mary Butts quite clearly though I only met her once [in the autumn of 1933]. She turned up one Sunday at St Just with the Manning-Sanders for Matins &/or Mass and you introduced me afterwards. The thing that impressed me most deeply about her was that she seemed to smell the business of living. The talk ranged over this aspect and that of human affairs and personal oddities; and at each prospect of man's endeavours to cope with his circumstances was Mary Butts, her nostrils twitching slightly, inhaling the savour of each situation; and I recall the smooth throaty voice defining each reaction."[304]

Having reconverted to Christianity, Mary Butts felt the need to justify her new position publicly. On the 16 April 1934 she experienced "the old rare sense as in the past that something good—a good fortune—is on the way." Five days later she declared: "That was right. Yesterday Ellis Roberts sent *Orthodoxy Sees It Through*. Domine, non sum digna." In late May (the day after a "Gay Sunday. Pentecost. Scarlet in Church as it should be") She considered writing a new pamphlet which would be "based on Huxley's criticism of George Herbert's 'And I replied—My Lord'. c.f. the Orthodoxy book. A statement of my position." She never published the pamphlet; but did discuss Aldous Huxley's "half-page gloss" on George Herbert's 'The Collar' in an article for *The Spectator* which came out a week after her death.[305]

She also gave a clear "statement of [her] position" in a long review of *Orthodoxy Sees It Through* (1934) for the May issue of *Time and Tide*. This book was "a collection of essays by nine authors [including Ellis Roberts] to show in effect what is the attitude and sometimes the answer of Catholic Christianity to nine aspects of the modern world. To Psychology, to the Arts of Music and Literature, to 'New' Religion, 'New' Morals, Economics and the re-shaping of peoples by Communism and Fascism. Also to the new myth which for some time now has been taught in advanced circles for history." She was particularly impressed by the essay on the latter subject: "The extraordinary perversion of the facts the people from my generation on swallow so easily and unlearn so painfully: that man alone was sufficient for man; that the process of evolution, by some unspecified virtue inherent in itself, would carry mankind through to a 'fantastic Utopia of easy money and easy virtue', without reference to the original source of all his past well-being, his faith in God, his practice of disciplined virtue, his awareness of the supernatural." She defended herself for having belonged to this crowd: "As to how this came about, it is only fair to say that the first was brilliantly taught us and mixed with much absorbing truth; the second as unintelligently as possible." Mary Butts believed it no more. On the contrary, she was "so angry now with Mr. Wells for misleading us, for taking the heart out of us with his evolving World-State and his pitiless technocrats, his hells of Materialism he tried to persuade us were heavens, that it is hard to be fair, to remember how much delight he gave when he set out not to preach but to please."

As for Darwin's discovery of natural selection, it had led to "a man-glorifying fairy-tale" with sciences evolving out of it being "squared to fit". As a result, mystical experiences were now "reduc[ed]...to a mere psychic abnormality, in sentences which leave the taste of death in the mouth." She then came to the "crux of the question":

> Are we to discover again, as man has hitherto believed and lived for, in a universe in which ours is a part, an image, a miniature, a "signature" of an infinitely great spiritual whole; in a natural world transfused by a supernatural; in a Power which has created the whole, and incarnated Itself for our salvation? Or are we as Julian Huxley...wants, to replace religion by ethical societies for the practice of moral self-abuse, sit with Mr. Shaw's corpses in "all the horrors of religion without revelation" and worship ourselves? And when that faith fails, worship nothing?... If we choose the former, then the Christian Faith contains the best statement of it.

In this review she cited Ellis Robert's essay because he had "shown with perfect understanding the effect all this has had on the art of letters". She quoted his words again when starting her last diary in May 1936 and, more publicly, in her autobiography: "Without God there is no man; without supernature there is no nature; without philosophy there is no psychology; without theology there is no science; without mysticism there is no commonsense. These axioms are the basis of all human endeavour. They are the condition of the arts. At first gradually, after the war catastrophically, they have been denied or ignored." For Mary Butts his words were "final" and the tone of her conclusion shows that she had undergone her own conversion back to the faith of her childhood: "Truth, realized again, is so quick in action and so serviceable, the same truth that, often mishandled and misconceived, has given Western man his glories, pulled Europe through the splendours and agonies of her history, that it would seem as though we had not much to fear. Yet there is one thing to remember—that the recovery for which we are preparing ourselves will be as dangerous as it is glorious."[306] Mary Butts's own battle would be to save the church of St. Hilary.

* * * * *

> *What brought [Mary Butts] to St Hilary? Was it Bernard Walke's personality or the religion he taught, or both? It hardly matters since it is obvious that here were the symbols of something she had almost lost and had to rediscover: a sanctification whose defilement she was then writing about in some of her stories... Perhaps Mary's intuition told her that St Hilary was coming to its last days; that here a significant battle was to be fought out, and one that she had to be in on.* —Frank Baker, *I Follow But Myself*[307]

The Church of St Hilary is "set among the tall gaunt trees and the few houses of St. Hilary Churchtown" just outside Marazion and 16 miles east of Sennen. Marazion may now be better known for its proximity to St Michael's Mount, yet it was only "in the 19th century that the township of Marazion was carved *out of* St Hilary to form a separate parish," explains Horace Keast in his pamphlet, *St Hilary of Cornwall: The Story of a Cornish Parish and its Church*. Built in the fourteenth century, the church was burnt down in the 1850s and rebuilt within a decade with only the tower and the spire remaining from the original edifice. No doubt Mary Butts would have delighted in the "tradition that a pagan temple stood on the site of the present church during the Roman occupation. It was converted into a Christian church by one of the Celtic saints and it was on this site that French monks of St. Michael's Mount built the first church of St. Hilary. The evidence is slim but it is feasible," concludes Keast, adding: "What is beyond dispute, however, is that the lanes and little roads leading to St. Hilary church were trodden by Celtic natives and by Roman soldiers, by French monks and by medieval farmers, by tin miners and bal maidens (who sorted out the tin ore on the surface) and by the modern pilgrims to this shrine of St. Hilary."[308] And by Mary Butts between 1934 and 1936.

Father Bernard Walke was the Vicar of St Hilary when she started to attend Sunday Mass "whenever she could afford a car to drive her from her Atlantic fastness to the gentler country of St. Michael's Mount, where the spire of the church tipped out above the trees, the spire which in the golden days of the mediaeval apotheosis had stood as a beacon for mariners."[309] He had come in 1913 and was by all accounts a holy and charismatic man. Baker wrote that "Ber Walke infected everybody who met him with his own unconditional love of life and of people. And more: they caught from him the awareness of a state of being which reduced materialism to dry ashes. Bernard Shaw had remarked on a visit to St Hilary that there he felt the presence of the Holy Ghost; and there was no Shavian barb in this."[310] A strong pacifist during the First World War, Walke was a man of integrity and strong Anglo-Catholic beliefs in an area where Methodism predominated.

He refurbished the church with the assistance of local people as well as artists of now-international fame, many of whom donated their work. To this day St Hilary contains a picture of St Joan of Arc by Walke's wife, the painter, Annie Walke, and one of St Francis by Roger Fry. The scenes depicted on the panels of the choir stalls are by Ernest Proctor, Annie Walke, Harold Harvey, Norman Garstin, Harold Knight, Alathea Garstin and Gladys Hynes—all members of the Newlyn School, 1900-1930. The reredos of the Lady Chapel is by Ernest Proctor and the pictures on the parclose screen are by Joan Manning-Sanders, completed when she was only ten years old. Since Mary Butts had known Roger Fry and Gladys Hynes well in her youth and had had her portrait painted by Fry and Joan Manning-Sanders, their work in the church probably contributed to her feeling that it was 'right' for her to be there. In late May 1936 she was shown a number of Annie Walke's pictures and was horrified that "all that genius [was] hidden away in a barn in that grove [near the church]." She was particularly interested in two which were for sale (although she could not afford to buy one), and decided to write to Jonathan Cape to draw attention to Annie Walke's work.

In the late 1920s the church became known nationally when Filson Young (occasional organist there) arranged for the BBC to broadcast the St Hilary Christmas plays. In August 1932 St Hilary made headline news: "PREACHERS STORM VILLAGE. Raid With Crowbars To Remove Articles Held Illegal: Verger Overpowered When Attempting To Ring Alarm. VICAR HELD PRISONER," declared *The Daily Mirror* on its front page. Keast gives an account of this attack, which was the culmination of a campaign by the Protestant sect of Kensitites against the high-church services: "The Protestant organisation found an embittered resident of St Hilary who agreed to act as 'aggrieved Parishioner' in an application to the Consistory Court for a faculty for the removal of all the altars, images and other ornaments in the church.... It was known in advance that Father Walke would refuse to recognise the jurisdiction of the court or plead before it." The Court gave the order and "the petitioner...armed with a legal document" came to the church in August 1932 with a "coachload of hired labourers [who] then began the work of destruction, demolition and sacrilege. Stone altars were attacked by axes and hammers, the baroque reredos and canopy of the high altar...were ruthlessly cut down and portable objects were taken away.... There was a large congregation of supporters at the Mass of Reparation on the following Sunday. Services were continued according to the traditional Catholic pattern but the persecution continued by one legal action after another for the next three years."[311] It was during this time that Mary Butts started to come regularly to St Hilary's. It was without doubt a situation which involved both danger and glory, as her review above had intimated.

It grieved her that Angus never accompanied her to St Hilary which became central to her life from then on. In 1935 Frank Baker became its organist and remembered how Bernard Walke compared Mary Butts to the Woman of Samaria (John, 3,4). For she:

> became one of that motley company who Sunday by Sunday went to Bernard Walke's invocation of the Holy Mysteries, finding in the Sacrifice of the Mass the patterns of their lives shifting into definable shapes. After Mass a number of us would stay for a while in Ber's study where, tray on desk, he would eat his boiled egg, coffee and toast breakfast while his friends drank sherry from Poole's in Penzance at two shillings a bottle, good even at that price. They were happy gatherings, with always the atmosphere of a festa about them. Bernard had the power of drawing out the essence of anyone in his company. This meant that to some extent we all played up, but it was no bad thing. In that calm room with its shelves of books and white walls and ash fire we had a sense of unity which is rare, and a feeling that we all had a unique role to play in the great adventure of living. Mary loved those Sundays as much as anybody.[312]

CHAPTER TWENTY-FIVE

Who Calls Country Life Dull?
1935

> *There are days when there is not enough time because Everything is significant with a next to intolerable interest and significance. I'd need to be seven or more persons to do justice to all that there is here to learn, to discover, to make, to 'approfondir', to enjoy. Bees hovering round an invisible Paradise-grown flower.*
> —MB, diary entry, 26.4.35

SEVERAL PEOPLE WHO WROTE to Mary Butts in January 1935 commented on Gabriel Aitken's latest Christmas card. "I meant to write you both at Christmas to thank you for your card. I enjoyed it even more than the one which you sent last year, and that is saying a great deal," wrote E.M. Forster on the 24 January.[313] Jack Lindsay liked it so much that he used it as "the only 'decoration' of my walls."[314] It is impossible to say whether Mary Butts passed on this praise to Gabriel Aitken, since by January he had left Tebel Vos and gone back to Newcastle where he was "living with an aunt and going to pieces, it is said, with drink".[315] It was uncertain when or even whether he would return to Sennen. There is a sense in which his three Christmas cards show in pictorial form the breakdown of the marriage. In the first Gabriel Aitken is kneeling before Mary Butts, offering her a lily. In the second they are sitting beside one another, albeit engaged in separate pursuits. In the final one they are standing apart, Gabriel Aitken looking disgruntled and Mary Butts aloof. They are no longer regarding one another. (See p. 556.) Throughout 1935 they did communicate, often through Angus Davidson, but none of their troubled correspondence has survived. Notwithstanding sometimes feeling lonely and being placed in a "socially difficult situation", Mary Butts felt only relief at her husband's absence and on the 4 January declared: "Out today. Tiepolo sky, north wind, the mist hardened out into marble, purple and grey and gold. The blue behind, as hard as lapis. As though I were on the edge, the earth's archetype, not the sea's. The under and overfrets nagged it aside. (My fault). Still it was nearer. Some day I may get there." Whilst she fretted over "what to do about Gabriel", she felt "underneath everything, the huge peace".

She was not alone in early January, since Angus Davidson had arrived in Sennen to organise his move into No Place. He had a large number of friends, many of them literary, and Mary Butts was introduced to a steady stream of writers who came to No Place, including Edward Sackville-West, Rosamund Lehmann and Alix and Ray Strachey.[316] In addition, he provided her with literary gossip such as the "*GOOD NEWS*.... E.M. Forster has got a policeman now."[317] On the 21 October, Angus described his time as assistant to the Woolfs at their Hogarth Press between 1924 and 1927: "On Leonard Woolf—who promised him 1/2 profits, and when he left, the profits [were] kept. (With new staff on another basis). V.W.'s cheque, £10. Given side-work on the *Nation*, and saleable art-books."[318] His presence also inspired Mary Butts to write: "FOR A STORY. Return of Angus from the sea. (Done)" (1.2). This became 'Look Homeward, Angel'. In contrast to 1934, when she did not leave Cornwall; in 1935 she would go on revitalising trips to London and friends' grand houses. All this social activity together with the new circle connected with St Hilary stimulated her to be ever more productive.

In a letter to Ezra Pound the previous October she had mentioned her involvement in collecting and editing a series of supernatural experiences to be published by Methuen. These experiences were sought via a questionnaire, sent out to writers in January 1935:

> Have you ever had a queer experience that you consider supernatural? The Editors are collecting authentic experiences for a book which Messrs. Methuen will publish if the response justifies it, and they would welcome any instance you could submit. Some of the headings under which these might fall are: prevision, and vision of the past; supernormal powers; magic; consciousness out of the body; awareness of the presence of a spirit; ghost stories etc. It is not intended to include experiences obtained through the agency of a medium, this wide field having been adequately dealt with elsewhere. Experiences must be first-hand, and any comment by way of alternative explanation of the occurrence would be valuable.
>
> Correspondence and contributions should be addressed to:
> Miss Mary Butts, Tebel-Vos, Sennen, Cornwall.

The response was, on the whole, disappointing: "Never," wrote Havelock Ellis. "Never," wrote E.M. Forster. The historical writer, Helen Simpson, replied: "Unfortunately, I can't in all honesty say that I have ever at any time been unable to account for incidents which impressed me, and which appeared at first sight to be out of the normal order of things." "I can't undertake what you require," declared the famous editor and teller of ghost stories, Lord Dunsany. Charles Williams, "gloomily contemplating exclusion", wrote: "I should very much have liked to have...contribute[d]...to your anthology of genuine supernatural experiences...but although I should be inclined to regard certain incidents as very nearly super-natural, I am compelled to add that all of them come under a perfectly natural heading." Ethel Colburn Mayne was sorry to say "I have to recognise that it is not given me to enter that sphere. A vague sense of dual being, which once came to me (in a bus!) and did at that moment deeply penetrate, has now become so confused a memory that I can't recapture it to any purpose." "All I've experienced," regretted Ross Williamson, "is the (I fear) too common 'anaesthetic revelation' under nitrous oxide. But the solution of the riddle of the universe in a dentist's chair (especially when one can't remember the solution afterwards—only it's something to do with splitting an apparently unsplittable interval: e.g. .999999999...and .99999999999...) wouldn't be any good for your book. To which the greatest success."[319] Naomi Royde-Smith and Jack Lindsay both promised to send accounts of their experiences.[320] Whilst amusing, the dearth of material meant that this fascinating project never saw the light, despite the wealth of Mary Butts's own supernatural data which she had described in 1930. She did have a rather strange experience in February, however, which was "*real* Dr [M.R.] James, including the usual inhibition about writing it down and I've *told* no one."[321] A fortnight later she confided to her diary "what happened, coming home that dark night":

> After dark, say 7-7.30, black as the crow's inside, so returned by the main-road, through 'the Bad Lands'. Walking briskly, without a light, and just before the top of the hill I saw, *not* visibly, but with awful distinctness across my mind's eye, a full size figure I wish I could forget. Facing me, taller than I, in black, with a white dead face, looking at me with a smiling stare of such malevolence as I would gladly forget. I had not been thinking of such things, I hurried home nearly in terror. I had, I think, been repeating a psalm, and there was a protection round me. Soon...as I felt I was out of its orbit, but sure that it belonged there, to that strip of road. What I said to myself was a hanged man who still cannot get away. If it was a man at all, and not an evil spirit who has a 'beat' along that road with the evil marshes behind and the wood.

Her vision is strangely like 'Feyther Dark' or other ghostly figures mentioned by Ruth Manning-Sanders in *The West of England*:

> Walk...in this little farthest corner of England...in the twilight of a wintry afternoon, when nothing is to be seen but the huge dim shapes of the silently withdrawing cliffs, and poised between a vagueness of sea and sky, a solitary watcher—the red, rhythmically winking eye of the Longships lighthouse. It is then that the drowned sailors can be heard 'hailing their names' above the moaning of the waters. It is then that the sense of the primordia, the strange and the savage, the

> unknown, the *very long ago*, fills the dusk with something that is akin to dread. It is then that the place becomes haunted.[322]

Mary Butts was not alone in sensing the supernatural in Sennen: Bernard Walke reported that when Walter de la Mare came to spend a weekend with him in Sennen in the 1910s: "On the way to St Hilary he told me that he thought Cornwall was a haunted land and that he would never venture to stay there again."[323]

Whilst the supernatural anthology came to nothing, it did give Charles Williams the "opportunity to write again" to Mary Butts. "Few things in life have given me more pleasure than our slightly dramatic acquaintance," he wrote of their previous year's correspondence.[324] This letter was particularly well-timed, as her newfound religious belief and fascination with Williams's work had become intertwined in her mind: "Those who believe what we believe and know what we know—with all that it implies—find our way to come out into the open. (This is clumsily put). In another way. Either spiritual value will become paramount again in England, or Brave New World is in prospect. Of the writers of our time yours is by far the best witness—to the heart of the matter. Would a critical...study of your work as a whole (*The Mercury* would take it or *Life and Letters*)...which I would submit to your approval and correction—be of any use?" To this draft of a letter to Williams, she added: "(Note—difficulty in writing this for which my heart has cried out.)"[325] Williams was "temporally gratified [by] and spiritually grateful" for her "extraordinarily moving suggestion" and sent her books, articles and poems dating back to his youth.[326] From his letters it is clear that he was a sensitive, witty and modest man with enough honesty to say: "Do believe that I am very deeply indebted to you for your suggestion and do make any use of me that you can. I will not say, like so many authors, that I don't care to talk about myself: like every other intelligent and sensitive person I like talking about myself."[327]

Along with copies of his *English Poetic Mind* (1932) and *A Myth of Shakespeare* (1928), Williams apologised for sending another "atrociously long letter" with the excuse that "other people's interest in middle age is a more thrilling thing even than their interest in youth". He added: "It may amuse you to know that Eliot has been reading the novels during the last year or so and wrote the other week after I had sent him *The Greater Trumps* to say that he did not like that as much as the others—like you, and you are both quite right—but that he simply ate them up and asked for more. I have always liked Eliot but for a moment I felt he was much more bright and good than I had supposed."[328] Such a comment could only have increased Mary Butts's belief (articulated eight years earlier) in the parallel between her and Eliot. There was, of course, a parallel in their lives also, for like Mary Butts, Eliot had become an Anglo-Catholic.

On the 24 January she noted "a hopeless letter from G;...found a magic stone on Grumbla Moor [and]...began the autobiography". There are very few comments about the actual writing of *The Crystal Cabinet*, probably because, unlike her other books, its writing was not difficult.[329] Mary Butts worked hard at it throughout 1935, mentioning in late August a sudden idea about how to give shape to her memories:

> Finally. This night. How the book is to be written. Not the development of *one* theme—...but the lot! Using the short-story technique—and fuse them *all*. I can do it, making it the living 'historiê'. Because it is one history, and my relations will be the making of what I have to say. Laus Deo. [I have an] intuition, none too pleasant per se, that...my Mother's hostility...[is] part of a pattern. Put one way, that at one time my Mother cursed me—yes, she did, raised up a hostility against her child.... Nor *can* I doubt that here I have hit—or been hit—by a statement of truth.

This added 'explanation' spurred her on with *The Crystal Cabinet* and on the 21 October she declared with joy: "The Book leaps ahead—Almost 'into the straight' now."

But this is leaping ahead. In the early months of 1935, *The Crystal Cabinet* was only one part of her busy life. The actor, Stephen Brocas, came to visit Angus Davidson in January and Mary Butts noted with glee how "in his car he flew off with me over Cornwall".[330] On the 30th she noted: "Remember—28.1.35. The Boxing at Penryn, and *all* that happened. Participation with Sennen and boxing in the bus, charging away through the night while we sang." She may well have been watching Zachy Nicholas, a Sennen man who began to box in this year and who went on to become the Western Area Heavyweight Champion.[331] Her interest extended beyond boxing; on the 8 March she attended "All-in-Wrestling...at Camborne. Beauty of the Black Panther—his animal head." Cornish wrestling is "an ancient sport," explains Ruth Manning-Sanders. "The Cornish wrestlers, with their socks, short drawers, and wide Chinese-looking canvas jackets, have a picturesque appearance. The hold is on the jacket only, and no part of the opponent's body must be grasped: 'Whosoever throweth his mate in such sort, as that either his back, or the one shoulder, and contrary heele do touch the ground, is accounted to give a *fall*. If he be indangered, and make a narrow escape...it is called a *foyle*.'"[332] Given Mary Butts's delight in discovering the customs of Cornwall, she probably learned these rules and terms.

"Angus is going to write to Gabriel—his image of The Ostrich only too true," she wrote in her diary on the 21 February. She was too busy to be disconsolate about her absent husband, however, for February brought the arrival in Sennen of her old friend, Harcourt Wesson Bull, who had come to live with Angus Davidson.

> Mary, for reasons of her own, had told Angus she wished our re-meeting to take place at the upper pub, and so, on my first evening there, we set eyes on each other once more at "The First and Last". I was surprised by her changed appearance. She was far less thin, almost stocky, and had really lost the beauty of the Villefranche days only seven years before. She wore no make-up to speak of, and the extreme paleness of eyebrow and eyelash in her somewhat freckled face gave me rather a shock. Her clothes also were decidedly countrified: beret, short, blue serge skirt and blouse, man's worn tweed jacket, "sensible" low shoes—costume that was rarely varied—and she carried a sturdy cane. She seemed nervous and keyed-up; her mind was working furiously, I suppose; she may have had qualms about my being there at all. I realized the importance of rebeginning on the right foot and took the cue to be perfectly natural. There was no doubt that we both preferred to be good friends again—and so we were.
>
> The next day Mary and I went for a walk, first to a rock where local tradition had it five kings (or was it more?) had gathered. She indicated barrows and pointed out the headland up the coast where Phoenicians and Romans had worked in tin mines—and Carn Brae, rounded hill in the distance where, she said, on a certain night all the drowned sailors crawled out of the sea to its summit. "It isn't a night to be out, Harcourt!" Her magic-making was with her still—and presently I saw the old lightness and gaiety too.[333]

The three friends spent a great deal of time together during Wesson Bull's stay in Sennen between February and July 1935. They were to be some of Mary Butts's happiest months and she called the "two tall, singularly handsome young men" the "Best Pair of Sirens". For his part Wesson Bull saw her as "Diotima (she of whom Socrates had said: 'perfectly skilled in this and many other doctrines'); Mary was pleased."[334] In recognition of their friendship, Mary Butts dedicated *The Crystal Cabinet* to Angus Davidson and offered to dedicate her next book to Wesson Bull. It was to be a historical narrative about Julian the Apostate. Stephen Brocas gave her the idea when visiting in July, and she began research for the book in September. "Julianus, a son of Julius Constantius, the brother of Constantine the Great, born at Constantinople [,]...showed his dislike for Christianity by secretly cherishing a desire to become one of the votaries of Paganism....[When he became] sole master of the Roman empire [in] A.D. 361 [,] Julian publicly disavowing the doctrines of Christianity, offered solemn sacrifices to all the gods of ancient Rome.... It has been observed of Julian, that like Caesar, he could employ at the same time his hand to write, his ear to listen, his eyes to read, and his mind to dictate."[335] While it exists in manuscript, Mary Butts would die before her completing her editing of the narrative.[336]

* * * * *

No Place

> *At No Place after tea,...here I'd made an idea flesh with a vengeance. That, in a way, it was all me. I found the house, was saved by it that night in the fog, fell in love with it; and when Angus started to come, foresaw my need, got it to fit with his need of a base, and that it should be near me. The rest did itself. Other places failed, my conviction about No Place carried weight, but somehow easily. Practical efforts and delays, but no exasperating ones—or even doubts.* —MB, diary entry, 30.3.35

IT IS CLEAR from this quotation that No Place was no ordinary dwelling, but had magical significance for Mary Butts. She helped Angus and Harcourt with all the arrangements for moving in, and described her first invitation to tea there on the 20 March as the "opening ceremony". Like Salterns before her father's death (see above, p. 18) it was, she felt, "a Perfectness. ...we had [tea] before the great stone hearth,[337] blessing Angus and Harcourt and Bolshie and I. His marvellous tea.... Then when Bolshie left, I turned on the Opus 131 quartette [by Beethoven], and we lay before the fire in blessedness while 'the sounds of beauty flowed and trembled' and I think Lytton blessed us from wherever he is." "REMEMBER ALL OF THIS," she wrote in the margin.

There were times, naturally, when she was not included in the plans of the No Place residents. Having invested the house with such sacredness, she felt the exclusion deeply, resenting what she saw as their refusal to allow what was hers by right. Her inevitable separateness was in many ways a repetition of her life amongst Cocteau and his entourage a decade earlier. At such times she sent Angus rather pathetic notes, in which she complained of loneliness and isolation. Fortunately these periods were infrequent and "the best pair of sirens" were fairly constant companions for her, as can be seen from Harcourt's account of the routine of the two households:

> When Angus and I had moved into 'No Place' to live, a wonderfully satisfying order in our days became established. We were both writing,[338] as was Mary, and spent the mornings at our desks. In the afternoons we always walked, sometimes took very long walks in that marvelous countryside, inland or along the coast, came back for tea

> and more work, with reading, writing letters, and so on, in the evening. But there was scarcely a day when we didn't see Mary: she came for lunch or tea or dinner, and we went to her together or separately. Well I recall her brief little notes brought up by Lucy, her devoted Cornish "daily", when it was my turn: "Harcourt, pink soup, wreck wine, seven o'clock!" Pink soup, wreck wine! The soup was a tomato bisque I had praised. "It's not just out of a tin," Mary said. "There's all sorts of things in it, herbs, and it takes a long time to prepare." The delicious and strong red wine came from bottles that had floated in on a certain ocean current from Portugal and been collected by fishermen, in this case Lucy's "wrecker" brothers who had a fascinating illegal cache of things from the sea.[339]

Mary Butts and Angus shared a love of gardening. They spent many hours in the gardens of No Place or Tebel Vos, sowing and tending plants, some of which were gifts from friends who owned the grand estates of Knole and Tidcombe. Harcourt mentions how the discovery of a garden slug had led him to regale Mary Butts with an anecdote about a printer's slug named after Gertrude Stein by a local newspaper in America, during one of her tours there. She was delighted by this and in her mind exchanged the printer's slug for a living version, chuckling to herself how "A new species of slug has been discovered and officially called 'The Gertrude Stein'."[340]

"Remember last night. Night of the storm," she wrote on the 18 May, adding a few days later: "My lovely garden, in its fourth year doesn't exist any more, neither flowers nor fruit nor tree." This was no ordinary storm to Mary Butts, who thought of the wind "as a curse...and kept crying over her garden" as the storm raged.[341] She described her experience of it in 'Spring Storm' for *The Manchester Guardian*: "The spring wind blew hard and long. For three days it had been blowing, veering from the pure north over Chapel Carn Brea to nor'-west over the Brisons and the full Atlantic." And then it got much worse:

> ...one saw, from under the join in the casement windows, bubbles rising, a perpetual fountain winking up; and soon the sills were running, overflowing into the rooms. Water there was no keeping back from every window that faced the storm. Trying to stem it, to soak it up with clothes, one looked out. Across the bay, now a square mile of raving water, in which could be seen neither ebb nor flow, but something like an agony of the contending strengths locked in a deadly embrace. Then suddenly there rose, spinning before one's eyes, as it might be midges dancing, a haze of little sticks, as a panel of hurdle melted into air. Small voices muttering against the glass, tapping on the panes, beneath the intolerable dialogue of wind and sea....
>
> Next morning, a wild, broken day, after a ninety-mile-an-hour gale, showed the fantastic damage, and outside this house the wheel of the iron water mill buckled and hanging sideways like a flower....

And of the garden there is nothing left of tree, or flower, or fruit
but a few sticks hung with rags, green slime, and blackening stalks.[342]

Although Harcourt Wesson Bull "could not read as much as Mary did in portent and auguries and changes, by queer coincidence we learned within a day or two that T.E. Lawrence had lost his life in a road accident, and I heard that my brother had been killed on the same day in much the same way. It was an unsettling time."[343]

By the time Wesson Bull came to Sennen in February 1935, Mary Butts no longer walked so far afield. It was in part because her knee had got worse. She habitually used a cane, but even so her "game knee... gave her trouble at stiles. She would lean on her stick and agitate her right leg in two or three little circles to fix her knee in its proper place before mounting any steps. After her first explaining that her knee could be thrown out easily, she didn't like to have it noticed or referred to."[344] As with other personal problems, Mary Butts was touchy about any comments and "didn't like to be teased", although she was quite free with her criticisms of others. Whilst her separation from Gabriel was "amicable", she claimed that one of his faults was that he "wouldn't wash his face. He said shaving cream on it in the morning was enough."[345] The increasing snobbishness she displayed (Mary Butts often liked to be "Lady Bountiful", and was paternalistic towards the villagers, especially Bolshie Burnett and his family) was in keeping with the persona she had quickly adopted after moving into Sennen. This was why she was excessively strict with Camilla when she came to stay and felt so let down by Gabriel, who would have to be brought home from his frequent drinking bouts in The First and Last and The Old Success. Once he was gone, she could become the Lady of the Manor, actively engaged with church and village matters. Except that instead of a manor, she had a "commonplace little villa."[346]

She continued to suffer a great deal from the sale of Salterns. Harcourt rightly characterised her writing of *The Crystal Cabinet* as "a way to resolve her past... When she read the description of her old home and what it had become, 'its back broken', her voice broke."[347] Her sense of loss was particularly acute at this time. In early March she learned that her mother no longer owned the 'family silver': "Do you really mean that you have [sold] it—that a large number of spoons and forks, marked with our crest are loose about the world?"[348] Her friends tried to make things easier by encouraging her as she wrote her autobiography: "She used to read chapters to Angus and me as they were completed, and very good we found them," remembered Harcourt.[349] They also gave her more material offerings, which delighted her: "Added to the house: Angus' gift, a large blue witch ball, probably new, but a good copy.[350] ...An ash-tray (Harcourt)—white porcelain with my Zodiac-sign, Sagittarius, on it in gold.... A hook-rug (Angus) black with 'stupid' yellow bird." Harcourt taught her how to hook her own rugs and she made several, including one with the Yin/Yang symbol in the centre and one depicting the Butts coat of arms. There was also a rug showing a "primitive Sennen Cove complete with boats, figures and a splendid sun".[351] She was offended when Angus refused the latter and still further when he showed a lack of enthusiasm at her offer to "work him 9,000 mortal stitches—at some expense and more time, in any pattern he wanted." She gave the rug of Sennen Cove to Bolshie Burnett. Apart from rug-making, she also continued to work at her patchwork quilt.

It is characteristic of Mary Butts, even in Sennen, that there were areas of her life which, though extremely important to her, were not shared with Wesson Bull (or Davidson). This was true of her zeal for St Hilary. Whilst Bernard Walke had become an influential figure in her life by this time, Wesson Bull mentions only vaguely how she "conversed at length with the excessively high church rector of a parish beyond Penzance. I went with her to one or two of his services and was not impressed by the general atmosphere, the silver witch balls that hung in every window."[352] Yet for Mary Butts St Hilary was a magical haven.[353] She bought Walke's autobiographical account, *Twenty Years at St Hilary,* in May and noted with disgust the "symptomatic insolence" of one review which described it as depicting "lost causes".

In early April Mary Butts's religious conviction informed her perception of everything. She recorded that a "vilely smashed knee" had brought "something like delight", when it forced her to rest. For out of that came "Lucy's kindness—everyone's. Books and work and quiet and prayer and tenderness and understanding." These periods of enforced "rest" would become more frequent and she did ever more work whilst sitting in bed, perceiving in them a "lovely necessary arrangement". Again, at the end of April she "fell ill and so helped to restore my knee, *just* as the Garden, plus Child, was fit to be left. She could water—while I meditated from bed, the E.P.M." This was Charles Williams's critical book, *The English Poetic Mind,* which Mary Butts described as "a fountain and a quarry":

> Glories of C.W. Since Coleridge what criticism have we to compare with it? The E.P.M....on Wordsworth is final. And what commentaries cd. be written on his comment (ending): 'Poetry has to do all its own work; in return it has all its own authority'.... Also—'the sweet but dangerous irony of the Muse' Blake... The 'single figure' lacking of Eliot. Then—On Solitude in the greatest of poets—Its lack in Tennyson and Browning.

She wrote to thank Williams whom she saw as "a star far-off" and both correspondents began to sign their letters "under the protection", a quotation from his *Many Dimensions*.

Just as February had brought an old friend 'back' to Mary Butts, so April brought her a new one. At Easter the writer, Edward Sackville-West, came to stay in Zennor, a village near Sennen better known for its associations with D.H. Lawrence, who stayed there during the First World War. Mary Butts spent a day of joy and magic there with Sackville-West on the 15 April and saw in him the reincarnation of the eighteenth-century writer, Horace Walpole. "Like the lovely portrait in the N P G [National Portrait Gallery]. The eyes, the voice, the extreme distinction, the way of speech, of approach. It was uncanny, for I've often played at learning the original talk—of the whole world of the XVIII C. he's embalmed for me."[354] She corresponded with Sackville-West from May onwards, partly about his novel, *Sun in Capricorn*, but principally on the subject of his religious doubts and worries over the future of Knole. This large country house in Kent is probably better known for its associations with the writer and gardener, Vita Sackville-West, who had written *Knole and the Sackvilles* in 1922. She was born in the house but on the death of her father in 1928 Knole passed to her Uncle Charlie (Edward's father), since her sex debarred her from inheriting it. Although Salterns was far less grand, there is a parallel between Mary Butts's sense of disinheritance and Vita Sackville-Wests's for whom the "loss of Knole seemed like a violation of her relationship to the feudal past that was...central to her life and work. She saw the Edwardian setting of her solitary childhood passing away...[and] the innovations at Knole were about far more than the adaptation of a living space. They meant a turning away from a way of life, from a history, and from an ideology."[355] Like Mary Butts, she reacted by writing about it in fiction and fact.

In her letters, Mary Butts advised Edward Sackville-West that "either Knowle [sic] is an idea in the mind of God 'made flesh' with you for its guardian and 'trésorier', with your body in every way, in every degree, the opposite of a museum-keeper!—or give it over to the public, in the name of Democracy, as a museum. Or, what is just as likely, let it be destroyed, by the rage to destroy. Which is a lust. A lust getting loose as the old sanctities and sanctions wane, *are over-drawn on without paying in*."[356] In trying to "save" Knole Mary Butts was living out what she had been unable to do for Salterns but had described in *Ashe of Rings*. It would have been all the more poignant since it came at the very time she was writing *The Crystal Cabinet* with the sense of loss it articulates. Unfortunately, although appreciating her concern, Edward Sackville-West did not agree:

> Though everything I love and admire is symbolised by the word Knole, yet the division in my nature—call it my intelligence, if you will—tells me that that order is irrevocably passing, *whether I like it or not*, and that it is not ultimately probable that humanity evolves in the wrong direction. I see no grounds for supposing it. Therefore, what will supersede Knole and Christianity (for they will be superseded) will ultimately prove beneficial to the mass of mankind.... A few years ago, I might have thought the Old System worth abiding by, but now it has been borne in upon me that the only way to do that is by Fascism—and a worse, a more utterly heinous machination is inconceivable. Such a witch's cauldron to revive the dead body of feudalism is essentially absurd.... Besides that body will not revive. ...and even if I could recapture my belief in Christianity as *true...*, I do not think it would justify one in adopting a cast-iron system of social beliefs—for ever and ever amen. Nothing is for ever, and one must face the fact.... The point is that the present position is hopelessly anomalous—people like my father in a certain position, yet *not* in it, expected to keep up a museum, yet deprived of the money to do so and the prestige which makes such a position valid. And what is Knole—a museum or a private house?[357]

Mary Butts visited him at Knole in June 1935 while it was still a private house. (Knole became a National Trust property shortly after the Second World War; a protracted business, in which Vita Sackville-West would be "irritated by the slowness of her Uncle Charlie and Eddy in making up their minds: 'Eddy is as floppy as an unstaked delphinium in a gale.'")[358] Edward Sackville-West concluded his letter to Mary Butts with the words "I am just about to open Cleopatra, Saluts! Eddy." *Scenes from the Life of Cleopatra* had come out on the 27 May.

CHAPTER TWENTY-SIX

The Last of the Lagidae

Age cannot wither her, nor custom stale her infinite variety.
—Shakespeare, *Antony and Cleopatra*

There was also a book on Cleopatra, whom Mary Butts saw as an intellectual, almost a bluestocking. —Sylvia Beach, *Shakespeare and Company*[359]

MARY BUTTS WAS GRATEFUL for Jack Lindsay's help as she worked on the final proofs of *Scenes from the Life of Cleopatra* at the beginning of 1935. They were sent off to the publishers on the 30 March and the book came out in its spare buff dust jacket, price 7s6d, less than two months later on the 27 May. What she described as a "preliminary puff" on the 2 May, was in fact a long article by Humbert Wolfe in *The Observer* which praised both *The Macedonian* and *Scenes from the Life of Cleopatra* in detail. She was pleased with the review, although in her appraisal of 1935 in late November, remarked sadly: "The Cleopatra book—contempt of it". Judging by the large number of reviews which, as for *The Macedonian* two years earlier, came from all over the British Isles, she was rather hard on herself. Lindsay's *Last Days With Cleopatra* had come out a few weeks earlier and several reviewers compared the two narratives, one going so far as to describe *Scenes from the Life of Cleopatra* as following "the Mitchison-Lindsay school of ancient-history-in-modern terms".[360] Lindsay himself had been unstinting in his response to the book the previous year, well aware that it was in no way derivative of his own: "I think you've done a really important bit of work in bringing out the atmosphere and meaning of Cleopatra, and I look on the book as a most vital contribution to that understanding of the graeco-roman world which is near to my heart."[361]

Scenes from the Life of Cleopatra received the same praise and criticism as *The Macedonian* had done for being difficult, high-brow and scholarly. In 'Preparing for the Autumn', Brother Savage wrote in *The Liverpool Post* that with "*Cleopatra...* Miss Mary Butts, an author,...working quietly and steadily down at her cottage in Cornwall, is surely winning the position to which a gifted application to art has given her...a just claim."[362]

For some, it was perhaps a little too "soaked with scholarship, soaked with extensive historical and mythological knowledge" for the "plain reader" wanting a "plain straightforward tale".[363] Yet Henry Baerlein writing in *Time and Tide* claimed that while "it would be absurd to call the work of Mary Butts either medium or low-brow. ...one is not without hope that a few thousand readers will, for their own sakes, appreciate this book. She is up against Plutarch and Shakespeare. Her knowledge of what we call ancient history is so profound and so imaginative that I am altogether on her side."[364] Mary Butts herself had raised the question, "How much knowledge on the part of the reader must the writers assume?", in her review of Compton Mackenzie's *Marathon and Salamis* the previous year:

> These [historical] books are fun to write and often fun to read, but it is on the reader's previous knowledge that their value almost entirely depends. If his idea of history can be compared to a vast fresco, sketched in, and his mind to that of a painter, filling in the design with perspective and chiaroscuro, then these books will be of use to him.
>
> The great question is: How much knowledge on the part of the reader must the writers assume? Now, it is particularly true of classical specialists that they are more than usually impatient with ignorance. Until lately *their* matter was the foundation of all education, its pattern and example. That to-day it is less so, ousted by vulgar or so-called "useful" studies, arouses in them grief and a very natural contempt.[365] ...Suppose [referring to Mackenzie's book] the only too common reader whose response to "Marathon" is "race", to "Salamis" a sausage?

Her answer to this dilemma is clear. There is no easy way to understand history; it takes time and effort: "to readers long spoon-fed on predigested food the result will make austere reading". Historical knowledge is worth having, but it is up to readers, whether they want to do the necessary work. As for writers of such books, they are "there—to tell the story, certainly, to be painstaking, to be accurate; also to give a carefully balanced view of historic probabilities in a story of infinite importance on some of whose vital details Time has closed his jaws."[366]

The reason that *Scenes from the Life of Cleopatra* attracted such vehement attention was because in it she was very much taking Cleopatra's "side". It was not the orthodox position:

> In this study...Miss Mary Butts has provided as lively and stimulating a work as one could wish. Down the ages so much has been written about Egypt's remarkable queen that probably the chief interest of every new book on the subject is the possibility of "new light", fresh facts and fancies, or the resurrection of hitherto un-discovered

> phases of the history of the ancient world. To use an Americanism that admirably suits the case, Miss Butts has debunked[367] all the notions, or misconceptions of Cleopatra as the most alluring "vamp" in creation. She pens a portrait that appears even more probable than any preceding it of the queen as a well-bred Greek girl, the one strong character remaining of an ancient family that was toppling to disintegration.[368]

Oswell Blakeston later commented: "Mary Butts did much to take the Queen out of her setting in a false Arabian Night, to move her into a world with a touch of Regency vitality to it; but she was herself, I think, too much of a romantic. I remember some admirers of her work exclaiming, on publication of this book, 'Oh I never realised Cleopatra was so like Mary Butts.'"[369]

Some reviewers, such as L.P. Hartley, "confess[ed] to a slight feeling of disappointment at finding Cleopatra's name cleared", but had to concede that "Miss Butts seems to have the facts on her side, and she pleads the cause of Cleopatra's virtue with an energy and an eloquence that every right-minded person must admire."[370] Ellis Roberts went much further: "Miss Mary Butts's Cleopatra is a thousand leagues nearer to what the historical Cleopatra must have been than any other interpretation of that Hellene intellect.... [Her] skill in re-creating the very sounds and colours, the magic and the faith, the policy and plotting of those ancient times is amazing. She is far better in this task, to my mind, than is Mr Graves in *Claudius*; and she has a far harder task. She can present the Romans' case against Egypt as justly as she does Egypt's case against Rome."[371]

The response of some reviewers was to present Mary Butts's account as the 'woman's angle'. *The Daily Herald* saw *Scenes from the Life of Cleopatra* first as a "serious gesture from one woman to another" and then "a serious attempt to get the truth about a remarkable human being".[372] Whilst it never seemed to occur to reviewers that men had been taking a 'man's angle' on historical figures since such books were first written, several headlines (whether teasing or serious) made explicit the coincidence that the author and subject were both women: 'The Last Pharaoh, A Modern Woman's View of Cleopatra'; 'Literary Ladies at a Tea Party'; 'Cleopatra through a Woman's Eyes'.[373] Notwithstanding such ribbing, the general reaction from critics was one of admiration; a rather hyperbolic review went so far as to maintain that "the world has waited 2,200 [sic] years for the first real effort to assess her character and life on the evidence remaining. It comes to us from the pen of a woman and a poet, Miss Mary Butts.... Miss Butts' story is an enthralling and thrilling portrait of the last of the pharaohs. It is something more than that; something more, even, than a vindication."[374]

Mary Butts provided an 'Appendix' to *Scenes from the Life of Cleopatra*, which is in fact more of an Afterword. In it she praised Arthur Weigall's recent *Life and Times of Mark Antony* and gave an account of the misconceptions about Cleopatra entertained by rather more famous predecessors, such as Chaucer (*The Legend of Good Women* (c. 1380s)), Shakespeare (*Antony and Cleopatra* (1606/7)) and, rather more recently, Shaw (*Caesar and Cleopatra* (1898)). She argued that "Mr Shaw...follows tradition, a maddening and what is worse, a vulgar version of it. It is one of his worst plays. His queen is a merry hussy, the kind of mindless, conscienceless woman he most dislikes. Ignoring history, he even has her ill-educated, a very young Aunt Sally for his crusade against sex-romance. In truth this canonical form of her legend as a strumpet rests on very little but a tragic story misunderstood and slander repeated."[375] Not surprisingly, some reviewers disagreed with Mary Butts's reading of Shaw; yet, as one remarked: "One may, or may not accept Miss Butts's Cleopatra as plausible reconstruction, but it is impossible to be insensible to its charm."[376]

Like *The Macedonian*, the form of *Scenes from the Life of Cleopatra* was difficult to characterise. In a review in *The Bystander* (which included a drawing of Mary Butts by Gabriel Aitken), the book was seen as belonging to "the form of semi-fiction, semi-history, [which] was a merry nineteenth-century sport. Flaubert was probably on the scratch mark in this event, with Bulwer Lytton getting a start of only a yard or two."[377] For J.M. Bulloch writing in *The Sunday Times*, *Scenes from the Life of Cleopatra* was "not a conventional biography, [but]...a series of crisp, cameo-like pictures".[378] The *Times Literary Supplement* saw it as "a novel, not an essay in revaluation. The ever-moving story is told subtly and well, in a series of vignettes and from a variety of angles. We start with a glimpse into the mind of Pompey before the civil war has begun, and end with a conversation between Antony and Cleopatra in the autumn of 37. It is through the eyes of his wife Cornelia that we watch Pompey being assassinated on the Egyptian shore; we learn of events in Rome while Cleopatra is there from the letters of Charmian and Iras."[379]

Inevitably, mistakes and inaccuracies occurred in the reviews. One which would probably have irked Mary Butts considerably, was the labelling of her work as "Bloomsbury".[380] This misappellation arose when discussing the style of the book and its Modernist combination of new and old. Yet notwithstanding minor reservations, the consensus was that *Scenes from the Life of Cleopatra* was "that kind of inexhaustible book that yields more, the more one brings to it, and convinces one that its apparent shortcomings are always the reader's rather than the writer's".[381] Certainly this was the view of her friends, whose praise poured in: "What a book!" declared Ellis Roberts (part of whose enthusiastic review has been quoted above).[382] "I thought it was extraordinarily good, although you had prepared me for a much less satisfactory work," commented Charles Williams.[383] Edward Sackville-West wrote from Knole: "How immensely I am enjoying Cleopatra. I am *really enthusiastic*. So beautiful and so imaginative. I love the sporadic style and the curious accuracy of the character-drawing. You seem to me to have done something really original and lovely. And what risks you ran.... Yet you have completely succeeded."[384] After her death he would go even further:

> It is for her two historical rhapsodies, *The Macedonian* and *Scenes from the Life of Cleopatra*, that Mary Butts best deserves to be remembered. I think I am not the only critic who is prepared to stake his literary judgement on the permanent value of these beautiful books. They are unique in their genre, being a remarkable blend of poetical rhapsody and exact historical information. Neither *biographies romancées* nor historical novels in the Ainsworth-Dumas sense, they are rather poetical reconstructions of character and event in which the scenes are imagined as if they had occurred yesterday, in the presence of the writer herself, and in which the dialogue—neither Wardour Street nor vulgarly "modern"—is imagined with brilliant success. There is no silliness, nothing overdone, nothing vague, no false romanticism and no striving after effect; yet everything in them is astonishingly unexpected. And they show fundamental greatness of mind.[385]

Most of Mary Butts's metropolitan friends were able to congratulate her in person, for she travelled to the capital in mid-June. As she wrote later, she "came away, heavy with treasure..., plans, memories. Life restored". Whilst in London she met Charles Williams at his O.U.P. office and visited the Ellis Roberts who were "utterly adorable".[386] She went to Windsor to visit her friend Betty Montgomery (the dedicatee of *Scenes from the Life of Cleopatra*).[387] She attended a production of *Hamlet* and a "new Irish play" in London as well as one of the first performances of T.S. Eliot's *Murder in the Cathedral* (1935) in the Canterbury Chapter House. There were also quieter, more reflective moments when she wandered around her old haunts in Bayswater: "...Through Kensington Gardens—the Palace, the kites, *the* Garden. Summer passion, and the loneliness getting worse.... O Sandy, Sandy my only love," she cried inwardly. She heard "the evening choir at the Abbey singing in descant" and attended a Russian Exhibition, whose "poignancy *sticks*. Will last all one's life. Fabergé toys and...remote splendours, and exotic variations on the 'Sergey-Boris' theme, dressed up in 18th Century clothes,...but their eyes, their eyes, giving it all away. The ikons of a Christianity we don't know... Scent of the past, and each separate object heavy with tragedy."[388] To offset the "anguish at Mother's of *our* not *my* humiliation and folly and defeat", there was the "sense of power, of work accomplished, after Heinemann, after my agents". One of her greatest pleasures was "luncheon" with Edward Sackville-West at "Knole 'which is sanctuary'. If rooms were prepared for me there, on the condition that I was never to leave them again or its precincts, I think I should say 'Yes'," she wrote ecstatically in late June.

The sense of exhilaration that summer did not end with "the last night at the Savoy" with old friends. She returned to Sennen for about two weeks during which time she received a letter from Hugh Ross Williamson: "My dear Mary, How foul to have missed you, as I found on my return to London I had done. I can't tell you how wretched I am about it." He had just finished reading *Scenes from the Life of Cleopatra* and exclaimed: "I...think it magnificent and do congratulate you so *very* much. Only, of course, it's too good: much too good. I doubt how many will really understand the history (none, of course, will see the technique—which seems to me your best.) You know all the characters so well that you can't realise that the library-public have probably never even heard of them (the real them, I mean). Anyhow, you don't write for the mob, so it doesn't matter. But the book ought to live."[389] *Scenes from the Life of Cleopatra* is in fact Mary Butts's most republished book: in 1974 the Ecco Press of New York published it with a dust jacket on which the silhouette of a woman belied the serious content. It was republished twice in 1994: by the Sun and Moon Press and earlier in the year by McPherson & Company in a volume with *The Macedonian*. Thomas McEvilley provides a fascinating preface to *The Classical Novels of Mary Butts*.

In mid-July Mary Butts went to Tidcombe in Wiltshire, at the invitation of Odo Cross and Angus Wilson. She found "a unity" in "the beech avenue, the vegetable garden, [the] bee-swarm in the little kitchen-garden and the cacti and Angus's persian irises.... The House...The arches in the panelling in the music room... The nine moons above the dome of the pavilion... The accumulating beauties." And with the place came the words: "There is what Odo said: the first night: 'I'm queer, but I so love you'. This friendship it has taken all these years to make. And his Angus when he came to see me that night: 'It's you who are the miracle'. And Odo, bless him, when I blamed him: 'this must be looked into' and that I was like a goddess with clothes on. I must remember these things. I can because I need them." Mary Butts had always been sensitive to language. It was not merely that she liked to hear herself praised, but there was almost a physical reaction. In March 1933 she had been upset at something Gabriel Aitken had said. "There is just one thing that people forget... Musical sound he can hear as I never could. Only, where words are concerned, people like me suffer just as truly.... [I am] driven to exasperation by mis-use of language. By cliché or coarseness: by vague, *slipshod* or inaccurate conveyance of meaning; or by mere infelicity of phrasing or even voyel [vowel] sounds." In *The Crystal Cabinet* she described her sensitivity and vulnerability to words from an early age:

> The musical intelligence I should have inherited from both sides of my family translated itself more and more into pleasure at verbal sound. I cannot remember a time when I was not enraptured at or tortured by words. Always there have been words which, sometimes for their sound alone, sometimes for their sound and sense, I would not use. From a loathing of their grossness or their sickliness, their weight or want of weight. Their inexactitude, their feeling of acidity or insipidity. Their action, not only on the intelligence but on the nerves, was instant: instant and constant, as my joy at other combinations, and also at what was nothing more nor less than our old friend *le mot juste*.... There were words. I could make words do things. But words could do things to me. Words would make me use them. Only of my own will I was afraid to begin, because once I had begun they would not let me stop. What was worse, I might not be able to do what they said. That would be a new pain, not being able to find what you must.[390]

Mary Butts travelled around with her hosts in a "long black and green and silver car"—a black Packard Eight—to the White Horse on White Horse Hill outside Calne and spent an evening in the village of Avebury, set in its ring of prehistoric standing stones as old as any in Cornwall. In thanks for her stay, Mary Butts wrote 'Ποτνι θηρον', a story which she dedicated to Odo Cross. It has never been published, although she sent it and others to Ellis Roberts who promised to try a find a publisher for them.

Whilst there is no mention of it in her diary she had a bad car accident on the way down to Tidcombe, just as foretold by the medium the previous year: "Car wrecked completely, (thank Heaven it was *no-one's* fault) and I'm still having rather a bad time with bruises and that slow, stupid business called 'shock'," she wrote to Ada on her return to Sennen.[391]

She returned to Tebel Vos with presents from Odo's travels abroad, including his "crystal and chain, which I hope to wear in my grave. The red and black and yellow lacquer stick from Java... The 'paru' of old batique, blue and petunia-rose." At that time her possessions from 14 Rue de Monttessuy were "restored to the House. The gold and black batique, the lacquer standish, the wood and ivory cigarette box. The leather book-box, the blue glass ink-bottle, Cedric's picture. The photographs... The books." Whether they had come by Tony's or her mother's agency, is unclear. Certainly their presence was a great consolation, since life in Sennen became much quieter when Harcourt had to return to

America in late July. "I had a last meal with Mary [of]...pink soup, wreck wine, candles on the table, an evening of easy and peaceful talk. ...little dreaming I would never see her again," he wrote of their last supper, although they corresponded up to her death.[392] Yet his departure changed things. She continued to see Angus Davidson, but it was no longer the happy daily occurrence of the previous months. "Am I to die soon?" she asked herself on the 6 August, feeling anxious the following day, that "despite a whiff this morning of what should be Sandy's blessedness,...I am becoming more and more sluggish." She expressed irritation at Camilla who was staying: "The child—disappointment there. The unconquerable egoism which—but that's a nightmare," she noted cryptically. The irritation was mutual: Camilla wrote to Ada that her mother was making her "mend her clothes and transcribe her notes; I have to do all the washing-up after supper and when we have people it sometimes takes an hour."[393] Unconcerned by her daughter's hardship, Mary Butts was preoccupied with her "great fear of Gabriel's return. My exit." She made a series of notes for Angus to include in a letter for her husband: that if he paid his way and changed his ways, she might accept him back. Despite Angus's obvious kindness, she often felt excluded from his life, although any disagreements were soon patched up. With her characteristic thoroughness, she ordered books about Scotland in order to understand his background.

As the summer passed and autumn came, she invested ever more energy in her work. In August, she wrote to Mr Beevers, the editor at *Time and Tide* who had taken over from Ellis Roberts, to ask for more reviewing and was sent several books.[394] She spent her days reading, writing *The Crystal Cabinet* and making extensive notes "for the Julian book—future reference". There were also memorable rambles, almost always with Angus: "Remember...the highly magic walk, instead of evensong... Magic because of the place.... The storm that blew up from the Scillies, our refuge between haystacks, on a barrow, at Trevescan Farm. *Then*, the whole rainbow, double and complete from horizon to horizon... Proscenium-arch of a stage that set Carn Brea and the inland moors, on grey thunder-rain driving up-country, flawless." In October there was "Angus' pic-nic on Skewjack...the woods dark with the storm and a gull floating across". And (again with Angus) her favourite trek to Penberth: "The best walk we have ever had. The colours in 'the wild glen sae green' and in the sky. The mystery in those meadows... Darkness gathering in on the way back. A great joy out of it."

Alongside these natural joys the "plain song from St Hilary rings in my ears," she wrote on the 21 October after one of her enjoyable meetings with her church friends. Yet, in spite of having almost completed her autobiography, she recorded many "sad days" and was relieved to leave Sennen in late October for a second stay at Tidcombe with her "frères, doues amys", Odo Cross and Angus Wilson.

* * * * *

Horae aureae Tidcomensis

> *All the things we have done—only here one never wants to put them down. 1st day—night rather—London. ER [Ellis Roberts]. Then 'in the Pit' (Cedric [Morris]). Next day, walk on the Downs once here. Trees on fire. Next day, walk in the rain. Sang all the way home. Visit to LS's [Lytton Strachey] house. Next day, Stonehenge and Wilton... To-day—morning down-walk. Afternoon, Church.... These are no more than the bones, an anatomy of the exquisite things that happen here.*
>
> —MB, undated diary entry, early November 1935

MARY BUTTS described her visits to Wilton and Stonehenge in great detail. She was enraptured by the proportions and interior decor of the Pembrokes' home in Wilton, although she felt there was "hardly enough time for *one* of these lovely things; or for the cedars 'who gave their shade to Sir Philip Sidney, underneath which Sidney Herbert walked before he died'." Stonehenge she found "rather overwhelming". It was not so much the stones themselves as the ravaged land around them, which in 1935 was occupied by the army:

> what wearied me...was—is—the horrors done to Salisbury Plain. The plague of blood red huts was/is bad enough, patch of blood on the green land. But the accompaniments, the slum purlieus of each camp. Hoardings and vile villas and petrol stations, and that most beastly sight, the rotting bodies of cars. As Odo said: 'they scream at you in a kind of pain.' Miles of barbed wire too over the green turf, and here and there a farm or an ancient cottage in a hollow, as if stranded, cut-off, abandoned from what had once been its own.
>
> I can give no idea of the pain it gave us—a septic wound on the earth's face and a scratch on our spirits that poisoned too. (It's not the Army so much, but the hideous accompaniments, the straggle along the ancient roads of a false civilisation.) Only, once out of it, the rest of the Plain received us and blessed us, unviolated. But from Stonehenge even, you could see the last out-post of the red huts.

The desecration of the land around Stonehenge embodied what Mary Butts spent a great deal of her writing life fighting against.[395]

She returned to Sennen in November with "two paperweights, a stone from the excavation at Stonehenge and a piece of green and turquoise glass-slag from the cactus-house at Tidcombe". Once back in Tebel Vos, she considered the following idea for a ghost story: "A room inside which you can hear a conversation. You think that there are persons inside, known or unknown, open the door, and the room is empty. Like [M.R.] James. I must find the right arrangement of this." She did not develop this idea, however, for that night she was overwhelmed by a "heart-breaking, body-destroying dream" in which she met Cecil Maitland. What gave the dream its disturbing quality was the fact that "he had not been dead, only abroad...and had thought it better for people to tell me he was dead. Lett [Haines] and Cedric [Morris], who were there, knew this. Lett enjoyed himself.... I was with them and we met, at a restaurant (London?). He [Cecil] was about to take Vita Sackville-West out to lunch.... He looked exceedingly handsome, but oddly dressed. Black Stetson hat, *dark* shirt and dark red tie. He was angry with me and brusque. I reason about it: 'How can it be true and all that happened, *after* I heard of his death, a fake, a lie?'" The dream left her "half-dead, [with] aching limbs and unspeakable *awareness* of longing for him." Whilst she had loved and lost several people during her life, she never felt their loss to the extent that she felt Cecil Maitland's. In her disturbed state, she tried to make sense of the dream. "Suppose the communicating power weak," she asked herself. "Might it not *have* to use common dream work, *change* its ordinary symbolism, and leave one to make what one can of it?" Her attempt to transform what she could of the dream conveys all the hopeless anguish of bereavement:

> There was a sensation that it *was* all symbolism, that there was something behind the dream-stuff I was meant to understand. A sort of 'this is the best we can do'.... As I lay awake, about 5.30, bleeding with sorrow, I remembered one or two things as tho' in significant relief.... There was a strength about him, power and beauty and poise; and the strange clothes I felt, in the dream, to be somehow significant. Then it was something in his eyes—his shoulders and their carriage. Longed to lay my hand across them, my arms around them. The thought of it now makes me half faint. Is it part—a continuation—of the other, sharp, profound, working, waking vision?

But she could not be sure, could only say: "Perhaps—probably—not. I must not fool myself through longing. I can only pray."

Haunted by such dreams, November in which "the Earth here is brooding herself away into Winter" was a bleak month.[396] She tried to keep busy and ordered, amongst other books, Evelyn Waugh's *Edmund Campion* (1935), Rudolph Steiner's *Fundamentals of Therapy* (1925) and Plutarch's *Opera Moralia*. She enjoyed reading Corvo's *Hubert's Arthur*, which she reviewed, and renewed her enthusiasm for Dorothy Sayers after the "catharsis" of reading her *Gaudy Night* (1935) with its claim that "if it ever occurs to people to value the honour of the mind equally with the honour of the body, we shall get a social revolution of a quite unparalleled sort—and very different from the kind that is being made at this moment."[397] In her enthusiasm for the book, she wrote about it to Angus Davidson, who was away in Brighton.[398] Both he and Harcourt were greatly missed by Mary Butts. In a bleak mood she looked back over 1935 and saw it as "The Terrible Year" in which not only had *Scenes from the Life of Cleopatra* been unsuccessful; but "I have failed in marriage because my mind was not on my job. Let it not be so in motherhood." There is no doubt, however, that as a mother she was found wanting.

Characteristically, such melancholic resolve did not last. Her interest in life was revived by reading: "30.11.35. Exquisite day—all day in this room by a fire, reading classics. Not dressed even, resting, resting, With only Tanaquil [Davidson's cat] for company. As easy a day as I've ever spent. Read *Phèdre*—as if that isn't joy enough; Pope, Lytton Strachey, and the précis of the Ruxton Case from *The News of the World*."[399] Enthusiasm made her add to her lists of books to be read: Conrad Aiken's *King Coffin* and Coventry Patmore's *Portrait of My Family*, both just published.

Her own family portrait dominated the few entries she made during December since the Holbein had finally, after six years, been sold in America. To Mary Butts, the sum of $50,000 (c. £12,000) seemed pitifully small and she wrote to Harcourt asking him to check the amount paid by the Boston Museum (only to find that the amount her mother had told her was correct). "Saddened by the bad price", she set about trying to persuade her mother to give her more than her £500 share.

> I shall of course be exceedingly glad to get your cheque. As I may have told you last Summer I was implored by Editors, publishers and people to come to London for a few months and *show* myself. Hardly anyone in the world has set eyes on me, all know *of* me, and for the last three years it's been time for me to get in touch. In fact I'm a sort of dark horse of letters, but for quite long enough. So H[einemann] begged, the Ellis Roberts, my Agent—every well-known person I met. Not for long, but properly dressed to be able to go about. Because, as they said, once in formal touch, I could get as much well-paid work as I want. Which I can't get here, in no personal contact and so far-off. ...I will of course pay A[unt] A[da]—but you know I have other debts. Nothing since my marriage, except A A, but some old ones, who all kindly said they'd wait till the picture was sold. ...for this reason...I've worked it out...[an] extra £100 would make all the difference in this coming to London on which, as anyone would tell you, my future depends. (Also, with it, I could have my knee seen to, which is giving me more and more trouble as time goes on.)[400]

The letter was a clever mixture of emotional blackmail about pressure from famous people (Heinemann, the Ellis Roberts); the certainty of future income ("once in formal touch I'd get as much well-paid work as I want") and physical disability added, as it were, as an afterthought in a quiet parenthesis. The draft of the letter formed her last entry for 1935. Yet it was unsuccessful. She did go to London, but it was only for a "dreadful little visit". On the 23 December she wrote to Ada that she had "caught a chill and had a doctor for once, who said it was *slight* congestion of the lungs. But I've been in bed ever since, really bad for once. Allowed now to sit up a little, but not to go out for Christmas—Not to Church or anything. Nor to any of our parties here.... Tell the lass—how glad she must be to have missed a wholly incapacitated mother."[401] For Camilla was not to come to Sennen for Christmas.

CHAPTER TWENTY-SEVEN

No, Not Bloomsbury

1936

Increase of irritability, not suffering fools, slight self-pity, irritated egoism, a 'fair' relief for a few seconds, taken with good humour, but degenerating into plain lies, sham scenes with myself. A danger also.

This is like my Father; also from living alone, without the discipline of another's constant company. —MB, diary entry, 29.5.36

NINETEEN THIRTY-SIX would be a grim year for Mary Butts. Troubled by periods of ill-health, publication problems over *The Crystal Cabinet* and renewed disagreements with her family over money, she would argue with the few friends she had in Sennen. On the 2 January, however, she was resolute about putting the period of ill-health at the end of 1935 behind her, noting in her diary: "an interlude for slight pneumonia, the thyroid and other gadgets found out of working order. Now to be set right and this phase of ill-health to pass DV, as we once said and had better go on saying." (Curiously, DV or God Willing, was a phrase which Mary Colville-Hyde tended to use...) She reread Arthur Symons's *The Romantic Movement in English Poetry* (1909) with much pleasure and ordered Boas's *Lytton Strachey* as well as a number of detective novels. In early January, she tried to allay her mother's fears about *The Crystal Cabinet*: "I don't quite understand why you should be worrying about a book that you don't know anything about—except what I told you—memories of my childhood, stopping short before I was twenty, seen, naturally, not through your eyes but through mine."[402] Given their difficult relationship this explanation would have done little to reassure Mary Colville-Hyde, who despite her letter of praise at the time, had been much discomforted by what she saw as thinly veiled portraits of herself and Tony in *Death of Felicity Taverner*. The following extract from a letter by Tony to his sister in late 1932 shows his complicity with Mary Colville-Hyde:

> ...there is something which I find a little confused, a little puzzling. Your characters, even when they are sometimes apparently drawn in duplicate, follow so closely in their objective attributes those of cer-

> tain of your relations, that an outsider, who did not know how you really felt about them, might scarcely help wondering how far your writing really represented your own personal attitude to these people. ...is it quite wise, from a purely worldly point of view, to present a portrait, or a series of portraits which might suggest to an outsider an interpretation of your relations with your family which is actually so false?... I only mention all this, because I can't help wondering whether you're quite wise in letting an outside world form so very false an opinion of how you feel about certain of your relatives. The only other interpretation which the world might make would be so unflattering to the intelligence that I hardly like to make it.... I really think, with all due respect, that you should be a little more careful about conveying so wrong an impression, and one which you so little intended, to the minds of the outside world.[403]

Far from evaporating, such concerns would increase during the year. Unaware of this Mary Butts noted on the 16 January that she was "feeling well again after so long" and able to go on a "hard, long walk with Angus on the moor road...Laus Deo." She spent the night of 21-22 January keeping "vigil" with him by the wireless, as King George V was dangerously ill. The next day she wrote, in a somewhat old-fashioned phrase to Harcourt that Edward VIII was proclaimed King in "every city of the kingdom". Mary Butts's views had altered dramatically since the First World War when she had shocked Stella Bowen with her anti-monarchist opinions. Indeed, her royalist sympathies were now so strong that she decided to wear a black armband as a decent mourning for George V—"let Bolshie and the MS's [Manning-Sanders] snigger. Even Angus raise his fine eyebrows." Her letter with its somewhat hyperbolic apostrophe to "my dear, loved, wise, kind, informed, informing, generous, intelligent Harcourt" also announced an improvement in her health due to the thyroid treatment she was getting. When he returned (hopefully the following winter), he would find her like a sylph, she declared, adding wryly: "Fit and gay and able to live on Rye-Vita—you know that kind of shrivelled bark—and apples and lean beef." She also wrote to say that *The Crystal Cabinet* was "almost ready" and that she was about to start on her next book, "Julian the Apostate".[404]

Mary Butts's support for the monarchy was surely prompted by her fear of Communism. She read G.K. Chesterton's *The Well and the Shadows* (1935) at this time and copied out a passage with which she was in agreement:

> The world is not going anywhere in the sense of the old optimistic progressives or even the old pessimistic reactionaries. It is not going to the 'B.N.W.' [*Brave New World*]...any more than to the 'New Utopia'. The world is what the saints and prophets saw it was, it is not getting better or getting worse; there is one thing the world does, it

> wobbles. Left to itself it does not get anywhere, tho' if helped by the right reformers of the right religion and philosophy, it may get better in many respects.... But in itself it is not a progress; it is not even a process; it is the fashion of this world that passeth away. Life...is not a ladder; it is a see-saw.
>
> ...We must not hate humanity or despise humanity, or refuse to help humanity; but we must not trust humanity; in the sense of trusting a trend in human nature... Be a Royalist...but do not trust a Monarch in the sense of expecting that a Monarch will be anything more than a man. ...but put not your trust in manhood suffrage or in any child of man. There is one little defect about Man, the Image of God...that he is not to be trusted. If you identify him with some ideal, which you choose to think in his inmost nature or his only goal, the day will come when he will suddenly seem to you a traitor.

Mary Butts wanted to use Chesterton's words as part of her argument against the rather more left-wing opinions of Bolshie Burnett, whom she was increasingly viewing as a "type" in the Jungian sense. She and Angus had provided a great deal of work for him in the previous two years and she admitted: "I like him rather well, even if in reaction against the type, which I know too well: whose opinion I once shared.... In the bad times one sees ahead—shall we ever be in *his* power, and what advantage will he take of it?" She was too astute not to see the disappearance before her eyes of her ideal of landed, benevolent patronage, which she was able to live out to a certain extent in Sennen, only because it was at "the world's End".

Isolated, as yet unable to translate critical success into financial security, alienated from her family and from Gabriel Aitken, often in poor health and spirits, Mary Butts was becoming ever more sensitive to slights, imaginary or real. Three years earlier she had written to Hugh Ross Williamson that she was "engaged in the fruitless war with the man from the Midlands who has bought up land in Sennen, and now is going to pull down the ruin of Chapel Idny [Idne],[405] where, traditionally, a Cornish saint rang a bell, with its old garden and chess board of veronica hedges; and on its site build a garage, complete with petrol pumps. I'm worrying the Cornish Archaeological Society, but I know he'll win, and my heart is sick to death."[406] Mr Barton (who had built Tebel Vos) did win, and there is now a car park on this ancient site. Mary Butts was grateful in March 1936 when the "personal public activity I asked for" materialised in the form of a controversy with Penzance over the efficiency of the Sennen Life Boat. As the year passed, she would take an increasingly active role in Sennen's fight against further development, especially by Mr Barton.

Yet this public activity did not blind her to her personal problems.

In early 1936 she began the regular practice of noting faults in her diary under the heading 'Sub Sigillo' (and later 'Confiteor') to discuss when she went to confession with Father Walke. As ever, she was accurate in recognising her weaknesses: from specific moments of bad temper with Camilla or Lucy and "inattention at prayers" to the more general "'arrangings' of truth to make things easier for me: to 'get me out' of things. Sloth. Inattention.... Self-pity.... Tendency to pretend to more knowledge than I have. Use of remote and learned sources, private information" in her work.

By March she was also aware of the hopelessness of her marriage and wrote to Tom Swan (who had been to the same school as Gabriel Aitken) for advice:

> To be brief, since Christmas, I have tried to bring him to a definite point...asking him to return for 6-8 weeks in the Spring: saying, frankly, that with so much less money coming in from reviewing, I can't say 'come back for good' because I *can't* shoulder 'in reduced circumstances', the whole burden again. Just, as I say, suggesting two months. To this, I after about 6 weeks' delay, got an answer to the effect that he couldn't manage the fare for so short a time.

Mary Butts admitted that Gabriel had been sending her £6 per month for the last "4-5-6 months", but felt his claims of poverty were unfounded, since he was working on a "ballet, dresses, decor etc. for the Dolin and Markova Season" in London. "Now, after 15 months I feel I should know how I stand. I don't want divorce, but feel the position must be defined. Do you think that a letter from you is advisable?"[407] She was finding herself in an increasingly difficult position socially. Misleading rumours abounded, even to the extent that Angus Davidson's presence was suspected for Gabriel's departure, which was particularly ironic given that Angus was a homosexual. The situation would not be resolved, however. In late September she noted that "Angus told Maynard Keynes about Gabriel. He was sorry, very sorry; and shocked. It is good to feel not quite alone." In fact, Gabriel Aitken returned to Sennen only for Mary Butts's funeral the following March.

In late February she received letters from Sackville-West and Ellis Roberts asking when *The Crystal Cabinet* was coming out. There were problems. In March, she minimised the reasons in her letter to Tom Swan, writing that *The Crystal Cabinet* had been finished "alas too late, after the touch of flu I had at Christmas, for publication till the Autumn."[408] Her description of the difficulties in a letter to Ada on the 11 April was closer to the truth: "My new book won't be out now till the early Autumn, alas. Red brackets in this present text round all the things which cannot yet be printed because of Mother."[409] A month later, she was still "working very hard on the book, its final revision, before it goes into type-proof".[410] On the question of possible offence to people still living, she had "taken the most careful opinion of two disinterested friends", Angus Davidson and Father Walke. This was not enough, however, to solve the problems.

In the meantime her attention was diverted by other bad news. As worship at St Hilary had continued to be a "sanctuary,...a blessedness" throughout these troubled months, she was distraught when Father Walke announced his imminent resignation (because of ill-health) on the 20 May. In the face of her conviction as to the danger of "our present state of disbelief", it was difficult to know who to turn to for comfort. Even her dear friend and "giver of blessings",[411] Angus Davidson, could be no help. He did not share the faith which had become so central to her life and she felt he did not appreciate the "horror" she was experiencing at Bernard Walke's departure. (She kept trying to convert Davidson; for example, urging him on the 21 May to read Christopher Dawson's *Religion and the Modern State* (1935), which she reviewed in the summer.[412] Since she had been brought back to her faith partly through reading, she hoped that he might find a similar illumination. All her attempts were unsuccessful.) "So one is driven back to one's solitude, work, books, thought," she lamented and was comforted by "John Buchan's *Witch Wood* [(1927)] found when it was a blessedness".

She sent Harcourt her version of the reasons for the coolness between Angus and herself (did he resent her? Was he jealous of her?).[413] He wrote back a reassuring, consoling and measured letter in which he judged her needs astutely. He agreed that she would feel the slight alienation more than Angus and that it came from a difference in temperament. That they were both complicated people and that she should speak to Angus about it. After all, Angus had come to Sennen "solely" because of her. Harcourt was looking forward to seeing her in the winter.[414] Such a letter did much to raise Mary Butts's spirits as she was missing Harcourt greatly. On the 29 June she sent him a short note announcing that she had done "what your letter bade me, and all is getting well."[415] She had also been cheered by letters, one from Edward Sackville-West, thanking her for her review of his book on Thomas de Quincey,[416] and one from Charles Williams, who sent her a copy of his new play for the Canterbury Cycle on Thomas Cranmer, which she would also review. And, as ever, she was consoled by gazing at the panorama of Sennen Cove: "Remember—the sea transparent and the sky transparent, and out of the salon window the top of the tree-mallow, just in flower, rising above the fence against them both."

By late June she had finished revising an essay which she had begun a month earlier. Prompted by "our present state of disbelief" (mentioned above), she had wondered about "a study, subsidiary to this, on Bloomsbury? ...*why* has it become synonymous with a sapless and slightly comic intellectualism, barrenness, the Waste Land? This with what it has done?" She offered the idea to Lord Gorell for *The Cornhill* on the 7 July. He replied two days later: "I will look at the article you mention with interest and it is quite possible that the material even will carry the length, but 10,000 words is rather long at first sight for this subject."[417] She sent him the essay, also suggesting an article on Charles Williams. However, on the 11 July she received "the worst news of all" which left her in a "fainting, paralysing surprise": "Evans [at Heinemann] has turned down *Childhood at Salterns*—with a three page schoolmaster's lecture on style, etc. With at the end, his real reason—fear of libel action. Behind this, I am nearly sure, lies some intrigue of my Mother's—through Tony... Angus is being very wise and kind." Heinemann offered to take "Julian the Apostate" instead yet she wrote of the rejection of *The Crystal Cabinet* to Ada at the end of July, blaming Tony ("I can't think of any other explanation") for "spreading unpleasant reports about the book. That it is the story of my whole life (instead of ending with my 19th year),[418] full of scandals about well-known people, my friends, etc. All of which is rubbish. I can't say for certain he did it, but these stories all originate in people in close touch with him, and whom I hardly know, or at least have not seen for years."[419] It would appear that she was wrong about Tony if the following account from Mary Colville-Hyde is true: "I am *quite certain* it was *not* Tony who wrote to your Publishers—some man did—saying, I am told, he would not 'put up with any more of your innuendoes' and should bring an action against your Publishers if they were not very careful. I do not know his name but *you* can very likely place him—it was not John Rodker."[420] Always anxious for Ada's approval, she offered to send her a copy of the manuscript to read for herself. There is no record that Ada did so.

No doubt Mary Butts was consoled by her friends in person, for she had organised a small holiday away from Sennen in mid-July. First she went to Magdalen College, Oxford, to work "with a don I know there" on "Julian the Apostate". As she admitted to her aunt: "We didn't do *much* work, but he wanted company...so gave me an *enchanting* time."[421] After Oxford there was a short visit to Badbury Rings and then on to Tidcombe, where in contrast to the sojourn of the previous year, she had "one of the most, strictly *dreadful* passages of my life. Not just sorrow, *dread*." Not clearly explained, Mary Butts's sense of dread seems to have arisen from a combination of Odo Cross's illness and Angus Wilson's worry about him and "two ghost books" she had bought in Blackwells bookshop in Oxford.[422] "Round the lawn the great tree, stirring and weeping in the rain. The hunch I had; the fulfillment of my desires, and, in sorrow over those two, almost their extinction." Thankfully, there had also been the "soulagements—and we needed them—the run round the enchanted country, Newbury to Ashmanshurst, across country to the wide green valley, and the acres of loosestrife. Where Angus Wilson stopped *the* car and picked me their mallow." Following her three days at Tidcombe there had been the "renouvellement" in London where she had visited the British Museum and met up with Charles Williams and Tom Swan. Still the feelings of some supernatural perception at Tidcombe "round the tail of my eye, yet unable to bring it out with conscious intellectual vision" haunted her after her return to Sennen on the 23 July.

In early August she was disappointed when she heard from Lord Gorell. *The Cornhill* would not accept an essay on Charles Williams because "I am afraid a writer of whom so very few have at present heard could not yet be the subject of an article."[423] This would have echoed all too closely Mary Butts's own comment in her review of Williams's *Thomas Cranmer* for *Time and Tide* which had come out the previous day: "One of the many curious things about the state of our letters today is the comparative obscurity of the fame of Charles Williams. His work with its range, its profundity, its scholarship, its unique beauties, its passion—you rarely hear it spoken of."[424]

* * * * *

Where the damp dark rot
Is never forgot
O bury 'em down
In Blooms
buree
Where the soup tastes like
Last night's gravee—

—MB, 'Bloomsbury' (1936), attributed to Ezra Pound

WITH REGARD TO Mary Butts's essay, 'Bloomsbury', Gorell wrote:

> I have read your article...with great attention and it is, as I should have expected from you, extremely well written, but, quite honestly, I cannot feel to-day that there is the amount of interest in many of the people of whom the article treats, that is suggested by the space that would be demanded.
>
> I tested out my own feeling by asking two friends of different ages, one of whom at least is very well versed in literature, their answers to the list of names, and in most cases it conveyed nothing to them.[425]

It seems hardly credible today that the names Roger Fry, Lytton Strachey, Aldous Huxley, Wyndham Lewis, Maynard Keynes, Clive Bell and T.S. Eliot should have been unfamiliar ones in 1936. A short account of this essay (to be published this year in *Modernism/Modernity*) will doubtless be of interest both because of the continuing fascination with Bloomsbury and the fresh perspective given by Mary Butts, who described herself as "some sort of an observer, some sort of witness, who [after a brief time spent in the company of Roger Fry] was never again so far as Bloomsbury *personalities* were concerned, to be wholly in or wholly out of touch." The essay provides an account of Bloomsbury's contribution to English culture and the attack on the group, made principally by Wyndham Lewis. It is not surprising, given her preoccupations in June 1936, that her discussion focuses on "what, if they had their way, would be the result, the pattern, the intelligible whole" of Bloomsbury's atheist culture. It opens with a description and the connotations in 1936 of this "group":

> 'Bloomsbury'—you hear people say today, and it is not a compliment. Applied correctly and incorrectly to a number of persons of the highest individual distinction, as a collective noun it is used to express a complicated reaction, including envy and dislike. Never wholly admiration or praise. And this essay is an examination, an explanation—or an attempt to show the justice and the injustice of this.
>
> Say 'Bloomsbury' and then, on the Freud Game, only too often a string of words will follow, varying with the player: 'The Intelligentsia in excelsis'. 'Oh, that lot', 'those barren leaves'. 'N.B.G.', 'faisandés' [high as in putrid], 'awful warnings', 'mental hermaphrodites', 'brittle intellectuals', '*that* bunch'. These applied to a group who, as individuals, are admitted to high distinction and a very real place in our national life. Yet, as a group, a picture-world follows them about, a popular film, of untidy figures in shapeless, expensive tweeds and horn-rimmed glasses, or of dark women, unfashionably bobbed. A fragment, quite worthless, except as a 'trailer' for a much more interesting picture. Or as light on the question—how a group of people, united by birth and training, who, after the War, made a startling bid—not in the arts only, but in most vital activities, to lead our culture, twenty years later, should have come to stand for something that has not succeeded; that is felt at once to be equivocal and portentous...

That this reads surprisingly easily to a late-twentieth-century eye, reveals Mary Butts's perceptive foresight with regard to Bloomsbury's lasting reputation.

Belonging to 'Old' or 'Upper' Bloomsbury were Roger Fry, Lytton Strachey, Clive Bell and Maynard Keynes. Mary Butts says very little about Virginia Woolf and nothing about Vanessa Bell, which may well have been for personal reasons.[426] She had a great deal of praise for Lytton Strachey and Roger Fry, both of whom she had known and both dead by 1936. Fry "with learning and wit, but with Quaker tenacity and conviction of aesthetic grace and sin,...[brought] over the new pictures that were being painted in France[,]...insisting that they were the only new pictures worth thinking about". As for Strachey, his *Eminent Victorians* (1918) was an "entrancing, brilliant" and seminal[427] work of art: "A piece of delicate explosive that, until quite lately, has still been going off in gay little bangs. Followed by the orgy of de-bunking which, with the tact of genius, Lytton Strachey saw how to lead off; though he little saw what it was to lead us to." She felt that his true significance had not been appreciated: "Everything of this new author's work was copied, except his learning, his intelligence, his wit, the essentials of his pure style; while his malice, his blind spots, his prejudices, his strange ignorance, his occasional sillinesses, these, to the discredit of our letters, have been put even to infamous use." Another result of his "genius, the genius of Old Bloomsbury in its highest form" was his transformation of the craft of biography, which he "smashed...to bits, and showed once and for all how to reassemble its fragments. Also, in the writing of history he illustrated the overwhelming importance of rhythm, design, a point of view, and above all, of scale."

In the early 1920s Old Bloomsbury "admitted to their numbers" T.S. Eliot ("the New Englander...the poet of Catholic Christianity") and Aldous Huxley ("of *Antic Hay*. A book that to many of us remains his best, with a tune to it and a pace, a design inherent in the action, as though there had passed into it something of the Ballet [Russe] itself").[428]

Here Mary Butts introduced herself to the English stage as one of the "other writers of England, who had survived the war, writers and artists whose names were known, or who would soon be known—what were they making of it?" Her reply was that:

> One was too young to judge, sitting in Roger's studio in Fitzroy Street, being painted by him, enjoying what one had never enjoyed before, contact with a superb and generous mind.... That was the writer's introduction to Bloomsbury, indeed the only time that one was in any deep and immediate contact with them, and then only through him. Yet, even then, even in these early years, there went with it an unequally divided judgement. Unequally but deeply divided between gratitude, affection and intellecual delight. These and the secret rapture of a country-bred child before the rich comic possibilities that seemed on one's own up-bringing inherent somehow in the whole situation.

Mary Butts writes of Wyndham Lewis's early collaboration in "that strange workshop, at once one of Bloomsbury's completest failures, yet which the world has never quite managed to forget"—Omega. And then how he left it and created his "anti-masque", the 1913 Rebel Art Centre, and wrote *The Caliph's Design* (1919) in which "loyalty apart, it was clear that a new formidable voice was speaking". Lewis was in no way a representative of "every other artist in England outside the Bloomsbury ring". His was a "lone voice speaking, a more violent gift, experimental, unfinished, 'futurist' was the current label; exceedingly male in quality, by no means free from the neuroticism of virility, and above all contemptuous of the intricacies, the private jokes...the snobberies, the pedantries of culture" which Bloomsbury embodied. Mary Butts was not a particular fan of Wyndham Lewis, for whom she had sat for her portrait, just as she had for Roger Fry. In fact she was well aware of the faults of the man ("who saw enemies everywhere (especially among his friends)"); notwithstanding these, she remained appreciative of his contribution, so different from that of Bloomsbury.

> He was crabbed, rude, unkind, ill-bred, unjust. He allowed for nothing that they could do, for Strachey's crystal style, for Roger Fry's magnanimity. He seems to have taken particular care that not more than one man in ten should understand what he has to say. He was uncharitable, bitter, unperceptive. He left most readers in a very dim state as to in what he himself put his trust.
>
> Yet, through it all from *The Caliph's Design* and *The Childermass*, from his drawings and his manifestos, he gives an overwhelming impression (much as he would blaspheme the imputation) of an intelligence at once powerful, searching, original, discontented, wounded, thwarted, maimed, unconquerable.

Already in 1936, she had to ask "What has been the succession from [Lewis's journal] *'Blast'*?"; whereas Bloomsbury could "in those first years...fairly claim that...nearly all the living art in England grew in their garden enclosed". By the mid- to late-1920s when she "was away on adventures of a very different kind, in another land, saving what could be saved of one's own youth from the war", there were the members of young Bloomsbury "and the term has widened, and the term has narrowed, and as individuals they have justified their fame".

Mary Butts gave several examples of the far-reaching contribution of Bloomsbury members which "it is impossible to under-estimate or...be ungrateful for". Yet there was the "ready, the obvious criticism" of their "private virtuosity", their tendency to intellectualism, an "ingenuous one for men and women of their intelligence", their despising "along with the Philistine (the Philistine is easy game)...the other world, the 'real' world, the larger world of men of good will". Also there was "a quality exceedingly hard to describe, that for all their learning, their science, their wit, their considerable art of living, that carried with it an all-pervading insufficiency. A kind of hole in the centre, into which the mind fell instantly, the moment the question was asked, and very soon it began to be asked 'what is the real meaning of all this?'"

The significant moment for Mary Butts was "when T.S. Eliot parted metaphysical company with" Bloomsbury, because of his faith.[429] She agreed, since: "the world, the intelligent world, whose beliefs and opinions filter down now to the mass of the people, to form the ambience of the social mind, must either abandon their scepticism or stick to it. Half beliefs, suspended beliefs, agnosticisms, modernisms, indifferences are becoming sensibly more impossible."

Bloomsbury was bound to be "liquidated" during this period when "cliché [though it is]...our civilisation is on its trial" because:

> to become what they have become they have lost—what to win again T.S. Eliot had to endure all that went to the making of *Ash Wednesday*. *Ash Wednesday* after *The Waste Land*. The thing that always gets lost when men set themselves to live as they have lived as Olympians playing, yet uncertain of the validity or the origin of their power. The quality we call among other things Simplicity of mind, by which alone values are preserved, by which alone the intelligence, out of the mixed heap of *virtu* we call the good life, knows how to pick out the stone of great price.

And, as with so much of her work, the essay ends on a warning note:

> Civilisation is their business. They have made it so. From them its Enemy, the Enemy, their's and the world's, and the Enemy of Wyndham Lewis, the old Enemy of the Intellectual Love, one of whose creatures they are, might get its *quietus*. Or it might not.
>
> One wishes to hear their answer.
>
> One wishes they knew it.

There is no doubt that Mary Butts's estimation in 1936 of the historical importance of Bloomsbury shows an extraordinary prescience.

Despite claiming in a letter to Harcourt that disappointment was bad for someone of her age, a week after Gorell's rejection of her essay Mary Butts considered writing a book containing "studies of modern tendencies". It would appear that a publisher had expressed interest in such a book as she wrote of "Methuen's suggestion of developing 'Bl[oomsbury]'—less as persons, more as cultural influences—their relations with Proust, Gide, the Ballet, etc". Another study might be "'What the Rose did to the Cypress'—ie. France to England, with the final reference to the Surréalistes and Picasso's last Period". Although she felt that writing such a book would be "fun" and completed the Rose and Cypress study, the other essays were never written.

Mary Butts was particularly lonely during August, for all that she wrote of an increased "understanding" between herself and Camilla, who was spending the summer in Sennen. Angus Davidson had let No Place and gone away until mid-September. Her reaction was to keep busy. Quite apart from her 'studies of modern tendencies', she was working hard on "Julian the Apostate": "As I had begun to despair, the éclaircissment came, the old 'r[apture] of the I[ntellect] at the approach of the fact'! I can't write steadily or decently about it. But I've got it now, the key to the Julian book. Gnosticism! Gnosticism—that was what he was after—Under the humanitarianism, the national humanism, there was Gnosis—*His* gnosis. What was his—Julian's—gnosis? That's what I have to find out—and all through—cf Us—Us—Us." In August she also had the idea "for a story. Two magic maps—Paris and London". This was to form the basis of 'Mappa Mundi', which she would complete the following January.

When not working, she reflected on her religious beliefs, noting on the 8 August: "Answer if I'm asked why I believe again—One answer: because it and it only corresponds to the deepest knowledge or intuition I've ever had—ever been given. Nothing but the Incarnation, however dimly but justly apprehended 'squares' with the other fragments of knowledge out of which everything of value in my life has been made."

On the 11 August Edward Sackville-West wrote to her: "I have read your memoirs [*The Crystal Cabinet*] with real pleasure. I do not like them as much as your purely imaginative work, but that is almost of course: you were not free. But I do think the book most remarkable and worthwhile and not to be lost. Omitting perhaps the passages in red brackets, I cannot see what there is to offend anyone. So do try and find another publisher."[430] This was the advice also given by Ellis Roberts who suggested "Gollanz, perhaps, or, at the other pole, Macmillan". Pleased about Methuen's interest in her "studies of modern tendencies", he reminded her that he also wanted her to "get to work on the volume of the series *In Defence of the Supernatural*. You remember that you are doing a volume covered by the words 'And was Crucified'; and you may write what you please. The books are to be 40,000, 45,000 or even 50,000 words: an advance of £50 and a decent royalty. The publishers—I once thought it an advantage," he inserted in deference to her problems with them, "are Heinemann—and if you let me know you are ready I'll have an agreement sent to you."[431] She did not reply, noting instead: "These last days, a dryness and a dullness and sloth and self-indulgence, making me ashamed and deficient." This may well have been an oblique reference to the large quantity of home-made opium which she was smoking at this time. Perhaps already "she had made [her alcoholic] discovery in Penzance. A new kick, very cheap, very efficacious. It was to be found in a herbalist's shop." In early 1937 Frank Baker went to the shop to try it for himself and found:

> On the counter in a large glass jar was a pale yellow liquid; a card propped up against it announced its inflated name. 'Champagne Wine Nerve Tonic'. The gaslight gave it a lambent glow, and on this cold evening it seemed to writhe and coil. Was this the ichor she had found?... The brew was sold, I think, for ninepence a medicine glass; and it soon became apparent that it had a potency one could not have expected in a place so woebegone. I cannot remember the taste. I only remember that at some period in the evening I was swinging from the gas bracket like a chimpanzee and then soaring over to the Cornish Arms to follow up this galvanizing chaser with as many pints of bitter as I could put down. Mary had been right about 'Champagne Wine N. T.'.
>
> But not for her at ninepence a glass. It was said that she had taken a whole jar of the stuff back to Tebel Vos.[432]

Whatever the reason, Mary Butts was not well in late August. She was also miserable after a visit from Apurva Kuma Chanda, an old friend from the 1910s: "Chanda 'du temps perdu'. The thing about his return that delighted and that hurt, the 'ambience' he brought with him of a lost world. A dearer, finer, more in the excellent sense—romantic world. Not only of youth, but of the world the War had not yet had time to kill." To meet him again after eighteen years brought "loveliness and sadness together".

September brought little to alleviate the sadness and she could only write: "How I need, as FB [Frank Baker] said, a living church close at hand." This did come, but not before November, by which time several friendships had foundered. The first was her precious relationship with Odo Cross and Angus Wilson. In mid-September she and Camilla went with them on a brief holiday to Dartmouth, where Cross and Wilson had rented a house overlooking the bay. Although there were some enjoyable moments, it seems to have been an unhappy visit, partly because Mary Butts had become "unstuck" with her bad knee, but mainly because her friends had refused to lend her money. The degree to which this refusal upset her is reflected in her heading the draft of her letter to them: "F.H.... now alas". They had joined her family, Gabriel Aitken and earlier Virgil Thomson in becoming the 'Family Horror'. She tried one last time to plead her need for the loan:

> God knows I would not be so importunate if I did not know that, in ways too long to explain and which I realise more day after day, my whole life—and C's [Camilla's] did not depend on this chance of getting to London and doing what I can for myself as a writer now. I've left it already almost too long. I'm absolutely alone in the world—

> My youth is going fast—that pull which a woman has up to a certain moment and then loses.[433]

The letter did no good. After Dartmouth, Mary Butts and Camilla were supposed to spend a few days with Father Cleribut (Walke's successor) in Bliesland on the Bodmin Moor, but it had to be cancelled because he had flu. On the 18th Camilla returned to school, leaving her mother alone in Sennen.

When Angus Davidson returned, he found her embroiled in yet another battle, this time with Marjorie Bagot, to which she had given the rather witty title 'Lizzie in Action'. It concerned her story 'The Warning' (published over eighteen months earlier), which had been inspired by a disagreement between Marjorie Bagot and Christine Ashcroft. Yet the former must only just have seen it since there was a stormy argument, threats of libel suits and the end of their friendship. Whilst Mary Butts felt that she was "in the wrong", it probably did not help when she could hardly remember the story. As to the "matter" of losing Marjorie Bagot's friendship, she did not "greatly regret [it]. You get no further with M[arjorie] and she's exhausting." Yet whatever her reaction, the disagreement did not do her reputation in Sennen any good. It was, therefore, a great relief to have Angus back, for whilst in her anger she felt that "at the moment I'd prefer to sock her one. That will pass.... [Angus said] that M[arjorie] had an I.C. [inferiority complex] (an old friend) about me. Also that I'd often shewed I'd no time—for women in general or half-baked minds. Also, that she certainly knew about the story long ago, liked it, liked herself in it; only said I'd been hard on C.A. [Christine Ashcroft]."

Now that Angus had returned, she took up some of her old routines. She worked hard at "Julian the Apostate", which she was writing in scenes, very much like *The Macedonian* and *Scenes From the Life of Cleopatra*. She took the occasional tea with Ruth Manning-Sanders, spent time with Frank Baker and his friend John Raynor at their mine-house in the nearby valley of Halamanning and resumed her habit of going for walks with Angus. Thus on the 1 October there was:

> a strange, 'charged' walk. First the valley's loveliness, the golds; then the garden where there were fifty or more butterflies. Red admirals, fritillaries and one small silver and mauve rarity, and bees. All on the superb clumps of Michaelmas daisies, the dahlias. We stood and adored and praised and swallowed it.
>
> Then that farm, up its lonely lane, a dingy, neglected, inside starveling place. Very silent, musty with vulgar little ornaments. Old... It was odd, I couldn't endure it, felt I was 'being poisoned'... Or should start 'seeing things'.
>
> Fall on my way back...the broken malachite [cigarette-case].

This sense of dread continued throughout October as her antagonism towards her mother came to another climax. It was partly due to the controversy over *The Crystal Cabinet* and partly to the Holbein settlement Mary Colville-Hyde had drawn up in May. On her death the money would go first to Tony and his children (if he had any) and only then to her daughter: "But, Mother, dear, it is most unlikely that I shall outlive Tony," reasoned Mary Butts.[434] Although the painting had belonged to Mary Colville-Hyde personally and not to the Butts Estate,[435] Mary Butts saw the whole matter as a rerun of the loss of Salterns, and she tried to get her mother to change the terms. "Throughout this business of the Settlement of the Holbein money and my own virtual dis-inheritance, Angus has been of the utmost help to me, both wise, just *and* understanding," she noted on the 31 October. She was "weak and desolate", therefore, when, on reading a letter from Mary Colville-Hyde which refused "to effect any change to my advantage...he seemed suddenly to become as it were Counsel for her defence." Since by this time she had come to see Mary Colville-Hyde as a "witch" and the last hope of her being able to go to London now gone, such a fair-minded approach was intolerable. The whole incident put her "in a strange state. Even to a shot of the usual unintelligible automatic writing!" They managed to resolve this further disagreement, however, for it was after "leaving No Place at dusk" a week later that she was struck by the violence of the waterscape as she walked home:

> The storm was still blowing strong, the third day's furious end. *Remember*—what frightened me, looking down as I hurried into the bay, was the dreadful whiteness of the surf. Surf on the reef, surf round the coast or lifting itself up behind the Brisons. Worst of all, the acres of seethed water in the curve of the bay, on the gently-descending sands. Broken over acres in arcs and fragments of arcs, torn and ravelled, and of that dreadful whiteness. White against ink-purple and ink-indigo and ink-slate. A Dreadfulness.... The whiteness in *Moby Dick*.

On the 17 November she wrote to Harcourt that her Introduction to "Julian the Apostate" was almost ready and would follow "by the next boat". In the quieter, calmer mood which accompanied the writing of this letter she was able to understand how "justifiably" irritating she was to Angus and confessed: "How vain we are! We don't mind being considered a great enemy, a curse, a danger, half so much as being an irritation or a bore." This letter also shows her sense of humour. After accidentally dropping the sagittarius ashtray which he had given her the previous year, "I had to pick up its twenty fragments and throw them down the hill-side for the benefit of future archeologists. 'The Sennen Saucer' B.M. A.D. 3,000".[436]

* * * * *

Our Curse—people trying to solve 4 dimensional problems in terms of 3; or 3 in terms of 2. —MB, diary entry, 15.12.36

After attending a mass given by Father Cleribut in late August, in which he had announced that he could no longer celebrate benediction, Mary Butts commented on "the end of St Hilary... And the beginning of the ugly little triumph" of the campaigners against high church services. On that particular Sunday she and Frank Baker stood in the churchyard, sorrowful and bewildered by the change. She later noted that Baker "helped" her to be strong, when he talked of the "weakness of his own soul and its needs". To his surprise Baker realised then that "without seeming to try to, Bernard had completely broken down my resistance to religion."[437] He decided to stay on as organist for a while. In late October he had what he thought was a vision in which he was commanded to "go on with what I had set myself to at St Hilary. Not to complain, not to lose faith, not to turn back."[438] When he asked Mary Butts for advice about the validity of his vision:

> I now began to discover her strength and her certainty. She accepted my story with neither surprise nor any hint of scepticism. She only urged me with all the force of her heart not to leave St Hilary until the right man—if ever there could be a right man to succeed Bernard—had been installed. 'We know, my dear, that there never can be another Bernard Walke. *Father* Bernard, yes? But that is not the point; and we know it. You—your work will wait. It will be the richer for this. You have had your instructions. You saw Him. He spoke to you. His eyes looked at you. You must act under command, however dreary, however unutterably boring it all might seem. Do you need me to tell you that? Very well, you do, and I do. There are these patches—these long, long arid patches...the *desert*. There is no possible way of putting the desert behind you except by going straight through it. You are the Captain. All who love St Hilary for what it *is*, not just for the sake of Father Bernard, will help you. You have to command us. Me. I will come to any meetings—do anything you think I should do. This thing—the *electoral* roll—it is necessary that I should be on it, yes? How do I do that?'[439]

Mary Butts continued to attend St Hilary for the rest of 1936, whenever she could afford to pay Mr Hills (the Sennen postmaster) the 14s 6d necessary for the fare. As Baker saw it: "There was a divine double-play in Mary. She liked the fun, very much. But she made me see that this tussle was much more than a parochial squabble in a remote Cornish parish. These divisions had racked the country at the time of the Reformation;

there was an historical significance to what was happening at St Hilary. So one had to believe; so she helped me to believe."[440] Baker organised meetings for all the parishioners who believed in the kind of service which Father Walke had conducted. He described one of them in late 1936:

> Mary's entrance...that winter night, watched by the curious eyes of these people, most of them having not the slightest idea who she was or where she came from, was one of her grandest, and had a dignity that hushed even the Protestant supporters of Miss King, the leader of those few in the parish who, even if they admired Bernard Walke as a man, saw in his 'Popery' the work of the Devil. Rightly she wore her most splendid clothes for the occasion, knowing that the Cornish love a bit of finery.[441] She must have been one of the very few there who did not live in the parish, yet could exercise a vote on the election of old Captain Hopes—a staunch friend of Bernard's—as People's Warden, on the grounds that she was a regular communicant member of the congregation. And he was elected; and the Church Council that was finally formed had a Catholic majority that was able to make its wishes known to the Patrons. It was a trivial little triumph, but we felt that the cause had been advanced.[442]

Alongside practical exertions to save the faith as preached by Father Walke, were her efforts in writing. She wanted to find a formula for the "whole of truth: not intellectual truth only, but a statement which takes his ['man's'] whole nature into account". In 'Bloomsbury' she had attempted to show the limitations of a purely intellectual formulation of existence, which she felt was based on a "false assumption". "We take man's 'infra-rational nature', emotional, imaginative and mystical, derive it, by assumption, from nothing but animal instinct—*Applying an intellectual process, and only an intellectual process*, to forces which the intellect cannot grasp at all. *Hence* our insistence that man's 'higher' or extra or infra-rational being is a development of his animal instinct *in order that* we may be able—or think we are able—to handle it that way." In September she had been engaged (for "Julian the Apostate") in understanding "what the world must have been like with paganism found wanting and the Christian synthesis not yet fully under way. In Julian's time." In November she realised that to do this she had to get the "'feel' of a world into which Christianity had not yet entered; culture without Christian Culture. Atmosphere. *That* is the hard thing to get, in a world saturated with both culture and religion. To-day not much help. For now...we are all inheritors of 19 centuries of Christian assumptions."

In order to find the right words, she read books dealing with the non-materialist aspects of existence, both Christian and occult. In addition to William du Bose's *The Gospel in the Gospels* (1906), she studied a variety of works published in 1936, including Hugh Ross Williamson's play, *The Seven Deadly Virtues, What is the Faith?* by Micklem, Philip Sergeant's *Witches and Warlocks*, Arthur Machen's *The Children of the Pool and other Stories* and Lord Halifax's *Ghost Stories*. She also praised Eunapius's *Vitae Sophistae* for "what one didn't expect! A late, second-rate classical author scattering wonder and interest and delight! Imagine—little cameos on the lives and adventures of men, once so important, now forgotten—Tales, if not always true, then 'like' truth." In this way she tried to free herself from the human desire, as she saw it, to intellectualise existence, to "try and reduce all things to order". She remarked on "how angry it made Blake" and agreed that "we cannot benefit. If only we could realise, under a formal definition, its limitations." Like Van Gogh, whose letters she had been reading that autumn, she was trying "to separate things in the dizzy whirl and chaos one can see in each little corner of Nature".[443]

She continued to be saddened by her inability to persuade Angus of the "tragedy" caused by the division between mind and spirit. Happily, however, they could still agree on the power of literature, and she noted in late November: "Angus impressed with *Burn, Witch, Burn!* [(1934), a novel by Abraham Merritt]. A curious parallel almost filled me with delicious fear that night." Such moments were all the more precious as she was increasingly afflicted by physical discomforts. During the last week in November she made "these dreary notes for the doctor, next time":

> Ill... Began Thursday, dim aches; knew I was in for it. Worse Friday, Sat., better Sunday but lay up. The only day I did. Just able to read and note things; no more. *Extra* symptoms, wind and *more* discomfort in bowels; less, on the whole, sickness. Slight pains between shoulder blades.... Did myself more good than at any other time with Epsom salts. 3 doses. Seemed to wash the dim sore feeling below the belt away.

Yet it did not really pass, for on the 9 December she wrote about her "health again: this time—pains in back, between shoulder blades etc. No wind. Aches in limbs, acute and spasmodic. Dislike of tobacco. *Much* less severe, no sickness, but great depression. Monday and Tuesday only *really* noticeable. Work of a sort possible. Slight griping pains in night especially." When she wrote to her mother on the 15 December to thank her for her Christmas gifts which included tulips, she remarked jokingly about an article of dress: "I am writing to Tony also—it is kind of him; only I am not *quite* as large as that! if I ever was, and I have lost a good stone lately." In fact she was very seriously ill, although no one realised then that she had less than three months to live.

When she could, she worked at "Julian the Apostate" and on the 16

December considered another idea: "FOR A BOOK: God, as we know Him as the ancient gods. Their verity—taken away for a time so that man should not only seek himself in Τα Θηιων.... Not only the Olympians, and not all for good." She was extremely demoralised by the abdication of Edward VIII on the 10 December: "One will not easily forget last night. As if a physical shadow is lying over the land, a natural and a supernatural sorrow and dread. You can feel the nation's pulse aching—as though a sword has gone through its side." The abdication led to yet another argument between herself and Angus, this time on the value of Kingship:

> He said that the only excuse today for the Throne was in its championing of the common man. This I hold superficial. Actually, a heresy. For there is more than that in kingship, and such an argument, like heresy, is a short cut. No more than a 'handling of the situation' for the moment. But great ideas, embodied in institutions, should not be so considered. With all allowance—for stresses at a particular time, judgement on them must be taken into consideration, their whole meaning and nature.

Perhaps because he was further away, Harcourt was better able to understand the painfulness of the abdication for Mary Butts and wrote her a long and sympathising letter.[444]

Another horror closer to home was the latest debacle concerning George Barton's development of Sennen. On the 14 December he called at Tebel Vos to accuse her of removing a fence he had put up. The allegation was unfounded, but she took the opportunity to write him a three-page letter in which she pleaded the case for the preservation of rural England:[445]

> ...like most persons whose life has been spent in or near towns, the country appears to you as a kind of raw material to which you can do what you like.... To me, as to others,...it is a matter of the deepest concern and distress, that, with your wealth and ability, you should elect to destroy Sennen rather than to preserve it. (Nor need I remind you that a national outcry is arising everywhere in England over the destruction of our natural beauties by reckless building for private gain.)
>
> You, as a landowner here, have had a great opportunity, yet it is a matter of general belief that you have not so regarded it, but have used your powers without thought for the ignorant and in most ways helpless people who do not want their ancient home destroyed, their ancient rights taken away.... (If I am right in believing, as I have heard, that once Sennen restored to you your health, it seems a poor return to make.)...[446]

Thus George Barton was carrying out in Sennen the very horrors Mary Butts had described and yet averted in *Death of Felicity Taverner* five years earlier. From our perspective sixty years on, her warnings have turned out to be all too dismally correct.

On the 18 December she made a series of notes about forebodings and clairvoyance which she had been experiencing in the preceding days: "Not because I believe now there is a word of truth in it, but to show me some of the ways, in imaginative persons, that delusions form; the snares into which the looking for (not always) or rather the observing of Signatures may lead one." Yet she did not completely discount the possibility that she was some kind of "receiver—an *exceedingly* imperfect receiver of what I can only describe as a real knowledge of what was going on." She saw the Manning-Sanders[447] and Angus only occasionally now and spent more and more time alone, until Camilla arrived for the holidays. Together they attended St Hilary on Christmas day and Frank Baker watched her walk in with her "magnificent wide black hat, her dark stick, her large intaglio ring, her cloak, her limping yet determined walk".[448] It was one of her last visits to the church. A letter from Ellis Roberts on the 23 December expressed concern "at [her] long silence" and especially the fact that she had not replied to his offer of a book for his *Defence of the Supernatural* series.

As for Mary Butts's diary, it is silent about what she was thinking and feeling during the last days of 1936.

CHAPTER TWENTY-EIGHT

Brightness Falls from the Air
1937

1937 is almost upon us. What will it bring?
—Harcourt Wesson Bull letter to MB, 26.12.36

HARCOURT ADDED AN ASTERISK to his 1936 letter: "It brought Mary's death."[449] But not immediately.

Camilla went back to school in early January and on the 9th Mary Butts pondered what title to give her now completed story about the "disappearance of an American in Paris", told in a "conversation in the first person in a café.... The title, I want, in Latin, 'magic maps'," she decided. "Now 'mappa' in medieval Latin, I can't find the correct word." She thought of "chartae" which meant "records or writing paper [and] 'magicus' meant magical", but this was not quite satisfactory. She did not give the precise date when she hit on the story's final title of 'Mappa Mundi'.

She considered several other ideas for stories during January, including "Barton and his Fence", "The Vampire Whose Corpse Disappeared With It" and "Maternal Mania". Whilst probably reflecting her state of mind at this time, they "remain unwritten". She did complete and sell one article, however, on T.S. Eliot and Aldous Huxley, which was published in *The Spectator*. Yet this provided only a small revenue and *The Sunday Times* had rather abruptly stopped sending her books to review so that she was desperate for new sources of income. Charles Williams wrote on the 15 January, offering sympathy and suggesting she try *The Criterion*. This may have been why she sent 'Mappa Mundi' to its editor, T.S. Eliot, shortly afterwards.

In the first few weeks of January she was still fairly sociable. She enjoyed a party at the Manning-Sanders' on the 5th and made several trips to Mousehole to see Oswell Blakeston and his friends. Lucy still came to Tebel Vos and Mary Butts made a note both of her kindness and the presents she had given in a list which has a strangely legalistic tone:

13.1.37. Gifts made to me during the past two years by my dear maid, Lucy Ellis of Van-an-Dreath.

1 antique white china dog, one of the best I have ever seen. Two bowls of flowered china, very old; one of lustre to hold pot-pourri.

A model of a full-rigged ship, about 12 in to 8 in high, perfect to the last detail, made for me by her brother, John Ellis of Val-an-Dreath.[450]

2 fire-proof glass dishes, for jam etc. 1 flower-vase of plain, blue-violet glazed Earthenware.

One antique glazed dish, green and orange leaves in high relief. Six or more glass floats off torpedo nets.

Angus Davidson appears to have been absent from Sennen for at least a month by the 19 January, and Frank Baker notes in his memoir that he rarely saw Mary Butts, who had "withdr[awn] from life and ceased to come to St Hilary".[451] He did try to see her one afternoon in February: "I stood by the gate looking down to the back windows of the bungalow. There was no sign of life. But she would be writing, I told myself; it was impossible to think of disturbing her. I had suffered invasions myself from friends, who had shattered a whole day's work without meaning to. So I called on George Manning-Sanders... No, he said; he had not seen her for some time either. Only in the garden, her head bent low over some poppy heads."[452] Although she did not mention it in her diary, Mary Butts was not just smoking opium; she was also drinking large amounts of Champagne Wine Nerve Tonic. In the absence of regular company, there was no one to impose any kind of check on her consumption.

On the 22 January she made one last bid to get to London, writing to her mother that with a loan of £300 (which she would repay with interest), she would be able to stay in the capital for two to three months and promote her work as well as introduce Camilla to some of her "older distinguished friends who are more than ready to do all they can, for us both."[453] This was quite true and might have saved her life, but she had asked once too often and Mary Colville-Hyde refused. Although Gabriel Aitken had now been gone for over two years, his wife still kept up the pretence to her mother that this was a temporary arrangement. In fact, by the time she wrote to Mary Colville-Hyde, Mary Butts had already heard from Tom Swan that her marital rights made her eligible to a third of her husband's income despite living apart. Whatever she said in public, privately she had few illusions, after Gabriel wrote her a letter in February to which she replied: "Thinking it over, I shouldn't wonder if your letter isn't meant to imply that you want a divorce."[454] Faced with his inability to make any definite decisions, she tried to find out from his Aunt Anne "what plans (if any) he proposes for the future... It is simply a matter of common fairness to let me know [where] I and my daughter stand."[455] This letter was a rather pathetic replay of June 1930, except that she was now six years older and more vulnerable. She received no reply and vainly wrote again three weeks later.

On the 27 January she drew up her will and sent it to Tom Swan. It is unclear exactly why she made final arrangements for her papers at this time. There are several references to ill-health, but no suggestion that she was aware of being terminally ill. On the 19 February she noted: "This past week's small miseries of illness, compulsory retirement to this chair, hot bottles, rugs, lazy,...weak, no energy for work and little for thought and less for contemplation and less for prayer." She tried to follow the advice she had given others and not "always practised. Always at these times read a classic, so it be the right one." The "right one" in February 1937 was James Boswell's diary. During these weeks she returned to the literature of the eighteenth-century, one of her favourite periods, also reading works by Samuel Johnson. Contemporary literature no longer satisfied her and on the 30 January she quoted in her diary from Micklem's *What is the Faith?*: "It is not surprising that modernism has been defined as 'the abandonment of the Christian faith coupled with the unwillingness to take the consequences'."

When she was well enough, she "made a practice of walking directly after lunch from the house to the 'Viking's Grave'". This "tumulus and a grave" situated "at the base of the next headland to Ped-men-dhu, on the left of the Irish Lady" became her favourite haunt, because from this promontory "you can see all that there is to be seen, from Cape Cornwall to the Longships." When she ventured there on the 3 February she felt that she had "tapped something. Something *sui generis* or unique, wholly external, strange, wholly *delightful*, strong." This effect was caused by:

> The silver bars and flashes out to sea; vast dead white waters hurling themselves on the Longships tower. The lighthouse,...black and menacing through foam and mist. On my right, on the look out, the black storm-cone swinging, menacing, sinister. The running water that had run with me, all down the turf path from the top of the moor to the barrow, crystal with small light plants under it. A clot of foam blown in on the grass at my feet; the empty grave, a wave breaking on the shore behind the Irish Lady, the strong hurrying air, violent to danger on the cliff-edge.
>
> All these and others which I have forgotten, each in their order fusing, poured into me—but rather like one drop distilled, filling my veins—with something entirely new.
>
> So that I can still say—'it is well with me'.

Yet, on the whole, all was not well with her. In Paris in the late 1920s she had noted an increase in perception due to lack of food. Once again, in February 1937, she remarked on "the clarity produced by a long fast". This 'vision' at Viking's Grave was not her only supernatural experience. The previous week at 10 o'clock in the evening she had walked down from Tebel Vos to the Cove:

> Then down onto the shore, against which and at the foot of the path, on the sands usually above high watermark several thousand tons of new rock have been thrown up.
>
> ...I walked across that space under the moon to the water's edge, the wave-wall high as a man; from where Cowloe Reef stands up like a small black deadly hill.
>
> I do not know what to say about it. One was on the edge of leaving the body and altogether in a different world. The break came at the sea's edge and with each sea. I never knew moonlight was blue before, but then it was all blue. And unspeakably blue—here where we see all the blues, and there is a daylight blue that is kin to it, when we think of the 'pearl-world'.
>
> The earth was blue, the light was blue—or rather the atmosphere through which the light passed. The cliffs were in black sapphire—the orange lights of the very few windows still lit, very agreeable to see.
>
> Of the rest, the less said the better, in these notes. Another move in perception? I think so, and oh but it was sweet.
>
> Returning I met a stone, a rock, about 3 feet high, round, standing on end. The shape and the marks on the face of a little old goddess, an idol, a Notre Dame de Sous Mer.... Perched on her haunches, not unfriendly, but strongly charged. Not so long ago we would have brought her up from the beaches, wreathed her in weed and shells and been very very careful in our tendance. As it was I saluted her with some reverence.

Such experiences gave Mary Butts temporary energy and inspiration. She no longer worked at "Julian the Apostate", considering instead: "2 NEW COLLECTIONS: I. Historic Mysteries" to include an article on "Dr Johnson's life, compare[d] with Buchan's" and "II. Heresies", to include the *Spectator* article on Aldous Huxley. She wanted to write one about "how right Kipling was...the intellectuals' contempt and his revenge." Unfortunately this idea was never fully sketched out.

On the 23 February T.S. Eliot wrote, rejecting 'Mappa Mundi' for *The Criterion*, but expressing interest in a book of short stories for Faber. Eliot claimed that this idea had first been mooted some time earlier in a discussion with her agent, Leonard Moore, but that nothing had come of it. Was she interested? It is unclear from the correspondence which followed whether or not Moore could have secured a contract for Mary Butts much earlier. He had sent three of her stories to Eliot in July 1934, which had been rejected. Whatever the truth of the matter, she replied immediately, offering to send a selection. In this letter she also wrote: "We are all very excited about Djuna Barnes' book. I have just heard from her. She was an old friend of mine in Paris."[456] She had ordered Djuna Barnes's novel, *Nightwood*,[457] when it had come out in 1936 and written to her expressing praise for it. Djuna Barnes had replied stating that an American edition was due out shortly with a preface by Eliot "which should make me happy for the rest of my life!"[458] In spite of the lightness of her reference to it in the letter to Eliot, this fact would no doubt have grieved Mary Butts, given his refusal to write an introduction to *Ashe of Rings* in 1932 on the grounds that, whilst liking the novel:

> I must be quite consistent with the principles I have adopted, and decline, except for very special reasons—as when I wrote an introduction to a selection of Ezra Pound's poems—ever to introduce in this way a living author.... I think myself that the value of prefatory commendations is over-rated. But the real point is, that if I did agree, as I should like to do, I should find it exceedingly difficult ever to refuse less welcome tasks of the same sort, particularly from people whose claim upon me would be rather personal than due to my admiration for their work.[459]

While she waited for Eliot's response, she wrote to Gabriel Aitken: "I would have tried to answer you before only for the last three weeks I have been really ill.... (Never mind about believing it—it just is so). You see, my dear, about the letter when you said: 'I'm a most unhappy man'. All this time I wouldn't have worried one tenth as much if you'd ever held out any hopes—of your affection, our reunion, or (and) that if ever you were in a position to make things easier, you would do so. Never a word for over two years to suggest either.... I won't write like this again. Try to put it down to sickness and most faint and dim sort of recovery."[460] A few days later she wrote to her mother expressing her regret at the failure of the couturier business which Tony had set up in London. "What a world! When talent like his can't unite itself, somehow, some way, with ability to market it.... Is he selling off stock? Perhaps he'd let me know and I'd try to afford something. If I ever wear anything again—which I don't feel I ever shall." As she remarked in her letter, Sennen "is not a good place to be really ill in".[461]

Perhaps Mary Butts had 'cried wolf' once too often. What is certain is that no one realised how ill she was until:

> One morning, March the 5th, the Feast of St Piran my telephone at Perran Downs rang. It was Angus Davidson, Mary's near neighbour and good friend, who was always close at hand should she have need of him.
>
> 'Frank, I have dreadful news. Our Mary is dead.'[462]

Mary Butts died at the West Cornwall Hospital in Penzance, where she was taken after Lucy found her collapsed in Tebel Vos. Tony wrote to John Rodker that she had died after "an operation for gastric ulcer—which should—one imagines have been diagnosed long before—but which was not."[463] Her death, which was registered in Penzance by Gabriel Aitken on the 8 March, gives as 'Cause of Death': "I.a. General Peritonitis. b. Perforated Duodenal ulcer. II. Diabetes Melitus." Her husband (like most of her friends) must have been unaware of her true age since he registered it as forty-four. It was actually forty-six.

EPILOGUE

The Legend of Mary Butts

1937/1997

A brief note in the Cornishman *had quoted from an obituary in* John O'London's Weekly, *which spoke of the 'noted novelist and classical scholar'; and the* Cornishman *had helpfully added in brackets, 'Mrs Atkinson'. Atkinson, Aitken, Atkins? What did it matter? She was already a legend.*

FRANK BAKER, *I Follow But Myself*

CHAPTER TWENTY-NINE

After the Funeral

1937-1938

We waited in the ice-dark, star-pierced church, under the sea of dead incense and winter-chilled stone. Under the sea of our sorrow and our memories. More memories than sorrow? More sorrow than memories? ...I must shape my memories of her. Hold on hard to something that would focus feeling; drill the memory-swarm.

—MB, 'After the Funeral' (1932)[1]

ANGUS DAVIDSON ASKED Frank Baker to play the organ at Mary Butts's funeral, which took place, not at St Hilary,[2] where she had been so happy, but at Sennen Church. Frank Baker played the twelfth-century canon, *Sumer is icumin in,* as her coffin was being brought into the church, because he felt she would have approved of the tune. Only a few people were in attendance, including Mary Colville-Hyde, Tony, Angus Davidson, Gabriel Aitken, George Manning-Sanders and Oswell Blakeston. It was felt that Camilla (who had exams coming up) should not interrupt her schoolwork to come to the funeral.

> Up the church came the box with Mary in it. I glanced at the mourners: the usual group of sad people who at any funeral become mysteriously more significant yet at the same time completely anonymous. The paradox of all funeral ceremonies was with us: that the only person who mattered was the one who was not here. I thought of Marcus, and the walk back from Sennen in the wild March wind, and the way we had laughed about the ridiculous woman we had met. I remembered her look when I had told her of his death. I saw her again, tilting up her head under her large hat and asking me if her make-up was all right, on a day when I called for her at Tebel Vos to take her to lunch in Penzance; recollected how I had hesitated for only two seconds, noticing a misplaced dab of lipstick and how she had quickly said thank you and gone up to her bedroom to put it right. Then the droning voice of the clergyman suddenly stopped and there was movement from the bearers. Something seemed to be needed to fill this shambling silence, and suddenly I realized I had almost missed my cue. I began Handel's March.[3]

After the service Mary Butts's body was interred in Sennen churchyard where she is to this day. Mary Colville-Hyde did not agree with Angus Davidson and Harcourt Wesson Bull's choice of epitaph from 'Pythian Ode'—"Truth is the heart's desire;... Be comforted"—because she felt it did not correspond with her view of her daughter. For their part, Davidson and Wesson Bull did not like Mary Colville-Hyde's choice of "some words from a poem on a child of wild fancies... So in the end the design went to the stonecutter provided with nothing but Mary's name and dates."[4] The dates were accurate but there was no mention of her being a writer; only that she was the "wife of Gabriel Aitken". Three decades later, Camilla generously added to the tombstone: "Mary Butts, Writer and Poet" and a line from Blake's poem, 'The Crystal Cabinet': "I strove to seize the inmost form."

On the 11 March Tony wrote to John Rodker to tell him of Mary Butts's death: "Dear Jimmy, We did not know how to get in touch with you... We have just returned from the funeral in Sennen. It was all over in about 18 hours."[5] Mary Butts was dead and buried.

But not yet forgotten

Everything that I want known about my life issues or my friends is in my diaries, a series extending over many years. These on my death become the property of my literary executor, Angus Davidson, to deal with as he thinks fit; and he is one of the most discreet of men.

—MB, draft of letter to Mary Colville-Hyde, 26.7.36

To some extent...I think I shall be remembered as an English writer.

—MB, draft of letter to Tom Swan, 21.1.37

THERE WERE ONLY A few notices following Mary Butts's death. *The Times*'s obituary continued the mistake that she had died at 44 rather than 46, and described her as "a writer who was especially interested in classical civilisation, the history of religions and mysticism." As mentioned earlier, mysticism was central to her beliefs. The notice went on to quote Charles Williams who said that her books "supplied the reader with provocation hidden in quietness. She concealed power in peace and made herself a style that was like burning glass."[6] In one of those horrible ironic twists, Williams had sent her a letter the day after her death which opened: "I had meant to write to you yesterday and the day before but many things intervened. It was extremely kind and lovely of you to write to me about what I suppose I must not call your most appalling morning. For the moment as I read it I thought you were going to say that the ceiling fell down and killed you and that you were writing from some more advanced state of being."[7]

In an open letter to *Time and Tide* on the 20 March, Naomi Royde-Smith spoke for several of her friends when she wrote of experiencing not only loss but:

> that unbearable sense of frustration usually associated with the death of younger writers of less mature performance than hers. Mary Butts had achieved so much; her work was so solid in foundation, so delicate in its mastery, that it seems ungracious to maintain that, coming from her, this was not enough. But the circumstances of her private life were such that she was often forced to lay aside plans which needed silence and concentration for their performance, before she could imprison the tremendous forces at her command in the network of words and phrases she never found it easy to handle. It had been our hope that, one day, the whole of her strength and generosity might have been at her own disposal and that then the full force of her genius might have been liberated in words of which the books we now possess give a foretaste of peculiar quality.

Naomi Royde-Smith also commented on the fact that Mary Butts's "imagination occupied itself with the subtleties of form, and, like her character, had heroic proportions proper to the work of a sculptor."[8] Charles Williams agreed with her: "It was very much to be hoped that style, mature with distance, and still developing its control of distance as of closeness, would have achieved a new intensity that would have brought it among the more remarkable of our time.... [Mary Butts] had considered a...novel on Julian who yet wants in English some nobility of the kind. There was every indication that her rich imagination would have surpassed itself in another 'turn of the event', of which she had already recorded two [*The Macedonian* and *Scenes from the Life of Cleopatra*]." Bryher, by contrast, did not agree and added, perhaps by way of consoling herself: "Nor do I think that [Mary Butts] had much more to do. Her last work already repeated itself."[9] Bryher is wrong here; to read Mary Butts's later works is to be made aware of the continuing development of her style. It is part of the tragedy that Mary Butts should die when she was at the height of her career and still had so much to contribute to the literature of this century.

Two other tributes were published shortly after her death. Both were inspired by her love of Shelley, as she had explained it in *The Crystal Cabinet*: "'Love and man's unconquerable mind.' Youth that so longs for one short passionate key to everything and still the years seem blessed when I was sure that in those five words I had found it.... There was simply everything Shelley had written to read. There, to obtain justice, one learned what happens to Fire-Bearers in this wicked world, and what they must expect and what they must endure."[10]

The first tribute was a poem by Frank Baker's friend, John Raynor, who had known Mary Butts in the mid-1930s. 'In Memoriam: Mary Butts' ends:

> There is a secret chamber set apart;
> The unlit lamp is held there, till a gleam
> Of sleeping fire lights upon the wick,
> Wakens to eager flame; and so at last
> The soul burns brightly, the dead heart is quick,
> He carries fire, the unlit days are past.
> In the hour when wavers the clear flame
> Bending towards his funeral pyre,
> He will remember whence the gift came
> And who, loving him, passed on the fire.[11]

The second was by David Hope (about whom nothing is known except that he was clearly a friend of hers in Sennen), who in June 1937 published *Mary Butts, Fire-Bearer*. In this five-page pamphlet Hope declared: "There is an old saying that every man is immortal till his work is finished, and if that be true then it is certain that sooner or later the value of Mary Butts's finished work will be realised, for her pen was certainly the instrument of a message which, though ended, is not yet fully known."[12]

On the 16 March Gabriel Aitken wrote to Ada Briggs (whom he had never met): "The whole thing seemed to come with tragic suddeness [sic] that I still feel rather stunned. I was in bed with the universal influenza at the time, and was forbidden to emerge. But I managed to escape: though I am afraid I was more dead than alive at the funeral. ... It was a terrible shock about poor Mary. I feel as if the roof had come off life: especially since there seemed every prospect of things improving financially, and our joint efforts proving a success."[13] Gabriel Aitken died on the 8 May (just over two months after Mary Butts) and a few days later Angus Davidson wrote to Ada Briggs:

> It was a shock to me...but not altogether a surprise. When he was down here for Mary's funeral it somehow seemed to me that he would not live long: he was like a person that had lost his hold on life, and he had gone so completely to pieces that one felt he had no resistance or vitality left. I think Mary's death really was a great shock to him: it seems strange that it should have been so after he had left her for over two years; perhaps regret had something to do with it. I cannot help feeling—much as I liked Gabriel in some ways—that his life had ceased to be of much use either to himself or to anyone else.[14]

* * * * *

ANGUS DAVIDSON and Tom Swan were named as joint-trustees of Mary Butts's estate and Angus Davidson as her literary executor. In late January 1937, she had sent Swan her will along with details of her wishes with regard to her literary papers. Given the present interest in such papers, her account was extraordinarily prescient:

> The actual MSS, if the interest in my work should continue, will have a value of their own. I think it would be best left to his [Angus Davidson's] judgement—he can get the best advice—whether to sell them for immediate profit (if there is any profit to be made) or to hand them over to Camilla, advising her to keep them in storage. It all depends on my future reputation. If it goes on as it is going now, they might be really valuable say fifty or more years from now. In that case we must arrange for their safe-keeping after Mr. Davidson's death.
>
> My letters to go to him also; those from well-known persons he had better put with the MSS, with, if suitable, a view for future sale. The family ones to hand over to Camilla when she is twenty-five, and presumably of an age to know what to destroy or what she had better keep.
>
> Then there are the volumes of my diary, kept on and off over the last ten years. Rather an explosive document in parts, especially as the persons sometimes mentioned in it get better known. I mean that an attempt was made once, quite unnecessarily, to steal part of it. Again, it all depends as to how far I am remembered—as to some extent I think I shall be remembered as an English writer. Also, apart from these, it has interesting pictures in it of the post-War world, in London and in Paris, and its actors. At all events, it must be kept. It has possible value (I) as (in part) as MS, i.e., original work in itself. (II) As a source for my own life. (III) As containing facts about our life and times. Mr. Davidson had better hold on to it carefully in the Child's interest.[15]

Mary Butts had no sooner died, than Angus Davidson had to act on her behalf, since, ignorant of her death, Eliot had written to her on the 9 March. Possibly fearful of a replay of the 1931 loss of Gabriel Aitken's drawings for *The Macedonian*, Eliot wrote to say that the short stories which he had requested to see for Faber had still not arrived. Was she or her agent sending them? Davidson wrote back promptly the next day, informing Eliot of her death and concluding: "I should like very much in the circumstances, that a volume of this kind should be published if possible."[16] Eliot was "very shocked and extremely sorry" to hear of Mary Butts's death, adding (like Naomi Royde-Smith) that he felt her best work was yet to come: "It is a good many years since I last saw her, but I felt that if she had lived she might have made some remarkable contributions to literature."[17] Eliot continued to wait for the stories to arrive. On the 22nd Davidson sent all the complete stories he could find amongst Mary Butts's papers to Leonard Moore to be forwarded to Faber. He sent a list of these thirteen stories to Eliot direct, announcing that the stories would follow shortly. The final letter from Eliot to Angus Davidson, dated the 24 March, acknowledged receipt of the latter's letter. No record seems to exist either of the stories arriving at Faber's (it is unlikely that they were not sent), or of Eliot's rejection (which also is improbable, since he suggested their publication originally). Had Faber published a volume of Mary Butts's stories, there is no doubt that her reputation, albeit posthumously, would have been secured.

* * * * *

The Crystal Cabinet

> *The secret places were better filled.... Yet still on the whole an empty cabinet, a crystal box like the one Blake wanted to live inside and outside of at once. Perhaps that was what learning to live meant; really learning. Anyone can live outside it, and a very few, like the duller saints, altogether inside. But to do what Blake said—and be inside and outside the cabinet at once? Wasn't that what someone called the "something and simultaneous possession of eternal life?" Wasn't that what Delphi had tried to show to the ancient world?* —MB, *The Crystal Cabinet*[18]

> *This fragment of autobiography must be the least self-centred work of its kind ever written: for Mary Butts was concerned not with herself as a child but with life as it revealed itself to a child.*
>
> —Naomi Royde-Smith, review of *The Crystal Cabinet*[19]

METHUEN PUBLISHED *The Crystal Cabinet* (10s 6d) in June 1937. Ironically, now that Mary Butts was no longer alive to enjoy the praise, it was her most popular book. Several of the reviewers used this occasion to pay tribute to her achievements as a writer.

"It is difficult to sum up such a book as this one," declared Naomi Royde-Smith in a long review in *Time and Tide*. Difficult because it was so many things at once, its very form defying an easy categorisation. Certainly for J.M. Hone, *The Crystal Cabinet* was "neither a collection of reminiscences nor a formal autobiography. The chapters are in chronological order, but within them we are brought back and forward in time, and everywhere early incidents and impressions become the occasion of hints and intimations bearing upon the mature life and mind of the narrator, her religion and her watching eye for the flag which blows between here and there. Her pages, as she put it, wrote themselves, 'winding in and out, like the streams of Poole Harbour, scouring their passages through mud to the mid-channel, and with the tide to the sea'—back to Salterns and to the hands time laid upon it."[20] Frank Baker described it in a more Blakean manner: "*The Crystal Cabinet* is the world of Innocence growing into the world of experience."[21] If it was not quite as formally 'finished' as the relationship played out between the fictional older and younger Pip in Charles Dickens's *Great Expectations*, this was because of Mary Butts's sudden death. "That she had planned a further statement of the meaning she had traced in life is as certain as it is lamentable that she had not lived to accomplish her purpose," declared Naomi Royde-Smith. It was nonetheless an "abiding joy" that Mary Butts "was able to close the doors on the crystal cabinet in which the treasure of her youth is set".[22]

There is no doubt that *The Crystal Cabinet* is a treasure trove, in which each reviewer found a different gem. Of the content of the book Edward Sackville-West wrote:

> Here she tells the story of her childhood in one of the loveliest parts of England—the country round Poole Harbour. It is a quiet story; but a sense of humour, a passionate love of landscape, and a wonderful eye for character, keep up the interest. Chiefly remarkable is the love of objects of virtu which informs the entire book. The Butts family had always been collectors of beautiful things (their collection of Blakes, now in the Tate Gallery, was made by one man), and Salterns—the house to which this book is a monument—contained a miscellany of works of art, each one of which seems to have had an all but human appeal for the child who grew up among them. More interesting to some will be the author's very amusing description of her stepfather and his family, the Hydes: this is a late-Victorian Conversation Piece of great brilliance. And the early chapters have all the vividness we are used to associate with earliest memories, heightened by the writer's poetical sense of significant detail.

Despite this glowing tribute Edward Sackville-West disliked the fragmentary form of her autobiography and was (perhaps inevitably) "disappointed", since he much preferred her historical books on whose enduring value he categorically staked his critical reputation. Even so, he praised "the essential quality of her vision" which he felt was "both true and worthy of record".[23]

There may or may not have been factual inaccuracies in the book, such as Mary Butts's claim that Salterns had since become a boarding-house,[24] and an occasion when Mary Colville-Hyde was supposed to have burnt some books belonging to the Captain, because she had considered them too suggestive. Tony was so upset by this account that he sent a letter to *The Spectator*: "My sister's memory seems to have failed her a little in her description of the burning of some of my father's books. Her reactions as a witness of this scene cannot be quite what she has described, since she did not participate in it, being in France at the time it took place. In point of fact these books were burned by my mother and myself alone.... My sister's book contains innumerable distortions or blunt misstatements of fact, which it would be out of place to single out here. Relations are everybody's literary capital, but it has hitherto been considered an act of grace and delicacy not to make the contents of one's passbook too undisguisedly public, more especially when the entries are so inaccurate."[25] One reviewer felt that *The Crystal Cabinet* "raises the question as to how far it may be seemly to make undisguisedly public what should perhaps remain private",[26] a question we are continually having to face to this day. Yet without the inside knowledge available to relatives and close friends, reviewers saw the disputed conflagration not as an opportunity taken by Mary Butts to attack her mother; rather as an example of social history: "The cult of feminine innocence and ignorance was represented for [Mary Butts] by the bonfire which her mother made from motives of prudery of all her father's finely illustrated books."[27] J.M. Hone went further: "In this book, so full of imaginative understanding, [Mary Butts] has shown no touch of rancour towards those who might be accounted responsible for her maladjusted upbringing. Indeed, all the people she writes about are lifted into an air of poetry and truth."[28]

This detached relationship to her experiences was attempted by Mary Butts throughout *The Crystal Cabinet*. There were of course "actors in her drama: the old scholarly father; her mother, the lovely and elegant young woman who was his second wife; the beloved ghost of his first wife's son—'all about the house the dead boy had left delicate signatures ... fishing-tackle; paint boxes; his violin...the garden, too, was full of him'; Nurse, no easy task hers tending the red-haired turbulent little girl; the graceful, inconsequent aristocrat who became her step-father; the brother, ten years younger than herself." Yet for Naomi Royde-Smith, the "great figures of the tale are the giants and immortals: William Blake ...; Athos, d'Artagnan...who stepped alive for her from the pages of Dumas; Shelley who became her god; Kipling, Macauley; George Macdonald from whom she learnt rhythm and her first reassurance about Natural Magic; the Heroes of Asgard, and behind and above and around them all 'a tall daimon standing beside a tree: his name I did not know: his address was the place called the Dark Tower: and he was the opposite of those who carry the Sanc-Grail.'"[29]

According to the reviewer in *The Listener*, it was neither the people nor the artists and writers who were the primary focus of *The Crystal Cabinet*: "It is for the sensuous perceptions of the landscape and the indoor as well as outdoor atmosphere of Salterns that the book is chiefly remarkable."[30] Equally, for Hone, "the principal characters of the story are the house at Poole and its treasures (there are many lovely things besides the Blakes) and its setting."[31] The reviewer in *The Times* went one step further: Mary Butts's "concern is less to describe her surroundings (though she does so with a poet's eye) than to trace their influence upon the growth of her imagination."[32] Ellis Roberts agreed, describing Mary Butts as "a rare genius" who "in this book...gives us the story of a girl for whom the invisible world existed, and the visible as the mirror or the form of that invisible."[33] This description brings us back to Naomi Royde-Smith's comment quoted in the epigraph above.

Edward Sackville-West and Hugh Ross Williamson reviewed *The Crystal Cabinet* as part of an overview of Mary Butts's life and work. For Edward Sackville-West, her death was "unnecessary and even appalling". His account highlights the disparity between the writer and the person:

> Intensely self-conscious, equally intensely conscious of the spiritual quality of those with whom she came in contact, she profited (as the autobiography shows) by a brave refusal of safety. She courted danger and unhappiness in personal relationships, not from a "ninetyish" desire for sensation, but because of her lively interest in the human soul. Yet few writers can ever have been more different from her books than she. In life she was diffuse, uneasy, awkward in friendship, impulsive in all the wrong as well as all the right ways, hopelessly generous. Clever discrimination, balanced judgement, sufficient scholarship, were not qualities which one associated with her living presence. Yet these were the very qualities which, together with a real and original poetical talent, combined to make her so remarkable a writer.[34]

Hugh Ross Williamson concentrated on Mary Butts, the writer, claiming that to say her death was "a calamity to literature" (as one of her publishers had done) was not

> interested overstatement...rather the simple truth. There are certain books, such as her projected work on the Holy Grail, which she and she alone of her generation could have written, and which will now be for ever lacking. And what she did achieve is sufficient to place her with D.H. Lawrence and T.S. Eliot.
>
> I choose these two names advisedly. Both are indisputably great writers; both are leaders of their time; both were sufficiently original to be "difficult" and consequently at first disproportionately neglected; and each is antithetical to the other.
>
> To say that Mary Butts was as "difficult", as original, as individual an artist, and that her work might be termed a mediation between their extremes, is perhaps the best way to introduce her writing to

> those ignorant of it. Her books combine Eliot's intellectual classicism with Lawrence's emotional romanticism; and it is that combination which makes them unique. For her fastidiousness, her scholarship, her aristocratic (in the best sense of the term) outlook saved her from the emotional vulgarity which infects so much of Lawrence's work, while her rich enjoyment of life, her frank acceptance of cosmopolitan experience made equally impossible the cloistered aridity which tinges much of Eliot.[35]

* * * * *

If they will remember this, take her as a historian of twenty years and poet of them, from 1910 to 1930.

—Bryher, 'Recognition not Farewell'[36]

IT WAS FRUSTRATION which drove Bryher to publish a long article on Mary Butts and her work in the autumn of 1937: "I do not know if we can speak, with poets, of tragedy or doom? They have their own reward. Yet when the notices of her death refer to a distinguished young writer, is silence possible? Mary was of the few who matter, a builder of English, and I have never doubted since I read her first short story that she belonged to the Immortals." Bryher wanted to redress the misrepresentation of Mary Butts's achievements: "Who has noticed that there is a spoken as well as a visual, quality in Mary's work? We call them stories because of the way they are printed, actually they are poems. ... If people are as blind to the quality of her mind as most of the reviewers have appeared to be, what else could she have done to make her readers believe in her?" And there was the unjust neglect: "Here was someone who so loved England that her chance words could push away one of the world's most famous landscapes [around Florence], yet nobody has commented on this quality, she is not recommended in the list of English authors distributed to foreign universities, she is unheard of in any school (for immortality this is just as well), and one reviewer even found her Dorset dull."

Bryher's account provides a commentary on Mary Butts's "relationship to her time":

> We can summarise her work: a happy childhood, this was the background for it all, then loss, loneliness and shock, a brief moment of uneventful development, war, and again upheaval. She clutched at Dorset and at the brother as a last barricade, attempted readjustment abroad, then found a home in the county nearest in spirit to her own and what was not surprising, in view of her experiences, renewed her early interest in religion. For her there was always the magic land,

> the visible one that was sometimes an echo of it, the fairy tale people, evil and good, hating and loving, that threatened and protected it.

It was a life, inevitably, with its own strengths and imperfections: "She forgave (that was like her) when she should not have forgiven.... It is true she was not 'left', not in any political sense, yet her life was communal enough; in spite of her own poverty she was always looking after people.... Her glorious sense of humour was too seldom in her stories..." Like Ross Williamson it was primarily her work which Bryher wanted to recognise in her tribute. A difficult writer ("her mixture of clarity and metaphysics, of charity and intolerance, made easy fame impossible"), Mary Butts's strength lay in her "pity and understanding and a new to literature sense of the psychological nuance of the emotions created by the [Great] war." According to Bryher, Mary Butts was "exploring the new type of emotion for which we have not yet words", and to this extent she was "a historian of twenty years and poet of them, from 1910 to 1930.... She was too close to the truth of art that is at once Gorgon's head and Perseus, not to come at last to her rightful place." Bryher concluded 'Recognition Not Farewell' with the regret that they had not met more in Mary Butts's last years. Had Mary Butts been alive when *The Crystal Cabinet* was published, Bryher would have "written to her"; instead "I can only prophesy, wonder what we could give her for memorial."[37]

In fact, Bryher gave Mary Butts the most apposite memorial for a writer. As well as *Life and Letters To-day* Bryher owned the Brendin Publishing Company which in 1936 had published Marianne Moore's *The Pangolin and Other Verse* and H.D.'s *The Hedgehog, a Tale*. In 1938 the Brendin Publishing Company published Mary Butts's *Last Stories*.

Last Stories

> *This book is one of the most interesting collections of stories published for ten years: it is interesting for its writing and its experiments, its faithful adherence to its writer's vision, its artistic integrity.*
>
> — Rhys Davies, review of *Last Stories*[38]

THE THIRTEEN STORIES contained in this volume (published in September 1938) with its striking green dust jacket were the same as those Angus Davidson had collected for Faber. They were Mary Butts's last in terms of being published, but not the last to be written; spanning, rather, the whole of her writing life. The collection did not include 'Magic' and 'Change' and a number of still unpublished stories. As the publisher's note announced, "none has previously appeared in book form", but a number had already been printed in small magazines, in the following chronological order: 'Lettres Imaginaires' (1919), 'After the Funeral' (1932), 'A Lover', 'The Warning', 'The Guest' (all 1934), 'A Roman Speaks' (1935).[39] Five were published posthumously in 1938 in *Life and Letters To-day*: 'In the House', 'Mappa Mundi', 'Honey Get your Gun', 'Look Homeward Angel', 'The House'.[40] The two remaining stories—'From Altar to Chimney-Piece' and 'With and Without Buttons'—never appeared in a magazine (although strangely, they have been the title stories in the two volumes of her stories published in the 1990s).

The collection was not reviewed widely, but the attention it did attract contained more praise than criticism. The reviewer for the *Times Literary Supplement* found in *Last Stories* "the wide range of subject and the intellectual distinction that marked everything she wrote". Quite apart from the strengths of specific stories, "the natural background of the sky, sea, earth, the seasons of the year, colour and sound and smell, is called up with something like genius."[41] Kate O'Brien in *The Spectator* found the stories "sentimental evocations without bones...'escapist' literature" even.[42] Margery Allingham, by contrast, considered them to be "delightful studies, most delicately penetrating... These stories express small truths so perfectly that no shade or contour is lost." She agreed with the publisher's notice that *Last Stories* was "a memorial to a fine writer",[43] stating that her favourite stories were 'The Warning' and 'A Lover'.[44] The latter was highly praised by Thomas Moult in the *Manchester Guardian*: "In the twenty-four pages covered by the story, Miss Butts's many admirable qualities are revealed, including an incisive portrayal of character, a cold-steely turn of phrase, and an all-round economy that enables her to convey an emotional crisis in a single sentence." Moult concluded by placing her writing at the forefront of her time: "Miss Butts carried on the psychological method in the short story that Henry James and Marcel Proust exploited in brief and long works alike, and she carried it on brilliantly."[45] For Rhys Davies, the best story in the collection was "'Mappa Mundi'...which is suffused with a mysterious poetry." Davies felt that Mary Butts had the "vision of the seer" who wrote difficult, allusive prose which was "almost menacing in its demands on the reader's intelligence". Yet if her "stories do not sink under this load of culture[,] this is because she was a poet".[46]

CHAPTER THIRTY

Remembering Mary Butts

There seems no need why literature, having lost the writer, should also lose the writings. — Hugh Ross Williamson, 'A Writer's Childhood', 1937[47]

> How could I be so foolish as not to believe
> that my great orange cat Boris (*Armed with Madness*)
> Butts loves me...
>
> —Frank O'Hara, 'Cantata'[48]

MARY BUTTS HAD BEEN INCLUDED in *The Author's and Writer's Who's Who 1934*, a sign that her work was beginning to be recognised while she was alive. Her death led to the start of the astonishing neglect. Edwin Muir did mention her in his 1939 *The Present Age from 1914*, but only to say that "her stories show a concern with 'mystical' evil which often declines into melodrama."[49] When W.J. Entwhistle and E. Gillett came to edit *The Literature of England AD 500-1942* only four years later, she was curtly dismissed "among other women writers who have written workmanlike and, at times, satisfying fiction".[50] As the decades passed, so Mary Butts's presence faded. David Daiches included her in *The Present Age: after 1920* (1958),[51] but when he edited *The Penguin Companion to Literature I: Britain and the Commonwealth* in 1971 she was left out. An incomplete list of her work was included in the *New Cambridge Bibliography of English Literature* the following year whilst there is no mention of her in the now-classic study by Malcolm Bradbury and James McFarlane, *Modernism 1890-1930* (1976) or in Bradbury's more recent study of *The Modern British Novel* (1993). As one critic of the Lost Generation put it: "The little magazines were a feature of the 20s... The same names—Joyce, Pound, Stein, William Carlos Williams—appeared from one issue to the next, crossed over from one magazine to another. They were names that survived the decade, others—Harold Loeb...Mina Loy ...Mary Butts—were to drift out of sight."[52]

One of the few literary historians of the interwar period to mention her work is Samuel Hynes. In *A War Imagined: The First World War and English Culture* (1990) he makes the following comment on women in England in the inter-war years:

> The lives of these young women offer a puzzling paradox: why are they at once so liberated and so unhappy? At a time when women were claiming freedom in their public and private lives, asserting their equality with men, and taking control of their own existences, one might expect to find a buoyant, affirmative literature of women. But one doesn't: the Modern women we meet in the Twenties Fiction are not free and not self-affirming, but bitter, sad cynical, wistful, lost. Look at some of the decade's most vivid and characteristic women characters: Iris Storm in *The Green Hat*...Lady Brett Ashley in *The Sun Also Rises*...the women in *The Waste Land*... And one could add many others that are similar, if less well known:...Helen Zenna Smith's *Not So Quiet*..., most of the women in Mary Butts's *Speed the Plough*.[53]

Notwithstanding the oversimplification of this statement, Hynes does at least pay Mary Butts the compliment of saying that her women characters are as shell-shocked as the male survivors of the First World War. As Claire Tylee points out: "people's lives are conditioned not merely by the objective, quantifiable facts of their existence, by their economic or political power. Their lives are conditioned also by how they understand themselves and their own position in society."[54] Despite her greater sensitivity to the complex and contradictory situations women found themselves in during and after the First World War, Tylee does not mention Mary Butts at all in *The Great War and Women's Consciousness* (1990), an otherwise in-depth study on "how British women imagined the Great War and their relation to it" in writings by women from 1914 to 1964.[55] This omission of Mary Butts is a measure of the difficulties involved when redressing inaccurate yet established literary genealogies.

If her work has not been given its proper place in Modernist histories and anthologies, it has never been entirely forgotten either. Until the late 1980s, articles, memoirs and the occasional republication of poems, stories and even books have led to scattered critical attention, ripples of recognition, usually introduced by the question 'Who was Mary Butts?'. On the whole it has been writers who have acknowledged their debt. As early as 1938, Virginia Woolf quoted from *The Crystal Cabinet* in *Three Guineas*, and when she saw Angus Davidson in September 1937 she "longed to ask [him] about Mary Butts, but had just not enough wine in my head for the purpose".[56]

From the 1940s onwards the American poet, Robert Duncan, was one of her greatest admirers: "Mary Butts was in 1941, when I was 22, an essential part of an initiation."[57] The term 'initiation' is not used lightly; in 1947 Duncan "collected signs and rumours" with his friends because "Mary Butts's *Armed with Madness* incited us to traffic in myths and to derive a 'scent' by charging every possibility with overtones and undertones, to make thunderheads, storm weather—but to hold it unreleased—

for the power's sake, living in actual life as if it were a dream."[58] A fellow poet, Robin Blaser, described the enormous influence her work had on their circle:

> Mary Butts was one of the many introductions Duncan prepared for us in those young days... Brilliant Jack Spicer gave his first lecture on *Armed with Madness* during the Fall term, 1949, even then interested in the "sacred game"[59] or an excuse for it such as the Grail. Thus, Mary Butts became a figure inside the imagination of what was later to be called the 'Berkeley Renaissance,' and then, with important changes of emphasis, the 'San Francisco Renaissance'.[60]

In her biography of H.D., *Herself Defined* (1985), Barbara Guest claimed that the pre-First World War fashion for all things Greek had fallen into disuse and that this was why H.D.'s work was less read by the mid-1930s. This would have been just as true of Mary Butts's work, although it does not account for the success of Robert Graves's and Mary Renault's writing. Oddly, given her friendship with H.D., their similar interests and mutual respect, Guest mentions Mary Butts only in passing and never considers her as having any literary importance.[61] Yet as early as 1963, Robert Duncan had raised the question of the unacknowledged influence of Mary Butts when discussing H.D.'s novel *Palimpsest*, which was published by McAlmon's Contact Editions in 1926, a year after *Ashe of Rings*. *Palimpsest* is made up of three parts or stories, 'Hipparchia', 'Murex' and 'Secret Name. "Excavator's Egypt"'. " Referring to the final chapter, Duncan declared:

> We too are excavators. In the vulgar eloquentia of our day [1960s] we have a valuable coinage 'to dig', that may mean in the popular sense 'to go in for'; that makes sense, deeper sense, in the light of how archaeology has awakened our imagination of origins or sources in time past, as meaning to dig thru layers of what a thing is, to get back to the roots and to reconstruct from fragments. Back of that, the love one must have for the idea of Troy or the Mayan thing to go digging for it.
>
> Here, anyway, is a last find for the day. Some glimpse of another precious world, though it was a contemporary also, seen in the genre of 'Secret Name'. 'Hipparchia' and 'Murex' may be compared with the novels and short stories of Mary Butts, to the life of *Speed the Plough*, which appeared in 1923, or of *Ashe of Rings*, which was published by Contact Editions, closely associated through McAlmon and Bryher with H.D.'s world. And in her later historical novels of the thirties, in *The Macedonian* and *Scenes from the Life of Cleopatra*, Mary Butts portrays the dawn and the height of the Hellenistic spirit. For the connoisseur of *The Little Review*, *The Dial*, *Pagany* or *Life and Letters To-day*, Mary Butts and H.D. appeared in one context and must have had their resonances.[62]

Duncan was surely right. Whilst H.D. had Hipparchia declare repeatedly in *Palimpsest* "we do not escape the dead',[63] Mary Butts wrote in her journal: "stronger than the living the dead surround me; figures and men-gods and I hardly need say, distinguo."

Throughout this account of her life, I have included numerous references to Mary Butts in the memoirs of her contemporaries. The problem is that the more time passed, the more she was misremembered if remembered at all. The English writer, Harold Acton, confirmed the myth of Mary Butts the socialite and would-be artist when he wrote in 1948: "Most Anglo-Saxon writers are preachers who have mistaken their profession. On the fringe of Montparnasse bars were a few talented story-tellers running to seed, like poor generous red-haired Mary Butts...[who] improvised the vivid stories one hoped she would write."[64] Yet Marianne Moore could still remember the "impact" of reading 'Speed the Plow' when she came to write her *Predilections* (1956) over thirty years later, and in 1962 Jack Lindsay wrote of their friendship in *Fanfrolico and After*.[65] Even *For Whom the Cloche Tolls: A Scrap-book of the Twenties*, the 1953 satirical account by Angus Wilson[66] and Philippe Julian, included an illustration of the terrasse of La Coupole in Montparnasse in 1925 allegedly showing amongst others: "Mary Butts and...Aleister Crowley (a terrible man!)".[67] In her memoirs published in 1960, Sylvia Beach mentioned "Mary Butts, who bounced in and out and was a personality of the twenties, with her red cheeks and red hair.... Cocteau's drawing of the authoress of *Traps for Unbelievers* is quite the Mary Butts of those days. But her life was tragic and her work, which was so promising, was interrupted suddenly by her death. All of her books that had appeared disappeared, too; they seemed to go out of print when she died."[68] These tantalising references could have little impact if such a close friend as Bryher chose to omit Mary Butts entirely from her own autobiography, *The Heart to Artemis* (1963). Perhaps Bryher felt that no one knew who Mary Butts was any more...

What made the neglect worse, was the active denigration of Mary Butts's work by William Plomer. In 1945 William d'Arfey's *Curious Relations* was published. In his introduction Plomer wrote: "William d'Arfey is the pseudonym of a man no longer living. He was a wonderful raconteur and in particular told many stories and anecdotes about his kinsfolk in late Victorian and Edwardian times."[69] The author's real name was Tony Butts, who had committed suicide in 1941. Plomer had suggested the title *Curious Relations* and he "published and cut [the] rough draft" which Tony left on his death. The book (which formed the basis of several episodes of the 1960s Granada television series, *The Liars*) describes

Mary Butts's "kinsfolk", especially her father and mother, but does not mention her directly.

However, seven years later Plomer published *Museum Pieces* (1952), which is a clear (fictional) sequel to *Curious Relations*. In this book the protagonist is Toby [William] d'Arfey himself and the antagonism Plomer felt towards Mary Butts is reflected in his biting portrait of her as Lydia Delap, "a girl with an opulent Edwardian background who had turned Bohemian in a nineteen-twentyish way and had written a couple of novels. I hadn't read them but imagined them to be decidedly precious."[70] Alongside unflattering physical descriptions of Lydia Delap, Plomer satirises some of her novels under the titles *Poisoned Milk* (*Ashe of Rings*), *Bones of Wonder* (*Armed with Madness*) and *Offlimits* (*Death of Felicity Taverner*). As an establishment critic and friend of the Woolfs (Wilson dedicated his *For Whom the Cloche Tolls* to him "in admiration"), Plomer revealed in his memoirs, *At Home* (1958), the level of his antagonism towards Mary Butts (who was, of course, no longer there to defend herself). Writing about Tony Butts, he declared:

> A complication was that he had an elder sister, Mary, who hated her mother and was neither liked nor trusted by Anthony himself. She wrote books. They had a tone of precious knowingness, and the fatal limitation of being too much of their period. In a sense they were vulgar: J.B. Yeats, writing of the paintings of Orpen, defined vulgarity as "the excess of the means of expression over the content". I do not mean to imply that the writings of Mary Butts had anything like the technical brilliance of Orpen's paintings, but they did show excess of manner over matter. They had for a time a certain vogue. She also wrote an autobiography, about which the most memorable thing was not modesty, nor good sense, nor veracity, but the frontispiece—a reproduction of a drawing of the author by Cocteau.[71]

* * * * *

YET THERE WERE more positive attempts to remember Mary Butts, quite apart from the substantial contributions by Goldring, Baker and Wesson Bull.[72] In 1951 the American writer, Louis Adeane, wrote a long article on her work in the *World Review*.[73] From the early 1960s until his death in 1984, Herbert Frank Ingram (a civil servant in Poole) devoted a great deal of time and energy to promoting her work. So much so, that "he became a leading expert…and carried on a large correspondence with scholars."[74] An excellent and meticulous researcher and archivist, Ingram shared all his findings with Camilla and bequeathed her his Mary Butts papers. His contribution is important; amongst other discoveries, is her acquaintance with Cyril Connolly.[75] Ingram collected references to Mary Butts in a number of biographies, as well as quotations in less obvious books, including Lilas Rider Haggard and Henry Williamson's *Norfolk Life* and Morrow McGrath's *Bus by the Brook*.[76] Ingram himself wrote a long article on Mary Butts, 'Poole's Forgotten Genius', in *The Poole and Dorset Herald* in 1966, where he also announced the interest of two American academics in her work in March of that year.[77]

The two American academics in question were Robert Byington and Glen Morgan, who undertook a great deal of research and a number of interviews of Mary Butts's contemporaries from the early 1960s. In 1965 John Ashbery published their initial findings in *Art and Literature* together with extracts from her journal.[78] Cedric Morris's 1924 portrait of Mary Butts accompanied the article. Byington eventually wrote a biography, "The Quest for Mary Butts", but it was never published.

Meanwhile the piecemeal republication of her work began. In 1969 her story 'Green' was reprinted in Stephen Halpert and Richard Johns's *A Return to Pagany*.[79] The 1970s saw the republication of some stories ('Look Homeward, Angel' and 'The Golden Bough'), poetry (including 'Avenue Montaigne', 'Corfe' and 'Heartbreak House') and two books: *Scenes from the Life of Cleopatra* (1974) and *Imaginary Letters* (1979). In 1984 Christopher and Barbara Wagstaff[80] organised a conference on 'The Life and Writings of Mary Butts' at the University of Davis, California, which led to the publication in 1995 of *A Sacred Quest*. This is an invaluable introduction to Mary Butts, including articles, essays and tributes to her as well as a selection of her work.

Mary Butts was also included in Gillian Hanscombe and Virginia L. Smyers's 1987 study, *Writing for their Lives: The Modernist Women 1910-1930*. Hanscombe and Smyers are to be praised for placing Mary Butts beside her contemporaries, although their portrayal does tend to reinforce the wilder, mythical aspects of her life at the expense of a more considered appreciation of her contribution to the literature of the period. Certainly this is the impression given by Sebastian Faulks in his reference to her in *The Fatal Englishman: Three Short Lives* (1996): "The English writer, Mary Butts, a devoted opium smoker with tangled red hair, wrote regional novels of the English West Country with mystic overtones."[81] A more recent critical chapter to be published on Mary Butts is 'Mary Butts: Mothers and War' by Mary Hamer in *Women's Fiction and the Great War* (1997). While it is right that Mary Butts's contribution to writings on the First World War should be recognized alongside those of Virginia Woolf, May Sinclair, Vernon Lee, Edith Wharton and others, Hamer's chapter unfortunately contains a number of factual errors. Rather than focussing on and celebrating the work, her depiction of Mary Butts echoes Hanscombe and Smyers' as well as Faulks's portrayals in a curiously antagonistic discussion whose tone is set by the opening sentence: "What kind of woman calls her own red hair scarlet?"[82] Oddly, given that the theme of the volume is the Great War, Hamer's chapter focuses on 'Speed the Plough' and *Imaginary Letters*, paying only cursory attention to Mary Butts's brilliant war-novel, *Ashe of Rings*.[83]

Recent readings which focus more positively on Mary Butts's work are those by Patrick Wright and Ruth Hoberman. In 1985 Wright drew attention to the importance of her Englishness and concern for the countryside in a long, insightful chapter, 'Coming Back to the Shores of Albion: The Secret England of Mary Butts (1890-1937)', in *On Living in an Old Country: The National Past in Contemporary Britain*.[84] In *The Village That Died For England: The Strange Story of Tyneham* (1995) Wright refers to the "retrospective mythologisation" in *The Crystal Cabinet*, whilst evoking her portrayal of the "hollow land" around Tyneham, south Dorset, with sensitivity and sympathy.[85] "She died young in 1937, but it is highly unlikely that she would have seen anything positive in the tanks' advance," he concludes, since this Dorset village was evacuated to make a training area for allied tanks during World War Two, and the inhabitants were never allowed to return.[86] In *The Crystal Cabinet* as well as in stories, novels and poetry, Mary Butts described and defended this very corner of England which vanished with the advance of the tanks. Wright adduces and explores her prophetic arguments and warnings from the 1920s and 1930s about the detrimental effects on our moral and cultural health of abusing England's countryside.

Ruth Hoberman is the first academic to give substantial critical attention to Mary Butts's historical narratives in her recent study, *Gendering Classicism: The Ancient World in Twentieth-century Women's Historical Fictions* (1997). In two separate chapters ('Mana and Narrative in Mary Butts's Greece' on *The Macedonian*, and 'When Mana Meets Woman: Mary Butts's Cleopatra' on *Scenes from the Life of Cleopatra*) Hoberman examines Mary Butts's work alongside that of Naomi Mitchison, Bryher, Phyllis Bentley, Laura Riding and Mary Renault. Her thesis is that "in writing historical fiction about Greece and Rome, Mitchison, Butts, Bryher, Bentley, Riding and Renault were working through the interrelationship of their gender, their desires, the possible roles with which reading history presented them, and the narrative power that the writing of history offered them."[87] Hoberman's account of Mary Butts's writing is sensitive, intelligent and insightful.

* * * * *

The stories have to be read carefully and slowly or you (I at least) will miss their very dense quality and darting imagination. I understand now as I didn't then, why she considered herself as indeed she was, an experimental writer. I am totally enthralled.

—Robert Medley on reading *With and Without Buttons and Other Stories* in 1994[88]

CARCANET PRESS led the English revival of interest in Mary Butts's work when they republished *The Crystal Cabinet* in 1988 (Beacon Press published the American edition) and *With and Without Buttons and Other Stories* in 1991. In America, McPherson & Company brought forth the following year another collection of stories, *From Altar to Chimney-piece,* and has since been steadily republishing Mary Butts's fiction, including *Armed with Madness, Death of Felicity Taverner, The Macedonian, Scenes from the Life of Cleopatra* and, concurrently with this biography, *Ashe of Rings.*[89] Over thirty-five years ago Sylvia Beach declared: "One day, let us hope, there will be a complete edition of the work of Mary Butts",[90] a wish that now looks nearer to fulfilment than at any time since her death. The 1990s have also seen an increase in the number of Mary Butts stories in anthologies: 'With and Without Buttons' in *The Virago Book of Ghost Stories Volume II* (1991); 'The Golden Bough' in *That Kind of Woman* (1991) and, most recently, 'Speed the Plough' in *Women, Men and the Great War* (1995). The result of such interest has meant that, once again, Mary Butts has an entry in a certain number of the more serious bibliographical histories of English Literature and is to be included in the *New Dictionary of National Biography.*[91] This general republication is part of a long-overdue recognition of her contribution to Modernism which places her firmly alongside her more well-known contemporaries.

NOTES

ABBREVIATIONS

Works by Mary Butts

AOR	*Ashe of Rings* (1925)
AOROW	*Ashe of Rings and Other Writings* (1998)
ASQ	*A Sacred Quest: The Life and Writings of Mary Butts* (1995)
AWM	*Armed with Madness* (1928)
DFT	*Death of Felicity Taverner* (1932)
FATCP	*From Altar to Chimney-piece: Selected Stories* (1992)
IL	*Imaginary Letters* (1928)
LS	*Last Stories* (1938)
SLC	*Scenes from the Life of Cleopatra* (1935)
SO	*Several Occasions* (1932)
STP	*Speed the Plough and Other Stories* (1923)
TCC	*The Crystal Cabinet* (1937); 2nd, expanded edition (1988)
TCN	*The Classical Novels of Mary Butts: The Macedonian, Scenes from the Life of Cleopatra* (1994)
TFU	*Traps for Unbelievers* (1932)
TM	*The Macedonian* (1933)
TTN	*The Taverner Novels: Armed with Madness, Death of Felicity Taverner* (1992)
WAWB	*With and Without Buttons: Selected Stories of Mary Butts* (1991)
WTH	*Warning to Hikers* (1932)

Libraries and Archives

Beinecke	The Beinecke Rare Book and Manuscript Library, Yale University
Bodleian	Modern Manuscripts, Bodleian Library, Oxford
Buffalo	Poetry/Rare Books Collection, State University of New York at Buffalo
Cocteau	Fonds Jean Cocteau/Fonds Mireille Havet du Centre d'Etudes du XXe Siècle, Université Paul-Valéry, Montpellier, France
Eliot archive	Correspondence held by Mrs V. Eliot
HRHRC	Harry Ransom Humanities Research Center, University of Texas at Austin
TGA	Tate Gallery Archive, London

Prologue

1. English dating is used throughout.

2. Shortly before her death, Mary Butts wrote *The Crystal Cabinet* (Methuen, 1938). This partial autobiography caused a certain amount of controversy and can only be relied upon as subjective.

3. *The Crystal Cabinet* (Carcanet Press, 2nd, expanded edn, 1988), p.94. Henceforth referred to as *TCC*.

4. Mary Butts letter to Ada Briggs, 27.9.15.

5. For an account of the desolating work undertaken by members of the Children's Care Committee, see Stella Bowen, *Drawn From Life* (Virago, 1984), p.385.

6. Bowen, *Drawn From Life*, pp.41, 39, 40.

7. For Phyllis Reid see, Bowen, *Drawn From Life*, pp.42-44. For Margaret Postgate, see Bowen, *Drawn From Life*, pp.52-53 and *TCC*, p.95, and her entry under 'Cole, Dame Margaret Isabel (1893-1980)' in the *Dictionary of National Biography*.

8. This first NCCL existed only between 1916-1919. The more well-known NCCL (now called Liberty), named after this first organisation, was founded in 1934.

9. Brian Dyson, *Liberty in Britain* (Civil Liberties Trust, 1994), p.1.

10. See Keith Robbins, *The Abolition of War: the 'Peace Movement' in Britain, 1914-1919* (U. of Wales Press, 1976), p.75.

11. *TCC*, pp.94-95.

12. Quoted in John W. Graham, *Conscription and Conscience* (Allen and Unwin, 1922), p.67.

13. See Robbins, *The Abolition of War*, pp.146-147.

14. Robert Calverley Trevelyan (1872-1951), brother of the historian, G.M. Trevelyan, and First World War active pacifist and MP, C.P. Trevelyan.

15. Jack White letter to Mary Butts, 22.5.16.

16. Mary Butts mentions that Eleanor was also working in an "office" (7.9.16)—it is unclear what her precise job was.

17. St Bride's off Fleet Street. Due to post-war rebuilding in this part of London, only the upper part of the church is now visible from Bride Passage. Originally a tenth-century church built on the site of a Roman crypt, St Bride's was extensively altered on six separate occasions before being badly damaged in the Great Fire of London of 1666. Christopher Wren redesigned the church which reopened for worship on the 19 December 1675. This was the church which Mary Butts saw from her office window in 1916. St Bride's was bombed during the Second World War (19.12.40), rebuilt in its present form and reopened in 1957.

18. Mary Butts's idiosyncratic spelling is retained throughout.

19. Mary Butts generally called menstruation either a haemorrage or, more typically, the curse. Only occasionally did she refer to it by its modern name of period.

20. Mary Butts wrote that her love of fine objects extended to semi-precious stones: "Today I cannot touch a lump of crystal, coral or amber, lapis or jade without the deepest sensuous joy." *TCC*, p.8. Jade in particular had a special resonance for her and she often wore an earring made of a wheel of jade; it was in some sense her 'signature', appearing in some form in almost all her works.

I : The Early Years 1890-1916

1. This 75-page document, which claimed among the Butts ancestry the famous Dr William Butt[e]s (c. 1485-1545), Royal Physician to Henry VIII and friend of Cranmer, was compiled and typed by Mary Colville-Hyde (early in their marriage) and amended by hand as late as the 1930s.

2. Mary Butts undated letter to Glenway Wescott, attributed to 1923, quoted in 'Three Letters', *A Sacred Quest: The Life and the Writings of Mary Butts*, ed. Christopher Wagstaff (McPherson & Co, 1995), p.145. Henceforth referred to as *ASQ*.

3. Frederick Butts letter to Sarah Briggs, 29.9.1888.

4. See chapter 'Aunt Monica' in *TCC*.

5. Camilla Bagg, 'Another View of Mary Butts', in *ASQ*, p.90.

6. Frederick Butts letter to Sarah Briggs, 29.9.1888.

7. Mary Butts no doubt also mentioned seeing the very "bullet taken from the foot of F.J. Butts [her father] after the attack on the Redan, and pieces of the Colours which he carried at Alma, cut off and sent to him by the Colonel of his regiment, when they were by the Queen's Command deposited in S. Paul's Cathedral." These would have been in Salterns when Mary Butts was a child. Mary Colville-Hyde, "Pedigree of the Butts Family", p.62.

8. Mary Butts's unusual second forename, Franeis, has consistently been misread as Frances. Frederick Butts entered it as "Franeis" in the family bible and it is spelt this way on MB's birth certificate. MB occasionally spelt it 'Franies'.

9. *TCC*, p.14. Details of its size were given in the Deed of Conveyance of the Salterns Estate (24th June 1863).

10. *TCC*, p.16.

11. Mary Colville-Hyde, 'Pedrigree of the Butts Family', pp.62-62A.

12. Peter Ackroyd, *Blake* (Sinclair-Stevenson, 1995), p.264. See this biography for more details on Thomas Butts.

13. Poem enclosed in a letter from William Blake to Thomas Butts, 2.10.1800 in *Blake's Complete Writings*, ed. Geoffrey Keynes (O.U.P, 1972), p.804.

14. In 1898 the Dorset Natural History and Antiquarian Field Club were "invited by Captain and Mrs Butts to tea and to see their unique collection of pictures by Blake". For a detailed description of the paintings and other Butts possessions see *Proceedings of the Dorset Natural History and Antiquarian Field Club*, ed. Nelson M. Richardson, Honorary Secretary, (Dorset County Chronicle Office, 1898), pp.lxvi-lxx. Mary Butts's description of the interior of Salterns in *The Crystal Cabinet* was the "strongest influence on ... [the] decor theme" of the owner of the property in the 1960s. See 'Where Time Stands Still', *Poole and Dorset Herald* (6.2.63), p.18.

15. Bryher, 'Recognition not Farewell', *Life and Letters To-day*, 17, no.9 (Autumn 1937), pp.159-164. Reprinted in *ASQ*, pp.3-10; pp.5-6.

16. *TCC*, p.96.

17. Ibid, p.98.

18. Ibid, p.36.

19. Ibid, p.31.

20. Ibid, p.31.

21. Ibid, p.76.

22. Mr F. Colville Hyde was among the "chief mourners" at Frederick Butts's funeral. See Funeral notice in *East Dorset Herald* (14.9.05).

23. *TCC*, p.180.

24. See *TCC*, pp.179-234.

25. Frederick Butts letter to Sarah Briggs, 29.9.1888.

26. *TCC*, p.13. The need for money seems to have been pressing. Less than three months after Frederick Butts's death his widow (on writing paper with black borders) wrote to a J. Sampson Esq: "My husband...has since I last wrote gone to his rest—and I am obliged by the great weight of the death duties—to the grief of myself and little daughter to part with our Blake collection. I do not wish to see it through a dealer—and though I have already been approached both from America and Vienna I should prefer it to remain in England—if possible.It comprises as you are doubtless aware, the *very* best of Blake's work—in absolutely perfect condition—they have none of them been re-produced and I would let the letters, manuscripts and relics go with them—but not the miniatures—and I should like to sell them as a whole. I won't break the collection up." Mary Butts [Mary Colville-Hyde] letter to J. Sampson, 14.12.[05] (Liverpool University Library, John Sampson Papers IV/20). Mary Butts, the "little daughter", was fifteen by this time; oddly, there is no mention of Tony.

27. Mary Butts [Mary Colville-Hyde] letter to Mr Warren, 26.2.[06].

28. The collection was exhibited soon after. See T. Sturge Moore's review, 'The Carfax Exhibition of Blake's Work. Including the "Butts Collection"', *The Outlook*, 17, no.438 (23.06.06), pp.845-846. Six months later an edition of Blake's letters was reviewed in the same journal. See 'The Letters of William Blake (Methuen) by A.G.B. Russell', *The Outlook*, 18, no.465 (29.12.06), pp.835-6.

29. MB wrongly claims that this was a private chapel, see *TCC*, p.154. In fact it had been built by public subscription on land donated by Frederick Butts. It later became the Church of the Holy Angels, Lilliput, Dorset. For more details see *Holy Angels, Lilliput, Centenary Year* (Poole Instant Print, 1974).

30. Mary Butts [Mary Colville-Hyde] letter to Sarah Briggs, 27.4.06.

31. [Mary Butts], 'The Poetry of Hymns', *The Outlook*, 18, no.461 (1.12.06), pp.696-7. This is an extraordinarily scholarly, sophisticated and well-written essay for a fifteen-year-old. She displays her poetic preferences when stating: "A poet is a very rare occurrence. But there are at present not a few living people who are able to write poetry. One is Mr. Rudyard Kipling. 'Sir Richard's Song,' for instance, in his new book, is the essence of poetry, the very soul of romance. Mr. A.E. Housman and Mr. Yeats have both a real vein; and their gift is to be preferred before thousands of gold and silver." Mary Colville-Hyde's reaction to this article remained a source of disappointment and resentment to Mary Butts, who wrote twenty years later in her autobiography (*TCC*, p.233):

> I had already had one article published. In the weekly Outlook; but pride in the event equally mixed with bewilderment, because of what had happened at home. I had written it one holiday, in the middle of my St Andrews years, a short essay, on hymns and how awful some of them were. Showed it to my aunt, and it was she who typed it for me and sent it in.
>
> When it was accepted, with a cheque for two guineas, our joy knew no bounds. I tore home... There would be a present for Aunt Ada and a present for Mother, and a Classical Dictionary for me. Till then I had kept it a secret, hoping to surprise my mother. And she was furious. How could I have been so unkind, so secretive (the implication was almost—so underhand) as not to have told her before?
>
> I could not see it. I have never been able to see it to this day. Who had, as I thought, prepared a joyful surprise. It was not as though Mother was interested in my ambitions.... So, on the whole, my first effort brought me more grief than anything else. What was worse perhaps, more and more confirmed me in the belief that from the majority of grown-up people I should get no help. From my mother least of all.
>
> Yet it is an episode with which she has not ceased to reproach me to this day.

32. Mary Butts, 'The Heavenward Side', *The Outlook*, 17, no.437 (30.6.06), p.504.

33. Ada Briggs letter to Mary Butts, 1.10.10.

34. *TCC*, p.238.

35. Ibid, p.240.

36. 'The Adventure' was written some time in late 1913 or 1914. The lines quoted show an affinity with the poetry of Francis Thompson (1859-1907), especially the poem, 'The Kingdom of God' which includes the verse:

> But (when so sad thou canst not sadder)
> Cry;—and upon thy so sore loss
> Shall shine the traffic of Jacob's ladder
> Pitched betwixt Heaven and Charing Cross.

Francis Thompson, *The Hound of Heaven* (Phoenix, 1996) p.50. This poem was first published posthumously in 1913 in a volume edited by the poet, Wilfred Meynell, who wrote: "'The Kingdom of God'...([was] found among his papers when he died). Francis Thompson might yet have worked upon to remove, here a defective rhyme, there an unexpected elision. But no altered mind would he have brought to the purport of it;—the prevision of 'Heaven in Earth and God in Man', pervading his earlier published verse, is here accented by poignantly local and personal allusion. For in these triumphing stanzas he held in retrospect those days and nights of human dereliction he spent beside London's River, and in the shadow—but all radiance to him—of Charing Cross." Wilfred Meynell, 'Notes' to, *The Poems of Francis Thompson* (O.U.P; 1937), p.354. Mary Butts mentioned reading 'The Hound of Heaven' in March 1921.

37. *TCC*, pp.17-19.

38. Mary Butts, *Death of Felicity Taverner* (Wishart, 1932). Republished in *The Taverner Novels: Armed with Madness/ Death of Felicity Taverner* (McPherson & Co, 1992), p.165. Henceforth known as *DFT* in *TTN*. Mary Butts was not alone in finding this myth resonant: E.M. Forster "asked [T.E.] Lawrence,...what he thought of the story of Polycrates and his ring. The story runs that Polycrates, tyrant of Samos, was so invarably successful in all his enterprises, that his friend the king of Egypt, fearing so much good fortune for him, told him he should sacrifice something of value to himself. Accordingly he threw a precious ring into the sea; but a few days later, a fish was brought to him at table and the ring was found in its stomach. At this, his friend abandoned him, as being clearly doomed by the gods. Forster told Lawrence he regarded it as an allegory, 'and more helpful than most'." E.M. Forster letter to T.E. Lawrence, 18.3.27, quoted in P.N. Furbank, *E.M. Forster: A Life: Volume Two, Polycrates' Ring 1914-1970* (O.U.P., 1978), p.132.

39. Virginia Woolf spoke for most (educated) women when she opened her 1925 essay, 'On Not knowing Greek':

> For it is vain and foolish to talk of knowing Greek, since in our ignorance we should be at the bottom of any class of schoolboys, since we do not know how the words sounded, or where precisely we ought to laugh, or how the actors acted, and between this foreign people and ourselves there is not only difference of race and tongue but a tremendous breach of tradition. All the more strange, then, is it that we should wish to know Greek, try to know Greek, feel for ever drawn back to the meaning of Greek, though from what incongruous odds and ends, with what slight resemblance to the real meaning of Greek, who shall say?

Virginia Woolf, 'On Not Knowing Greek', in *The Common Reader* (Harcourt, Brace & World Inc., 1953 reprint), p.24. In stark contrast to Woolf's, Mary Butts's knowledge and experience of Greek literature was closer to that of many of her male contemporaries, including T.S. Eliot and Ezra Pound. Nonetheless Mary Butts and her work was omitted from Hugh Kenner's *The Pound Era* (1971). Julian Symons did mention Mary Butts (albeit only briefly) in his more recent *Makers of the New: The Revolution in Literature, 1912-1939* (André Deutsch, 1987), pp.131, 233.

40. Woolf, 'On Not Knowing Greek', in *The Common Reader*, p.24. See also, p.501, n.365.

41. Shari Benstock, *Women of the Left Bank: Paris 1900-1940* (Virago, 1994), p.25.

42. Mary Butts's undated poem, 'On Reading Jane Harrison's *Prolegomena*' ([1912/13]) opens:

The City thunders on, bound to the wheel
Of the past red with blood, or bright with fire,
Men catch a few stars and have dared to steal
A little near to the world's desire.

Our Gods in our own likeness wax or wane
Our soul like thin flames waving in the air
Blown out to fire the universe—again
Sink to draw colour from our lover's hair.

43. Ezra Pound, 'Psychology and Troubadours' (1916) in *The Spirit of Romance* (2nd edition, Peter Owen, 1970), p.92. See Hugh Ross Williamson's comment on Mary Butts's attitude to Dorset, p.302.

44. This untitled poem was no. III of Mary Butts's 'In London' cycle (1913).

45. *TCC*, pp.22, 10-11. In the 1910s Mary Butts wrote a number of poems about the Dorset landscape including: 'Aphrodite on Purbeck' (undated, possibly 1913) and 'Warbarrow Bay' (Summer 1911). These poems remain unpublished.

46. *TCC*, pp.41-42. In addition to numerous references to Frazer's study throughout her writing, Mary Butts wrote a short story called 'The Golden Bough'. First published in her collection of stories, *Speed the Plough* (1923), it has been reprinted twice since: in *Antaeus*, 13/14 (1974), pp.88-97, and in *That Kind of Women: Stories from the Left Bank and Beyond*, ed. Bronte Adams and Trudi Tate (Virago, 1991), pp.16-28.

47. Amongst Mary Butts's books there are several volumes by Rudyard Kipling in which she dated their purchase, including *Barrack-Room Ballads* (1892), "8.1.09", and *Rewards and Fairies* (1910), "Penzance, end Feb. 1936". Despite her lifelong admiration for Kipling, she was disappointed in her teens when she read *The Light that Failed* (1891): "Story again, as I saw, of the Wounded Prince, only I could not forgive Kipling his contempt for the woman who wanted to be a painter. He, an idol, only one less sancrosanct than Shelley, wrote of women as though they were not quite human beings, creatures only of the flesh, the flesh touched with a kind of bad magic; creatures always, in their essence, inferior to men. That was woe. It wasn't, it couldn't, it shouldn't be true; and horrible to think of one's idol telling one that one had no business to learn things and become a writer. That it wasn't even any use trying, because one couldn't. Sturdily I threw it away from me. It was going to be true. For me anyhow, and Kipling and Co. would have to put up with it." *TCC*, p.222.

48. Mary Butts letter to Ada Briggs, 21.7.11.

49. Constance Maynard, unpublished private diary, 10.6.12 (Queen Mary & Westfield College).

50. Marion Delf Smith, early staff member of Westfield College, 'Afterthoughts: 1. The Race Meeting', unpublished memoirs, 1969 (Queen Mary & Westfield College).

51. Constance Maynard, unpublished private diary, 15.6.12 (Queen Mary and Westfield College). Not getting a degree was only a handicap if Mary Butts had wanted to become a teacher, which she did not. See *TCC*, p.238.

52. Twenty years later Mary Butts gave her account of the incident: "...in my third year, Westfield and I had parted, none too kindly, because of my intention to go to the Derby. Accident, not virtue, had prevented me at the last moment, nor had it so much as occurred to me to hold my tongue. All of which had given a charming, jealous, elderly don, to whom I owed much, a chance for a little exasperated intrigue. It was all very silly, and mercifully not a crime for which my family would reproach me." *TCC*, p.252.

53. Ada Briggs letter to Sarah Briggs, 21.9.12.

54. Mary Butts undated letter to Ada Briggs, 1923/1924.

55. Bowen, *Drawn From Life*, p.39.

II : The London Years 1916-1920

1. Bowen, *Drawn From Life*, p.39.

2. "Mrs Colville-Hyde was a great and important lady in the district... Her daughter, Mary Butts, was often with her mother, and she was the first lady I ever saw smoking. I remember being shocked and thinking it quite dreadful," Mildred Holmes, *Parkstone Recollections* (W.E.A. Southern District Publication, 1983), p.9.

3. *TCC*, p.103.

4. Corfe Castle was one of Mary Butts's favourite places and inspired both her poetry and fiction.

5. Harcourt Wesson Bull, '"Truth is the Heart's Desire"', in *ASQ*, p.56.

6. Tony did not live in the college itself, but had rooms in Eton town.

7. Bowen, *Drawn From Life*, pp.39-40.

8. Tony Butts, letter to Cedric Morris, Friday 28 March. No year given—1940-41. (TGA 8317.1.1.352)

9. Ada Briggs letter to Mary Butts, 1.10.10.

10. Mary Butts also wrote a novel called "Unborn Gods" in these early years. Still among the MB papers, it was never published.

11. 'Ashe of Rings I', *The Little Review*, 7, no.4 (Jan-Mar 1921), pp.2-14; 'Ashe of Rings II', *The Little Review*, 8, no.1 (Autumn 1921), pp.97-106.

12. Mary Butts undated letter to Hugh Ross Williamson, Sunday, June 1932 (HRHRC).

13. John Rodker's novel, "The Switchback", was never published in English. It was, however, published in France with the title *Montagnes Russes*, translated by Ludmila Savitzky (Librairie Stock, 1923). For a rather extraordinary coincidence, see below, p.470, n.141.

14. For Goldsworthy Lowes Dickinson's role during the First World War see Robbins, *The Abolition of War*, pp.48-51.

15. Mary Butts letter to Ada Briggs, 27.9.15. The cat may also have been named after Wyndham Lewis's explosive magazine, *Blast*, which first appeared on the 20 June 1914.

16. John Middleton Murry, *Fyodor Dostoevsky: A Critical Study* (Secker, 1916).

17. [John Rodker], *Memoirs of Other Fronts* (Putnam, 1932), pp.119-121.

18. Bowen, *Drawn From Life*, p.42.

19. This may have been 1, Glenilla Studios, NW3, to which Mary Butts moved a few months later.

20. This was presumably Anna Wickham's *The Man with a Hammer* (Grant and Richards, 1916).

21. Mary Butts may be referring here to Havelock Ellis's chapter (10), 'The Art of Love', in his *Studies of the Psychology of Sex (Volume VI). Sex in Relation to Society* (1910).

22. It has not been possible to trace where the story (not among MB's papers) was published. On the 19 February 1919 Mary Butts wrote that she had been "unburdened" of her feelings for Agnes Helen (who appears to have been Australian—perhaps Stella Bowen herself?) through the writing of 'Agnes Helen' and "Unborn Gods", her unpublished novel.

23. In her autobiography Mary Butts was no doubt referring to Jack White when she wrote of "the man who was looking up the war's progress in the Book of the Prophet Daniel". *TCC*, p.95.

24. Cecil Boulton, 'Mary Butts' Bright Novel *Ashe of Rings*, Dostoevski served with a Little Milk', *New York Evening Post* (5.6.26), p.5.

25. Nina Hamnett's "remarkable gifts have rarely been as fully revealed as in her portrait of Miss Mary Butts". P.G. Konody, 'The London Group', *The Observer* (12.5.18), p.3. Review of the eighth exhibition of the London Group at the Mansard Gallery. Also exhibiting were Roger Fry, C.R. Nevinson and Mark Gertler. The portrait has not been traced.

26. Mary Butts, *Ashe of Rings*, (1925). Reprinted in *Ashe of Rings and Other Writings* (McPherson & Co., 1998), p. 82. Henceforth referred to as *AOR* in *AOROW*.

27. When attending a Tribunal one CO was told: "Yours is a case of an unhealthy mind in an unwholesome body." Graham, *Conscription and Conscience*, p.71.

28. [Rodker], *Memoirs of Other Fronts*, pp.129-131.

29. Ibid, pp.145-146.

30. Ibid, pp.148-151.

31. Ibid, p.155-6.

32. Graham, *Conscription and Conscience*, p.235.

33. Ibid, pp.235-237.

34. The song 'A Broken Doll' (1916) was a music hall hit. Words by Clifford Harris and music by James W. Tate.

35. Quite apart from his work as a classical scholar, Professor Gilbert Murray was instrumental in 1916 in drawing attention to the plight of absolutist COs (those who would accept no alternative to imprisonment, such as work of National Importance). In May and June army authorities had secretly started to arrange the transfer of a number of absolutists to France, where the penalties were more extreme (including execution). Gilbert Murray headed a group of Liberals who informed P.M. Asquith of this covert operation. Appalled, the P.M. ordered its immediate halt.

36. Iris Barry wrote that in 1916 "another regular diner [at Pound's table] was Mary Butts, with her long white Rossetti throat and vermilion red hair...just married to John Rodker at the other end of the table" (Charles Norman, *Ezra Pound* (McDonald & Co, 2nd edn, 1969), p.197.) Since this came from an article by Iris Barry in *The Bookman* of October 1931, no doubt she was misremembering the year. Certainly Mary Butts and John Rodker were not married in 1916. Ford Madox Ford refers to Mary Butts as part of "les jeunes". Ford Madox Hueffer undated letter to Stella Bowen, August 1918. See this and editorial note in *The Correspondence of Ford Madox Ford and Stella Bowen*, ed. Stang and Cochran (Indiana U.P., 1993), pp.6-7.

37. See *Pound/Ford: The Story of a Literary Friendship*, ed. Brita Lindberg-Seyersted (Faber, 1982), pp. 34, 36, 77, 186 and Norman, *Ezra Pound*, p.267.

38. Not only did Ezra Pound recommend Mary Butts's work to the American poet, Charles Olson (who visited him in St Elizabeths Hospital), he also "wildly jotted down...[the] ms for Laughlin's attention, Mary Butts' *The Death of Felicity Taverner...*" James Laughlin was the editor of the publishing house, New Directions. Charles Olson, 'Canto 2, January 15, 1946', *Charles Olson and Ezra Pound: An Encounter at St Elizabeths*, ed. Catherine Seelye (Grossman, 1975), p.48.

39. See [Rodker], *Memoirs of Other Fronts*, where Muriel stays several days, pp.166-169.

40. Mary Butts, 'Lettres Imaginaires', *The Little Review*, 6, no.6 (October 1919), pp.8-12; and 6, no.7 (November 1919), pp.27-32.

41. Mary Butts letter to Ada Briggs, 17.5.18.

42. [Rodker], *Memoirs of Other Fronts*, pp.191-193.

43. Mary Butts letter to Ada Briggs, 17.5.18.

44. Mary Butts letter to Ada Briggs, 22.5.18.

45. A reference to William Wordsworth's poem, 'Michael' in *Lyrical Ballads* (1800).

46. Arthur Machen, 'The Secret of the Sangraal' (1907), in *The Shining Pyramid* (Martin Secker, 1925), p.86.

47. *TCC*, p.33. It is unclear exactly which book Mary Butts is referring to. The 'matter of Britain' (matière de Bretagne) was "the traditional designation of literary material deriving from Britain (in the broadest sense, including Brittany) and of presumed Celtic ancestry. The term,

which is a convenient and accepted label if something of a misleading oversimplification, comes from lines written by the French poet Jean Bodel in *Les Saisnes* (late twelfth century). Bodel divides acceptable literary material into the Matter of France (the epics or chansons de geste), of Rome (the romances of antiquity), and of Britain (the Breton lais and romances). The usual, but not exclusive, subject of much of the Matter of Britain is Arthur." *The New Arthurian Encyclopedia* ed. Norris J. Lacy (St James Press, 1991), p.315.

48. Mary Butts would describe this term in her pamphlet *Traps for Unbelievers* (1932). Reprinted in *AOROW.* Henceforth referred to as *TFU* in *AOROW*, p.326.

49. The Grail was a popular subject for writers of this period; see Arthur Machen's story 'The Great Return' (1915). Mary Butts's novel *Armed with Madness* (1928) predates both Charles Williams's *War in Heaven* (1930) and John Cowper Powys's *A Glastonbury Romance* (1933).

50. Mary Butts undated letter to Ada Briggs, autumn 1918.

51. This may well have been Johann August Strindberg's *Legends. Autobiographical Sketches* (Andrew Melrose, 1912 (English translation of 1898 text)).

52. Debussy, *L'Après-midi d'un Faune* (1892-1894), inspired by Mallarmé's poem of that name (1876).

53. Mary Butts undated letter to Ada Briggs, autumn 1918. See Richard Buckle, *Diaghilev* (Weidenfield, 1993).

54. Mary Butts, 'Vision', *The Egoist*, 5, no.8 (September 1918), p.11. On her copy of the published poem, she added "*1st* attempt! (to please JR)".

55. Mary Butts undated letter to Ada Briggs, autumn 1918.

56. The portrait is unfortunately not among her papers. Yet this experience may well have inspired Mary Butts's short story, 'Magic', in which a woman sitting for her portrait declares: "Painters are not concerned with youth or age. They are not finally interested in your phenomena extended in time and space. They use it to present appearance in reality. Reality swallows phenomena and puffs them out in patterns discerned in the arrangement of antitheses. A good painter is free of the pain of opposites. He leads out the arrangement in reality by hand or claw. He was examining her pattern." 'Magic', *The Little Review*, 7, no.2 (Jul-Aug 1920), pp.3-6, p.3.

57. Mary Butts wrote in the idiom of her time, where "man" stands for men *and* women.

58. In fact Tony did die young, at the age of forty, see p.436.

59. Dr C.G. Jung, *Psychology of the Unconscious: A Study of the Transformations and Symbolisms of the Libido: A Contribution to the History of the Evolution of Thought* (Kegan Paul, Trench, Trubner & Co, Ltd, 1916), p.330.

60. See Stella Bowen letters to Ford Madox Ford, 23.4.19, 28.4.19, 7.5.19. Quoted in *The Correspondence of Ford Madox Ford and Stella Bowen*, ed. Stang and Cochran, pp.97, 108, 125. Walter Sickert was Stella Bowen's teacher, but she hoped through Mary Butts and John Rodker to arrange a more personal meeting with him.

61. Eliphas Lévi (pseudonym of Alphonse Louis Constant) (1810-1875), was a defrocked priest. He greatly influenced the French Surrealist, André Breton. "Lévi believed in 'an occult science with true power, able to work miracles and compete with the miracles of authorized religion'. In a masterly synthesis [*Dogme et rituel de haute magie* (1861)], he set out all of hermeticism (astrology, Cabala, and so on) and turned it into a weapon for freedom, capable of explaining both the meta-political world and the meta-poetical world. At the same time,...he was drawn towards operational magic as a source of practical exercises which could 'give power' to those who studied them. His ritual involved spells, exorcisms and clairvoyance, but—and herein lies his originality—it always relied on explicit symbols. In this way, the sign of the cross, or prayer, became a means of rousing the psyche of the experimenter and acting, mysteriously, on matter." André Nataf, *The Wordsworth Dictionary of the Occult* (Wordsworth Reference, 1994), p.152. *Dogme et rituel de haute magie* was translated by A.E. Waite, *Transcendental Magic: Its*

Doctrine and Ritual (George Redway, 1896).

62. See below, p.263, for Mary Butts's review of a biography of Philip Heseltine/Peter Warlock.

63. Charles Baudelaire, 'Correspondances' in *Les Fleurs du Mal*, translated Richard Howard (Harvester Press, 1982), p.15. The original reads:

> La Nature est un temple ou de vivants piliers
> Laissent parfois sortir de confuses paroles;
> L'homme y passes à travers des forêts de symboles
> Qui l'observent avec des regards familiers.

Charles Baudelaire, 'Correspondances', in *Les Fleurs du Mal* (Flammarion, 1991), p.62.

64. "I by the way sent you the name of subscriber. Miss M[ary] Butts, 1 Glenilla Studios, Glenilla Road. N.W.3.... If not, put her down. I have just sent her Sept. Sub runs. May to May. She has earlier nos. from me." Ezra Pound letter to Margaret Anderson (8.10.17), quoted in *POUND/The Little Review: The Letters of Ezra Pound to Margaret Anderson: The Little Review Correspondence*, ed. Thomas L. Scott and Melvin M. Friedman with the assistance of Jackson R. Bryher (Faber, 1988), p.133.

65. Mary Butts, 'Aldington's Images of Desire', *The Little Review*, 6, no.4 (August 1919), pp.35-36; '*The Works of Thomas Vaughan*', *The Little Review*, 6, no.10, (March 1920), pp.47-48. (See also 'Thomas Vaughan', Mary Butts's reply to S. Foster Damon, *The Little Review*, 7, no.3 (Sep-Dec. 1920), p.58; '*The Wind-Flowers of Asklepiades, and Poems of Poseidippos* and *The Poems of Meleager of Gadara*', *The Little Review*, 7, no.4 (Jan-Mar 1921), pp.45-47.

66. When the American edition of *Georgian Stories, 1922* was published by G.P. Putnam & Co in 1923, photographs of the authors represented in the anthology accompanied each story. The only author not to have her photograph included was Mary Butts. No explanation is given for this anomaly.

67. In her autobiography, Mary Butts relayed a conversation between herself and another schoolgirl, Doria, about the importance of handing on knowledge. Doria was being prepared for her confirmation and was doubtful until Mary Butts reminded her that (*TCC*, p.208):

> She was only to think of the infinite ways there were of knowing God.
>
> 'If I could believe it was true—out here with you it looks as if it was.' Then she grinned: 'Keep me to it. I'll need it. You don't know what a difference you've made.'
>
> The difference she had made. Did she know that—my life was suddenly filled and brimming over? It was all right. How simple it was. I'd come up north simply to be able to do this. Hand on a little of the lovely things I had learned to someone else who needed them. It was as simple as that.
>
> 'Keep me to it'—I did not know that to nine people out of ten it would not be a sacred word. Or rather that they go back on it because it is a sacred word.

68. Bowen, *Drawn From Life*, p.65.

69. Ibid, p.68.

70. Ibid, pp.40-41.

71. Ford Madox Ford letter to Ezra Pound, 20.7.20. Quoted in *Pound/Ford*, ed. Lindberg-Seyersted, p.34.

72. Douglas Goldring, *South Lodge: Reminiscences of Violet Hunt, Ford Madox Ford and the English Review Circle* (Constable & Co, 1943), p.147.

73. See Bowen, *Drawn From Life*, pp.65-68. The conditions at Red Ford may have been basic; Ford Madox Ford's cooking was not: "We were away for Christmas, and got back late last night. We spent it with a friend four miles from a station who is so proud of his cooking that we were never left in peace a moment because of the fresh things he had brought us to eat. He cooks à la Provençal with cream and oil and garlic, and stuffs quiet birds like chickens with almonds and chestnuts soaked in rum. He loses his temper if you don't go on and on." Mary

Butts letter to Ada Briggs, 29.12.19. Perhaps Ford also served up his breed of potato which he had good-humouredly named after her; see Ford Madox Ford, *It was the Nightingale* (Heinemann, 1934), p.108.

74. Bowen, *Drawn From Life*, p.164.

75. Ibid, pp.40-41.

76. Wyndham Lewis, *The Apes of God* (Penguin, 1965), p.147. As Edgell Rickword's biographer points out: "*The Apes of God*, [was] Wyndham Lewis's *roman à clef* in which many of the leading figures of the literary world appeared under thin disguises—the Sitwells, Lytton Strachey, Sidney Schiff and many now forgotten." Charles Hobday, *Edgell Rickword: A Poet at War* (Carcanet, 1989), p.217.

77. May Sinclair letter to Mary Butts, 7.1.20.

78. Edward Wadsworth (1889-1949) was a painter and Fanny Wadsworth a violinist.

79. In late December 1919 Mary Butts wrote to her aunt about Eliot's book: "We are sending you down something from the press directly it comes from the binders—a book of poems by a friend of ours. They will interest you I think—he's a very remarkable man." Mary Butts letter to Ada Briggs, 29.12.19. 264 copies of *Ara Vos Prec*, the first book of poems published by the Ovid Press, came out in early February 1920. Whilst it is not well-known today, the contents of this second book by Eliot were identical (in a different order) to those published a few weeks later in *Poems*, by the American publisher, Knopf. (They included 'Portrait of a Lady' and 'Gerontion'.) See Donald Gallup, *T.S.Eliot: A Bibliography* (Faber, 1952), pp.4-5; *The Letters of T.S. Eliot. Volume 1. 1898-1922*, ed. Valerie Eliot (Harcourt, Brace, Jovanovich, 1988), pp.294, 312, 314, 338, 348, 356-7, 363, 384.

80. "This edition of 190 copies is the second book of the Ovid Press: was printed by John and Mary Rodker: and completed April 8th 1920." John Rodker, in *Hymns* (The Ovid Press, 1920).

81. Edward Wadsworth's *The Black Country* and *Fifteen Drawings* by Wyndham Lewis were published in 1920 as well as *Twenty Drawings from the Note-books of H. Gaudier-Brzeska* the previous year. For more details about John Rodker and the publications of his short-lived Ovid Press, see Andrew Crozier's Introduction to John Rodker, *Poems and Adolphe 1920*, ed. Andrew Crozier (Carcanet, 1996); *The Letters of T.S. Eliot*, ed. Eliot, pp.299, 383, 463.

82. For a description of the café, nicknamed "the Armenian", see Douglas Goldring, *The Nineteen Twenties: A General Survey and Some Personal Memories* (Nicholson & Watson, 1945), pp.155-156. Dora Carrington described Rodker as the "Armenian" in a letter to Lytton Strachey, 10.12.16. *Carrington: letters and extracts from her diaries*, ed. David Garnett (O.U.P., 1979), p. 49.

83. This may well have been Arthur Machen's story, 'The Children of the Pool', collected in *The Children of the Pool and other stories* (Hutchinson & Co, 1916).

84. In addition to the particular connotations the word "abyss" had for MB and in Aleister Crowley's system of magic, it was doubtless also informed by Jack London's account of poverty in London's East End, *The People of the Abyss* (1903). Rodker's Whitechapel origins were never forgotten.

85. Goldring, *South Lodge*, p.137.

86. Ibid, pp.158-164. Oddly, Cecil Maitland is not mentioned in the Public Records Office at Kew.

87. Probably the Margaret of Mary Butts's Westfield poems. See above, p.23.

88. See '"Athenaeum" Prize Competition', *The Athenaeum*, 4703 (18.6.20), p. 801.

89. Interestingly John Rodker republished Scot's *The Discoverie of Witchcraft* in 1930, with an introduction by Montague Summers.

90. Mary Butts was omitted from Edward F. Ellis, *The British Museum in Fiction* (Buffalo, 1981), although the British Museum features in several of her stories, including 'Widdershins' and 'In Bloomsbury'.

91. She did buy her own copy of Yeats's *Per Amica Silentiae Lunae;* see below, p.466, n.76.

92. Mary Butts's transcription was accurate; see William Butler Yeats, *Per Amica Silentia Lunae* (Macmillan & Co, 1918), pp.30-31.

93. M.R. James, 'Canon Alberic's Scrap-book', in *The Ghost Stories of M.R. James* (Edward Arnold, 1974, 2nd edn.), p.1.

94. Mary Butts undated letter to Ada Briggs, end May/early June 1920.

95. Mary Butts letter to Ada Briggs, 9.6.20.

96. Mary Butts letter to Ada Briggs, 23.6.20.

97. Mary Butts letter to Ada Briggs, 10.7.20.

98. Mary Butts, 'Taking Thought', *Time and Tide,* 14, no.2 (1933), p.738.

99. Sigmund Freud, *Psychopathology of Everyday Life* (Penguin, 1938), p.197.

100. Sigmund Freud, 'The Uncanny' in *Art and Literature,* Pelican Library 14, ed. Albert Dickson (Penguin, 1985), pp.352, 363 and 365.

101. Freud, *Psychopathology of Everyday Life,* pp.195-6.

102. Ibid, p.195; Freud's italics.

103. J.E. Harrison, *Themis: A Study of the Social Origins of Greek Religion* (C.U.P., 1912), p.63.

104. Mary Butts undated letter to Ada Briggs, 21/22 July 1920.

105. Mary Butts letter to Ada Briggs, 16.7.20.

106. Mary Butts letter to Ada Briggs, 27.7.20.

107. Mary Butts, 'Change', *The Dial,* 72 (May 1922), pp.465-470.

108. Mary Butts undated letter to Ada Briggs, 4.8.20.

109. Mary Butts undated letter to Ada Briggs, postmarked 5.8.20.

110. Mary Butts undated letter to Ada Briggs, postmarked 13.8.20.

111. Mary Butts undated letter to Ada Briggs, mid-August 1920.

112. Mary Butts undated letter to Ada Briggs, Wednesday, early autumn 1920.

113. Mary Butts letter to Ada Briggs, 24.9.20.

114. For an indirect influence, see Mary Butts's discussion of Middleton Murry's essay on Dostoevsky above, p.38.

115. Edward Wadsworth was independently wealthy and may have considered buying the press; the actual machinery was a realisable asset.

116. Mary Butts undated letter to Ada Briggs, Monday, late October 1920.

117. There is controversy surrounding Camilla's date of birth. Mary Butts claimed in her diary that it was the 7 November; yet she told Camilla that it was the 11th because she remembered hearing the traffic come to a stop for the Armistice Day ceremonies...

118. Bowen, *Drawn From Life,* pp.73-74.

III : The Wild Party in London and on the Continent 1921-1925

1. On the 20 February 1918 Mary Butts had tried to articulate her dissatisfactions with John Rodker: "What analysis? Again the short circuit, the broken rhythm. A noble intellect, a noble impulse, uncorrelated—barren. His women who are to have no souls.... His demand for a temporal absolute.... Like the inconclusive anguish of Tchekov his master—Am I so far the wiser?"

2. Mary Butts letter to Ada Briggs, 13.1.21.

3. Cecil Maitland letter to Ada Briggs, postmarked 3.2.21.

4. Advice from the Rector, Clarence May, in a letter to Ada Briggs, 25.5.22.

5. Goldring, *The Nineteen Twenties*, p.193.

6. Nina Hamnett, *Laughing Torso* (Virago, 1984), p.177.

7. John Symonds, *The Great Beast: The Life and Magick of Aleister Crowley* (Mayflower Books Ltd, 1973), p.270.

8. Symonds, *The Great Beast,* p.13.

9. Robert Medley interview with Nathalie Blondel, July 1994.

10. Symonds, *The Great Beast*, p.270.

11. This unpublished play by Rodker was called "Orpheus." It is among his papers at the HRHRC.

12. The Alkmaionids were a noble family in Ancient Athens involved in rebuilding the Delphic Temple and the Eumolpidae were guardians of the Eleusian mysteries. See Jack Lindsay's comment on Mary Butts, pp.352-3.

13. *TCC*, pp.12-13.

14. In 1923 Mary Butts wrote to Douglas Goldring from Rapallo: "By the way, my dear, has there been recently published *An Anthology of English Ghost Stories,* edited, I think, by Eliot O'Donnell? If there has, could you get it for me up to 7s 6d... I want to get ideas from it.... The ghost-story is a form with which there remains a lot to do." Quoted in Goldring, *The Nineteen Twenties,* p.214.

15. Ezra Pound letter to Margaret Anderson, 21.5.21. Quoted in *POUND/The Little Review*, ed. Scott et al., p.274.

16. James Joyce undated card to Cecil Maitland, May 1921.

17. Mary Butts draft of letter to John Rodker, 1.6.21.

18. Symonds, *The Great Beast*, p.270.

19. Ibid, p.299.

20. Hamnett, *Laughing Torso,* p.177.

21. Crowley was mistaken; Cecil Maitland's initials were actually J.A.C., see p.229.

22. Symonds, *The Great Beast*, pp.299-300.

23. *The Confessions of Aleister Crowley*, ed. John Symonds and Kenneth Grant (Bantam, 1971), p.1018.

24. Ibid, p.969.

25. A fellow resident, Frank Bennett, read it on the 1 September. See Symonds, *The Great Beast*, p.310. Symonds thinks it is published at this point, although he then corrects himself; *Ashe Of Rings* was published only in 1925.

26. Mary Butts, 'Bellerophon to Anteia'. First published in *Speed the Plough* (1923). Republished in *With and Without Buttons: The Selected Stories of Mary Butts*, ed. N. Blondel (Carcanet, 1991), pp.185-187, p.186. Henceforth referred to as *WAWB.* It was also reprinted in the appendix of three stories to *The Classical Novels* (McPherson, 1994), pp.349-351.

27. *DFT*, in *TTN*, p.364.

28. See below, p.464, n.26 for Mary Butts's Yi King poem.

29. Symonds, *The Great Beast*, p.312.

30. Hamnett, *Laughing Torso*, p.177.

31. For an account of the case see Symonds, *The Great Beast*, chapter 30 'Mr Justice Swift is Surprised', pp.434-437.

32. Val's identity is unknown; she may have been Yanko Varda's partner, see above, p.62.

33. "In love with Bertrand Russell... As I have always been. Am now—Ever shall be. I shall never be so much as introduced. Couldn't stand those circles—or they me." Mary Butts, diary entry, 6.12.21.

34. The story in the States would have been 'Change' which was published in *The Dial* in May 1922. It is not clear which stories Mary Butts had published in England in 1922. (Perhaps she was referring to the inclusion of 'Speed the Plough' in *Georgian Stories 1922*.)

35. Mary Butts letter to Ada Briggs, 19.12.21.

36. Goldring, *South Lodge*, p.159.

37. Goldring, *The Nineteen Twenties*, pp.156-7.

38. Mary Butts undated letter to Douglas Goldring, August 1922. Quoted in Goldring, *The Nineteen Twenties*, p.212.

39. See Douglas Goldring, *Odd Man Out: The Autobiography of a 'Propaganda Novelist'* (Chapman & Hall, 1935), p.281.

40. *The Sketch* claimed that Alec Waugh invented the cocktail party to fill the gap in London social life between 5.30 and 7pm. There are several accounts of a party he threw at Mary Butts's maisonette at 43 Belsize Park Gardens (September 1923 or 1924). See Goldring, *The Nineteen Twenties*, p.212, and Selina Hastings, *Evelyn Waugh: A Biography* (Minerva, 1995), p.119.

41. Editor's Preface, *Georgian Stories 1922* (Chapman & Hall Ltd, 1922), p.6.

42. 'The Art of the Short Story,' *The Daily News* (24.8.22).

43. 'Georgian Stories,' *Times Literary Supplement* (6.7.22), p.440.

44. Winifred Blatchford, 'Nasty Georgian Fiction', *The Clarion* (4.8.22), p.4.

45. 'The Best Short Stories of 1922', *The Observer* (4.2.23), p.4 and 'The Short Story', *The Weekly Westminster Gazette* (9.6.23), p.20.

46. Elsa Lanchester, *Elsa Lanchester Herself* (Michael Joseph Ltd, 1983), p.66.

47. Goldring, *The Nineteen Twenties*, pp.147-8.

48. Lanchester, *Elsa Lanchester Herself*, p.65.

49. Ibid, p.67.

50. Ibid, pp.65-66.

51. Ibid, p.70.

52. Ibid, pp.67, 70.

53. Anton Dolin [Patrick Kaye], *Autobiography* (Oldbourne Book Co Ltd, 1960), p.25.

54. Ibid, p.23.

55. Mary Butts undated letter to Ada Briggs, June 1922.

56. Mary Butts undated letter to Ada Briggs, April 1922.

57. Mary Butts letter to Douglas Goldring, 9.4.22. Quoted in Goldring, *The Nineteen Twenties*, p.210.

58. Mary Butts's use of the word 'web' seems oddly reminiscent of Frazer's deployment of it in *The Golden Bough*: "Without dipping so far into the future, we may illustrate the course

which thought has hitherto run by likening it to a web woven of three different threads—the black thread of magic, the red thread of religion, and the white thread of science, if under science we may include those simple truths, drawn from observation of nature, of which men in all ages have possessed a store. ...what will be the colour of the web which the Fates are now weaving on the humming loom of time? Will it be white or red? We cannot tell. A faint glimmering light illumines the backward portion of the web. Clouds and thick darkness hide the other end", J.G. Frazer, *The Golden Bough: A Study in Magic and Religion* (Macmillan abridged edn, 1980), pp.713-714.

59. Lanchester, *Elsa Lanchester Herself*, p.65; Constance Maynard, unpublished diary entry, 15.6.12; Goldring, *South Lodge*, p.148 and *Odd Man Out*, p.281; Bowen, *Drawn From Life*, p.39; Norman, *Ezra Pound* p.197; Symonds, *The Great Beast*, p.299.

60. Mary Butts letter to Ada Briggs, 19.5.22.

61. See J.G. Lockhart, *The Life of Sir Walter Scott*, Vol I (Adam & Charles Black, 1898), pp.248-249.

62. John Milton, 'Comus', in *The Poetical Works of John Milton*, ed. Helen Darbishire (O.U.P., 1958), p.463, line 182.

63. Whilst little is known about Cecil Maitland's writing, Goldring wrote: "Cecil had made a profound study of [James Joyce's] work and had reviewed *Ulysses* in the *New Witness* of August 4th 1922. ...beyond a number of ribald verses which were never printed, this review, part of which is quoted in Herbert Gorman's *James Joyce*, is the only example of Cecil's writing which seems to have survived." Goldring then quotes an extract from this review, possibly written whilst in the Schwarzwald. See Goldring, *South Lodge*, pp.162-163.

64. William Blake, No. 11 'Of the Gates' in *For the Sexes: The Gates of Paradise*, in *Blake's Complete Writings*, ed. Keynes, p.771.

65. Mary Butts, 'In the Street', in *Speed the Plough and Other Stories* (Chapman & Hall Ltd, 1923), pp. 162, 163, 165. Henceforth referred to as *STP*.

66. See *TCC*, p.102. In his 1995 study of the village of Tyneham in Dorset, Patrick Wright is categoric that Corfe Castle is the setting for 'In the South'. See Patrick Wright, *The Village that Died for England: The Strange Story of Tyneham* (Vintage, 1996), p.84.

67. Mary Butts, 'In the South' in *STP*, pp.200-201.

68. This may have been S. Egliston Cottage in Kimmeridge which is very close to Tyneham Cap.

69. Mary Butts undated draft of letter to Tony Butts, July 1922.

70. Mary Butts undated letter to Douglas Goldring, August 1922. Quoted in Goldring, *The Nineteen Twenties*, pp.211-212

71. Douglas Goldring, 'A London Bookman's Day Book', *The Sunday Tribune* (October 1922).

72. Virginia Woolf, diary entry, 29.10.22, in *The Diary of Virginia Woolf. Volume II: 1920-1924*, ed. Anne Olivier Bell (Penguin, 1978), p.209; Virginia Woolf letter to Katherine Arnold-Foster, 29.10.22, in *The Question of Things Happening: The Letters of Virginia Woolf. Volume II: 1912-1922*, ed. Nigel Nicolson (Hogarth, 1976), p.576. Anne Olivier Bell claims that it "was probably at Carrington's suggestion that [Mary Butts] had sent her novel to Virginia Woolf to read" (op. cit., p.209). This was because in a letter to Dora Carrington on the 24 August 1922, Virginia Woolf declared: "Miss Mary Butts has never answered." (*The Question of Things Happening*, p.552.) There is no evidence amongst Mary Butts's papers to support this claim.

73. Aleister Crowley, *Diary of a Drug Fiend* (Sphere Books Ltd, 1972), p.34. Crowley states with regard to Peter Pendragon that "the worst elements in his character are drawn accurately from one, Cecil Maitland". Ibid, p.23n1.

74. Ibid, p.335. See also p.336

75. Mary Butts letter to Ada Briggs, 19.5.22.

76. 'Complete Exposure of "Drug Fiend" Author', *The Sunday Express*, (26.11.22), p.7. See also the account given in G. Hanscombe and V. Smyers, *Writing for their Lives* (Women's Press, 1987), pp.108-109.

77. See Symonds, *The Great Beast*, p.332.

78. Ethel Colburn Mayne letter to Mary Butts, 1.12.22.

79. 'Unpleasant Court Cases', *The Pall Mall Gazette* (20.12.22), p.5.

80. 'Court of Appeal', *The Times* (17.2.23), p.4.

81. Mary Butts letter to Kirk Askew, 25.2.23 (HRHRC).

82. 'Books of the Week', *The Daily Telegraph* (24.3.23), p.10.

83. *Country Life* (17.3.23)

84. '*Speed the Plough* by Mary Butts', *The Daily Express* (20.3.23).

85. 'Short Stories', *The Nation and Athenaeum*, 33, no.1 (7.4.23), p.23.

86. '*Speed the Plough*', *The Irish Times*, (29.5?.23).

87. Brodie Fraser, 'untitled', *The Sunday Times* (11.3.23). Quoted on the book jacket of *Speed the Plough*.

88. Rose Macaulay, 'Stories Old and New', *The Daily News* (12.4.23), p.7.

89. J.B. Priestley, 'Fiction', *The London Mercury*, 8, no.43 (May 1923), pp.97-99 and '*Speed the Plough* by Mary Butts', *The Bookman* 64, no.384 (Sept 1923), p.298.

90. Gerald Gould, 'New Fiction', *The Saturday Review*, 135, no.3517 (24.3.23), p.406.

91. Gerald Bullett, '*Speed the Plough* by Mary Butts', *The Challenge* (4.5.23).

92. '*Speed the Plough* by Mary Butts', *The Scotsman*, (25.6.23).

93. 'Literary Surgery', *The Liverpool Post and Mercury* (11.4.23), p.9; 'Disintegration', *The Observer* (25.3.23).

94. 'The "Georgian" Short Story', *Bolton Evening News* (22.3.23), p.3.

95. K.K., 'How to "see": Quite the Silliest thing in Short Stories', *The Evening Standard* (12.4.23), p.12; '*Speed the Plough*', *Westminster Gazette*, (28.4.23).

96. Conal O'Riordan, 'So far as I can see: Ideas in the light of Experience—Of a new author', *The New Witness* (16.3.23). O'Riordan was a playwright and novelist whose publications include *Rope Enough* (1914) and *Adam of Dublin* (1920).

97. Rose Macaulay, *The Daily News*, loc. cit.

98. Bryher, 'Recognition Not Farewell', in *ASQ*, p.3. 'Angele au Couvent' was republished in both *WAWB* and *ASQ*.

99. *The London Mercury*, loc. cit.; *The Westminster Gazette*, loc. cit.

100. *The Westminster Gazette*, loc. cit.; D.L., 'In a Napkin', *Review of Reviews*, 67 no.402 (June 1923), p.632; *The Evening Standard*, loc. cit.

101. Robert McAlmon, *Being Geniuses Together* (Martin Secker & Warburg, 1938), p.131. When McAlmon claimed he did not like 'Madonna of the Magnificat' ("I insisted that her story was a stunt, not worthy of her"), Mary Butts apparently agreed, saying to him: "Of course you are right about that story. I did it as a space-filler. The publisher thought the book too short." McAlmon, *Being Geniuses Together*, p.132. Given the months that Mary Butts spent on this story, her dismissal of it does not ring quite true.

102. A.N.M., 'A Bookman's Notes: Change for Change's Sake', *Manchester Guardian Weekly* (16.3.23), p.212.

103. Conal O'Riordan, *The New Witness*, loc. cit.

104. *The Liverpool Post and Mercury*, loc. cit.; D.L., *Review of Reviews*, loc. cit.; 'Book Banned', *Daily Courier* (16.3.23).

105. Frank Vernon, 'Books We'd like to Burn', *John Bull*, 33 no.882 (28.4.23), p.18.

106. Advertising Catalogue for Auction by Messrs. Hankinson & son, By direction of Mrs. Colville-Hyde.

107. There is an undated letter from Mary Butts to Glenway Wescott, sent while she was on holiday with Cecil Maitland in Kimmeridge, Dorset. Reprinted in *ASQ*, pp.145-146. According to the editors, this letter dates from 1923; Mary Butts and Cecil Maitland must therefore have returned to the spot they had so liked in the spring of 1921.

108. Glenway Wescott, 'The First Book of Mary Butts', *The Dial*, 75 (September 1923), pp.282-284.

109. Tony Butts undated letter to Mary Butts, late 1923.

110. Goldring, *The Nineteen Twenties*, p.177.

111. Mary Butts undated letter to Douglas Goldring, late October/early November 1923. Quoted in Goldring, *The Nineteen Twenties*, pp.212-213.

112. Goldring, *Odd Man Out*, p.281.

113. Carlos Baker, *Hemingway: The Writer as Artist* (Princeton University Press, 1963), p.17.

114. "I learned about Harold Stearns from Duff Twysden, the vivacious lady with whom Hemingway fell in love, and on whom he modeled the character of Brett Ashley in his novel, *The Sun also Rises*. She and Mary Butts were close friends, and I was Mary's friend. Mary introduced me to Duff and we got on perfectly." Glenway Wescott, Foreword to Hugh Ford, *Four Lives in Paris* (North Point Press, 1987), p.xix.

115. Mary Butts undated letter to Douglas Goldring, November/December 1923, quoted in Goldring, *The Nineteen Twenties*, pp.213-214.

116. Ford Madox Ford, quoted in Goldring, *South Lodge*, pp.144-145.

117. Goldring, *South Lodge*, p.145.

118. Mary Butts undated letter to Douglas Goldring, November 1923. Quoted in Goldring, *The Nineteen Twenties*, p.213.

119. The Pension Balestra was so popular with English and American tourists, that its card was printed in English.

120. Mary Butts undated letter to Ada Briggs, late 1923/early 1924.

121. Bryher, 'Recognition Not Farewell', in *ASQ*, p.3.

122. Tony Butts letter to Mary Butts, 12.1.24.

123. Tony Butts undated letter to Mary Butts, February 1924.

124. Tony Butts undated letter to Mary Butts, late February 1924.

125. Morley Callaghan, *That Summer in Paris* (Coward McCann, 1963), pp.89-90.

126. Goldring, *The Nineteen Twenties*, p.156.

127. Arlen J. Hansen, *Expatriate Paris: A Cultural and Literary Guide to Paris of the 1920s* (Little, Brown & Co, 1990), p.99. See also Mary Butts's 'Tune I', p.136.

128. William Carlos Williams, *The Autobiography of William Carlos Williams* (New Directions, 1967), p.211.

129. Cedric Morris painted portraits of most of his friends, including Mary Butts (1924), Rupert Doone (c. 1923), Arthur Lett-Haines (1919, 1925, 1928), Gladys Hynes (1936). For reproductions, see Richard Morphet, *Cedric Morris* (The Tate Gallery, 1984), pp.43, 98, 105, 111.

130. Bowen, *Drawn From Life*, p.120.

131. Ibid, p.121. For a rather different version of events see Harold Loeb, from his autobiography, *The Way It Was*, quoted in Alan Judd, *Ford Madox Ford* (Flamingo, 1991), p.343.

132. Daniel Halpern, 'Interview with Edouard Roditi', *Antaeus*, 2 (1971), p.104.

133. Mary Butts, 'Deosil', *the transatlantic review*, 1, no.3 (March 1924), pp.40-50; Ezra Pound letter to Ford Madox Ford, 17.5.24. Quoted in *Pound/Ford*, ed. Lindberg-Seyersted, p.77.

134. Mary Butts, 'Pythian Ode', *the transatlantic review*, 2, no.3 (September 1924), pp.235-239. Republished in *ASQ*, pp.150-154. Part of the poem is quoted in Ruth Hoberman, *Gendering Classicism: The Ancient World in Twentieth-Century Women's Historical Fictions* (State U. New York Press, 1997), p.47.

135. McAlmon, *Being Geniuses Together*, pp.170-171.

136. See Mary Butts letter to Mr Seldes (the (previous) Editor), 25.10.24 and Alyse Gregory letter to Mary Butts, 28.11.24 (Beinecke; Dial/Scofield Thayer Papers YCAL MSS 34).

137. The anthology was published simultaneously in England and America: Mary Butts, 'Speed the Plough' in *Stories from the Dial* (Jonathan Cape, 1924), pp.152-166; 'Speed the Plow', *Stories from the Dial* (Linclon MacVeagh, The Dial Press, 1924), pp.152-166.

138. Paul Morand, 'A Notable Collection', *The Dial* 78 (1925), pp.51-53.

139. See Mary Butts letter to Mr Seldes, 14.4.24 (Beinecke; Dial/Scofield Thayer Papers YCAL MSS34).

140. *The Sketch*, (4.11.25).

141. *The Diaries of Evelyn Waugh*, ed. Michael Davie (Phoenix, 1995), p.185. According to Goldring, Cecil Maitland dined with him in London on the 13 November 1924, the day the newspapers announced E.D. Morel's death. See Goldring, *The Nineteen Twenties*, pp.159-160.

142. Patrick Wright, who quotes from 'Corfe', points out that Mary Butts's term "Hollow Land" originates from William Morris's long prose narrative, 'The Hollow Land: A Tale' (1856). For his discussion of this term, see Wright, *The Village that Died for England*, pp.84-88. Mary Butts would no doubt have been amused by the following reference to a great bell "which was called Mary. Now this bell was never rung but when our House was in great danger; and it had this legend on it: WHEN MARY RINGS THE EARTH SHAKES; and indeed from this we took our war-cry, which was "'Mary rings';..." *The Collected Works of William Morris*, Introductions by his daughter May Morris, Volume 1 (Routledge/Thoemmes Press, 1992), p.264. Perhaps this was the subconscious reason why, as she noted in October 1931, "bells affect me". See p.271.

143. Some of these 'House Rhymes' were published as part of 'Selections from the [Mary Butts] Journal', ed. with introduction by Robert H. Byington and Glen E. Morgan in *Art and Literature*, 7 (winter 1965), pp.167-169.

144. It is unclear exactly when and with whom this event is supposed to have taken place.

145. The title would be changed to 'The Later Life of Theseus, King of Athens'. See p.144.

146. *The Diaries of Evelyn Waugh*, ed. Davie, p.198.

147. 'Abstruse Tales in "Best" Collection', *The Yorkshire Evening Post* (19.2.25).

148. Mary Butts, 'Deosil', in *The Best Short Stories of 1924*, ed. Edward J. O'Brien and John Cournos (Small, Maynard and Co, 1924), pp.27-37. "O'Brien had tremendous influence in determining the quality of American story. He had first published his annual collection *The Best Short Stories* as early as 1915... For many authors his assessment of quality meant acceptance not only by other little magazines but by the larger commercial publishers as well." Introduction to *A Return to Pagany 1929-1932: The History, Correspondence, and Selections from a Little Magazine*, edited by Stephen Halpert with Richard Johns (Beacon Press, 1969), pp.25, 33. In 1923 O'Brien and Cournos had entered Mary Butts's name for her stories 'Change' (1921) and 'Magic' (1922) in their 'Roll of Honour', because they were included in "a group of stories which possess, we believe, the distinction of uniting genuine substance and artistic form in a closely-woven pattern with such sincerity that they are worthy of being reprinted". Edward O'Brien and John Cournos, 'The Best British and Irish Short Stories: A Year's Survey', *The Bookman*, 63, no.376 (Jan 1923), p.202. Despite this praise, these two stories by Mary Butts are her only ones to be published in a little magazine and not reprinted.

149. 'New Fiction', *The Scotsman* (28.5.25).

150. *Cassell's Weekly* [date unknown].

151. Henry Baerlein, 'Short Stories', *The Bookman* 68, no.403 (April 1925), p.32; 'Best Short Stories 1924', *Times Literary Supplement* (20.3.25), p.385.

152. Lanchester, *Elsa Lanchester Herself*, p.62.

153. Mary Butts, 'The Later Life of Theseus, King of Athens', *The Calendar of Modern Letters* (June 1925) 1, no 4, pp.257-265. The entire journal (1925-7) was reprinted in three volumes in the 1960s: *The Calendar of Modern Letters*, eds. Edgell Rickword and Douglas Garman; new impresssion with 'A Review in Retrospect' by Malcolm Bradbury, (Frank Cass & Co., 1966).

154. 'The Magazines', *The Saturday Review*, 139, no.3633 (10.6.25), p.652.

155. Mary Butts, 'The Later Life of Theseus, King of Athens', *Georgian Stories 1927*, ed. Arthur Waugh (Chapman & Hall, 1927), pp.66-75. There were complimentary reviews of this anthology and Mary Butts in particular in 'Short Stories', *Morning Post* (25.10.27) and '*Georgian Stories 1927*', *The Nation and Athenaeum* 42, no.4 (29.10.27), p.162.

156. Ford Madox Ford, *It was the Nightingale* (Heinemann, 1934), p.317.

157. Robert McAlmon and Bryher had married on the understanding that he would get money for his publishing ventures, in return for the freedom for Bryher to be with H.D. which being married gave her from her family. In 1923, Bryher's father, Sir John Ellermann, gave McAlmon £14,000.

158. Robert McAlmon, quoted in Hugh Ford, *Published in Paris: American and British Writers, Printers, and Publishers in Paris, 1920-1939* (Garnstone Press, 1975), p.45.

159. McAlmon, *Being Geniuses Together*, p.78. McAlmon wrote an unpublished vignette-à-clef called 'History of Encounters' which featured Neil [himself], Amy [Mary Butts], Hubert [John Rodker] and Frank [Cecil Maitland]. This manuscript is now in the Beinecke. For more information and extracts see Hanscombe and Smyers, *Writing for their Lives*, pp.109-110.

160. McAlmon, *Being Geniuses Together*, p.57.

161. *AOR* in *AOROW*, p.44.

162. Ibid, p.13.

163. Ibid, p.44.

164. Ibid, p.5

165. See above, p.454, n.12.

166. *AOR* in *AOROW*, p.213.

167. Sanford J. Smoller, *Adrift Among Geniuses: Robert McAlmon, Writer and Publisher of the Twenties* (Pennsylvania State U.P., 1975), p.127.

168. John Wieners, letter published in *Floating Bear*, guest ed. Billy Linich, No.26 (1963), p.287.

169. '*Ashe of Rings* by Mary Butts', *The Manchester Guardian*, (31.7.25).

170. J.E., 'Futurism in Fiction; The Nightmare Prose of the Moderns', *The Liverpool Courier* (17.9.25).

171. Elinor Wylie (1885-1928), American poet and novelist.

172. 'The Story of a Family', *The Saturday Review* (14.8.26), p.37.

173. Cecil Boulton, 'Mary Butts' Bright Novel *Ashe of Rings*: Dostoevski served with a little Milk', *New York Evening Post* (5.6.26), p.5.

174. 'London after the War', *New York Times Book Review* (9.8.25), p.7.

175. '*Ashe of Rings*', *The Boston Transcript* (2.6.26), p.4.

176. Edwin Muir, '*Ashe of Rings* by Mary Butts', *The Calendar of Modern Letters*, 1, no.6 (Aug. 1925), pp.476-478.

177. *'Ashe of Rings* by Mary Butts', *The New Criterion*, 4 no.1, (January 1926), p.209; *The Saturday Review* (29.8.25), p.7; ibid, (14.8.26), p.37; *The Philadelphia Inquirer* (10.7.26).

178. *The Boston Transcript* loc. cit.; '*Ashe of Rings* by Mary Butts', *The Dial*, 82 (1927), p.164; Edward Fitch Hall, 'Modern Witchcraft', *New York Herald Tribune* (8.8.26), p.8.

179. *The Saturday Review* (1926) loc. cit.

180. *New York Evening Post*, loc. cit.

181. *New York Herald Tribune*, loc. cit.; *The Manchester Guardian*, loc. cit.; *The New Criterion*, loc. cit.

182. *New York Times Book Review*, loc. cit.; *New York Evening Post*, loc. cit.

183. Muir, *The Calendar of Modern Letters*, loc. cit.

184. '*Ashe of Rings*: Story of Archeology and the Remote English Countryside', *Springfield Republican* (27.6.26), p.7.

185. 'Literary Intelligence', *The London Mercury*, 12, no.71 (September 1925), p.454. *Contact Collection of Contemporary Writers* (Contact Editions, Three Mountains Press, 1925).

186. See Ford, *Published in Paris*, p.60.

187. It is unclear exactly who this refers to; perhaps Lett Haines and Cedric Morris were present at the party.

188. Evelyn Waugh, diary entry, 15.9.25. Quoted in *The Diaries of Evelyn Waugh*, ed. Davie, p.221.

189. Mary Butts must have refused to cut the story, since 'A Week-End', which has been lost, was not published in *The Dial*. It is not clear which poem was offered.

190. Marianne Moore letter to Mary Butts, 10.11.25 (Beinecke).

IV : The Years in France 1925-1930

1. Essie Robeson letter to Carl van Vechten and Fania Marinoff, 16.11.25. Quoted in Martin Bauml Duberman, *Paul Robeson* (The Bodley Head Ltd, 1989), p.94.

2. Alec Waugh, *My Brother Evelyn and Other Profiles* (Cassell & Co, 1967), p.75. Jocelyn Brooke, *Conventional Weapons* (Faber & Faber, 1961), p.147.

3. "L'hôtel Welcome, de Villefranche-sur-Mer...aux chambres bleu pale ouvertes sur le golfe ... est une source de mythes, un lieu que la jeunesse, éprise de lyrisme, devrait transformer en autel et couvrir de fleurs. Des poètes de toute sorte, de toutes les langues y vécurent et, par un simple contact de fluides, firent de l'extraordinaire petite ville dont le désordre à pic s'arrête au bord de l'eau, une véritable Lourdes, un centre de fables et d'inventions." Jean Cocteau, *Portraits Souvenirs* (Grasset, 1935), p.121.

4. On occasion Glenway Wescott and Monroe also "stayed at the Welcome Hotel, in Villefranche with co-residents that included, at various times, Mary Butts, Clive Bell, Paul Robeson and his wife, and most important for me, Jean Cocteau..." Glenway Wescott, Foreword to Hugh Ford, *Four Lives in Paris*, p.xxi. See also Robert Phelps, Introduction to *Continual Lessons: The Journals of Glenway Wescott 1937-1955*, ed. Robert Phelps with Jerry Rosco (Farrar Straus Giroux, 1990), p.xii.

5. "Your friend Robeson triumphs at Drury Lane and sings like all the celestial choirs." Tony Butts letter to Mary Butts, 13.6.28.

6. In January or February 1926 Mary Butts sat for a portrait by Eugene MacGown, but it has not survived. When Robert Byington interviewed him and asked: "Had he painted a portrait of Mary? He couldn't remember." Robert H. Byington, 'Interview with Eugene MacGown', in *ASQ*, p.41.

7. Perhaps this thought was inspired by Wallace Stevens' poem, 'Thirteen Ways of Looking at a Blackbird', *Harmonium* (1923), republished in *The Collected Poems of Wallace Stevens* (Faber, 1955), pp.92-95. *Armed with Madness* includes the phrase "fifteen ways of looking at a finch" and in Mary Butts's poem, 'Two Ways of Not Seeing the World', there is the line, "*seven* ways of looking at a piece of jade". Although she does not mention Stevens's poem, it is hard to believe that she had not read it...

8. For Eugene MacGown's account disputed by Robert Byington, see Byington, 'Interview with Eugene MacGown' in *ASQ*, p.41.

9. Mary Butts also gave the name Picus to one of her characters in *Armed with Madness* and *Death of Felicity Taverner*, because of the rich resonances, as described by Harrison: "Picus was an oracular bird, a tree guardian, a guardian of kings; he was also a king, king over a kingdom ancient and august.... In the figure of Picus are united, or rather as yet undifferentiated, king and daimon, if not god... Finally, Picus enshrines a beautiful lost faith, the faith that birds and beasts are mana other and sometimes stronger than the mana of man. The notion that by watching a bird you can divine the weather is preceded by the far more primitive notion that the bird by his mana actually makes the weather, makes and brings the rain, the thunder, the sunshine and the spring. Beasts and birds in their silent, aloof goings, in the perfection of their limited doings are mysterious still and wonderful. We speak of zoomorphic or theriomorphic or ornithomorphic *gods*, but again we misuse language. Birds are not, never were, gods; there is no definite bird-cult, but there are an infinite number of bird sanctities. Man in early days tries to bring himself in touch with bird-mana, he handles reverently bird-sanctities." Harrison, *Themis*, pp.104-110.

10. "Fallait-il le suivre dans tous ses déplacements du nord au sud, entre 1924—date de son premier séjour à Villefranche—et 1963—il quitte Santo Sospir pour la dernière fois en mars de cette année-la? Tâche impossible dans l'état actuel de nos connaissances sur la biographie de Cocteau et de surcroit assez vaine.

Le poète nous l'a souvent répété en effet: l'essentiel échappe à l'histoire—celles des peuples ainsi bien de celle des individus—même s'ils se construisent à travers elle, car 'l'histoire est faite de vérités qui deviennent à la longue des mensonges et la mythologie est faite de mensonges qui deviennent à la longue des vérités'." *Jean Cocteau et le Sud*, Notice and chronology by Pierre Caizergues (A Barthélemy, 1989), p.9.

11. This is a reference to Mary Butts's unpublished story, 'A Week-End'. See above, p.150.

12. "Plus je vais, plus je crois que l'étrange haine des surréalistes ne se contente pas d'être la haine toute simple et qu'ils y mêlent de la magie, de l'envoutement. C'est depuis leur apparition leur apparition (dada) que ma vie a commencé à prendre cet aspect invivable. Seule la prière me sauvera. Prie. Priez. Prions." Jean Cocteau letter to his mother, 1926. Quoted in Monique Lange, *Cocteau: Prince sans Royaume* (Jean-Claudes Lattès, 1989), p.21.

13. Goldring, *The Nineteen Twenties*, pp.199-200.

14. "In *Le Mot* and elsewhere he identified with the cockerel, the bird which heralds the dawn and spells out its name syllable by syllable. In his *Monologues* he quotes Apollinaire who stated that Cubism found its origin in the 16th century Italian artist Paolo di Dono whose talent for painting birds earned him the nickname Uccello (Italian for bird)."

["Dans *Le Mot* et ailleurs, il s'est identifié au coq, l'oiseau qui annonce l'heure matinale et lance son nom par bribes. Dans ses *Monologues*, il cite Apollinaire, qui déclara que le Cubisme prenait sa source chez l'artiste italien du seizième siècle Paolo di Dono, dont l'habileté à peindre des oiseaux lui valut le nom d'Uccelllo (oiseau en italien)."] William A. Emboden, *Jean Cocteau: Dessins, Peintures, Sculptures* (Nathan Image, 1989), p.37.

15. "L'ami le plus respecté qui existe". Mary Butts, 'The Little Party' (1926). The concluding words from two letters by Georges Auric (one of "Les Six" composers) to her confirm that they became close friends: "Work hard. Have fun. Dear Mary, write to your friend. [Travaillez bien. Amusez-vous. Ecrivez, ma chère Mary à votre ami.]" And: "Do not forget me. Believe in my gratitude for all you have done—and in my affection for you. [Ne m'oubliez pas. Croyez à ma gratitude pour ce que vous avez fait—et à mon affectueux souvenir.]" Georges Auric undated letters to Mary Butts, summer 1926. Despite this friendship, he (like so many of her friends), does not mention her in his autobiography, *Quand j'étais là* (Bernard Grasset, 1979).

16. It is difficult to know exactly what Cocteau meant by "vous cherchez, comme moi, les mots sculptés, pas les mots colorés."

17. Cocteau was clearly an amusing person, as Mary Butts noted in the following anecdote: "*Remember* JC as one thought, reading a tragic letter really a demand for income tax." MB, undated diary entry, Jan/Feb 1926. Monique Lange points out that Cocteau was never responsible about money ["n'entretint jamais de rapport adult avec l'argent"], Lange, *Cocteau*, p:259. This was yet another characteristic he shared with Mary Butts.

18. "L'opium se fumait beaucoup en ce temps-là, si l'on était riche, colonel ou marin. Il fut une des malédictions de la vie de Cocteau. Sa place a autant d'importance dans la biographie du poète que l'enfance, l'écriture et l'amour." Lange, *Cocteau*, p.211.

19. "Les opiomanes aiment à faire des adeptes avec qui partager ce qui'ils prennent pour le bonheur." Ibid, p.213.

20. Robert Medley interview with Nathalie Blondel, July 1994.

21. Harcourt Wesson Bull, '"Truth is the Heart's Desire"', in *ASQ*, p.56.

22. Quentin Bell, 'Robert Medley and Mary Butts', in *Elders and Betters* (John Murray, 1995), p.196.

23. The poems Mary Butts translated for Cocteau included the anonymous fifteenth-century lyric, 'I sing of a maiden', William Browne's dirge, 'On the Countess Dowager of Pembroke' (1623) and William Blake's 'Introduction' (1794) to his 'Songs of Experience'.

24. "I guess my native land can do without me for a bit, while I make the best career I can in Paris, where Jean is helping me.... As a writer, he's just getting into his form. He says good things all the time." Mary Butts undated letter to Rupert Doone, spring 1926.

25. "Malédiction sur votre traducteur. J'ai corrigé 40 pages. Il invent, il ment, il fait une recherche des mots maladroits. Il aime les guillemets. Il se passionne pour les fautes de style. Vos phrases, beau[sic], correct, élégant comme Edgar Poe se montre comme si elles avaient été trempées en melasse. J'ai beaucoup changé. Je reste votre amie fidèle et furieuse, Marie." Mary Butts undated draft of letter to Cocteau, April 1926; the mistakes are Mary Butts's.

26. Mary Butts wrote the following short unpublished poem, 'Advice of the Yi-King' [1925/6], to this effect:

> ACT WITH FIRM CORRECTNESS
> And I have acted with firm correctness.
> And it was amusing.
> And as amusing as it had been to act with complete impropriety.
> Some-day, O diamones, let it be necessary
> To indulge my senses and my heart again.

27. Poppy Vanda letter to John Rodker, 13.5.27.

28. Mary Butts letter to John Rodker, 1.5.26.

29. John Rodker letter to Mary Butts, 10.5.26.

30. Mary Butts later reviewed Arthur Weigall's *Alexander the Great* in 'Alexander the Great, the Claim to Divinity', *The Sunday Times* (24.9.33), p.10 and 'Alexander the Great', *The Bookman*, 85, no.504 (Autumn supplement), pp.78-79.

31. Robert Medley, *Drawn from The Life* (Faber, 1983), pp.68-69.

32. Robert Medley letter to Nathalie Blondel, 15.8.94.

33. McAlmon, *Being Geniuses Together*, p.59.

34. Elizabeth Sprigge and Jean-Jacques Kilm, *Jean Cocteau: The Man and the Mirror* (Victor Gollanz, 1968), p.84.

35. Maurice Sachs, quoted in Sprigge and Kilm, *Jean Cocteau*, p.85.

36. Hansen, *Expatriate Paris*, p.203.

37. James Harding, *The Ox on the Roof* (Macdonald, 1972), p.83. See also Cocteau's description of the nightclub in Pierre Chanel, *Album Cocteau* (Tchou, 1970), p.52.

38. Medley, *Drawn from the Life*, p.72.

39. See Ford, *Four Lives in Paris*, p.270.

40. 'Questionnaire', *The Little Review*, 7, no.2 (May 1929), pp.21-22. Reprinted in *ASQ*, pp.126-128. This attitude was characteristic of Mary Butts, see above, pp.64, 144.

41. Mary Butts spells his name both as Sergei and Sergey; since it is only a transliteration from the Russian, I have followed her variations.

42. Augustus John on Tony Gandarillas, quoted in Sebastian Faulks, 'Christopher Wood', in *The Fatal Englishman: Three Short Lives* (Hutchinson, 1996), p.10. See this chapter for an insightful account of the life of Christopher [Kit] Wood as well as essays by Michael Tooby and Françoise Steel-Coquet, in André Cariou and Michael Tooby, *Christopher Wood: A Painter between two Cornwalls* (Tate Gallery: St. Ives, 1997). A drawing of Christopher Wood by Jean Cocteau (undated but signed) exists in the Mary Butts archive.

43. Jeanne Bourgoint, see p.249.

44. Mary Butts, 'Avenue Montaigne', *Antaeus*, 12 (Winter 1973), pp.151-152. For a description of Gandarillas's grandiose flat which contained a "Louis XIV *lit de repos*...[and] a big open fireplace in which a fire burned all day", see Faulks, *The Fatal Englishman*, p.27.

45. I have written an article (unpublished) showing that in her story, 'Brightness Falls', Mary Butts is providing in a literary form a reply to and refutation of Freud's *Psychopathology of Everyday Life*.

46. Benvenuto [surname unknown] letter to Lett Haines, [15].6.26. TGA. 8317.1.1.174.

47. Robert Medley interview with Nathalie Blondel, July 1994.

48. *DFT*, in *TTN*, pp.314-315.

49. Bowen, *Drawn From Life*, p.157.

50. *DFT*, in *TTN*, pp.309-310.

51. "Son caracter [sic] est curieux, comme le roi de Suède, qui s'appellait 'Le Roi à deux visages'. Le[sic] plus part du temps il me rends assez malheureuse, et tout d'un coup il montre un aspect de lui-même, moitié saint, moitié enfant, moitié prince. Sur ça j'ai beaucoup joué, comme vous savez." Mary Butts undated letter to Mireille Havet, July 1928.

52. The title of the poem 'Frère Doue Amye', was inspired by the medieval French romance, *Aucassin et Nicolette*, which features the line "Soeur Douce Amye". Mary Butts studied this anonymous poem when in Villefranche in the spring of 1927.

53. This image was very like Mary Butts's diary entry of 11.2.22; see above, p.110.

54. "'Comme vous aimez vous plaigner, Marie.' ...'Surement, vous m'avez enguelée trop. Comme vous ne savez pas tirer les belles choses des gens.'" Mary Butts, diary entry, September 1926.

55. Harcourt Wesson Bull,'"Truth is the Heart's Desire"', in *ASQ*, p.61.

56. Medley, *Drawn from the Life*, p.104.

57. "I suppose I should explain what Russia means to us...Dostoevski, Turgenev, Sologub, Chekhov. Every variation of the Ballet, and what I have seen during my life of your people. Your first batch of exiles and their successors in such remarkable opposition. Odd by-product of the victory of principles, this crowd of émigré boys." Mary Butts, *Imaginary Letters* (At the Sign of the Black Manikin, 1928). Republished by Talonbooks in 1979 with an Afterword by Robin Blaser. Most recently republished in *AOROW*, p.236. Henceforth referred to as *IL* in *AOROW*.

58. Although the date printed on the story is Autumn 1924.

59. Gertrude Stein was also interested in Whitehead's work, see *Autobiography of Alice B. Toklas* (Penguin, 1983 (originally published 1933)), pp.158-9.

60. Robin Blaser, Afterword, *Imaginary Letters* (Talonbooks, 1979) , p.75.

61. *IL* in *AOROW*, p.236.

62. Benvenuto [surname unknown] letter to Lett Haines, 7.12.26. TGA. 8317.1.1.175.

63. This term suggested by Ian Patterson in his unpublished doctorate aptly encapsulates the elusive form of *Imaginary Letters*.

64. Whilst they may not have liked each other a great deal, Mary Butts and Virginia Woolf always read each other's books. In 1919 Mary Butts read *Night and Day* and in October 1928 she noted: "damn style in Virginia Wolfe's [sic] *Common Reader*, where exquisite sentences float by round no single concept, or group of concepts." See also pp.337, 434.

65. Goldring, *South Lodge*, p.153.

66. "Comme je suis changé. J'étais comme un appartement en désordre, et vous entrez, et m'avez fait les portes en crystal qui donnent sur un jardin plein de belles choses. Maintenant, j'ai de l'air." Sergei Maslenikof to Mary Butts. Mary Butts, undated diary entry, late October 1926.

67. Mary Butts used the term 'knight's move' frequently: "At dinner she sat between the man who had invited them and his brother. Neither of them spoke to her. ...she...talked at an angle like a knight's move with the archaeologist's wife." 'The Dinner-Party' in *Several Occasions* (Wishart & Co, 1932), p.62; In *Death of Felicity Taverner* Scylla Taverner quickly realises that there is an "oblique help in Boris". If he is able to save them and their land, it is because he understands the oblique forces which are acting through Nick Kralin, who has "learned the attack which looks as though it were part of a different war about something else; and [whose]

move is like the knight's move in chess". *DFT*, in *TTN*, pp.167, 318. "...things to be crossed to get out/ Corners in chess the knights turn." 'Rites de Passage'(1931); In 'Ghosties and Ghoulies', her study of supernatural fiction, Mary Butts described this term which conveys "the interaction of other worlds with ours" and praised E.M. Forster's supernatural tales for the very fact that "Mr Forster knows the knight's move, its oblique turns in human adventure." 'Ghosties and Ghoulies' II, *The Bookman*, 83, no.497 (February 1933); IV, *The Bookman*, 84, 499 (April 1933). Similarly, "Colonel Buchan knows the first law—for whatever it may mean, the law is there—of the interaction of other worlds with ours; that it can be somehow described by a parallel with the knight's move in chess. The other moves are comparable with ordinary activities. Only the knights move two squares and a diagonal, on and sideways and can jump." 'Ghosties & Ghoulies' II, *The Bookman*, 83, no.497 (February 1933). Republished in AOROW. Henceforth referred to as 'G&G' in *AOROW*, p.347; p.364; p.347. In a sense this corresponds with her 1921 description of the artist "as the true, because the oblique, adept". See above, p.100.

68. This may well have been John William Navin Sullivan's *The Bases of Modern Science* (Ernest Benn, 1928).

69. Mary Butts letter to Hugh Ross Williamson, 1934. Quoted in *ASQ*, pp.148-149.

70. *AOR* in *AOROW*, p.20.

71. "'Dear, delightful Mary Butts' exclaims Sisley Huddleston without further elaboration, and his tantalizingly brief reference is characteristic of many, many more." Byington and Morgan, 'Mary Butts', p.163.

72. See Stella Bowen letters to Ford Madox Ford, 9.11, 22.11, 30.11.26. On the 25 January 1927 she wrote: "On Sunday the Storrs with Monica & Ionides, Mary with Camilla, & Ann Drake with Betsy, all came to the studio to play with Julie. My Sundays for children are getting quite famous, & I have got into quite an easy system of running them." Quoted in *The Correspondence of Ford Madox Ford and Stella Bowen*, ed. Stang and Cochran, pp.218, 232, 242, 305.

73. This pet name for Camilla came from the Edmund Spenser's *The Shepheardes Calendar* (1579):
Cuddie, the prayse is better than the price,
The glory eke much greater than the gayne.

74. See p.389 where Mary Butts feels that Cecil Maitland has found peace.

75. Virgil Thomson, *Virgil Thomson* (Knopf, 1966), pp.86-87. Thomson inscribed a copy of his autobiography for Camilla Bagg "whom I remember as a very pretty child and in memory of the imperishable Mary Butts".

76. W.B. Yeats *Per Amica Silentiae Lunae* (Macmillan, 1918), p.69. Mary Butts underlined the words in her own copy. (I am very grateful to Andrew Crozier for sending me the relevant passages.)

77. There would be other such occasions: "TE [Tommy Earp] and I were in touch over Cecil. Conversation to-day and he said that a book left below in the book-case of the little Foyot salon, *The Power House* [(1916)] by John Buchan was tolerable because of its decent writing and a favourite of Cecil's. So I stole it and read it in swallows between callers." Mary Butts, diary entry, June 1927.

78. *The Macedonian* (Heinemann, 1933). Republished in *The Classical Novels*. All page references from this edition, henceforth referred to as *TM*, in *TCN*, p.4.

79. Goldring, *The Nineteen Twenties*, p.216.

80. No doubt Mary Butts was thinking of Saki's story, 'The Unrest-Cure':

"What you want," said the friend, "is an Unrest-cure."

"An Unrest-Cure? I've never heard of such a thing."

"You've heard of Rest-cures for people who've broken down under stress of too much worry and strenuous living; well, you're suffering from overmuch repose and placidity, and you need the opposite kind of treatment."

Saki, 'The Unrest-Cure', originally in *The Chronicles of Clovis*, (1911). Reprinted in *The Short Stories of Saki (H.H. Munro)*, with an introduction by Christopher Morley (John Lane, The Bodley Head Ltd, 1956 reprint (1930)), p.149. In one of her stories Mary Butts has a character reflect on the "death of Saki's Clovis and Comus Bassington". 'A Lover', in *Last Stories*. Reprinted in Mary Butts, *From Altar to Chimney-piece: Selected Stories*, preface by John Ashbery (McPherson & Co, 1992), pp.172-191, p.183. Henceforth referred to as *FATCP*.

81. Mary Butts, 'Two ways of not seeing the world', 'Thinking of Saints', 'Parenthesis', 'Corfe', 'Heartbreak House' and 'Avenue Montaigne', *Antaeus*, 12 (1973), Introduction by Glen E. Morgan, pp.140-150.

82. "A small hotel up above near G[lenway] and M[onroe], and much better and cheaper than the Welcome". ["Un petit hotel en haut près de G et M, beaucoup mieux que le Welcome et moins cher."] Mary Butts undated draft of letter to Jean Cocteau, late March 1927.

83. Thomson, *Virgil Thomson*, p.86. The misconception about Mary Butts is similar to that which her acquaintance, C.R.W. Nevinson, felt the need to defend himself against in his autobiography: "It might be imagined that my life had been all fun, associating as I was on the one hand with actors, clowns, dancers, 'society people', men-about-town, and on the other with extremists who were reacting against puffy vulgarians stagnating in complacency and commercial expediency. Actually I was a serious, and even a grim, hard-worker, often doing eighteen hours on end and sometimes painting as many as three pictures a day. ...work has always been my lodestar." C.R.W. Nevinson, *Paint and Prejudice* (Methuen, 1937), p.65.

84. Mary Butts's "lever" seems to have been another term for the "yardstick" of sophrosynê, which she described in 1917, see above, p.48 . She wrote the poem, 'Heartbreak House', at this time in which she described the "tall tight boys" which made up her new aristocracy. See p.214

85. This quotation comes from an essay by R. Ellis Roberts; see pp.363-4.

86. *TCC*, p.275.

87. Thomson, *Virgil Thomson*, p.86.

88. Mary Butts undated draft of letter to Tony Butts, Spring 1927.

89. 'Juan-les-Pins' was included in the manuscript of poems Mary Butts sent to the publisher, Edward Titus, in 1928, see p.212.

90. "The effect of the south on the poet's sensibility was to refine it to such an extent that he was transported to the very heart of Greek mythology which is the greatest. 'Sea-air which inspires poetry explains the lyricism of the Greeks,' wrote Cocteau to his mother from the Lavandou in May 1922." ["Car le sud aiguise, de son propre aveu, la sensibilité du poète, au point de le mettre de plain-pied au coeur de la grande mythologie: entendez la grècque. 'L'air de mer qui excite à la poésie explique le lyrisme grec,' écrit-il à sa mere de Lavandou, en mai 1922."] Caizergues, *Jean Cocteau et le Sud*, p.10.

91. Thomson, *Virgil Thomson*, pp.86-7.

92. Sir Paul Harvey, *Oxford Companion to Classical Literature* (O.U.P., 1984), p.447. The *Sortes Virgilianae* also figure in a story by M.R. James. See 'The Ash-Tree' (1904) in *The Ghost Stories of M.R. James*, pp.61-62.

93. Peggy Guggenheim, *Out of this Century* (André Deutsch, 1979), p.62.

94. Ibid, p.68.

95. Mary Butts may well have chosen the title 'The House-Party' in deference to her love for the ballet, since it was the English translation given to *Les Biches*, Diaghelev's ballet, composed by Francis Poulenc with costumes by Marie Laurencin. It was first performed in 1924. See Buckle, *Diaghelev*, pp.417-419, 453.

96. Mary Butts draft of letter to Virgil Thomson, 23.7.27.

97. Guggenheim, *Out of this Century*, p.74.

98. Ibid, p.73.

99. Mary Butts described this most westerly coast of France in 'Two Land's Ends', *The Manchester Guardian* (28.5.34), p.9.

100. Mary Butts undated letter to Douglas Goldring, late summer 1927, quoted in Goldring, *The Nineteen Twenties*, pp.216-217. She also sent a postcard to Virgil Thomson, dated the 30 August 1927 on which she declared: "Never attend a pardon!" In Virgil Thomson Papers at the Yale University Music Library.

101. The suicide of Val Goldsmith's wife was reported in an article in *The Observer* (5.12.27).

102. For more information about money Thomson lent to her, see Mary Butts undated letter to Virgil Thomson, 1927. In Virgil Thomson Papers at the Yale University Music Library.

103. As a basis for comparison, the English painter, Christopher (Kit) Wood, was smoking five to six pipes each evening by November 1928. (Cocteau introduced him to this habit, which despite its Greek name, Nepenthe, meaning 'destroyer of grief', caused a great deal of anguish.) See Faulks, *The Fatal Englishman*, pp.70, 88.

104. 'Picus Martius: Here lies the Woodpecker who was Zeus', *Hound & Horn* 3, no.2 (Jan-Mar 1930), pp.230-232. It was one of Mary Butts's poems to be published in Dr Bhat's *Soma* (1932). See pp.293-4.

105. Marianne Moore letter to Mary Butts, 2.11.27 (Beinecke).

106. Richard Johns, announcing *Pagany*, quoted in *A Return to Pagany*, ed. Halpert with Johns, p.40.

107. Ibid, p.20.

108. Cecil Rickword, who died in an accident in 1931, was actually Edgell's cousin.

109. Harcourt Wesson Bull may well be thinking of Mary Butts's poem 'Corfe', ['A poem to Keep People out of Dorset'], which includes the lines:

> Turn back our folk from it, we hate the lot
> Turn the American and turn the Scot;
> Make unpropitious the turf, the dust
> If the sea doesn't get 'em then the cattle must.

110. Harcourt Wesson Bull, '"Truth is the Heart's Desire"', in *ASQ*, p.65.

111. Humphrey Carpenter, *Geniuses Together* (Unwin Hyman, 1987), p. 199. The source for Carpenter's quotation was McAlmon's memoir, *Being Geniuses Together*, and referred to a conversation between himself, Mary Butts and Scott Fitzgerald whilst crossing the channel to France in the mid-1920s. See McAlmon, *Being Genuises Together*, p.203. Elsewhere in his memoir, McAlmon declared: "Mary breathed in an exalted ecstacy of being. 'My lamb,' she would sigh. 'You clean, pure, young American. You are a gentleman, one of us, but you don't know the depths, the depravity of Europe. There are sinister forces, there is a black cloud gathering to overwhelm us all, and we must combat it with the good, the pure, the sweet, and the true." *Being Geniuses Together*, pp.78-79.

112. Mary Butts, 'Americans on England: Pilgrims of the Past', *The Sunday Times* (2.2.36), p.13.

113. Mary Butts, 'Mappa Mundi', in *WAWB*, p.189. Of course Mary Butts is not alone in presenting this difference between Americans and Europeans, a subject central to the work of Henry James and Edith Wharton amongst others.

114. Mary Butts, *Armed With Madness* (Wishart & Co, 1928; republished in 1932). The novel was reprinted in *The Taverner Novels* (1992). All page references are to this edition, henceforth referred to as *AWM*, in *TTN*, pp.23 and 15.

115. John Ashbery wrote the Preface to *From Altar to Chimney-piece*, the 1992 American edition of stories by Mary Butts. For Mary Butts's influence on Frank O'Hara's and John Wieners' poetry see John Wieners, untitled review, *Floating Bear*, 26 (1963), p.287; John Wieners, 'Klugwerth' in *Selected Poems 1958-1984*, ed. Raymond Foye (Black Sparrow Press, 1986), p.245;

Frank O'Hara, 'Cantata' in *The Collected Poems of Frank O'Hara*, ed. Donald Allen (Knopf, 1972), p.489 (see epigraph, p.433). Furthermore, O'Hara's poem 'Blue Territory' was originally entitled 'For Mary Butts', see O'Hara, *Collected Poems*, p.539.

116. See p.435.

117. Stella Bowen letter to Ford Madox Ford, 18.11.27. Quoted in *The Correspondence of Ford Madox Ford and Stella Bowen*, ed. Stang and Cochran, p.355.

118. See Mary Butts undated letter to Virgil Thomson, 11.12.27. In Virgil Thomson Papers at the Yale University Music Library.

119. "JC said: 'Virgil, c'est un type qui a rien à faire, ce sont ces gens la qui font les scenes...cres [sic] les difficultés...imaginent les pieges qui n'existent pas.'" Mary Butts, undated diary entry, late November 1927.

120. It is uncertain what the "books" might be. Boni had certainly published *Ashe of Rings* (1926) and would publish *Armed with Madness* (1928). Perhaps they were considering a volume of stories or poems. See p.216.

121. Lion Feuchtwanger, *The Ugly Duchess: A Historical Account* (Martin Secker, Nov. 1927). Trans. by Willa and Edwin Muir from 1926 German edition. Mary Butts would later review Feuchtwanger's *Josephus* in '*Josephus*', *The Bookman*, 83, no.496 (January 1933), p.405.

122. See Mary Butts's letter to Douglas Goldring from the Hotel Antipolis, quoted in Goldring, *The Nineteen Twenties*, pp.217-218. One of Mary Butts's life-maps could be stretched between Vauban's fortresses, from the one she watched being destroyed in Brest in the summer of 1927 to this one in Antibes and the one in St Malo in Nov 1929.

123. A fact she incorporated into her poem, 'Waiting'; see p.184.

124. McAlmon, *Being Geniuses Together*, p.264.

125. In 'A Lover', Alan Courcy describes Anne Clavel as "Anna Perenna, the moon-in-and-out...the Moon-Woman". Mary Butts, 'A Lover', in *FATCP*, pp.177-181. See also her story-cycle, 'What the Moon Saw', p.307.

126. Douglas Garman quoted in Jack Lindsay, *Fanfrolico and After* (The Bodley Head, 1962), p.138.

127. Whilst staying at the Hotel Antipolis, Mary Butts declared that she had written "several poems, and another of my perennial worryings at the origin of the Greek Civilisation; a fruitful one this time, only I haven't half the books I need." Mary Butts undated letter to Douglas Goldring, January 1928, quoted in *The Nineteen Twenties*, pp.217-218. 'On An American Wonder-Child who Translated Homer at Eight Years Old' was first published in 1933, see p.294.

128. See Frazer's discussion of the concept of 'sympathetic magic' in *The Golden Bough*, pp.11-20.

129. As she paraphrased from Shakespeare's play, *Richard II* (Act 2, scene iii, line 171): "Things past redress may be 'now for me past care'. But not thank God, past curiosity." Mary Butts, diary entry, April 1928.

130. Mary Butts undated draft of letter to H.G. Wells, early February 1928.

The editors, Kenneth Irby and Christopher Wagstaff, claim in *A Sacred Quest* that in 1918 Mary Butts was responsible for the translation of and introduction to *Dieu L'Invisible Roi* by H.G. Wells. See *ASQ*, p.252. This mistake is understandable given that the translator's name was *Marie* Butts. However, the latter was an established French writer, editor and translator by the 1910s (her works include *Roland le Vaillant Paladin*, *Au Temps des Chevalier* and *Héros! Episodes de la Grande Guerre* as well as several other translations of books by Wells). A similar confusion has arisen regarding the French translation by Marie Butts of Ford Madox Hueffer [Ford]'s collection of essays, *Between St Dennis and St George*. See Alan Judd, *Ford Madox Ford* (Flamingo, 1991), p.286; *The Correspondence of Ford Madox Ford and Stella Bowen*, ed. Stang and Cochran, p.46. This translation was already in existence by July 1916 (see Max Saunders, *Ford*

Madox Ford: A Dual Life (O.U.P., 1995), p.494). In these essays Hueffer "set out to confront various pacifist writers or other writers who were opposed to the Government of this country entering upon a war side by side with France". Preface to *Between St Dennis and St George: A Sketch of Three Civilisations* (Hodder & Stoughton, 1915), p.v. The confustion may have arisen in part from a letter attributed to Mary Butts in the Special Collection at Cornell University Library, dated 24.7.16, in which the writer hopes that Ford likes her translation. This letter is, however, by *Marie* Butts. Notwithstanding the fact that Mary Butts had probably not met Ford by 1916, it would have been very highly improbable for her to translate such a pro-war publication when working for the NCCL. Also, her French would hardly have been good enough at the time!

131. "He [JC] said: 'ca vaut la peine d'avoir écrit quelque chose en ce que j'ai écrit m'a trouvé Jean Desbordes' I said, 'Dear Jean, wish a Jean Desbordes for me.'" Mary Butts, diary entry, February 1928.

132. Until, a few years later, W.H. Auden wrote his wonderful poem *Night-mail* (1935), commissioned by the G.P.O.

133. A reference to the sculpture of Nina Hamnett by Gaudier-Brzeska done in the 1910s. Hamnett called the first volume of her autobiography *Laughing Torso* (1932).

134. Francis Rose, *Saying Life: The Memoirs of Sir Francis Rose* (Cassell, 1961), p.58.

135. See Goldring, *The Nineteen Twenties*, pp.232, 240.

136. On the 19 April 1928, Mary Butts recorded in her diary the "exquisite pleasure, dressing with the proper tools again, creams, essences, lipsticks of orange wood, frozen scent, orange-down puffs, canary sponges".

137. Harcourt Wesson Bull, '"Truth is the Heart's Desire"', in *ASQ*, p.53.

138. Harcourt Wesson Bull's title is a quotation from Mary Butts's 1924 poem, 'Pythian Ode':

Truth is the heart's desire.
A stone instead of the heart's desire
Is given you for truth.
Truth is a mean between extremes.
Be comforted.

139. Harcourt Wesson Bull, '"Truth is the Heart's Desire"', in *ASQ*, pp.86-7.

140. Ibid, p.56.

141. Insight into the significance of Mary Butts's relationship with Mireille Havet would have been impossible, had it not been for the generosity of Dominique Tiry, who provided photocopies of Havet's journal and letters between the two women. I am very grateful also for the time and trouble she took in our subsequent discussions and correspondence. Dominique Tiry had Mireille Havet's papers because her grandmother, Ludmila Savitzky, had informally adopted Havet. Close friends with her at that time, Mary Butts sent a copy of her *Imaginary Letters* with a dedication to Ludmila Savitzky in June 1929. By a strange coincidence which would have appealed to Mary Butts, Savitzky had translated Rodker's novel, "Switchback" (see p.448, n.13), and her daughter, Marianne, became his third wife. As a result letters belonging to both Mary Butts and John Rodker were amongst Dominique Tiry's papers.

142. According to Mary Butts's diary, she had met Mireille Havet in Tréboul the previous summer.

143. Mary Butts's family motto read: *Soyez sage et simple* (Be wise and simple). In June 1928 she gave Harcourt Wesson Bull a photo of herself on which she drew her crest and motto. See also p.377.

144. Eugene MacGown interviewed by Robert Byington in *ASQ*, p.38.

145. "J'ai rêvé de Norma et de son retour à Paris—Nous sortions ensemble—...et je battais Norma avec une bougie qui se cassait en deux. Puis nous dinions ensemble au cimetière de Passy entre les tombes voilées d'herbes folles." Mireille Havet, diary entry, 16.9.29. (Cocteau)

146. Mireille Havet, 'Carnaval', in *Les Oeuvres Libres*, 17 (1922), pp.251-344, pp.252-253.

147. "...la lourde charge que je peux être... Je n'accepte—ni ne supporte *quand je suis là* ...que l'on m'oublie—Je veux être beaucoup ou rien!" Mireille Havet letter to Mary Butts, 13.6.28.

148. "C'est vraiment ce calme-ci—ce cadre-ci—cette chambre-ci—cette vue directe sur la mer et mon cher Cap Ferrat sans faubourgs ni trop de toits intermédiaires—qu'il me faudrit ... V.—des attaches particulières pour moi ... depuis 8 ans j'aime et je connais V—j'y fais hélas des séjours de plus en plus courts et intermittents—mais c'est malgré tout là ... dans ce vieux pays que j'ai laissé quelque chose et quelque chose que je comprends être maintenant de mon vivant et différent et sans rapport." Mireille Havet, diary entry, 3pm, 13.6.28. (Cocteau)

149. "Et depuis la vague amitié et tendresse de Germaine—il y a eu Mary—oh rien de trouble—beaucoup moins qu'avec Germaine certes! mais la douceur bouleversante dans la franchise et sincérité non déguisée ni réprimée de 2 nuits côte à côte—dans la chaleur et la fraternité d'un corps aimé...et le silence d'une petite chambre—ou seul—le ciel clair de la nuit confie le clair de lune—nous regardait par la paupière à demi soulevée de ces volets d'ici—la douceur—de deux bras noués chastement et si tendrement à la fois autour de moi et sous ma joue... Ayant ce sommeil à deux...ds les bras de Mary—que je n'avais jamais imaginée si délicatement tendre...je n'avais jamais songé que je pourrais passer 2 nuits et parmi les plus douces de ma vie même..." Mireille Havet, diary entry, 30.5.28. (Cocteau)

150. "Je trouverai un moyen un jour de vous remercier pour certaines des plus belles heures de ma vie." Mary Butts undated letter to Mireille Havet, 20.6.28.

151. "...je n'aime nullement Mary d'amour—il y en ait pas question une seconde ni pr elle—ni pr moi..." Mireille Havet, diary entry, 30.5.28. (Cocteau)

152. "Si je rêve communiquer avec vous...autrement tout de même que par mon corps, pour ce qu'il nous arrive...en ce moment parce que je ne *peux pas vous parler.* Je ne peux pas vous en parler, et je sens qu'il ne faut pas que je m'y oblige et ne brise avant son temps, le silence inoui—la paie miraculeuse et entièrement nouvelle pour moi qui nait dans vos bras...qui nous enferme dans la nuit, comme une cage magique, un cercle tracé autour de notre bonheur... Mon bien, Mary...c'est le ciel vraiment qui vous a envoyée sur ma route—et je le crois que c'est Dieu lui même—sans aucune profanation—qui m'a mise dans vos bras à vous..." Mireille Havet letter to Mary Butts, 10.30pm, 4.6.28.

153. Eugene MacGown quoted in interview with Byington, *ASQ*, p.38.

154. Mireille Havet described these three volumes in a letter to Lud Savitsky (dated "Easter Monday, 9th April 31—I think") as follows: "*The Islands*—Non-fictional accounts of the Greek and Roman landscapes of the South; *Past Times*: A volume of reminiscences—dedicated to mother—about people I knew as a child; and finally the book...about the Maleissyes—and which will probably be eponymous...? which is too beautiful, too much about them not to give it a very plain title such as *My Friends the Maleissyes*—(??)" [" le lundi de pâcques 9 avril 31—je crois... *Les Iles*—volume pur d'intrigue et uniquement de paysages grecs et latins du Sud; Un volume de souvnirs [sic] sur ceux que j'ai connus, enfant, à *la mémoire de Maman*: *Les Saisons Passées*; et enfin le livre...sur les Maleissye—et qui portera sans doute leur nom...? qui est trop beau, trop eux pour ne pas le mettre ds un titre tres simple comme *Mes Amis Maleissye*—(??)".]

155. 'A Small Town', Mary Butts's unpublished essay on Villefranche, see above, p.153.

156. "Je n'admets pas 5 minutes la supposition odieuse et absurde pour moi que Mary—soit partie sans me revoir—sans seulement me faire signe—me dire au revoir... Elle n'est pas folle—elle ne m'aime pas d'amour et ne me craint pas comme hélas mon pauvre Robbie—je n'admets pas—je ne peux admettre et cependant je tremble d'inquiétude—et suis bouleversée d'une angoisse—d'une crainte réelle. Ah si Mary—mon amie que je croyais cette fois—amie et fidèle de coeur et d'esprit—Si Mary a fait cela—ose faire cela—à bas l'Angleterre... Mary, est-il vrai que vs m'ayez quittée sans me revoir—si cela est vrai—en effet—vous ne me reverrez plus..." Mireille Havet, diary entry, 1am, Wed 20.6.28. (Cocteau)

157. "Mireille, si vous consentez d'être patiente avec moi, nous aurons une tres belle amitié. Les choses s'arrangeront 'magiquement' pour nous. (Je connais plus des arrangements magiques que vous.)" Mary Butts undated letter to Mireille Havet, late June 1928.

158. "Revenez à Paris—reprenez votre travail. (Tous que j'écris me semble si dur). Mais vous êtes si douée, si fière, si belle, si adorable, si bien née, que vous devez être dur avec vous même." Mary Butts undated letter to Mireille Havet, late June/early July 1928.

159. "Ma Mireille:

Ecoutez, chérie et n'oubliez pas comme c'est difficile de vous répondre en français.

Premièrement beaucoup de ce que vous avez écrit est *illisible*. Mais vous m'est si chère que je comprends par une espèce de divination, et surtout je sais que vous êtes fachée avec moi à cause de mon départ à Paris.

Mireille, je suis une amie loyale à vous. Mes jours et mes nuits sont pleins des pensée de vous. Mais 'small love' vous avez su, depuis le commencement, que j'étais forcée de revenir à Paris le plus vite possible. C'était à cause de vous que j'avais resté si long là bas, pour le plaisir esquis de votre compagnie.

Mais, pensez un moment sur ma situation. Je suis écrivain...je suis mère de Camilla...mon devoir...est de mener une vie très réglée ici, de travailler régulièrement, reprendre toutes mes relations avec les éditeurs et les gens qui pourraient être utile pour moi." Mary Butts undated letter to Mireille Havet, July 1928.

160. Marianne Moore, 'A House-Party', *The Dial*, 85 (Sept 1928), pp.258-260; republished in *The Complete Prose of Marianne Moore*, ed. Patricia C. Willis (Faber, 1987), p.147.

161. *AWM*, in *TTN*, p.9.

162. In addition to the 'ordinary' print-run of *Armed with Madness*, Wishart published a deluxe edition in 1928, printed on hand-made paper and limited to a hundred copies. This edition was illustrated with three drawings by Jean Cocteau: his earlier line drawing of Mary Butts (done in 1926 or 1927) and two sketches, 'Je suis un mensonge qui dit toujours la vérité' (I am a lie which always speaks the truth), 'La vérité du jeu d'échecs' (the truth of chess). Wishart also reissued the novel in a cheaper edition in 1932. On the dust jacket of the A.& C. Boni edition, it was claimed that Mary Butts was born in 1891 (rather than 1890)—the myth continued... It is uncertain exactly who the dedicatees were, but they may well have been her friends, Peter Morris and Paul Odo Cross. Cedric Morris painted a portrait of Cross in 1925. See Richard Morphet, *Cedric Morris*, p.61.

163. Elizabeth Madox Roberts letter to Messrs. Albert and Charles Boni, 3.6.28. The American writer, Elizabeth Madox Roberts (1886-1941), had work published in *The Dial*, where (as he had done for Mary Butts's first book in 1923) Glenway Wescott reviewed 'Miss Roberts' First Novel' in July 1927.

164. 'Sophisticated Fantasy', *New York Times Book Review* (13.5.28), p.9.

165. *The Complete Prose of Marianne Moore*, ed. Willis, p.147.

166. 'New Fiction: Entanglements not easily untied: Tales of sorts', *Morning Post* (17.7.28); Eugene Lohrke, 'Cups and Spears', *New York Herald Tribune* (10.6.28), p.16; Gerald Gould, 'Novelists and a Humorist: Queer Birds', *News Chronicle* (18.6.28).

167. '*Armed with Madness*. A Novel. By Mary Butts', *The New Age* 43, no.1866 (14.6.28), p.83. This parody of Mary Butts's style makes her sound more like Gertrude Stein.

168. '*Armed with Madness* by Mary Butts', *Aberdeen Free Press* (14.5.28).

169. *New York Times Book Review*, loc. cit.

170. 'Butts (Mary) *Armed with Madness*', *The Librarian* (July 1928).

171. Libbian Benedict, 'Decadence in England', *New York Sun* (26.5.28).

172. Lohrke, *New York Herald Tribune*, loc. cit.; Mary Shirley, 'Join the Ladies', *Time Magazine* (22.8.28).

173. *New York Times Book Review*, loc. cit.

174. '*Armed with Madness* by Mary Butts', *Times Literary Supplement* (24.5.28), p.397.

175. Lohrke, *New York Herald Tribune*, loc. cit.; *A de S.*, '*Armed with Madness* by Mary Butts', *The Manchester Guardian* (15.6.28), p.7; Shirley, *Time Magazine*, loc. cit.

176. *Aberdeen Free Press*, loc. cit.

177. Benedict, *New York Sun*, loc. cit.

178. 'A Psychological Study', *Natal Mercury* (18.6.28); Lohrke, *New York Herald Tribune* loc. cit.; *Morning Post*, loc. cit.

179. Gould, *News Chronicle*, loc. cit.

180. *The Complete Prose of Marianne Moore*, ed. Willis, p.148.

181. Mary Butts undated draft of letter to Mary Colville-Hyde, May 1928.

182. Harcourt Wesson Bull, '"Truth is the Heart's Desire"', in *ASQ*, p.58; see also Douglas Goldring's description above, p.172, and Mary Butts's inclusion of the Man Ray sculpture in her poem, 'Frère Doue Amye' above, p.173.

183. A pun on Kolle's name sounding like 'collar' as faux-col means false collar and the 'head' or froth on the top of a beer.

184. Harcourt Wesson Bull, '"Truth is the Heart's Desire"', in *ASQ*, pp.59-61.

185. Mary Butts submitted a manuscript to the Hogarth Press in 1927. On the 7 August Virginia Woolf noted "The Press is going on. Novels are the great bloodsuckers.... So in the past two days I have rejected Butts." *The Diary of Virginia Woolf: Volume 3 1925-1930*, ed. Anne Olivier Bell (Penguin, 1980), p.150. The editor suggests that it was the manuscript of *Armed with Madness*; it could however, just as easily be that of *Imaginary Letters*.

186. Tony Butts undated letter to Mary Butts, autumn 1928.

187. Mary Butts undated letter to Edward Titus, Autumn 1928 (Buffalo).

188. "Existe-t-il de l'amour autre que son amour? Il y à des heures d'amour rien que sur mon papier. Où es-tu toi qui saurais aimer comme j'aime avec mon encre?" Jean Desbordes, 'La Faiblesse des Forts', *J'adore* (Bernard Grasset, 1928), p.163.

189. "Celui qui n'aime pas, qui n'adore pas suivant son coeur et son sens a seul besoin du pain leger de notre Maison l'Eglise.
La prudence du coeur insulte Dieu. Dieu a-t-il donne la secheresse comme regle de son amour? Dieu donne l'amour parce qu'il est amour aveugle."
Desbordes, 'Suite aux Coulisses d'Antigone', *J'adore*, p.132.

190. "Le sexe n'entre pas dans les lois de l'amour, mais le sexe est amour parce qu'il est vie et chaleur et simplicité. Il se donne, il exalte, et l'état où il met les êtres est un état d'ange extenue, d'ange tout de même.... Savoir que d'aimer l'amour c'est aimer Dieu et gouter son calme sur une épaule.
Il vous poussera des ailes et vos mains confondront les anges avec les hommes."
Desbordes, 'La Faiblesse des Forts', *J'adore*, p.164.

191. See John Ashbery, Preface to *FATCP*, p.xii.

192. Mary Butts is referring to the jury she sat on in December 1922, see above, pp.123-4.

193. *AWM*, in *TTN*, p.92.

194. "Sous mes cuisses, la terre cedait pour laisser pénetrer mon corps dans son corps.... Mon corps entourait la terre et la terre emplissait ma nuit." Desbordes, 'L'amour au Jardin Solitaire', *J'adore*, p.170.

195. "Ils diront: «Qu'avez-vous? Vous avez de la peine? Je vous aime, soyez tranquille... Vous êtes content?» Ils ne montreront pas qu'ils sont bons mais ils montreront de l'amour. On ne saura pas qu'ils sont intéressés parce qu'ils feront comme s'ils ne l'étaient pas. Magnifiques et

silencieux ils viendront combler les vides, aggrandir les coeurs, hausser la vie sans savoir ce qu'ils font, ce qu'ils sont, ce qu'ils aiment; et puis ils iront se faire lire les lignes de la main. Ils diront: «Je vais essayer de tout comprendre. Je voudrais tant vous obliger! Avec tellement d'amour, je pense bien en donner un peu...»
Ce seront les plus beaux garçons de la terre."
Desbordes, 'Les Plus Beaux Garçons de la Terre', *J'adore*, pp.144-145.

196. See Mary Butts's poems: 'Pythian Ode' (1924); 'Heartbreak House'(1930); 'Picus Martius' (1930); 'Thinking of Saints & Petronius Arbiter' (1931).

197. "Existes-tu? Est-ce à quelqu'un que je m'adresse? Est-ce que je ne fais pas qu'appeler le vide? Peut-être est-ce une étoile que j'entoure de mes rêves." Desbordes, 'Lettre Anonyme', *J'adore*, p.177.

198. "Comme tout se ressemble...et comme on vous parle, mon Dieu, de la même manière que l'on fait l'amour ou que l'on se souvient ou que l'on est malade, aussi désesperément, avec une même solitude. Celui qui aime, aime seul. Celui qui fait l'amour, fait l'amour seul et celui qui prie, prie seul." Desbordes, 'La Maison', *J'adore*, p.184.

199. "Aspire les étoiles que l'amour fait filer de toi. Prends l'amour à ses racines. Sois assez hors la vie du monde, assez calme dans le feu, assez ordonné dans le ciel meme, pour absorber l'amour où est l'amour." Desbordes, 'La Faiblesse des Forts', *J'adore*, p.165.

200. Tony Butts letter to Mary Butts, 10.8.28. A letter to Harcourt Wesson Bull sent in June 1930 reflects her attitude to money. She claimed in a note "scribbled out unrevised, in a little restaurant, full of food, thanks to you" that she had spent the last few months living quietly alone. "Worked enormously: eaten little, borrowed nothing. Lived on my psychic-physical capital...if you like. All these last months I've needed money and what money does *and prevents* more than ever in my life. An easier life would—might—have saved me." Mary Butts undated letter to Harcourt Wesson Bull, June 1930 (Beinecke).

201. Mary Butts draft of letter to Mary Colville-Hyde, 1/2.7.29.

202. Gabriel Atkin undated letter to Mary Butts, June 1928. Quentin Bell recorded in *Elders and Betters* that Sebastian Sprott was employed for a time as his tutor at Charleston. See also below, p.38, n.266.

203. Mary Butts letter to Mireille Havet, 5.8.28.

204. *DFT*, in *TTN*, pp.184-185.

205. See above, pp.176-7.

206. Mary Butts, 'In the House', in *Last Stories* (Brendin Publishing Company, 1938), p.246. Henceforth referred to as *LS*.

207. Throughout her adult life Mary Butts alluded to this feeling of being "war-shocked". In late Feb 1928 she had written in her diary: "I belong to the war-ruined generation; those years lie like a fog on my spirit, mud, slough of despair, cynicism, panic." In her autobiography she mused: "It is the most wistful of all speculations what life would have been like if there had been no war, if one age had passed tranquilly into the next; how blessed it would seem, how full of possibilities of achievement. How many—and this is the worst of all—dead or maimed in body and spirit would now be at the height of their ripened powers." *TCC*, p.54.

208. Perhaps Mary Butts was thinking of Blake's Song of Innocence 'The Lamb' in which the line "Little Lamb God Bless Thee" occurs.

209. *AWM*, in *TTN*, pp.104-105.

210. "I know that your life is not centred in the Boeuf," Tony reassured his sister. Tony Butts letter to Mary Butts, 21.6.28.

211. Medley, *Drawn from the Life*, p.79.

212. Mary Butts would have an equally strong reaction to paper in July 1935: "FOR A POEM OR WHATNOT: All the bits and ends and kinds and forms of *paper* which pour even into this house—brown parcel paper—the kind that goes without packing; the tissue stuff, bill paper, invoice paper, butter-paper, parcel pens, newspapers—Ad inf[initum]." Mary Butts, diary entry, 13.7.35. The poem was not written.

213. Mary Butts, 'Mappa Mundi', *WAWB*, p.188.

214. Compare the Sortes Virgilianae mentioned above, p.182.

215. It is not clear exactly when Mary Butts met this "young journalist, Walter Shaw" who drove down from Paris to Nice with Isadora Duncan in the summer of 1926. (Irma Duncan and Allan Ross Macdougall, *Isadora Duncan's Russian Days: and her last years in France* (Victor Gollancz Ltd, 1929), p.338.) Robert Medley, who looked after Shaw when when he was undergoing detoxification with Mary Butts, described him as "the great hulk…a handsome American gigolo". Medley, *Drawn from the Life*, p.79.

216. Mary Butts, 'Chartres—The Symbol', *Time and Tide*, 17, no.24 (13.6.36), p.856.

217. While Camilla was in Cannes, Mary Butts only sent her the occasional postcard with pathetic messages, which implied that work was depriving her of her daughter: "Heart's girl. Demain je vais te chercher quelques livres. Plus tard les livres que j'ai écrit moi-même. J'ai écrit un livre pour toi, mais je n'ai pas trouver [sic] un editeur encore. [I will get you some books tomorrow. Later, you'll get the books I wrote myself. I have written a book for you, but I haven't found a publisher for it yet.] Mother (undated, early summer 1928). "Little Love, J'espère que tu aime [sic] les livres. Nous lirons l'anglais ensemble, si tu a [sic] trop oublié. [I hope you like the books. We will read the English one together, if you've forgotten it], Mother" (undated, early summer 1928); "Little Love, Maman travaille comme tout. Bientôt nous serons ensemble. [Mummy is working hard. Soon we will be together]. Your own Mother" (27.6.28); The most extraordinary example of Mary Butts's self-deception was a postcard she sent to Camilla on the 31 July 1928. It was a reproduction of Cazin's painting, 'Ishmael' and depicted the banished Hagar covering her face with her hands as her small child tries to comfort her. The message reads: "Maman separée de toi [Mum separated from you]. Your own Mother."

218. Mary Butts letter to Marianne Moore, 7.11.28 (Beinecke).

219. Pendant longtemps… J'ai dit et pourrais dire sans exagération…ni vantardise…que…les drogues ne sont pas un danger pour moi. J'ai encore ma tête sur mes épaules et dans cette tête un [?] suffisant d'instinct et de conscience raisonnable et pouvant ordonner à mon corps et être obéi sans difficulté pour savoir exactement ce que je consomme, pouvoir le déclarer honnêtement à peu de choses près à un médecin…qui pourra s'en servir comme base et aussi en se fiant pour une fois à son malade—me soigner facilement et en collaboration avec moi-même…et même me supprimer toute seule, s'il ne s'agit que de l'opium…. Je sais qu'il n'en est plus de même maintenant pour la 1ère fois de ma vie—je tiens à l'écrire ici s'il m'arrivait par hasard et plus rapidement que je ne pense…d'en mourir accidentellement et non par suicide—ce qui me vexerait beaucoup et serait sans doute mon chatiement suprême et celui que mon infernel orgueil mérite! Je ne m'avoue plus me doses…ne veux plus les contrôler ni les connaitre…et ne les avouerai à aucun médecin—ni ami—pour la bonne raison que je ne les sais pas d'une part et ne veux pas les savoir—et qu'ensuite…je sais très bien que je ne suis plus complice…mais prisonnière liée par le sang et le souffle à mon toxique favori—et que dans cette inhumaine liaison aux débuts pourtant si agréables…comme les sourds qui ne veulent pas entendre ou les conducteurs qui s'égarent exprès mais connaissent leur itinéraire par coeur—et volontairement sont ceux qui l'oublient—j'ai perdu mon libre arbitre—et ne suis plus qu'un animal, esclave entre tous les esclaves…. Ma vie n'est plus qu'une série de manque et d'abus!… Je n'écrirai plus d'histoires Mary! j'aimais trop les histoires—j'ai voulu avant de les écrire en avoir—et la réalité s'est substituée à la création—ma vie—à l'ouvrage que je devais faire ds la vie—Ma mort…à la mort imaginaire de nos fins de chapitres et pour finir sur un mauvais jeu de mots l'héroine à mes héros!" Mireille Havet, diary entry, Monday, 10pm, 10.6.28. (Cocteau)

220. In *Drawn from the Life*, p.79, Medley claimed that he helped Mary Butts in 1926; in an interview with Nathalie Blondel in 1994, shortly before his death, he agreed that he had been mistaken and that it was indeed in 1928.

221. Mary Butts letter to John Rodker, 28.12.28.

222. Mary Butts letter to John Rodker, 3.1.29.

223. Harcourt Wesson Bull, in *ASQ*, p.66.

224. Marianne Moore to Mary Butts, 15.3.29 (Beinecke).

225. Mary Butts, 'Mr Wescott's Third Book', *The Dial*, 82 (May 1929), pp.424-427.

226. Mary Butts letter to John Rodker, 20.4.29: "I am tired of being half-crippled, and wish to avoid if possible becoming lame for life—which seems likely—violent steps seem indicated."

227. Mary Butts undated letter to John Rodker, March 1929.

228. 'Aldous Huxley' was published in Edgell Rickword's second volume of *Scrutinies* (1931) See p.265.

229. It is not known whether Mary Butts did buy this painting or exactly which one it was. When she died, a painting of a house by Cedric Morris, rather than one of two gulls and a duck, was among her possessions.

230. Mary Colville-Hyde undated letter to Mary Butts, 1929.

231. Paul Ganz, 'An Unpublished Holbein Portrait', *The Burlington Magazine: for Connoisseurs*, 56, no.324 (March 1930), p.118.

232. Laurence Vail wrote to Charters: "As you changed premises every year or so, your bar-room was always a novelty, *le dernier cri de Paris*. It is the little bar near the Pantheon that I remember best. Tommy Earp lived at Foyot's then. So did Mary Butts, Max Beerbohm, Maitland, Dobson, Iris Tree, so it was easy for them to drop in for a dozen whiskies and sodas from nine to three." Vail quoted in James Charters, *This Must be the Place* (Herbert Joseph Ltd, 1934), p.294. Mary Butts ordered a copy of Charters's autobiography in June 1934.

233. Charters, *This Must be the Place*, p.115. Charters is referring to a fabulous offer made to Mary Colville-Hyde for the Holbein by Duveen, see p.314.

234. Mary Butts undated letter to Harcourt Wesson Bull, June 1930 (Beinecke): "I was promised a fortune which would one day arrive and put me out of my material difficulties."

235. Harcourt Wesson Bull commented on Mary Butts having a "high lilting voice." Harcourt Wesson Bull, '"Truth is the Heart's Desire"', in *ASQ*, p.55. Douglas Goldring remembered "her high treble". Goldring, *South Lodge*, p.149.

236. Four years later Mary Butts paid tribute to the "debt" the world owed Gilbert Murray in her review of his *Aristophanes* in 'Aristophanes, the laughing Philosopher', *The Bookman*, 84, no.501 (June 1933), p.152. She again reviewed it as part of a longer article in December 1933, 'Magic of Person and Place', see p.485n.44.

237. Mary Butts's bibliophilia resembled Walter Benjamin's. See his essay, 'Unpacking my library: a talk about Book collecting' [1931], in *Illuminations* (Fontana, 1982).

238. This lunch may well have taken place as a result of a note from Carlo [sic] van Vechten in which he suggested "a rendez-vous" and concluded: "Petunias, verbena, and fuschias to you!". Carl van Vechten letter to Mary Butts, 4.8.[29].

239. This fact is omitted from Hugh Ford's account of Edward Titus's editorship of *This Quarter*, see Ford, *Published in Paris*, pp.139-146.

240. Mary Butts, work notebook, Paris, August 1929.

241. A reference to Gilbert Murray's *Ordeal of our Generation* (1929), which Mary Butts was then reading.

242. Mary Butts letter to Ada Briggs, 10.9.29.

243. "Chez Mary Butts 14 Rue de Monttessuy pendant mon 5ème abcès au genou ouvert par le Dr Tivel." Title page of Mireille Havet's diary, 10.9.29 (Cocteau).

244. "le 11 sept 1929 % Mary 14 rue de Montessuy Paris, 9h matin mercredi:...sans l'admirable bonté de Mary je n'aurais eu que l'hôpital et son lit de fer anonyme comme refuge.
le 13 sept minuit:...la chance ne m'abandonne pas vraiment—j'ai trouvé cette amitié fraternelle et si dérouté de Mary me soignant chez elle—malgré sa pauvreté et sa fatigue—avec un inaltérable dévouement et bonne humeur—qu'aurais'je fait seule chez moi—l'hôpital seul me restait.
samedi 14 sept 29 Paris Matin:...Cher Docteur Tivel. Miracle...mon genou...il y a huit jours...qu'il a fait gicler au bout de la lancette...et merveilleusement fait panser et vider toute cette semaine par Mary."

Mireille Havet, diary entries, 11-14.9.29 (Cocteau).

245. Mary Butts letter to Ada Briggs, 10.9.29.

246. "Mais la confiance et tout au moins la curiosité et l'intérêt ds la vie et ma propre vie est presque retrouvée grâce au génie de Mary et à ce qu'elle me fait entrevoir et moralement contourner comme issue subite et secrète en cela qu'elle n'ait imaginée peut être que d'elle seule—à ce degré *de la Poésie*. Je ne comprends pas encore et l'avoue mais je sais je suis que de la seconde où j'aurais compris ce sera transformer ma jeunesse—ma foi—mon audace—mon courage batailleur retrouvés et que je n'aurais pas assez de minutes ds une journée pour m'exprimer, servir mon nouveau devoir et accomplir—ds tous les autres—sociaux, amicaux, littéraires enfin en l'écrivant pour en donner peut être une des premières traductions et versions au monde, mon travail inspiré dès lors et ordonné de Dieu seul et de mon ange gardien. Mais d'ici la—c'est tellement formidable et un angle si nouveau et inaccoutumé pour ma tête de concevoir ce service poétique de notre vie et univers—Ma tâche enfin! que je suis gauche et à tatons ds ce qui devient pour moi et mon ignorance l'ombre des formules éblouissantes et inerrantes de vérité céleste que me donne Mary comme la chose la plus naturelle et coutumière du Monde.

Son génie foudroie ma pauvre intelligence qui n'a rien appris depuis des années et tous les rouages sont rouillés par l'inaction ou le plus bas et vulgaire visage de la pensée et des seules préoccupations et déceptions sentimentales.

Il faut qu'à cet alphabet magique je me fasse et que doucement le temps créant en moi la théorie des nouveaux signes qui me serviront à épeler puis transmettre moi-même le nouvel usage poétique du Monde et de ses vraies vérités éternelles."

Mireille Havet, diary entry, 16-17.9.29 (Cocteau).

247. In late September Mary Butts recorded her belief that "it is for art to take over the anthropologists' material—Vivian said it was for me to do also". A few days later she added: "And here let me say, if for the first, surely not for the last time, that there are the makings of a very wise man in Vivian Ogilvie." Mary Butts, diary entries, 30.9.29 & 2.10.29.

248. Recording a seance on the 14 September 1929 Mary Butts wrote: "Mother's initials ... tu es en désespoir [you are despairing]."

249. Mary Butts undated draft of letter to Tony Butts, 22.9.29.

250. See p.340. Whilst Mary Butts did not review this book, in 1933 R. Ellis Roberts asked her to review Merezhkovsky's *Jesus the Unknown* and *The Secret of the West*. She did so in 'A Russian Prophet', *Time and Tide*, 14, no.4 (14.10.33), pp.228-230.

251. Mary Butts defined the term: "the thread of life, in Heimarmenê, the fine strand running through existence, stringing spirits and their activities like pierced stones." *TCC*, p.98. See pp.157, 277.

252. Mary Butts draft of letter to Anne Weir, 30.10.29.

253. Also known as the Hôtel Central-Benoit.

254. Known variously as the Grande Rue.

255. Always conscious of improving her style Mary Butts wrote 2 and 1 under "scarlet" and "cold green" respectively, indicating that they should be reversed. There are many other examples of this technique in her diary, e.g. when describing the attic at 14 Rue de Monttessuy she wrote "there our builder's subhuman malice$_3$, incompetence$_1$, boredom$_2$ found its expression" (28.1.30).

256. See *TCC*, pp.233-234 for an equally striking description of the train ride when Mary Butts left St Andrew's.

257. "Mary est là aussi pr 2 jours—...M. m'excite—me tend les nerfs, m'agite et me fait tripler mes piqures et je l'aime pourtant de tout mon coeur aussi et elle m'a sauvée de la mort." Mireille Havet, undated diary entry, 14.10.29 (Cocteau).

258. "Je suis tentée de demander de l'argent pour aller à St Malo me reposer—mais je crains la fatigue, la tension nerveuse née de ce voisinage des deux, Mary et son ami anglais qu'il faut empêcher de boire." Mireille Havet, diary entry 1.30pm, Tuesday 15.10.29 (Cocteau).

259. "Mary remue tout le temps, son insomnie d'intoxiqué trop semblable à la mienne l'excite—elle entre ds ma chambre sous tous les prétextes et me parle. Oh! que je suis fatiguée—" Mireille Havet, diary entry, 3am 16.10.29 (Cocteau).

260. Rather a biassed and understated comment on Mary Butts's part. Robert Surcouf (1773-1827), son of one of the three most important St Malo families, was among the most powerful, bravest and most venerated Malouins. His courage led him to be called the King of the Corsaires and he was feared by the English and given the title 'Baron of the Empire' by Napoleon.

261. Algernon Blackwood, 'Ancient Sorceries' in *John Silence* (Eveleigh Nash, 1908) and collected in *Ancient Sorceries and Other Tales* (Collins, 1927), p.20.

262. See below, pp.271; 492, n.167.

263. This would not be the only time Mary Butts analysed his stories. On the 18 January 1930 she examined E.F. Benson's *Room in the Tower* (1929) and on the 22 May 1934 his *More Spook Stories* (1934) with the same rigour. She also 'found' *Visible and Invisible* on the 23 March 1936 when it was a great comfort.

264. Gabriel Atkin undated letter to Mary Butts, late Summer 1928.

265. Osbert Sitwell, Foreword to *Catalogue of the Loan Exhibition of Paintings and Drawings by Gabriel Atkin* (Laing Art Gallery, 1940).

266. Bell, 'Maynard Keynes' in *Elders and Betters*, p.88. "Another of Keynes's serious young men was Gabriel Atkin, an artist, who appears to have been the only person other than Sebastian [Sprott] whom Keynes took down to Charleston. Their relationship did not last after 1920." D.E. Moggridge, *Maynard Keynes: An Economist's Biography* (Routledge, 1992), p.354.

267. Gabriel Atkin undated letter to Mary Butts, June 1928.

268. Gabriel Atkin letter to Mary Butts, SS Pierre and Paul [29.6] 1928.

269. Gabriel Atkin undated letter to Mary Butts, Sunday June 1928. His sociability can be glimpsed in the pages of Irma Duncan and McDougall's biography of Isadora Duncan. In early 1927 when she arrived in Nice, "two young men were there to greet her, Gabriel Atkin, a charming English artist, and his friend Sewell Stokes, an English journalist, who was hanging about Isadora for material for one of the chapters in his book on Riviera personalities... Atkin was to do the caricatures for the book." *Isadora Duncan's Russian Days*, ed. Duncan & McDougall, p.343. This was a reference to Sewell Stokes, *Pilloried!* illustrated by Gabriel Atkin (Richards, [1928]). In 1926 Odo Cross saw Atkin in France with "three fragile aunts as he called them...and certainly he looked depressed enough to have martialed [sic] a band of missionaries here." Paul [Odo Cross] undated letter to Cedric Morris, postmarked March 1926. TGA.8317.1.1.697.

270. Mary Butts draft of letter to Anne Weir, 30.10.29.

271. Mary Butts undated draft of letter to Mary Colville-Hyde, early December 1929.

272. Mary Butts draft of letter to Trevor Stevenson, 13.11.29.

273. Three weeks later Mary Butts added cryptically: "On the 17 [December], the Sergey news. Have pity on him and on us, O God. (While I also remember G[abriel]'s comment : his comparison between SS and the Captain in *Decline and Fall*.)"

274. Mary Butts had met the French spiritualist and author, Pierre Corneiller, in 1928. Initially she was impressed by his ideas but by the end of December 1929 (perhaps as a result of his sudden coolness towards her) she rejected them.

275. Unaware that Mireille Havet had died five years earlier, when Bryher wrote her memorial to Mary Butts, 'Recognition Not Farewell' in 1937, she alluded to both Mireille and Sergei when she asked: "The girl she nursed, the boy she kept out of prison, will they remember her, do they even know that she has died?" Bryher, 'Recognition Not Farewell', in *ASQ*, p.10.

276. 'A Journey's End' was the working title Mary Butts gave a short story begun the following spring and which was published in 1932 under the title 'In Bloomsbury'.

277. Einstein's theory of relativity and the theory of quantum mechanics. In *Armed with Madness* Scylla Taverner remarks on the relationship between scientific and moral relativism: "If the materialist's universe is true, and not a working truth to make bridges with and things, we are a set of blind factors in a machine. And no passion has any validity and no imagination. They are just little tricks of the machine. It either is, or it isn't. If you hold that it isn't, you corrupt your intellect by denying certain facts. If you stick to the facts as we have them, life is a horror and insult. Nothing has any worth, but to tickle our sensations and oil the machine. There is no value in our passions and perceptions, or final differences between a life full of design and adventure and life crawled out in a palace or a slum. The life of Plato or Buddha, apart from the kick of illusion, was as futile as the lives of the daughters of Louis XV. Old talk, you say, and remember IN MEMORIAM. But notice what is happening now people have become used to the idea. Any little boy in a Paris bar, who had never heard of physics knows. Everyone gets the age's temper. With results on their conduct—'Why be good any more' they say, and the youngest ones not that. And it's not intellectual beauty the culture-camp admire. It's themselves for having such fine subconciousnesses. Such an elegant sublimation of their infant interests. Watch the world with the skeleton acclimatised! Even when I was new we tried the bad to see if it might not be good. But the new lot aren't interested. Don't give a button for the good any more. "*AWM*, in *TTN*, pp.89-90. In the January-March 1930 issue of *Hound and Horn* Mary Butts "announced an essay on relativity and the artist in general". Mike Weaver, *William Carlos Williams: The American Background* (C.U.P., 1977), p.65. The essay is not among her papers and does not seem to have been published. Perhaps this was a reference to her unpublished "View of Civilisation in the West".

278. Mary Butts undated draft of letter to Mary Colville-Hyde, 1.1.30.

279. Robert McAlmon, 'Truer than Most Accounts', *The Exile*, 2 (1927), pp.40-86, pp.42-43.

280. Benjamin Franklin V, Introduction to Wambly Bald, *On the Left Bank 1929-1933*, ed. by Benjamin Franklin V (Ohio University Press, 1987), p.xiii.

281. Ibid, pp.140-141.

282. T.S. Eliot quoted in Ford, *Published in Paris*, p.38.

283. John Rodker letter to Mary Butts, 9.1.30.

284. Mary Butts draft of letter to Mary Colville-Hyde, 29.1.30.

285. Bertrand Russell, 'The Philosophical Consequences of Relativity', in *Encyclopedia Britannica*, (13th edn, 1926).

286. Edith Nesbit may well have read H.G. Wells's *A Modern Utopia* (published in 1905, but first serialised in the *Fortnightly Review* (October 1904–April 1905)), where Wells and a friend, "the Botanist", get transported to a parallel, Utopian world.

287. Mary Butts's interest would continue. In December 1932 she ordered Doris Langley Moore's *E Nesbit: A Biography* (Benn, 1933).

288. Mary Butts, 'Widdershins', in *WAWB*, p.152.

289. The original passage from E. Nesbit's *The Story of the Amulet* (1906) occurs in the chapter, 'The Queen in London':

> Anthea took the [Babylonian] Queen's hand and gently pulled her away. The other children followed, and the black crowd of angry gentlemen stood on the steps [of the British Museum] watching them. ...[the Queen's] eyes fell on the bag where the Psammead was. She stopped short.
>
> 'I wish,' she said, very loud and clear, 'that all those Babylonian things would come out to me here—slowly, so that those dogs and slaves can see the working of the great Queen's magic.'
>
> 'Oh, you *are* a tiresome woman,' said the Psammead in its bag, but it puffed itself out.
>
> Next moment there was a crash. The glass swing doors and all their framework were smashed suddenly and completely. The crowd of angry gentlemen sprang aside when they saw what had done this. But the nastiest of them was not quick enough, and he was roughly pushed out of the way by an enormous stone bull that was floating steadily through the door. It came and stood beside the Queen in the middle of the courtyard.
>
> It was followed by more stone images, by great slabs of carved stone, bricks, helmets, tools, weapons, fetters, wine-jars, bowls, bottles, vases, jugs, saucers, seals, and the round long things, something like rolling pins with marks on them like the print of little bird-feet, necklaces, collars, rings, armlets, earrings—heaps and heaps and heaps of things, far more than anyone had time to count, or even to see distinctly.

E. Nesbit, *The Story of the Amulet* (Puffin, 1959 reprint), p.144.

290. This was a reference to Mary Butts's poem, 'Picus Martius', inspired by Roy Martin and just published in *Hound and Horn*, 3, no.2 (Jan-March 1930), pp.230-233.

291. Bell, 'Robert Medley and Mary Butts', in *Elders and Betters*, p.196.

292. Erich Maria Remarque, *All Quiet on the Western Front*, trans. A.W. Wheen (Putnam, 1929).

293. Mary Butts did not appreciate it, however, when John Rodker told her about a newspaper report of a scandal in a French nightclub (unnamed) in which her name had been mentioned. MB, diary entry, 26-7.4.30.

294. On the 26 May 1930, Mary Butts's diary read: "Lunch at Agathe Paléologue: translation nearly done." No indication is given as to which of her books was being translated. Since she wrote to Cocteau in March 1932 about a French edition of *Imaginary Letters*, it may well have been this narrative. See p.304.

295. In writing this Harcourt Wesson Bull may well have been thinking of two undated letters Mary Butts sent him in June 1930. In one she wrote "Very dear Harcourt... We Must Not Quarrel." In a second letter she advised: "It's as you like, but I think you're wrong. Friendship such as I hold ours *can* weather such misunderstandings, *should* do so.... I need you now.... Harcourt mio, don't make life worse than it is—you who are my pride and my delight." (Beinecke).

296. Harcourt Wesson Bull, '"Truth is the Heart's Delight"', in *ASQ*, pp.67-68.

V : Back to England 1930-1931

1. Mary Butts draft of letter to Anne Weir, 30.6.30.

2. E.M. Forster, 'The Machine Stops'. In 1947 Forster wrote that "The Machine Stops is a reaction to one of the earlier heavens of H.G. Wells." E.M. Forster, Introduction, *Collected Short Stories of E.M. Forster* (Sidgwick and Jackson Ltd, 1948), p.vii. This may well have been why Mary Butts liked it so much.

3. Rudyard Kipling, 'A 3-part Song' in 'Dymchurch Flit', *Puck of Pook's Hill* (Macmillan & Co, 1924 reprint of 1908 edn.), p.277.

4. Goldring, *The Nineteen Twenties*, p.218. Witnesses at the wedding were Nina Hamnett, Terence Loudon and Charles H. Gray. Mary Butts's age on the marriage certificate is given as 36—she was in fact almost 40...

5. The name entered on the marriage certificate is "Aitken" and Goldring provides the following anecdotal explanation: "He had been born Aitken, but when he first dazzled London with his good looks and shared a house with the Sitwell Brothers, Siegfried Sassoon and Tommy Earp, he had modifed this to Atkin. One of his uncles, to whom he was attached, was a watercolour painter called Park. Mary decided that his new surname should be 'Park-Aitken', and it was as 'Mrs Gabriel Park-Aitken' that she settled down, her wild oats sown and forgotten, to establish herself as a respected local resident." Goldring, *South Lodge*, pp.149-150. Gabriel used both Atkin and Aitken in his work as an illustrator, see below, p.454, n.227.

6. Rudyard Kipling, 'Tommy' (March 1890), reprinted in T.S. Eliot, *A Choice of Kipling's Verse* (Faber, 1941), p.172. Interestingly the prevalence of this nickname for soldiers in the First World War can be seen in 'Tommy Atkins et les Paysans de France' in Marie Butts, *Héros! Episodes de la Grande Guerre* (1915), p.70. Douglas Goldring referred to "Atkins senior" and "Thomas Junior" in his Postscript to *The Nineteen Twenties*, pp.254-266.

7. Goldring, *The Nineteen Twenties*, p.218. Apparently Gerald Reitlinger was a friend of Christopher Wood's, see Faulks, *The Fatal Englishman*, p.24.

8. Mary Butts draft of letter to the landlord of 14 Rue de Montessuy, 11.1.31.

9. For an explanation of Mary Butts's understanding of the "hollow land", see pp.439; 459n.142.

10. Mary Butts quotes the last two verses. The first one reads:

> Had thine art not skill to change
> Dream into deed of sense?
> Did the baffled heart recoil
> On itself in penitence?

Æ, 'Ancestry' in *Enchantment and other Poems* (Macmillan & Co, 1930), p.17.

11. Mary Butts's enjoyment of detective fiction may well have influenced her choice of the detective-sounding title for her third novel, *Death of Felicity Taverner*. Her taste for this genre was characteristic of the period. See chapter 2, 'Agatha Christie and conservative modernity', in Alison Light's *Forever England: Femininity, literature and conservatism between the wars* (Routledge, 1991), pp.61-112. She was one of the lead reviewers, for example, in the slim quarterly entitled *Crime* devoted to detective fiction which began in late 1935. The first issue included her review of Nigel Morland's *The Phantom Gunner* ('This Season's Best Thriller', *Crime* 1, no.1 (Winter 1935-6), p.5) as well as the promise that "*Crime* No. 2 (Feb., 1936) will contain articles by several famous writers...the leading review by Mary Butts" (ibid, p.11). Despite research in the British Library and long interesting conversations with several specialist booksellers of modern first editions, periodicals and crime fiction, it proved impossible to track down any further issues of *Crime* beyond no.1. Mary Butts's other reviews of detective fiction include: 'Seven Detective Stories, New Poirot Novel', *The Sunday Times* (14.7.35), p.8; 'Four Detective Novels', *The Sunday Times* (21.7.35), p.8; 'Adventure and Detection, Stories by Beginners', *The Sunday Times* (1.9.35), p.7; 'Conspiracies and Crime', *The Sunday Times* (8.9.35), p.7. In turn, Margery Allingham was one of the reviewers of *Last Stories*, see below, p.432.

12. Mary Butts letter to Frosca Munster, 16.6.31. TGA. 723.106.

13. For an account of Frosca Munster's attempt to compile a book of recollections see Faulks, *The Fatal Englishman*, p.104. See also Richard Ingleby, *Christopher Wood: An English Painter* (Allison & Busby, 1995), p.283 where he lists a number of still unpublished memoirs, including contributions by Mary Butts, Jean Cocteau and Max Jacob, collected by Frosca Munster.

14. Mary Butts, 'Two Artists', *Time and Tide*, 15, no.45 (10.11.34), p.1430. On the 12 December 1930 Mary Butts also commented in her diary on a conversation with Gabriel Aitken about the death of Jacques de Malleissye: "That strip of our tragedy had become tolerable because I had reduced it to art. And I saw that only by that way would the others become tolerable also."

15. Mary Butts invited Douglas and Malin Goldring to Sussex, but they could not come (see Goldring, *The Nineteen Twenties*, p.218). She also mentions more or less pleasurable visits from John Steedgeman, JD [unknown], and Charles Griffin.

16. Mary Butts draft of letter to Mary Colville-Hyde, 5.2.31.
17. Mary Butts draft of letter to Mary Colville-Hyde, 19.2.31.
18. Mary Butts draft of letter to Mary Colville-Hyde, 6.3.31.
19. Mary Butts draft of letter to Mary Colville-Hyde, 12.3.31.
20. Mary Butts draft of letter to Tom Swan, 6.3.31.

21. See p.475, n.217.

22. At this time Mary Butts wrote in her diary "For a title-page. Eddington *Nature of the Physical World* (p.344). 'We are bound to claim for human nature that, either by itself or as inspired by a power beyond, it is capable of making legitimate judgments of significance.'" This quotation was never used for an epigraph.

23. Mary Butts draft of unsent letter to Harold Nicolson, 25.4.30.

24. Mary Butts, 'Aldous Huxley', in *Scrutinies. Volume II*, collected by Edgell Rickword (Wishart & Co, 1931), pp.73-98. This collection included essays on Virginia Woolf by William Empson, on James Joyce by Jack Lindsay and on Wyndham Lewis by Edgell Rickword and received favourable reviews, including one which described Mary Butts's article as having "point and insight". 'Significant Criticism', *Times Literary Supplement* (19.3.31), p.226; 'The Rising Literary Generation', *The Spectator* (14.3.31), p.427; one reviewer wrote: "Mary Butts, the author of that strangely talented novel *Ashe of Rings*, writes...on Aldous Huxley. Her essay is a remarkable example of feminine patience and pertinacity. But to attempt to define or de-limit Mr. Huxley as *The Perfect Writer*! Even if his critic achieved this—fortunately she has not—how much wiser would anyone be? The whole discussion would, at a less serious moment of time, be comically like a merry-go-round. *Cui bono?* says Mr Huxley, contemplating life in general. *Cui bono?* says Mary Butts, contemplating Mr. Huxley. And all we can add, after gathering the threads of her brilliant discussion, is: *cui bono*?" H.P. Collins, 'Books of the Quarter', *The Criterion*, 10, no.41 (July 1931), p.746.

25. A.J.A. Symons letter to Mary Butts, 5.5.34.

26. "I have, by the way, done a good deed to the locality at the Library by gaining influence among the Committee (a formidable collection of Conservative dunderheads, hedged in by prejudice and convention) and getting them to order *Speed the Plough*. This is no ordinary library, you must understand, but a vast, ancient, and exclusive institution called the Literary and Philosophical Society, with a limited membership. It is commonly referred to as the "Lit. and Phil." I always feel that I want to set up a restaurant in the shade of its Corinthian porticos and call it "The Sit and Fill"—or else, perhaps, a pub, "The Sit and Swill," but I think the rest of the members drink only Horlicks malted milk..." Gabriel Aitken undated letter to Mary Butts, June 1928. See *Warning to Hikers* (Wishart, 1932). Reprinted in *AOROW*. Henceforth referred to as *WTH* in *AOROW*. p.287.

27. This was probably Alan Porter's *The Signature of Pain and other Poems* (Cobden-Sanderson, 1930).

28. Mary Butts, 'A Story of Ancient Magic', *The Bookman*, 80, no.478 (July 1931), p 210. For a more detailed description of the novel and its reception, see Jill Benton, *Naomi Mitchison: A Biography* (Pandora, 1993), pp.63-69. Mitchison remembered that Mary Butts had reviewed *Corn*

King and Spring Queen, but never met her. Naomi Mitchison letter to Nathalie Blondel, 23.9.92.

29. Mary Butts, 'Antiquity', *The Bookman*, 81, no.482 (Nov 1931), p.137.

30. See Mary Butts letters to Mr Warner, 20.8.31 and 1.9.31 and Mr Warner to Mary Butts, 21.8.31. University of Reading Library, Chatto & Windus file MS2444.

31. It may well have been in contradistinction to herself that Mary Butts made the following quotation from Evelyn Waugh's *Rossetti* in late July 1931 (see above p.267). "He was typically Bloomsbury bred in his attitude to the country. When he tries to express his delight in some natural beauty it is nearly always by comparison with something artificial." Mary Butts then adduced "old [William] Morris" as being closer to her own view: "'O me! O me! How I love the earth and the seasons and the weather, and all things that deal with them, and all that grows out of them.'"

32. Hugh Ross Williamson, *The Walled Garden* (Michael Joseph Ltd, 1956), p.95.

33. Hugh Ross Williamson gives a detailed account of the "demise" of *The Bookman* in *The Walled Garden*, pp.95-6.

34. Towards the end of her Preface to *The Macedonian* Mary Butts thanked "Mr. Ross-Williamson for his encouragement". *TM* in *TCN*, p.5.

35. Hugh Ross Williamson letter to Mary Butts, 16.9.31.

36. Mary Butts draft of letter to Hugh Ross Williamson, 19/20.3.31.

37. Val Goldsmith, whose wife committed suicide, see p.468n101. On the 6 July 1931 Mary Butts noted that she should buy *An Adventure*. Originally published in 1911, it was reissued by Faber in 1931 with 'further additional material' and a Preface by the now-neglected but extremely powerful writer, Edith Olivier and (a fact which would have particularly interested Mary Butts) 'A Note' by J.W. Dunne. It is the record of "a unique experience [at Versailles]. Two women of the twentieth century found themselves walking together in the Trianon of 1789, and, there, coming upon figure after figure unaccountably arisen from that unfamiliar past." Edith Olivier, 'Preface' to C. Anne E. Moberly and Eleanor F. Jourdain *An Adventure* (Faber, 1932 edn.), p.9.

38. Whilst in Sussex in January 1931 Mary Butts copied out some lines from the folk song, 'When the Boat comes in':

> He shall have a fish,
> He shall have a fin,
> He shall have a haddock
> When the boat comes in.

She later incorporated these into her story, 'The Guest', in *LS*, p.29.

39. See pp.436-7; For a more detailed discussion see Harcourt Wesson Bull, '"Truth is the Heart's Desire"', in *ASQ*, pp.85-86 and Peter F. Alexander's *William Plomer: A Biography* (O.U.P., 1989). Whatever Mary Butts's personal feelings, she continued to buy and read his work. For example, in February 1933 she ordered Plomer's *Cecil Rhodes*, see p.494, n.217.

40. Ethel Colburn Mayne letter to Mary Butts, 20.10.31.

41. The previous month Mary Butts had written to Violet Hunt after a gap of some years hoping that they would renew their friendship. See MB letter to Violet Hunt, 7.10.31 (Special Collection, Cornell University Library).

42. Ethel Colburn Mayne letter to Mary Butts, 22.12.31.

43. "For a long time I've wanted to ask you if I might dedicate my next book to you...in memory of our long friendship and of all I owe you, and all my work owes you, and all that the people I love owe and have owed to you." Mary Butts undated letter to Douglas Goldring, November 1931. Quoted in Goldring, *The Nineteen Twenties*, p.219.

44. Hugh Ross Williamson undated letter to Mary Butts, November/December 1931.

45. Hugh Ross Williamson undated letter to Mary Butts, early December 1931.

46. Ethel Colburn Mayne letter to Mary Butts, 31.12.31.

VI : The Cornish Years 1932-1937

1. Ruth Manning-Sanders, *The West of England* (B.T. Batsford Ltd, 1949), pp.40-41.

2. Manning-Sanders, *The West of England*, p.38.

3. *Black's Guide to the Duchy of England* (A.& C. Black, 1870), p.366.

4. Mary Butts, 'Look Homeward, Angel' in *LS*, p.20.

5. John Corin, *Sennen Cove and its Lifeboat* (Sennen Cove Branch of the R.N.L.I., 1985), p.16.

6. Mary Butts, 'Look Homeward, Angel', in *LS*, pp.9-10.

7. The Newbons would complete several successful rescues after Mary Butts's arrival in Sennen. In 1935 she described in a letter to the novelist, Charles Williams, just how treacherous the Cornish coastline could be in a storm: "In one way or another no one has yet got over that storm.... The Mousehole men still won't speak, not about that night, nor what they met in mid-Atlantic. Also an ugly story is only too certain here. At 6 o'clock that night the Welcome of Gloucester got out of control, engine shot, just off the out pass of the L[izard?/Longships?]. Only just kept off the reef. Passed a night in hell off Nanjizal, to be finally saved and towed to Penzance by a Brixham fishing boat, dependent on sail—a superb piece of seamanship.... I have never seen a horror to match—who have spent most of my life in country places, and great parts of it in [the] wild." Mary Butts undated draft of letter to Charles Williams, late May 1935.

8. Daphne du Maurier, *Vanishing Cornwall* (Penguin, 1972), p.53.

9. Mary Butts letter to Ada Briggs, 17.12.32.

10. Mary Butts letter to Ada Briggs, 29.3.33.

11. Filson Young was the Programme Consultant for the BBC from September 1926 until his death in 1938. He had been responsible for the broadcast of the programmes from St Hilary (a church in Marazion which would become central to Mary Butts's life from 1934) in the late 1920s. For more details see Bernard Walke's *Twenty Years at St Hilary* (Anthony Mott Ltd, 1982), pp.242-255; Asa Briggs, *The History of Broadcasting in the UK, vol II: The Golden Age of the Wireless* (O.U.P., 1975 revised edn.); Frank Baker's chapter, 'Filson Young' in his autobiography, *I Follow But Myself* (Peter Davies, 1968).

12. Instrument of Transfer, P.9898 (H.M. Land Registry, 14.6.32), Third Schedule, paragraph 1.

13. Mary Butts letter to Hugh Ross Williamson, 29.1.32, quoted in *ASQ*, p.147.

14. Mary Butts letter to Angus Davidson, 8.2.32 (Beinecke).

15. du Maurier, *Vanishing Cornwall*, p.48.

16. Manning-Sanders, *The West of England*, p.39.

17. Ibid, p.42.

18. Ethel Colburn Mayne letter to Mary Butts, 7.2.32.

19. See below pp.285, 346, for Mary Butts's descriptions of the sea as a green and grey tiger respectively.

20. In Jennifer Clarke's *Exploring the West Country: A Woman's Guide* (Virago, 1987), Mary Butts is mentioned only in the Dorset section, in spite of being buried in Cornwall and, as this biography shows, writing a great deal about the Cornish landscape.

21. Mary Butts undated letter to Hugh Ross Williamson, quoted in *ASQ*, p.278.

22. Manning-Sanders, *The West of England*, p.4.

23. The Manning-Sanders had a studio down in Sennen Cove behind the Old Success pub. Shortly after Mary Butts's arrival in Sennen, they moved into 'Esther's Field', a house built on Maria's Lane almost opposite Mary Butts's house, Tebel Vos.

24. Mary Butts, 'Our Native Land', *The Bookman*, 84, no.5C3 (Aug. 1933), p.252.

25. Mary Butts letter to Hugh Ross Williamson, 29.9.32 (HRHRC); see also *TCC*, p.22.

26. Manning-Sanders, *The West of England*, p.39.

27. Ethel Colburn Mayne letter to Mary Butts, 29.5.32.

28. du Maurier, *Vanishing Cornwall*, p.53.

29. Bryher, 'Recognition Not Farewell', in *ASQ*, p.9.

30. Mary Butts wrote the same thing in a letter to Angus Davidson: "... there are things which come out at night which had better have stayed in. I noticed that the first evening, when I went for a walk in the full moon and got rather lost and saw its light glaring through the wheel of the keltic crosses". Such repetition shows both the impact of the experience and how she used her diary and letters to constantly develop and refine her style. Mary Butts letter to Angus Davidson, 8.2.32 (Beinecke).

31. Transfer of Sale, P.9898, First Schedule, paragraph 1.

32. Mary Butts letter to Hugh Ross Williamson, 4.6.32 (HRHRC).

33. Baker, *I Follow But Myself*, p.119.

34. Gabriel Aitken painted the boards in Camilla's room after Wyndham Lewis designs. He also painted the square table and small corner cupboard in the salon (as well as Mary Butts's workbox) in the style of the Omega workshop.

35. Tony Butts undated letter to Mary Butts, November/December 1932. In June 1930 she had commented on how objects from her childhood were alive, see above, p.259.

36. Reviews by Mary Butts on gardening books include: 'On Gardens: Gardens and Gardening', *The Bookman*, 82, no.487 (Apr 1932), p.40; 'Our Native Land', *The Bookman*, 84, no.503 (Aug 1933), p.252; 'The Pleasures of Gardening', *The Sunday Times*, (3.12.33), p.15; 'On Gardens: Holding the Right Emotion', *The Sunday Times* (10.12.33), p.3; 'Gardens and Gardening', *The Bookman*, 86, no.513 (June 1934), p.161. 'Green Fingers', *Sunday Times* (8.12.35), p.12.

37. Mary Butts, 'On Gardens: Gardens and Gardening', loc. cit.

38. Mary Butts meant this quite literally. On the 12 March 1933 she noted that a morning's gardening made her "hungry for lunch and thirsty; bowels right".

39. This was very like her description of the house in 'The Guest' which was "perched like a wart on an eyebrow of flowery cliff 300 feet up from the Atlantic". Mary Butts, 'The Guest', in *LS*, p.19.

40. Mary Butts, 'Spring Storm', *The Manchester Guardian* (11.6.35), p.16.

41. "Life is in layers—where does this come in, the sensation of pleasure when the full teapot is lighter by the cup you are pouring out? 'Cup' here is not the china cup, but the idea of a quantity." Mary Butts, diary entry, 16.5.21. The following year she described Badbury Rings as a "a cup to hold me". Mary Butts, diary entry, 8.3.22. The opening sentence of *Ashe of Rings* ("Rings lay in a cup of turf.") is just one of many examples of her use of the word throughout her writing.

42. Mary Butts, 'The Warning', in *FATCP*, pp.117-118.

43. Mary Butts, 'The Guest', in *LS*, p.35; 'The Warning', in *FATCP*, p.126; 'Look Homeward, Angel, in *LS*, pp.14, 10, 15.

44. Mary Butts, 'Magic of Person and Place', *The Bookman*, 85, no.507 (Dec 1933), pp.141-143. In the Spring of 1934 she wrote a review of *Cornish Homes and Customs* by A.K. Hamilton Jenkins. Her laudatory account of the book reveals how the mores of the people of Cornwall fascinated her just as much as the land on which they lived: The "way of life [of the Cornish] is a very complete thing in itself, as Mr Jenkins shows. In a really interesting book, a collection of things seen and delighted in—food and fashions, anecdotes and snatches of song, tracing the varieties of ancient custom and usually, alas, their disappearance. It is highly local. He is showing Cornwall and nowhere else on earth." Mary Butts, 'Cornish Homes and Customs',

The Bookman 86, no.511 (April 1934), p.72. She also wrote longer articles about the customs of West Cornwall, e.g. 'Vandal Visitors to the West', Everyman, 39 (22.6.34), p.484, and 'The Seine Net: Community Fishing in Cornwall', *The Manchester Guardian* (8.3.35), p.9—for discussion see p329. Like Corin's *Sennen Cove and its Lifeboat*, these articles depict some of the features and the customs of West Penwith which have now disappeared.

45. Mary Butts draft of letter to Douglas Goldring, 2.2.32.

46. Mary Butts letter to Angus Davidson, 8.2.32 (Beinecke).

47. Baker, *I Follow But Myself*, p.135.

48. Mary Butts reviewed H.L. Mencken's *Treatise of Right and Wrong* in 'Mr Mencken Again, A Question of Ethics', *The Sunday Times* (30.9.34), p.12.

49. Tree potencies also figure in 'The Ash-Tree' by M.R. James, 'The Tree of Life' by Arthur Machen and 'The Man whom the Trees Loved' by Algernon Blackwood.

50. See Goldring, *The Nineteen Twenties*, p.199 and Bowen, *Drawn From Life*, pp.129-130.

51. On the 11 October 1931 Mary Butts recorded that she had "sent to Zukofsky, 50 Morton St. N.Y., 'Corfe', 'Thinking of Saints' and 'The American Child'". Only 'Corfe' was accepted for *An "Objectivists" Anthology*, ed. Louis Zukofsky (To Publisher, Le Beausset, Var, 1932), pp.36-39. John Wieners cited part of it in his 1963 article (see p.460, n.168) as did Patrick Wright in *The Village That Died For England*, pp.87-88. The poem was reprinted in full in *Antaeus* 12 (see p.467, n.81) and by Robin Blaser at the end of his Afterword to the 1979 reissue of *Imaginary Letters*, pp.77-80.

52. Mary Butts, 'Picus Martius', 'Thinking of Saints and of Petronius Arbiter', 'Douarnenez', 'Heartbreak House', *Soma*, 3 (1932), pp.41-48. Three of the poems had already been published: 'Heartbreak House', *Pagany* 1, no.3 (Jul-Sept 1930), pp.1-4; 'Thinking of Saints and of Petronius Arbiter', *Pagany*, 2, no.1 (Jan-March 1931), pp.95-7; 'Picus Martius', *Hound & Horn*, 13, no.2 (Jan-May 1930), pp.235-239.

53. "It is difficult to write anything about Oswell Blakeston, because he has spent most of his short life trying to avoid a label. Yesterday he was working in movies and founding a film society for the London proletarian, and to-day he is writing personally involved poems. He has composed a two movement sonatina for the organ, has designed book jackets, writes art criticism and (under a pseudonym) articles on comparative religion.

His greatest achievement, I think, was to make the film *Light Rhythms*, with Francis Bruguière.... He is an assistant editor of *Close-Up*, the only magazine devoted entirely to cinematograph aesthetics, experiment and development.... At the moment Blakeston is writing detective novels, with a collaborator, under the name 'Simon'. This list may give the reader some idea of the not inconsiderable achievement of a young artist still in his early twenties." Editorial on Oswell Blakeston, 'The Cinema in 1933', *The Bookman* (Dec. 1933), p.163.

Blakeston's reviews of Mary Butts's work include 'Plutarch's Siren', *Books and Bookmen* (March 1971), p.29. and 'Dangerous Enchanter', *Gay News*, 245 (25.11-8.12.82), pp.30-31. For comments by Blakeston on Mary Butts, see Hanscombe and Smyers, *Writing for their Lives*, pp.112, 241.

54. Mary Butts 'On an American Wonderchild who translated Homer at 8 years old', *Seed*, 1 (1933), pp.9-10. See Oswell Blakeston's letter under the heading "Seed" to *The New English Weekly* (May 1933).

55. In 1931 Mary Butts renamed 'Deosil' (meaning in the direction of the sun; clockwise) 'Widdershins' to reflect its rather contrary nature (Widdershins/Withershins—in the opposite way to the sun; anti-clockwise; with the secondary meaning of against the grain). It was published as 'Widdershins' in *Several Occasions*.

56. H.D. letter to editor, 14.3.[30]. Quoted in *A Return to Pagany*, p.444; Ezra Pound letter to Mary Butts, 2.12.31.

57. Hugh Ross Williamson letter to Mary Butts, 10.3.32.

58. Edward Crickmay, 'Latest Fiction: A Beautiful German Novel', *Sunday Referee*, 2845 (13.3.32), p.6.

59. 'Sophisticated Short Stories', *Northern Echo* (16.3.32).

60. Review of *Several Occasions*, *The Saturday Review* (26.3.32); '*Several Occasions* by Mary Butts', *The Observer* (20.3.32).

61. 'Realm of the Woman Novelist', *Glasgow Herald* (10.3.32).

62. '*Several Occasions* by Mary Butts', *The Yorkshire Post* (16.3.32); 'Critic's Commentary', *Time and Tide*, 13, no.13 (26.3.32), p.352.

63. R. Ellis Roberts, 'Short Stories', *The New Statesman & Nation*, 3, no.5 (12.3.32), pp.338, 340.

64. Mary Butts reviewed R.E. Mantz and J. Middleton Murry's *The Life of Katherine Mansfield* in 'A Biographical Problem, Katherine Mansfield's Early Life', *The Sunday Times* (31.12.33), p.6.

65. J.C. Squire, 'The Modern Revival of the Short Story: Miss Mary Butts's Success', *The Daily Telegraph* (8.3.32), p.16.

66. Ethel Colburn Mayne letter to Mary Butts, 13.4.32.

67. Editorial appended to Naomi Royde-Smith's letter to the editor, 'Mary Butts', *Time and Tide* 18, no.12 (20.3.37), p.378.

68. Possibly their acquaintance went back as far as the early months of 1916 (before Mary Butts began to keep a diary), when Lytton Strachey, like Virginia Woolf, Adrian Stephen and others did occasional office work in the Fleet St offices of the NCCL. They certainly knew one another in Paris in the 1920s: "Everybody here seems to be very trying nowadays and absolutely inescapable.... Mary Butts even pushed Lytton Strachey into me at the Boeuf the other night: he seems catastrophic. And asked me if *really* (you know how they talk from Cambridge—frankly I prefer what somebody called my 'dialect') I was amused." Benvenuto [surname unknown] letter to Lett Haines, 8.6.26. TGA. 8317.1.1.173.

69. Both were written in late 1931. *Warning To Hikers* was started on the 17 October, and with respect to *Traps for Unbelievers* Mary Butts wrote to Winifred Henderson [at Harmsworth]: "As for the pamphlet: ... what about this idea—my mind's been running on it for months. Substitutes to-day in the popular mind and in all our minds for the ideas and practices of religion, community-singing, cults of success or antiseptics or sex, psycho-analysis (that would get in 'pathological prose'). More especially, worship of daimons and old gods rediscovered in figures of aviators and movie-stars and athletes. A study of our world, perhaps for the first time—a world with the faith left out of it. What do you think? I know I could do it well." Mary Butts draft of letter to Mrs Henderson, 6.11.31 (headed 'The Family Fortune').

70. In early August 1931 Mary Butts noted "*Remember*: Rebecca West in the D.T. [Daily Telegraph] on the film-star substitutes for the gods". Afterwards she added "[Used later: 'Traps for Unbelievers'] Done".

71. *DFT* in *TTN*, p.179.

72. Mary Butts, *Traps for Unbelievers* (Harmsworth, 1932). Republished in *AOROW*. Henceforth referred to as *TFU* in *AOROW*, pp.299, 306, 312, 317.

73. Hugh Ross Williamson letter to Mary Butts, 10.3.32.

74. Hugh Ross Williamson, 'Religion and Science', *The Bookman*, 82 (April 1932), p.5.

75. George Pendle, '*Traps for Unbelievers*', *Twentieth Century*, 3, 15 (May 1932), pp.29-30. Other reviews of *Traps for Unbelievers* include '*Traps for Unbelievers*', *Public Opinion* (22.4.32); *The Church Times* (1.1.33); Philemon, 'A Monograph', *Scots Observer* (17.3.32); 'Modern Paganism', *Western Mirror[?] News* (19.3.32); 'Whither Shall We Worship?', *The Tatler* (4.5.32); 'Human "Gods"', *Sheffield Independent* (20.6.32); 'Religion and Life', *Oxford Mail* (6.4.32); '*Traps for Unbelievers*', *Times Literary Supplement* (9.6.32); '*Traps for Unbelievers*', *Liverpool Evening Express* (16.4.32); 'For the Library List', *Birmingham Mail* (27.4.32).

76. 'Tyneside: "A Public Catastrophe"', *Northern Echo* (19.4.32).

77. Mary Butts, *WTH* in *AOROW*, pp.272, 271.

78. The Taverners in *DFT*, for example are "country-bred, they went to capital cities in the same way as their ancestors, for their amenities and for the people they would find there. To the country they returned, as head-hunters or sea-raiders to examine spoil, but never as though their home could be anywhere else." Town-tuned Kralin is, by contrast, at a loss in the country: "geraniums and lobelias...as a Londoner was as far as his [botanical] vocabulary if not his imagination went." *DFT*, in *TTN*, pp.299, 244.

79. Tony Butts undated letter to Mary Butts, June 1932.

80. Louis Wilkinson letter to Mary Butts, 27.8.32.

81. James Agate, 'Good Writing', *Daily Express* (14.4.32), p.6. Agate reviewed several other books by Mary Butts; see bibliography.

82. Mary Butts draft of letter to Mary Colville-Hyde, 25.6.32. The reviews of *Warning to Hikers* reveal the extent of the interest in hiking at this time, e.g.: John Hargreave, 'Happy when they're hiking?', *The New Age* (9 May 1932), pp.69-70; C Henry Warren, 'Love of Nature?, *The Bookman*, 82, no.488 (May 1932), pp.116-7; 'A Bag of All Sorts', *The Manchester Guardian* (19.4.32); 'Townsmen and the Countryside', *The Glasgow Herald* (7 April 1932), p.8. B.D.N., 'On and off the English Roads', *The Week-end Review*, 5, no.117 (4.6.32), p.714.

83. Hugh Ross Williamson, 'Portrait of Mary Butts', *The Bookman*, 81 (Xmas 1931), pp.188-189. The article was accompanied by a drawing of Mary Butts by Archibald Ziegler.

84. "Rappelez-vous—(je suis en train d'écrire à mes amis à Paris) qu'il y avait une traduction de moi—de cette livre I.L. [*Imaginary Letters*] pour qui vous avez fait les desseins adorable, pour qui vous avez dit que vous m'écirez une préface—Est ce que c'est fait? J'ai entendu que cette Américaine qui édite l'Echéance, a annoncé leur publication avec cette préface de vous. Si c'est vrai, je vous remercie de tout mon coeur; si non, pouvez vous me renseigner?... Jean Desbordes, comment va-t-il? Et Jeannot [Bourgoint]? Mireille (sur quelle j'ai peur de poser les questions) Georges Auric? J'ai entendu par J.G. [Jean Guérin?] la fin atroce des de Malleissyes. Parmi nos amis en commun, Napier Alington fleurisse encore. Et surtout vous, Jean." Mary Butts undated draft of letter to Jean Cocteau, 2/3.3.32. This translation has not been found.

85. Mary Butts draft of letter to Duff Twysden, 25.6.32.

86. Mary Butts letter to Hugh Ross Williamson, 4.4.32 (HRHRC).

87. Ethel Colburn Mayne letter to Mary Butts, 19.4.32.

88. Mary Butts undated letter to Angus Davidson, dated June 1932 by Davidson (Beinecke).

89. Mary Butts, 'From Altar to Chimney-Piece', in *WAWB*, p.183.

90. Mary Butts letter to Hugh Ross Williamson, 5.12.32 (HRHRC).

91. Hugh Ross Williamson undated letter to Mary Butts, June 1932.

92. Hugh Ross Williamson, *The Poetry of T.S.Eliot* (Hodder and Stoughton Ltd, 1932), p.151.

93. Hugh Ross Williamson undated letter to Mary Butts, July 1932.

94. Gabriel's book was a thriller—a "shocker" as Mary Butts called it. Heinemann expressed interest in the novel, but it was never published.

95. J.C. Squire, who had so favourably reviewed *Several Occasions* in March 1932 (and would praise *DFT*), published 'After the Funeral' in the December 1932 issue of *The London Mercury*, which he edited. Mary Butts had a few doubts about the story 'The House'—was it "good enough" she asked herself in her journal. It was published posthumously in *Life and Letters To-day* in the summer of 1938. 'The Guest' was published at Ellis Roberts's invitation in *Life and Letters To-day* in the spring of 1935 (it originally had the working title of 'The man who could have been a painter'). 'With and Without Buttons' was never published in a small magazine during Mary Butts's lifetime, yet along with 'Speed the Plough' has been the most often re-

printed story since the 1980s, being included in four separate anthologies: *Ghosts in Country Villages* (1984); *With and Without Buttons and Other Stories* (1991); *The Virago Book of Ghost Stories: II* (1991) and *From Altar to Chimney-piece: Selected Stories* (1992).

96. This was not the first time that Mary Butts wrote to M.R. James; they corresponded in 1928 about his book, *Five Jars*. "I've at last managed to write a ghost story myself, which should come out soon—in *The Adelphi* or something like that and anyhow in a book—and since any quality it may have it owes to your influence, I want to be allowed to dedicate it to you.... And if I do not hear from you to forbid me, I shall understand that I may acknowledge my debt to you on the title page." Mary Butts undated draft of letter to M.R. James, 23.9.32. There is no reply from James among Mary Butts's papers, but 'With and Without Buttons' was published posthumously without a dedication. "It was inevitable that she should have admired the work of M.R. James, and one of her ghost stories, 'With and Without Buttons' (*Last Stories*) is equal to almost anything written by the master himself." Louis Adeane, 'Mary Butts', *World Review* (September 1951), pp.23-27. Reprinted as 'An Appraisal of Mary Butts' in *ASQ*, p.105.

97. Joan Manning-Sanders letter to Nathalie Blondel, 17.7.90.

98. Mary Butts draft of letter to Mary Colville-Hyde, 24.7.32.

99. Baker, *I Follow But Myself*, p.116.

100. Louis Wilkinson letter to Mary Butts, 27.8.32.

101. In a diary entry for late November 1931 when Mary Butts had first decided to dedicate *Several Occasions* to Douglas Goldring, she had written "D G Dedication. 'O saisons , O châteaux'; 'Go and catch a falling star'." On the 17 September 1932 she added: "None of the lovely or enchanting words or 'fancies chaste and noble' would do. It went without. The answer is in this last August." From the correspondence between Mary Butts and Wilkinson, it is clear that Goldring also quarrelled (temporarily) with Wilkinson.

102. This actually happened after Mary Butts's death when William Plomer parodied her work in his *Museum Pieces* (1952). See p.437.

103. No doubt it was Mary Butts's interest in the moon which led to the description of Anne Clavel as Anna Perenna in 'A Lover'. See above, p.469, n. 125.

104. The title comes from the anonymous Scottish prayer: "From ghosties and ghoulies and long-leggety beasties/And things that go bump in the night,/Good Lord, deliver us." *The Penguin Dictionary of Quotations*, ed. J.M. and M.J. Cohen (Jonathan Cape, 1960), p.6.

105. There is no record of the original dedication.

106. Hugh Ross Williamson undated letter to Mary Butts, October 1932.

107. Mary Butts letter to Hugh Ross Williamson, 28.10.32 (HRHRC).

108. Patrick Wright locates "the house and garden over which Mary Butts had superimposed the racially threatened ancestral home of Felicity Taverner". See Wright, *The Village That Died for England*, pp.85 and 234.

109. Wynyard Browne, 'A Great Novel: *Death of Felicity Taverner*', *The Bookman*, 83, no.695 (Xmas 1932), p.306.

110. Hugh Ross Williamson undated letter to Mary Butts, mid-late Oct 1932.

111. Forster was no doubt amused by Mary Butts's quotation from his novel, *A Passage to India* (1924), in *Death of Felicity Taverner*. See *DFT* in *TTN*, p.295 and E.M. Forster, *A Passage to India* (Penguin, 1960 reprint), p.175.

112. Filson Young letter to Mary Butts, 28.11.32.

113. Ethel Colburn Mayne letter to Mary Butts, 13.12.32.

114. Mary Colville-Hyde letter to Mary Butts, 28.11.32.

115. Tony Butts undated letter to Mary Butts, Nov/Dec 1932.

116. Gwendolin Raverat, 'New Fiction', *Time and Tide* 13, no.49 (3.12.32), p.1348.

117. L.A.G. Strong, 'Fiction', *The Spectator* (23.12.32), p.900.

118. 'A Tale No Man Can Tell', *London Evening News* (29.11.32).

119. Ethel Colburn Mayne letter to Mary Butts, 30.12.32.

120. *'Death of Felicity Taverner'*, *Times Literary Supplement* (29.12.32), p.988.

121. Strong, loc. cit.

122. Browne, loc. cit.

123. I have only quoted from some of the many reviews of *Death of Felicity Taverner*. Others included: Geoffrey Grigson, *Yorkshire Post* (14.12.32); Storm Jameson, 'Recent Novels', *New English Weekly* (5.1.33), p.281; 'The Soul in Fiction', *Observer* (12.2.33), p.8; Helen Moran, 'Fiction II', *London Mercury*, 27, no.159 (January 1933), p.273; 'Sophisticated Melodrama', *Punch* (18.1.33); '*Death of Felicity Taverner* by Mary Butts', *Evening Standard* (December? 1932); T.M., 'A Memorable Novel', *The Manchester Guardian* (9.12.32), p.7; '*Death of Felicity Taverner* by Mary Butts', *Birmingham Post* (13.12.32); Lilian Arnold, 'Novel of the Week: Russian and English', *John O'London's Weekly* (10.12.32), p.438; Gerald Gould, 'Two Strange Novels by Women', *News Chronicle* (29.12.32), p.4; F.J. Mathias, 'Plumbing the Depths', *The Western Mail* (15.12.32), p.11. There was also a review in Italian by the poet, Basil Bunting, 'Uno dei Mali dell'Inghilterra', *Il Mare* (1933). Work by Bunting and Mary Butts had been published in the January-March 1931 issue of *Pagany* and she referred to Bunting's review in a letter to Ezra Pound. See Mary Butts letter to Ezra Pound, 10.11.34 (Beinecke).

124. Mary Butts, 'G & G' in *AOROW*, p.343.

125. Mary Butts letter to Hugh Ross Williamson, 5.12.32.

126. Edgell Rickword letter to Mary Butts, 5.12.32.

127. R.R. Tatlock, 'X-Rays Reveal a Masterpiece', *The Daily Telegraph* (27.2.30), p.13 (three photographs of the Holbein painting on p.16); Frank Davis, 'A Page for Collectors: The Newly Discovered Holbein portrait of Sir William Butts: A Triumph for X-Rays and Scholarship', *The Illustrated London News* (8.3.30), pp.394-396; *Bulletin of the Museum of Fine Arts*, 34 (1930), pp.19-20. See also p.476, n.231. In 1935 Mary Colville-Hyde wrote her own article to try and promote the sale of the portrait: 'The Boston Holbeins, Sir William Butts and Lady Butts', *Apollo: the Journal of the Arts for Connoisseurs and Collectors*, 22, no.127 (July 1935), pp.36-38.

128. His biographer described Joseph Duveen "who became Lord Duveen of Millbank before he died in 1939, at the age of sixty-nine" as "the most spectacular art dealer of all time". S.N. Behrman, *Duveen* (Hamish Hamilton, 1952), p.1.

129. Mary Butts letter to Ada Briggs, 8.3.33. This incident forms the basis of James Charters's anecdote, see above, pp.222-3.

130. Mary Colville-Hyde letter to Ada Briggs, 9.8.32.

131. Mary Colville-Hyde undated letter to Mary Butts, Sept-Oct 1932.

132. Mary Colville-Hyde undated letter to Mary Butts, Nov-Dec 1932.

133. Tancred Borenius (1885-1948). Finnish art historian who settled in England around 1910. Lectured at University College London where he was Professor of History of Art from 1922-1947.

134. Tony Butts undated letter to Mary Butts, Nov 1932.

135. Mary Butts letter to Hugh Ross Williamson, 5.12.32 (HRHRC).

136. Mary Butts had been reading the recently published second edition of T.S. Eliot's *Essays* a few weeks earlier and had been greatly impressed by them. 'Tradition and the Individual Talent' (1919) was included.

137. Hugh Ross Williamson undated letter to Mary Butts, early Dec 1932.

138. Hugh Ross Williamson undated letter to Mary Butts, Nov 1932. See also pp.429-30.

139. Mary Colville-Hyde letters to Ada Briggs, 9.8.32 and 15.11.32.

140. Mary Colville-Hyde letter to Ada Briggs, 15.7.32.

141. Mary Colville-Hyde undated letter to Mary Butts, Autumn 1932.

142. Mary Butts draft of letter to Mary Colville-Hyde, 12.10.32.

143. Mary Butts letter to Ada Briggs, 2.1.33.

144. Mary Butts letter to Ada Briggs, 10.1.33.

145. An increasing number of accounts by the children of writers and artists (e.g. Angelica Garnett, *Deceived with Kindness: A Bloomsbury Childhood* (1984)) now exist. See also Smyers and Hanscombe, *Writing for their Lives*, a study which shows that Mary Butts was not, unfortunately, untypical in her attitude to her child.

146. Mary Butts letter to Ada Briggs, 10.1.33.

147. Mary Colville-Hyde undated letter to Mary Butts, Jan-Feb 1933.

148. Mary Colville-Hyde letter to Ada Briggs, postmarked 16.12.32.

149. Mary Butts letter to Hugh Ross Williamson, 11.12.32 (HRHRC).

150. Baker, *I Follow But Myself*, p.115. Perhaps the lily in Gabriel's card reminded Mary Butts of the final verse of her poem, 'December 1912' (see pp.28-9):

O London streets, O lights of Picadilly,
Voice of the Strand, O watchers of my loss!
London, O Mother, have you not seen a lily
Spring shining from the mud at Charing Cross?

151. Mary Butts letter to Ada Briggs, 10.1.33.

152. "Chapel Carn Brea was the site of at least eight barrows and seems to have been of some funerary importance. During the early Bronze Age, a burial cist was set on the side of the barrow...on the top of the 'First and Last' hill [Carn Brea] and the whole site was buried beneath another stone mound.... In the thirteenth century, the tiny hermitage of the chapel of St. Michael of Brea was built on the very top of the cairn. Here the hermits kept a beacon for the guidance of local fishermen and for land-travellers (a major ancient trackway passes the hill). The chapel was demolished in 1816, having become a dangerous ruin, and its stone was used to build a barn at the foot of the hill. ...traditional midsummer bonfires...are still lit there, with full ceremony spoken in Cornish, each midsummer's eve." Craig Weatherhill, *Belerion: Ancient Sites of Land's End* (Alison Hodge, 1989), p.9. For more details about the 740 feet high Carn Brea, see also C. Lewis Hind, *Days in Cornwall* (Methuen, 1924), pp.136-7

153. Mary Colville-Hyde letter to Mary Butts, 10.1.33.

154. Mary Butts letter to Ada Briggs, 22.1.33.

155. Mary Butts letter to Ada Briggs, 31.1.33.

156. Mary Butts letter to Ada Briggs, 3.2.33.

157. Mary Butts's dedication was "To Gabriel, χᾷριδτριον [a thank-offering]".

158. Mary Colville-Hyde letter to Ada Briggs, 7.12.32.

159. Harcourt Wesson Bull, '"Truth is the Heart's Desire"', in *ASQ*, p.74.

160. Hugh Ross Williamson undated letter to Mary Butts, February 1933. Actually Hugh Ross Williamson did marry; Margaret Ross Williamson was one of the many people who generously gave me a great deal of their time and shared with me their relevant papers when I was researching this biography.

161. Mary Butts letter to Ada Briggs, 16.1.33.

162. In a laudatory review of Vera Brittain's *Testament of Youth* in October 1933, Mary Butts particularly praised this autobiography for its "directness, its naiveté, its candour, its utter sincerity.... For the people who lived through what she tells...a cry is wrung out of one's heart: 'Yes, it was like that'... No one else has better realised than Miss Brittain the hideous

danger, the awful futility of war as it is likely to come upon us now. Or of our late experience, men refer to correctly as 'The War'." Mary Butts, 'It was Like That', *The Bookman*, 84, no.505 (Oct 1933), p.44. See p.343 for corresponding reaction to *Ashe of Rings*.

163. Mary Butts, Preface to *TM*, in *TCN*, p.5.

164. Margaret Anderson, *My Thirty Years War* (Covici, Friede, 1930), pp.210-211. For more information see poems by Else von Freytag-Loringhoven in *The Little Review*, 7, no.2 (July-Aug 1920), pp.28-30, 37-40, and John Rodker's discussion of her work in which he claims: "It is possible that Else von Freytag-Loringhoven is the first Dadaist in New York" (ibid, pp.33-36). (This same issue of *The Little Review* also contained Mary Butts's short story, 'Magic', and an extract from Joyce's Ulysses.) See also the entry on Baroness Elsa von Freytag-Loringhoven in Francis M. Naumann, *New York Dada, 1915-1923* (Harry N. Abrams Inc., 1994), pp.168-175.

165. Mary Butts letter to Hugh Ross Williamson, 20.1.33 (HRHRC).

166. Mary Butts may well be referring to Conan Doyle's story, 'Charles Augustus Milverton', in *The Return of Sherlock Holmes* (1905). See p.195.

167. Mary Butts letter to Hugh Ross Williamson, 1932. Quoted in *ASQ*, p.147. She had had a similar feeling about a spot in east Sussex when staying at Little Thornsdale. "The day I found the waterfall and the small anemone valley, the stream choked with rotten wood, the dead boughs that snapped, the pool below the rock that was not quite pure, the slight taint about the place made me a little uneasy." Mary Butts, diary entry, 24.4.31. She described the spot in more detail in *WTH* in *AOROW*, pp.281-2.

168. Mary Butts, 'The Guest' in *LS*, pp.22, 19, 22, 30, 35, 44, 45.

169. Mary Butts, 'The Sanc Grail', *The Bookman*, 84, no.499 (Spring 1933), pp.72-4. Six years earlier Mary Butts had quoted from "Machen on the study of occultism: 'But I would advise any curious person who desires to investigate this singular character of the mind to beware of over-thoroughness...avoid all deep and systematic study... For if you go too far, you will be disenchanted.'" Mary Butts, diary entry, 22.7.27. In 1935 she wrote: "Re-read Machen on the Sancgrail. Understood again—and its principle—that it is the rule of great mystical and magical experiences that it cannot be told *directly*. It must be expressed by an indirection. In the matter of the Grail, art, 12th century art, the art, for example of Salisbury came in contact with the experience, the existence in the tangible world of that Sanctity, and expressed it by means of a translation." Mary Butts, diary entry, 11.8.35. Here is another (oblique) allusion to her use of the knight's move.

170. Mary Butts, 'The Seine Net: Community Fishing in Cornwall', *The Manchester Guardian* (8.3.35), p.9. See Harcourt Wesson Bull, '"Truth is the Heart's Desire"', in *ASQ*, p.78; Manning-Sanders, *The West of England*, p.48. For the kind of description that Mary Butts might have read on the subject, see J. Harris Stone, *England's Riviera: A Topographical and Archaeological description of Land's End, Cornwall and adjacent spots of Beauty and Interest* (Kegan Paul, Trench, Trubner & Co, 1912), pp.45-47.

171. Ethel Colburn Mayne letter to Mary Butts, 30.12.32.

172. R. Ellis Roberts letter to Mary Butts, 24.1.33.

173. R. Ellis Roberts, 'Tale of Two Worlds', *The New Statesman and Nation* (24.12.32) 4, no.96, p.837.

174. Mary Butts letter to Ada Briggs, 16.2.33.

175. R. Ellis Roberts, *Portrait of Stella Benson* (Macmillan, 1939). "Isn't it terrible about Stella Benson. Just my age, and dead with her lovely gifts. From her eyes I never thought she'd stay here long—tho' I never knew her." Mary Butts undated letter to Hugh Ross Williamson, November/December 1933 (HRHRC).

176. See letter from R. Ellis Roberts to Gilbert Murray, 8.10.34 (Bodleian). Mary Butts's stories published in *Life and Letters To-day* were 'A Lover', 'The Warning', 'The Guest', 'In the House', 'Mappa Mundi', 'Look Homeward, Angel', 'The House' and 'Honey, get your Gun'.

177. Douglas Goldring letter to Mary Butts, 14.3.33. See anon (Douglas Goldring), 'Alexander the Great', *Sunday Referee* 2900 (2.4.33), p.9. It is odd that there was no recommendation, since Hugh Ross Williamson wrote to Mary Butts: "Hugh Walpole tried to persuade the Book Society to choose *The Macedonian*" (undated letter [May 1933]). Hugh Walpole certainly chose it amongst the books which had "given [him] pleasure" in 'Some books I have enjoyed in 1933', *The Bookman*, 85, no.507 (Dec 1933), p.137.

178. Hugh Ross Williamson undated letter to Mary Butts, May 1933.

179. Naomi Royde-Smith undated letter to Mary Butts, March 1933.

180. Ethel Colburn Mayne letter to Mary Butts, 14.4.33.

181. R. Ellis Roberts, 'Reviews and Impressions of Alexander', *The Guardian* (28.4.33).

182. *TM*, in *TCN*, pp.3-4. For his "lead" see E.M. Forster, 'The return to Siwa', *Pharos and Pharillon* (Hogarth, 1923), pp.20-22. Jack Lindsay commented on this aspect of *The Macedonian*: "It seems to me that after Siwa [Alexander's] image of himself changed from Achilles to Osiris ... It's not merely a bit of antiquarianism since it sheds light on A's aims and the effect of Egypt on him: which Forster and you seem alone to have fully appreciated." Jack Lindsay letter to Mary Butts, 19.6.34.

183. E.M. Forster letter to Mary Butts, 14.3.33.

184. E.M. Forster, *Alexandria, a History and a Guide* (Whitehead Morris & Co, 1922).

185. Robin Blaser, Afterword to *IL*, p.64.

186. *'The Macedonian'*, *Times Literary Supplement* (20.7.33), p.494.

187. T.M., 'A Study of Greatness', *The Manchester Guardian* (16.3.33), p.5.

188. Wynyard Browne, 'Greek and Barbarian', *The Bookman*, 84, no.499 (April 1933), pp.44-5.

189. Humbert Wolfe, 'King of the World', *The Observer* (12.3.33), p.5.

190. See W.J. Blyton, 'Far Past Revived: Men are Enemies', *Sheffield Independent* (13.3.33); T.M., *The Manchester Guardian*, loc. cit.; *'The Macedonian'*, *The Leytonshire Express* (13.8.33); Joseph Sell, 'Plus something Plutarch Had Got?', *The Manchester Evening News* (16.3.33); John Coghlan, 'The Macedonian', *Everyman* (29.8.33).

191. See 'A Great Book by A Woman', *Bristol Evening World*, (1.4.33) and Helen Moran, 'Fiction II', *The London Mercury*, 28, no.163 (May 1933), p.78.

192. Edmund Blunden, 'Alexander', *Time and Tide*, 14, no.17 (29.4.33), pp.501-502.

193. See *'The Macedonian'*, *The Sketch* (17.5.33); *'The Macedonian'*, *The Scotsman* (27.3.33); L.P. Hartley, 'New Books', *The Week-end Review*, 7, no.166 (13.5.33), pp.539-540.

194. Sell, op. cit.; 'Selected Novels', *Nottingham Guardian* (22.3.33); untitled review, *Inverness Courier* (24.3.33); Mary Butts letter to Hugh Ross Williamson, 4.4.33 (HRHRC).

195. John Coghlan, 'A Letter of Appreciation to Miss Mary Butts', *The Bookman*, 84, no.499 (April 1933), p.69.

196. Helen Moran, loc. cit.

197. The terms were the same as for *The Macedonian*: An advance of £50 and a print run of 1,500. It was sold at 7/6d. Unfortunately the record of the sales figures has not survived.

198. Mary Butts letter to Ada Briggs, 8.3.33.

199. Hugh Ross Williamson undated letter to Mary Butts, late April 1933.

200. *'Ashe of Rings'*, *Philadelphia Inquirer* (10.7.26).

201. Mary Butts letter to Hugh Ross Williamson, 4.4.33 (HRHRC).

202. Mary Butts incorporates her own signature into the review when giving an account of the different earings worn through the ages: "a gold bird on a perch, a cluster of pearl grapes, a button of diamond, jet, enamel, a cartwheel of jade..." Harcourt Wesson Bull remarked on her striking wheel-shaped jade earring in Villefranche, see above, p.197.

203. For a delicate story in which a father would "rather see [his] daughter in her coffin than going about in the streets as those fallen women do, their shameless heads uncovered", see 'The Green Cupboard' (1952) in Frances Bellerby, *Selected Stories* (Enitharmon, 1986), p.116.

204. Virginia Woolf, *Three Guineas* (Penguin, 1993), pp.118-119. Originally published by the Hogarth Press in 1938, a year after Mary Butts's death.

205. Whilst Tony was sent to Eton, Mary Butts went to a minor public school in St. Andrew's. See *TCC*, pp.179-185.

206. Mary Butts, 'The Girl through the Ages', *The Bookman*, 84, no.500 (May 1933), p.110.

207. Denys Val Baker, *The Spirit of Cornwall* (W.H. Allen & Co, 1980), p.57. Oddly, given his friendship with Frank Baker and the fact that he would publish one of Mary Butts's stories, Val Baker does not mention Mary Butts in this lyrical account of the effect of Cornwall on its inhabitants and visitors, particularly writers and artists.

208. Mary Butts letter to Ada Briggs, 5.4.33.

209. Mary Butts undated letter to Ada Briggs, early April 1933.

210. Mary Butts, 'Cornish Homes and Customs', *The Bookman*, 86, no.511 (Spring 1934), p.72. See Val Baker, *The Spirit of Cornwall*, pp.89-90; Harris Stone, *England's Riviera*, p.397.

211. Naomi Royde-Smith sent Mary Butts a card the following week: "The irises or irides are still living and tall in vases and remind me of Penzance and Cleopatra. I hope she is striding through her chapters. We dined with the Ellis Roberts and spoke of you and your work in *such* terms..." Naomi Royde-Smith postcard to Mary Butts, 20.5.33.

212. For the source of Mary Butts's short story, 'One Roman Speaks', see 'The Life of Julius Caesar' in *Plutarch's Lives*, volume 7, englished by Sir Thomas North (J.M. Dent, 1899), p.120.

213. Theo Bartholomew was probably A.R. Bartholomew, a friend of A.J.A. Symons. See Donald Weeks, *Corvo* (Michael Joseph, 1971), p.432.

214. Little is known about Sir Roderick Meiklejohn (possibly a neighbour of Mary Butts's), except that he was a friend of A.J.A. Symons.

215. Mary Butts draft of a letter to an unnamed friend [Edgell Rickword], 27.8.33.

216. Mary Butts letter to Angus Davidson, 30.8.33 (Beinecke).

217. William Plomer's *Cecil Rhodes* (1933), see below, p.509, n.71

218. This would not have been a random guess by Tony, since in late 1924, Mary Butts's interest in this subject had led her to read Breasted's *History of Egypt* and copy into her diary a list of the various reigns within the Akhnaton dynasty.

219. Tony Butts letter to Mary Butts, 27.3.33.

220. Tony Butts undated letter to Mary Butts, April 1933.

221. Mary Butts letter to Angus Davidson, 3.9.33 (Beinecke).

222. Tony Butts undated letter to Mary Butts, Sept. 1933.

223. Ibid.

224. Mary Butts letter to Angus Davidson, 8.9.33 (Beinecke).

225. Mary Butts's first review was of David Gascoyne's *Opening Day*, D.M. Low's *Twice Shy* and Peter Hall's *Midnight Sun* in 'For Special People', *John O'London's Weekly*, 30, no.756 (7.10.33), p.22. David Gascoyne was unaware of this review. David Gascoyne letter to Nathalie Blondel, 1993.

226. Mary Butts draft of letter to Leonard Moore, 2.11.33.

227. On this cover his name is given as 'Gabriel Atkin'; he uses both spellings in the 1930s. E.g.: '"Now I'm worth 20,000 a year."' (illustration), *The Bookman* (Nov 1931) which is signed "Gabriel Aitken".

228. Henry Fraser, 'Printed in Paris', *Everyman*, 10, no.242 (16.9.33), p.320.

229. Hugh l'A. Fausset, 'A "War Fairy-Tale"', *The Manchester Guardian* (22.9.33), p.5; 'Seven New Novels: Conflicts and Follies of the War', *The Glasgow Herald* (28.9.33). A week later Mary Butts reviewed l'Anson Fausset's *A Modern Prelude* in 'The Dark Tower', *Time and Tide*, 14, no.39 (30.9.33), pp.1153-1154.

230. See M.J., '*Ashe of Rings* by Mary Butts', *The New Age* (30.11.33), pp.58-59; '*Ashe of Rings*', *The Northern Echo* (27.?.33); E.B.C. Jones, 'New Novels', *The New Statesman and Nation*, 6, no.136 (30.9.33), pp.388-389.

231. Edward Crickmay, 'The Latest Novels', *Sunday Referee*, 2927 (8.10.33), p.11; E.M. Delafield, *Morning Post* (29[?].9.33); Gerald Gould, *The Observer*, (29.8.33); *News Chronicle* (16[?].10.33).

232. See reviews in *Northern Echo*, loc. cit. and William Plomer, 'Fiction', *The Spectator* (29.9.33), p.420; also '*Ashe of Rings*', *Times Literary Supplement* (5.10.33), p.673. Crickmay's review in the *Sunday Referee*, loc. cit., and Richard Church's 'Grim Fairy Tale', *John O'London's Weekly*, 30, no.754 (23.9.33) , p.889-890, wrongly described *Ashe of Rings* as a "new" novel.

233. William Plomer, loc. cit.

234. Clifford Bax letter to Mary Butts, 2.10.33. When he came to write his autobiography after the Second World War, Bax only said in passing: "A few people may still even remember the strange and somewhat obscure books that were written by...[the] handsome...Mary Butts—a big-hearted bohemian who died young." Clifford Bax, *Rosemary for Remembrance* (Frederick Muller Ltd, 1948), p.196.

235. R. Ellis Roberts letter to Mary Butts, All Helwas [1.11] 1933.

236. R. Ellis Roberts letter to Mary Butts, 19.11.33.

237. It is not known exactly when Mary Butts started employing Moore as her agent; perhaps when she stayed in London in 1931.

238. Mary Butts draft of letter to Leonard Moore, 2.11.33.

239. Ibid.

240. Ethel Colburn Mayne letter to Mary Butts, 8.11.33.

241. Tony Butts letter to Mary Butts, 11.8.33.

242. Mary Butts's desk which stood in the living room salon. It was reproduction Queen Anne.

243. Mary Butts described her reaction to the biography of Nijinsky in great detail in an undated letter to Angus Davidson, Thursday, added in his handwriting: Late 1933 or early 1934, pp.2-3 (Beinecke).

244. Mary Butts undated card to Angus Davidson, Xmas 1933 (Beinecke).

245. Douglas Goldring letter to Mary Butts, 29.12.33.

246. The writer and art critic, Adrian Stokes, made the same link between Cornwall and Hellas: "I was attracted later to the peninsula between the two seas, extending on the north from St Ives to Land's End. I thought of it as the only part of Britain belonging to the geography of the ancient world. It was certainly a fount of tin and so, perhaps, of Greek bronzes. Hills of Celtic and Stone-Age traces were once Phoenician land-marks, traversed for long after by the single file of pack-mules. On the north coast near Zennor, a wide pasture-land spreads between the surf and the hills, of Homeric scale it seems to the observer who is picking out the farm communities and noting the inhospitable sea, the isolated perpendicular stones and the network of bright walls. Warm fertile valleys that run down the other side to Mount's Bay where, they say, Phoenician tin was shipped, would accord with a sense, particularly in autumn, of ancient fire." Adrian Stokes, *Smooth and Rough* (Faber, 1951), p.17.

247. Mary Butts, 'The Art of Montagu James', *The London Mercury*, 29, 172 (Feb 1934), pp.306-313. For James's response, see Michael Cox, *M.R. James: An Informal Portrait* (O.U.P., 1986) p.141.

248. Mary Butts's enthusiasm for Charles Williams's work had led her to write to him. He wrote back on the 10 January to say that he was "indebted" for her letter which he had found thought-provoking.

249. Mary Butts letter to Angus Davidson, 20-22.1.34 (Beinecke).

250. Mary Butts letter to Angus Davidson, 5.3.34 (Beinecke).

251. Although there is no reference to *The Macedonian* in Mary Renault's *The Nature of Alexander* (1975), the very form of Renault's novels, *Fire From Heaven* (1970) and *The Persian Boy* (1972) do echo that of Mary Butts's life of Alexander...

252. Baker, *I Follow But Myself*, pp. 117-118. Baker also commented on the influence of Mary Butts's work on his own: "I do not exaggerate the effect *The Macedonian* had upon me; for it drew me into the main stream of historical tradition, exposed my lack of scholarship, and taught me that the true writer must call upon powers he may not even know exist in him. *The Macedonian* became the gateway to my own work, a key book for me." Baker, *I Follow But Myself*, p.121.

253. Not only did he pay tribute to Mary Butts in a long chapter devoted to her in *I Follow But Myself*; Baker was also responsible for republishing Mary Butts's work: 'Look Homeward, Angel' was reprinted in *The Cornish Review*, no. 16 (Winter 1970), pp.9-14, prefaced by 'A Note on Mary Butts' by Baker, pp.4-8; *The Cornish Review* was edited by Denys Val Baker, whom Baker persuaded to include 'With and Without Buttons'in his 1984 supernatural anthology, *Ghosts in Country Villages*. He also mentions Mary Butts in his Introduction to the re-issue of Bernard Walke's *Twenty Years at St. Hilary*, [p.v], and *The Call of Cornwall* (1976).

254. Baker, *I Follow But Myself*, pp.114-115.

255. Ibid, pp.122-123.

256. MB undated letter to Hugh Ross Williamson, September 1933 (HRHRC).

257. Mary Butts letter to Angus Davidson, 4.2.34 (Beinecke).

258. See also Bryher's comment on Mary Butts, p.431.

259. *TCC*, p.180.

260. Mary Butts letter to Harcourt Wesson Bull, 1.10.35 (Beinecke).

261. Mary Butts, 'A Man Possessed', *Time and Tide*, 15, no.7 (17.2.34), pp.212-214, p.212. The interest in Corvo was fairly wide-spread at this time. Three months later Leonard Moore (her agent) himself published 'More about Corvo' in *The Bookman*, 86, no.511 (April 1934), pp.8-11.

262. A.J.A. Symons letter to Mary Butts, 18.1.34.

263. Mary Butts, 'Baron Corvo', *The London Mercury*, 30, no 175 (May 1934), pp.619-624.

264. This is a reference to Mary Butts's story, 'Scylla and Charybdis'.

265. A.J.A. Symons letter to Mary Butts, 5.5.34.

266. See Donald Weeks, *Corvo*, p.432. There are a few notes about it in Mary Butts's diary in early April 1936, but otherwise there is no trace of this operatic version of Rolfe's *Don Tarquinino: A Kataleptic Phantasmatic Romance*, described in A.J.A. Symons's *The Quest For Corvo* (Penguin, 1950 reprint), pp. 132-133. Apparently Gabriel Aitken was "a great and early admirer of [Rolfe]" and lent Osbert Sitwell a book by Rolfe in 1919. See *The Scarlet Tree: Being the second volume of Left Hand, Right Hand. The Autobiography of Osbert Sitwell* (Macmillan, 1946), p.244.

267. Mary Butts, 'The Finer Corvo', *Time and Tide*, 16 no.49 (7.12.35), pp.1800, 1802. See Mary Butts's letter to A.J.A. Symons, 22.11.35 (Bodleian, 1935 MS.Don.c.149).

268. Mary Butts did contribute articles to the *Everyman*, including a general discussion of 'Alexander the Great', *Everyman*, 29 (13.4.34), pp.209, 224 and 'Vandal Visitors to the West', *Everyman*, 39 (22.6.34), p.484.

269. R. Ellis Roberts letter to Mary Butts, 8.4.34. In a letter later in the year in which he praised her story, 'The Warning', he asked: "have you ever tried a play? Yeats was here at lunch today, and he's helping to start a new theatrical venture (he is 70 next year) with T.S. Eliot and W.H. Auden, and... suprisingly, Ashley Dukes. They will need plays, and look for them to be 'modern' to use a foolish word. I believe you could write an exciting play." R. Ellis Roberts letter to Mary Butts, 22.12.34. There is no evidence that she took up his suggestion to submit a play to the Group Theatre, established by Rupert Doone in 1932, which published its own manifesto in January 1934. See Medley, *Drawn from the Life*, pp.145-153.

270. Mary Butts letter to Hugh Ross Williamson, 6.10.33 (HRHRC).

271. Mary Butts, 'King Harry', *Time and Tide*, 15, no.13 (31.3.34), pp.412-413; 'Scandal or History', *Time and Tide* 15, no.18 (5.5.34), pp.584-586; 'The Past Lives Again', *The Bookman*, 86, no.511 (April 1934), pp.44-45.

272. Una Broadbent letter to Mary Butts, 17.5.34.

273. Jack Lindsay undated letter to Mary Butts, April 1934.

274. Jack Lindsay letter to Mary Butts, 1.5.34.

275. Lindsay, *Fanfrolico and After*, p.145.

276. But not always. Jack Lindsay recommended his brother Philip Lindsay's historical novels to Mary Butts. In fact, Mary Butts had already reviewed one in: 'King Richard III Defended', *The Sunday Times*, (8.10.33), p.8. She did, however, review another in 'King Henry the Fifth: Behind the Curtain of History', *The Sunday Times*, (6.1.35), p.8.

277. Jack Lindsay letter to Mary Butts, 1.5.34. She explained her position in her autobiography: "What is our difficulty in writing about the past? When we have gathered together the clothes and the toys, the beliefs and the disbeliefs; the states of the weather, trade, agriculture, the arts, the diseases, the disasters and the dreams—what is it then we have to do which is impossible or almost impossible for us? Get the temper that went with those, the ambience in which they moved. Not what they did—and that is hard enough—but how. In what humour, with what half-realized values behind? These debates are facile, but it is not easy to get to the heart of them." *TCC*, pp.53-54.

278. Jack Lindsay undated letter to Mary Butts, May 1934.

279. Jack Lindsay was not alone in thinking *The Macedonian* superior to *I, Claudius*. Writing of Mary Butts's two historical narratives, Ellis Roberts claimed: "I think her work in this kind...reconstructions of the past...is better than Robert Graves's and Jack Lindsay's. Her lamp of learning has a clearer wick than theirs." R. Ellis Roberts, 'A London Letter', *The Saturday Review of Literature* (11.1.36), p.17.

280. Ibid.

281. Mary Butts, *The Classical Novels: The Macedonian and Scenes from the Life of Cleopatra*, (McPherson & Company, 1994), Preface by Thomas McEvilley.

282. Jack Lindsay undated letter to Mary Butts, June 1934.

283. Jack Lindsay undated letter to Mary Butts, late May 1934.

284. Mary Butts letter to Angus Davidson, 3.5.34 (Beinecke).

285. Lord Gorell letter to Mary Butts, 1.8.34.

286. Mary Butts, 'One Roman Speaks', *The Cornhill*, 152, no.910 (Oct 1935), pp 448-465.

287. Mary Butts draft of letter to Mary Colville-Hyde, 3.6.34.

288. Bryher, 'Recognition Not Farewell', in *ASQ*, p.3.

289. Mary Butts, 'The Warning', *Life and Letters* 11, no.61 (Jan 1935), pp.396-404.

290. Mary Butts letters to Angus Davidson, 23.10, 28.10, 9.11, 19.12.34 (Beinecke).

291. Dod Proctor and Gladys Hynes studied art together at the Newlyn School of Art. Dod Proctor painted a striking portrait of Gladys's younger sister, Sheelah Hynes, in the 1910s. See

Dod Proctor RA 1892-1972 (Tyne and Wear Museums, 1990), pp.38-39.

292. Tony Butts undated letter to Mary Butts, Sept/Oct 1934.

293. Mary Butts letter to Angus Davidson, 13.9.34 (Beinecke).

294. Mary Butts, '"Mr Ezra Pound is the Goods"', *The Sunday Times* (28.10.34), p.12.

295. Ezra Pound letter to Mary Butts, 5.11.34.

296. Ezra Pound and Mary Butts were not alone in thinking this; the much younger Oswell Blakeston had written the previous year that "there is no small magazine on a plane with Margaret Anderson and Jane Heap's *Little Review*". Oswell Blakeston, 'The Responsibility of the Public', *The Bookman*, (October 1933), pp.15-16.

297. Mary Butts letter to Ezra Pound, 10.11.34. This letter and one she sent him on 2.6.34 are both in the Beinecke. In the earlier letter, she teased her old friend by describing him as "the only person who types worse than I do".

298. Margaret W.J. Jeffrey, 'The Trend of the Modern Novel', *The Glasgow Herald* (9.11.33), supplement.

299. Mary Butts, '*The New Child* By Quentin Bell', *The Bookman*, 87, no.519 (Xmas 1934), p.152. This miskaten attribution of Adrian Bell's *The Balcony* to Quentin Bell is mysterious (he never wrote a book called *The New Child*). Perhaps it was a joke on the part of some sub-editor at *The Bookman;* certainly there is no evidence that MB was aware of this 'mistake'.

300. Frank Ingram made notes about an interview he conducted with Ruth and Joan Manning-Sanders on the 4 September 1984, in which he noted that the latter was "much more fond of the husband Gabriel Atkin the artist—usually slightly drunk. Illustrated his stories with appropriate actions. Always kind. Mary treated him badly."

301. Mary Butts draft of letter to R. Ellis Roberts, 25.2.35.

302. *AWM*, in *TTN*, p.10.

303. Mary Butts draft of letter to the writer, Robert Goodyear, 29.7.36. They corresponded about religion and their work (Goodyear had published two novels under the initials, 'R.G.G.': *I Lie Alone* and *The Mirtle Tree* (1936)) during the second half of 1936 after Mary Butts had been "angelically kind" to Goodyear and his wife during their visit to Sennen in June. He wrote to her on the 18 January 1937, a few weeks before her death:

> I have just been reading *Armed with Madness* again. I don't know how you feel about it, but I like it best of your novels. I can re and re and re-read it. And never tire. It enchants me—That house and the wood and the secret place below the cliff, and the brilliant, vivid people.... Your prose fills me with envy. So taut, and magically evocative.
>
> And then from that I went on to *Several Occasions*. Some of those stories (why on earth aren't you writing more?) are superb. 'Friendship's Garland' for instance, and 'Dinner Party' and 'In Bloomsbury'. I wish I had written them. You are still, and have been for years, one of my favourite authors. It's a constant source of pleasure to me to know that I know you....

304. Patrick Harvey undated letter to Frank Baker. Quoted in Baker, *I Follow But Myself*, p.122.

305. Mary Butts, 'The Heresy Game', *The Spectator*, 158 (12.3.37), pp.466-467.

306. Mary Butts, 'A New Vision', *Time and Time* 15, no.21 (26.5.34), pp 584-586.

307. Baker, *I Follow But Myself*, pp.128-129.

308. Horace Keast, *St Hilary of Cornwall: The Story of a Cornish Parish and its Church* (no publisher [isbn: 0951114409], 1986), pp.6, 14.

309. Baker, *I Follow But Myself*, p.129.

310. Ibid, pp.127-128.

311. Keast, *St Hilary of Cornwall*, pp.8-9.

312. Baker, *I Follow But Myself*, p.129.

313. E.M. Forster letter to Mary Butts, 24.1.35.

314. Jack Lindsay undated letter to Mary Butts, January 1935.

315. Harcourt Wesson Bull, '"Truth is the Heart's Desire"', in *ASQ*, p.70.

316. In mid-April 1935 Mary Butts ordered Ray Strachey's [Rachel Costelloe's] *Careers and Openings for Women: A Survey of women's employment and guide for those seeking work* (1935) as well as *Our Freedom and its Results* (by five women) (1936), ed. Ray Strachey, on the 11 December 1936.

317. This was a reference to E.M. Forster's relationship with Bob Buckingham. See Furbank, *E.M. Forster: A Life*, p.188, n.1.

318. For the difficulties Angus Davidson had in working with Leonard Woolf see Angus Davidson, 'Angus Davidson', *Recollections of Virginia Woolf*, ed. Joan Russell Noble (Peter Owen, 1972) p.55, and J.H. Willis, Jr in *Leonard and Virginia Woolf as Publishers: The Hogarth Press 1917-1941* (University Press of Virginia, 1992), pp.163-165.

319. Havelock Ellis undated response to questionnaire; E.M. Forster letter to Mary Butts, 24.1.35; Helen Simpson, response to questionnaire, 11.1.35; Lord Dunsany, letter to Mary Butts, 11.1.35; Charles Williams letter to Mary Butts, 25.1.35; Ethel Colburn Mayne letter to Mary Butts, 26.1.35; Hugh Ross Williamson undated letter to Mary Butts, Jan/Feb 1935. Mary Butts had an experience similar to Ross Williamson's on the 4 July 1936: "Gas at the Dentist's. It *is* queer stuff. Just as one comes round, the sense that one has knowledge, that an answer has been given, that a form of the 'Secret of Secrets' is known. Yet utterly un-recallable—and it is always like that."

320. There is no trace of Naomi Royde-Smith's account; Jack Lindsay sent Mary Butts the manuscript of "A Possession of Some Visions".

321. 'Mappa Mundi', a story which Mary Butts wrote between the end of 1936 and the beginning of 1937, describes an inexplicable supernatural experience of the narrator: "It is one of the curious things about such experiences, whatever their reality, their ultimate significance or insignificance, that no one can discuss them for long. (It has been years before I could bring myself to write this.)" Later in the story the narrator refers to M.R. James directly: "This dumbness Montagu [sic] James describes as 'common form' still held me." Mary Butts, 'Mappa Mundi', in *WAWB*, pp.192-3, 197.

322. Manning-Sanders, *The West of England*, p.39.

323. Walke, *Twenty Years at St. Hilary*, p.10.

324. Charles Williams letter to Mary Butts, 25.1.35.

325. Mary Butts undated draft of letter to Charles Williams, end January 1935.

326. Charles Williams letter to Mary Butts, 31.1.35.

327. Charles Williams letter to Mary Butts, 7.2.35.

328. Charles Williams letter to Mary Butts, 21.2.35.

329. See p.423 for Naomi Royde-Smith's comment on the difficulty Mary Butts had in writing.

330. Mary Butts undated draft of letter to Charles Williams, 29.1.35. Little is known about the actor, Norman Steven Brocas Harris, other than that he was also friends with Cedric Morris from the 1920s and moved permanently to Africa in the 1950s. See letter from Harris to Morris (TGA 8317.1.1.1923).

331. See Michael Williams, *Around Land's End*, (Bossiney Books, 1983), p.92.

332. Manning-Sanders, *The West of England*, p.47.

333. Harcourt Wesson Bull, "Truth is the Heart's Desire"', in *ASQ*, pp.68-69. See description of Carn Brea, p.491, n.152.

334. Ibid, p.77. For Diotima, see Plato's *Symposium*, 201b-212b.

335. Lemprière, *Lemprière's Classical Dictionary*, pp.237-238.

336. Llewelyn Powys wrote an account, 'Julian the Apostate', in *The Rationalist Annual* (1936), pp.75-80. Mary Butts does not mention this essay and may not have known of its existence. She does however mention an anecdote about him on the 8 November 1935: "Angus today on Llewelyn Powys 'twined about with tartan shawls' and his distressing 'literary diarrhoea'". She was probably then writing a review of Llewlyn Powys's *Dorset Essays*, printed a few weeks later as: 'Dorset Essays, Scenes and Memories', *The Sunday Times* (24.11.35), p.16. (She had already reviewed this book eighteen months earlier for the same newspaper in 'Mr. Powys's Dorset', *The Sunday Times* (18.2.34), p.11.

337. In her letter to Angus Davidson on the 25 September 1934, Mary Butts described how she had done "appropriate magics" before the three stone slabs which were to form the hearth. (Beinecke).

338. Angus Davidson may well have been writing his biography of Edward Lear, which was published in 1938. Interestingly, the first edition opens with a sketch by Lear of Villefranche made on the 29 January 1865 (10.45 a.m.). Perhaps it was included by Davidson as a tribute to Mary Butts?

339. Harcourt Wesson Bull, '"Truth is the Heart's Desire"', in *ASQ*, p.70.

340. Ibid, p.72. Perhaps it also reminded Mary Butts of the line from her poem, 'Corfe': "Make many slugs where the stranger goes"...

341. Ibid, pp.72-73.

342. Mary Butts, 'Spring Storm', *The Manchester Guardian* (11.6.35), p.16.

343. Harcourt Wesson Bull, '"Truth is the Heart's Desire"', in *ASQ*, pp.73-74.

344. Ibid, p.71.
345. Ibid, pp.77, 69.
346. Ibid, p.71.
347. Ibid, p.77.

348. Mary Butts draft of letter to Mary Colville-Hyde, 2.3.35.

349. Harcourt Wesson Bull, '"Truth is the Heart's Desire"', in *ASQ*, p.76.

350. This gift would have been particularly significant for Mary Butts, since she had owned one in the early 1920s, see above, p.114

351. Harcourt Wesson Bull, '"Truth is the Heart's Desire"', in *ASQ*, p.71.

352. Ibid, p.76.

353. Walter de la Mare shared this feeling about St Hilary: "The fear that had haunted him in Cornwall was absent from this place and that within its trees was a magic circle of peace." Walke, *Twenty Years at St Hilary*, p.10.

354. Mary Butts draft of letter to Colin [friend with whom Edward Sackville-West stayed in Zennor], 15.4.35. Her interest can be seen in her review 'The 18th Century', *Time and Tide*, 16, no.38 (21.9.35), pp.1337-1340.

355. Suzanne Raitt, *Vita and Virginia* (Clarendon press, 1993), p.102.

356. Mary Butts undated draft of letter to Edward Sackville-West, mid-May 1935.

357. Edward Sackville-West letter to Mary Butts, 8.6.35.

358. Vita Sackville-West, quoted in Victoria Glendinning, *Vita: The Life of V. Sackville-West* (Weidenfeld and Nicolson, 1983), p.326.

359. Sylvia Beach, *Shakespeare and Company* (Plantin, 1987), p.113.

360. Geoffrey West, *'Scenes from the Life of Cleopatra'*, *Fortnightly Review* (July 1935). See also J.M. Bulloch, 'Defence of Cleopatra', *The Sunday Times* (26.5.35); untitled review, *Dundee Evening Telegraph* (20.6?.35); A.T.G. Edwards, 'Literary Ladies at a Tea Party', *Northern Echo* (14.6.35).

361. Jack Lindsay undated letter to Mary Butts, early summer 1934.

362. Brother Savage, 'Preparing for the Autumn', *Liverpool Post* (11.5.35).

363. 'Cleopatra', *John O'London's Weekly*, 33, no.844 (15.6.35), p.356.

364. Henry Baerlein, 'New Fiction', *Time and Tide*, 16 (24.8.35), pp.1226-7.

365. In a review of T.R. Glover's *Greek By-Ways* three years earlier, Mary Butts had made it quite clear where her sympathies lay: "One reason why we study the classics, why we assume, or used to until lately, that whatever an educated man did or did not know, he must know something about the language and thought of the antique world, is because we feel that we are dealing there with men who had the same assumptions as our own." 'The Past in the Present', *The Bookman*, 83, no.490 (July 1932), p.206. Perhaps this view was not surprising from someone who wrote in her autobiography of "the sanctuary of Hellas". *TCC*, p.218. By contrast, when Virginia Woolf read the classics she did not feel at home: "When we read Chaucer, we are floated up to him insensibly on the current of our ancestors' lives, and later, as records increase and memories lengthen, there is scarcely a figure which has not its nimbus of association, its life and letters, its wife and family, its house, its character, its happy or dismal catastrophe. But the Greeks remain in a fastness of their own." Virginia Woolf, 'On Not Knowing Greek', *The Common Reader*, p.24.

366. Mary Butts, 'Jigsaw History', *The Bookman*, 87, no.517 (October 1934), p.62.

367. "It's the bunk" was a phrase often on Mary Butts's lips. She explained it as "a feeling I called 'the hollow feeling', and am blessed and cursed with to this day. A feeling which tells me, besides the facade of proper feeling and the expected emotion, that 'it is all my eye'. That what is true is something quite different, not necessarily the very opposite of the side one is asked to applaud, but something implying deeper values, something imperative and pitiless and ironic. That is the hollow feeling. And a voice saying: 'It's the Bunk.' No help, no compromise. Only it is impossible to revere the Bunk any more." *TCC*, p.100. See also accounts by Baker, *I Follow But Myself*, p.136; Williamson, 'Mary Butts', *The Bookman*, 81 (Xmas 1931), p.188 and his 'A Writer's Childhood. The Testament of Mary Butts', *John O'London's Weekly* (11.6.37), p.388.

368. 'Egypt's Romantic Queen', *Worcester Evening News* (13.6.35).

369. Oswell Blakeston, 'Plutarch's Siren' [review of Jack Lindsay's *Cleopatra* (1971)], *Books and Bookmen*, 16, no.6, (March 1971), p.29.

370. L.P. Hartley, 'The Literary Lounger', *The Sketch* (3.7.35) p.40.

371. R. Ellis Roberts, 'The Real Cleopatra', *News Chronicle* (19.6.35), p.4.

372. *The Daily Herald* (22.6.35).

373. 'The Last Pharaoh, A Modern Woman's View of Cleopatra', *Stratford on Avon Herald* (19.7.35); A.T.G. Edwards, loc. cit.; 'Cleopatra through a Woman's Eyes', *Liverpool Echo* (18.6.35).

374. 'The Last Pharaoh, A Modern Woman's View of Cleopatra', loc.cit.

375. Mary Butts, Appendix to *Scenes from the Life of Cleopatra* (Heinemann, 1935). Republished in *The Classical Novels*. All page references to this edition henceforth referred to as *SLC*, in *TCN*, p.345. Oddly, two recent studies which concentrate on images of Cleopatra do not pay a great deal of attention to Mary Butts's narrative. Lucy Hughes-Hallett writes "only cursorily about...*Scenes from the Life of Cleopatra*, even though it is very fine" in *Cleopatra: Histories, Dreams and Distortions* (Bloomsbury, 1989), p.4. Mary Hamer's only reference is its inclusion in the bibliography of *Signs of Cleopatra: History, politics, representation* (Routledge, 1993).

376. 'Two Famous Women: Catherine the Great and Cleopatra', *The Scotsman* (20.6.35).

377. A.G. Macdonell, 'Biography and Wit, Greater and Less', *The Bystander*, 126, no.1643 (12.6.35), p.490.

378. J.M. Bulloch, loc.cit.

379. '*Scenes from the Life of Cleopatra*', *Times Literary Supplement* (27.6.35), p.414.

380. *'Scenes from the Life of Cleopatra'*, *The London Mercury*, 32, no.189 (July 1935), p.301; James Agate, 'Cleopatra as a Schoolmistress', *Daily Express* (6.6.35), p.4; P. Quennell, 'New Novels', *The New Statesman and Nation* (1.6.35), pp.829-830.

381. 'New Novels: Footnotes to history', *Northern Daily Mail* (30.5.35).

382. R. Ellis Roberts letter to Mary Butts, 9.6.35.

383. Charles Williams letter to Mary Butts, 25.6.35.

384. Edward Sackville-West letter to Mary Butts, 11.6.35.

385. Edward Sackville-West, 'A Poetical Autobiography', *The New Statesman and Nation*, 13, no.329 (12.6.37), p.974.

386. Mary Butts letter to Harcourt Wesson Bull and Angus Davidson, 17.6.35 (Beinecke).

387. For a comment on Mary Butts's visit to Betty Montgomery, see Harcourt Wesson Bull, '"Truth is the Heart's Desire"', in *ASQ*, pp.75-76.

388. Mary Butts letter to Harcourt Wesson Bull and Angus Davidson, 24.6.35 (Beinecke).

389. Hugh Ross Williamson undated letter to Mary Butts, July 1935.

390. *TCC*, pp.119-120.

391. Mary Butts undated letter to Ada Briggs, August 1935.

392. Harcourt Wesson Bull, '"Truth is the Heart's Desire"', in *ASQ*, p.78.

393. Camilla Rodker letter to Ada Briggs, 25.8.35.

394. See Mary Butts letter to Mr Beevers, 12.8.35 (HRHRC). Her reviews were 'The Eighteenth Century', *Time and Tide*, 16, no.38 (21.9.35), pp.1337-1340; 'Imperial Rome', *Time and Tide*, 16 no.40 (5.10.35), pp.1403-1404; 'The Funeral March of a Marionette', *Time and Tide*, 16, no.41 (12.10.35), p.1450; also, her review of Corvo's *Hubert's Arthur*, see p.496, n.267.

395. Patrick Wright discusses this relationship in detail in his chapter on Mary Butts in *Living in an Old Country* and in his more recent book, *The Village That Died for England* (1995), see p.439.

396. Mary Butts letter to Harcourt Wesson Bull, 22.10.35 (Beinecke).

397. Mary Butts reread *Gaudy Night* with even greater interest shortly before her death: "Strange how it hurts and pleases, being about, among other things, a real love-affair. And that is over for me, for ever, now that I might have learned a little wisdom. Only memories left, some bitter, some sordid, stupid, ridiculous, sad." Mary Butts, diary entry, 5.2.37.

398. See Mary Butts letter to Angus Davidson, 25.11.35 (Beinecke).

399. Dr Buck Ruxton was accused of the brutal murder of his wife and maid. He was hanged at Strangeways Prison, Manchester, on the 12 May 1936.

400. Mary Butts undated draft of letter to Mary Colville-Hyde, December 1935.

401. Mary Butts letter to Ada Briggs, 23.12.35.

402. Mary Butts letter to Mary Colville-Hyde, 4.1.36.

403. Tony Butts undated letter to Mary Butts, late 1932. This letter reads oddly given the enthusiastic responses to the novel from both Tony and his mother; see above, p.311. However, Mary Butts's family were not alone in seeing *Death of Felicity Taverner* as a roman à clef. Hugh Ross Williamson had been curious about this novel: "Of course I can't help (being human) wondering how far it's autobiographical...there must be...something of you and your mother in Felicity and hers; and (guessing) something of Rodker in Kralin. And Tony and Adrian? You've depersonalised it, though; completely. More, universalised it." Hugh Ross Williamson undated letter to Mary Butts, late October 1932. "Autobiography? Well, none of the events occured," she replied, although she agreed with several of his guesses, except about Kralin who was not based on "poor old John". For more details see Mary Butts letter to Hugh Ross Williamson, 2.11.32 (HRHRC).

404. Mary Butts letter to Harcourt Wesson Bull, 22.1.36 (Beinecke).

405. "Entering the Cove by the road, the first cottage near the bottom of the valley on the right-hand side is an old and pretty thatched abode, behind which is all that remains of Chapel Idne, or the 'narrow chapel.' The Lord of Goonhilly, a proprietor of Lyonnesse, the fabled land fair and fertile stretching from Land's End to Scilly and now submerged,...is said to have escaped the catastrophe of the great overflowing of the sea in 1029, and built as a thank-offering for his escape this Chapel Idne on the little plateau overlooking Whitesand Bay. Before his time there was no doubt an oratory or hermitage on the spot where the saint dwelt, and therefore the spot was considered holy ground. Now the sole remnants of the chapel consist of a rounded arch with some tracery upon it and some shaped granite stones behind it." Harris Stone, *England's Riviera*, p.32. This would have been what Mary Butts saw of Chapel Idne in the 1930s. Her interest in saving it started only a few months after her arrival at Sennen when she noted Bolshie Burnett's "Barton-story: his wife said to the man: 'But you know it's an old chapel, don't you?' Answer: 'Yes, there's lots of Wesley's old places left about'... (Campaign to be begun)." Mary Butts, diary entry, 10.9.32.

406. Mary Butts letter to Hugh Ross Williamson, 28.2.33 (HRHRC). Quite apart from in her pamphlets and a great deal of her fiction and poetry, she expressed her views about the destruction of the countryside whenever she could, including in her reviews: '"Back to the Land", A Plea to the Town Dweller', *The Daily Telegraph* (21.11.33), p.15; 'Roads Through the Centuries: Track to By-Pass', *The Sunday Times* (22.4.34), p.12; 'Vandal Visitors to the West', *Everyman*, 39 (22.6.34), p.484. As to the dangers of increased tourism, she declared of motorists at Land's End: "The mysterious land to left and right of them lies empty. While in their hurry to arrive and depart, they have made life in Sennen Churchtown, the last village in England, about as safe as in Piccadilly Circus, without benefit of men on point duty or traffic lights." 'Two Land's Ends', *The Manchester Guardian* (28.5.34), p.9.

407. Mary Butts undated draft of letter to Tom Swan, March 1936.

408. Ibid.

409. Mary Butts letter to Ada Briggs, 11.4.36.

410. Mary Butts letter to Ada Briggs, 15.5.36.

411. Mary Butts addressed Angus Davidson in this way in her letter to him, 4.2.34 (Beinecke).

412. Mary Butts, 'Modern World and Religion', *The Sunday Times* (18.8.35), p.9.

413. Mary Butts letter to Harcourt Wesson Bull, 17.5.36 (Beinecke).

414. Harcourt Wesson Bull letter to Mary Butts, 4.6.36.

415. Mary Butts letter to Harcourt Wesson Bull, 29.6.36 (Beinecke).

416. Mary Butts, 'Flickering Genius', *Time and Tide*, 17, no.19 (9.5.36), pp. 680-681.

417. Lord Gorell letter to Mary Butts, 9.7.36.

418. This was rather disingenuous on Mary Butts's part, since there are numerous references to later years in *TCC*.

419. Mary Butts letter to Ada Briggs, 30.7.36. This letter may have been prompted by the reassurance she had received from her old friend, Cedric Morris, to whom she had anxiously written for information: "Dear Mary, Yours just arrived forwarded here.... I don't know what you are talking about—I may have said as a joke that your autobiography had 14 libel suits in it. I don't remember—I certainly had heard it all over the place, but only as a joke. I do not mean a malicious one. You know I have the greatest respect and admiration for your work—I always have had—so have most other people that I know. If only you would realise this and leave all this nonsense alone... Good luck to you and please don't take all that rubbish seriously." Cedric Morris undated letter to Mary Butts, early summer 1936.

420. Mary Colville-Hyde undated letter to Mary Butts, summer 1936.

421. Mary Butts letter to Ada Briggs, 30.7.36. It is not clear who the don was.

422. Mary Butts described the books as: "*In Ghostly Company* and its companion volume". The former could be Amyas Northcote's novel, *In Ghostly Company* (John Lane, 1922).

423. Lord Gorell letter to Mary Butts, 31.7.36.

424. Mary Butts, 'Great Drama and Small', *Time and Tide* 17, no.31 (1.8.36), p.1103.

425. Lord Gorell letter to Mary Butts, 31.7.36.

426. "There seems to be a view that Mary was in some way thwarted if not actually persecuted by what is called Bloomsbury. My own impression is that she was hardly in touch with Bloomsbury except of course in her relationship with Roger Fry. In later years, Virginia Woolf was clearly interested in Mary and questioned me about her. She relied for her information on Mary Butts's brother whom I never knew." Quentin Bell letter to Nathalie Blondel, 14.11.95. Given the difficulties between Mary Butts and Tony as well as his relationship with William Plomer, who was always scathing about Mary Butts, this may well explain the rather negative comments about her in Virginia Woolf's diaries and letters. See Bell, 'Robert Medley and Mary Butts', in *Elders and Betters*, and p.508, n.56.

427. Mary Butts referred to Lytton Strachey's influence in her review of Helen Simpson's *Henry VIII*, 'King Harry', *Time and Tide* 15, no.13 (31.3.34), pp.412-3. She also commented on Strachey's "exquisite genius" in *TCC*, p.51.

428. "In the swinging frolic of the twenties, Aldous Huxley's *Antic Hay*, there is a character who insists on coming into my mind whenever I try to imagine the young Mary Butts I never met: Mrs Viveash—Myra Viveash…[with] 'a cloak of flame-coloured satin, and in bright, coppery hair a great Spanish comb of carved tortoiseshell.'" Baker, *I Follow But Myself*, p.119. There is no evidence that this character is modelled on Mary Butts, who described Myra Viveash as "an image of suffering and beauty with its heart torn out". Mary Butts, 'Aldous Huxley', in *Scrutinies*, ed. Rickword, p.84. Nevertheless this 'fact' has been incorporated into the Mary Butts myth. Another contender was suggested by Huxley's first biographer who speculated on the possibility of Nancy Cunard's being the original of Myra Viveash. See Sybille Bedford, *Aldous Huxley. Volume One: The Apparent Stability* (Quartet, 1979 edn), pp.143-144. This coincidental bringing together of Mary Butts and Nancy Cunard is odd, given that after their marriage broke down John Rodker had a relationship with Nancy Cunard. Mary Butts reviewed the anthology, *Negro* (1934), compiled and edited by Cunard (to which Tony Butts contributed an essay). See Mary Butts, 'Negro', *The Adelphi*, 3rd series, 9, no.1 (October 1934), pp.185-187.

429. In March Mary Butts had ordered *The Use of Poetry and the Use of Criticism* (1933) by T.S. Eliot. On the 28 July she would copy out in her diary his poem, *The Hollow Men* (1925).

430. Edward Sackville-West letter to Mary Butts, 11.8.36.

431. R. Ellis Roberts letter to Mary Butts, 26.8.36.

432. Baker, *I Follow But Myself*, pp.137-138.

433. Mary Butts draft of letter to Odo Cross, 15.9.36.

434. Mary Butts draft of letter to Mary Colville-Hyde, 26.7.36.

435. See above, p.222; In The Butts Pedigree Mary Colville-Hyde had added in her own hand, that she had bought the portrait *for* Tony…

436. Mary Butts letter to Harcourt Wesson Bull, 17.11.36 (Beinecke).

437. Baker, *I Follow But Myself*, pp.130-131.

438. Ibid, p.132.

439. Ibid, pp.132-133.

440. Ibid, p.133.

441. Harcourt Wesson Bull gives another account of Mary Butts rising to the occasion in Sennen in 1935: "A group of four or five American college girls touring England had stopped to see me, and Angus and I gave them an elaborate Cornish tea, inviting Mary to meet them. She did not appear early, but then a knock at the door and Mary stood framed there wearing a wide-

brimmed hat turned up on one side and a dark silk dress I had never seen, in her arms and a gloved hand an enormous sheaf of long-stemmed flowers. 'Mary!' I'm afraid I gasped. And to what perfection she played the part of lady bountiful, terribly interesting to me, for there were other roles she might have chosen and this one, for the young females from overseas, was so different from the everyday Mary we were accustomed to." Harcourt Wesson Bull, '"Truth is the Heart's Desire"', in *ASQ*, p.75.

442. Baker, *I Follow But Myself*, p.134.

443. See Vincent van Gogh, *Letters* (Constable & Co, 1927-29).

444. See Mary Butts letter to Harcourt Wesson Bull, 11.12.36 and his reply, 26.12.36 (Beinecke).

445. The Society for the Protection of Rural England had been set up in 1926, but did not really become active until after the Second World War. See Camilla Bagg, 'Another View of Mary Butts' in *ASQ*, pp.89-96, p.94.

446. Mary Butts draft of letter to George Barton, 14.12.36.

447. After her mother's death, when Camilla asked Ruth Manning-Sanders to choose one of Mary Butts's possessions to remember her by, Ruth Manning-Sanders chose the silver bangles, so famously photographed by Man Ray. Mary Butts made no adverse comments about Ruth Manning-Sanders in her diary and letters and seems to have thought of her as a close friend. However when interviewed by Frank Ingram in September 1984 (when she was 96 years old), Ruth Manning-Sanders was wholly negative about Mary Butts: "Remembered quite a deal of the past in Sennen but regarded this as part of her life that was to be left in the *Past*. Mary Butts a clever woman but not to be trusted—spiteful and treacherous—treatment of that poor child Camilla was disgraceful and quite unforgivable.... Saw quite a bit of her because she could not be avoided living just across the Rd from Esthersfield [at] Tebel Vos." Frank Ingram, unpublished interview with Ruth and Joan Manning-Sanders, 4.9.84. This antagonism may well explain why Ruth Manning-Sanders did not refer to Mary Butts in her study, *The West of England*.

448. Baker, *I Follow But Myself*, p.135. Perhaps she had also been carrying her eighteenth-century Bible (inscribed "Mary Franies Butts. Sennen St Hilary. October 1936) and her English missal (inscribed "Mary Butts Sennen St Hilary Sept 1935").

449. After Mary Butts's death, Angus Davidson returned to Harcourt Wesson Bull all the latter's letters to her; it was some time later that Wesson Bull added this asterisked comment.

450. It was in fact called Vel-an-Dreath; Mary Butts's spelling was never very good.

451. Baker, *I Follow But Myself*, p.137.

452. Ibid, pp.138-139.

453. Mary Butts draft of letter to Mary Colville-Hyde, 22.1.37.

454. Mary Butts undated draft of letter to Gabriel Aitken, mid-January 1937.

455. Mary Butts draft of letter to Anne Weir, 1.2.37.

456. Mary Butts letter to T.S. Eliot, 24.2.37 (Eliot archive).

457. Whilst living in Paris in the 1920s Mary Butts had known Dan Mahoney, the model for "Dr Matthew O'Connor, an Irishman from the Barbary Coast ..., whose interest in gynaecology had driven him half around the world." Djuna Barnes, *Nightwood* (Faber, 1979), p.29.

458. Djuna Barnes letter to Mary Butts, 8.2.37.

459. T.S. Eliot letter to Mary Butts, 1.1.32.

460. Mary Butts draft of letter to Gabriel Aitken, 26.2.37.

461. Mary Butts undated draft of letter to Mary Colville-Hyde, end Feb/early March 1937.

462. Baker, *I Follow But Myself*, p.140.

463. Tony Butts letter to John Rodker, 11.3.37.

EPILOGUE : THE LEGEND OF MARY BUTTS 1937-1997

1. Mary Butts, 'After the Funeral', *The London Mercury*, 27, no.158 (Dec. 1932), pp.111-115. Published in *LS* and *WAWB*, pp.202-3.

2. As a tribute to her role in the the life of St Hilary in the 1930s, Frank Baker arranged for Mary Butts's name to be added the list of souls to be prayed for which hangs to this day in the Church. In recent years other souls, including that of her friend, Bernard Walke, were added.

3. Baker, *I Follow But Myself*, p.144.

4. Harcourt Wesson Bull, '"Truth is the Heart's Desire"', in *ASQ*, p.81. The choice of epitaph seems to have been a difficult one. In response to a letter from Camilla in November 1937 Angus Davidson wrote back on the 25th:

> I do feel there ought to be a quotation, but I find it extremely difficult to think of exactly the right thing—especially as it has to be something that we all like!
>
> Your grandmother sent me two or three quotations, but I can't say that any of these seemed to me entirely satisfactory. I quite like your suggestion of "A soul that pity touched"—but I feel that it doesn't go quite far enough and that it might be said of many people. I have another idea, from a poem by Yeats (a poet your mother was very fond of):..."Be you still, trembling heart;/ Remember the wisdom out of the old days."

5. Tony Butts letter to John Rodker, 11.3.37.

6. Charles Williams quoted in 'Miss Mary Butts: Imaginative Gift', *The Times* (13.3.37), p.14.

7. Charles Williams letter to Mary Butts, 6.3.37.

8. Naomi Royde-Smith, letter to Editor, *Time and Tide*, 18, no.12 (20.3.37), p.378. Oddly enough, in December 1921 Mary Butts had pondered the difference between sculpture and literature in terms which seem to confirm Naomi Royde-Smith's comparison:

> *Illuminations*. Why am I so moved by Brancusi's egg and bird forms?[9] Because they are forms of quintessential eggness and birdness, and *what that* is, is something which is a subject for a god's speculation.
>
> The sculpture's truth to be retranslated *into itself* for the writer's material.
>
> A word is not sculptor's mass or plane—a word is no more than a grain in the stone.
>
> The quintessential shape of each word must be held faster than any detail however witty.
>
> How long have I known that to discover each time what it *means*?
>
> Sit on the stone of that shape and see a long way down the people, weather, properties, passions, and cut them fine and small. Or large and loose—it will not matter. Story-telling cannot—does not—need not abstract like sculpture? ...
>
> Note. 'Shape' in writing does not quite mean sculptural in shape—the line drawn round the story—it is something conveyed in the texture of language.

In referring to "Brancusi's egg and bird forms", Mary Butts is probably referring to the sculptures, *Sleeping Muse* (1910), *Bird* (1913), *Bird in Space* (1919) by Constantin Brancusi (1876-1957).

9. Charles Williams quoted in *The Times* obituary, loc.cit. Bryher, "Recognition Not Farewell", in *ASQ*, p.4.

10. *TCC*, p.115-116. Mary Butts devotes an entire chapter in her autobiography to the importance of Shelley on the development of her imagination, see Chapter 18, 'Shelley', pp.111-118.

11. John Raynor, 'In Memoriam: Mary Butts', *Time and Tide* 18, no.13 (27.3.37), p.408. Reprinted by Frank Baker in *The Cornish Review*, 16 (Winter 1970), p.8. On 2 July 1946 when he was "ill, and longing for Cornwall", Raynor wrote and dedicated his song, 'Lelant', "In Memorium Mary Butts". The notes to the song read: "Here we have Cornwall put down in memory of Mary Butts, the writer, who was a close friend of the composer. The poem [by E.K. Chambers] described Lelant, near St Ives, but to John Raynor it meant Mary's grave at Sennen." *Eleven Songs* by John Raynor, Introduction and note by Olwen Picton-Jones (Galliard Ltd, 1971), pp.5, 27-29.

12. David Hope, *Mary Butts, Fire-Bearer* (Sennen Pamphlet Series, no. 1 [There were no others] June 1937). Republished in *ASQ*, pp.21-24, p.21.

13. Gabriel Aitken letter to Ada Briggs, 16.3.37.

14. Angus Davidson letter to Ada Briggs, 11.5.37.

15. Mary Butts letter to Tom Swan, 21.1.37.

16. Angus Davidson letter to T.S. Eliot, 10.3.37 (Eliot archive).

17. T.S. Eliot letter to Angus Davidson, 12.3.37 (Eliot archive).

18. *TCC*, p.237.

19. Naomi Royde-Smith, '*The Crystal Cabinet* by Mary Butts', *Time and Tide*, 18, no.21 (5.6.37), p.756.

20. J.M.Hone, 'Mary Butts', *The Spectator* (4.6.37), p.1060.

21. Baker, *I Follow But Myself*, p.147.

22. Naomi Royde-Smith, loc. cit.

23. Edward Sackville-West, 'A Poetical Autobiography', *The New Statesman and Nation*, 13, no.329 (12.6.37), p.974.

24. There is a brief correspondence between Angus Davidson and Ada Briggs relating to a complaint by a Mr Armstrong about Mary Butts's claim. Angus Davidson concluded: "... though it seems very ridiculous—the [publishers] seem to think they must insert a slip in future copies and also send a letter to the local paper apologising." Angus Davidson letter to Ada Briggs, 15.9.37.

25. Tony Butts letter to the Editor, '*The Crystal Cabinet*', *The Spectator* (18.6.37), p.1149.

26. '*The Crystal Cabinet: My Childhood at Salterns*', *The Listener* (9.6.37), p.1159.

27. Armide Oppé, 'Mary Butts', *The Bookman*, 36, no.212 (June 1937), p.200.

28. J.M. Hone, loc. cit.

29. Naomi Royde-Smith, op. cit., p.757.

30. *The Listener*, loc. cit.

31. J.M. Hone, loc. cit.

32. 'A Novelist's Memoirs', *The Times* (8.6.37), p.22.

33. R. Ellis Roberts, 'Childhood', source and date unknown.

34. Edward Sackville-West, loc. cit.

35. Hugh Ross Williamson, 'A Writer's Childhood: The Testament of Mary Butts', *John O'London's Weekly* (11.6.37), p.388.

36. Bryher, 'Recognition Not Farewell', in *ASQ*, p.9.

37. Ibid, pp.3-10.

38. Rhys Davies, 'A Note on Mary Butts', *Wales*, 6/7 (1939), p.207.

39. Originally published as '*One* Roman Speaks' in *The Cornhill Magazine* in 1935, the story was called '*A* Roman Speaks' in *Last Stories*. It was republished under this title alongside 'Bellerophon to Anteia' and 'The Later Life of Theseus, King of Athens' in the Appendix to *The Classical Novels*, pp.349-384, pp.362-384.

40. Mary Butts, 'In the House' and 'Mappa Mundi', *Life and Letters To-day*, 18, no.11 (Spring 1938), pp.83-85 and 86-96; 'Look Homeward, Angel', 'The House' and 'Honey, Get Your Gun', *Life and Letters To-day*, 18, no.12 (Summer 1938), pp.56-60, 61-73, 74-80. 'The House' had already been written by 1924; see Mary Butts letter to Douglas Goldring, quoted in Goldring, *The Nineteen Twenties*, pp.213-214.

41. '*Last Stories* by Mary Butts', *Times Literary Supplement* (8.10.38), p.649.

42. Kate O'Brien, 'Fiction', *The Spectator* (16.12.38), p.1062.

43. Margery Allingham, 'New Novels', *Time and Tide* (1.10.38), p.1336. The blurb on the inside flap of the austere yet stylish green and cream dust jacket of *Last Stories* reads: "This book comprises the thirteen stories which the author left uncollected at her death in March, 1937.... In addition to being a memorial, *Last Stories* of Mary Butts is a testimony to the development of her art."

44. 'A Lover' was written when Mary Butts knew Geoffrey Dunlop (see pp.143-4). According to Camilla Bagg, When *Last Stories* was published, he threatened Mary Butts's estate with a potential libel suit. Tom Swan paid him a sum of money and the matter went no further. 'A Lover' is the first story to have been translated: 'Der Geliebte', in *Das grosse Frauenlesebuch IV,* trans. Blanca Dahms (Goldmann Verlag, 1994), pp.109-131.

45. Thomas Moult, 'The Art of the Short Story', *The Manchester Guardian* (14.10.38).

46. Rhys Davies, loc.cit.

47. Hugh Ross Williamson, 'A Writer's Childhood', *John O'London's Weekly* (11.6.37), p.388.

48. *The Collected Poems of Frank O'Hara*, ed. Donald Allen (Alfred A. Knopf, 1972), p.489.

49. Edwin Muir, *The Present Age from 1914: Introductions to English Literature,* 5 (Cresset Press, 1939), p.25.

50. W.J. Entwhistle and E. Gillett, *The Literature of England AD 500-1942* (Longmans & Co, 1943), p.341.

51. Mary Butts's entry is incomplete and inaccurate; her dates are given as 1892-1935. Daiches repeats Edwin Muir's description of her stories. David Daiches, *The Present Age: after 1920* (Cresset Press, 1958), p.286.

52. James R. Mellow, *Charmed Circle: Gertrude Stein and Company* (Avon, 1975), p.341.

53. Samuel Hynes, *A War Imagined: The First World War and English Culture* (The Bodley Head, 1990), p.378.

54. Claire M. Tylee, *The Great War and Women's Consciousness: Images of Militarism and Womanhood in Women's Writings 1914-1964* (Macmillan, 1990), p.251.

55. Ibid.

56. See Virginia Woolf, *Three Guineas* (Penguin, 1993), p.146; Virginia Woolf letter to Vanessa Bell, 17.9.37. Quoted in Virginia Woolf, *Leave the Letters Till We're Dead: Collected Letters VI, 1936-41*, ed. Nigel Nicolson (Hogarth, 1994), p.168. Virginia Woolf also mentioned Mary Butts to William Plomer on two separate occasions during 1937. On the 17 June she told him: "I've been meeting Tony Butts and hearing the story of the malignant Mary which I want to discuss with you." On the 23 September she repeated how she "met Tony Butts, and discussed Mary's autobiography." Ibid, pp.138 and 172. There is no doubt that her friendship with Plomer and Tony would have influenced her personal acquaintance with and attitude to Mary Butts, especially if Woolf regarded her as an important writer.

57. 'Re Mary Butts', *The Writings and the World of Mary Butts* (conference brochure, February 1984). Reprinted in *ASQ,* p.157.

58. Ekbert Fass, *Young Robert Duncan* (Black Sparrow Press, 1983), p.227.

59. Mary Butts used the term "sacred game" throughout her work; see *WTH* in *AOROW*, p.289, *AWM,* in *TTN*, p.43; *DFT* in *TTN*, p.283.

60. Robin Blaser, Afterword to *IL* (1979), p.67. Mary Butts's work also inspired the American artist, Jess's 'Mary Butts Landscape' (1952), in *Jess: A Grand Collage 1951-1993,* organized by Michael Auping (Albright-Knox, 1993), p.109. "Of course, it was Duncan who had set me to reading her stories and novels, first one was *Death of Felicity Taverner* (from which the subscript for the painting was taken) and next *Armed with Madness*. The painting was made (1953) shortly after reading the latter novel." Jess letter to Nathalie Blondel, 17.1.94.

61. Barbara Guest, *Herself Defined: The Poet H.D. and her world* (Collins, 1985), pp.155, 215, 232.

The references are mainly concerned with Mary Butts's drug-taking.

62. Robert Duncan, 'Night and Days. Chapter 1', *Sumac*, pp.144-145.

63. H.D., *Palimpsest* (Southern Illinois U.P., 1968; 2nd edn), p.37.

64. Harold Acton, *Memoirs of an Aesthete* (Hamish Hamilton, 1984 reprint), p.174.

65. Moore, *Predilections*, p.104; Jack Lindsay, *Fanfrolico and After*, pp.145-146, 249.

66. Although they shared the same name, this is not the Angus Wilson who was the partner of Odo Cross.

67. Angus Wilson and Philippe Julian, *For Whom the Cloche Tolls: A Scrap-Book of the Twenties* (Methuen, 1953), p.44.

68. Beach, *Shakespeare & Co*, p.113.

69. William d'Arfey, *Curious Relations*, ed. William Plomer (Jonathan Cape, 1945), p.7. Interestingly, this echoes Edward Sackville-West's comment on Mary Butts in his review of *The Crystal Cabinet*; see above, p.427.

70. William Plomer, *Museum Pieces* (Jonathan Cape, 1952), p.12.

71. William Plomer, *At Home* (Jonathan Cape, 1958), p.67. He might have been even more scathing had he read a passage omitted from the 1937 edition of *TCC* (and restored in 1988). Having praised Lytton Strachey for his contribution to the art of biography, Mary Butts turns to "the deadly club of his imitators. We all know them now, the pert young men, scurrying like earwigs under the feet of their betters, and charting the thin places in the sole. Books like Plomer's *Cecil Rhodes*, ephemeral as pastry, for the reason that they never come to grips with their subject at all; and spreading far and wide the notion that human greatness is all a matter of luck, of showmanship, of a conditioned reflex: isn't there." *TCC*, p.51.

72. Notwithstanding Harcourt Wesson Bull's knowledge of Mary Butts's life and work, even he mistakenly referred to the the early 1930s as "fallow years". Harcourt Wesson Bull, '"Truth is the Heart's Desire"', in *ASQ*, p.76.

73. Louis Adeane, 'Mary Butts', *World Review* (Nov. 1951), pp.23-27. It is republished as 'An Appraisal of Mary Butts' in *ASQ*, pp.97-106.

74. H.F.V.J., letter on the death of H.F. Ingram in *Newsletter of the United Reform Church Poole* (September 1984).

75. Among Ingram's papers there is a letter from Cyril Connolly to Frank Ingram, 27.8.69.

76. Lilas Rider Haggard and Henry Williamson's novel, *Norfolk Life* (Faber, 1943), quotes from *TCC* on p.197; Morrow McGrath, *Bus by the Brook* (Cape, 1964), quotes Mary Butts in the Preface.

77. H.F. Ingram, 'Poole's Forgotten Genius', *Poole and Dorset Herald* in two parts: (23.2.66), p.2 and (2.3.66), p.2; H.F. Ingram letter, *Poole and Dorset Herald* (23.3.66), p.16.

78. Byington and Morgan, 'Mary Butts', pp.162-179.

79. Mary Butts, 'Green', in *A Return to Pagany*, ed. Halpert with Johns, pp.344-356. For his reaction to this story, see William Carlos Williams letter to the editor, Richard Johns, 6.1.30, quoted in *A Return to Pagany*, p.93. A letter Mary Butts sent to Johns on the 8 November 1931 is also printed, p.339. Stephen Halpert describes the influence of her writing on the editor's: "Johns was pleased with his own story, 'Solstice' [published in October-December 1930 issue of *Pagany* alongside Mary Butts's story, 'Scylla and Charybdis']. He felt that now he was beginning to add texture to a constantly changing and improving style.... 'Solstice' was fashioned after the style of Mary Butts.... Johns felt that he had successfully made use of Butts' intricacies of style to give his story the glossy overlay he had to discover outside of himself." *A Return to Pagany*, pp.161-162.

80. Barbara Wagstaff (pseudonym Leslie Rivers) has been influential in the recent republication of Mary Butts's work. See Wagstaff's 'Alchemist of Reality: Recovering Mary Butts', *Poetry Flash* (April 1984), pp.4, 9; the Afterword to both editions of *The Crystal Cabinet* (Beacon,

1988), pp.275-282 and (Carcanet, 1988), pp.275-282; 'Brightness Falls from the Air', Afterword to *The Taverner Novels*, pp.367-373.

81. Faulks, *The Fatal Englishman*, pp.29-30.

82. Hamer, 'Mary Butts, Mothers and War', *Women's Fiction and the Great War*, eds. Raitt and Tate, p. 219.

83. For a much more sensitive and in-depth analysis of Mary Butts's "work of exploring the mental and spiritual worlds of damaged or traumatised men and women", particularly in *Ashe of Rings*, see Ian Patterson, 'Mary Butts', ch.5, in "Cultural Critique and Canon Formation: 1910-1939" (Cambridge, Unpublished PhD, 1997). Part of this chapter which focuses on *Death of Felicity Taverner* is forthcoming in 'The Plan Behind the Plan: Russians, Jews and Mythologies of Change' in *Modernity, Culture and "the Jew"*, eds. Laura Marcus and Brian Cheyette (Polity Press/Stanford University Presss, 1998).

84. Patrick Wright, 'Coming Back to the Shores of Albion: The Secret England of Mary Butts (1890-1937)', in *On Living in an Old Country* (Verso, 1985), pp.93-134. Despite the very strong case made by Wright, Mary Butts was omitted from Gillan Tindall's *Countries of the Mind: The Meaning of Place to Writers* (Hogarth, 1991).

85. Wright, *The Village That Died For England*, p.84. One odd thing in this later study is that despite accurately citing Mary Butts's birthdate in his earlier work, Wright cites it here as 1891—the myth persists...

86. Ibid, p.89.

87. Hoberman, *Gendering Classicism*, p.2.

88. Robert Medley letter to Nathalie Blondel, 15.8.94.

89. See Mary Butts, *Ashe of Rings and Other Writings* (McPherson & Co, 1998), Preface by Nathalie Blondel. See Mary Butts bibliography at the end. These recent republications have provoked a certain amount of critical attention:

On *The Crystal Cabinet*:

Joy Grant, 'Glimpses and Grievances', *Times Literary Supplement* (23-29.12.88); Meg Spilleth, 'The Effects of Childhood', *The Minnesota Daily* (28.9.88); N. Blondel, '*The Crystal Cabinet*', *P.N.R.*, 15, no.5 (1988), pp.53-55; '*The Crystal Cabinet: My Childhood at Salterns*', *Publishers Weekly* (24.6.88), p.104; '*The Crystal Cabinet: My Childhood at Salterns*. Mary Butts', *Studies on Women Abstracts*, 7 (1989), p.5.

On *With and Without Buttons* and *From Altar to Chimney-piece*:

Nicholas Wollaston, 'Emma and Mr. Elton don't get laid—again', *The Observer* (20.10.91); Anne Duchêne, 'Landowners and Lasses', *Times Literary Supplement* (18.10.91), p.1; Patricia Beer, 'Very like Poole Harbour', *London Review of Books* (5.12.91), p.16; 'Easy going', *Gay Times Monthly* (Jan 1992), p.57; Norman Shrapnel, 'New Fiction', *The Guardian* (1991); Mary Ann McKinley, 'Rediscovering an English Femme Maudit', *New Letters Book Reviewer*, 4 (Autumn 1993), p.14; Oliver Conant, 'Countryside Modern', *New York Times Book Review*, VII (26.7.92), p.23.

General articles on recent republications of Mary Butts's works:

Chris Goodrich, 'Early Modernists Olive Moore, Mary Butts Back in Print', *Publishers Weekly* (17.2.92); Michael Upchurch, 'Rediscovering Mary Butts', *Washington Post Book World* (20.9.92), p.11; Brenda Wineapple, 'Shadow of the Left Bank', *Belles Lettres* (Summer 1992), pp.32, 34; Harvey Pekar, 'Butts is Back', *Los Angeles Reader* (24.4.92), untitled review, *Review of Contemporary Fiction* (Autumn 1992), pp. 181-182 and 'The Classical Novels', *Chicago Tribune* (1.1.95), p.4; Jascha Kessler, 'Beauty and the Beast: Rediscovering Mary Butts', *The Bookpress* 3.7 (Oct. 1993), pp.1, 12-14; David Seed, 'Extending the Modernist Canon', *Bête Noire* 14/15 (1994), pp.405, 407-412; Bruce Hainley, 'Quite Contrary: Mary Butts's Wild Queendom', *Voice Literary Supplement* (May 1994), pp.21-23; Elizabeth Shostak, 'Mary Butts: The Permanent behind the Impermanent', *The Boston Book Review* (August 1995), p.28-29.

90. Beach, *Shakespeare & Company*, p.130.

91. Mary Butts is now included in Virginia Blum, Patricia Clements, Isobel Grundy, *The Feminist Companion to Literature in English: Women Writers from the Middle Ages to the Present* (B.T. Batsford Ltd, 1990); Rodney Legg, *Literary Dorset* (Wincanton, 1990); Joanne Shattock, *The Oxford Guide to British Women Writers* (O.U.P., 1993); *The Bloomsbury Guide to Women's Literature*, ed. Claire Buck (Bloomsbury, 1992).

She is omitted from *British Women Writers*, ed. Janet Todd (Routledge, 1989); *The Dictionary of National Biography: Missing Persons*, ed. C.S. Nicholls (O.U.P., 1993) although she is now to have an entry by Nathalie Blondel in the *New DNB* (O.U.P., 2002); *The Reader's Companion to Twentieth Century Writers*, ed. Peter Parker (4th Estate Publishing Ltd & Helicon Publishing Ltd, 1995); *The Cambridge Guide to Literature in English*, ed. Ian Ousby (C.U.P., 1995, new edition).

BIBLIOGRAPHY

A. Works by Mary Butts

I: *Single Works*

Speed the Plough and other Stories (Chapman & Hall, 1923).

Ashe of Rings (Contact Editions, 1925); A. & C. Boni, 1926; Wishart & Co, 1933, rev. edn.

Armed with Madness (Wishart & Co, 1928); a deluxe edition of 100 copies with drawings by Jean Cocteau (Wishart & Co, 1928); A. & C. Boni, 1928; republished in a cheaper edition by Wishart & Co, 1932.

Imaginary Letters, illus. Jean Cocteau (Edward Titus: At the Sign of the Black Manikin, 1928). Republished with an Afterword by Robin Blaser (Talonbooks, 1979).

Several Occasions (Wishart & Co, 1932).

Traps for Unbelievers (Desmond Harmsworth, 1932).

Warning to Hikers (Wishart & Co, 1932).

Death of Felicity Taverner (Wishart & Co, 1932).

The Macedonian (Heinemann, 1933).

Scenes from the Life of Cleopatra (Heinemann, 1935); republished by Ecco Press, 1974; Sun and Moon Press, 1994.

The Crystal Cabinet (Methuen, 1937). Second expanded edition, with Foreword by Camilla Bagg and Afterword by Barbara O'Brien Wagstaff (Carcanet, 1988; Beacon Press, 1988).

Last Stories (Brendin Publishing Co, 1938).

With and Without Buttons and other Stories, selected with an Afterword by Nathalie Blondel (Carcanet, 1991)

From Altar to Chimney-Piece: Selected Stories of Mary Butts, Preface by John Ashbery (McPherson & Co, 1992).

The Taverner Novels: Armed with Madness and Death of Felicity Taverner, Preface by Paul West and Afterword by Barbara O'Brien Wagstaff (McPherson & Co, 1992).

The Classical Novels: The Macedonian/Scenes from the Life of Cleopatra, Foreword by Thomas McEvilley (McPherson & Co, 1994).

Ashe of Rings and Other Writings, Preface by Nathalie Blondel (McPherson & Co., 1998).

II: *Fiction and Poetry in Little Magazines and Anthologies*

'The Heavenward Side', *The Outlook*, 17, no.437 (30.6.06), p.504.

'Vision', *The Egoist*, 5, no.8 (Sep 1918), pp.111.

'Lettres Imaginaires' [in two parts], *The Little Review*, 6, no.6 (Oct 1919), pp.8-12; 6, no.7 (Nov 1919), pp.27-32.

'Magic', *The Little Review*, 7, no.2 (1920), pp.3-6.

'Speed the Plow', *The Dial*, 71 (Oct. 1921), pp.399-405.

'Speed the Plough', in *Georgian Stories 1922* (Chapman & Hall, 1922), pp.46-54; 'Speed the Plow', in *Georgian Stories 1922* (G.P. Putnam's Sons, 1923), pp.44-54. 'Speed the Plough'/'Speed the Plow', in *Stories from the Dial* (Jonathan Cape, 1924; Lincoln MacVeagh, The Dial Press, 1925), pp.152-166; in *Women, Men and the Great War: An anthology of Stories*, ed. Trudi Tate (M.U.P., 1995), pp.45-51. Due to be reprinted in *Women's Writing of World War I*, eds. D. Goldman, A. Cardinal, T. Hathaway (OUP, 1998).

Ashe of Rings [first five chapters in two instalments], *The Little Review*, 7, no.4 (Jan-Mar 1921), pp.3-14; 8, 1 (Autumn 1921), pp.97-106.

'Change', *The Dial*, 72 (May 1922), pp.465-470.

'Deosil', *the transatlantic review*, 1, no.3 (Mar 1924), pp.40-50. Collected in *The Best Short Stories of 1924*, eds J. O'Brien and J. Cournos (Small, Maynard & Co, 1924), pp.27-37. Renamed 'Widdershins' when included in *Several Occasions*.

'Pythian Ode', *the transatlantic review*, 2, no.3 (Sep 1924), pp.235-239. Reprinted in *A Sacred Quest*, ed. Christopher Wagstaff (McPherson & Co, 1995), pp.150-154.

'The Later Life of Theseus, King of Athens', *The Calendar of Modern Letters*, 1, no.4 (Jun 1925), pp.257-265. Collected in *Georgian Stories 1927*, ed. Arthur Waugh (Chapman & Hall, 1927), pp.66-75. Reprinted in *The Calendar of Modern Letters* , eds. Edgell Rickword and Douglas Garman, with 'A Review in Retrospect' (preface) by Malcolm Bradbury, (Frank Cass & Co, 1966), I, pp. 257-265..

'Friendship's Garland', in *Contact Collection of Contemporary Writers* (Contact Editions, Edward Titus, 1925), pp.30-40.

'Surprise Song' and 'On Vexin', *Larus*, 1, no.3 (May 1927), pp. 10-13.

'Picus Martius', *Hound and Horn*, 3, no.2 (Jan-May 1930), pp.230-233. Reprinted in *Soma*, 3 (1932), pp.41-43.

'The House-Party', *Pagany*, 1, no.1 (Jan-Mar 1930), pp.7-24.

'Heartbreak House', *Pagany*, 1, no.3 (Jul-Sep 1930), pp.1-4; reprinted in *Soma*, 3, (1932),pp.46-48; in *Antaeus*, 12 (Winter 1973), pp.147-150.

'Scylla and Charybdis', *Pagany*, 1, no.4 (Oct-Dec 1930), pp.6-17.

'Thinking of Saint Petronius Arbiter', *Pagany*, 2, no.1 (Jan-Mar 1931), pp.95-97. Reprinted as 'Thinking of Saints and of Petronius Arbiter', *Soma*, 3 (1932), pp.43-45. As 'Thinking of Saints and Petronius Arbithe', *Antaeus*, 12 (Winter 1973), pp.141-142.

'Rites of Passage', *Pagany*, 2, no.2 (Jul-Sep 1931), pp.62-63.

'Green', *Pagany*, 2, no.4 (Oct-Dec 1931), pp.1-13. Reprinted in *A Return to Pagany*, ed. Stephen Halpert and Richard Johns (Beacon Press, 1969), pp.344-356.

'Corfe' ['A Song to Keep People out of Dorset'], in *An 'Objectivists' Anthology*, ed. Louis Zukofsky (To Publishers, le Bausset, Var, France, 1932), pp.36-39. Final section of 'Corfe' reprinted at end of John Wieners' note, in *The Floating Bear*, 26 (Oct 1963), p.3. Reprinted in full in *Antaeus*, 12 (Winter 1973), pp.151-152; appended to Afterword by Robin Blaser to 1979 reprint of *Imaginary Letters*, pp.77-80.

'Douarnenez', *Soma* , 3 (1932), pp.45-46.

'After the Funeral', *The London Mercury*, 27, no.158 (Dec 1932), pp.111-115.

'On an American Wonderchild who translated Homer at eight years old', *Seed*, 1 (Jan 1933), pp.9-10.

'A Lover', *Life and Letters To-day*, 12, no.58 (Oct 1934), pp.26-37. Reprinted as 'Der Geliebte', trans. Bianca Dahms, in *Das grosse Frauenlesebuch IV* (Goldmann Verlag, 1994), pp.109-131.

'The Warning', *Life and Letters To-day*, 12, no.61 (Jan 1935), pp.396-404.

'The Guest', *Life and Letters To-day*, 13, no.1 (Sep 1935), pp.101-115.

'One Roman Speaks', *The Cornhill Magazine*, 152, no.910 (Oct 1935), pp.448-465.

'Alexander the Great, 325 BC' [extract from *The Macedonian*], in *The Imaginary Eye-witness*, ed. C.H. Lockitt (Longmans, Green & Co, 1937), pp.14-20.

'In the House', *Life and Letters To-day*, 18, no.11 (Spring 1938), pp.83-85.

'Mappa Mundi', *Life and Letters To-day*, 18, no.11 (Spring 1938), pp.86-90.

'Look Homeward, Angel', *Life and Letters To-day*, 18, no.12 (Summer 1938), pp.56-60. Reprinted in *The Cornish Review*, no.16 (Winter 1970), pp.9-14.

'The House', *Life and Letters To-day*, 18, no.12 (Summer 1938), pp.61-73.

'Honey, Get your Gun', *Life and Letters To-day*, 18, no.12 (Summer 1938), pp.74-80.

Mary Butts and Cecil Maitland, 'The Douglas Credit System'; 'Hutson's Meals'; 'Love'; 'The Bath', from 'House Rhymes by Cecil and Mary', 'Selections from the Journal', ed. Robert H. Byington and Glen E. Morgan, *Art & Literature*, 7 (Winter 1965), pp.167-169.

'Two Ways of Not Seeing the World', *Antaeus*, 12 (Winter 1973), p.140.

'Parenthesis', *Antaeus*, 12 (Winter 1973), p.143.

'Avenue Montaigne', *Antaeus*, 12 (Winter 1973), pp.151-152.

'The Golden Bough', *Antaeus Double Fiction Issue*, 13/14 (Spring-Summer 1974), pp.88-97. Reprinted in *That Kind of Woman*, ed. Bronte Adams and Trudi Tate (Virago, 1991), pp.16-28.

'With and Without Buttons', in *Ghosts in Country Villages*, ed. Denys Val Baker (William Kimber, 1984), pp.9-23; in *The Virago Book of Ghost Stories, Volume II*, ed. Richard Dalby (Virago, 1991), pp.15-26.

'Bellerophon to Anteia', 'The Later Life of Theseus, King of Athens', 'A Roman Speaks' reprinted in 'Appendix: Three Stories' to *The Classical Novels*, op.cit., pp.349-384.

'Angele au Couvent' in *A Sacred Quest*, ed. C. Wagstaff, pp.109-125.

III: Essays and Articles

[anonymous], 'The Poetry of Hymns', *The Outlook*, 18, no.461 (1.12.06), pp.696-697.

[anonymous] interview in 'Complete Exposure of "Drug Fiend" Author [Aleister Crowley]', *Sunday Express* (26.11.22), p.7.

'Unpleasant Court Cases, Facts of Life, Plea for Rank and Adequate Knowledge' [Interview], *Pall Mall Gazette* (20.12.22), p.5.

'Confessions and Interview', *The Little Review*, 7, no.2 (May 1929), pp.21-22. Reprinted in *A Sacred Quest*, ed. C. Wagstaff, pp.126-128.

'Aldous Huxley', in *Scrutinies II*, ed. Edgell Rickword (Wishart & Co, 1931), pp.73-98.

'Ghosties and Ghoulies', *The Bookman*, 83, no.469 (Jan. 1933), pp.386-389; 83, no.497 (Feb. 1933), pp.433-435; 83, no.498 (Mar. 1933), pp.493-494; 84, no.499 (Apr. 1933), pp.12-14.

'The Art of Montagu [sic] James', *The London Mercury*, 29, no.172 (Feb. 1934), pp.306-317. Extracts reprinted in *Twentieth-Century Literary Criticism*, ed. Sharon K. Hall (Gale Research Co), 6 (1982), pp.206-208.

'Alexander the Great', *Everyman*, 29 (13.4.34), pp.209, 224.

'Baron Corvo', *The London Mercury*, 30, no.175 (May 1934), pp.619-624.

'Two Land's Ends: The French and the English', *The Manchester Guardian* (28.5.34), p.9.

'Vandal Visitors to the West', *Everyman*, 39 (22.6.34), p.484.

'The Seine Net: Community Fishing in Cornwall', *The Manchester Guardian* (8.3.35), p.9.

'Spring Storm', *The Manchester Guardian* (11.6.35), p.16.

'The Heresy Game', *The Spectator*, 158 (12.3.37), pp.466-467.

IV: Reviews

'Aldington's Images of Desire', *The Little Review*, 6, no.4 (Aug 1919), pp.35-36. On Richard Aldington, volume of Imagist poetry.

'The Works of Thomas Vaughan', *The Little Review*, 6 no.10 (Mar 1920), pp.47-48. On *The Works of Thomas Vaughan*, ed. A.E. Waite. See 'Thomas Vaughan', letter by Mary Butts in *The Little Review*, 7, no.3 (Sep-Dec 1920), p.58, in reply to comment by S. Foster Damon.

'The Wind-Flowers of Asklepiades', *The Little Review*, 7, no.4 (Jan-Mar 1921), pp.45-47. On Meleagar of Gadara, *The Wind-Flowers of Asklepiades* and *Poems of Poseidippos*.

'A Correction' [Letter], *the transatlantic review*, 2, no.1 (1924), p.98.

'Mr Wescott's Third Book', *The Dial*, 82 (May 1929), pp.424-427. On Glenway Wescott, *Good-bye Winconsin*.

'A Story of Ancient Magic', *The Bookman*, 80, no.478 (Jul 1931), p.210. On Naomi Mitchison, *The Corn King and the Spring Queen*.

'France and Classicism', ibid, p.211. On H. Caudwell, *Introduction to French Classicism*.

'Antiquity?', *The Bookman*, 81, no.482 (Nov 1931), p.137. On Douglas Sladen, *The Greek Slave*.

'Rousseau', *The Bookman*, 81, no.483 (Xmas supplement), pp.51-52. On John Charpentier, *Jean-Jacques Rousseau*.

'On Gardens: Gardens and Gardening', *The Bookman*, 82, no.487 (Apr 1932), p.40. On *Studio Gardening Annual 1932*.

'A Glimpse of the Victorian Scene', *The Bookman*, 82, no.488 (May 1932), p.119. On Mark Perugini, *Victorian Days and Ways*.

'The Past in the Present', *The Bookman*, 82, no.490 (Jul 1932), p.206. On T.R. Glover, *Greek By-ways*.

'The Real East End', *The Bookman*, 83, no.493 (Oct 1932), p.24. On Thomas Burke, *The Real East End*.

'Hesiod, an Hellenic Prophet', *The Bookman*, 83, no.494 (Nov 1932), p.113-114. On *Hesiod: Works and Days*, ed. T.A. Sinclair.

'Vision of Asia', *The Bookman*, 83, no.495 (Xmas 1932), pp.223-225. On L. Cranmer Byng, *Vision of Asia*.

'Rome: of the Renaissance and Today', ibid, p.254. On Sir Rennell Rodd, *Rome: of the Renaissance and Today*.

'This England', ibid, p.274-80. On S.P.B. Mais, *This Unknown Island and The Highlands of Britain*; T.A. Coward, M.Sc., *Cheshire: Traditions and History*; Fred S. Thatcher, *Kennet Country*; Anthony Steele, *Jorrocks's England*; Rhoda Leigh, *Past and Passing: Tales of Remote Sussex*; Edward Thomas, *The South Country*. See 'This England', letter by Mary Butts in *The Bookman*, 85 (Xmas 1932), p.202, in response to comment by L.M. Claisen on this review.

'Josephus', *The Bookman*, 83, no.496 (Jan 1933), p.405. On Lion Feuchtwanger, *Josephus*.

'The Sanc Grail', *The Bookman*, 84, no.499 (Spring 1933), pp.72-4. On A.E. Waite, *The Holy Grail*.

'The Girl Through the Ages', *The Bookman*, 84, no.500 (May 1933), p.110. On Dorothy Margaret Stuart, *The Girl Through the Ages*.

'Aristophanes, the laughing Philosopher', *The Bookman*, 84, no.501 (Jun 1933), p.152. On Gilbert Murray, *Aristophanes*.

'Taking Thought', *Time and Tide*, 14, no.24 (17.6.33), pp.738-740. On Harry Roberts, *Thinking and Doing*.

'A History of Delos', *The Bookman*, 84, no.502 (Jul 1933), p.212. On W.A. Laidlaw, *A History of Delos*.

'Our Native Land', *The Bookman*, 84, no.503 (Aug 1933), p.252. On Horace Annesley Vachell, *This was England;* Thomas Burke, *The Beauty of England;* Henry Williamson, *On Foot in Devon.*

'Alexander the Great: the Claim to Divinity', *The Sunday Times* (24.9.33), p.10. On Arthur Weigall, *Alexander the Great.*

'The Dark Tower', *Time and Tide*, 14, no.39 (30.9.33), pp.1153-1154. On Hugh l'Anson Fausset, *A Modern Prelude.*

'Alexander the Great', *The Bookman* 84, no.504 (Autumn supplement 1933), pp.78-79. On Arthur Weigall, *Alexander the Great.*

'Ancient Greek Literature, ibid, p.84. On C.M. Bowra, *Ancient Greek Literature.*

'It was Like That', *The Bookman*, 84, no.505 (Oct 1933), p.44. On Vera Brittain, *The Testament of Youth;* Violet M. MacDonald, *Up the Attic Stairs.*

'For Special People', *John O'London's Weekly*, 30, no.756 (7.10.33), p.22. On David Gascoyne, *Opening Day;* D.M. Low, *Twice Shy;* Peter Hall, *Midnight Sun.*

'King Richard III Defended', *The Sunday Times* (8.10.33), p.8. On Philip Lindsay, *King Richard III: A Chronicle.*

'A Russian Prophet', *Time and Tide*, 14, no.4 (14.10.33), pp.228-230. On Dimitri Merezhkovsky, *Jesus the Unknown* and *The Secret of the West.*

'Gods and Men', *Week-End Review*, 8, no.190a (21.10.33), pp.411-412. On Arthur Weigall, *Alexander the Great.*

'Homage to Bertrand du Guesclin', *The Sunday Times* (5.11.33), p.8. On M. Coryn, *Black Mastiff.*

'"Back to the Land": A Plea to the Town Dweller', *The Daily Telegraph* (21.11.33), p.15. On A.G. Street, *Country Days.*

'The Real Wordsworth', *Time and Tide*, 14, no.48 (2.12.33), pp.1446-1448. On Edith C. Batho, *The Later Wordsworth.*

'The Pleasures of Gardening', *The Sunday Times* (3.12.33), p.15. On H.N. Wethered, *A Short History of Gardening.*

'On Gardens: Holding the Right Emotion', *The Sunday Times* (10.12.33), Xmas supp. p.iii. On Marian Cran, *I know a Garden.*

'This England', [letter], *The Bookman*, 85, no.507 (Dec 1933), p.202.

'Poet and Artist in Greece', *The Bookman*, 85, no.507 (Xmas 1933), p.218. On E.A Gardner, *Poet and Artist in Greece.*

'Magic of Person and Place', *The Bookman*, 85, no.507 (Dec 1933), pp.141-143. On Gaston B. Means, *The Strange Death of President Harding;* Leon Feuchtwanger, *Josephus;* Gilbert Murray, *Aristophanes;* T.R. Glover, *Greek By-Ways;* Ruth Manning-Sanders, *The Crochet Woman;* H. O'Neil Hencken, *West Cornwall;* Aldous Huxley, *Texts and Pretexts;* E.F. Benson, *King Edward VII;* E. Channon, *The Ludwigs of Bavaria.*

'The Herschel Chronicle', *The Bookman*, 85, no.507 (Xmas 1933), pp.252-253. On *The Herschel Chronicle: The Life Story of William Herschel and His Sister Caroline*, ed. Constance A. Lubbock.

'England', *The Bookman*, 85, no.507 (Xmas 1933), pp.256-258. On S.P.B. Mais, *Week-Ends in England*; Lukin Johnston, *Down English Lanes*; A.G. Street, *Country Days*.

'The Drama of the Weather', *The Bookman*, 85, no.507 (Xmas 1933), pp.309-310. On Sir Napier Shaw, *The Drama of the Weather*.

'A Biographical Problem: Katherine Mansfield's Early Life', *The Sunday Times* (31.12.33), p.6. On R.E. Mantz and J. Middleton Murry, *The Life of Katherine Mansfield*.

'Unparalleled Swift', *Time and Tide*, 15, no.2 (13.1.34), pp.44-45. On Mario M. Rossi and J.M. Hone, *Swift or the Egoist*; W.D. Taylor, *Jonathan Swift*.

'Values', *John O'London's Weekly*, 30, no.772 (27.1.34), p.656. On Nora Stevenson, *Whistler's Corner*; Martin Boyd, *Scandal of Spring*; Monica Curtis, *Landslide*.

'Where are we going?', *John O'London's Weekly*, 30, no.773 (3.2.34), p.690. On Anne Stretton, *Camilla*; Philip Keeley, *Corner Shop*; Campbell Nairne, *Stony Ground*.

'The New Gods', *John O'London's Weekly*, 30, no.775 (17.2.34), p.766. On Raymond Otis, *Fire Brigade*; Richard Baker, *Night-Shift*; Margaret Dale, *Maze*.

'A Man Possessed', *Time and Tide*, 15, no.7 (17.2.34), pp.212-214. On A.J.A. Symons, *The Quest for Corvo*.

'Mr Powys's Dorset', *The Sunday Times* (18.2.34), p.11. On Llewelyn Powys, *Earth Memories*.

'Alexander the Great: the Real Dilemma', *The Sunday Times* (25.2.34), p.11. On F.A. Wright, *Alexander the Great*.

'The Isles of Greece', *The Bookman*, 85, no.510 (Mar 1934), p.505. On F.L. Lucas and Prudence Lucas, *From Olympus to the Styx*.

'King Harry', *Time and Tide*, 15, no.13 (31.3.34), pp.412-413. On Helen Simpson, *Henry VIII*.

'The Past Lives Again', *The Bookman*, 86, no.511 (Apr 1934), pp.44-45. On Jack Lindsay, *Rome for Sale*; Una Broadbent, *Perilous Grain*; F.A. Wright, *Alexander the Great*.

'Cornish Homes and Customs', *The Bookman*, 86, no.511 (Apr 1934), p.72. On A.K. Hamilton, *Cornish Homes and Customs*.

'The Happy Elizabethan: A Reconstruction of Old Country Life', *John O'London's Weekly*, 31, no.782 (7.4.34), p.19. On *The Countryman's Jewel*, ed. Marcus Woodward.

'Roads Through the Centuries: Track to by-Pass', *The Sunday Times* (22.4.34), p.12. On T.W. Wilkinson, *From Track to By-Pass*.

'The Grandeur of Rome', *The Bookman*, 86, no.512 (May 1934), p.119. On G.P. Baker, *Twelve Centuries of Rome*.

'Scandal or History', *Time and Tide*, 15, no.18 (5.5.34), pp.584-586. On Robert Graves, *I, Claudius*.

'A New Vision', *Time and Tide*, 15, no.21 (26.5.34), pp.675-677. On *Orthodoxy Sees It Through*, ed. Sidney Dark.

'Gardens and Gardening', *The Bookman*, 86, no.513 (Jun 1934), p.161. On *The Studio*

Gardening Annual 1934, ed. F.A. Mercer.

'The Great Dumas', *Time and Tide*, 15, no.23 (9.6.34), pp.732-734. On G.R. Pearce, *Dumas, Père*.

'"A Waste of Shame"', *Time and Tide*, 15, no.25 (23.6.34), pp.802-803. On Hesketh Pearson, *The Fool of Love: A Life of William Hazlitt*.

'Country', *The Bookman*, 16, no.514 (Jul 1934), p.189. On H.J. Massingham, *Country*.

'The Bull and the Fighter', *Time and Tide*, 15, no.27 (7.7.34), p.860. On Roy Campbell, *Broken Record*.

'A Man Set Apart', *John O'London's Weekly*, 31, no.796 (14.7.34), p.545. On John Lindsay, *Tenderness*; Allan Govan, *Children of the Hill*; Joan Temple, *Duologue*.

'Sir Philip Gibbs's New Book', *John O'London's Weekly*, 31, no.797 (21.7.34), p.576. On Sir Philip Gibbs, *Paradise for Sale*; Barbara Goulden, *Slings and Arrows*.

'An Artist in a New World', *The Sunday Times* (22.7.34), p.12. On Van Wyck Brooks, *The Ordeal of Mark Twain*.

'Two Blind Mice', *The Bookman*, 86, no.515 (Aug 1934), p.255. On Victor Canning, *Mr Finchley Discovers His England*.

'An Old Song Re-written', *John O'London's Weekly*, 31, no.801 (18.8.34), p.705. On Eden Philpotts, *Portrait of a Gentleman*; Jacob Wassermann, *The Goose-man*; Beatrice Tunstall, *The Long Day Closes*.

'Simple and Ambitious', *John O'London's Weekly*, 31, no.803 (1.9.34), p.770. On Peter Brook, *Arden Vales*; George Woden, *Sowing Clover*; Col. T.W. Tweed, *Blind Mouths*.

'An older America', *John O'London's Weekly*, 31, no.804 (8.9.34), p.808. On Dubose Heyword, *Peter Ashley*; Arnold Armstrong, *Parched Earth*; Ralph Bates, *Lean Men*.

'Mr. S.P.B. Mais in America', *The Sunday Times* (9.9.34), p.9. On S.P.B. Mais, *A Modern Columbus*.

'Mr Mencken Again: A Question of Ethics', *The Sunday Times* (30.9.34), p.12. On H.L. Mencken, *Treatise on Right and Wrong*.

'Jig-saw History', *The Bookman*, 87, no.517 (Oct 1934), p.62. On Compton Mackenzie, *Marathon and Salamis*.

'Negro', *The Adelphi*, 3rd series, 9, no.1 (Oct 1934), pp.185-187. On *Negro*, ed. Nancy Cunard.

'Dostoievsky: An Interpretation', *Life and Letters To-Day*, 11, no.58 (Oct 1934), pp.120-121. On Nicholas Berdyaev, *Dostoievsky: An Interpretation*.

'"Mr Ezra Pound is the Goods"', *The Sunday Times* (28.10.34), p.12. On Ezra Pound, *Make it New*.

'Five also Ran', *The Bookman*, 87, no.518 (Nov 1934), pp.129-130. On Joseph Hergesheimer, *The Foolscap Rose*; K. de B. Codrington, *The Wood and the Image*; Humphrey Parkington, *In Company with Crispin*; Archibald Marshall, *Nothing Hid*; Tennyson Jesse, *A Pin to see the Peepshow*; Charles Braibant, *Dead Woman's Shoes*.

'Two Artists', *Time and Tide*, 15, no.45 (10.11.34), p.1430. On Daphne du Maurier, *Gerald, A Portrait*; Cecil Gray, *Peter Warlock: A Memoir of Philip Heseltine*.

'Mr. Graves's Rome', *The Bookman*, 87, no.519 (Xmas 1934), p.36. On Robert Graves, *Claudius the God*.

'The New Child', *The Bookman*, 87, no.519 (Xmas 1934), p.152. On Adrian Bell, *The Balcony*.

'King Henry the Fifth: Behind the Curtain of History', *The Sunday Times* (6.1.35), p.8. On Philip Lindsay, *King Henry V*; J.D. Griffith Davies, *Henry V*.

'A Swedish Childhood', *Time and Tide*, 16, no.2 (12.1.35), p.55. On Selma Lagerlöf, *Memories of my Childhood*.

'Seven Detective Stories: New Poirot Novel', *The Sunday Times* (14.7.35), p.8. On Agatha Christie, *Death in the Clouds*; Nigel Morland, *The Moon Murder*; A.E.W. Mason, *They wouldn't be Chessmen*; Sydney Hales, *Lord of Terror*; J.J. Connington, *In Whose Dim Shadow*; R.A.J. Walling, *The Cat and the Corpse*; J. Jefferson Farjeon, *Holiday Express*.

'Four Detective Novels', *The Sunday Times* (21.7.35), p.8. On Anthony Gilbert, *The Man Who Was Too Clever*, Clive Ryland, *The Blind Beggar Murder*, Leonard R. Gribble, *Murder at Tudor Arches*, Richard Hull, *Keep it Quiet*.

'Modern World and Religion', *The Sunday Times* (18.8.35), p.9. On Christopher Dawson, *Religion and the Modern State*; C. Scott, *Outline of Modern Occultism*; R.L. Smith, *John Fisher and Thomas More*.

'Adventure and Detection: Stories by Beginners', *The Sunday Times* (1.9.35), p.7. On Louis Christie, *Better than Warfare*; John Rowlands, *Bloodshed in Bayswater*; N. Toye, *The Twice-Murdered Man*.

'Conspiracies and Crime', *The Sunday Times* (8.9.35), p.7. On Inez Haynes, *Murder in Fancy Dress*, Henry Kitchell, *The Alleged Great Aunt*, Frank A Clement, *Picture Him Dead*, Charles Vivian, *Cigar for Inspector Head*, Van Wyck Mason, *The Vesper Service Murders*, John Halstead, *The Black Fear*.

'The Eighteenth Century', *Time and Tide*, 16, no.38 (21.9.35), pp.1337-1340. On Stephen Gwynn, *Oliver Goldsmith*; Gilbert Thomas, *William Cowper*.

'American Unemployed', *John O'London's Weekly*, 34, no.859 (28.9.35), p.898. On Edward Anderson, *Hungry Men*, James Hanley, *Stoker Bush*; Anthony Bertram, *Men Adrift*. See correspondence between Anthony Bertram and "Our Reviewer" [M.B.] on this review in '"Men Adrift"', *John O'London's Weekly*, 34, no.862 (19.10.35), p.139.

'Imperial Rome', *Time and Tide*, 16, no.40 (5.10.35), pp.1403-1404. On Gunther Birkenfeld, *Augustus, A Novel*; Sulamith Ish-Kishor, *Magnificent Hadrian*.

'Fantastic Tales', *John O'London's Weekly*, 34, no.861 (12.10.35), pp.91-92. On Thomas Burke, *Night Pieces*; L.A. Pavey, *Moving Pageant*; Margaret Irwin, *Madame Fears the Dark*.

'The Funeral March of a Marionette', *Time and Tide*, 16, no.41 (12.10.35), p.1450. On Susan Buchan, *The Funeral March of a Marionette*.

'America in the "Gilded Age"', *The Sunday Times* (20.10.35), p.16. On Elizabeth Drexel Lehr, *'King Lehr' and the Gilded Age*.

'This Season's Best Thriller', *Crime*, 1, no.1 (Winter 1935-6), p.5. On Nigel Morland, *The Phantom Gunman*.

'Dorset Essays, Scenes and Memories', *The Sunday Times* (24.11.35), p.16. On Llewelyn Powys, *Dorset Essays*.

'The Finer Corvo', *Time and Tide*, 16, no.49 (7.12.35), pp.1800-1801. On Rolfe, Baron Corvo, *Hubert's Arthur*.

'Green Fingers', *The Sunday Times* (8.12.35), p.12. On E.J. Salisbury, *The Living Garden*.

'"Parzival"', *Time and Tide*, 17, no.2 (11.1.36), pp.57-58. On Wolfram von Eschenbach, *The Story of Parzival and the Grail*, interpreted and discussed by Margaret Fitzgerald Richey.

'Americans on England: Pilgrims of the Past', *The Sunday Times* (2.2.36), p.13. On R.B. Mowat, *Americans in England*.

'Queen Victoria's "Wicked Uncle"', *The Sunday Times* (9.2.36), p.11. On Herbert van Thal, *Ernest Augustus, Duke of Cumberland and King of Hanover*.

'Mount Athos', *Time and Tide*, 17, no.11 (14.3.36), pp.385-386. On R.M. Dawkins, *The Monks of Athos*.

'American Scene', *John O'London's Weekly*, 34, no.883 (14.3.36), pp.936, 938. On R.T.S. Stribling, *The Sound Wagon*; E.F. Bozman, *X Plus Y*; Mary Mitchell, *Maidens Beware*.

'The Lady on a Black Horse', *Time and Tide*, 17, no.12 (21.3.36), pp.417-418. On M.A. Sinclair Stobart, *Miracles and Adventures*.

'Land and Liberty', *John O'London's Weekly*, 34,no.884 (21.3.36), pp.980-981. On Kristmann Godmudsson, *The Meaning of Life*; A. Dan Doolaard, *Express to the East*; W. Townend, *The Top Landing*.

'The Fortunes of a Family', *The Sunday Times* (29.3.36), p.11. On Col. A.C. Murray, *The Five Sons of "Bare Betty"*.

'Cleopatra's Daughter', *Time and Tide*, 17, no.14 (4.4.36), pp.488-489. On Beatrice Chanler, *Cleopatra's Daughter*.

'Flickering Genius', *Time and Tide*, 17, no.19 (9.5.36), pp.680-681. On Edward Sackville-West, *A Flame in Sunlight: Thomas de Quincey*.

'Caesar and His times', *The Sunday Times* (24.5.36), p.10. On Ferdinand Mainzer, *Caesar's Mantle*, trans. Eden Paul & Cedar Paul.

'Chartres—The Symbol', *Time and Tide*, 17, no.24 (13.6.36), p.856. On Henry Adams, *Mont-Saint-Michel and Chartres*.

'Great Drama and Small', *Time and Tide*, 17, no.31 (1.8.36), p.1103. On Charles Williams, *Thomas Cranmer*; John Drinkwater, *Garibaldi*.

'The Real Voltaire', *Time and Tide*, 17, no.46 (14.11.36), p.1596. On Alfred Noyes, *Voltaire*.

'Eminent Romans', *Time and Tide*, 18, no.15 (10.4.37), pp.470, 472. On F.A. Wright, *Marcus Agrippa*; Bernard M. Allen, *Augustus Caesar*.

SECONDARY BIBLIOGRAPHY

A. UNSIGNED OR UNTRACED REVIEWS OF WORKS BY MARY BUTTS (CHRONOLOGICAL)

'Georgian Stories', *Times Literary Supplement* (6.7.22), pp.440.

'The Art of the Short Story', *Daily News* (24.8.22).

'"The Best Short Stories of 1922"', *The Observer* (4.2.23), p.4.

'Court of Appeal', *The Times* (17.2.23), p.4.

'Book Banned', *Daily Courier* (16.3.23).

'*Speed the Plough* by Mary Butts', *The Daily Express* (20.3.23).

'The "Georgian" Short Story', *Bolton Evening News* (22.3.23), p.3.

'New Novels: *Speed the Plough*', *Times Literary Supplement* (22.3.23), p.196.

Review of *Speed the Plough, The Outlook* (24.3.23).

'Books of the Week', *The Daily Telegraph* (24.3.23), p.10.

Untitled Review of *Speed the Plough, The Weekly Review* (24.3.23).

'Disintegration', *The Observer* (25.3.23).

'Chaotic Studies', *Aberdeen Free Press* (28.3.23).

'Short Stories', *The Nation and Athenaeum*, 33, no.1 (7.4.23), pp. 22-23.

'Literary Surgery', *The Liverpool Post and Mercury* (11.4.23), p.9.

'*Speed the Plough*', *Weekly Westminster Gazette* (28.4.23).

'The Short Story', *Weekly Westminster Gazette* (9.6.23), p.20.

'*Speed the Plough* by Mary Butts', *The Scotsman* (25.6.23).

'*Speed the Plough* by Mary Butts', *The Bookman*, 64, no.384 (Sep 1923), p.298. Reprinted in the final issue of *The Bookman*, 87, no.519 (Dec. 1984), pp. 214-215.

'Our Book of the Week': Abstruse Tales in "Best" Collection', *The Yorkshire Evening Post* (19.2.25).

'*Best Short Stories 1924*', *Times Literary Supplement* (20.3.25), p.385.

'New Fiction', *The Scotsman* (28.5.25).

'The Magazines', *The Saturday Review*, 139, no.3633 (10.6.25), pp. 650, 652.

'*Ashe of Rings* by Mary Butts', *The Manchester Guardian* (31.7.25).

Review of *Ashe of Rings, The Saturday Review of Literature* (29.8.25), p. 7.

'Literary Intelligentse', *The London Mercury*, 12 no.71 (Sept 1925), p.454.

'London after the War', *New York Times Book Review* (9.8.25), p.7.

'*Ashe of Rings* by Mary Butts', *The New Criterion*, 4, no.1 (Jan 1926), p.209.

'*Ashe of Rings*', *The Boston Transcript* (2.6.26), p.4.

'*Ashe of Rings*: Story of Archeology and the Remote English Countryside', *Springfield Republican* (26.6.26), p.7.

'Ashe of Rings', *Philadelphia Inquirer* (10.7.26).

'The Story of a Family', *The Saturday Review* (14.8.26), p.37.

'Briefer Mention: *Ashe of Rings* by Mary Butts', *The Dial*, 82 (1927), p.164.

'Short Stories', *Morning Post* (25.10.27).

'*Georgian Stories 1927*', *The Nation and Athenaeum*, 42, no.4 (29.10.27), p.162.

'Sophisticated Fantasy', *New York Times Book Review* (13.5.28), p.9.

'*Armed with Madness* by Mary Butts', *Aberdeen Free Press* (14.5.28).

'*Armed with Madness* by Mary Butts', *Times Literary Supplement* (24.5.28), p.397.

'*Armed with Madness*. A Novel. By Mary Butts', *The New Age, 43, no.1866* (14.6.28), p. 83.

'A Psychological Study', *Natal Mercury* (18.6.28).

'Books worth reading: The best of the new novels: Hard Playing', *John O'London's Weekly*, 19, no.475 (26.5.28), p.222.

'Butts (Mary) *Armed with Madness*', *The Librarian* (Jul 1928).

'New Fiction: Entanglements not easily untied: Tales of sorts', *Morning Post* (17.7.28).

'The Rising Literary Generation', *The Spectator* (14.3.31), p.427.

'Significant Criticism', *Times Literary Supplement* (29.3.31), p.226.

'Realm of the Woman Novelist', *The Glasgow Herald* (10.3.32).

'Sophisticated Short Stories', *Northern Echo* (16.3.32).

'*Several Occasions* by Mary Butts', *The Yorkshire Post* (16.3.32).

'Modern Paganism: Have the Film Star & Athlete Displaced Christianity?', *Western Morning News* (19.3.32).

'*Several Occasions* by Mary Butts', *The Observer* (20.3.32).

'Critic's Commentary', *Time and Tide*, 13, no.13 (26.3.32), p.352.

Review of *Several Occasions, Saturday Review* (26.3.32)

'*Several Occasions* by Mary Butts', *The Spectator* (2.4.32).

'Studies in Adjustments', *Birmingham Post* (6.4.32).

'Religion and Life', *Oxford Mail* (6.4.32).

'Townsmen and the Countryside', *The Glasgow Herald* (7.4.32), p.8.

'Memorabiblia: Books of the Road', *Publishers' Circular* (9.4.32).

'*Several Occasions* by Mary Butts', *Times Literary Supplement* (14.4.32), p.273.

'*Traps for Unbelievers*'. *Liverpool Evening Express* (16.4.32).

'A Bag of All Sorts', *The Manchester Guardian* (19.4.32).

'Tyneside: "A Public Catastrophe"', *Northern Echo* (19.4.32).

'*Traps for Unbelievers*', *Public Opinion* (22.4.32).

'For the Library List', *Birmingham Mail* (27.4.32).

'Whither shall We Worship?', *The Tatler* (4.5.32).

'*Traps for Unbelievers*', *Times Literary Supplement* (9.6.32).

'Human "Gods"', *Sheffield Independent* (20.6.32).

'A Tale No Man Can Tell', *London Evening News* (29.11.32).

'*Death of Felicity Taverner* by Mary Butts', *Birmingham Post* (13.12.32).

'*Death of Felicity Taverner*', *Times Literary Supplement* (29.12.32), p.988.

'*Death of Felicity Taverner*', *Good Housekeeping* (Jan? 1933).

'Sophisticated Melodrama', *Punch* (18.1.33).

'The Soul in Fiction', *The Observer* (12.2.33), p.8.

'New Novels: Alexander the Great', *The Glasgow Herald* (?).

'Interval', *Close-Up* (Mar 1933).

'Alexander the Great', *The Birmingham Post* (14.3.33).

'Selected Novels: Woman Writer's Picture of Alexander the Great: Legend and Life', *Nottingham Guardian* (22.3.33).

Untitled review, *Inverness Courier* (24.3.33).

'A Great Book by A Woman', *Bristol Evening World* (1.4.33).

'Alexander Made Real', *Punch* (5.4.33).

'New Fiction', *The Church Times* (8.4.33).

'The Macedonian', *The Spectator* (17.4.33).

'Mary Butts' Success', *The Daily Telegraph* (18.4.33).

'The Great Alexander', *The Liverpool Echo* (19.4.33).

Review of *The Macedonian*, *The Listener* (10.5.33).

'*The Macedonian*', *The Methodist Times* (11.5.33).

'"The Macedonian"', *The Sketch* (17.5.33).

'*The Macedonian*', *Times Literary Supplement* (20.7.33), p.494.

'The Macedonian', *The Leytonshire Express* (13.8.33).

'"Ashe of Rings." By Mary Butts', *The Observer* (29.8.33).

'Seven New Novels: Conflicts and Follies of the War', *The Glasgow Herald* (28.9.33).

'*Ashe of Rings* by Mary Butts', *Times Literary Supplement* (5.10.33), p.673.

'Egypt's Romantic Queen', *Edinburgh Evening News* (28.5.35).

'New Novels: Footnotes to history', *Northern Daily Mail* (30.5.35).

'Among the New Books: Egypt's Romantic Queen', *Worcester Evening News* (13.6.35).

'Cleopatra', *John O'London's Weekly, 33, no.844* (15.6.35), p.356.

'Cleopatra Through A Woman's Eyes', *Liverpool Echo* (18.6.35).

'Two Famous Women: Catherine the Great and Cleopatra', *The Scotsman* (20.6.35).

'*Scenes from the Life of Cleopatra*', *Times Literary Supplement* (27.6.35), p.414.

'*Scenes from the Life of Cleopatra*', *The London Mercury*, 32, no.189 (Jul 1935), p.301.

'The Last Pharoah, A Modern Woman's View of Cleopatra', *Stratford on Avon Herald* (19.7.35).

'The Real Cleopatra', *The Southport Guardian* (4.3.36).

'Miss Mary Butts: Imaginative Gift', *The Times* (13.3.37), p.14b (Charles Williams cited).

'A Dorset Childhood', *Times Literary Supplement* (29.5.37), p.404.

'A Novelist's Memoirs', *The Times* (8.6.37), p.22c.

'*The Crystal Cabinet: My Childhood at Salterns* by Mary Butts', *The Listener* (9.6.37), p.1159.

'A Writer and Early Contributor, *Life and Letters Today*, 17, no.8 (1937), pp.3-4.

'*Last Stories* by Mary Butts', *Times Literary Supplement* (8.10.38), p.649.

'Where Time Stands Still', *Poole and Dorset Herald* (6.2.63), p.18.

'*The Crystal Cabinet: My Childhood at Salterns*', *Publishers Weekly* (24.6.88), p.104.

'*The Crystal Cabinet: My Childhood at Salterns*. Mary Butts', *Studies on Women Abstracts*, 7 (1989), p.5.

'Easy going', *Gay Times Monthly* (Jan 1992), p.57.

'The Classical Novels', *Chicago Tribune* (1.1.95), p.4.

B: Sources, Essays, Reviews, Citations

Ackroyd, Peter, *Blake* (Sinclair-Stevenson, 1995).

Acton, Harold, *Memoirs of an Aesthete* (Hamish Hamilton, 1984).

Adeane, Louis, 'Mary Butts', *World Review* (Sep 1951), pp.23-27. Reprinted as 'An Appraisal of Mary Butts', in *A Sacred Quest*, ed. C. Wagstaff, pp.97-106.

Agate, James, 'Good Writing', *The Daily Express* (14.4.32), p.6.

__________'Over-Writing', *The Daily Express* (1.12.32), p.8.

__________'Before the Curtain falls: Good-Bye to the Books of 1932!', *The Daily Express* (27.12.32), p.6.

__________'Cleopatra as a Schoolmistress', *The Daily Express* (6.6.35), p.4.

__________*Ego 7: Even More of the Autobiography* (George G Harrap & Co Ltd, 1945).

Aldington, Richard, *Death of a Hero* (Chatto & Windus, 1929).

Alexander, Peter F., *William Plomer: A Biography* (O.U.P., 1989).

Allingham, Margery, 'New Novels', *Time and Tide* (1.10.38), pp.1335-1336.

Anderson, Margaret, *My Thirty Years War* (Covici, Friede, 1930).

Arnold, Lilian, 'Novel of the Week: Russian and English', *John O'London's Weekly* (10.12.32), p.438.

Arrowsmith, J.E.S., 'Fiction', *The London Mercury*, 25, no.150 (Apr 1932), p.594.

Ashbery, John, Preface to *From Altar to Chimney-piece* (McPherson & Co, 1992), pp.vii-xii.

Auric, Georges, *Quand j'étais là* (Bernard Grasset, 1979).

Baerlein, Henry, 'Short Stories', The Bookman, 68, no.403 (April 1925), pp.31-32.

__________'New Fiction', *Time and Tide*, 16 (24.8.35), pp.1226-1227.

Bagg, Camilla, 'Another View of Mary Butts', in *A Sacred Quest*, ed. C. Wagstaff, pp.89-96.

Baker, Carlos, *Hemingway: The Writer as Artist* (Princeton University Press, 1963).

Baker, Denys Val, *The Spirit of Cornwall* (W.H. Allen & Co, 1980).

Baker, Frank, 'A Note on Mary Butts', *The Cornish Review*, 16 (Winter 1970), pp.4-8.

__________*I Follow But Myself* (Peter Davies, 1968).

__________*The Call of Cornwall* (Robert Hale, 1976).

Bald, Wambly, *On the Left Bank 1929-1933*, ed. Benjamin Franklin V (Ohio University Press, 1987).

Barnes, Djuna, *Nightwood* (Faber, 1979).

Bax, Clifford, *Rosemary for Remembrance* (Frederick Muller Ltd, 1948).

Beach, Sylvia, *Shakespeare and Company* (Plantin, 1987).

Bedford, Sybille, *Aldous Huxley. Volume One: The Apparent Stability* (Quartet, 1979).

Beer, Patricia, 'Very like Poole Harbour', *London Review of Books* (5.12.91), p.16.

Behrman, S.N., *Duveen* (Hamish Hamilton, 1952).

Bell, Quentin, *Elders and Betters* (John Murray, 1995).

Bellerby, Frances, *Selected Stories* (Enitharmon, 1986).

Benedict, Libbian, 'Decadence in England', *New York Sunday[?]* (26.5.28).

Benstock, Shari, *Women of the Left Bank: Paris 1900-1940* (Virago, 1994).

Benton, Jill, *Naomi Mitchison: A Biography* (Pandora, 1993).

Black's Guide to the Duchy of England (A. & C. Black, 1870).

Blackwood, Algernon, *John Silence* (Eveleigh Nash, 1908).

__________ *Ancient Sorceries and Other Tales* (Collins, 1927).

Blake, William, *Blake's Complete Writings*, ed. Geoffrey Keynes (O.U.P., 1972).

__________*The Blake Collection of W. Graham Robertson*, ed. Kerrison Preston (Faber, 1952).

Blakeston, Oswell, 'The Responsibility of the Public', *The Bookman* (Oct 1933), pp.15-16.

__________'Plutarch's Siren', *Books and Bookmen*, 16, no.6 (March 1971), p.29.

__________'Dangerous Enchanter', *Gay News*, 245 (25.11-8.12.82), pp.30-31.

__________'The Lady Who Enchanted Cocteau', *Little Caesar*, 12 (1982), pp.19-22.

Blaser, Robin, Afterword, *Imaginary Letters* (Talonbooks, 1979), pp.61-76.

__________ Pῖκοσ ὸ καὶ Ζενσ, *The Writing and the World of Mary Butts* [conference brochure] (University of California, 1984).

__________ '"Here Lies the Woodpecker Who was Zeus"', *A Sacred Quest*, ed. C. Wagstaff, pp.159-223.

Blatchford, Winifred, 'Nasty Georgian Fiction', *The Clarion* (4.8.22), p.4.

Blondel, Nathalie, '*The Crystal Cabinet*', *P.N.R.*, 15, no.5 (1988), pp.53-55.

Blum, Virginia, Clements, Patricia & Grundy, Isobel, *The Feminist Companion to Literature in English: Women Writers from the Middle Ages to the Present* (B.T. Batsford Ltd, 1990).

Blunden, Edmund, 'Alexander', *Time and Tide*, 14, no.17 (29.4.33), pp.501-502.

Blyton, W.J., 'Far Past Revived: Men are Enemies', *Sheffield Independent* (13.3.33).

Botkin, B.A., 'Mary Butts Tortures Reader', *Oklahoma City* (14.10.28).

Boulton, Cecil, 'Mary Butts' Bright Novel *Ashe of Rings*, Dostoevski served with a little Milk', *New York Evening News* (5.6.26), p.5.

Bowen, Stella, *Drawn From Life* (Virago, 1984).

Brooke, Jocelyn, *Conventional Weapons* (Faber & Faber, 1941).

Browne, Wynyard, 'A Great Novel: *Death of Felicity Taverner*', *The Bookman*, 83 , no.495 (Xmas 1932), p.306.

__________ 'Greek and Barbarian', *The Bookman*, 84 (Apr 1933), pp.44-45.

Bryher [Winifred Ellerman], 'Recognition not Farewell', *Life and Letters To-day*, 17, no.9 (Autumn 1937), pp.159-164. Reprinted in *A Sacred Quest*, ed. C. Wagstaff, pp.3-10.

__________*The Heart to Artemis* (Collins, 1963).

Buck, Claire, ed., *The Bloomsbury Guide to Women's Literature* (Bloomsbury, 1992).

Buckle, Richard, *Diaghilev* (Weidenfield, 1993).

Bull, Harcourt Wesson, '"Truth is the Heart's Desire"', in *A Sacred Quest*, ed. C. Wagstaff, pp.53-88.

Bullett, Gerald, '*Speed the Plough* by Mary Butts', *The Challenge* (4.5.23).

Bulloch, J.M., 'Defence of Cleopatra', *The Sunday Times* (26.5.35).

Bunting, Basil, 'Uno dei Mali dell'Inghilterra', trans. Maria Agosti, *Il Mare* (1933).

Butts, Tony, letter to the Editor, *'The Crystal Cabinet'*, *The Spectator* (18.6.37), p.1149.

_________ [pen name] William d'Arfey, *Curious Relations*, ed. William Plomer (Jonathan Cape, 1945).

Byington, Robert & Morgan, Glen E., 'Mary Butts', *Art and Literature*, 7 (1965), pp.162-179. Mary Butts's Journal extracts reprinted as 'From the Journals' in *A Sacred Quest*, ed. C Wagstaff, pp.129-136.

Byington, Robert, 'Interviews with Virgil Thomson, Eugene MacGown, Quentin Bell and Hugh Ross Williamson', in *A Sacred Quest* , ed. C. Wagstaff, pp.25-52.

C., V.C., *Alexander of Macedon*, *Liverpool Post* (3.4.33).

Caizergues, Pierre, ed., *Jean Cocteau et le Sud* (A Barthélemy, 1989).

Callaghan, Morley, *That Summer in Paris* (Coward McCann, 1963).

Cariou, André & Tooby, Michael, *Christopher Wood: A Painter between two Cornwalls* (Tate Gallery St Ives, 1997).

Carpenter, Humphrey, *Geniuses Together* (Unwin Hyman, 1987).

Carrington, Dora, *Carrington: letters and extracts from her diaries*, ed. David Garnett (O.U.P., 1979).

Chanel, Pierre, *Album Cocteau* (Tchou, 1970).

Charters, James, *This Must be the Place* (Herbert Joseph Ltd, 1934).

Church, Richard, 'Grim Fairy Tale', *John O'London's Weekly, 30,* no.754 (23.9.33), pp.889-890.

Clarke, Jennifer, *Exploring the West Country: A Woman's Guide* (Virago, 1987).

Cocteau, Jean, *Portraits Souvenirs* (Grasset, 1935).

Coghlan, John, 'A Letter of Appreciation to Miss Mary Butts', *The Bookman*, 84, no.499 (Apr 1933), p.69.

_________ 'The Macedonian', *Everyman* (29.8.33).

Cohen, J.M and M.J., eds., *The Penguin Dictionary of Quotations* (Jonathan Cape, 1960).

Collins, H.P., 'Books of the Quarter', *The Criterion*, 10, no.4 (Jul 1931), pp.745-747.

Colville-Hyde, Mary, 'The Boston Holbeins, Sir William Butts and Lady Butts', *Apollo: the Journal of the Arts for Connoisseurs and Collectors*, 22, no.127 (Jul 1935), pp.36-38.

Conant, Oliver, 'Countryside Modern', *New York Times Book Review*, VII (26.7.92), p.23.

Corin, John, *Sennen Cove and its Lifeboat* (Sennen cove Branch of the R.N.L.I, 1985).

Cox, Michael, *M.R. James: An Informal Portrait* (O.U.P., 1986).

Crickmay, Edward, 'Latest Fiction: A Beautiful German Novel', *Sunday Referee*, 2845 (13.3.32), p.6

_________'The Latest Novels', *Sunday Referee*, 2927 (8.10.33), p11.

Crosbie, Mary, 'A Cromwellian Interlude', *John O'London's Weekly*, 27, no.677 (1932), p.21.

__________ 'Alexander of Macedòn', *John O'London's Weekly*, 28, no.728 (25.3.33), p.1021.

Crowley, Aleister, *Diary of a Drug Fiend* (Sphere Books Ltd, 1972).

__________ *The Confessions of Aleister Crowley*, eds. John Symonds & Kenneth Grant (Bantam, 1971).

D., H., [Hilda Doolittle], *Palimpsest* (Southern Illinois University Press, 1968, 2nd edn).

Davidson, Angus, 'Angus Davidson', in *Recollections of Virginia Woolf*. ed. & intro. Joan Russell Noble (Peter Owen, 1972), pp.53-61.

Davies, Rhys, 'A Note on Mary Butts', *Wales*, 6/7 (1939), p.207.

Davis, Frank, 'A Page for Collectors: The Newly Discovered Holbein Portrait of Sir William Butts: A Triumph for X-Rays and Scholarship', *The Illustrated London News* (8.3.30), pp.394-396.

Delafield, E.M., Review of *Ashe of Rings*, *Morning Post* (29[?].9.33).

Desbordes, Jean, *J'adore* (Bernard Grasset, 1928).

Dolin, Anton, [Patrick Kaye] *Autobiography* (Oldbourne Book Co Ltd, 1960).

Doyle, Charles, *Richard Aldington: A Biography* (Macmillan, 1989).

Duberman, Martin Bauml, *Paul Robeson* (The Bodley Head Ltd, 1989).

Duchêne, Anne, 'Landowners and Lasses', *Times Literary Supplement* (18.10.91), p.1.

Duncan, Irma & Macdougall, Allan Ross, *Isadora Duncan's Russian Days: and her last years in France* (Victor Gollancz Ltd, 1929).

Duncan, Robert, 'Night and Days. Chapter 1', *Sumac*, pp.101-146.

__________ 'Re Mary Butts', *The Writings and the World of Mary Butts* [Conference Brochure] (University of California, Feb 1984). Reprinted as 'Re Mary Butts', *A Sacred Quest*, ed. C. Wagstaff, pp.157-158.

Dyson, Brian, *Liberty in Britain* (Civil Liberties Trust, 1994).

E., J., 'Futurism in Fiction; the Nightmare Prose of the Moderns', *The Liverpool Courier* (17.9.25).

Edwards, A.T.G., 'Literary Ladies at a Tea Party', *Northern Echo* (14.6.35).

E.A. [George Russell], *Enchantment and other Poems* (Macmillan & Co, 1930).

Eliot, T.S., *The Letters of T.S. Eliot. Volume 1. 1898-1922*, ed. Valerie Eliot (Harcourt, Brace, Jovanovich, 1988).

Ellis, Edward F., *The British Museum in Fiction* (Buffalo, 1981).

Emboden, William A., *Jean Cocteau: Dessins, Peintures, Sculptures* (Nathan Image, 1989).

Entwhistle, W.J., & Gillett, E., *The Literature of England AD 500-1942* (Longmans & Co, 1943).

Faas, Ekbert, *Young Robert Duncan* (Black Sparrow Press, 1983).

Faulks, Sebastian, *The Fatal Englishman: Three Short Lives* (Hutchinson, 1996).

Fausset, Hugh l'A., 'A "War Fairy-Tale"', *The Manchester Guardian* (22.9.33), p.5.

Fitch, Noel Riley, *Sylvia Beach and the Lost Generation* (Penguin, 1988).

Ford, Ford Madox, *It was the Nightingale* (Heinemann, 1934).

_________ *Between St Dennis and St George: A Sketch of Three Civilisations* (Hodder & Stoughton, 1915).

_________ *The Correspondence of Ford Madox Ford and Stella Bowen*, eds. Sondra J Stang & Karen Cochran (Indiana University Press, 1993).

Ford, Hugh, *Published in Paris: American And British Writers, Printers, and Publishers in Paris, 1920-1939* (Garnstone Press, 1975).

_________ *Four Lives in Paris* (North Point Press, 1987).

Forster, E.M., *Pharos and Pharillon* (Hogarth, 1923).

_________ *The Collected Short Stories of E.M. Forster* (Sidgwick & Jackson Ltd., 1948).

Fraser, Brodie, Review of *Speed the Plough, The Sunday Times* (11.3.23).

Fraser, Henry, 'Printed in Paris', *Everyman*, 10, no.242 (16.9.33), p.320.

Frazer, J.G., *The Golden Bough: A Study in Magic and Religion* (Macmillan abridged edn, 1980).

Freud, Sigmund, *Psychopathology of Everyday Life* (Penguin, 1938).

_________ 'The Uncanny', in *Art and Literature*, Pelican Library 14, ed. Albert Dickson (Penguin, 1985), pp.335-376.

Furbank, P.N., *E.M. Forster: A Life: Volume Two, Polycrates' Ring 1914-1970* (O.U.P., 1978).

G., D.M. [Douglas Garman], '*Contact Collection of Contemporary Writers*', *Calendar of Modern Letters*, 1, no.6 (1925), pp.487-488.

Gallup, Donald, *T.S. Eliot: A Bibliography* (Faber, 1952).

Ganz, Paul, 'An Unpublished Holbein Portrait', *The Burlington Magazine: for Connoisseurs*, 56, no.324 (Mar 1930), p.118.

Gernon, Robert, 'A "Fairy" Story', *New Briton* (4.8.33).

Glendinning, Victoria, *Vita: The Life of V. Sackville-West* (Weidenfeld and Nicolson, 1983).

Goldring, Douglas, 'A London Bookman's Day Book', *Sunday Tribune* (Oct 1922).

_________[anon.]'Alexander the Great', *Sunday Referee*, 2900, (2.4.33), p.9.

_________*Odd Man Out: The Autobiography of a 'Propaganda Novelist'* (Chapman & Hall, 1935).

_________*South Lodge: Reminiscences of Violet Hunt, Ford Madox Ford and the English Review Circle* (Constable & Co, 1943).

__________ *The Nineteen Twenties: A General Survey and some Personal Memories* (Nicholson & Watson, 1945).

Goodrich, Chris, 'Early Modernists Olive Moore, Mary Butts Back in Print', *Publishers Weekly* (17.2.92).

Gould, Gerald, 'New Fiction', *The Saturday Review* 135, no.3517 (24.3.23), p.406.

__________ 'Novelists and a Humorist', *News Chronicle* (18.6.28).

__________ 'Two Strange Novels by Women', *News Chronicle* (29.12.32), p.4.

__________ Review of *Ashe of Rings*, *The Observer* (29.8.33).

Graham, John W., *Conscription and Conscience* (Allen & Unwin, 1922).

Grant, Joy, 'Glimpses and Grievances', *Times Literary Supplement* (23.-29.12.88).

Grigson, Geoffrey, Review of *Death of Felicity Taverner*, *Yorkshire Post* (14.12.32).

Guest, Barbara, *Herself Defined: The Poet H.D. and her world* (Collins, 1985).

Guggenheim, Peggy, *Out of this Century* (André Deutsch, 1979).

Hadfield, Alice Mary, *Charles Williams* (O.U.P., 1983).

Haggard, Lilas Rider & Williamson, Henry, *Norfolk Life* (Faber, 1943).

Hainley, Bruce, 'Quite Contrary: Mary Butts's Wild Queendom', *Voice Literary Supplement* (May 1994), pp.21-23.

Hall, Edward Fitch, 'Modern Witchcraft', *New York Herald Tribune* (8.8.26), p.8.

Hall, Marshall, *The Artists of Northumbria* (Marshall Hall Assoc, 1973).

Halpern, Daniel, 'Interview with Edouard Roditi', *Antaeus*, 2 (1971), pp.99-114.

Halpert, Stephen & Johns, Richard, eds., *A Return to Pagany 1929-1932: The History, Correspondence and Selections from a Little Magazine* (Beacon Press, 1969).

Hamer, Mary, *Signs of Cleopatra: History, politics, representation* (Routledge, 1993).

__________ 'Mary Butts, Mothers and War', in *Women's Fiction and the Great War*, ed. Suzanne Raitt & Trudi Tate (O.U.P., 1997), Ch.10, pp.219-240.

Hamnett, Nina, *Laughing Torso* (Virago, 1984).

Hamovitch, Mitzi Berger, ed., *The Hound and Horn Letters* (University of Georgia Press, 1982).

Hanscombe, G. & Smyers, V., *Writing for their Lives* (Women's Press, 1987).

Hansen, Arlen J., *Expatriate Paris: A Cultural and Literary Guide to Paris of the 1920s* (Little, Brown & Co, 1990).

Harding, James, *The Ox on the Roof* (Macdonald, 1972).

Hargreave, John, 'Happy when they're hiking?', *The New Age* (9.5.32), pp.69-70.

Harrison, J.E., *Themis: A Study of the Social Origins of Greek Religion* (C.U.P., 1912).

__________ *Prolegomena to the Study of Greek Religion* (Princeton University Press, 1991).

Hartley, L.P., 'New Books', *The Week-end Review*, 7, no.166 (13.5.33), pp.539-540.

__________'The Literary Lounger', *The Sketch* (3.7.35), p.40.

Harvey, Sir Paul, *Oxford Companion to Classical Literature* (O.U.P., 1984).

Hastings, Selina, *Evelyn Waugh: A Biography* (Minerva, 1995).

Havet, Mireille, 'Carnaval', *Les Oeuvres Libres*, 17 (1922), pp.251-344.

Hind, C. Lewis, *Days in Cornwall* (Methuen, 1924).

Hobday, Charles, *Edgell Rickword: A Poet at War* (Carcanet, 1989).

Hoberman, Ruth, *Gendering Classicism: The Ancient World in Twentieth Century Women's Historical Fictions* (State University of New York Press, 1997).

Holmes, Mildred, *Parkstone Recollections* (W.E.A. Southern District Publication, 1983).

Hone, J.M., 'Mary Butts', *The Spectator* (4.6.37), pp.1059-1060.

Hooker, Denise, *Nina Hamnett: Queen of Bohemia* (Constable & Co Ltd, 1986).

Hope, David, *Mary Butts, Fire-Bearer* (Sennen Pamphlet Series, no.1, June 1937). Reprinted in *A Sacred Quest*, ed. C. Wagstaff, pp.21-24.

Hughes-Hallett, Lucy, *Cleopatra: Histories, Dreams and Distortions* (Bloomsbury, 1989).

Huxley, Aldous, *Antic Hay* (Chatto & Windus, 1936).

Hynes, Samuel, *A War Imagined: The First World War and English Culture* (The Bodley Head, 1990).

I.-C., G., '*Ashe of Rings*. By Mary Butts.' *The Manchester Guardian* (31.7.25).

Ingram, H.F., 'Poole's Forgotten Genius', *Poole and Dorset Herald*, in two parts: (23.2.66), p.2; (2.3.66.), p.2.

__________Letter, *Poole and Dorset Herald* (23.3.66), p.16.

J., H.F.V., Letter on the death of H.F. Ingram, *Newsletter of the United Reform Church Poole* (Sep 1984).

J., M., '*Ashe of Rings* by Mary Butts', *The New Age* (30.11.33), pp.58-59.

__________'*Several Occasions*. By Mary Butts', *The New Age* (31.3.32).

James, M.R., *The Ghost Stories of M.R. James* (Edward Arnold, 1974, 2nd edn.).

Jameson, Storm, 'Recent Novels', *New English Weekly*, 2, no.12, (6.1.33), pp.279-281.

Jeffrey, Margaret W.J., 'The Trend of the Modern Novel', *The Glasgow Herald* (9.11.33), supplement.

Jess, *Jess; A Grand Collage 1951-1993*, organised by Michael Auping (Allbright-Knox Buffalo, 1993).

Jones, E.B.C., 'New Novels', *The New Statesman and Nation*, 6, no.136 (30.9.33), pp.388-389.

Judd, Alan, *Ford Madox Ford* (Flamingo, 1991).

Jung, Dr C.G., *Psychology of the Unconscious: A Study of the Transformations and Symbolisms of the Libido: A Contribution to the History of the Evolution of Thought*

(Kegan Paul, Trench, Trubner & Co Ltd, 1916).

K., F.H., 'The Book World', *John O'London's Weekly*, 32, no.830 (9.3.35), p.870.

K., K., 'How to "see": Quite the Silliest thing in Short stories', *The Evening Standard* (12.4.23), p.12.

Keast, Horace, *St Hilary of Cornwall: The Story of a Cornish Parish and its Church* (no publisher [isbn: 0951114409], 1986).

Kenner, Hugh, *The Pound Era* (Faber, 1972).

Kessler, Jascha, 'Beauty and the Beast: Rediscovering Mary Butts', *The Bookpress*, 3, no.7 (Oct 1993), pp.1, 12-14.

__________ 'Mary Butts: Lost and Found', *The Kenyon Review* (1995), pp.206-218.

Kipling, Rudyard, *Puck of Pook's Hill* (Macmillan & Co, 1924).

__________ *A Choice of Kipling's Verse*, ed. T.S. Eliot (Faber, 1941).

Knoll, Robert E., *McAlmon and the Lost Generation* (University of Nebraska Press, 1976).

Konody, P.G., 'The London Group', *The Observer* (12.5.18), p.3.

Kunitz, Stanley J. & Haycraft, Howard, eds., *Twentieth Century Authors: A Biographical Dictionary of Modern Literature* (The H.W. Wilson Co, 1942).

L., D., 'In a Napkin', *Review of Reviews*, 67, no.402 (June 1923), p.632.

L., E., 'Irritating', *Liverpool Post* (16.5.28).

Lacy, Norris J., ed., *The New Arthurian Encyclopedia* (St James Press, 1991).

Lanchester, Elsa, *Elsa Lanchester Herself* (Michael Joseph Ltd, 1983).

Lange, Monique, *Cocteau: Prince sans Royaume* (Jean-Claudes Lattès, 1989).

Lansing, Gerrit, 'Foreword' to *A Sacred Quest*, ed. C. Wagstaff, pp.xvii-xix.

Legg, Rodney, *Literary Dorset* (Wincanton, 1990)

Lewis, Wyndham, *The Apes of God* (Penguin, 1965).

Light, Alison, *Forever England: Femininity, Literature and Conservatism between the Wars* (Routledge, 1991).

Lindsay, Jack, *Fanfrolico and After* (The Bodley Head, 1962).

Lockhart, J.G., *The Life of Sir Walter Scott*, Vol I (Adam & Charles Black, 1898).

Lohrke, Eugene, 'Cups and Spears', *New York Herald Tribune* (10.6.28), p.16.

M., A.N., 'A Bookman's Notes: Change for Change's Sake', *The Manchester Guardian* (16.3.23), p.212.

M., T., 'A Memorable Novel', *The Manchester Guardian* (9.12.32), p.7.

__________ 'A Study of Greatness', *The Manchester Guardian* (16.6.33), p.5.

Macaulay, Rose, 'Stories Old and New', *The Daily News* (12.4.23), p.7.

Macdonell, A.G., 'Biography and Wit, Greater and Less', *The Bystander*, 126, no.1643 (12.6.35), p.490.

Machen, Arthur, *The Shining Pyramid* (Martin Secker, 1925).

Manning-Sanders, Ruth, *The West of England* (B.T. Batsford Ltd, 1949).

F.J. Mathias, 'Plumbing the Depths', *The Western Mail* (15.12.32), p.11.

__________'Alexander the Great As Hero in a Novel: Revealing Story', *The Western Mail* (16.3.33), p.13.

du Maurier, Daphne, *Vanishing Cornwall* (Penguin, 1972).

Maynard, Constance, Unpublished private diary (Queen Mary and Westfield College).

McAlmon, Robert, 'Truer than Most Accounts', *The Exile*, 2 (1927), pp.40-86.

__________ *Being Geniuses Together* (Martin Secker & Warburg, 1938).

McEvilley, Thomas, Preface to *The Classical Novels of Mary Butts* (McPherson & Co, 1994), pp.vii-xi.

McGrath, Morrow, *Bus by the Brook* (Cape, 1964).

McKinley, Mary Ann, 'Rediscovering an English Femme Maudit', *New Letters Book Reviewer*, 4 (Autumn 1993), p.14.

Medley, Robert, *Drawn from the Life* (Faber, 1983).

Mellow, James R., *Charmed Circle: Gertrude Stein and Company* (Avon, 1975).

Milton, John, *The Poetical Works of John Milton* ed., Helen Darbyshire (O.U.P., 1958).

Moberly, C. Anne E. & Jourdain, Eleanor F., *An Adventure* (Faber, 1932, 2nd edn.).

Moggridge, D.E., *Maynard Keynes: An Economist's Biography* (Routledge, 1992).

Moore, Marianne, 'A House-Party', *The Dial*, 85 (Sep 1928), pp.258-260. Reprinted in *The Complete Prose of Marianne Moore*, ed. Patricia C. Willis (Faber, 1987), pp.146-148.

__________ *Predilections* (Faber, 1956).

Moore, T. Sturge, 'The Carfax Exhibition of Blake's Work. Including the "Butts Collection"', *The Outlook*, 17, no.438 (23.06.06), pp.845-846.

Moran, Helen, 'Fiction II', *The London Mercury*, 28, no.163 (May 1933), p.78.

Morand, Paul, 'A Notable Collection', *The Dial*, 78 (1925), pp.51-53.

Morgan, Glen E., 'Mary Butts', Intro. to six poems by Mary Butts, *Antaeus*, 12 (Winter 1973), p.139.

Morphet, Richard, *Cedric Morris* (The Tate Gallery, 1984).

Morris, William, *The Collected Works of William Morris*, I (Routledge/Thoemmes Press, 1992).

Moult, Thomas, 'The Art of the Short Story', *The Manchester Guardian* (14.10.38).

Muir, Edwin, '*Ashe of Rings* by Mary Butts', *The Calendar of Modern Letters*, 1, no.6 (Aug 1925), pp.476-478.

__________ *The Present Age from 1914: Introductions to English Literature, 5* (Cresset Press, 1939).

Murry, John Middleton, *Fyodor Dostoevsky: A Critical Study* (Secker, 1916).

N., B.D., 'On and off the English Roads', *The Week-end Review*, 5, no.1171 (4.6.32), p.714.

Nance, R. Morton, *A New Cornish Dictionary / Gerlyver Noweth Kernewek* (Dyllansow Truran, 1990).

Nataf, André, *The Wordsworth Dictionary of the Occult* (Wordsworth Reference, 1994).

Naumann, Francis M., *New York Dada 1915-1923* (Harry N. Abrams, 1994).

Nesbit, E., *The Story of the Amulet* (Puffin, 1959).

Nevinson, C.R.W., *Paint and Prejudice* (Methuen, 1937).

Norman, Charles, *Ezra Pound* (McDonald & Co, 2nd edn, 1969).

O'Brien, Edward J. and Cournos, John, 'The Best British and Irish Short Stories: A Year's Survey', The Bookman, 63, no.376 (Jan 1923), pp. 199-203.

O'Brien, Kate, 'New Novels: The family "under fire"', *The Sunday Referee*, 2883, (4.12.32), p.7.

__________ 'Fiction', *The Spectator* (16.12.38), p.1062.

O'Hara, Frank, *The Collected Poems of Frank O'Hara* ed. Donald Allen (Knopf, 1972).

Oppé, Armide, 'Mary Butts, *The Crystal Cabinet*. By Mary Butts', *The London Mercury and Bookman*, 36, no.212 (Jun 1937), p.200.

Olson, Charles, *Charles Olson and Ezra Pound: An Encounter at St Elizabeths*, ed. Catherine Seelye (Grossman, 1975).

O'Riordan, Conal, 'So far as I can see: Ideas in the light of Experience - Of a new author', *The New Witness* (16.3.23).

P., W., 'The Real Cleopatra', *Glasgow Evening News* (15.6.35).

Patterson, Ian, Ch.5: 'Mary Butts', in "Cultural Change and Canon Formation: 1910-1939" (Cambridge, unpublished PhD, 1997).

Pekar, Harvey, 'Butts is Back', *Los Angeles Reader* (24.4.92).

__________ untitled review, *Review of Contemporary Fiction* (Fall 1992), pp.181-182.

Pendle, George, *'Traps for Unbelievers'*, *Twentieth Century*, 3, no.15 (May 1932), pp.29-30.

Philemon, 'A Monograph', *Scots Observer* (17.3.32).

Plomer, William, 'Fiction', *The Spectator* (29.9.33), p.420.

__________ *Museum Pieces* (Jonathan Cape, 1952).

__________ *At Home* (Jonathan Cape, 1956).

Plutarch, *Plutarch's Lives*, 7, englished by Sir Thomas North (J.M. Dent, 1899).

Pound, Ezra, 'Psychology and Troubadours', in *The Spirit of Romance* (Peter Owen, 2nd edn., 1970).

__________*Pound/Ford: The Story of a Literary Friendship*, ed. Lindberg-Seyersted, Brita, (Faber, 1982).

__________*POUND/The Little Review: The Letters of Ezra Pound to Margaret Anderson: The Little Review Correspondence*, eds. Thomas L. Scott, Melvin M. Friedman and Jackson R. Bryher (Faber, 1988).

Powys, Llewelyn, 'Julian the Apostate', *The Rationalist Annual* (1936), pp.75-80.

Priestley, J.B., 'Fiction', *The London Mercury*, 8, no.43 (May 1923), pp.96-99.

Pritchett, V.S., 'New Novels', *The New Statesman and Nation*, 5, no.110 (1.4.33), pp.419-420.

Proctor, Dod, *Dod Proctor RA 1892-1972*, Catalogue produced by The Laing Art Gallery, Newcastle upon Tyne in collaboration with Newlyn Orion, Penzance (Tyne and Wear Museums Service, 1990).

Quennell, Peter, 'New Novels', *The New Statesman and Nation* (1.6.35), pp.829-830.

Raitt, Suzanne, *Vita and Virginia* (Clarendon Press, 1993).

Raverat, Gwendolin, 'New Fiction', *Time and Tide*, 13, no.49 (3.12.32), p. 1348.

Raynor, John, 'In Memoriam: Mary Butts', *Time and Tide*, 18, no.13 (27.3.37), p.408. Reprinted in *The Cornish Review*, 16 (Winter 1970), p.8.

__________ *Eleven Songs by John Raynor*, Intro. & Notes Olwen Picton-Jones (Galliard Ltd, 1971).

Richardson, Nelson M., ed., *Proceedings of the Dorset Natural History and Antiquarian Field Club* (Dorset Country Chronicle Office, 1898).

Rickword, Edgell & Garman, Douglas eds., *The Calendar of Modern Letters*, new impression in 3 vols. with Malcolm Bradbury, 'A Review in Retrospect' (Frank Cass & Co, 1966).

Roberts, R. Ellis, 'Short Stories', *The New Statesman and Nation*, 3, no.5 (12.3.32), pp.338-340.

__________'Tale of Two Worlds', *The New Statesman and Nation*, 4, no.96 (24.12.32), p.837.

__________'Reviews and Impressions of Alexander', *The Manchester Guardian* (28.4.33).

__________'The Real Cleopatra', *News Chronicle* (19.6.35), p.4.

__________'A London Letter', *The Saturday Review of Literature* (11.1.36), p.17.

__________'Childhood: "*The Crystal Cabinet*"', [source and date unknown], 1937.

__________*Portrait of Stella Benson* (Macmillan, 1939).

Robbins, Keith, *The Abolition of War: the 'Peace Movement' in Britain, 1914-1919* (University of Wales Press, 1976).

Rodker, John, *Hymns* (Ovid Press, 1920).

__________ [anon], *Memoirs of Other Fronts* (Putnam, 1932).

__________ *Poems and Adolphe 1920*, ed. Andrew Crozier (Carcanet, 1995).

Rose, Francis, *Saying Life: The Memoirs of Sir Francis Rose* (Cassell, 1961).

Royde-Smith, Naomi, 'Mary Butts', *Time and Tide*, 18, no.12 (20.3.37), p.378.

__________ '*The Crystal Cabinet* by Mary Butts', *Time and Tide*, 18, no.21 (5.6.37), p.756-757.

de S, A., '*Armed with Madness* by Mary Butts', *The Manchester Guardian* (15.6.28), p.7.

Sackville-West, Edward, 'A Poetical Autobiography', *The New Statesman and Nation*, 13, no.329 (12.6.37), p.974.

Saki [H.H. Munro], *The Short Stories of Saki (H.H. Munro)* (John Lane, The Bodley Head Ltd, 1956).

Saunders, Max, *Ford Madox Ford: A Dual Life* (O.U.P., 1995).

Savage, Brother, 'Preparing for the Autumn', *Liverpool Post* (11.5.35).

Scott, Bonnie Kime, ed., *The Gender of Modernism: A Critical Anthology* (Indiana University Press, 1990).

Seed, David, 'Extending the Modernist Canon', *Bête Noire*, 14/15 (1994), pp.405, 407-412.

de Selincourt, B., 'A Haunted Childhood', *Times Literary Supplement* (30.5.37), p.5.

Sell, Joseph, 'Plus Something Plutarch Hadn't Got?', *The Manchester Evening News* (16.3.33).

Shanks, Edward, 'Miss Mary Butts's Farewell', *The Sunday Times* (30.5.37), p.12.

Shattock, Joanne, *The Oxford Guide to British Women Writers* (O.U.P., 1993).

Shirley, Mary, 'Join the Ladies', *Time Magazine* (22.8.28).

Shone, Richard, *Bloomsbury Portraits: Vanessa Bell, Duncan Grant and their circle* (Phaidon Press Ltd, 1993).

Shostak, Elizabeth, 'Mary Butts: The Permanent behind the Impermanent', *The Boston Book Review* (Aug 1995), pp.28-29.

Shrapnell, Norman, 'New Fiction', *The Guardian* (1991).

Sitwell, Osbert, *The Scarlet Tree: Being the second volume of Left Hand, Right Hand. The Autobiography of Osbert Sitwell* (Macmillan, 1946).

__________ Foreword to *Catalogue of the Loan Exhibition of Paintings and Drawings of Gabriel Atkin* (Laing Art Gallery, 1940).

Smith, Marion Delf, Unpublished memoirs, 1969 (Queen Mary and Westfield College).

Smoller, Sanford J., *Adrift Among Geniuses: Robert McAlmon, Writer and Publisher of the Twenties* (Pennsylvania State University Press, 1975).

Spilleth, Meg, 'The Effects of Childhood', *The Minnesota Daily* (28.9.88).

Sprigge, Elizabeth & Kilm, Jean-Jacques, *Jean Cocteau: The Man and the Mirror* (Victor Gollanz, 1968).

Squire, J.C., 'The Modern Revival of the Short Story: Miss Mary Butts's Success', *The Daily Telegraph* (8.3.32), p.16.

_________ 'A Subtle Pen' *The Sunday Times* (27.11.32).

Steegmuller, Frances, *Cocteau: A Biography* (Constable, 1986).

Steen, Marguerite, 'Novel of the Week: The Glory That Was Greece', *Everyman*, 9, no.216, (18.3.33), p.341.

Stevens, Wallace, *The Collected Poems of Wallace Stevens* (Faber, 1955).

Stokes, Adrian, *Smooth and Rough* (Faber, 1951).

Stone, J. Harris, *England's Riviera: A Topographical and Archaeological description of Land's End, Cornwall and adjacent spots of Beauty and Interest* (Kegan Paul, Trench, Trubner & Co, 1912).

Strauss, Ralph, 'Alexander the Great', *The Sunday Times* (23.4.33).

Strong, L.A.G., 'Fiction', *The Spectator* (23.12.32), p.900.

Symonds, John, *The Great Beast: The Life and Magick of Aleister Crowley* (Mayflower Books Ltd, 1973).

Symons, A.J.A., *The Quest for Corvo* (Penguin, 1970).

Symons, Julian, *Makers of the New: The Revolution in Literature, 1912-1939* (André Deutsch, 1987).

Tatlock, R.R., 'X-Rays Reveal a Masterpiece', *The Daily Telegraph* (27.2.30), pp.13, 16.

Thompson, Francis, *The Hound of Heaven* (Phoenix, 1996).

_________ *The Poems of Francis Thompson*, ed. Wilfred Meynell (O.U.P., 1937).

Thomson, Virgil, *Virgil Thomson* (Knopf, 1966).

Tindall, Gillian, *Countries of the Mind: The Meaning of Place to Writers* (Hogarth, 1991).

Tylee, Claire M., *The Great War and Women's Consciousness: Images of Militarism and Womanhood in Women's Writings 1914-1964* (Macmillan, 1990).

Upchurch, Michael, 'Rediscovering Mary Butts', *Washington Post Book World* (20.9.92), p.11.

Vernon, Frank, 'Books We'd like to Burn', *John Bull*, 33, no.882 (28.4.23), p.18.

Wagstaff, Barbara, Untitled statement, *The Writings and the World of Mary Butts* [Conference brochure] (University of California, 1984).

_________ [Leslie Rivers], 'Alchemist of Reality: Recovering Mary Butts', *Poetry Flash*, 133 (Apr 1984), pp.4, 9.

_________ Afterword to *The Crystal Cabinet* (Carcanet & Beacon, 1988), pp.275-282.

_________ 'Brightness falls from the Air', Afterword to *The Taverner Novels* (1992), pp.367-373.

_________ 'The Effectual Angel in *Death of Felicity Taverner*', *A Sacred Quest*, ed. C. Wagstaff, pp.224-242.

Wagstaff, Christopher, ed., Preface to *A Sacred Quest: The Life and the Writings of Mary Butts* (McPherson & Co, 1995), pp.xi-xv.

Walke, Bernard, *Twenty Years at St Hilary* (Anthony Mott Ltd, 1982).

Walpole, Hugh, 'Some Books I have enjoyed in 1933', *The Bookman*, 85, no.507 (Dec 1933), p.137.

Warren, C. Henry, 'Love of Nature?', *The Bookman*, 82, no.488 (May 1932), pp.116-117.

Waugh, Alec, *My Brother Evelyn and Other Profiles* (Cassell & Co, 1967).

Waugh, Evelyn, *The Diaries of Evelyn Waugh*, ed. Michael Davie (Phoenix, 1995).

Weatherhill, Craig, *Belerion: Ancient Sites of Land's End* (Alison Hodge, 1989).

Weaver, Mike, *William Carlos Williams: The American Background* (C.U.P., 1977).

Weeks, Donald, *Corvo* (Michael Joseph, 1971).

Wescott, Glenway, 'The First Book of Mary Butts', *The Dial*, 75 (Sep 1923), pp.282-284. Reprinted in *A Sacred Quest*, ed. C. Wagstaff, pp.11-14.

__________ *Continual Lessons: The Journals of Glenway Wescott 1937-1955*, eds. Robert Phelps & Jerry Rosco (Farrar Straus Giroux, 1990).

West, Geoffrey, '*Scenes from the Life of Cleopatra*', *Fortnightly Review* (Jul 1935).

Wickham, Anna, *The Man with a Hammer* (Grant & Richards, 1916).

Wieners, John, letter published in *Floating Bear*, 26 (1963), p.287.

__________ *Selected Poems 1958-1984*, ed. Raymond Foye (Black Sparrow Press, 1986).

Williams, Michael, *Around Land's End* (Bossiney Books, 1983).

Williams, William Carlos, *The Autobiography of William Carlos Williams* (New Directions, 1967).

Williamson, Hugh Ross, 'Portrait of Mary Butts', *The Bookman*, 81 (Xmas 1931), pp.188-189. Reprinted as 'Who is Mary Butts?', *A Sacred Quest*, ed. C. Wagstaff, pp.15-20.

__________ 'Religion and Science', *The Bookman*, 82 (Apr 1932), p.5.

__________ *The Poetry of T.S. Eliot* (Hodder & Stoughton Ltd, 1932).

__________ 'A Writer's Childhood. The Testament of Mary Butts', *John O'London's Weekly* (11.6.37), p.388.

__________ *The Walled Garden* (Michael Joseph Ltd, 1956).

Willis Jr, J.H., *Leonard and Virginia Woolf as Publishers: The Hogarth Press 1917-1941* (University Press of Virginia, 1992).

Wilson, Angus & Julian, Philippe, *For Whom the Cloche Tolls: A Scrap-Book of the Twenties* (Methuen, 1953).

Wineapple, Brenda, 'Shadow of the Left Bank', *Belles Lettres* (Summer 1992), pp.32,34.

Wolfe, Humbert, 'King of the World', *The Observer* (12.3.33), p.5.

__________ '"Her Infinite Variety": Cleopatra of Alexandria', *The Observer* (2.5.35).

Wollaston, Nicholas, 'Emma and Mr. Elton don't get laid - again', *The Observer* (20.10.91).

Woolf, Virginia, 'On Not Knowing Greek', in *The Common Reader* (Harcourt, Brace & World Inc., 1953).

__________ *The Question of Things Happening: The Letters of Virginia Woolf. Volume I: 1912-1922*, ed. Nigel Nicolson (Hogarth, 1976).

__________ *The Diary of Virginia Woolf. Volume II: 1920-1924*, ed. Anne Olivier Bell (Penguin, 1978).

__________ *The Diary of Virginia Woolf: Volume III: 1925-1930*, ed. Anne Olivier Bell (Penguin, 1980).

__________ *The Diary of Virginia Woolf. Volume IV: 1931-1935*, ed. Anne Olivier Bell (Penguin, 1982).

__________ *Three Guineas* (Penguin, 1993).

__________ *Leave the Letters Till We're Dead: Collected Letters VI, 1936-1941*, ed. Nigel Nicolson (Hogarth, 1994).

Wright, Patrick, 'Coming Back to the Shores of Albion: The Secret England of Mary Butts (1890-1937)', ch.3 of *On Living in an Old Country: The National Past in Contemporary Britain* (Verso, 1985), pp.93-134.

__________ *The Village that Died for England: The Strange Story of Tyneham* (Vintage, 1996).

Yeats, W.B., *Per Amica Silentiae Lunae* (Macmillan, 1918).

INDEX

THE AUTHOR

NATHALIE BLONDEL was born in Stoke-on-Trent in 1960 and grew up in Colchester, Essex. She was educated at Colchester Girls' High School and Liverpool University, where she completed a doctorate on the fiction of Mary Butts and the American writer, Jane Bowles, in 1989. In the same year she married Paul Evans, and their daughter Cecily was born. Subsequently she has edited three of Jane Bowles's unpublished stories in collaboration with Bowles's husband, the writer/composer Paul Bowles, and has worked as a writer and translator: her subjects have included Jean Cocteau, Arthur Symons, Frances Bellerby, Patrick Hamilton, and Jocelyn Brooke, as well as Mary Butts. Widowed in 1991, she married Charles Butler in 1994: they, Cecily, and their son Nathaniel, now live in Bristol. Nathalie Blondel currently holds a lecturship at the University of the West of England, where she is Mary Butts Research Fellow.